THE HISTORY OF MORRIS DANCING, 1458–1750

John Forrest

Morris dancing, one of the more peculiar of the English folk customs, has been greatly misunderstood. Traditional scholarship on this custom has been based on the assumption that morris dancing is one of the pagan calendar rituals, a preconception held by many folklorists of the late nineteenth and early twentieth centuries.

Now, building on his previous work with Michael Heaney of the Bodleian Library in *Annals of Early Morris*, John Forrest carefully analyses a wealth of evidence to show that morris dancing does not, in fact, have pagan or ancient origins. His examination of early documentation draws morris traditions into the wider area of communal customs and public celebrations, showing the passage of dance ideas between groups of people who until now have been considered folklorically distinct.

Careful, detailed, and encyclopedic, *The History of Morris Dancing, 1458–1750* is an essential reference work for specialists in English drama and social historians of the period.

(Studies in Early English Drama)

JOHN FORREST is a professor of Anthropology, State University of New York at Purchase. He is also co-author of *Annals of Early Morris* with Michael Heaney and the author of *Morris and Matachin: A Study in Comparative Choreography*.

STUDIES IN EARLY ENGLISH DRAMA 5
General Editor: J.A.B. Somerset

JOHN FORREST

The History of Morris Dancing, 1458–1750

James Clarke & Co Ltd
Cambridge

James Clarke & Co Ltd
P.O. Box 60
Cambridge
CB1 2NT

British Library Cataloguing in Publication Data:
A catalogue record is available from the British Library.

ISBN 0227 67943 1 cased
ISBN 0227 67944 X paperback

First published in Great Britain by James Clark & Co Ltd 1999

First published in the USA & Canada by University of Toronto Press Inc. 1999

Copyright © University of Toronto Press 1999

Printed in Canada

This book is dedicated to:

ROYSTON WOOD, who was struck by a car while assisting a fellow motorist in need on 17 March 1990. He died three weeks later without regaining consciousness. Go in peace friend.

and to

JOHN ROYSTON FORREST-BLINCOE, who was born on 12 October 1991. Welcome son.

Contents

viii   Contents

Acknowledgments

A glance at the acknowledgments section of my joint work with Michael Heaney, *Annals of Early Morris*, will reveal the number of people who have been involved with the early morris project since its inception. Without the generous support of these people the current work would not have been possible. In addition to thanking them all again I must add a note of indebtedness to others who have helped specifically with this volume.

Without question, Mike Heaney and Keith Chandler deserve an enormous vote of thanks. Both have been magnanimous with their data, open and challenging with their commentary, and unfailingly hospitable.

Likewise I have received help from all manner of quarters. Even since the publication of *Annals* REED editors have been turning up new sources. For providing me with these new materials prior to publication, and also for lively discussion, I would like to thank my series editor, Alan Somerset (who also deserves credit for clearing away many of the usual prepublication obstacles), Sally-Beth MacLean, Alexandra Johnston, James Stokes, and Anne Brannen. In addition, a considerable vote of thanks is due to my copy editor, Miriam Skey, whose energy, enthusiasm, meticulousness, and patient detective work went well beyond the bounds of her duty. The text is smoother and kinder to the reader because of her absolute thoroughness, intelligence, and grace.

I taxed the resources of many librarians at different institutions in the course of checking sources for publication. Special thanks go to the professionals at the Bodleian, SUNY Purchase, the School of American Research, the Museum of New Mexico, the Museum of International Folk Art in Santa Fe, and the University of New Mexico. I also had individual help in checking obscure materials from Ivor Allsop, Stephen Corrsin, Stephanie Hall, and Roy Judge.

The foreign language texts, particularly from the early modern period, caused endless head scratching because of unusual orthographies and idiosyncratic syntax.

I received invaluable aid in decipherment from Rossanna Chille, Anabella Domingos, Anna Iwaschkin, John Kidman, Maria Lara-Netto, and Rob and Sandra Ogden.

Then, of course, there are the myriad crucial details involving specialized knowledge. Thanks go to John Dawson for geological materials, Chris Sheffield for legal work, Martin Sykes for information on brewing techniques, and Bill Young of Krauss Photo in Port Jervis, NY, for photographic assistance. The Ancient Men provided me with aid in reconstructing certain aspects of historic morris tours, as well as injecting sufficient hilarity into my researches to counterbalance my occasional lapses into seriousness.

As the early morris database and archive were forming it became clear that the work of storage and retrieval, coding, editing, and discussion among interested parties would be greatly facilitated by computer technology. At the outset, and as the computer world has gone through endless revolutions, Rob Ogden has been an unfailing aid and guide in hardware and software problems.

Computing also opened up the possibility of being in touch with other interested souls, and it was a great help that the RENDANCE discussion list started when I was wrestling with the chapter on country dance. Various members of that list helped in tracking down and interpreting foreign sources. In particular I would like to thank Allan Terry, who provided the transcription of Feuillet notation found in appendix C, and Mary Railing for her aid in interpreting Italian sources.

I am delighted that even in a world greatly impoverished by the need to know the current market value of everything there are still institutions and individuals willing to provide financial support for a definitive history of morris dancing. Heartfelt thanks go to the National Endowment for the Humanities, the School of American Research, SUNY Purchase, Roy Judge, Chris Sheffield, Roy Dommett, John Dawson, John Price, St Albans Morris Men, Greg Finch, Andrew Leleux, Gerard Robinson, Steve Corrsin, and the Ancient Men for grants large and small.

Finally, I would like *not* to acknowledge the invaluable help I have received from Deborah Blincoe, because she expressly asked me not to.

Illustrations

Tables

Introduction

This book has been growing and developing in my head for over thirty years, although I was not really aware of what I was embarking on when I first began collecting and sorting primary materials. At the outset I started gathering snippets of source materials unsystematically just for the fun of having the information. What I really wanted was a great big book that had the whole history of morris dancing laid out in it in exquisite detail, backed up with copious exotic quotations, my odds and ends of data being a poor substitute for me until the real thing should show up. Quite early in the process of collecting I realized that the book I was looking for did not exist, but it was only about ten years ago that I decided that I had to write it myself. Thus, what I have done here is to write just exactly the kind of book that, had I not written it, I would love to read and reread.

Yet in a strange sense I did not exactly write the book. Other scholars will understand me when I say that great sections of this book wrote themselves, with me simply acting as the vehicle for getting the ideas on paper. The fact is that the primary sources tell their own story when they are probed deeply enough. What I have tried to do here is put those sources together in a way that they belong naturally, and put a framework around them so that they can tell their own story.

It was the sources themselves that first pulled me away from that old chestnut, 'What are the origins of morris dancing?' – which is not a very good question anyway – to the much more interesting study of how morris dances have evolved and developed over the centuries. In fact, trying to discover the 'origins' of any long-standing and complex tradition is undoubtedly a lost cause from the outset.

Most important, the problem of 'origins' is almost impossible to formulate in such a way that makes sense. What counts as the 'origin' of any traditional custom? Is there such a thing as an ancestorless ancestor? What criteria does the scholar use to say, 'Further back I need not go'? And even if these questions had answers, what ultimately would be the point in finding some remote forebear of painting eggs at

Easter or hanging up mistletoe at Christmas? We cannot justifiably argue that people paint eggs at Easter, for example, *because* the egg was sacred to Eostre, the Anglo-Saxon goddess of spring. This is patently not true. Most people have never heard of Eostre. There may be a temporal link between the two but not a causal one. There may be cultural links as well – the egg can symbolize regeneration and renewal for the modern Christian and the pagan of antiquity – but there are as many differences in the meanings of the customs of the two eras as similarities.

Modern anthropologists and folklorists avoid the problem of origins by focusing their efforts on discovering the meaning of contemporary customs (the 'texts') by virtue of their place in their current social and cultural milieu (the 'context'). This text-in-context approach has been extraordinarily successful in exploring the riches of symbolic behaviour, but just because of its evident achievements we need not tip the balance all the way to one side, concentrating all our energy on the present to the complete exclusion of the past. There is a considerable theoretical and methodological difference between seeking *the* origin of custom and tracing its development over time.

Nor need a developmental approach to customs be at odds with the text-in-context school; on the contrary, it can benefit from the methods. There is no theoretical impediment to studying the role of eggs at Easter in 1990, 1890, 1790 ... and so on (or 1990, 1980, 1970 ...) as far back as one wishes to go, noting changes in the 'texts' and 'contexts' along the way, and perhaps suggesting mechanisms to explain the changes. Such an approach must inevitably provide fresh insights into the nature of customs and their role in society, and contribute to a better understanding of human history. Many anthropologists do this as a matter of course, returning to the field at regular intervals so as to add a temporal dimension to their works.

In analysing customs developmentally the problem is not theoretical but empirical: the data simply do not exist, at least not in any convenient form. The would-be student of Easter egg history has too many gaps to fill between 1990 and 599 AD to make the project more than a speculative fantasy. To be sure there is a glimpse here or there – maybe a diary entry made by a visiting prelate from Rome in 1520 noting an example of egg rolling on his perambulations, or a line in a domestic account book for 1635 for egg dye – but these are paltry in comparison with the ocean of ignorance.

Such was the case for morris dancing in Britain for most of this century. The date of the earliest reference to a dance called 'morris' has long been set at 1458, but data for the next 500 years are sparse and hard to come by, with almost all the detailed information belonging to the period 1890 onward. Thus, attempts in the past to recreate anything approximating a developmental history have been woven from fine gossamers indeed. To rectify the data shortfall I began to rationalize my collection of odds and ends into a formal database of all known primary sources, whatever their quality or size. After several years of conflating bibliographies, search-ing old documents, and scanning likely texts, it became clear that a complete listing from 1458 to the present was beyond my individual resources; the period would have to be divided up somehow.

In the end it was the source materials themselves that suggested a chronological division in the middle of the eighteenth century. After around 1750 the dances and their contexts described in the sources tend to be like the forms that are familiar to contemporary researchers. Prior to that time they are generally quite different, even though some strands are reasonably continuous. Basically the dances prior to 1750 are considerably more diverse in form and context than those afterwards. Thus began the 'Early Morris Archive and Database' – a listing and bibliography of all sources from 1458 to 1750. In the process of compiling sources I discovered that Michael Heaney of the Bodleian Library was attempting something similar, and so we pooled our resources and worked jointly to produce *Annals of Early Morris* (Heaney and Forrest 1991).

Although primary sources will no doubt continue to trickle in forever (right now they appear at the rate of about one per month), it is clear that the archive is com-prehensive enough to begin the task of creating a developmental history of morris dancing that is founded on a solid base of primary materials, and not, as in the past, dependent more on imagination than on empirical substance.

Because of these data riches I can set certain critical goals for the current work. First, I can avoid all anachronistic analysis. It has been common in past histories to use descriptions of the dance from one era to flesh out sources from another. This approach would be legitimate only if it could be definitively proven that the dance had not changed from century to century, but because *changes* in the dance are the principal subject of inquiry, it is ruled out. All data are to be rigorously confined to supporting descriptions and analyses within appropriate time periods. Second, I can generalize concerning dance forms without being simplistic. In some eras the data suggest a complex picture, and I intend to explore this picture without the kind of harmful reduction that eliminates inconvenient data for the sake of a neat hypothesis.

Beyond these methodological aims my concerns are straightforward. I wish to chart the flow of dance ideas in time and space. Most particularly I wish to docu-ment the passage of dance ideas between groups of people who are conventionally thought of as quite distinct when talking about folk customs. There is no question that in the sixteenth century, for example, dance ideas passed between nobles and peasants. The study of the mechanism for the transmission of these ideas, and how they were changed in the process, ought to be of intrinsic interest to all historians.

Yet this study is much more than an exploration of the diffusion of a dance. To begin with, even a cursory examination of the database shows that there was never a time when one could speak of *the* morris dance (nor is this true today). Under the rubric 'morris' have been included solo jigs, country dances for couples, maypole dances, sword fighting dances, and mimes, to name a few. Thus a simple analysis of the geographic spread of 'morris' would not be appropriate. Rather, what is needed is a detailed investigation of the evolution of each dance idea and how these strands affected one another. Furthermore, a simple spatial diffusion model would miss the critical importance of the social contexts of the dances, which varied from royal courts to village streets, but not in absolute correlation with dance types. There were probably at least three different morris dance types performed on the stage in the early seventeenth century, for example.

Following the many threads and their contexts reveals a rich tapestry woven into England's history and, just as important, elaborates and often challenges a number of cherished ideas concerning English culture at critical junctures. Therefore, this work spreads its analytic and empirical net well beyond the mere recounting of the evolution of choreographic forms. It is often necessary to delve deeply into the form and function of the contexts of the dances in order to understand fully the ways the dances are structured into these contexts, and to gain further clues from this contextual information concerning the nature of the dances. As such, the work is as much about the social history of dance contexts as of the dances themselves.

Above all these specific goals, I wish to use the fine-grained details of the developmental history of morris dancing as a case study for reflections on a much more general and analytic plane concerning the cultural transmission of ideas over time and space, evolution in the arts and aesthetic forms, the sources of creativity and innovation in culture, and the interplay between aesthetics and other arenas of cultural life. These reflections permeate the work and are drawn together at the end. My hope is to show, in principle, how the most exacting dissection of the smallest events on the most local of scales can open out into visions of the universal.

THE HISTORY OF MORRIS DANCING, 1458–1750

1

Theories of Origin

Few modern academics have been willing to undertake a thorough analysis of morris dancing in its historical context because the field has been hopelessly dogged by a series of preconceptions imposed upon it by folklorists of the late nineteenth and early twentieth centuries. These preconceptions stem from an almost obsessional concern for *the* origin of the dances, which quest has in turn led generation after generation of devotees into extravagant flights of fantasy. As a prelude to the analysis of the historical materials it is useful, therefore, to consider why the concern for origins has been so perennially attractive, where this concern has taken generations of scholars, and what its many pitfalls are.

Interest in the origins of morris dancing is almost as old as the oldest of primary sources themselves; all theories of origin, old and new, come with political or social or ideological or intellectual agendas attached, although these agendas are rarely acknowledged explicitly by their authors. What is certainly a continuing curiosity is that morris dancing's own history had been forgotten almost as soon as the dances appeared in the primary record in England, so that the earliest hypotheses varied greatly and seem to consist largely of unsupported armchair theorizing. From these earliest days speculation has been endless and wildly diverse, although some themes have proven enduring.

Possibly the oldest belief concerning origins, and the most doggedly persistent in contemporary popular consciousness, comes from attacks on morris dancing by Elizabethan Puritans in the last quarter of the sixteenth century. Theirs was an argument of guilt by association; that is, morris dancing is the work of the devil, paganism is the religion of the devil, therefore morris dancing is pagan. This argument has neither logic nor evidence on its side but its conclusion has had an endless appeal.

Actually the Puritan polemicists were not concerned with morris dancing specifically but, rather, were railing against a whole raft of customs including Whitsun ales, May games, maypoles, and the like, which they found ungodly and reprehensible. The following diatribe from 1585 is a representative example of the kind of polemical argument by assertion used by the Elizabethan Puritans to link all these customs together and to associate them with paganism:[1]

whereas a heathenish and ungodly custom hath bene used before time in many partes of this lande about this season of the yeare [Whitsun] to have Church Ales, May games, morish dances, and other vaine pastimes upon the Sabath Dayes, and other dayes appointed for common prayer, which they have pretended to be for the relief of theire Churches, but indede hath bene only a meanes to feed the mindes of the people and specially of the youth with vaine sight which is a strange perswasion among Christians, that they cannot by any other means of contribution repaire theire churches but must first do sacrifice to the Devil with Drunkenes and Dancing and other ungodly wantonnes.   (Atkinson 1963, 245)[2]

Throughout the period of Puritan struggle for the control of the English church the same perception of morris and other customs was continually reasserted with no more evidence or logic, but with the growing certitude born of endless repetition, as in this extract from the Quarter Sessions Order Book of 1655 from Henley in Arden:

... the court was informed that vsually heretofore there haue beene att Henley in Arden in this County severall vnlawfull meeteings of idle & vain persons about this time of yeare for erectinge of MayPoles and mayBushes and for vseinge of Morris dances and other heatheanish and vnlawfull Customs ...
                    (Warw RO QS 40/1 f 202v; see also Ratcliff and Johnson 1937, 275)

A century later some clerics were still making the same argument, as in this fragment of a now lost open letter from a minister in Stow on the Wold to his parishioners, dated 1736:

Morris Dances, so called, are nothing else but reliques of Paganism.   (Brand 1849, 1:227)

In the nineteenth century this and kindred references were used by John Brand in his *Observations on the Popular Antiquities of Great Britain* (Brand 1849) as 'evidence' that many of the folk customs of Britain originated in paganism. But of course it is no evidence at all, merely the continued repetition of unsupported assertions from bygone eras.

From Brand the notion of pagan origins became entrenched in popular works that used him as a source, and thus it entered the mainstream of twentieth-century folklore. This notion has been by far the most popular speculation on origins, persisting in popular works down to the present day, and is also the most commonly articulated point of view by revivalist morris dancers at the present time. Nowadays the notion of pagan origins has a mysterious and romantic appeal, even though now, as in the sixteenth century, there is absolutely no evidence to support the belief, and a mounting body of evidence to suggest that it is quite mistaken.

Almost as soon as the idea of pagan origins was developed, competing hypotheses emerged, based on very different agendas. The classicism of the seventeenth century, for example, sought an origin for morris in classical antiquity, the commonest hypothesis being that it was invented by Pyrrhus, son of Achilles. This idea seems to have been ventured first by Philemon Holland in his translation of the works of Pliny the Younger:

> The Curets taught to daunce in armour; and Pyrrhus the Morisk, in order of battell; and both of these were taken up first in Crete … In the late solemnitie of tournois and sword-fight at the sharpe, which Germanicus Caesar exhibited to gratifie the people, the elephants were seen to shew pastime with leaping and keeping a stirre, as if they daunced, after a rude and disorderly manner. A common thing it was among them … to encounter and meet together in fight like sword-fencers, and to make good sport in a kind of Moriske dance.
>
> (Holland 1601, 189, 192–3)

From this conjecture of translation came the general idea, to be found in dictionaries throughout the seventeenth and eighteenth centuries, that the classical dance called *saltatio pyrricha* (i.e., the Pyrrhic – the war dance in armour of the ancient Greeks) was either a precursor of, or identical with morris. John Minsheu gives a characteristic interpretation:

> Saltatio Pyrricha. Πυῤῥίχη ὄρχησις, a Pyrrho inuentore, & authore vnde πυῤῥιχίζω, pyrricham salto, & πυῤῥιχισῆς, i. pyrrhicho saltator, i. *a Morice-dancer. Nota* Pyrrhum *hanc saltationem in armis militibus instituit.*   (Minsheu 1617, 315)

An origin for the morris in antiquity was highly desirable for classicists because it elevated the dance in the eyes of the learned from something rude and unworthy of interest to an object worthy of admiration akin to a newly unearthed marble statue, now broken and fragmentary but still showing all the beauty of classical lines.

Towards the middle of the seventeenth century the theory of classical origins for the morris found competition in a speculation (based on the etymology of the words 'morris' and 'morisco') that the dance came to England from Spain, but ultimately derived from the Moors. Contemporary supporters of the Pyrrhic origin explicitly rejected reasoning based on names and etymology, as in Edward Phillips's dictionary:

Morisco, (Span.) a moor, also a kind of Dance which seemeth to be the same as that which the Greeks call Pyrrhica, we vulgarly call it the Morris Dance, as it were the Moorish Dance.

(Phillips 1658a, sig. Cc4)

Phillips implies here that the name is part of the popular debasement of the classical form, thus prefiguring later intellectual discussions of popular entertainments as corruptions of earlier elite forms. Nonetheless, the notion of a Moorish genesis was attractive, imputing an exotic quality to the dance. The first attempt to expound the Spanish/Moorish origins appears in Christopher Wase's commentary on his transla- tion of *Grati Falisci Cynegeticon*:

Those of the East us'd to wear bells about their legs in ornament: thus the Jews, Isa. 3.16.18. And the leaping about with bells ty'd on the legs after an Hoboy, and a Horse, is not origin- ally an European frolique, though brought amongst us by Spaine, but the name imports to dance Alla Moresca.

(Wase 1654, 76)

The hypothesis that the dance came to England from Morocco via Spain became a mainstay of dictionaries and commentaries from the mid-seventeenth century on- wards, and represents an attempt to apply scientific reasoning to cultural data. The speculation of origins in the Greek pyrrhic, by contrast, was no more than armchair reflection with little or no data to support it. First, there are no primary sources for descriptions of the classical pyrrhic, so there is no way to determine whether sev- enteenth-century morris was like it or not. Second, there is no clear mechanism by which a classical Greek dance, with semimythic origins of its own, travelled to and became rooted in rural England.

The reasoning behind the Spanish/Moorish hypothesis is largely implicit in the sources and is flawed in several respects. But it represents a step forward in historical theorizing. The argument may be summarized in a series of steps:

- Cognate forms of the word 'morris' exist in most European languages.
- All the cognates appear to mean 'Moorish.'
- Dances using these cognate names must, therefore, be Moorish in origin (espe- cially since in some languages cognates are construed in phrases such as *danza alla moresca*, or *dance à la moresque*, meaning 'dance in the style of Moors').
- Moorish customs in general – moresque work, Moorish architecture, etc. – came to Europe via Spain during the Moorish occupation.
- Morris/Moorish dances are, therefore, likely to have come to Europe via Spain.

To some extent the inference that the morris was Moorish in origin carried the implication that it was wild and exotic (certainly a suitable origin and prototype for rustic dances), but the theory also conveniently fit an aesthetic impulse of musicians and dancing masters in the mid-seventeenth century to expropriate non-Western forms or, at least, to incorporate into their inventions their notion of what these forms should be like. The 'morisco' was a conventional exotic piece for a number of Caroline dancing masters. There are, for example, five moriscoes in the 1670 edition of John Playford's violin tutorial and compendium, *Apollo's Banquet* (Playford 1670).

The Moorish origins theory is thus in direct contrast to the pyrrhic theory. The latter argues that the morris originated in an elite form that over time was debased and corrupted until it became the contemporary rural tradition, whereas the former proposes that contemporary 'primitive' dances must have a primitive origin. Thus, speculations on the origin of the dance in particular regions or eras veil more complex social notions of the development of traditional customs – notions which continued in relatively similar form into the twentieth century.

It is interesting to note that while simplistic theories of origin held sway in the seventeenth and eighteenth centuries (that is, imputing a single point and place of origin), there was at least one attempt to introduce the possibility of syncretism and evolutionary development, albeit in slightly scoffing manner. Francis Peck commenting on Milton's masque *Comus*, in which there is a metaphorical allusion to morris, repeats the Spanish/Moorish theory with a slight twist:

> The *morris* or *moorish* dance was first brought into *England*, as I take it, in *Edward* III. time, when *John* of *Gaunt* returned from Spain, where he had been to assist his father-in-law, *Peter* K. of *Castile*, against *Henry* the bastard. This dance was usually performed *abroad* by an *equal* number of young men, who danced in their shirts with ribands & little bells about their legs. But *here* in *England* they always have an *odd* person besides, being a boy dressed in a girl's habit, whom they called *Maid Marian* ... I cannot forbear observing on the boy dressed in girl's cloaths introduced into this dance, that tho' the young folks of *England* had, by this *Spanish* expedition, got a new diversion, yet they could not forbear dashing it with their old favorit one of *Maid Marian*.   (Peck 1740, 135–6)

This analysis suffers from a lack of primary data to support it (John of Gaunt was in Spain in the mid-fourteenth century, yet morris dancing does not show up in the English records until the second half of the fifteenth), but it does attempt to address some critical questions in the diffusionist model of dance development. First, he proposes an answer to how and when the dance got from Spain to England – previous theorists had simply assumed that it had, based on the indirect evidence at their disposal. But Peck envisages English and Spanish troops meeting in friendly circumstances and exchanging fads and fashions (as they are generally wont to do). Furthermore, he imagines a direct trade of peasant customs (including morris dance) between men of the agricultural working classes, who formed the backbone of medieval armies. Thus he initiated the general search for ways and means for the 'folk' to act as vehicles for the transmission of 'folk arts' across Europe, working on the assumption that such arts always existed in a particular socioeconomic plane and tended to diffuse laterally between similar classes in different regions, rather than vertically between different classes. Second, Peck provides a solution to the question of how a Spanish import could involve such an 'obviously' English character as Maid Marian. The answer, which seems to have eluded his predecessors (and was ruled out of court by many later scholars), was syncretism – even if his statements are hopelessly anachronistic and his tone towards English practitioners condescending.

Peck was responding to trends in antiquarianism that appeared in rudimentary form in the eighteenth century – to be greatly refined and elaborated in the nineteenth – that allowed for traditional forms to change and develop as they diffused and migrated across cultures. Thus Francis Douce in his classic essay, 'A Dissertation on the Ancient Morris Dance' (Douce 1807), proposes that the morris was not carried directly from Spain to England (because there is a lack of data to support this hypothesis) and, instead, proposes a general diffusionist model whereby the dance travelled slowly up through France and the Low Countries, arriving in England in the mid-fifteenth century (when primary sources begin to show up). Syncretism and evolution are inevitable associates of the process of diffusion:

The genuine Moorish or Morisco dance was, no doubt, very different from the European *morris*; but there is scarcely an instance in which a fashion or amusement that has been borrowed from a distant region has not in its progress through other countries undergone such alterations as have much obscured its origin.   (Douce 1807, 433)

Douce thus brings us into the nineteenth century where the investigation of the origins and evolution of forms spanned almost all academic disciplines. Douce's arguments might have been accepted by late-nineteenth- and early-twentieth-century scholars because of their evolutionary flavour – but many branches of folklore, for political reasons, bucked the academic trend of the times and became antievolutionary and antidiffusionist.

Indeed, in the late-nineteenth century folklorists had the choice of whether to treat folk materials in an evolutionary framework or not, and they mostly chose not to. The clue to why is given by the name that folk materials had had before the coinage of the term 'folk-lore,' that is, 'popular antiquities.' Folk practices, under the rubric popular antiquities, had long been treated by collectors and scholars of culture as something like cultural atavisms – behaviours that had had a specific meaning and purpose in bygone eras but which had largely been forgotten.

This point of view had been popular in anthropology in the nineteenth century spawning some of the classics of the era, such as *The Golden Bough* by James George Frazer and *Primitive Culture* by E.B. Tylor. Tylor proposed a general evolutionary theory of culture, but suggested that running counter to cultural development was a conservative force that ensured the survival of a great many 'primitive' customs into later evolutionary stages. This became known as the 'doctrine of survivals' and was his way of explaining seemingly irrational cultural practices such as modern superstitions. They appear irrational only because their primitive origins are lost to us, and their status as 'survivals' from more archaic cultures has been forgotten.

Frazer's analysis of the origins of morris is a typical example of the doctrine of survivals in practice:

It is ... worth observing that in some places the dancers of Plough Monday, who attended the plough in its peregrinations through the streets and fields, are described as morris-dancers. If the description is correct, it implies that they had bells attached to their costume ... for the chief characteristic of the morris-dance is that the performers wear bells fastened to their legs which jingle at every step. We may suppose that if the men who ran and capered beside the plough on Plough Monday really wore bells, the original intention of this appendage to their costume was either to dispel the demons who might hinder the growth of the corn, or to waken the spirits of vegetation from their long winter sleep.

(Frazer 1907–15, 9: 250–1)

Although anthropology subsequently rejected Tylor's and Frazer's theories, folk-lore (especially in Britain), continued to embrace them, thereby retaining the general notion of folk behaviour as atavistic. Cecil Sharp, the great twentieth-century collector and revivalist of morris dances, whose theories of origin still reverberate throughout popular literature, is entirely Frazerian in tone:

There is reason to believe that the Mumming-play and the Sword-dance are no more than survivals of different aspects of the same primitive rite; and the fact that both are often called by the country people 'Morris-dances' is, perhaps, evidence that the tradition of this common origin still lingers in the minds of the country people. Little more than a cursory examination is needed to see that the same central idea permeates all three of them. Originally expressions of religious belief, in which the idea was as essential as the form, they have passed by various stages and along devious paths into the inspiriting dances and quaint dramas with which we are now familiar.

(Sharp 1912–24, 1:13)

The reasons why folklore took an essentially nonevolutionary, nondiffusionist stance are complex; the sociopolitical climate in which the discipline was founded requires exploring. This will also help to explain why morris dance scholarship took the peculiar path that it did (and also how a great many misunderstandings about

English traditional customs have come to be so deeply embedded in popular consciousness).[3]

The nineteenth-century search for origins in numerous disciplines was part of
the scientizing of social and behavioural science. Within this context it is possible
to tease out two, not entirely mutually exclusive, models. The first, as typified by
stories in the biblical book of Genesis, takes the principle of 'origin-as-essence' as
fundamental. Take the following story from Genesis concerning Jacob's change of
name to Israel:

> And Jacob was left alone; and there wrestled a man with him until the breaking of the
> day.
> And when he saw that he prevailed not against him, he touched the hollow of his thigh;
> and the hollow of Jacob's thigh was out of joint, as he wrestled with him.
> And he said, Let me go, for the day breaketh. And he said, I will not let thee go, except
> thou bless me.
> And he said unto him, What is thy name? And he said, Jacob.
> And he said, Thy name shall be called no more Jacob, but Israel: for as a prince hast thou
> power with God and with men, and hast prevailed.
> And Jacob asked him, and said, Tell me, I pray thee, thy name. And he said, Wherefore
> is it that thou dost ask after my name? And he blessed him there.
> And Jacob called the name of the place Peniel: for I have seen God face to face, and my
> life is preserved.
> And as he passed over Penuel the sun rose upon him, and he halted upon his thigh.
> Therefore the children of Israel eat not of the sinew which shrank, which is upon the hollow
> of the thigh, unto this day: because he touched the hollow of Jacob's thigh in the sinew
> that shrank.   (Genesis 32:24–32, KJV)

The crux of this story lies in the fact that the Hebrew word 'Israel' can be read as
meaning something roughly equivalent to 'the man who will prevail with God.'
The putative origin of the name, embedded in this narrative, thus has profound
meaning for descendants of Jacob/Israel (father of the twelve men who gave their
names to the twelve tribes), because their eponymous ancestor has bequeathed them
a racial geist – they are the people who can claim a special personal relationship
with God (he prevailed in a personal way, so they will *always* prevail with Him) –
and this fact is rooted in not only their personal identity, which can seem somewhat abstract, but also in a sacred place name, in a dietary practice, and in a national
name tied to a specific parcel of land.

Following this kind of analysis, the world – culture, history, ritual, everything –
is a giant intelligible *pattern* created as the intersections of the traces of a series of

significant events. Although these events took place in time, such a perspective tends to be synchronic, or outside the framework of time (at least from a contemporary perspective). That is, all significant events which laid down the pattern that we now know are in the past and so can be viewed as a whole in relation to one another. These events have a teleological purpose (i.e., laying down the pattern) and we see the meaning of the pattern because we can now see the whole.

According to this model the pattern, and the past that it represents, are immortal and all powerful, so that working within such a system – that is, accepting such premises – the past can never be disempowered – if anything, its power increases with time. The language of the Christian Bible, for example, is of fulfilment of the past or of revelation of the meaning of events in the past. The past does not *change*, in the sense of being *diminished* or made irrelevant by later actions; it comes to *fruition*. The words of the prophets were fulfiled in Jesus, and thus their place, and his, in the pattern were revealed. Their meaning may appear to change to us – what looked like a prophecy limited in time and space to a certain people at a certain time, for example, became applicable to the salvation of all humankind – but that is because our view of the overall pattern was incorrect or incomplete, not that the prophecy itself was subject to change.

The second model, typified by evolutionary biology, does not treat origin as essence, or as a static fact at all, but as a small component in a diachronic *process*, which is *nonteleological*. The main emphasis of this approach is change over time, and is concerned primarily with the mechanisms of change. Within this model, origin points may be fluid, and may rise and fall in significance as current interests change. So, for example, in *Descent of Man* Darwin's endeavour was to show – mainly via comparative anatomy – that *homo sapiens* shared an origin point with primates, but more recent investigations (spurred by Darwin's original work) have continued to change and augment Darwin's notions of what this origin point was. Contemporary physical anthropology suggests that there are few, if any, monolithic origin points or events, but rather identifies nodal points in a general evolutionary process. *Australopithecus africanus* and *homo erectus* may be ancestral to *homo sapiens* (i.e., in some sense origin points), but the issues of fundamental intellectual interest in physical anthropology are the process of evolution from one morphological type to another, how and when the transformations occurred, and so on. Did *homo erectus* evolve into *homo sapiens* at one place at one time and then radiate out globally, or did multiple analogous transformations occur on different continents at roughly the same time? Different methodologies – comparative DNA studies versus comparative fossil studies, for example – yield different kinds of results, and often different nodal points in the general process.

Furthermore, an evolutionary model allows for the transformation of the meanings of origin points or for their becoming irrelevant as the systems that they are part of change. An example from etymology illustrates the point. The word 'moot' has completely *reversed* meanings from its original use. The word is derived from Anglo-Saxon and is a generic term for legislative bodies, that is, groups who debate matters of profound significance to the community. Common current American usage, as in 'moot point,' is that 'moot' means an issue that could be debated but over which there is little point in discussion because the matter has no practical value. This is a complete reversal of meaning from the origin point, probably via the words 'moot' and 'moot court' – used first at Gray's Inn and then at American universities to signify mock legal discussions for educational purposes, that is, legal discussions with no direct practical application beyond practice and instruction.

In this case, the origins in the past have been changed or disempowered by current usage, and no pleading of origins will change present practice (although some pedants seem endlessly willing to try). The power of the origin point has been absorbed in the process of the evolution of meanings. Such origin points, therefore, are useless as timeless sources of meaningful patterns. At best they are indices of the flow of processes.

The evolutionary model thus stresses process and change over time. An 'origin' point (of a species, ritual, word, and so on) is only of significance inasmuch as it is a marker for the flow of process, and the meanings of origins can change as present circumstances change, or as new methods are brought to bear on the analysis of process.[4]

One might expect that late-nineteenth-century folklore would have been inclined towards the evolutionary model, given the boost in that direction the discipline was given by the Grimms, whose work in linguistics and folklore was entirely evolutionary in perspective (see especially Grimm 1811, 1822–37, and Grimm and Grimm 1812–15). Certainly a few practitioners appear to have been moving in that direction – or a simulacrum thereof. But analysis of morris (and other dances) and ultimately much of general folklore tended to follow the Genesis model, perhaps for sociopolitical reasons. If, for example, Sharp's personal motive as a Fabian socialist in reviving the near extinct traditional dances of England was to raise the esteem of the English peasant in the eyes of the middle class (as seems likely), then the Genesis model would have suited his purposes best because it empowered the past to enchant and enrich the present. The English peasant could be made to be the *fulfilment* and bearer of a glorious past.

The point can be best understood by examining part of a description of a collecting session by Cecil Sharp with the Rolfe brothers in Bucknell, Oxfordshire. The narrative is presented by E.V. Lucas in *London Lavender*:

[Cecil Sharp] in his search for primitive English music had tidings of two old Morris dancers in an Oxfordshire village, survivals from the past when the whole of that country fostered the art, and he took me to see them. Never have I spent a more curious evening.

We left the train at Bicester late on a golden afternoon, and were driven to a little hamlet a few miles distant where the old fellows lived. They were brothers: one a widower of seventy, still lissom, and the other a bachelor of sixty-seven, bent and stiff...

Together, or alone, they went through several of the old favourites – 'Shepherd's Hey,' 'Maid of the Mill,' 'Old Mother Oxford,' 'Step Back,' 'Lumps of Plum-pudding,' 'Green Garters' – and it was strange to sit in that little, flagged Oxfordshire kitchen, with its low ceiling and smoky walls, and watch these simple movements and hear those old tunes. For the Morris dance is like nothing else. It is as different from the old English dance as that is different from the steps of the *corps de ballet*. It is the simplest thing there is, the most naive. Or, if you are in that mood, it is the most stupid; jigging rather than dancing, and very monotonous. But after a little while it begins to cast its spell, in which monotony plays no small part, and one comes in time to hope that nothing will ever happen to interrupt it and force one back into real life again.

The feeling became positively uncanny when old Jack, the bent one, jigging alone, with his eyes fixed on the musician, but seeing nothing nearer than 1870, began to touch his body here and there in the course of the movements of the dance, every touch having a profound mystical meaning, of which he knew nothing, that probably dated from remotest times, when these very steps were part of a religious or ecstatic celebration of fecundity. Odd sight for a party of twentieth century dilettanti in an Oxfordshire kitchen. (Lucas 1912, 220–2)

Lucas's immediate impression of the dance, as would have been typical of the gentry of his day, is that it is (like other peasant customs) crude and debased. Many of his descriptions are openly patronizing: the dance is 'stupid,' 'naive,' 'very monotonous.' But through generous application of the Genesis model (the dances are the trace of a fabulous prehistoric fertility ritual) – coming directly from Sharp – he is forced to reappraise his initial view. Under that aegis the dance is mesmeric, profoundly mystical, uncanny, and unreal; its ritual qualities show through the un-promising surrounds. Thus the same physical forms are able to provide both (seem-ingly contradictory) interpretations by completely changing the frame of reference of the onlooker.

To apply the evolutionary model to the dance would have been supremely danger-ous for Sharp's overall agenda, and on the occasions when he applied it himself, he did so to marginalize dancers who he, himself, thought had a debased attitude to morris. The arguments involved are complex and require considerable knowledge of the relationships between Sharp and his key informants (as well as between Sharp and other teachers such as Neal); but they can be simplified for present purposes. Most nineteenth-century 'dilettanti' in the Lucas mould could not help but see peasant dances as crude and primitive, but the question is: what could they be made to see beyond the perceived crudity? Applying the evolutionary model is of little help; it simply confirms the dilettanti in their opinion that what they are seeing bears little relation – physical or spiritual – to anything of value in the past. That is, even if they were told that the dances had an origin point in primitive ritual, they could argue that in the hands of crude peasants the dances had evolved into grotesqueries barely worthy of their ancestors. The Genesis model, on the other hand, does not allow this counter.

By applying the Genesis model the worst that the dilettante can say is that the dance *appears* debased because of the context in which it is presented. But strip away these superficialities and the original shines through. The origin point still controls the presentation and meaning of the dance, even though the practitioners are ignorant of it. Lucas makes this latter point clear farther on in the narrative:

The brothers described, each fortifying the other and helped by the promptings and leading questions of the Director, the ritual of the Morris as they remembered it. A lamb would be led around by a shepherd, and behind this lamb they danced. At night the lamb was killed and the joints distributed. Most was eaten, but portions were buried in the fields. Why the old men had no notion; they had never heard. But the Director knew, although he did not explain.   (Lucas 1912, 223)

In this sense, the Genesis model seems to be empowering the collector – and onlooker – as well (he is the bearer of arcane knowledge to rival the dancers').

Sharp had harsh words for those dancers (and teachers) who thought that they could transform the dances in whatever fashion they saw fit, as if they were the dances' owners. Using an evolutionary model one could quite easily justify the dancers' attitude here: things evolve to meet present needs. But using the Genesis model, we see that such action is heresy; the dances have an autonomous nature that should not be tampered with. Sharp's feud with the social activist and dance teacher Mary Neal on exactly this issue is discussed below. In addition to battling with other dance teachers he also vilified dancers who accepted evolutionary principles. Chief villains in this respect were D'Arcy Ferris of Bidford on Avon and Sam Bennett of Ilmington. Both were showmen (of very different backgrounds) intent on creating a money-making spectacle, and had no qualms about manipulating morris events to this end. Ferris was a semiprofessional pageant master who revived the Bidford morris and used it as a component in larger events around 1886–7 (see Judge 1984 for details). The venture was successful enough to spark revivals in neighbouring towns, including Ilmington (nine miles distant). But Ferris made no bones about inventing dances – such as Bluff King Hal to the old tune Stanes morris – to suit his purposes and Bennett, who could be considered a kind of rustic protégé of Ferris (as well as an associate of Neal's), did the same in Ilmington.

Sharp, while still a tenderfoot collector, notated the Ferris and Bennett dances and even included some of them in the first edition of *The Morris Book* (Sharp and MacIlwaine 1907, 57, 71–5). But these were the days when he was flirting with a kind of evolutionary model for morris (with Morocco as the origin point). As soon as he had settled on the Genesis model of ancient pagan origins reaching out across the centuries, he expunged all these 'heretical' materials. Even by 1910 he was writing in dogmatic tones that suggested the fixed, ritualized character of the dance (to which only he held the key of interpretation):

... if the spirit of the dance is to be caught and its traditional character accurately reproduced, our instructions must be scrupulously followed and, whenever possible supplemented by the explanations of a qualified teacher. On this point we feel it necessary once more to offer a word of advice and warning, for we have seen again and again how easily the Morris may degenerate into a disorderly romp. Slovenly dancing of this sort can only create a false and mischievous impression of the aesthetic nature of the Morris dance, and thereby retard the progress of the movement in which we are so deeply interested.

Now, to dance the Morris ungracefully is to destroy it ... [T]he impression left on the minds of those who, like ourselves, have constantly seen the dance performed in country places, is one first of beauty, solemnity and high restraint, then of vigour.

(Sharp and MacIlwaine 1910, 8)

Any attempt at fostering natural evolution was thus anathema to Sharp, but one also sees here another reason why the Genesis model appealed. The ritual past of the dance, according to Sharp, is manifest in its 'ritual' present. The dance is not any old entertaining romp, but a serious endeavour, not to be lightly copied or profaned. The dance is the kernel of a present-day aesthetic spirituality now domiciled only in peasant villages, but which was once the birthright of all English people. If it can be shown that the dances (and their spirit) are the invention via evolutionary process of these same peasants, then Sharp's romantic argument falls apart.

Therefore, what the Genesis model did, perhaps not entirely wittingly, was make folklore fixated on origins and the past. It grounded present practice in the past, and thus scholars sought out the past as a way of validating and comprehending the present. The model also inspired in collectors such as Sharp a quasi-religious fervour in recording and preserving dances accurately – because, like rituals, they must be performed correctly to be efficacious.

For Sharp this fixation meant seeking out older practitioners in places where he had his doubts about contemporary dancers. Therefore, at Ilmington he eventually shunned Bennett in favour of older men, from whom he reconstructed what he took to be normative and 'purer' dance practices of *c* 1867 – the principle being, the further back one seeks, the less corrupted dances are likely to be by modern evolutionary influences. One could, in other words, attempt a method of triangulation from the present to the past, to distil out the pure form that was inherent in all 'true' morris. Sharp was not able to pursue this idea very far because for many village traditions he had but one or two aged dancers to rely on for all his information, and in others, where he might have compared the styles of older and younger dancers (at Bampton and Headington Quarry, for example), he was satisfied that his key informants were 'true' morris men, and so looked no further afield.

One of the main weaknesses of the Genesis model is that you can use it to support just about any political view that you favor. In the main this is because in folklore this model tended to rely on unsupported assertions and circular reasoning. The veiled reasoning is somewhat as follows:

- If (past) origin leads to (present) essence, then present essence can indicate past origin.
- Present essence of morris is ritualistic.
- Therefore, morris originates in primitive ritual.

But the middle point is a subjective, highly selective opinion. More accurately Sharp was saying that the 'true' morris dancer danced ritualistically. Others, such as Bennett, he discounted as not true to the essence. But what if we accepted Bennett and his peers as the true exemplars and discounted the others? Then we could construct a different syllogism:

- If (past) origin leads to (present) essence, then present essence can indicate past origin.
- Present essence of morris is a merry romp.
- Therefore, morris originates in secular fun and games.

The whole issue hinges on the analyst's perception of the nature of the dance in present times. To go beyond this kind of reasoning requires some knowledge of the earliest forms of the dance so that the analyst need not use present essence to hypothesize past form. Sharp did not possess such knowledge. The best he had were the conjectures of the Puritans; these speculations were no better than his because they were based on the same reasoning, viz., the dance is ungodly now, therefore it must originate in ungodly (pagan) ritual.

It is also important to remember that Sharp's arguments were of much more than academic interest to him. For a dance collector, teacher, and social activist they had a clear practical application. In fact Sharp's passionate concern for the 'purity' of performance of morris (as defined by its origins) led him into a celebrated conflict with a contemporary morris dance teacher and activist, Mary Neal, who also took an 'origin equals essence' point of view, but used it in absolute opposition to Sharp's position. Investigation of their quarrel illuminates many more of the problems with the 'origin equals essence' model.

In the introduction to the second part of *The Morris Book* Sharp wrote:

In our Morris Book, Part I., we said in describing the Morris that it was '... essentially a manifestation of vigour rather than of grace.' This, and other similar remarks of ours in the description of the dance, while they are strictly correct have in some instances been given a too-liberal interpretation. Here and there we have noticed in the would-be Morris-dancer a tendency to be over-strenuous, to adopt, upon occasion, even a hoydenish manner of execution. These are utterly alien to the true spirit of the dance; for although it is characterized by forcefulness, strength, and even a certain abandonment, it is at the same time and always an exposition of high spirits under perfect control. When he is dancing, the true Morris-man is serious of countenance, yet gay of heart; vigorous, yet restrained; a strong man rejoicing in his strength, yet graceful, controlled, and perfectly dignified withal.

(Sharp and MacIlwaine 1909, 6)

This was a direct attack on Neal, appealing to an essence of the dance (derived from its ritual origins) that defines the 'true spirit' of the dance and the 'true Morris-man.' What Sharp is trying to convey here is his sense of the authentic spirit of the true Englishman, that is, strong, gay, energetic, light-hearted, but held in control by the majesty of the morris tradition; and it is that tension between the dancers' (wilder) nature and the (domesticating) essence of the dance form (created by its origins) that manifests itself in the form that a contemporary audience sees.

Mary Neal had approached Sharp in 1905 because she ran a recreational association for young London seamstresses, the Espérance club, and was interested in finding music and dance for them to perform for their amusement that was beyond the normal parlor fare of the time. Sharp introduced her to some traditional dancers who agreed to teach the dances to the club members, and it was the resultant 'hoydenish' spectacle that he objected to. But Neal responded in equally vigorous terms:

... if folk music is the spontaneous expression of a people's life, we of our generation too have a contribution to make to it. And it is this contribution which I believe these Espérance instructors have given to the movement for the revival of folk music which is going on to-day.

There must be nothing in this revival which cannot be done by the average boy and girl; it must be kept, in the true sense of the word, a 'vulgar' movement, understood of the common people.

I am only afraid of the hindering touch of the pedant, of the professional dance and music teacher. The movement must be kept clear of all pedantry and of everything *précieux*. These dances must from time to time be learnt direct from the peasant, and be handed on by the simple-minded, the musically unlettered, the young and the happy.   (Neal 1910, 5)

She approached the dance from the point of view that origin is essence also but chose to see the 'origin' not in surmised, far-off, pagan ritual, but in traditional peasant custom of the more recent past. Its essence, therefore, was 'vulgar,' and its true spirit could be evoked by anyone whose class affinity was also vulgar. More simply put all folk traditions were by origin, and by definition, the property of the working class to do with as they pleased.

Another weakness of the Genesis model therefore concerns what the theorist takes as the true origin point of the dance. Both Sharp and Neal were arguing from their contemporary needs and motivations, and chose suitable origin points to support their positions. Sharp was attempting to ennoble the peasant in popular consciousness while Neal was straightforwardly enriching the lives of working-class women. Neither teacher possessed or used primary historical data to support their conjectural origin points.

Other agenda of early-twentieth-century folklorists associated with assertions about the origins of the morris and related to the notion of origin as essence were strictly nationalist. Sharp's insistence on the pagan origins of the morris basically followed a line of argument laid out by E.K. Chambers in *The Mediaeval Stage* (Chambers 1903), who in turn was doing no more than following the doctrine of survivals espoused by Tylor and Frazer. For Sharp one of the practical implications of Chambers's theory of ritual pagan origins was that English folk music and dance were more thoroughly English in essence than any other more recent performance forms. That is, long before the invasions of Normans, or Danes, or Romans the true Brit was engaged in the business of morris dancing as part of ritual central to communal life. Traces of this fact remain in the cultural memory of every true Englishman as implied in the following memoir by Mary Neal of the halcyon days before her split with Sharp:

I went to see Mr. Cecil Sharp to ask his advice as to whether [folk] songs would be suitable for a Working Girls' Club. In ten minutes we were deep in the subject of Folk Song, and I was told that I would be surprised at the way in which English boys and girls would understand and appreciate their own Folk music. 'They will learn it,' said Mr. Sharp, 'by a sort of spiritual sixth sense.'

(Cited in Fox Strangeways and Karpeles 1955, 69)

Elite and popular music and dance of more recent times are either foreign imports or the result of syncretic influences, but folk traditions are pure in their national character and can therefore be learned instinctively by those with the necessary national/genetic credentials. Thus was justified the many movements across Europe to link folk performance with nationalist endeavours and ambitions. Any attempt to argue or assert that folk traditions themselves were subject to the same syncretic forces as any other kind of aesthetic form (or that a particular form derived ultimately from another nation) would have demolished the emotional appeal of folk traditions to nationalists, and so were vigorously denied; hence Sharp's quick retreat from the Moorish hypothesis when he realized what it entailed.

Likewise Violet Alford, a disciple of Sharp, speaks of syncretic 'foreign' influences on pure ritual folk traditions as 'taints' to be removed if possible (Alford 1962). Sharp's school was following a general aspiration, common throughout Europe at the time (and still a powerful force), of giving a people its own unique form of expression – an aspiration made especially sociopolitically potent by such cataclysmic events as the collapse of the Austro-Hungarian Empire and the outbreak of the Great War.

For all the preceding reasons the Genesis model has had a strong emotional appeal among the general public. But barely a decade after Sharp's death, scholars had little choice but to explore alternative theories because of the profound weaknesses of the Genesis model. Evolutionary and diffusionist thinking could be held back no longer. In ballad and tale scholarship the idea developed that one could combine knowledge of present forms with basic theory of evolution and diffusion to generate hypotheses concerning originating archetypes. This thinking spawned a generation of analysis using the so-called Finnish, or historic/geographic, method (see Krohn 1926).

The method is based on a theory of the spatial diffusion of cultural innovations that once had a widespread vogue, but is now rather more limited in its applications (see Hägerstrand 1967 for classic examples). The basic idea is that an innovation (a new song or tale or dance) has a single point of origin, and as the form is transmitted from person to person, examples of the form will be found further and further away from this point of origin. All variables being equal, the forms would ripple out in a series of concentric rings all centred on the point of origin. But various factors – geographic or cultural barriers, main lines of communication, complex patterns of interregion marriage or commerce, and so forth – cause lines of diffusion to be rather more irregular. Nonetheless, in principle, these factors can be controlled so that certain normative patterns of diffusion should recur.

The historic/geographic school started from the premise that new ballads, tales, and the like had diffused out from discrete origin points, so that it ought to be possible to plot the occurrences of individual examples in order to work back to the origin point and to the archetype that spawned the spatial diffusion pattern in the first place. In the process of experimentation they discovered that many forms could be classified into subtypes, and these subtypes were usually associated with local geographic regions. The method thereafter combined spatial plotting with typological sorting to produce patterns of diffusion.

Stith Thompson's analysis of the Native American 'Star Husband Tale' is a classic examplar of the method (Thompson 1953). For typological purposes Thompson reduced the variants of the tale to a series of motifs lettered A to N:

A. Number of women; B. Introductory action; C. Circumstances of introductory action; D. Method of ascent; E. Identity of husband; F. Distinctive qualities of husband; G. Birth of son; H. Tabu broken in upper world; I. Discovery of skyhole; J. Assistance in descent; K. Means of descent; L. Results of descent; M. Explanantory elements; N. Sequel.

(Thompson 1953, 420)

Each motif has a number of variants (K1, K2, K3, ...), each of which may have subvariants (K3a, K3b, K3c, ...) as well. Thus, each variant of the tale as a whole may be reduced to a sequence of motif variants and subvariants. Having divided all of the variants of the tales into strings of motif types Thompson then plotted the spatial distribution of each individual motif, looking in particular for widespread versus regionally confined variants (as well as examining the date of recording of each). It is a basic premise of the method that widespread (and older) variants are more likely to be archetypical, and regionally confined (and newer) variants to be evolutionary branches from the archetype. Thus, an archetype for each motif can be hypothesized, which when strung together with the archetypes of the other motifs produces a hypothesized archetypical (i.e., ur-type) whole tale. In the process regional groupings of variants of motifs may be noted producing prototypic subtypes, or evolutionary branches, of the tale.

In this way Thompson derived a taxonomy of seven categories of the whole tale. Thence he plotted these variants geographically, demonstrating that most of the categories are regionally distinct; this led him to develop hypotheses concerning lines of historical diffusion and evolution. For example, he notes that the variants found in the central Plains are close to the hypothesized archetype and show little variation among one another, whereas tales on the periphery of the zone of distribution – such as the northwest coast – are farther from the archetype and show a great deal of variation (as if multiple variants diffused there in different periods). Thus, he proposes the central plains as the origin point of the original tale.

In spite of relatively subjective methods of classification Thompson's basic typology seems to stand up to rigorous testing. For example, Andrew Abbott and I used a computer-based sequence matching algorithm and cluster techniques to examine the typology, and discovered that while we might argue about the placement of individual tales in categories, the overall classificatory scheme was sound, as was the general hypothesis of spatial diffusion (Forrest and Abbott 1990:165–7).

But even with the application of sophisticated techniques, the basic method suffers from a general inability to break free from a descriptive, pattern-based (i.e., Genesis model) modality. It can suggest lines of evolution by constructing categorical prototypes and indicating 'bridge' tales that link the various prototypes. But the best it can do is to indicate *that* evolution or diffusion have taken place; it cannot explain *how* or *why* they have taken place, because it proposes no mechanics (on the order of natural selection) of diffusion or evolution that explain variation and spatial configuration. As such, the method edges in the direction of an evolutionary model but is, nonetheless, primarily a classificatory framework (with spatial overtones) and not fundamentally process oriented.

Just how rooted in classificatory pattern this method is can be seen by reviewing the few, relatively rudimentary, attempts to use it in the analysis of morris and other traditional dance forms in England. Joseph Needham started the ball rolling with his 'Geographical Distribution of English Ceremonial Dance Traditions' (Needham 1936). His typology of dances is based on a choreographic equivalent of motifs, that is, dance elements such as number of dancers, basic costume, accoutrements, extra characters, and so forth. In plotting a variety of dance types, the most obvious discovery was that they were all regionally distinct, with virtually no overlap of forms (see figure 1).

The extreme regional clustering of forms suggested to Needham a cultural/historical explanation:

The zonation of the ceremonial dance traditions, seen as one looks at them on the map, is indeed striking. Chancing to look some years ago at an historical atlas, I was much impressed to find that the frontier between Danish Mercia and Saxon Mercia at the end of the ninth century traced a line remarkably like that separating the Morris from the Sword traditions. This frontier was settled at a variety of dates, but the two principal agreements were the Treaty of Wedmore (represented on the map by a dotted line) and the Peace of Alfred and Guthrum (represented on the map by a continuous line).   (Needham 1936, 23)

Thus, he proposes a historical/geographical spatial correlation which, in turn, suggests a Saxon origin for the English morris and a Scandinavian origin for the English hilt-and-point sword dance. This was something of a blow aimed at the nationalists, who wished to see all traditional dance as originating in early British pagan ritual (the sword dance being an older or more primitive form, and the morris a later).

Needham completes his theorizing by adding in another dance type, namely processionals – those that are essentially perambulations of streets or villages:

[I]t seems to me highly significant that the most primitive surviving Processionals are found in Celtic parts of the country, namely, Cornwall and N. Wales. In the east country there are absolutely no traces of Processionals. In the Morris country there are very strong processional

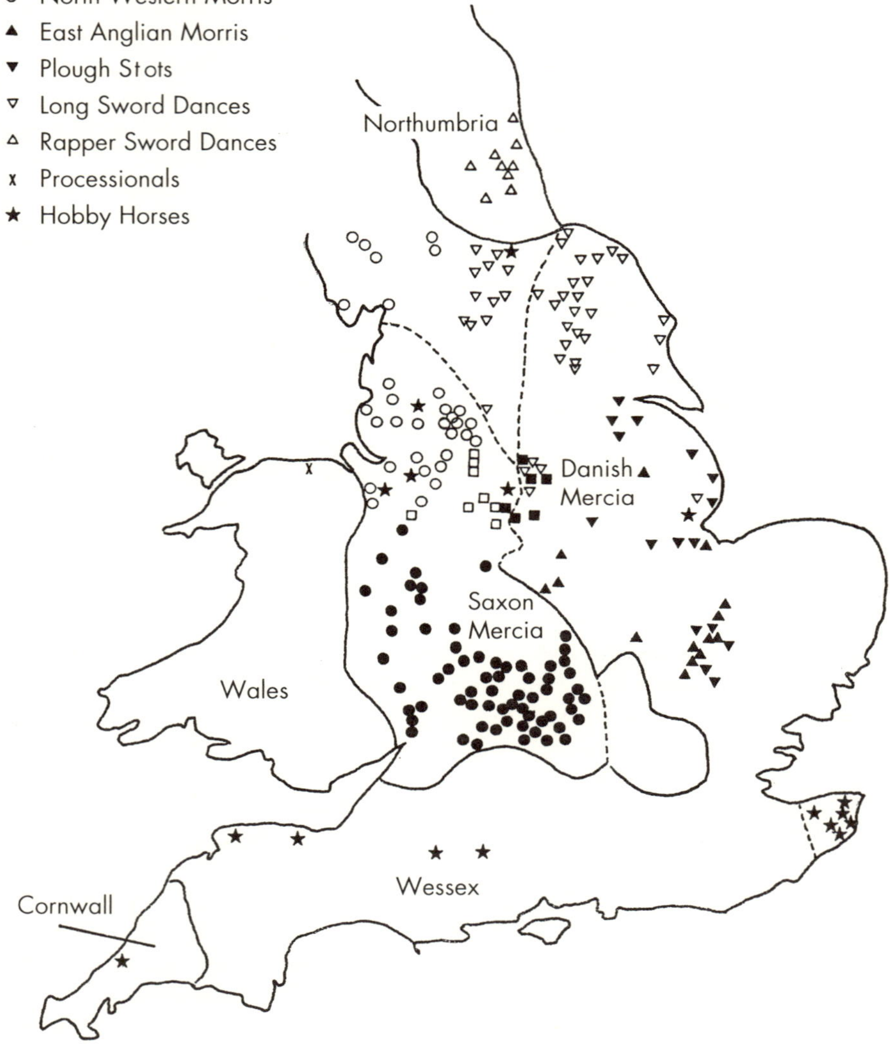

● Cotswold Morris
■ Derbyshire Morris
□ Well Dressing
○ North Western Morris
▲ East Anglian Morris
▼ Plough Stots
▽ Long Sword Dances
△ Rapper Sword Dances
x Processionals
★ Hobby Horses

Figure 1: Joseph Needham's map of the general distribution of morris events (Needham 1936)

elements, and the North-western Morris is essentially processional. Remembering that we are only speaking of England, then, we may arrive at the working hypothesis that the Processionals are in origin Romano-British or Celtic, and that the Morris is what the Saxons made of the earlier Processionals. The later coming of the Danes and Norwegians brought the Sword dance to our country.   (Needham 1936, 29)

Needham's method is fundamentally flawed in that his data are only from 1800 onwards – he excluded all earlier material – yet he used this historically late dataset to establish hypotheses concerning the ninth century AD, with an inexplicable gap of a thousand years in between. However, within the temporal limits that he set, some less chronologically improbable interpretations might be found. One might suggest reasons why in the nineteenth century certain dance types clustered in particular regions, which means correlating *nineteenth-century* sociopolitical and geographic factors with nineteenth-century dance data. This work has yet to be accomplished, although Needham's basic database was greatly expanded by a team working under the general direction of E.C. Cawte (Cawte et al. 1960) and by Michael Heaney and myself (Heaney and Forrest 1991).

Cawte's typology and regional studies are a considerable refinement on Needham's but cannot break out of the classificatory mode either. His analysis of the morris of the Welsh border counties (Cawte 1963), for example, involves a very precise typing of forms based on dance elements, coupled with geographic plotting that indicates a regional basis for the typology:

[T]hree areas may be distinguished as North, West, and East. The east group has both handkerchief and stick dances, though the figures are normally the same for both, while the north and west teams only had one dance, always with sticks. Singing during the dance is mainly a feature of the north and west teams.

In other respects the contrast is between north and the rest. The dancers often wore bells in the east and west, but never in the north ... The characteristic tune 'Not for Joe' was common in the north, but otherwise is only recorded from ... John Locke [of Herefordshire (in the west)], one of a gypsy family which was also well known in the Broseley district [i.e. in the north]. The Clown is an almost invariable member of the team in the east, commonly in the west, but only at Hodnet in the north ...   (Cawte 1963, 208)

Cawte suggests that there is something of clinal variation here (akin to conspecific variation in biology) with character gradients over two axes: north versus east/west, and east versus north/west. This direct analogy from evolutionary biology implies that morris in the Welsh borders has diffused and subsequently evolved locally (presumably because of local factors). And the idea for this analogy comes directly from Needham:

I cannot conclude this paper without drawing attention to the close logical resemblance between the problem of the ceremonial traditional dances and the problems of biology. These dances are, in effect, sociological organisms obeying their own curious laws of persistence, and we are faced with the necessity of classifying them into species and genera. Like living organisms, too, they have been subject to an evolutionary process ... (Needham 1936, 38)

So both Needham and Cawte are sensitive to the evolutionary model, yet the work of both remains largely a matter of classificatory schemes mapped spatially, which in some ways is a necessary precursor to a process orientation; Linnaeus et al. found the pattern of species that Darwin transformed into the process of evolution.

Although pattern and process (and analogue dichotomies such as synchronic/diachronic) are generally treated as polar opposites, it seems clear in the history of ideas that the two have regularly been interrelated in certain critical ways, the one tending to precede and predict the other. That is, the first item on the agenda has been to find order in a dataset (i.e., pattern) and the next has been to seek the cause of the order (i.e., process). Generally the second step is revolutionary (a paradigm shift in current Kuhnian terminology), because those seeking pattern have trouble reaching beyond what their typological vision allows them to see. Linnaeus, for example, was working on a Genesis model assumption that the pattern in species had been laid down by God, and so could not see the evolutionary implications of his work. But without the pattern laid out, Darwin would not have been able to take the next step to see the process inherent in the pattern.

There is a definite (though logically anachronistic) symbiosis at work here, because it is clear that the initial typological work has to somehow capture the essence of process even before the process is known, as, in a sense, the process is latent in the pattern. This may sound mysterious, but what it comes down to is that the taxons chosen for the initial typology, as well as the general ordering of the typology – although laid out for the purposes of evoking pattern – must be amenable to a process orientation. Thus the decision by Linnaeus to define species (the critical taxon) in terms of sexual reproduction and breeding populations meshed perfectly with the mechanics of natural selection and inheritance proposed by Darwin (even though evolutionary biology has subsequently considerably modified the details of the Linnaean scheme): evolution works at the species level via sexual reproduction.

What is needed in morris dance analysis (and by extension in folklore in general) is the revolutionary leap from pattern to process, but that leap can be nothing but an optimistic tumble into the void if the typology that is the springboard does not have process latent in it. This, I believe, is the problem with the kinds of typologies proposed by Needham, and Cawte et al. Such typologies are limited in two related respects. First, and of greatest importance, they are based entirely on superficial dance elements such as number of dancers, equipment, costumes, and the like and, as such, are much like pre-Linnaean typologies based on superficial (i.e., visual) likeness. Purely visual likeness is rarely a clue to process and may be more misleading than edifying (a moth whose camouflage colouring resembles tree fungus can hardly be said to be biologically related to that fungus). Second, their typologies, because of their general structure, cannot easily handle pre-1800 material. Needham excluded such data out of hand but Cawte, who tried to include it, ended up with a pre-ponderance of items in the pre-1800 period labelled 'doubtful' (i.e., unclassifiable), because there is not enough direct evidence in the primary record of visual form of the dances to make a firm typological decision about them. Therefore the spatial patterns of diffusion drawn by both scholars have almost no time depth to them, and mostly reflect an image of affairs in the nineteenth century only. Or, in more general terms, their typologies are so rooted in surface form, and in a narrow his-torical period, that it is impossible for them to provide clues to long-term process. And in the last analysis, this may be the fatal weakness of the historic/geographic method overall. Yet all is not lost.

The energy driving historic/geographic studies dissipated upon the rise of the text-in-context school, whose most damning critique of the method (and of diffu-sion studies in general) was that it wrested objects out of their cultural context and so robbed them of meaning. It is a basic premiss of the text-in-context school that cultural forms derive meaning from the ways in which they are structured into a particular culture, and every form has multilayered metaphoric and metonymic connections to other parts of the culture. Lauriston Sharp's classic paper 'Steel Axes for Stone Age Australians' (Sharp 1952), for example, demonstrates that for the Yir Yiront of northeastern Australia the traditional stone ax was a focal artefact in a wide arena of cultural affairs – ritual, trade, work, gender, power, law, language. When missionaries brought in steel axes to 'help' the Yir Yiront, their culture col-lapsed because this act was not a simple matter of replacing one object with another, as if cultural forms were interchangeable in modular fashion, but of undercutting the entire meaning system of the culture.

Thus, what looks like the same object can be structured into two different cul-tures in such completely different ways that the surface likeness is insignificant in comparison with the deeper symbolic differences. Imagine, for example, the myriad differences in meaning that a cow has to a Hindu, a Masai, and a Muslim. Or on a more specific level, consider the fact that in the variants of the 'Star Husband Tale' of both the Chehalis of the northwest Pacific coast and the Assiniboine of the northern plains contain the subvariant motif of the descent from the sky by the wife by means of a spider rope. Does this surface congruence indicate an underly-ing connection between the two cultures (which seems unlikely), or is it a product of diffusion that is interpreted quite differently in the two cultures (which seems more likely)? If the latter is the case, then the surface resemblance of the two tales at this point is of little or no cultural significance, and a typology based on this surface resemblance produces patterns of little analytic use.

There is, however, nothing intrinsically wrong with starting from a different point and building typologies that are sensitive to context. Michael Heaney and I began on this new track by working first with dance context, and building typologies and spatial plots that took context, rather than dance form, as central (Forrest and Heaney 1991). The results (figures 5–13) are very different from the kinds of images produced by Cawte and Needham. For one thing, they have adequate time depth, which adds considerable complexity to the picture; there are, for example, no neatly bounded regional zones of context type. Furthermore, the maps (and their typologies) are much more inclusive of primary data; there are many fewer 'doubtful' cases.

The next step is to use these contexts as a framework for understanding the total *dance event* – that is, dance form plus dance context – which is what the substantive body of the present work attempts to effect. The dance event as a single unit is a complex matrix of dance form (such as gestures, figures, costumes, and accoutrements) and contextual factors (such as the venue, rewards, patrons, audience, performers); in other words, it is a synthesis of the multiplex variables coded into the database that is at the heart of this work (see appendix A). It is this taxon (that is, *types* of dance events) that is the cultural equivalent of species for evolutionary purposes.

It is easy to see that a change in a single component of the context of a dance can change the character of the entire dance event, even though the choreographic form may be the same in both cases. Household servants dancing for their master, for example, is a very different dance event from visiting craftsmen from a far-off village performing for the same man. It is also easy to see how changes in one aspect of the dance context can cause coevolutionary changes in other aspects. Moving from dancing in the churchyard to dancing in village streets, for example, created a variety of changes (over time) throughout the dance event (see chapter 9).

What I attempt in this work is to build a set of images of types of dance events, piece by piece out of fragmentary data – much as the fossil hunter builds images of prehistoric species out of odds and ends of stones and bones (with a fair degree of extrapolation based on correlative data). The aim is to find pattern in types of dance events, beginning with context as a foundation and working out from there. Occasionally it is possible to glimpse evolutionary process at work, but the initial and primary goal is the taxonomic description of types of dance-in-context wholes.

This work is, therefore, divided into a number of sequential steps. First, it is necessary to devise a cogent list of dance contexts (chapter 2). Second, it is then possible to describe the dances within those contexts (chapters 3–11). Third, we may step back and see if any evolutionary process emerges from the described patterns, and try to extract the mechanism whereby this evolutionary development occurs (chapter 12).

Using this method the following will be abundantly clear:

- morris has no single origin point.
- morris is not and never has been a single or simple phenomenon.
- morris has evolved continuously throughout its documented history.
- morris is not especially 'folk' or rural.
- styles of morris from different contexts have had a constant evolutionary influence on one another.

2

The Contexts

With the advent of microcumputer technology and database management software Michael Heaney and I were able not only to create an electronic archive of morris dance sources, but also to index and access data from the files in sophisticated ways. The first product of the database and archive was the annotated bibliography *Annals of Early Morris* (Heaney and Forrest 1991). Those readers interested in the technical aspects of the construction of the database and archive, including the principles of inclusion and exclusion employed, should consult the original or appendix A.

In the indexing system for the early morris database there is a section labelled *Type of Venue* that contains the following subheadings:

- *court/noble's estate*: the dance took place at the royal court or on the property of a noble with sufficient prominence to be part of the royal sphere.
- *special group's premises*: the dance took place on the property of a secular organization (e.g., a guildhall).
- *church property*: the dance took place on property owned by the church.
- *urban streets*: the dance took place out of doors in a city or large borough.
- *public house*: the main site of dancing was in or around a public house.
- *out of doors in village*: the dance took place out of doors in a nucleated settlement smaller than a main township.
- *open country*: the dancing took place away from settlements.
- *private house*: dancing took place in or around a private house. This may include large rural estates, but not the houses of nobles covered under the first subheading.
- *unlocalized*: a dance took place but no locale can be attributed owing to imprecise description.

Not every source, by any means, indicates a venue. In some cases this is simply a

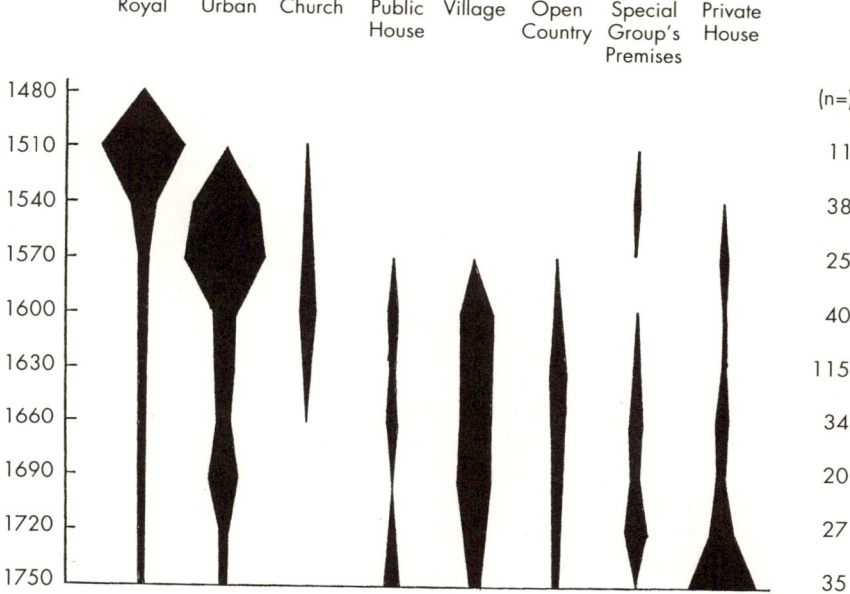

Figure 2: Seriation of venue

fault of the source, and in others a venue designation is not appropriate. But even given the fragmentary nature of much of the data, *type of venue* is one of the best represented variables overall. As such it is amenable to some kind of modest statistical treatment to determine trends.

To reduce the mass of information coded under variables in a fragmentary database of this kind, I devised a modification of a seriation technique invented by archaeologists to produce a graphic presentation of trends over time. The details of this method may be found in appendix A. Essentially the technique produces 'bars' (or, more accurately, 'curves') that vary in width over time. The wider the bar, the more frequent the occurrence of the variable at that point in time. The widest points in the bars are designated as 'peak' occurrences. The widths of the bars represent relative percentages and not absolute values, so that the sum of the widths of the bars is always the same at any point in time. A majority fashion thus is represented by a bar that is wider than the others at a particular point (see also Forrest 1985b and Forrest and Heaney 1991).[1]

Figure 2 shows a graphic seriation of *type of venue* for the period 1480–1750. The earliest years of the database, 1458–1479, have been excluded because there are only two references for this period, which is not a fair sample for graphing purposes. Thirty-year units were chosen as convenient, and because that span represents a generation. The statistics for the coding Ii (*unlocalized*) have also been excluded as irrelevant and likely only to produce 'noise' in the graphing process, because sources so coded are by their nature imprecise.

From the peaks in each curve a tentative chronology may be proffered. Royal venues peak very early (1480–1510); then Urban (1541–70); then Church (1571–1600); then Village, Public House, and Open Country are simultaneously strong with no clear peaks from 1601–90; then Special Group's Premises has a small peak (1691–1720); then Private House expands in importance to the end of the period (1721–50).

Looking at the overall shapes of the curves also helps in general interpretation. The curves for Royal, Urban, Village, and Private House venues all peak to a point where each is in the majority for one period of time, whereas those for Church, Public House, Open Country, and Special Premises may have significant peaks, but are always in the minority. Furthermore, the three venues separated out in the database as Public House, Village, and Open Country appear to run in parallel, which may indicate that in some sense the three, analytically separable, venues are part of a complex, that is, a rural morris tradition. The curves would then suggest a seriation of majority references from Royal to Urban to Rural to Private. It may also be noted that the periods of relative popularity of these venues are unequal in length. Royal/noble venues peak and decline within a thirty-year period around 1510; urban street venues show a somewhat longer period of importance, roughly from 1525 to 1585 with a slight renaissance around 1690; and village venues sustain their majority position for 120 years, from 1600 to 1720.

One 'venue,' the stage play, has not been included here because its place in any typology of venues is problematic and likely to confuse the chronology. A small number of publicly performed plays in the late sixteenth and early seventeenth centuries contain stage directions for the performance of a morris dance.[2] The main problem is that there are several contexts within which the analyst could choose to view these dances. One could, for example, consider a dance within a play to be a replica or emulation of a 'real' dance, in much the same way that a sword fight in a play is an imitation of the real thing. There is no question that some playwrights included morris dances to give an air of rusticity or to set a village scene. Treated in this way, a dance in a play is analogous to a description in a literary source; a play that showed a morris dance at a country fair in May would be evidence that morris was performed at *country fairs in May* even though the immediate context might be a play performed on a public stage in the middle of a city in September. Under this supposition *type of venue* would be recorded as 'village.'

A stage morris is not completely analogous to a stage sword fight, however. Professional actors may play the parts of villagers, but when they dance they are really dancing. They may parody or otherwise copy the kinesics of the people they are

TABLE 1

Stage plays containing a morris

Date	Number of Plays
1571–1600	5
1601–30	6
1631–60	2
1661–90	1

playing, so that what might be serious when performed in a village becomes comic on the stage. But the dance is still a dance, and can be legitimately called a stage morris dance. A dance in imitation of a dance is also a dance, whereas a fight in imitation of a fight is not a fight. This is a critical point because, of course, the diffusion and evolution of dance styles is based on imitation and replication. One cannot, a priori, rule out one form of imitation – stage morris – because it has 'literary' qualities. A morris seen in a play could stimulate changes in local dance customs, or even inspire a new tradition. Taken in this light a stage morris has the venue 'public theatre.'

The picture is further complicated by the fact that companies took their plays out into the provinces, and so it is not possible to give simple dates and places of performance for stage morris as for other types. Much of this information is lost or fragmentary, and what survives cannot be handled statistically in a straightforward manner without clouding the general picture. Let us suppose a town has a local morris team that performs once a year, and in a particular year a London company of players arrive with a play that includes a morris dance. They perform the play ten times and move on. Counting each performance separately would make stage morris the overwhelming norm (10 to 1) in the town for that year. Or one could count the visit of the players as a single performance even though it was repeated several times, and this might embody the feeling of the event better from a local point of view. Then again the play probably has only one dance in it, whereas the local dancers might perform thirty or more times on their one day out, tipping the balance in the other direction if each separate dance is to be counted.

Generally these problems point to the need to isolate the play data as likely to create noise in any statistical analysis, but not to exclude it entirely since it is clearly potentially relevant to issues of evolution and diffusion. Stage morris is to be dealt with at length in due course. For now it should be noted that there are only a few plays that have an actual dance in them (although there are many that *mention* a morris as part of the plot or as an aspect of the scene setting). These plays were written between 1589 and 1664, so that if they were tabulated according to the thirty-year periods on the graphic seriations strictly according to date of composition they would group as in table 1.

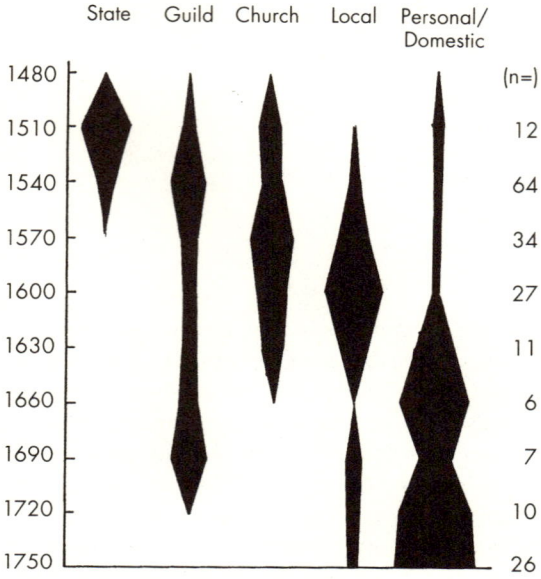

Figure 3: Seriation of financial support

If added to the graphic seriation these data would make a very slender curve peaking with *church property* at the beginning of the long 'rural' period. On this basis it might be argued that visits to the provinces by play companies may have had an effect on the spread of rural morris, but this whole question must be dealt with by reviewing the performance histories of the individual plays in conjunction with what data there are on the geographic spread of morris.

Thus, these data on plays do not alter the chronology of majority venues, but they could be added to the complete chronology to produce a sequence: Royal → Urban → (Church and Stage) → (Village, Public House, and Open Country) → Special Group's Premises → Private House. Such a linear sequence is at present nothing more than the result of an exploratory method and acts simply as a signpost on the twisted path to social meaning. Further graphic seriations and other methods of data reduction must be added to create additional milestones.

Figure 3 is based on financial records over the period, and indicates who was supporting morris dancers with hard cash in some way or another. Not all payments represented here are direct fees for services; some are payments for costumes and accoutrements, or general expenses incurred in performing. Nonetheless all may be grouped under the general rubric of 'financial support.' In many ways the curves match the trends discovered in the *type of venue* curves. State records (representing primarily royal expenditures) dominate early for a brief period (1481–1510), followed – in order – by the guilds (1511–40), the church (1541–70), local towns and villages (1571–1600), and finally, after a transition period with no clear peaks (1601–30), individuals and small households (1631–1750). The trend is again from the urban to the rural, and from the centralized/public to the localized/private.

The shapes and lengths of the *financial support* curves are significantly different from those for *type of venue*, however. Royal support peaks and declines in much the same way on both graphs, but financial support by the church, the guilds, and private individuals also show up from the earliest period graphed, even though they are not represented in any way in this era on the venue graphs. This discrepancy is a function of fragmentary data, and sounds a cautionary note. The financial sources on which the second graph is built indicate *that* a dance took place and *who* paid for it, but not *where* it happened. More complete sources would certainly extend one or more of the urban streets, church property, or private premises venue curves back to the earliest period to challenge the complete supremacy of the royal courts.

Such differences as the comparatively wide curve for church financing as against the thin curve for church venue also serve to indicate that the two graphs draw on two overlapping but different samples of sources from the entire database and, therefore, must be seen side by side as different views on the same historical reality, to be used in conjunction in order to see the general picture more clearly. It may be that the church supported morris dances in a variety of venues other than church property, and hence the different widths of the curves; or sampling error (or methodological strategy) may account for the differences. Such cautionary tales merely underscore the fact that these data reduction techniques are the beginning, not the end, of analysis.

Another warning bell also needs to be sounded concerning the relationship of the curves to the sources themselves. It is always a possibility that the curves exist purely as an artefact of the nature of the sources, and do not accurately reflect the underlying historical realities. Thus, for example, the apparent rise in the number of morris events at private houses at the end of the period might simply be a statistical artefact produced by virtue of the fact that domestic account books were kept with greater regularity (and have survived in greater numbers) from the late-seventeenth century onwards than from earlier periods. More sources of a certain type in one era could therefore mean more *reports* and not necessarily more *events*.

With fragmentary data there are no easy solutions to this problem, and it must remain as a caution throughout. However, there are several reasonable responses. First, and most important, the analysis presented here does not rely exclusively, or even primarily, on statistical reductions of this sort. The latter are merely used as signposts to direct conventional exegetical use of sources. Second, no variable in the database corresponds isomorphically with a single type of source. Thus, for example,

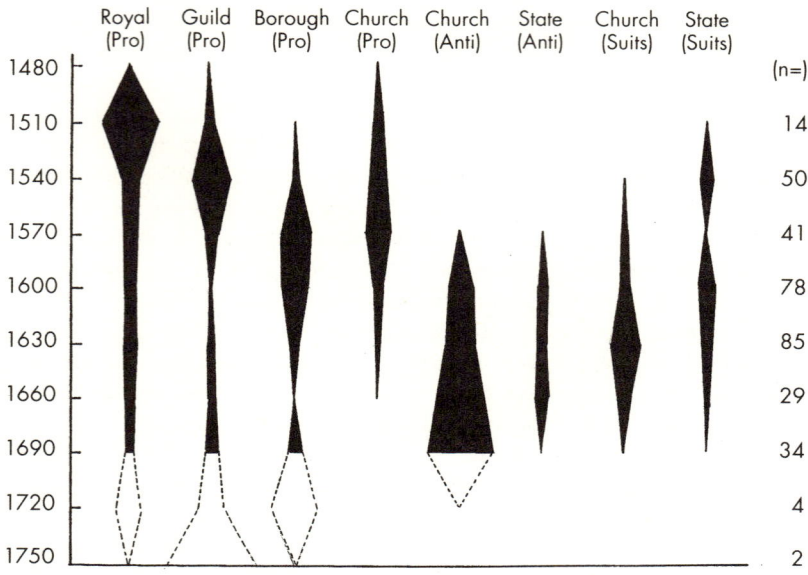

Figure 4: Seriation of official actions

not all references to events at private houses come from domestic account books. Of the data on private houses synthesized in the seriation curves 37 per cent comes from sources other than domestic accounts. Therefore the rise and fall of a single variable cannot be entirely the product of the rise and fall of a certain type of source. Third, seriation is not responsive to the *absolute* rise in the number of reports of a particular kind of event, but to the *relative* rise of such events in relation to events of a different sort. For the apparent late rise of morris events at private houses to be an artefact of the rise in the number of extant domestic account books would also require that all sources that reported morris events at places other than private houses (church documents, legal papers, royal records, etc.) suffered a severe decline in numbers in the same period.

The potentially compromising effects of the nature of the sources themselves on statistical analysis can also be diminished by developing multiple strategies for viewing the database. One possiblity is to take numerous views of the variables (as above) in an attempt to collate data that cuts across types of sources. Another is to use methods other than the statistical (such as geographic mapping), which not only call on different subsets of the database but are also less sensitive to the particular nature of the sources.

To follow the first of these strategies we may draw another set of curves, those for what I have labelled *official actions*, to add a further historic dimension to the details exposed by the other two graphs (figure 4). State and local governments, the church, and other official bodies actively supported or opposed morris dancing by, for example, sending representatives to dance events on the one hand, or creating legislation to ban them on the other. The various actions for and against dancing by these official groups are summarized on the graph as royal support, guild support, borough support, church support, church legislative opposition, state legislative opposition, prosecutions under church law, and prosecutions under state law. Actions defined as 'support' here do *not* include financial support although a single source may include both an official action and a payment.

In the period roughly covered by the sixteenth century, royal, guild, church, and borough support follow on from one another in that order, exactly concurring with the curves for financial support. Then in the seventeenth century there is an expansion of church legislation against dancing, increasing as the century progresses (with an exaggerated bulge in the curve due to the general issue of new visitation articles in 1662). This trend is mirrored, but only modestly, by secular legislation. It is also interesting to note that actual prosecutions under church and state laws occur early in the century and do not continue. In fact prosecutions show up prior to the appearance of legislation aimed against morris dancing specifically, usually under more general laws against sabbath breaking and the like.

Comparison with the *type of venue* seriations shows that the rise of church legislation coincides precisely with the shift of dancing from urban to village settings. Once church opposition has died, at the beginning of the eighteenth century, royal, guild, and borough (but not church) support emerge again. Thus the evidence presented by the curves from this graph leads to the hypothesis that the church played a pivotal role in the overall developmental history of the dance. But without further data this is no more than a generalized theoretical beginning.

To assist interpretation of seriated data, locations of dancing taken from the database can be mapped geographically. In this way the seriation curves are given a spatial dimension. (It should be noted, however, that the curves and the maps draw on somewhat different subsets of data from the database – the maps, for example, do not plot prohibitions.) The nine maps shown in figures 5 to 13 (starting on p. 37) have been derived from the primary dataset, and follow the thiry-year divisions of the seriations. Entries have been made on the maps to indicate when and where there is evidence of morris activity. Rather then indicating geographic location only, the symbols give some indication of the nature of the source, so that the spatial information presented in them can be compared with the temporal information derived from the seriations. This method is based on a system devised by Michael Heaney (see Forrest and Heaney 1991).

Before comparing the maps directly with the seriation curves some related trends may be noted. There are intimations of classic patterns of diffusion at work. The maps show a general expansion outward from the London region, with only a few outliers in each period. That is, from 1481 to 1630 there is a consistent expansion of the geographic area covered by relatively densely plotted points. Then figures 10 and 11 show a sharp diminution in support covering the period 1631–90, the plotted points thinning drastically over the region that saw maximal expansion (as represented by figure 9). Figures 12 and 13 witness a clustering and renewal of support in regions away from London, most notably in the south Midlands.

In terms of the absolute number of recorded events, then, there is a form of temporal symmetry around the 1601–1630 axial period, that is, growth to a zenith followed by decline (with some renewed growth at the tail end). Spatially the picture is slightly more complex. Over time the area of popularity expands but as the number of events diminishes after 1630, the area of maximal expansion does not collapse; rather the distance between events thins out until a new focal point, in the south Midland counties, emerges.

One way to map the focus of dancing activity as it diffuses outward is to use centroids. A centroid is literally a centre of gravity, and is determined by averaging the x and y coordinates of all the points on a particular map (multiple events in a single location counting as distinct points in the averaging process) in order to produce a single point. Figure 14 shows the centroids for the periods represented by the individual maps. The centroids cluster in the London area from 1481 to 1540, and then move west and north from 1541 to 1630, the period of expansion and diffusion outward from London. From 1631 to 1750 they concentrate in a small area in the south Midlands.

These diverse methods of data reduction all appear at first glance to confirm and illuminate one another, suggesting a number of trends, notably a shift from the urban to rural, and from large public displays to smaller localized events, hinging on the support or opposition of the church. Yet these generalized observations need careful investigation in the light of data drawn directly from the sources, because it is not fair to assume that we are dealing with a single or simple phenomenon called 'morris' that is spreading as an innovation in the same kind of way as, say, a new type of plough. As noted in the next chapter, morris was from the earliest times a diverse entity, and could well continue so over time. Indeed it could become more diverse as it spread outward into new physical and social environments. Its spread is likely to have been accompanied with evolutionary change more like the spread and speciation of an organism than of a new piece of technology. To understand this process requires a detailed account of each of the environments into which morris became adapted.

This study of dances in their social and historical contexts begins with a detailed study of the earliest sources – those from the fifteenth century. They are dealt with as a single group because they are so fragmentary. Subsequent chapters deal with later materials and are divided into the contexts that are indexed in the Early Morris Database and archive.

Figure 5: General distribution of morris events by type, 1466–1510

Domestic records

Guild records

State records

Prose nonfiction

Ecclesiastical records

Local records

Secular prosecutions

Personal records

Ecclesiastical prosecutions

Ecclesiastical legal records

Legal records

Interludes and masques

Other entertainments

Polemical attacks

Nontheatrical advertisements

Theatrical advertisements

Figure 6:   General distribution of morris events by type, 1511–40

□   Domestic records
◀   Guild records
☆   State records
—   Prose nonfiction
●   Ecclesiastical records
★   Local records
✪   Secular prosecutions
■   Personal records
○   Ecclesiastical prosecutions
◁   Ecclesiastical legal records
▷   Legal records
❀   Interludes and masques
Ⅱ   Other entertainments
—   Polemical attacks
❖   Nontheatrical advertisements
◂   Theatrical advertisements

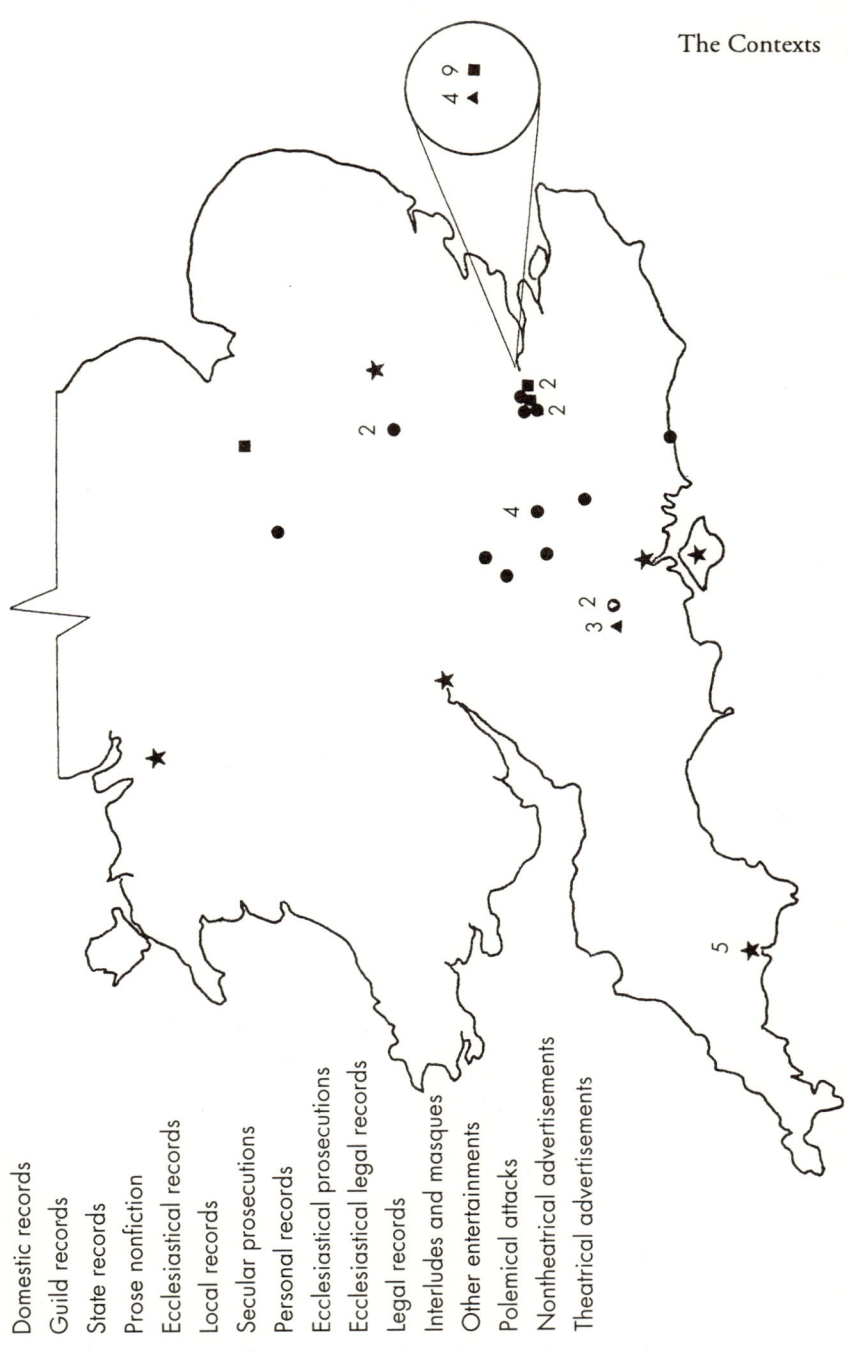

Figure 7: General distribution of morris events by type, 1541–70

□   Domestic records
◄   Guild records
☆   State records
▬   Prose nonfiction
●   Ecclesiastical records
★   Local records
✪   Secular prosecutions
■   Personal records
○   Ecclesiastical prosecutions
△   Ecclesiastical legal records
▽   Legal records
❀   Interludes and masques
⧓   Other entertainments
▬   Polemical attacks
❖   Nontheatrical advertisements
◄   Theatrical advertisements

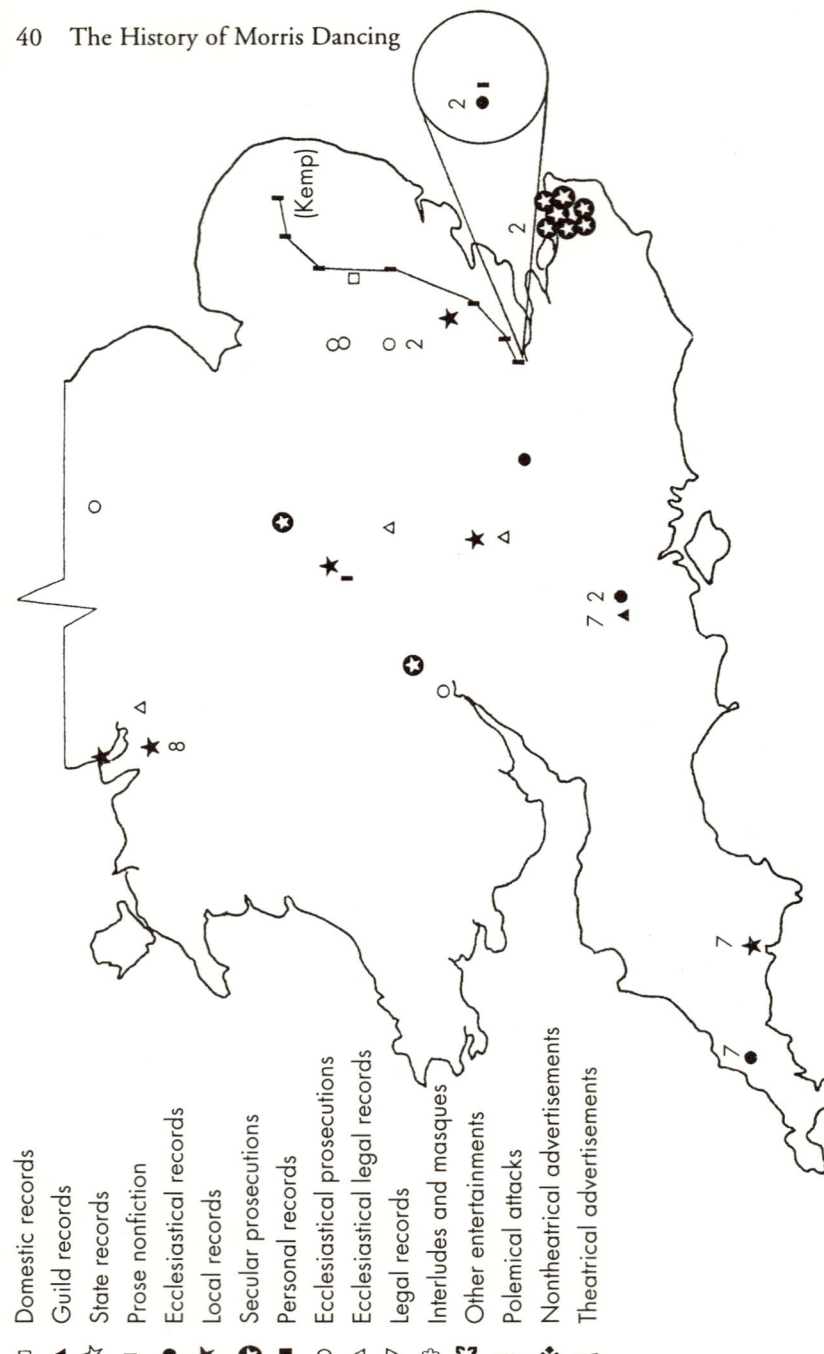

(Kemp)

Domestic records   □
Guild records   ◄
State records   ☆
Prose nonfiction   ▬
Ecclesiastical records   ●
Local records   ★
Secular prosecutions   ✪
Personal records   ■
Ecclesiastical prosecutions ○
Ecclesiastical legal records △
Legal records   ▷
Interludes and masques   ✿
Other entertainments   ⧓
Polemical attacks   ▬
Nontheatrical advertisements ❖
Theatrical advertisements ◄

Figure 8: General distribution of morris events by type, 1571–1600

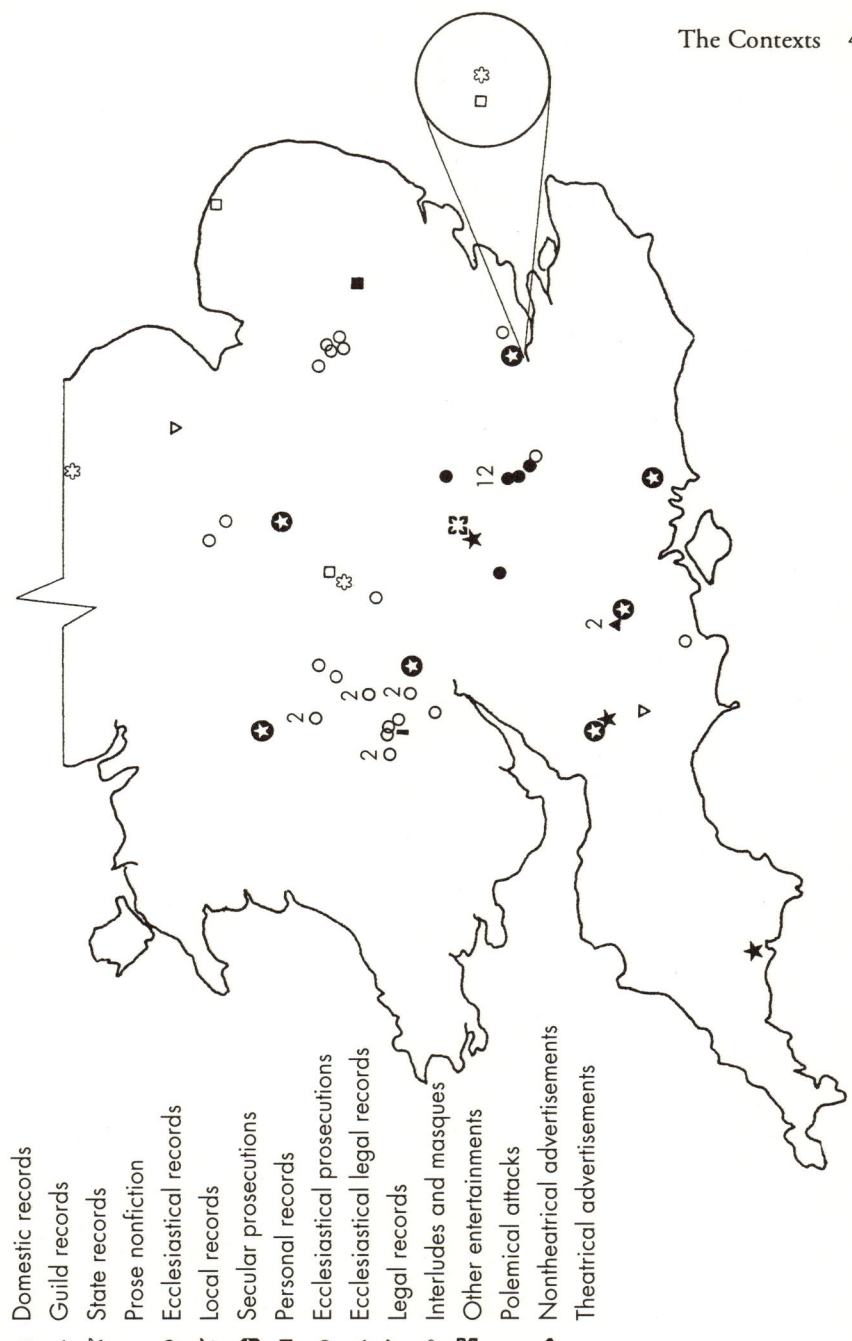

Domestic records □
Guild records ◀
State records ☆
Prose nonfiction ▬
Ecclesiastical records ●
Local records ★
Secular prosecutions ✪
Personal records ■
Ecclesiastical prosecutions ○
Ecclesiastical legal records △
Legal records ▷
Interludes and masques ✿
Other entertainments ⚶
Polemical attacks ▬
Nontheatrical advertisements ❖
Theatrical advertisements ◀

Figure 9: General distribution of morris events by type, 1601–30

Figure 10: General distribution of morris events by type, 1631–60

□ Domestic records
◄ Guild records
☆ State records
– Prose nonfiction
● Ecclesiastical records
★ Local records
✪ Secular prosecutions
■ Personal records
○ Ecclesiastical prosecutions
△ Ecclesiastical legal records
▽ Legal records
✿ Interludes and masques
𝄪 Other entertainments
– Polemical attacks
❖ Nontheatrical advertisements
◄ Theatrical advertisements

Figure 11: General distribution of morris events by type, 1661–90

□   Domestic records
◄   Guild records
☆   State records
–   Prose nonfiction
●   Ecclesiastical records
★   Local records
✪   Secular prosecutions
■   Personal records
○   Ecclesiastical prosecutions
◁   Ecclesiastical legal records
▽   Legal records
✿   Interludes and masques
Ӡ3   Other entertainments
—   Polemical attacks
❖   Nontheatrical advertisements
◄   Theatrical advertisements

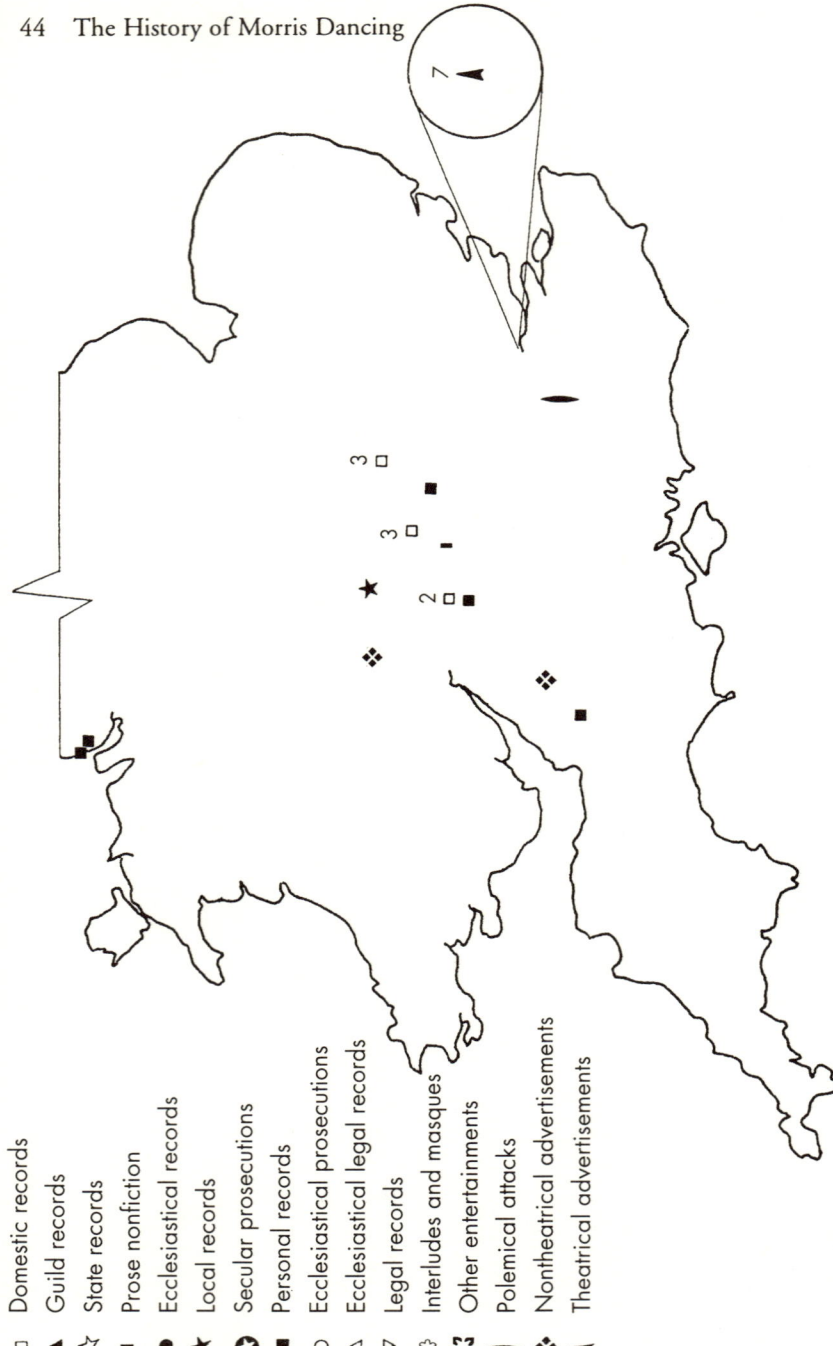

Figure 12: General distribution of morris events by type, 1691–1720

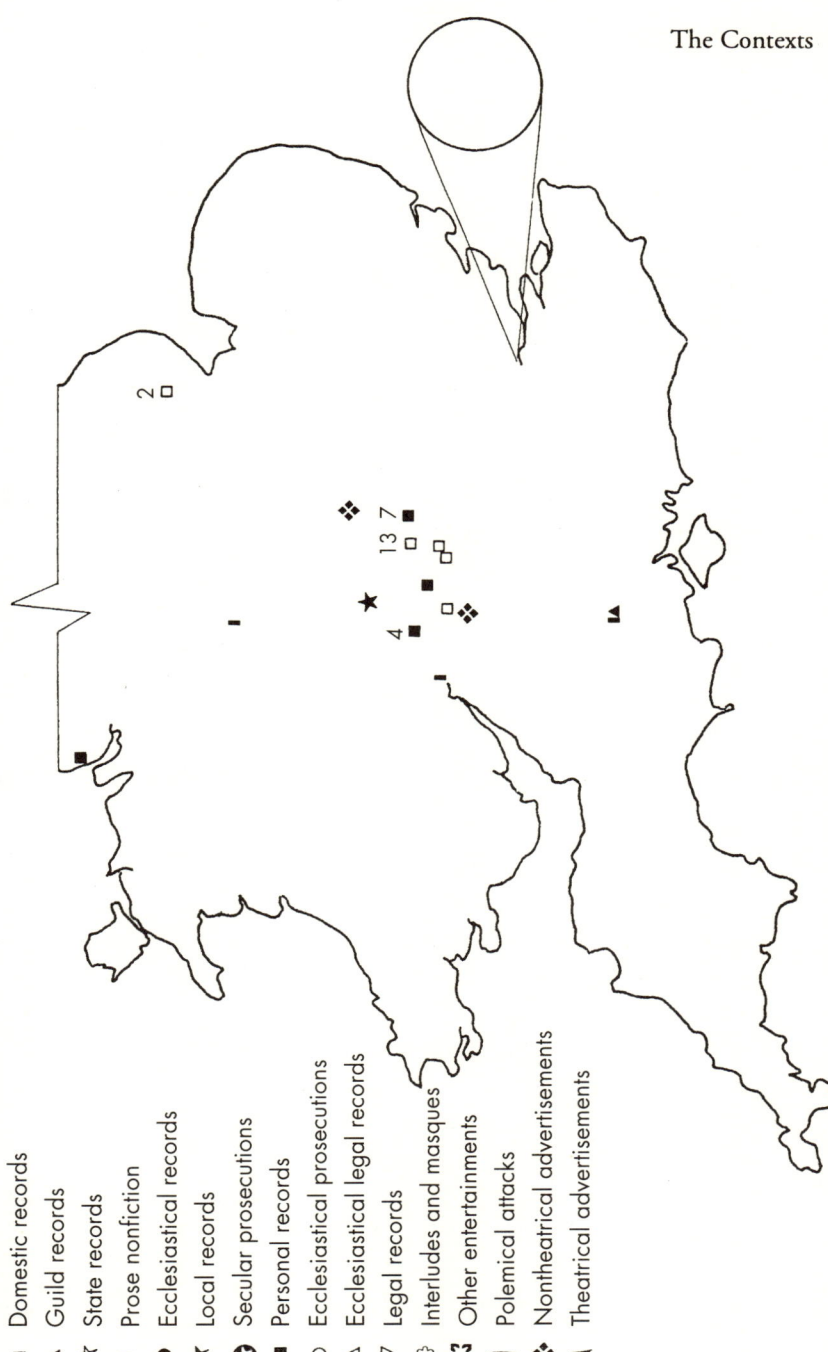

Figure 13: General distribution of morris events by type, 1721–50

□ Domestic records
◄ Guild records
☆ State records
▬ Prose nonfiction
● Ecclesiastical records
★ Local records
✪ Secular prosecutions
■ Personal records
○ Ecclesiastical prosecutions
△ Ecclesiastical legal records
▽ Legal records
✿ Interludes and masques
⧓ Other entertainments
▬ Polemical attacks
❖ Nontheatrical advertisements
◄ Theatrical advertisements

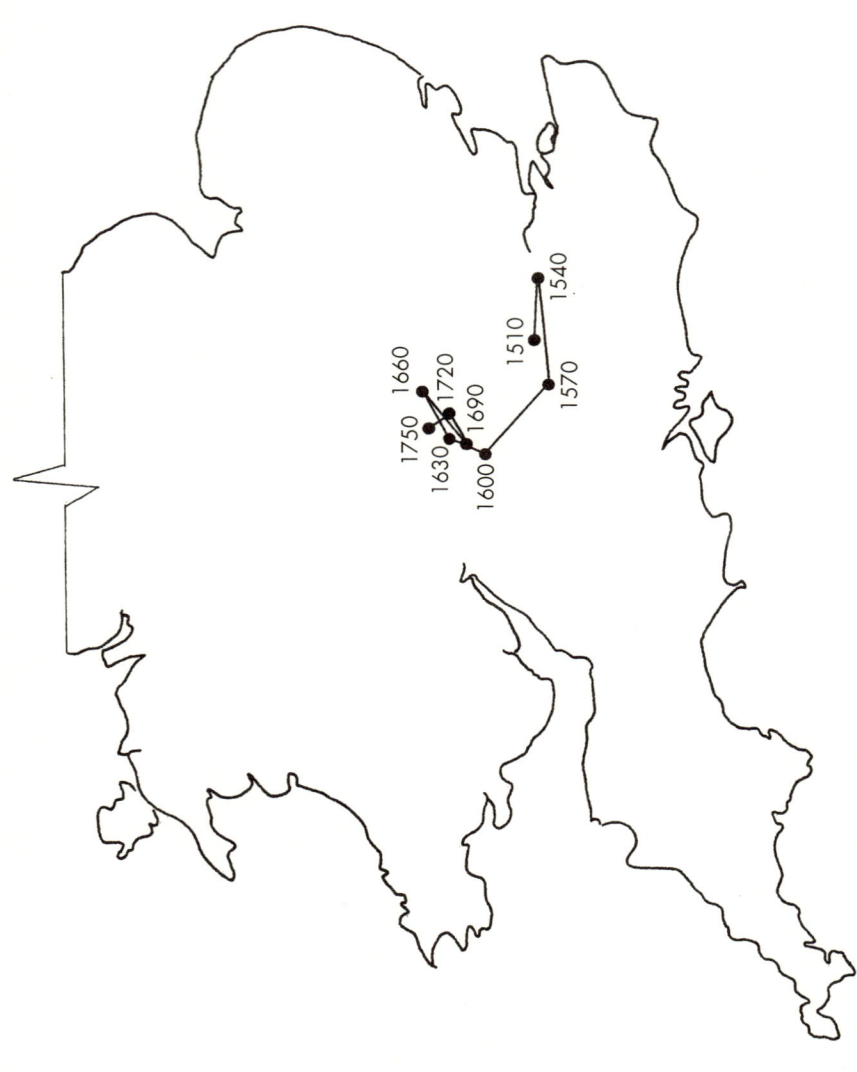

Figure 14: Map showing centroids for figures 5–13

3

Earliest References

The first unequivocal reference to a morris dance of any sort comes from the will of Alice Wetenhale, a widow from Bury St Edmunds, dated 1458:

lego Caterine filie mee ... iij ciphos argenti sculptos cum moreys daunce cum unico cooperculo ad eosdem.   (PRO, Prerogative Court of Canterbury Records 24–5)

[I leave to my daughter Catherine ... 3 silver cups, sculpted with a morris dance, with one lid for them.][1]

There are only two other references to morris in the fifteenth century that are incontrovertible. In 1477 the Drapers' guild paid for a morris as part of its contribution to the Midsummer Watch in London:

Payment of the costis don on seint Petre Nycht for the Wache Wayting vppon the Meyre. ffirste paid for the morisse daunce and for the costs of the ix worthi as it aperith by a bill of parcells of the same. xxviij s. ix d.   (Johnson 1915, 273)

In 1494 Henry VII's account books record as part of the Christmastide celebrations:

Item for pleying of the mourice dance xl^s.   (Anglo 1960, 28)

To these can be added two references to a morisk.[2] The first, by coincidence, is a will from the same year as Alice Wetenhale's and also concerns images made on silver:

Sir Thomas praith his seid executors that ... thai delyvere to William Chaworth ... iij peces of silver ... the which oon of thaym coveryth, another with a flatt knoppe and with a Moresk yeron.   (Raine 1855, 226)

The second is excerpted from domestic accounts from Lanherne in Cornwall for Christmas activities over the winter of 1466/7:

It. di. li. vermelen of Betty xij d.
It. di. li. orsedy of Betty xij d.
It. viij quayars of paper for disgysynge ij s. ...
It. ij whit Bonetts for mynstrells on newe yer ys day of Betty xx d.
It. ij ellis of holond cloth for Melionek the same day xxij d.
Itm. iiij dosyn bellis for the Moruske of Betty iij s.
It. ij quayers paper for the moruske of Betty vij d.
It. v ellys of holond cloth for disgysing whan ye were avysid to go to my lord Stafford of Betty wheche was delyvered to my Lady ij s. vj d.
It. di. li. glewe of Betty for the Moruske ij d.
It. iij yerdis Blak Bokeram whan ye wolde to my Lord with disgysing whech y delyverid to my lady of Betty ...   (Douch 1953, 27–9)

That is the sum total of primary material relating to morris (or morisk) in the fifteenth century. A number of inferences may be drawn from these sources and a few conjectures appended, but it is as much a matter of declaring what *cannot* be inferred.

To begin at the beginning, Alice Wetenhale's will does not say much, but it provides a few clues to get started with, and is important in the context of the other sources. The fact that the image of a morris dance is mentioned in a will at all is significant. The executor of this will had to be able to identify all of the property in it and distribute it to the right hands without muddle and without undue research into the meaning of its specific terms. Therefore, in order for the executor to identify three silver cups by virtue of an image of a morris dance, there must have been a reasonable expectation at the time that an educated person would know what a morris looked like. This in turn suggests that morrises had been known in England for some (perhaps not long) period of time, and they had a readily identifiable form, or some visual component that was unmistakable.

Also the fact that the image was carved on silver cups is important. There is a connotation here that the dance image is worthy of precious (and lasting) objects – things destined as heirlooms. What is more, this is not an isolated object: Thomas Chaworth's will contains something similar, and into the sixteenth century there are references to expensive items depicting a morris. The will of Richard Jackson in 1510 mentions a cup:

My cuppe wt the morres daunce   (PRO, Prerogative Court of Canterbury Records 31)

An inventory of royal valuables in 1532 mentions a gold salt:

A gold salt, called the Moresdaunce, with 5 Moresdauncers and a tabrett …
(Gairdner 1880, 5: 739)

This is more carefully described in the 1547 inventory made when Edward VI succeeded his father Henry VIII:

Item one Salte of golde called the morres daunce having the foote garnished with vj greate Saphires xv course diamounts xxxviij course rubies xlj small garnishing perles having vppon the border about the shanke xij course dyamounts xviij course rubies and xlix garnishing perles and standing aboute the v morres dauncers and a tabrell having amonge all the saide morres dauncers and tabrell xj small garnishing perles and one rubie the Ladie holding the salte having vppon her garmentes from her foote to her face xix course garnishing perles and x course small rubies or glasses the foote of the saide salte having iiij course rubies or glasses and iiij course diamountes or glasses the border aboute the middle of the saide salte having v course dyamountes or glasses and vij rubies or glasses and vij perles and vppon the knopp of the saide salte iiij diamountes iiij rubies and iij greate perlis having vppon her attyer on her hed xiiij course rubies xij course dyamountes and xxiij course garnishing perles …
Cxlvij oz.   (Society of Antiquaries MS 129, vol.A, f.18)

I would be getting ahead of myself to study these later references in detail now. The point is simply that the two cups recorded in the fifteenth century are not isolated objects. In fact one even shows up in a 1606 inventory of some of James I and VI's valuables:

A note of such gold plate & Jewelles [belonging to James I] as Sr Willm Hericke hath took into his charge … A cup with a morris dance 68 oz.
(Bodleian Lib. MS Eng. hist. c. 479, f.239)

The first reference is, therefore, the beginning of a slim thread in the overall developmental history, which can be followed wheresoever it leads. Other fifteenth-century references similarly begin paths that continue and widen later, namely, those relating to the craft guilds and to the royal court. Only the Lanherne domestic accounts stand out as at all singular.

The reference to the Drapers' guild sponsoring a dance at the Midsummer Watch in 1477 is the first source to mention a specific dance event categorically identified as 'morris.' The Lanherne account is earlier but refers to a 'moruske,' and the image on Alice Wetenhale's cup cannot now be treated as anything more than a general depiction, rather than a picture of a datable event. But the dance performed at the drapers' expense can be located in time and space.

The London Midsummer Watch for the first half of the sixteenth century was a common context for the performance of morris, often under the patronage of the drapers, and is to be discussed at length in due course. This watch was essentially a parade that went in procession around London's streets, celebrating yearly in glorious pageantry the more mundane circuits on other evenings of the night watch (the men who perambulated the night streets calling the hours and keeping the peace). The mayor provided and attended on one section of the procession, and the sheriffs one each, accompanied by vast contingents of supporters, musicians, dancers, armed men, and exotic displays provided by the guilds of the city.

Conventionally there were two ceremonial watches, the first on the night of the eve of the feast of St John the Baptist (that is, 23 June), also known at that time as Midsummer's eve because it was around the summer solstice. The second was on the eve of the feast of St Peter (28 June), and it is this watch that is recorded in the Drapers' account books ('Payment of the costis don on seint Petre Nycht for the Wache Wayting vppon the Meyre'). So the first specific morris dance event on record was part of a procession through the streets of London in the late night hours of 28-06-1477.[3]

This specific reference reveals little about the dance itself. It is not even possible from this source alone to get a sense of the economics involved, because the expenses of the dancers are grouped in with the 'costs of the ix worthi' (men dressed to represent the so-called Nine Worthies of Antiquity, possibly on horseback) whose percentage of the total is indeterminable. Unfortunately this habit of parcelling the morris costs with other display items continues well into the sixteenth century, so that comparative expenditures from which to make some kind of speculation do not exist. The best that can be offered are the Drapers' expenses for a morris at the watches in 1521:

It' to Robert Greves for a morysdance & ij mynstrelles riding at there own coste except ij sylk cotes & ij hors trappers that we lent them and we gave the said mynstrelles ij white hattes & paid for the mores daûnce for both nyghtes xiiij s.(Robertson and Gordon 1954, 10)

This reference is close to an accounting of a single payment for morris alone, but it covers two nights, and costumes are supplied by the drapers themselves. And it is forty-four years later than the source to be compared. So, an estimate of seven shillings for a night's dance (that is, fourteen shillings divided by two nights and not counting the costs of the minstrels' hats) is no more than a stab in the dark; but given that the line item in the 1477 accounts came to twenty-eight shillings and nine pence it might, if anything, be a low estimate.

Such funding is a good amount of money and conveys a sense that the dancers were paid well, and may even have been professionals. To give some sense of the value of money at the time in terms of contemporary prices and wages the following are extracted from sources that bear on the year 1477:

Earnings:

building laborer	4 d. per (10-hour) day	
craftsman	6 d. per day	(Darby 1973, 198)

Prices (averages rounded to the nearest penny):

wheat	6s. 4d. per quarter (i.e., eight bushels)	
cows	8s. 6d. each	
geese	4d. each	
butter	1s. 4d. per doz. lb.	
eggs	8d. per 10 doz	(Finberg 1967, 869)

Statistics on prices and wages for this period are scarce and not totally reliable, but at least some relative sense of what a payment of nine shillings would imply can be gleaned from these figures. What cannot be known is among how many people the sum had to be split, nor what other expenses had to be paid. And, of course, the actual sum awarded is strictly a guess.

Similar problems arise in drawing conclusions based on the only other datable and locatable reference to a 'morris' in the fifteenth century, the record of an amount paid by Henry VII to dancers at his Christmas revels in 1494. The account book simply states that forty shillings was paid 'for pleying of the mourice dance,' with no indication of the number of people involved, their expenses, or any other hint as to how the money was apportioned. Even so, the sum is substantial and, even more than the guild accounts, suggests an elaborate professional performance, which the royal court would naturally expect of festivities at one of the great annual holidays (although by comparison with what Henry's son Henry VIII spent on revelling, this forty shillings is a mere *pourboire*). It should also be noted that the costs of the royal court are absolutely higher than those of the Drapers' guild, being nearly twice as much as the drapers paid all told, including the expenses of the 'ix worthi.'

The royal Christmas revels at which the morris makes its first known appearance were a long-standing tradition of the Tudor monarchs, and their account books provide extensive records of morris dancing and its context (which receive their due in later chapters). Thus this last source in the fifteenth century, like the others, founds a soon-to-be venerable tradition of kings, queens, and nobles feasting in glittering halls and enjoying morris dancing as part of their midwinter's sport.

Only one other fifteenth-century source remains to be considered, that of the household accounts from Lanherne for Christmas 1466/7. I have left this reference until last because in several respects it is singular and difficult to interpret. To begin, the performance is called a 'moruske,' so that by the principles established in appendix A it is not a fully applicable source. Nor can it be considered especially representative. Morris dances at private houses appear in the records sporadically 100 years later, and after another 100 years have passed become quite frequent. But for this era, the reference is unique. Thus, complete trust cannot be placed in what may be deduced from its particulars. However, it being only one of a bare handful of sources, it must be considered.

The items in the Lanherne account book that relate explicitly to the morisk are brief but give a few clues as to the nature of the performance. There are actually only three line items specifically linked to the morisk: two quires of paper (7d), a half pound of glue (2d) and four dozen bells (3s). So, the total cost directly attributable to the morisk is three shillings and nine pence. And there are no expenditures for dancers themselves, nor for turning the raw materials into costumes. Taken together these facts seem to indicate a home-made performance of some sort.

Conjectures on how the paper and glue were turned into costumes or other dance gear – if indeed that was even their use – must necessarily be hedged around with caveats, but a few points may be established. At the outset it must be remembered that paper was not the commodity then that it is today. Paper for writing and wrapping was not unheard of in England in the fifteenth century, but general demand was low and all paper was imported until the tail end of the century. When Caxton set up his press in 1476 he used nothing but imported paper, and although the establishment of the printing of books increased the need for paper over parchment, vellum, and other manuscript materials, it was not until the second half of the sixteenth century that English paper mills were able to turn a profit (see Coleman 1958: 1–88, and Shorter, 1971: 13–19 for details). Thus paper might well have made a suitable temporary costume or staging material as befits its physical properties, but it would, nonetheless, have had a rarity value, making it at least minimally exotic.

The quantity of paper and its quality are not easily deduced from the Lanherne accounts. A quire is twenty-four (sometimes twenty-five) sheets, but the size of a sheet can vary according to the type of paper and its use. Thus absolute area (on which to hazard a guess concerning the number of costumes made therefrom) cannot be known. Comparison with the accounts of Winchester College – the only reliable series of records for establishing a base price for paper in the fifteenth century (see Beveridge 1939, 69–70 and 85–6) – are very difficult to make. Using calculations based on parcelled entries in the accounts, and extrapolations from later years, it would seem that there were two basic prices for paper – 2d and 3d per quire – suggesting perhaps two different sizes, or, more likely, different qualities. In 1540 – when basic paper prices were unchanged from their fifteenth century levels – there is an entry for Imperial sheets (22" x 30" for writing paper) at 6d per quire. Thus, Demy sheets (15.5" x 20" for writing paper) at 3d per quire would be reasonable, with a poorer grade selling for 2d. But sizes and qualities were not standardized in the fifteenth century and are almost never specified in accounts. Nevertheless, it is within the bounds of reason to hypothesize that the morisk at Lanherne used no less than forty-eight Demy sheets (a total of approximately 103 square feet), assuming, among other things, that it was all used.

If for no other reason it might be argued that the paper used at Lanherne was of a standard writing size such as Demy or Medium (17.25" x 22.5") because the larger sizes were special stocks, hard to come by. Then again it is not inconceivable that the paper used was not writing paper at all, but some other, perhaps coloured stock, sold in sizes that cannot now be determined. And it cannot be ruled out that the 7d for the two quires was a parcelled item with, say, one quire valued at 4d and the other at 3d, the two prices representing two different sizes or qualities. Whatever the case, unless the paper were of some exorbitant quality, which seems unlikely given the modesty of other expenses, there was a sizable quantity of it from which to make the gear for a household entertainment.

Possibly of as much use for comparative purposes is the fact that Winchester College throughout the fifteenth century used only between three and six quires of the more expensive paper in a *year* (and one to two reams, i.e., twenty to forty quires, of the cheaper), all purchased at one time. Thus a sense can be gained of the cultural value and rarity of paper as a commodity.

There are actually two entries for paper used at Lanherne's Christmas celebrations – the one already mentioned for two quires at 3.5d per quire in regards the morisk, and eight quires 'for disgysynge' at 3d per quire. If the paper for the morris is a significant amount, that for the disguising is enormous (possibly over 400 square feet by the above calculations). Other entries connected with the Christmas celebrations may refer to the disguising, the morisk, or both. For example, there are payments of 12d each for half a pound of vermilion and the same weight of orsidue (or arsedine), a gold-coloured alloy of copper and zinc used in thin sheets as a base substitute for gold leaf on toys and the like. Both could have been used to add colour to costumes or other performance gear, although no specific mention of their use is made in the accounts themselves.

It is also worthy of note that in the early sixteenth century, court records often speak of 'disguisings' and 'morisks' (rather than 'morrises') in a way that suggests a close relationship between the two, and generates some ideas concerning the nature of the Lanherne Christmas entertainments. For example the court accounts for 1501 record:

Item, that Jacques Hault and William Pawne ... devise and prepare disguisings and some morisks after the best manner they can. (Kipling 1977, 100)

and for Christmas 1508:

Also, Henry Wentworth asketh alowauns for his costes, being abought the besyness of the disguising and moreske by the kinges commaundement, from the 27th day of September to the 27th day of December, at 8d be the day for 80 days 53s 4d.   (Myers 1981, 127)

'Disguising' was the name given at this time to the forerunner of the courtly masques and antimasques and, as such, was concerned more with spectacular display than drama. That is, disguisings emphasized costume and extravagant exhibition over narrative content. The court records above seem to indicate that it was the fashion to include in the disguising a dance or other performance *à la moresque*, or, in the Moorish style, and this is confirmed by a contemporary source – an eyewitness description of the marriage of princess Mary to Charles of Castille in 1508:

His igitur cenis, tam lautis tamque opiparis ut nihil omnino egregium quod vel terra vel freto aut flumine crescat illis abfuerit, non defuerunt ludi Maurei quas morescas dicunt, et saltan-tium juvenum generosa virensque propago, simul et comediarum tragediarumque hystrionica et ludicra queque spectacula previsa sane prius ac sumptuose preparata.
There lacked no disguysynges, moriskes nor entreludes made and appareilled in the beste and richest maner.   (Gairdner 1893, 30)

The original gloss links disguising and morisks, but the Latin on which it is based goes further in saying that what are called 'morescas' are 'ludi Maurei,' that is, Moorish spectacles. The meaning of all of this in terms of courtly morris and the develop-ment of the dance in general is to be explored in due course. For the moment the issue is that disguisings and morisks were associated with each other in the courtly setting. It is possible, therefore, to imagine that the Lanherne Christmas celebrations are analogous to the courtly ones.

    Were it not anachronistic from the point of view of sources, one might even sug-gest that the Lanherne morisk and disguising were home-made versions of the grander public spectacles. But the Lanherne accounts are dated 1466, and the first court reference to the two together is not until 1501. So unless it is to be concluded that the courtly shows were descendants of local household fun and games (which cannot be ruled out), then the courtly and the local must simply be deemed ana-logues with no lineage preferred. Given the general absence of data, this is as far as the sources support speculation.

    One more point may be made in connection with Lanherne, however. If the morisk was indeed a performance in the Moorish style, then the item for bells has a ready explanation. Moors who appeared in disguisings had certain stereotyped costume elements, one of the most significant being bells and other paraphernalia that caused rhythmic jangling as the performer moved. If, indeed, the Lanherne performance was 'Moorish' it is difficult to assess the number of performers from the number of bells bought. The account book records an order of four dozen bells. If the performers wore them strapped to their calves (as more recent morris dancers did) then scarcely fewer than six per leg would suffice to produce a sound that could be heard over the musical accompaniment. Under those conditions there could be no more than four dancers. But Moorish characters often wore bells attached to their clothes to create a general jingling, rather than a rhythmical sound specifically associated with leg motion. In this case there could have been more than four performers (the bells being a mere token), or as few as one (laden with bells). But a single dancer would scarcely have needed such a large amount of paper, whereas four could conceivably have done so.

None of the above conjectures based on these earliest of sources is meant to be definitive or exhaustive. The inquiries are merely to point the way and indicate trends to be explored in more depth as the data grow richer. Yet certain general propositions about the nature of the performances may be made.

First, the comparative absence of sources may itself be meaningful. Partly this reveals a general problem, that of dwindling primary resources the further into medieval history one delves. But the overall scarcity of appropriate materials cannot alone explain why one century is represented by a thimbleful of data. It must, at least tentatively, be held that morrises were a rare novelty in England until the sixteenth century and were unknown before the fifteenth.

Second, the actual dance events recorded are associated with major calendar festivals – Christmas and Midsummer – but not with one time of year in particular.

Third, the dances were sponsored by the nobility and wealthier merchant/middle class, although the class status of the performers themselves is, from these documents alone, unclear. The silver cups with images of morris on them add further evidence for the elite status of the dance.

Fourth, the dances are unlikely to be all of a single type. Perhaps the royal and Lanherne performances shared similarities because they were performed in large halls, but the guild morris must have been different because it was part of a procession. Then again the guild and royal morrises were great public spectacles, and the entertainment at Lanherne was a private affair.

Fifth, the three references to actual performances are widely dispersed. Two are from London, but the third is from Cornwall, 340 miles away. Admittedly the Cornish reference concerns a morisk, but given courtly analogues in the following century it cannot be excluded out of hand as not applicable or not representative.

What is revealed, in effect, is some general unity and some diversity, bespeaking not a single dance type, but at best an underlying thread linking the several forms. The combination of (implied) diversity of dance type and geographic dispersal of the locations of the dance is sufficient to defeat any effort at discovering the single, monolithic 'origin' of British morris, the mythical ancestor of all later forms. A promiscuous assortment of ideas and places is evident from the beginning of the dance's recorded history, hinting at multiple influences over time and space. Each of the threads begun in the fifteenth century leads out into a variety of dance contexts in later centuries.

4

Royal Court

Royal interest in and support of morris dancing took two distinct directions at the time of the Tudors. Some morrises were performed as integral components of disguisings and masques enacted in large banqueting halls before the court during seasonal revels; others were part of urban processions honouring dignitaries or providing some holiday pageantry and mirth. Although both types had royal patronage, this chapter deals only with the former, and chapter 5 incorporates the latter; the division of interest here is based initially on *type of venue*. The main idea is to explore the dance in different physical environments on the supposition that these are likely to influence the nature of the performance. An outdoor processional dance must necessarily be different from an indoor circumscribed one, and some aspects of their forms may be inferred from these contexts. What follows, thus, concerns only indoor dances sponsored by royalty.

Although kings and queens have formed part of the audience for morris dances from its earliest years to the present century, their most active patronage for dances performed at the royal court seems to have come during the reigns of Henry VII and Henry VIII (and in Scotland under James IV), specifically, between the years 1494 and 1522. The primary sources consist largely of extracts from the royal account books, which are often terse, and when they are not, the main details they supply concern costumes, scenery, and other accoutrements. These sources are also not completely reliable in the sense that absence of a recorded payment does not necessarily mean absence of a morris. For example, the royal accounts that cover the Lord of Misrule's midwinter processions of 1552 and 1553 are quite detailed, and yet no mention is made anywhere in them of a morris (Feuillerat 1914, 56–61, 77–81, 89–94, and 117–25). However, Henry Machyn's diary clearly states that a morris was part of both processions (Machyn 1848, 13 and 28–9).

The accounts of Henry VII, Henry VIII, and James IV vary quite considerably in terms of the details given about the financing of the dance, all the way from those that are a single relatively uninformative line item to those that include page after page of exquisite detail. As Sydney Anglo (Anglo 1960, 26) quite rightly points out, it is a mistake to assume too much about the entertainments themselves directly from the writing styles of the record keepers, and it is almost certainly true that the image of Henry VII's court as flat and workaday in comparison with Henry VIII's has been overplayed because of this kind of interpretation. There is no question that Henry VIII, in comparison with his father, was an extravagant spender, and that his court spectacles were often conducted on a scale scarcely to be believed. But Henry VII took care, as his accounts show, to impress foreign and local dignitaries as necessary, with some degree of ostentation and spectacle. So underneath the differences of scale represented by money spent, or ink spilled to record expenditures, entertainments and spectacles show many similarities between the reigns of the first two Tudors.

Morris dancing certainly exhibits general continuities in this era, and yet, at the same time, there are some indications that it was not a single, simple phenomenon. In fact it is possible to divide the court morris references into two (or more) groups based, in part, on the context in which the dance was found. One context, namely the disguising, holds a paramount position and should be explored at length because of the effects such a context may have had on the form of the dance. But there seem to have been other, less spectacular contexts as well, and because these are earlier, it is reasonable to start with them.

Actually to say that there are other 'contexts' is overstating the case. Rather, it should be said that there are occasions when no context is mentioned, and there are no other payments nearby in the account books to suggest one. Such is the payment of 1494 already noted in the previous chapter. There are also the following in England in Henry VII's time from 1501 and 1502 respectively:

Item to theym that daunced to mores daunce xxvj^s viij^d (Anglo 1960, 37)
Item to one Lewes for a mores daunce liij^s iiij^d (Anglo 1960, 38)

and in Scotland under James IV (1502):

Item, the viij day of Februar, to the men that brocht in the morice dance, and to thair menstrales, in Strivelin, be the kingis command xlijs   (Mill 1927, 318)

These references are noteworthy for several reasons. Most particularly, they appear to document performances of a morris for its own sake, as it were, rather than as a part of some larger presentation. True, the dances would almost certainly have accompanied general festival events, given that the payment in 1494 is dated in the Christmas season and those for 1502 at Shrovetide, the two great yearly celebrations for all the Tudor monarchs. But the absence of records in the contemporary accounts of disguisings or interludes or other entertainments with which these morrises could have been involved, suggests they were shown as separate and complete acts in and of themselves.[1] Although it must be conceded that given the threadbare and obviously fragmentary nature of the account books, the absence of such records is not proof conclusive that these dances did not have some broader dramatic or choreographic context. If there were only one reference to morris without any performance context, it could be treated as idiosyncratic or evidently incomplete. But because there are four, all within eight years of each other, and from accounts kept by different men for different courts (that is England and Scotland) the case is strengthened that the dance so recorded existed as an independent entity.

The payments for these dances also indicate a degree of uniformity. The costs range from 26s 8d to 53s 4d, a latitude which is not wide enough to represent different kinds of performances. In addition these costs say something about the social status of the dancers. Although a little higher in general, the payments to morris dancers are commensurate with those made to the minstrels and other professional players who made special appearances in court, as the following extracts from Henry VII's accounts demonstrate:

Item to iiij pleyers of Essex in rewarde	xx^s
Item to the pleyers of Wymbone Mynystre	xx^s
...	
Item to iij straunge mynystrelx	xx^s
...	
Item to the Quenes mynystrelx in rewarde	xl^s (Anglo 1960, 28, 29, 31)

The costs for elaborate shows or disguisings in the same period are substantially higher:

Item to Walter Alwyn in full payment for the disguysing made at Christenmes	xiiij^{li} xiij^s iiij^d
...	
Item Jaks Haute in full payment of his bille for his disguysings	xiij^{li} x^s vj^d
...	
Item to Lewes Adam that made disguysings	x^{li}
	(Anglo 1960, 28, 29, 39)

Admittedly these items have been selected from a long list where some of the payments to players and minstrels are much higher and some for disguisings are lower, but those presented here are quite representative. Thus the actual costs themselves bespeak a professional company of dancers and musicians putting on an exhibition of morris that was complete in itself and did not require the level of funding commanded by more elaborate spectacles with their scenic and other decorative props.

What such a morris might have looked like cannot be conjectured from such paltry evidence, although many scholars have ventured an opinion. Sandra Billington (1978), for example, following a well-worn path (Welsford 1927, Chambers 1903), asserts that the dance was a courtly version of a rustic morris. It is already clear that direct evidence in the form of primary sources does not exist to support such an hypothesis; no rural morris is known in this era. This is not to say that the primary sources are infallible, and in the absence of a contemporary source definitively stating that there was *no* rustic morris prior to the courtly version, we must at least entertain the possibility that such a dance existed. Lacking both positive and negative evidence our only reasonable course is silence.

What we cannot do is assert, as did Chambers and Welsford (and, therefore, numerous subsequent scholars) that the courtly dance must have evolved from a folk model on the grounds that all elite performance forms have their origins in traditional ones, and then – heaping anachronism on dubious premises – use descriptions of twentieth-century folk performance to assist in the description of the old courtly forms. Such a method is no method at all; it is proof by assertion coupled with circular reasoning. That courtly dances developed out of folk dances is something to be demonstrated, not to be assumed, and the demonstration must be made afresh for each dance type using primary sources. In many cases an argument, sometimes tenuous, can be made. But there are no data to support even the flimsiest of such contentions for morris.

As it happens there is the opportunity to inspect an analogous line of reasoning, because the next context in which courtly morris is found is the festive performance commonly called a 'disguising,' and much evidence has been set forward to justify the opinion that these shows developed in direct line from folk mumming (see especially Welsford 1927). More recent researches have, however, cast serious doubt on this hypothesis and suggest instead a more complex developmental history. Glynne Wickham in *Early English Stages* (Wickham 1959, 1, 191–228), for example, considers the various theories of folk (and other) origins of the courtly disguising in some detail, and argues that the disguisings of the late Middle Ages are a hybrid descendant of several complex performance types – the two most significant being the knightly tournament and courtly mumming (which latter may or may not have roots in traditional performance). The track of the evolution of courtly disguising is critically important for a history of morris because the form of the one provides clues as to the form of the other. I shall, however, merely point out the salient facts presented by Wickham and others inasmuch as they are germane to morris dancing, rather than attempt a comprehensive overview of an argument that can easily be consulted in the original (see especially Wickham 1959, 1: 13–50 and 191–228, and also Ferguson 1986, 19–65).

The tournament form underwent many changes over its long history stretching into a remote past, but because we are primarily concerned here with its spectacular and dramatic qualities we need extend our view no further back than the late-thirteenth century. Prior to this time tournaments were little more than simulacra of battles, often with similarly fatal results. As such they had been outlawed by successive generations of popes on pain of excommunication, and were banned in England until the accession of Richard I. General edicts did not stop tournaments in England entirely, however, and occasionally limited royal licences were granted. Even so, for much of the thirteenth century English knights travelled abroad, especially to France, for their sport. Here they might meet combatants from across Europe and, thus, styles of spectacular display diffused quickly through the length of the continent.

Two related innovations of the later thirteenth century served both to make the tournament less dangerous and to assist in the transformation of its nature from pure combat to a more stylized entertainment, which eventually found its way indoors. First, there was a gradual linkage of tournamenting with elements from the Arthurian cycle and with the principles of chivalry enshrined in popular prose and metric romances. Partly this came about through a synthesis of the tournament proper (that is, a general mêlée of fully armed men divided into small armies) with the Round Table, a social occasion involving music and feasting, and individual bouts or 'jousts' between knights using light armour and blunted instruments. This in itself was enough to begin the process of transforming the tournament into a dramatic spectacle, aided and abetted by the second change, a series of statutes limiting the number and type of weapons used in tourneying to those that were least likely to cause fatalities.

The classic *Pas d'Armes* developed out of this new tournament style and, in turn, bequeathed much to other courtly entertainments. At first this form of bout was staged on a bridge or other narrow pass, defended against a challenger who had to defeat his opponent to get through. By the fifteenth century such natural settings had been replaced by artificial ones, such as stage castles or gateways elaborately decorated. Furthermore, the simple bout of defender and challenger was replaced by a narrative structure, often highly fanciful and rich in symbolism, that 'explained' the combat. As befitted the chivalric code of the Arthurian romances, the central figure of this allegory was quickly established as a lady who had a mission to be accomplished, and, on its completion, prizes to present to the most accomplished knights. The prize-giving was carried out as part of the evening festivities when the participants feasted, sang, and danced together. The Lansdowne manuscripts provide the general format for such events:

Then comys foorth a lady by the avise of all the ladys and Gentilwomanys and gevis the dia-monde unto the best juster withoute ... This shall be doon with the Rubie and with the saufre unto the othir two next the best Justers. This doon than shall the heraude of armys stonde up all an high. And shall sey wt all an high voice. John hath wele justid, Ric[har]d hath justid bettir and Thomas hath justid best of all. Then shall hee that the diamount is geve unto take a lady by the hande and begynne the daunce. (Cited in Wickham 1959, 1:22)

At first blush the *Pas d'Armes* might appear to be no more than a species of mime, but it is important to remember that the centrepiece was an actual fight whose out-come was not assured, and might yet prove fatal to one of the participants even into the sixteenth century, although by then such occurrences were rare. In the course of time several factors caused the dramatic structure of the tournament to outweigh and eventually supercede the combat as the focus of attention, in the process draw-ing the whole event indoors as an elaborate prelude to the prize-giving and dance. Not least of these factors was the advent of firearms, initially causing a need for heavier armour (which, in turn, made tilting and other jousts less dangerous), and ultimately leading to the demise of the armed knight as a potent force in warfare.

Changes in the state of warfare had a profound effect both on the form of the tournament and its meaning. Although allegorical and symbolic elements had been present from the fourteenth century, they took a dominant role in Tudor times be-cause the martial component had less and less practical justification (even though it still had the capacity to thrill an audience). Thus the tournament became essentially festive, and served to mark significant courtly events such as coronations, wed-dings, and the induction of new knights into orders of chivalry.

Several dramatic features of the later tournaments concern us directly because they contributed to the development of the disguising, and later of the masque – both significant contexts of the morris. First, there are the scenic devices employed to dramatize the entrance of combatants to the lists. In an English tournament in 1501, for example, the College of Arms records indicate that the earl of Essex entered 'in a great mountayn' and his opponent, William de la Ryvers came forth 'in his pavylion, in a goodly shippe' (Wickham 1959, 1:44). Such cars and other elements of scenery not only acted as the basic staging for the tournament but also contributed to the symbolic meaning of the whole. Heraldic flora and fauna, for example, or trees festooned with heraldic 'fruit,' indicated the genealogies of the contestants (or who they purported to represent). These meanings were supple-mented by costumes and props which followed an enormously complex code laid down and interpreted by heralds.

Indeed, it was the tournament itself that gave a major impetus to the develop-ment of heraldry, the chief method by which participants identified themselves, for the benefit of the general audience (which included all ranks) and for each other.

In addition there was a tradition of entering the lists in symbolic disguise. For example Holinshed reports that in 1343,

> there was solemne justs proclaimed by the Lord Robert Morley, which were holden in Smithfeeld, where for challengers came foorth one aparelled like to the pope, bringing with him twelve other in garments like to cardinals.   (Cited in Wickham 1959, 1:20)

Whether used as a disguise or not, the costumes and dress of all participants answered to a well-developed system of meanings intertwined with standardized Christian doctrine, cosmology, and iconography. The heraldic tinctures, for example, while obviously serving the practical purpose of distinguishing one knight from another, were also codified into constellated patterns of significance. Likewise, particular costume elements had codifiable meanings (see Wickham 1959, 1:47).

What all of this suggests is that the tournament in the fifteenth century, with its declining emphasis on the strictly martial elements and an attendant rise in spectacular and dramatic display, was able to make the transition from an outdoor to an indoor setting with relative ease, where mimed action, pure and simple, replaced the combat. But it would be unfair to see the rise of Tudor disguisings as no more than the metamorphosis of the tournament form under the pressures of a changing military and courtly world. Other traditions, especially mumming, were folded into the matrix as well.

Before exploring the evolution of mumming it is as well to be clear on what the words 'mumming' and 'mummer' originally meant, because there has been considerable confusion here, which in turn has clouded historical theories. Wickham inclines towards *Oxford English Dictionary* in equating 'mummer' with the echoic 'mum,' meaning 'to be silent,' but Welsford prefers a derivation from the Old French *mômer*, 'to wear a disguise' or 'to masquerade' (favoured also by Eric Partridge in *Origins* [Partridge 1958]). The former etymology leads to the general inference that mumming was originally a form of mimed action without words, whereas the latter emphasizes the use of masks and costume.

The etymological problem arises because early references to mumming could be interpreted as dumb shows, or masquerades, or both. However, historical data and comparative etymology seem to support Welsford's case (Welsford 1927, 32–3). All French sources agree in deriving the modern *momer* from a root meaning a 'face mask' (and, also, a prize for the winner of a dicing game, *mumchance*, acted by disguised people). Likewise the German *mumme*, which may be the root for the French, means a 'face mask' or 'masked visage' (and is related to *mummenschantz*).

Also, French uses of *momer* antedate the English word 'mummer' and generally indicate disguising as the principal attribute, as in this edict issued in Lisle in 1395:

Defense de mommer de nuit a tout faulx visage ou le visage couvert de mascarure ou autrement.

[It is forbidden to *mommer* at night with a false face or face covered by a mask or such thing.]
(Cited in Welsford 1927, 37)

This is matched by a decree in England from 1418 in which it is ordered:

that no manere persone, of what astate, degre, or condicioun that euere he be, duryng this holy tyme of Cristemes be so hardy in eny wyse to walk by nyght in any manere mommyng, playes, enterludes, or eny other disgisynges with eny feynyd berdis, peyntid visers, diffourmyd or colourid visages in eny wise.   (Cited in Welsford 1927, 38)

It seems fair, therefore, to take the primary meaning of the English words as referring to *disguise*. One of the purportedly earliest uses of the English 'mumming' (see below) speaks of '130 men disguizedly aparailed ... to goe on mumming,' in keeping with the French usage. Yet this same text, by Wickham's lights, could be treated as an example of mumming as dumb show. Here I believe that Welsford's argument is sound, viz., it is more reasonable historically (and causally) to imagine being masked requiring being silent than the reverse; that is, that 'masking' is logically prior to 'silence.' The silence of the masked performers could subsequently lead to a confusion between the Anglo-French term 'mummer,' meaning 'masked performer' and the echoic English word 'mum,' meaning 'silent.'

If the derivation of 'mummer' as 'disguised person' is accepted, then the synthesis of elements from mumming with the tournament as it was evolving into a dramatic form makes sense. Some history of mumming as it developed in England in the late Middle Ages helps support this point of view.

The earliest record of a performance called a mumming in England appears to date from 1377 when ten-year-old Prince Richard (to be crowned Richard II later in the year) was treated to an elaborate show.[2] For present purposes several elements of this mumming can be highlighted.[3] The event began with a mounted procession through London of the participants in elaborate disguises representing a pope with a retinue of cardinals, an emperor with a following of knights and squires, and a legation of devils – all vizarded. On arrival at the prince's festal hall the mummers showed Richard a pair of dice that he was to use to cast for prizes ('first a ball of gould, then a cupp of gould, then a gould ring') in a game of some sort – the dice being rigged so that he would win. The implication of the text here seems to be that these events were acted out in mime. After the game there was a general dance with the courtiers dancing together on one side of the hall and the mummers on the other.

The initial procession is strongly reminiscent of processions that preceded tournaments, which included men equipped as knights, esquires, and cardinals. This form of mumming and the tournament, therefore, drew on a common stock of performance ideas and images, making it possible for the two to develop hybrid forms. In this light it is also important to note that this is by no means a folk entertainment. Although it was managed by 'ye Comons,' these men should be understood as the most powerful members of English society outside of the nobility.

Broken down into basic units, the mumming before prince Richard apparently consists of:

- a procession in costume through the town
- mimed action
- a (rigged) dice game
- a general dance

The first has already been discussed as parallel to the procession to the lists. The second, mimed action, is largely an inference from the text which is not really clear on this point. There are no set speeches described, and the natural implication from the statement 'ye said mummers saluted them, shewing a pair of dice upon a table to play with ye prince' is that the mummers could not, or would not, speak on account of their disguises (that is, either their masks prevented speech, or they wished to preserve their incognitos), and instead mimed what actions were required on the part of the prince and other participants. The third, the apparent game of chance that is loaded in the prince's favour, is the centrepiece of the whole affair. It would seem most likely that the dicing game that is feigned here is the French *mumchance*, given that the prize in this game was traditionally a gold ring in a gold cup (Welsford 1927, 32). The fourth, the general dance, follows the awarding of prizes in somewhat similar manner to the festivities after prize-giving at the tournament.

A good case could be made, therefore, for seeing this courtly mumming and the tournament (particularly the *Pas d'Armes*) as parallel performance forms – involving a costumed procession, a contention, a prize-giving, and a general dance – making the cross-fertilization of forms perfectly feasible. Further evidence as to the character and evolution of these courtly mummings is supplied through the ballads of John Lydgate.

Several poems written by Lydgate around 1430 are now understood to be the texts of mummings that were acted out (Wickham 1959, 1:191–228). The titles of these pieces alone indicate a number of the dramatic features of these mummings. For example:

a *lettre* made in wyse of balade by ledegate daun Johan, of a mommynge, whiche the Goldesmythes of the Cite of London mommed in Right fresshe and costele welych desguysing to theyre Mayre Eestfeld, vpon Candelmasse daye at nyght, affter souper; brought & presented vn to the Mayre by an heraude cleped ffortune   (Welsford 1927, 52)

tells us that the piece was introduced by a herald (in other words, a convention taken straight from the tournament), and that the actors were guild members performing in elaborate and expensive disguises. The poem itself contains no dialogue, or any other text that could be interpreted as speech for the actors, so it must be inferred that the act was a species of narrated dumb show.

At one time, this piece was taken by historians to be the usual medieval misconception of the structure of Greek drama, but Welsford and Wickham both interpret it as a description of the fifteenth-century mumming, although possibly an unwitting one. That is, it may well be Lydgate's idea of a Greek drama but, at the same time he may have based his own mummings on this form; thus, an inaccurate account of the one becomes a faithful rendering of the other, due to Lydgate's creative use of the form.

The main points of this performance are that the 'poet' stands at a pulpit and recites a verse narrative of momentous events, while actors in masks proceed from a stage house and perform the actions thus specified. Again the relation between this action and the action of tournament heralds announcing combatants who appear from pavilions in response to the announcement is apparent.

The only other feature of Lydgate's mummings that needs to be mentioned for the moment is the giving of gifts, often symbolic, by the mummers to the eminent person for which the show is being enacted (Wickham 1959, 1:199). In fact, the central purpose of Lydgate's species of mumming remained the giving of gifts. In the days of Richard II the central action was no more than a rigged game justifying the presentation of the gifts, but sixty years later this has evolved into a complex allegory with borrowings from the tournament and from medieval notions of Greek drama.

Several of Lydgate's texts use the word 'disguising' rather than 'mumming' in the title, and thus give us some idea of the development of the dramatic form that eventually evolved into the masque, and which was the main context for the courtly morris in the Tudor period. In many formal respects Lydgate's disguisings are like his mummings; basically a presenter introduces costumed characters who act out their parts largely in mime, followed by a general dance. But there are also key differences.

If anything the early disguising, as represented by Lydgate's texts, is closer in overall form to the later tournament with its symbolic trappings than to the mumming, because at its centre, in place of the gift-giving spectacle, is a formal conflict between two parties that must be resolved. In Lydgate's texts the conflict is pursued verbally, rather than physically – in one instance presenting the favourite drama of husband and wife in dispute over control in the house, and in another presenting a more symbolic encounter between Fortune and the Virtues. But in other disguisings for which we have detailed descriptions the enacted conflict comes straight out of the chivalric *Pas d'Armes* tradition. The following extract is taken from an eye-witness account of the festivities that marked the wedding of Prince Arthur to Katherine of Aragon in 1501, an occasion significant in morris history because it was the first time that disguisings and morisks appear together:

Upon the Friday at nyght ... when the Kyng and Quene hade takyn their noble seats undre their clothis of Estate ... then began and entrid this moost goodly and pleasaunt disguysing, conveyed and shewed by iii pagens p[ro]per and subtil: of whom the furst was a castell ... sett uppon certain whelys, and drawen into the seid hall of iiii^{or} great bestis w^t cheynys of gold ... There were w^{t}in this Castell, disguysid, vii goodly and fresshe ladies, lokyng owt of the wyndowes of the same ... The secunde pagent was a shippe in like wise sett upon whelys, w^{t}out any leders in sight, in right goodly apparell, havyng her mastys, toppys, saylys, her taclyng, and all other app[ur]ten[au]ns necessary unto a seemly vessell, as though it hade been saylyng in the see ... In the which shipp there was a goodly and a faire lady, in her apparell like unto the P[ri]ncess of Hispayne. Owte and from the seid shippe descendid down by a ledder two weelbeseen and goodly p[er]sons, callying themsilf Hope and Desire, passyng toward the rehersid castell, w^t their baners in maner and forme as ambassadours from Knights of the Mownte of Love unto the ladies w^{t}in the castell ... for th'entente to ateigne the favouris of the seid ladies p[re]sent; The seid ladies gave their final answere of uttrly refuse and knowledge of any such company ... The two seid ambassadours, therew[ith] takyng great displeasure, shewed the seid ladies that the Knights wolde for this unkyend refusall make bataill ... Incontynent cam in the thirde pagent, in liknes of a great hill ... in whom were enclosid viii goodly Knights w^t ther ban[ers] spred and displaied ... they toke their stondyng upon the other sid of the shipp ... they alited from the sid mount ... and hastely spede them to the rehersed castell, which they forthw[ith] asaultid so and in such wise that the ladies, yeldyng themselvys, descendid from the seid castell. The knights right freshly disguysed and the ladies also, iiii^{or} of them afte[r] th'englisshe fachyon and th'other iiii^{or} afte[r] the man[ner] of hispayne ... and dauncyd togyders dyv[er]s and many goodly daunces.   (College of Arms MS, 1st M13, cited in Wickham 1959, 1:208–9)

Here the relationship to the tournament is abundantly clear. In fact, pageant cars in the shape of a hill (with a castle) and a ship were used to bear the main protagonists in a tournament earlier in the same year. They were, however, not the same vehicles; the descriptions of them by eyewitnesses are quite distinct (see Wickham 1959, 1: 218). The cars used for the disguising were presumably special indoor vehicles. The sending of ambassadors, the official challenge, display of banners, and so forth are all taken directly from the tournament proper.

This description of a disguising does not indicate that a morisk, as such, took place, but the accounts of the wedding clearly indicate that disguisings and morisks were to be intrinsic parts of the festivities:

Item, that Jacques Hault and William Pawne ... devise and prepare disguisings and some morisks after the best manner they can ...   (Kipling 1977, 100)

This reference by itself could be considered equivocal in that it is not clear whether the disguisings and morisks are part of the same event. But a review of other accounts and consideration of the nature of the morisk itself makes it clear that they do indeed belong together. For example, at the celebration of the proxy marriage of princess Margaret and James IV of Scotland, one year after the wedding of Prince Arthur, a disguising and morisk appeared together using familiar pageant machinery:

Incontinent after the Pryses [for jousting] were given, there was in the Hall a goodly Pageant, curiously wrought with Fenestralles, having many Lights brenning in the same, in the manner of a Lantron out of wich sorted divers Sorts of Morisks. Also very goodly Disguising of Six Gentlemen and Six Gentlewomen, which danced divers Dances.   (Anglo 1960, 23–4)

Disguising and morisks are again spoken of together in the principal description of the wedding of Henry VII's daughter, Princess Mary (see p. 54). And, similarly, they appear together in the royal accounts of the same year:

Henry Wentworth asketh alowauns for his costes, being abought the besyness of the disguising and moreske by the kinges commaundement, from the 27th day of September to the 27th day of December, at 8d be the day for 80 days 53s 4d   (Myers 1981, 127)

So, although no single reference is unambiguous, taken together there is some reason to suppose that disguisings and morisks were linked in some manner. This hypothesis is reasonably confirmed by exploring the nature of the morisk itself. Before doing so, however, it is necessary to consider one problem of nomenclature, in order to draw on the widest range of data.

It is not entirely clear whether, when performed at the Tudor court, 'morisk' and 'morris' are the same kind of dance with a slightly different name, but there are some indications that the two words could be used interchangeably, and, of course, this whole section of the evolutionary history of morris is predicated on the belief that the two words are, in some measure, synonymous (see also appendix A). At least one pair of references helps confirm this supposition. Edward Hall in his *Chronicle* gives an account of the events of Epiphany 1511 that includes the following statement:

Agaynste the xii. daye or the daye of the Epiphanie at nighte, before the banket in the Hall at Richemond, was a pageaunt deuised like a mountayne ... & out of the same came a ladye, appareiled in cloth of golde, and the chyldren of honor called the Henchemen, whiche were freshly disguised, and daunced a Morice before the kyng.   (Hall 1809, 516–17)

Richard Gibson in his financial summary of the same events states:

For pastyme the kynges plesyr was to havf sum revelles the weche devysyd by master harry gyllforth that ys to under stond an hyll somet ther oon a golldyn stoke branchyd with rosyes and pom garnetes kround ... ought of the weche hyll yssewd a morryske dancyd by the kynges yong gentyllmen as hynes men and ther to a lady ...   (PRO E 36/217, ff.21–8)

The one calls the dance a 'Morice' and the other, a 'morryske.' It could be argued that Hall's account is not exactly contemporaneous with the event, but he does use primary documents and the accounts of eyewitnesses (and he was Henry VIII's contemporary), so his observations cannot be brushed aside as anachronisms.

Although there may be quibbles to contend with, it is reasonably certain that 'morisk' and 'morris' were originally related word forms and, as such, could have been used as synonyms in the Tudor court (although this does not mean that they were identical in meaning). On this argument, the following extracts from John Heron's account book could be included with the references to disguisings that involved morisks:

Item delyuered to Master Wentworth for to make a dysguysing for a moryce daunce xiij^{li} vj^s viij^d

Item to Master Wentworth towarde the makyng of a disguysing for a moryce daunce c^s

          (PRO E 36/214 in Anglo 1960, 43)

Very little direct evidence exists in the English sources to determine the precise nature of the courtly morisks/morrises associated with the custom of disguising. But judicious use of European sources can, tentatively at least, fill in some of the blanks. First, however, we must glean what we can from the English materials. We have already seen that the dancers entered on or in a pageant car from which they issued to perform the morisk. Only two sources give further details, but these provide important clues linking the English forms with Italian and other European models.

The first text is Richard Gibson's accounts of the Epiphany 1511 disguising performed before Henry VIII and devised by his master of revels Sir Harry Guildford (PRO E 36/217, ff.21–8). The second text also concerns a morisk devised by Sir Harry Guildford for Epiphany, three years later:

For to do pleser the Kyngs grace, and for to pas the tyme of Chrestemas, by sir Harry Gyllfurth Master of the Revells, was devysed an Interluit, in the wheche conteyned a moresks of vj persons and ij ladys [called Beauty and Venus]: wherfor by hys commandement, of our soveraine lord the Kyng, and at appointment of Sir Harry Gylforth, was preparyd, had and wrought dyvers and sundry garments ... Item ... bowght of satten of bregs, whyte & gree, xlviij yards, the yard 2s 6d, wherof spent in 6 jakytts for gentylmen, to every jakytt 6 yards. These jakyyts had wyd slevys pendent. Itm bought ... of yowlow sarsenet xxxviij yards, the yard 4s wherof spent & imployd for a foolys kote 4 yards ... Item bowght ... xxiiij dozyn of bells, the dosyn 12d spent for the said morysks, as well as 5 dosyn of the Kyngs store that were also spent ... Item bowght 38 yards of blake sarssenet, the yard 3s wherof spent in vj gownys for the sayd gentylmen to kever ther garmentts, to every gowne v yards, 30 yards ... item spent for vj payer of slop hosyn for kevyring of ther bells, 4 yards. (PRO E 36/217, ff.74–6)

These accounts, while full of information concerning costumes and props, do not contain enough narrative detail to reconstruct the dances based on them alone. They do, however, contain sufficient clues to find possible analogues elsewhere. To begin, it is evident that the morisks were performed by specific characters, sometimes named. The first involved four knights – green, white, red, and black – a fool, and a lady, and the second, six dancers, a fool, and two ladies identified as Beauty and Venus.

In the 1511 production the costumes would have turned the scene around the mountain into a riot of reflected light and jangling bells. The four knights, presumably identified by the underlying colours of their jackets, had sewn on their clothing hanging spangles ('spanges hyngeres') and set spangles ('setteres'), as did the lady. In all, Gibson bought 29,000 spangles, or 5,800 per costume. In addition the knights had white bullions ('bolyones'), or little baubles – 200 per man – attached to their hose. The accounts do not indicate that the coat – a confection of crimson and white sarsenet – had spangles attached, but he and the knights were weighted down with bells. The fool, in place of spangles, had twelve dozen bells attached to his coat, and he and the knights had, in addition, nine dozen bells each, attached to leather garters buckled to arms and legs.

It is hardly to be imagined that such volatile garments were in the service of a sedate and measured choreography. Rather we can envisage the dancers cavorting and leaping in order to shower the audience with kaleidoscopic images and frenzied tinklings. This conjecture is possibly strengthened by the fact that Gibson reports that the costumes (with the exception of that of the lady, who may have moved more graciously) were ruined by the end of the performance, to the point of not being worth saving in the king's store. Baubles, spangles, and bells attached to flimsy silken fabrics would easily tear loose under the stress of constant gyration. Apparently the costumes were used only once (for the actual performance) because Gibson had to hire bells for practice sessions. This adds further weight to the notion that the sound of the bells chinking along with the motions of the performers was an intrinsic component of the choreography.

There is also the possibility that the use of bells on costumes added a specifically Moorish connotation to them. For example, at Shrovetide festivities in 1548 King Edward VI and a troupe of young lords performed a masque of Moors. Included in the accounts is the following:

> To Wi*ll*iam hobson of london hab*e*rdassh*er* ... ffor xij doss*en* of bell*es* to hange at the skyr*tes* of the mores ga*r*ment*es* at v^d ob doss*en*   (Feuillerat 1914, 31)

The materials (and payments for craftsmen) for Gibson's costumes are also reminiscent of specifically Moorish costumes for a morisque designed by Hue de Boulogne in the fifteenth century:

A *Hue de Boulongne*, varlet de chambre et paintre de MdS, pour, par l'ordonnance d'icellui S, avoir fait de son mestier VII habis de drap de soye de plusieurs coulleurs et estrange fachon, propices à danser la morisque et iceulx enrichiz d'ouvrage de peaulx de Bresil d'or et d'argent, de lettres sarasinoises et de tourbettes faictes à maniere de frap d'or, et avec ce, fait toutes les bordures et manches et lez enrichiz d'or clinquant de trois doubles dehachées à manières de franges d'or et d'autres ouvrages non samblables l'un à l'autre, et avec chascun habit une coqueluce de samblable soye et de pareilles façon et estoffes, estoffées les unes de elles de serpens et ung long col à manière d'une beste tout chargiée de fremailles et d'or tramblant, le plus dru que faire se peut, et les autres d'autres devises, ensamble avec chascun d'iceulx habis, une paire de chausses de toille, où sont faictes testes de serpent de bature d'or parcy, qui mordent de dessus jusques aux genoulx dont saillent gouttes comme de sang et autres devises et fait à chascun une barbe et chevelure estranges, sollers et sonnettes pour, à tous iceulx habiz, danser la morisque ...

[To Hue de Boulogne, manservant and painter of MdS, by the order of said S, having made according to his need seven costumes in silken cloth in several colours and foreign fashion, suitable for dancing the *morisque*, the latter made more luxurious by workmanship in skins from (Bresil), in gold and silver, saracen letters, and turbans made in the manner of cloth of gold with all the borders and sleeves enriched with gold leaf, three doublets slashed to give the effect of golden fringes, and other outfits all different from one another, and with each costume a hood of similar silk and in similar fashion and materials, some of them filled out with serpents and with a long *col*, fashioned like a beast all covered with gold spangles as thick set as it can be made, and the others made with other devices, and together with each of these costumes, a pair of cloth hose, on which are serpent heads in gold lacquer biting from the top down towards the knees whence drops like blood spurt out, and other devices, and each one with foreign beard and coiffure, shoes and little bells for all these outfits for dancing the morisque ...]   (LaBorde 1849–52, 1:252–3)

Gear other than costumes entered in Gibson's records provides further insight into the nature of the dance. In particular, his accounts show that the performance re-quired four targets (round shields) and six darts (light projectiles such as spears or lances), all highly embellished with bells and streamers. Four armed knights sug-gests a mock contest perhaps for the purpose of winning the lady's favour or some prize. Certainly this would be in keeping with the tournament and mumming tra-dition from which the disguising evolved and would also be in line with European analogues discussed below.

The knights dancing using a combination of dart and target may also have a Moorish connection. At the installation of the mayor of Norwich in 1556, described in the manuscript, Mayor's Book of Oaths, there were three standing pageants, two of which involved images of Moors with dart and target:

This paggeaunte was doone by the waightes off the Cytte of Norwich. There was a skaf-fowllde made at Sainte Peters of Howndegate cherche styelle Rownnde Lyke a pavyllioun Richelie adorned full of targettes with A morien [i.e., Moor] on the toppe staunding naked with a targett and a greate darte in his haunde ...

There was in the parrsshe of St Iohns a greate pageant*nt* stonndinge betwene Mr persses and Richard Bat*es*, *whi*chwas like a greate Castell w*i*th a greate gate thervnd*er* like a Cytte gate & ou*er* the gate a greate Castell w*i*th towers ... & vppon eu*ery* tower a Morrian w*i*th his darte & his targett ...   (Cited in Galloway 1984, 38–9)

Also, Edward VI's masque of Moors mentioned above required darts for the Moors (but no targets). Likewise, Machyn describes a May game in London in 1557 that involved Moors with dart and target (Machyn 1841, 137).

The role of the fool is not immediately obvious. According to the accounts he carried a turned ladle decorated with the ubiquitous bells, and which was 'spent' during the performance. In much later depictions from England, such as Vincken-boom's 'Thames at Richmond' (*c* 1620) the morris fool uses a ladle as a device to col-lect money from the audience, but in the Tudor period Gibson's account is the sole reference, and it seems unlikely that the fool was going around collecting at the banquet. It is more usual at this time for the court fool to be shown carrying a bauble or marotte, but it is quite possible that the ladle served a similar function. In one of the Burgundian masquerades represented in the Freydal Codex (*c* 1512) commis-sioned by the Holy Roman Emperor Maximilian I – admittedly not an English source, but roughly contemporary with the English morisks – there is a court fool dancing brandishing what appears to be a leather covered ladle as if it were a marotte (Leitner 1880–2, n.p.) Also, in the accounts for the Lord of Misrule for the Christ-mas celebrations of Edward VI in 1551/2 (see next chapter) there is an entry for:

a ladle w*i*th a bable pendant ... deliv*er*id to the Lorde of mysrules foole ... (Feuillerat 1914, 73) suggesting a conflation of the bauble and ladle into one symbol. The fool's costume alone, however, does not permit speculation on his place in the dance. But, further use of European analogues may give insight into the dance in general and shed some light on the fool in particular.

The morisk accounts from 1514 at first blush appear merely to replicate those of 1511 with different numbers of performers – two ladies, six men, and a fool – and somewhat less detail concerning their costumes. But one set of items is curious and may provide a link to European morisks of the period. Although the men had fashionable jackets of green and white satin with pendant sleeves, the accounts call for black sarsenet to make 'vj gownys for the sayd gentylmen to kever ther garmentts' and also 'vj payer of slop hosyn for kevyring of ther bells.' This appears to indicate that the men entered with disguises over their disguises, and that at some point they tossed off the black gowns and hose to reveal themselves in their gaudy splendour. If this is the case, the performance is highly reminiscent of a moresca performed before Pope Leo X in 1521 at the court of Castel San Angelo:

Prima uscì una donna, che con certe stanze in ottava rima pregò Venere che le volesse dare un amante degno. Poi a suon di tamburi, una moresca di otto eremiti uscì di sotto un padiglione di raso berrettino che avevan rizzato, e circondarono un Amore privo della faretra, percotendolo come nemico del mondo. Amore fece orazione a Venere perchè lo liberasse dalle loro mani: Venere invocata scese, e diede a bere un certo liquore agli eremiti, rendendo ad Amore l'arco e la faretra, sicchè egli cominciò a «saetare quei poveri frati,» i quali, svegliati, si lamentavano forte, e pur ballando intorno ad Amore, cominciarono a dir parole amorose alla donna che aveva invocato Venere. Essa li pregò di dimostrare il valor loro, e quelli buttata via la schiavina, restarono giovani, ben vestiti «in abito di galanti» e presero a combatter fra loro, rimanendone uno solo che fu l'amante destinato.

[First, a woman entered and in stanzas of *ottava rima* prayed Venus to give her a worthy lover. Thereupon, to the sound of drums, a *moresca* of eight eremites came out of a grey-green satin pavilion that they had put up, and surrounded a Cupid, deprived of a quiver, beating him like an enemy of the world. The Cupid prayed to Venus to free him from their hands. Venus evoked, came down and gave a potion to the eremites, and restored to Cupid his bow and quiver, with which he began to shoot these poor friars. Thus aroused, they lamented exceedingly, and while dancing around Cupid began to sing loving words to the woman who had invoked Venus. She bade them demonstrate their valour. They threw off their religious habits and showed themselves to be young and well dressed in the garments of gallant gentlemen, and began to fight among one other, the one remaining being the destined lover.]

(D'Ancona 1891, 2:92)

Although it would be an unwarranted leap to equate the English performance with this

Italian version, the coincidences of characters and costumes do suggest the possibility of parallels. And if we accept the reasonable assertion that English morisks drew on models from Italy and France (and vice versa), then more detailed accounts from contemporary Europe can tentatively be drawn on to complement the English records.

Certainly there is evidence that performers from England, Burgundy, Flanders, and Italy, where the morisk was popular in courtly festivities, had the opportunity to meet and exchange ideas. For example, at the wedding of Charles the Bold, duke of Burgundy, to Margaret of York in Bruges (Flanders was at the time under the control of Burgundy) in 1468, English and local musicians worked together. Olivier de la Marche records in his *Mémoires* that when Margaret entered Bruges she was greeted by

… clairons, menestreulx et trompettes, tant angloix comme bourguignons …

[… as many English as Burgundian clarionists, fiddlers, and trumpeters.]

(de la Marche 1883–8, 3:110)

De la Marche also provides lengthy descriptions of several morisks given to entertain the wedding guests.

However, when making comparisons with European materials several limitations should be observed. First, it is important to remember that the morisk often does not comprise the entire performance described in a primary source, but is, rather, a dance element within it. The English accounts of 1514, for example, say that the revels consisted of an interlude 'in the wheche conteyned a moresks.' That is, the morisk was not the whole performance, merely a component of it. Therefore, statements concerning the nature of the morisk must be confined to descriptions that are clearly connected to dancing and not drawn randomly from the elements of the overall performance which is the context for the dance. Second, it is essential not to fall into the trap, so common in morris history and in theatre history in general, of believing that European court morisks were entirely homogeneous. Sources suggest quite the opposite. Finally I should make it quite clear that the following rehearsal of European morisks is not exhaustive by any means; that study would deserve a book in its own right.

Bearing in mind these caveats, a few prototypical characteristics, or 'family resemblances,' of European morisks may be identified tentatively: high leaping, fighting, mimed action, individual rather than concerted or figured action, dancing in a circle or around the room, rhythmic stepping, beating time with implements, and the use of dancing bells.

Eyewitnesses frequently refer to the leaping of morisk dancers, sometimes even indicating that the style of leap is definitive of the dance. At the wedding of Charles the Bold, for example, sirens issued from a whale pageant,

ayant pignes et mirouers à leurs mains, qui commencerent une chanson estrange ... et au son de celle chanson saillirent l'ung après l'aultre, en maniere de morisque.

[having combs and looking glasses in their hands, who began a strange song ... and at the sound of this song cavorted one after the other, in the style of a *morisque.*]

(de la Marche 1883–7, 3:198)

Here the recorder, who was also the organizer of the spectacles and therefore a firmly reliable authority, clearly indicates that there is a style of saltation that is peculiar to the morisk, as does the following description of a performance in 1524:

poi stringendosi su alcuni punti moreschi, butarono molti belli salti schiavoneschi con certe fortezze di schena, che fu bellissimo veder.

[then, limiting themselves to certain features of moresca [*punti moreschi*], they sprung with many beautiful leaps in the manner of slaves, with some strength of the back, which was most beautiful to see.]   (D'Ancona 1891, 2:125)

These leaps are supposedly so vigorous that in the farce *Troys galans et un badin* it is stated that 'morisque' dancers will not get into heaven because their movements will break through the floor (see Brown 1963, 162).

The moresca of eremites cited above also indicates a very common theme, namely, that of the moresca as a fighting dance. The following description by Castiglione of an intermezzo with morescas, performed during a performance of Bibbiena's comedy *Calandra* at the court of Urbino during Carnival 1513, supplements the first in this regard:

La prima fu una moresca di Jason, il quale comparse nella scena da un capo ballando, armato all'antica, bello, con la spada e una targa finissima: dall'altro furon visti in un tratto due tori simili al vero, che alcuni pensorno che fosser veri, che gittavano fuoco dalla bocca. A questi si accostò il buon Jason, e feceli arare, posto loro il giogo e l'aratro, e poi seminò i denti del dracone, e nacquero a poco a poco dal palco uomini armati all'antica, tanto bene, quanto credo io che si possa; e questi ballorno una fiera moresca, per ammazzar Jason, e poi quando fûrno all'entrare s'ammazzavano ad uno ad uno ...

[First there was a *moresca* of Jason, who appeared on the scene on one side dancing, armed in the old style, beautiful, with a very fine sword and shield. On the other side one could see two bulls that almost looked real, – some believed they were real – and that were throwing fire from their mouths. The good Jason approached them, and made them plough, placing on them a yoke and plough. He sowed the dragon's teeth and little by little from the stage, men, armed in the old style, were born – so well done that I believe it could not have been done better. These men danced a good *moresca* to kill Jason, and when they went at it they killed one another, one by one ...]   (D'Ancona 1891, 2:103)

An anonymous manuscript records another moresca at the same carnival, also with a sword-fighting motif:

In la detta commedia di Nicola per uno degli intermezzi comparse una Italia, tutta lacerata da genti barbare, et volendo dire alcuni lamentevoli versi, perdui fiate, come per duolo extremo, firmosse nel recitare, et cosi come smarrita, partì dil palco, lasciando ai spettatori oppinione che la si fussi persa nel dire. Ma nel representarsi gli altri giorni poi la commedia del Rugiero, fu remesso questo medesimo intermezzo, e nel chiamare in suo ajuto Francesco Maria, cum bellissimo attizare di moresca, comparse uno armato cum nuda spada in mano, il quale come a stoccate et altri colpi, cacciati d'intorno essa Italia tutti quelli barbari che l'avevano saccheggiata, et tornato a lei pur a tempi di suono in bellissima moresca.

[For one of the intermezzi in Nicola's commedia appeared Italy, all lacerated by barbarians and wishing to recite some verses in lament. She took two deep breaths, as if in extreme pain, stopped reciting, and, as if she were lost, left the stage, leaving the spectators to believe or think that she had lost her power to speak. But, in presenting Rugiero's commedia on the other days the same intermezzo was introduced, and in calling to her assistant, Francesco Maria, with a beautiful enactment of *moresca*, one appeared armed with a naked sword in hand. This one with stoccados and other thrusts, having driven away from around Italy all the barbarians that had ravaged her, returned to her with rhythmic sounds in a most beautiful *moresca*.]   (D'Ancona 1891, 2:105)

Indeed this swordplay aspect of the dancing is so well known that contemporaries are known to have spoken of the moresca in the same breath as the matachin, a sword-fighting dance:[4]

Escan fuor quattro vestiti da mattaccini, con sonagliera a' piedi e spade ignude in mano, con gran strepito; e sarebbe buono che facessino due o tre atti di moresca e, non li sapendo fare, scorrino per la scena e rientrino.

[Four entered dressed as *mattacini* with bells on their feet naked swords in their hands, and a great noise; and it would have been good if they had done two or three turns of moresca. But not knowing how to do it, they strolled on the scene and left.]

(*Rappresentazione di Santa Uliva* 34, 795, cited in Battaglia et al. 1961– , 10:899)

In this regard it is also worth noting that John Florio, in his Italian/English dictionary, gives the following definition for the Italian cognate of matachin:

Mattacíni, as Atteláni, *a kinde of antique moresco or mattacino dance.*   (Florio 1611, 304)[5]

When the dancers are not specifically identified as fighting there are, nonetheless broad hints that gestured action is of considerable importance to the dance. References commonly speak admiringly of the dancers' 'dexterity' and 'gestures.' In 1542 a moresca designed by Giulio Romano is described in part:

... et cosi, et con gli habiti che riuscirono maravigliosi, et con la musica, che fu dolcissima, et con la lor agilità et destrezza, che non fu poca, diedero grandissima pastura agli spettatori ...

[... they gave a great deal to the spectacle with their costumes which were beautiful, with the music which was most sweet, and with their not little agility and dexterity ...]
(D'Ancona 1891, 2:439)

And the description from 1524 cited above concerning the beautiful leaping ability of the dancers continues:

... et sopra tutto gesti et moti tanto lassivi, che facevano liquefar li marmi ...

[... and most of all with gestures and forms so lascivious they would arouse statues ...]
(D'Ancona 1891, 2:125)

The iconic primary sources of the period appear to confirm the importance of gestured action. Ten 'maruscka tanntz' figures survive from an original set of sixteen commissioned in 1480 for the Tanzsaal of the Rathaus in Munich and carved in limewood by Erasmus Grasser (see Müller-Meiningen 1984). Each figure is, in many ways, distinct but all definitely depict a style of dancing that emphasizes dramatic gestures of the hands, limbs, and torso accompanied by intense facial expressions. All the dancers are contorted or twisted in some way. Some are bent at the torso, while others show exaggerated postures of the legs and carefully articulated positions of the fingers on each hand. Two engravings by Israel van Meckenem that are traditionally associated with moresques (figures 15 and 16) show much the same twists and contortions of the body and limbs of the dancers.

The interest of the written sources with gestures and dexterity combined with the clear indications of precise finger movements in the iconic is reminiscent of certain dictionary references to morris and moresque in England. Under the entry 'chironomia' appears the following in Thomas Cooper's 1552 revision of *Bibliotheca Eliotae*:

Figure 15: Engraving of the ring dance by Israel van Meckenem

Chironomia, foe. ge., a facion of gesture with the hands, used in dauncynge, as in a morys daunce, or in kervyng of meate ...
Chironomia saltatio, the morys daunce.
Chironomus, i, mas. ge., he that teacheth one to make gesture, or he that daunceth with gesture of the handes in a morys.   (Cooper 1552, sig. O vi recto)

The link with moresques is expressly made by John Higins in his translation of Junius's *Nomenclator*:

Chironomus, Iuuen., gesticulator, ... danseur de morisques. A morise danser, or danser of the morisques ...   (Higins 1585, 521)

The Latin word *chironomus*, and its cognate forms, is a direct transliteration of the Greek *cheironomos*, which means an actor noted for mimed gestures. The term is also specifically used to designate gestures that are rhythmic or regular (as when performed to music).

It is also implicit in these descriptions and depictions that the emphasis of the dance is on individual action and prowess, rather than on group action or motions based on figured evolutions (although there are clearly moments of group activity). In Giulio Romano's moresca, for example:

Oltre a questi otto pastori, eravi il Dio lor Pan vestito nella medesima maniera, ma con la corna, si come si figura. Questo è uno Giudeo, che suona l'arpa, il quale fu il primo ad uscir in sala come lor Dio, si che se ne usci in modo di moresca con l'arpa in mano, dietro al quale uscirono ad uno ad uno gli otto pastori, con una hasta per uno nella man destra, facendo la medesima moresca, che haveva fatta il lor Dio.

[In addition to these shepherds was their god Pan, dressed in the same way, but with horns just as you would imagine him. He was a Jew who played the harp, and was the first person to come into the room as their god. He came out in the *moresca* style, harp in hand. Behind him the shepherds came out one by one, each a stick in the right hand, doing the same *moresca* that their god had done.]   (D'Ancona 1891, 2:439)

That is, the moresca movements can be and are performed by a single individual – Pan – and then the shepherds imitate his motions.

It is also worthy of note that the description of the dancers coming out in view or performing motions 'one by one,' as in the last citation, is frequently repeated. The following description of a moresca, for example, is extracted from a letter by Lodovico Genovesi concerning a feast given by Cardinal Pietro Riario at carnival time, 1473:

E ne la corte era aparechiato uno carro triumphale, del quale usivano a una una persone che fecero la morescha ...

[In the courtyard there was constructed a decorated car out of which issued, one by one, characters who performed a *morescha* ...]   (D'Ancona 1891, 2:67)

Note also that the description of the moresca at the wedding of Charles the Bold, cited above, speaks of the sirens dancing, 'one after the other, in the style of a *morisque*' (de la Marche 1883–8, 3:198). These accounts are, in turn, reminiscent of standing orders concerning the protocols of performance of an English aristocratic morris:

And when the saide moris cummes in the Midst of the Hall Than the said Minstrallis to play the daunces that is appointid for theim And when they Here the saide Minstrallis play than

Figure 16: Book engraving by Israel van Meckenem

to com out oon aftir an outhir as they be apointid And when they Haue doon to go furth in like caas as they cam into the saide towr or thing devisid for theim ...

(Lancashire 1980, 35–6)

Even though the dancers appear to perform individual rather then figured evolutions there is strong evidence that the loose formation of the dancers in a circle or of dancing single file in a circle around an object or character was commonplace. The shepherds that danced with Pan in Giulio Romano's moresca are typical:

Poichè tutti furono usciti, et si hebbero radunati in cerchio girando intorno alla sala ...

[As they entered they gathered in a circle going around the room ...]

(D'Ancona 1891, 2:439)

A moresque of monkeys, performed as an *entremets* at the wedding of Charles the Bold, contains this element:

et le cinge, qui avoit le tabourin, commença à jouer une morisque, et en dansant celle morisque, firent le tour autour de la tour ...

[and the monkey who had the tabor began to dance a *morisque*, and in dancing that *morisque*, made a circle around the tower ...]   (de la Marche 1883–8, 3:154)

The two van Meckenem engravings also strongly suggest the importance of a circular formation, and have in the past been used as primary evidence (along with similar representations from Germany and Italy) for the existence of a type of moresca known rather confusingly as the 'ring dance' – not because the dancers stand in a ring but because a central character sometimes holds a ring.[6] Barbara Lowe's sketch has often been taken as reasonable:

The theme is always the same – a group of dancers, including a Fool, compete for the favours of a Lady, who stands in the centre holding a ring, apple, or other symbol of her favour. The prize conventionally goes to the Fool. The dance is generally grotesque, or 'antic,' even when it is not specifically a 'moresk.' This appellation seems to depend chiefly on two things – bells, and chironamia (sic) or 'dancing with the hands.'   (Lowe 1957, 65)

This, like so many other of Lowe's conjectures, probably contains a germ of truth but needs to be handled circumspectly because of her cavalier use of sources. On the positive side, it is quite clear that dances involving a central lady around whom male dancers cavort grotesquely, often using elaborate gestures of the hands, are well documented in Europe in the late fifteenth and early sixteenth centuries. Whether *all* depictions of such dances should be called morisks is open to doubt, although some definitely are. Many of them are not labelled as such so that the kind of circular reasoning alluded to in previous chapters appears to be in operation. That is, Lowe has abstracted certain elements that she takes to be typical (i.e., bells, chironomy, central lady, dancing in a circle) from a limited number of images designated specifically as morisks, and then put together a list of other images that conform to this general picture. From this list she then argues that the ring morisk was commonplace.

Furthermore, it is difficult to assess the reliability of sculptures, drawings, and engravings as accurate renderings of actual morisks because these depictions so clearly draw heavily from each other and from images outside the dance. Joan-Baptista Vrints' Chorea Mundi, for example, is highly reminiscent of Daniel Hopfer's ring morisk (figures 17 and 18) in composition, characters, and gestures, suggesting either that one is a direct copy of the other, or that both rely on a third earlier source. In addition, the head of the kneeling character in Hopfer (not in the Vrints) is a copy of a drawing Scaramuccia (i.e., scaramouche from commedia dell'arte) by Leonardo.[7]

In addition, the morisk itself clearly combines components that can be found in other contemporary dance and masquerade forms. In Maximilian I's Freydal Codex (Leitner 1880–2), for example, what appears to be a classic ring morisk is depicted as one of over sixty masquerades, with which it shares many elements, particularly of costume. In fact it is hard to distinguish the morisk from other masquerades using pictorial evidence alone. The morisk's male dancers, for example, wear black gauze on their faces and so do the men in many of the other engravings (at least all who are not wearing masks or other apparel to hide their faces).

Bells on legs and arms, often used as indicative of morisk or morris dance, are common costume elements in the fifteenth and sixteenth centuries for dancers who are definitely not performing morisks. Many of the Schembartläufer at the Nuremburg Schembart Carnival, for example, are shown in contemporary manuscripts wearing bands of bells identical with those worn by morisk dancers (Sumberg 1941, 215–17). It is unwise, therefore, to infer too much about a dance in a depiction, seeing that elements were freely traded between dance types.

It is also difficult to know whether the ring dance (or dances) ever featured in British courtly morrises or morisks; there is only the most circumstantial evidence to support such a claim. Gibson's inventories, for example, indicate that one morisk involved four dancers, a fool, and a lady, and another, six dancers, a fool, and two ladies. In 1504 in Stirling there was a morris presented to the Scottish king comprising six dancers and a lady (Paul 1900–2, 2:414). Likewise the gold salt detailed in the sixteenth-century catalogues of royal jewels was said to depict five dancers and a lady (see p 49). But without more concrete testimony, no more can be said

Figure 17: *Chorea Mundi* by Joan Baptista Vrints

Figure 18: Etching of the ring dance by Daniel Hopfer

than that the European 'ring' dances and English courtly morrises and morisks shared certain characters and costume elements.

The final set of points that can be made about European morisks in general is that they involved a variety of rhythmic or metrical movements, keeping time with the music. There are both general allusions and detailed accounts of unique stepping patterns, for example. In Giulio Romano's moresca the dancing around the room was apparently performed to a pace complicated enough that an interested observer could not record it accurately:

Poichè tutti furono usciti, et si hebbero radunati in cerchio girando intorno alla sala con certi lor contrapassi, ch'io non so discerner nè far.

[As they entered they gathered in a circle going around the room with a certain step, which I can neither explain nor do.]   (D'Ancona 1891, 2:439)

The sixteenth-century dancing master Jehan Tabourot, canon of Langres (under the pseudonymous anagram Thoinot Arbeau), gives a more detailed account of the stepping of one kind of 'morisques' that he says was fashionable when he was young. He was born in 1519, so it would be fair to date this description at around 1540:

Les Morisques se dancent par mesure binaire: Du commencement on y alloit par tappements de pieds, & parce que les danceurs les treuuoient trop penibles, ils y ont mis des tappements des talons seullement, en tenant les arteils des pieds fermes: Aulcuns les ont voulu dancer auec des marque-pieds, & marque-talons meslés ensemble ... Ie ne laisseray de vous en donner l'air, auec les mouuements d'vn passage ...

frappe talon droit	Le danceur de Morisques tient
frappe talon gaulche	le bout des arteils tousiours
frappe talon droit	ferme cependant qu'il frappe des
frappe talon gaulche	talons, pour faire resonner ses
frappe talons	sonnettes, & les frappe talons
souspir	sans dire a droit ni a gaulche,
	equipolent pieds ioincts.
frappe talon droit	
frappe talon gaulche	
frappe talon droit	
frappe talon gaulche	
frappe talons	
souspir	
frappe talon droit	

> frappe talon gaulche
> frappe talon droit
> frappe talon gaulche
> frappe talon droit
> frappe talon gaulche
> frappe talon droit
> frappe talon gaulche
> frappe talon droit
> frappe talon droit
> frappe talon gaulche
> frappe talons
> souspir

Il fault bien qu'il marche tousiours auant, iusques au bout de la salle: Et pour ce faire, notterez qu'aprez le frappe talons qui equipole à pieds ioincts & cadance, auant le frappe talon droit, le danceur auance légerment ses deux pieds, & en mesme instant, fait le dit frappe talon droit ...

[*Morisques* are danced in duple meter. Originally they were performed with taps of the whole foot, but because the dancers found this too tiring, they executed heel taps only, keeping their toes still. Others chose to dance with the movements *marque-pieds* (lit. mark feet) and *marque-talons* (lit. mark heels) mixed together ... I will give you the melody plus movements of one sortie only ...

> tap right heel
> tap left heel
> tap right heel
> tap left heel
> tap both heels
> rest
>
> tap right heel
> tap left heel
> tap right heel
> tap left heel
> tap both heels
> rest
> tap right heel
> tap left heel
> tap right heel

The *Morisques* dancer always keeps the tips of his toes still as he strikes his heels in order to make his bells ring. 'Tap both heels' is equivalent to *pieds ioincts* (lit. feet together).

tap left heel
tap right heel
tap left heel
tap right heel
tap left heel
tap right heel
tap left heel
tap right heel
tap left heel
tap both heels
rest

The dancer must continuously advance to the end of the hall. To do this note that after the *frappe talons*, which is equivalent to *pieds ioincts* and cadence, before the *frappe talon droit*, the dancer moves both feet forward slightly, and at the same time performs *frappe talon droit* …]

(Fonta 1888, 94–5)

The emphasis here is on rhythmic alternation of heel motions designed to create a sustained, pulsing ringing of the leg bells in the following metre (where / represents a heel strike and − a pause):

$$/ \ / \ / \ / \ / \ -$$
$$/ \ / \ / \ / \ / \ -$$
$$/ \ / \ / \ /$$
$$/ \ / \ / \ /$$
$$/ \ / \ / \ / \ / \ -$$

The use of bells on the legs to accentuate the dance metre is a common theme in descriptions of the morisk, as in the following account of the intermezzi at the first performance of Ariosto's *i Suppositi* in February 1509 taken from a letter from Bernardino Prosperi to Marchesana Isabella d'Este:

Li intermeci furono tuti canti et musiche, et in fine de la comedia, Vulcano cum Ciclopi baterno saete a sono de piffari, battendo il tempo cum martelli et cum sonagli che tenivano a le gambe, et facto questo acto de la saette col menar de'mantici, fecero una moresca cum dicti martelli.

[The intermezzi were all songs and music, and, at the end of the commedia, Vulcan with the Cyclops forged thunderbolts to the sound of pipes [i.e., flageolets], beating time with their hammers and with bells that they had on their legs; and while forging the thunderbolts and working their bellows, they danced a *morescha* with their hammers].

(Italian original cited in D'Ancona 1891, 2:395n)

Equally important here, though, is the indication of the use of other implements (in this case hammers) to beat time along with the bells. Several other accounts confirm the use of hand-held instruments used to beat time with the music. From another of Prosperi's letters concerning an Ariosto commedy comes this account:

... poi fo ornata de honorevoli et boni recitatori, tuti di fuori, de vestimento bellissimo et dolce melodie de intermeci, et de una moresca de cochi scaldati de vino, cum pignate cinte inanzi, che battevano a tempo cum canne de legno del sono de la musicha del Cardinale.

[It was played by honorable and good actors, all from outside, with most beautiful costumes and sweet melodies for intermezzi, and with a *moresca* of cooks heated up with wine, with earthenware pots strapped in front of them and beating time with their wooden sticks to the cardinal's music.]   (D'Ancona 1891, 2:394n)

The second intermezzo in the performance of Bibbiena's *Calandra* in 1513, following the morisk of Jason cited above, was described by Castiglione:

La seconda fu un carro di Venere bellisimo, sopra il quale essa sedea con una facella sulla mano nuda: il carro era tirato da due colombe, che certo pareano vive; e sopra esse cavalcavano due Amorini, e drieto quattro altre, pur con la facelle accese al medesimo modo, ballando una moresca intorno, e battendo con la facelle accese.

[The second was a beautiful pageant of Venus, which she was sitting on top of with a dim light in her bare hand. The pageant was pulled by two doves that really seemed alive, and on top of them rode two Cupids. Behind came four more women, also with lights lit in the same manner, who danced a *moresca* around, clashing with the lit lights.]   (D'Ancona 1891, 2:103)

There are also intimations in the European sources that 'moresca time' was readily identifiable as a specific tempo. In describing intermedii Leone de' Sommi says:

... et per un altro intermedio fece comparir poi quattro fachini, che dopo breve contese di parole rusticali nel partir un nolo tra loro, venivano a darsi co' pugni et calci et guanciate, a tempo di moresca.

[... and in another intermedio he called for four porters, who after a brief dispute in rustic language over the division of some money, came to blows and kicks, in *moresca* time.]

(Sommi 1968, 70)

In una tragicomedia poi nella città nostra, vidi, non ha molto, rappresentar la battaglia delli tre Orazii con li tre Curiazii, con tanto arteficio condotta a tempo di moresca ...

[In a tragicomedy presented here in our city not long ago, I saw enacted the battle between the three Horatii and the three Curiatii, produced so effectively in *moresca* time ...]

(Sommi 1968, 71)

In addition to these general characteristics of the dance actions, a few themes emerge that are worth noting because of their implications for interpreting the meanings and actions of the dances. The actual use of Moors as characters in the dance is conspicuously rare, so that whatever Moorish-ness the titles *moresque, morescha, maruscka,* and so forth imply, the reference is somewhat indirect. But the characters are, in the main, representative of the non-Christian world: Jews, pagans, barbarians, Turks. In a general sense, therefore, the dances may be said to be outlandish – symbolic of the remote and exotic worlds at the fringes of Europe.

Coupled with outlandishness is the common use of grotesque imagery in depictions of the morisk, Daniel Hopfer's engraving of a ring morisk being a prime example. There is a sense that the morisk is, or can be, a caricature form, possibly cross-fertilizing with other genres such as commedia dell'arte (again hinted at by Hopfer's use of a scaramouche figure in his morisk).

Perhaps linked to the alien nature of the characters is the tinge of the erotic found in some of the dance forms. The Turkish moresca dancers of 1524, for example, are specifically described as 'lascivious,' and there is the implication in the intermezzo in Rugiero's commedia of 1513 that the barbarians had sexually assaulted the figure of Italy. Likewise morisks frequently appear in farces or other plays whose basic plots turn on sexual motifs.[8] Prosperi describes Ariosto's play, in which the moresca of cooks appears as an intermezzo, as follows:

Lo suggieto fu bellissimo, de due inamorati in due meretrice conducte a Tarantho da uno ruffiano, dove ge andoe tante astutie et ingani et tanti novi accidente et tante belle moralita et varie cose, che in quelle de Terentio non ge n'è a mezo.

[The theme was beautiful – two men in love with two whores brought to Taranto by a pimp – in which there was so much shrewdness and deception and so many novel events, and so many fine moralities and different things, that in the commedies of Terence there are not half of them.]

(D'Ancona 1891, 2:394n)

It is also possible to see in the ring morisk the general themes of courtly love (or rather a parody thereof). The lady stands aloof as the image of beauty at the centre of the dance, while the men cavort and display in competition for her affections. The final ironic twist is enacted when she chooses the fool as the winner, thus implying that men's amorous gestures – particularly in elaborate courtly manner – are inherently foolish, and that the fool's blatant sexuality (symbolized by his phallic marotte) is to be preferred.

In some respects this last theme brings us back to the discussion of the genres that gave rise to morisks and disguisings – in particular, the wooing or courting images of the tournament and *Pas d'Armes*. My earlier discussion of the latter has already drawn out a skeleton form or typical chronology of events: a costumed procession, a contention, a prize-giving, followed by a general dance. The morisk can be seen as a choreographic elaboration and transformation of this skeleton, with the addition of elements from elsewhere. From the prototypic elements of the morisk defined above we may re-emphasize these points:

- the appearance of elaborately costumed dancers one by one from a stage machine, who proceed on a circular path as they enter (costumed procession)
- the feigned combat of the prospective lovers of a beauty, defeating one another by force of arms, or the competition for the favour of the lady through dance actions themselves (contention)
- the offering of a ring or apple or some other 'favour' to the victor (prize-giving)

In one light, therefore, the morisk could be seen as a dance/mime version of the fifteenth-century *Pas d'Armes*.

This metamorphosis has several important aspects from the point of view of the developmental history of the dance. What is happening here is that basic forms of medieval combat have gradually become surrounded by dramatic trappings until the aesthetic forms have completely usurped the martial. The morisk is pure theatre: the outcome of any contention is preset, all action is stylized and rehearsed, and the attention of the audience is on the affective qualities of the aesthetics of the execution of planned motion. The transformation is so complete that many of the morisk forms are parodies or grotesqueries; that is, they are yet one step further abstracted from genuine combat actions.

In addition, many of the morisks have a well defined narrative structure that, unlike the narratives of the *Pas d'Armes* (which are simply excuses for combat and other displays) is of theatrical and symbolic importance in its own right. The dances themselves are vehicles of narrative meaning. As such, morisks are quite distinct from other courtly dances of the time, and destined to evolve in different directions.

Apart from this narrative component, morisks have several other qualities that mark them off from the courtly dances of the day, and it should be noted in passing that Baldessare Castiglione in his *Book of the Courtier* specifically admonishes the would-be courtier not to dance morescas in public unless in mask and costume, because to do otherwise would be undignified. If he wishes to dance unmasked the courtier should confine himself to his own private quarters (Castiglione 1528, 102–3). The bulk of the courtly dances of the era are partner dances that have a social or participatory quality; the courtiers are meant to dance and not simply watch, whereas morisks are spectacular dances intended specifically for an audience's delectation. The social and participatory qualities of the courtly dances are indicated by the fact that they are primarily partner dances, where morisks are unpartnered. The emphasis of the partner dances is on style and grace, couples working in league or in counterpoint, balancing and complementing the skills of the other. The morisks, on the other hand, involve violent, often competitive exertion, in which grace may gave way to rude and grotesque action.

Both the function and form of the court morisks thus separate them from other dances performed in the same milieu. In this regard they can be viewed as the beginnings of a broad theatrical dance tradition that would eventually develop in a number of different directions. One major thread in this evolution takes the morisk beyond the scope of this work, namely, its transformation into early forms of ballet in Europe, particularly in France and Italy. Monteverdi's *Orfeo* (1607), for example, ends with a moresca of shepherds, so that this piece forms one of many links between the older court morisks and the operatic ballet.[9]

The emergence of the masque in England as a discrete form also gave morisk/morris a new context and caused further transformations. In particular, morris became a standard feature of the grotesqueries of the antimasque. The masque, although it had roots in courtly disguisings, opened up a theatric tradition that became available to wider audiences. At the same time, the public stage was rapidly rising to prominence and morrises became, for a few decades, interludes in the action of the plays (see chapter 8). Therefore, the courtly morris/morisk, itself the product of a number of performance traditions, did not simply die out, but became the source of inspiration for a number of dance types outside the courtly sphere.[10]

5

Urban Streets

Throughout the period of record covered by this work, morris dancing was popular in cities, but there was a particular span of time, roughly from 1520 to 1580, when urban street settings predominated. Subsequently the focus shifted from cities to smaller towns and villages. As is true throughout the evolution of morris dancing in Britain, urban street morris cannot be characterized as a single phenomenon, or even as a series of clearly related dance types. The events at which morris appeared varied in kind of location, sponsorship, duration, and basic justification, all of which affected the dance. Even so, there are one or two common threads that can be followed. The strongest of these is that the urban celebrations of which morris was an element more often than not involved, or were exclusively, processions.

Urban street morris was associated with different kinds of events, but they may be grouped into two broad categories, midsummer guild processions and May games. These kinds of events are fundamentally distinct because of who sponsored them and who participated in them, the time of year they occurred, specific locations, course of events, and raison d'être. I will treat them separately here. There is a third, smaller category – Lord of Misrule processions – which is distinct from the other two in many ways but which contains elements of parody of the Midsummer processions, and so I will discuss them along with that category. For the first half of the sixteenth century urban morris is attested in primary materials almost exclusively in London. Subsequently its popularity there decreased, and it is recorded more commonly in regional centres such as Salisbury (where the tradition continued through the nineteenth century) and Chester (locus of an ongoing tradition).

GUILD PROCESSIONS IN LONDON

The references to morris at the Midsummer processions in London come mostly from records of expenditures kept by the guilds, which are brief and minimally informative. Therefore a careful consideration of the nature of the events themselves and European analogues is necessary in order to make inferences concerning the form of the dance.

The early development of the Midsummer Watch processions in London – on the eves of the feast of the Nativity of St John the Baptist (i.e., 23 June) and SS Peter and Paul (i.e., 28 June) – is not fully clear and can only be speculated on. Their form in the sixteenth century, when they were associated with morris dancing, is reasonably well documented, however.

Stow in his 1603 *Survey of London* (1908, 92) records that watches were inaugurated by Henry III in 1253 because of a rise in violence and robbery in the night. Organized groups, such as the guilds, were charged with raising and maintaining an efficient watch at their own expense. Such watches might either stand guard in a designated location (the standing watch), or perambulate a specified area (the marching watch).

In 1377 in London there was a

Precept for a proper watch and ward to be kept on the eves of the nativity of St. John Bapt. and the Feast of SS. Peter and Paul, and for precautions to be taken against fire.

(Sharpe 1907, 308)

This entry may provide some insight into the raising of special watches at Midsummer, which ultimately became part of the general pageantry. There was, apparently, an especial need for a close watch on Midsummer's eve because it was a particularly hazardous time of year for several reasons; it was associated with general licence, and there was a concern about festival bonfires getting out of control.

Given the possibilities for social disorder on this night it is understandable that the civic authorities should make redoubled efforts to maintain law and order. Even so, order at Midsummer was sufficiently precarious that the very attempt to preserve it might undo itself. According to a contemporary manuscript, there was in 1474,

a grete watche upon Seint Petres nyght, the kyng [Edward IV] beyng in the Chepe; and ther fill affrey bitwixt men of his household and the constablis, wherefore the kyng was gretely displeasid with the cunstablis.   (Cited in Withington 1918, 1:38)

And an eyewitness to the 1521 watches notes at the end of his description, that mayhem caused by the soldiery was normal:

Poi vene una banda di alabardieri da 2000, li qual passati et tutti acompagnati, sì li primi come li novissimi, da lumiere, li spectatori *utriusque sexus*, che erano in grandissimo numero, se ritornorono *ad propria*. Questi veramente di la terra dubitando di queste gente armate non facesseno qualche tumulto, come è suo costume, fecero grandissime guardie per tutta la terra.

[Then came a band of some 2000 halbardiers, all accompanied from first to last by cresset bearers; and when they [the end of the watch] had passed, the spectators of both sexes, who were in very great number, returned home. The inhabitants, being apprehensive lest, as usual, these armed men should raise some tumult, kept very strict watch throughout the city.]

(Spinelli 1521, 96, translated in Brown 1869, 137)

It is also understandable how the marching watch was transformed from a troop of constables parading the town to keep order to a more splendid procession, ultimately becoming the glorious spectacle described in Stow's famous account:

Then had ye besides the standing watches all in bright harness [body armour], in every ward and street of this city and suburbs, a marching watch, that passed through the principal streets thereof ... The marching watch contained in number about two thousand men, part of them being old soldiers of skill, to be captains, lieutenants, serjeants, corporals, etc., wiflers, drummers, and fifes, standard and ensign bearers, sword players, trumpeters on horseback, demilances on great horses, gunners with hand guns, or half hakes, archers in coats of white fustian, signed on the breast and the back with the arms of the city, their bows bent in their hands, with sheaves of arrows by their sides, pikemen in bright corslets, burganets, etc., halberds, the like billmen in almaine rivets, and apernes of mail in great number; there were also divers pageants, morris dancers, constables, the one-half, which was one hundred and twenty, on St. John's eve, the other half on St. Peter's eve ...   (Stow 1908, 93)

It is evident that this is primarily a military spectacle, akin in some respects to the tournament processions described in the previous chapter. The emphasis is on the maintenance of social order through the constabulary and the militia, and no expense is spared to show them off to their best advantage. The watch was not only an emblem of civic order and the means of keeping it, but was in itself supposed to be a model of the order that it was raised to uphold. In 1585 John Mountgomery[1] wrote a small treatise on the procedures for the Midsummer Watch (seemingly from memory and documentary evidence) to encourage its restoration, entitled 'A Booke conteyning the Manner and Order of a watch to be used in the Cittie of London, upon the even at Night of Sainct John Baptist and Sainct Peeter, as in tyme past hath bene accustomed' (BL Harl. MS 3741, reprinted in Mountgomery 1585). Its instructions show in great detail the precise formations involved in the marching watch, and also confirm its military nature. An extract of its directives is sufficient to establish this point:

ITEM, that the Chamber provide XX olde soldyers of skille, to be hyred for wages to serve in the martchinge watche, to wete, 4 of the most skillfullest to be made captaynes, two to be lieutenants, and 14 to be corporalls. The captaynes and lieutenants to take the charge and leadinge of the two battayls of footmen, as to saie of the shott and pikes according to th'order sett downe in the martche, and the 14 corporalls, to goe all alonge on th'one side of the saide footmen, to put them in remembraunce of good order, and true martche

(Mountgomery 1585, 9:393)

The marching watch, although ostensibly a civic amusement, had the serious purpose of keeping the watch and its equipage in readiness and, as important, *showing* the populace that it was prepared, the combination of sheer numbers and ostentatious display of polished weapons and armoury creating the sense of security.

This message must at best of times been ambiguous, however. Mountgomery remarks at the end of his pamphlet:

Thus maie the saide wattche be donne honorably, and after a true and warrelike manner, and I suppose with as small charge nowe as in tyme past when it was not so orderly done.

(Mountgomery 1585, 9:408)

This, plus his detailed plans for ensuring the strictly military mien of the watch, suggests that in times past the watch could turn into a revelling rabble; and a dangerous one, given that hundreds of the participants had loaded guns, as well as stores of black powder, shoulder to shoulder with spluttering and flaming cresset lights. But with proper control and foresight the watch could serve its original purpose of displaying and maintaining order.

In an age that had no other efficient methods of mass communication, the civic procession was a critical ingredient in the establishment and maintenance of civil order. On the one hand, rulers, temporal and spiritual, took every opportunity to parade through the streets to reinforce their authority; on the other, a key component in the punishment of miscreants was their public display. Henry Machyn's *Diary* (Machyn 1848), which covers the period 1550 to 1563, records a procession of some sort on virtually every page. Admittedly Machyn had a special interest in street processions, because he was a furnisher of funerals, and the funeral procession – highly structured in Tudor England according to rules relating to rank and family – was his stock in trade. Nonetheless it is clear that civic processions and perambulations were a fundamental component of daily law and order in sixteenth-century England.

During the troublous times after the death of Edward VI in 1553, for example, it was critical that Mary Tudor show herself publicly to the people of London, so that it was clear, by virtue of the fact that she was able to ride in procession – bearing the symbols of authority, and accompanied by noble supporters and a powerful guard – that she was the lawful successor. In return, the livery companies, by officially watching the parade gave their overt assent to her rule (see Machyn 1848, 38–9).

On the other side of the coin, the procession was an important aspect of punishment. In some cases lawbreakers were processed around the streets so they might be identified and avoided in the future (in addition to their public shaming), as in the case of a woman caught illegally selling small fish:

The xxij day of Marche [1561] dyd a woman ryd a-bowt Chepesyd and Londun for bryng-yng yonge frye of dyvers kynd of fysse unlafull, with a garland a-pone her hed hangyng with strynges of the small fysse, and on the horse a-for and be-hynd here, led by on of the bedylls of Brydwell.

(Machyn 1848, 253)

Or a punishment might be carried out in a procession, as in a whipping at the cart's tail. The marching watch thus fits into a general pattern of urban displays of the tools of social control in an era when the social order was often precariously balanced.

The form of the marching watch, judging from the account books of the livery companies, varied over its history, being almost exclusively a parade of men in armour until the beginning of the sixteenth century when other elements, such as pageants and morris dancers, were added with regularity. The addition of such elements does not, I believe, indicate a lessening of the military quality of the parade in favour of 'pure' entertainment, but rather marks changing tastes in martial displays, especially as Henry VIII's reign progressed.[2] As indicated in the previous chapter, the old tournament proper was, by the sixteenth century, transformed into an elaborate spectacle with pageants, larded with allegory and symbolism. Combatants entered the lists accompanied by pageants that displayed the emblems of their lineage, and by retainers in costume. But the core of the event remained the martial arts, the spectacular elements contributing to, not distracting from, the combat.

The transformation of the Midsummer Watch can be seen in the same light. As the tournament procession became increasingly embellished, so too did its civic analogue. The pageants, for example, were not simply decorative tableaux to punctuate the marching troops, but were specifically accoutrements of the three civic dignitaries – the mayor had three (or so) and the sheriffs, two each – like their knightly counterparts. These pageants indicated the livery company of each dignitary and sometimes involved a visual pun on the man's name. Others were straightforwardly or symbolically military, or taken directly from the tournament. In 1512, for example, the Drapers paid for several pageants for the mayor Roger Acheley, a draper:

It' for the charges of iij pagentes that is to say Saynt Blythe. Achilles. and thassumpcion and also a Morish daunce besides the Castell of were that the Bachillers paid for them self of our Charges as aperys in 220 parcelles Sm^a xij^{li} xvij^s ix^d (Robertson and Gordon 1954, 2)

The Assumption was the Drapers' main pageant, used in many watches when the mayor or sheriff was a draper, and symbolized their patron saint, the Virgin Mary; Achilles was a classic warrior (as well as a pun on Acheley); and the castle is a direct transplant from the *Pas d'Armes*.[3] So that although it is possible to categorize the provenances of the pageant themes as biblical, religious, and classical, or the like as some historians have done (see, for example, Robertson and Gordon 1954), such a taxonomy is anachronistic (that is, it is based on a modern conception of history and mythology) and misses the point of their underlying unity of theme.

I do not mean to suggest, however, that the Midsummer Watch was merely a civic replica of the tournament procession, nor that its themes were drawn exclusively from that, or any other, direction. This is clearly not the case. Royal entries, progresses, triumphs, and miracle plays all contributed something (see Wickham 1959 and Withington 1918), and furthermore, the watch changed considerably in character through the first half of the sixteenth century. But I do wish to assert the primacy of the martial and to avoid dichotomizing, or otherwise classifying, the elements of the procession into the martial and the 'other.' Accepting this argument leads, a fortiori, to the conclusion that the morris dance in the procession was somehow martial. Hints throughout the literature tentatively support this position, as do comparisons with continental materials.

Dorothy Gardiner in her history of the town of Sandwich, for example, relates the following story from 1526:

Booll during his term of office [as Mayor, in 1522 and 1525] had been in the habit of parading the town at night, with 16 or 20 'light and wyld persons' whom he called his Beagles ... These ruffians were now called into action ... Booll taunted Sir Edward, boasting that he had the town at his whistle and defying the King's authority. On St Clement's Day [23 November] when Ringeley attempted to gather the King's tolls at the annual fair, his three adversaries arranged for twenty men, led by John Redde and armed with swords, daggers and clubs, to walk up and down the fair all day long, 'craking and swearing to kill ... whosoever durst presume to gather any penny that day for the King'. The same night the rioters danced a morrice about the town, with swords and bucklers, and Henry Booll gave them wine at a tavern.   (Gardiner 1954, 153–4, citing *White Book* [1488–1526], f. 368d)

So there is incontrovertible evidence of at least one street morris dance in the era of the London guild morris, in the service of a man of mayoral rank, that was performed with sword and buckler. There is also clear evidence from a considerably later period (1607) from Wells that street morris there was a martial dance with sword and daggers. This morris is to be considered in detail later in the chapter so for the moment I will simply cite a sample of one of the depositions from the Star Chamber proceedings against the dancers:

[Christopher Croker] ... saieth That hee doethe knowe that on the tenthe daye of Maye ... being sondaye there were greate number of people assembled in the streetes of wells afore-sayed, with drumbes & an auncyente [i.e., ensign], gunns and powder, Morryce dauncers then dauncinge vpp and downe the stretes with naked rapyers and daggers in theire handes.

(PRO STAC 8/16/1 f.39 in Stokes 1996, 1:347)

But neither source can do more than hint at the possiblity that the London morris was a martial dance, because the first is not from a formal borough-sponsored proces-sion and the latter is outside the appropriate time span. Even if the Wells dance is a descendant of the London type of street morris one would expect substantial changes over a period of one hundred years.

Looking to European analogues of the era may strengthen the case, however. In the northern Portuguese town of Braga there were guild-sponsored processions in and around Corpus Christi in the fifteenth and sixteenth century that included mouriscas. Violet Alford (1933) cites a local history of Braga festivals ('O ão João em Braga' (1904) by José Gomes) that seems to indicate that the sixteenth-century mourisca in Braga was straightforwardly military:

A master-shoemaker was the King, and he modelled his ... Mourisca on those of Guimarães and other cities where 'the said Mourisca was well done.' He succeeded in making a *boa Mourisca* with twenty persons counting the King. They were gallantly dressed and also had a Dragon ... [T]he Braga young men were armed with little shields and sticks like lances – long swords perhaps – 'and to the sound of the drum advanced against each other as though to battle.'

(Alford 1933, 223–4)

Similar mouriscas (or mouriscadas) are recorded throughout Portugal (see, for example, Chaves 1941 and 1942, Figueiredo 1886, 286–9, and Ribeiro 1829, 201).

These European dances may legitimately be seen as analogues to the English dances in part for the reasons given in the previous chapter concerning court morisks, and in part because at least one contemporary writer connected European dances with the English urban morris. Lodovico Spinelli, secretary to the Venetian amabassador in England, saw the Midsummer Watch in 1521 and wrote in a letter:

Et poi sequiva una banda di alabardieri con uno soler sopra el qual era san Zorzi armato che soffocava uno grande dracone et liberava Santa Margarita. Poi a piedi sequivano alcuni che faceano la morescha, et drieto questi, cum bella banda di contestabeli de la terra ...

[Next came a band of halberdiers with a stage, on which was Saint George, in armour, chok-ing a big dragon and delivering Saint Margaret. Then followed on foot a company dancing the *morescha*, preceding a fine band of the city constables ...]

(Spinelli 1521, 95, translated in Brown 1869, 136)

Spinelli used the Italian word *morescha* for the morris dance that he saw, indicating that what he knew from Venice was sufficiently like what he saw in London to use the same noun. This does not imply tremendous similarity between the two dances, but simply that the coincidences were sufficient for him to apply the Italian term to the English dance.

The European processional morescas may well be descendants of the widespread medieval dance/drama Moros y Cristianos, but without a European database equivalent to the early morris archive it is difficult to proffer more than tentative conjectures. Supposedly the first Moros y Cristianos was performed in Lérida in 1149 as part of the celebration of the betrothal of Petronilla, queen of Aragon to Ramon of Barcelona (see Alford 1962, 150–2, for an overview history). The previous year Moors had been defeated in the region and the dance/drama was apparently invented to celebrate the victory. As the Moors were pushed further south, Moros y Cristianos was instituted as a custom in their wake, some Spanish towns performing a version to this day.[4] Numerous variants exist historically but the underlying theme is the same: two armies, one of Moors and one of Christians meet and, having delivered long speeches, attack one another, the Christians ultimately winning the day.

It is a fair conjecture, therefore, to see the European processional morescas as derivative of this older form stripped of narrative drama and, instead, emphasizing pure dance. It is equally possible to imagine the court morescas evolving from the same root but in a different direction. The processional morescas concentrated on dance elements from Moros y Cristianos that were suitable for performing while travelling down a street, while the court morescas focused on narrative, dramatic action. Thus, both forms could have arrived in England independently even though both had a common European ancestor. In that way both might share certain elements – notably choreographed conflict and the name 'morris' – without being descendants of, or derivative of, each other *in England*. Indeed, it is possible that there were multiple stages of importation from European descendants of the older Moros y Cristianos dance/dramas.

That London Midsummer Watches borrowed such exotic customs from European processions is well documented. In 1521, for example, the Drapers' company included in their mayor's (Sir John Brugges's) train a king of Moors and followers:

It' to the said Godfrey for a Reward And for the lone of a dymy lawnce that the kyng of the Moores pavillion was born vppon over his hede. & for a long swerd for the said king & a chyldes harnes & for all his laboures Sm^a iij^s iiij^d …

It' for wages to lx moryans grete & small w^t *seruants* & all & a woman morian iiij^d a pece for bothe nyghtes & the woman morian viijd for bothe nyghtes Sm^a xx^s iiij^d

It' for the lone of lx dartes to Godfrey for the said moryans ij^s & for the losse of iij dartes xij^d Sm^a iij^s …

It' for fyre for the moryans aft' they had put of ther clothes & were nakyd vj^d

(Robertson and Gordon 1954, 6–7)

The king of the Moors and his train appeared again in 1536 when the draper Humfrey Monmouth was sheriff:

Agreed w^t Iohn Leedes paynter the xvth daye of Iune for the garnyshyng of the Kyng of the Moores well trymmed w^t all thynges that shalbelong vnto hym as well his wages as horsse Trapper & leder and also of X moores & trymmyng of them aft' the best ffascyon & the hyer of them & gonstones of paper sufficyent soe that ther lack none for defens of the Castell & and for makying of v harness of sylver paper for the Champyon & childern in the Castell & for new trymmyng & paynting of x Targates for the Moores & for trymmyng of the Kynges pavylyon of Moores & of the iiij Men that shall bere hym and for their wages he to have for All the premysses sm^a xxvj^s viij^d   (Robertson and Gordon 1954, 27)

Both these records seem to indicate that the Moors in the procession were engaged in some minimal dramatic action, although it is difficult to determine the scale and the particulars from the way the items are parcelled and detailed. In the first example, from 1521, the Moors are provided with darts but they also carried 'wild-fire' (an incendiary chemical mixture used primarily in siegecraft but also employable as a firework when held at the end of a staff), which they let off 'aft' they had put of ther clothes & were nakyd.' My suspicion is that rather than being literally naked they had body-tight suits made of black leather, or other suitable material, under their outer garments which were revealed when they disrobed and which gave the appearance of nudity. Such skin-tight, skinlike costumes are described in the accounts for a Masque of Young Moors at court in 1548 (Feuillerat 1914, 30–1).

Spinelli's letter to his brother provides us with an eyewitness account of the 1521 watches in London, but unfortunately his description of the part of the procession involving the Moors is obscure, due to his misinterpretation of the characters:

… da poi una altra man de soni con 50 homeni et putti nudi et tineti di negro in forma di diavoli, con il dardo et scuto in mano et quelli percotendo. Li quali sopra uno pulpito sequiva Pluton sotto una umbrela, qual sedeva sopra una serpe che getava foco da le fauce, et lui nudo con uno gladio evazinato in mano, quello vibrando; qual in tal modo era disposto, che come si movea faceva al serpe getaruno globo di faville molto fetente de sulfure. Sopra al qual pulpito eravi *etiam* avanti Pluton uno bove, uno lione, et alcuni serpi formati.

[Next came another band of musicians, with 50 men and naked boys dyed black like devils, with dart and target in their hands, goading the followers of Pluto, who was on a pulpit under a canopy seated on a serpent that spat fire; he himself being naked, with a drawn sword in his hand so contrived that, when he brandished it, it made the serpent vomit very fetid sulphuric fire-balls: and on the pulpit in front of Pluto were figures of an ox, a lion, and some serpents.]   (Spinelli 1521, 95, translated in Brown 1869, 136)

He calls the Moors 'devils,' and their king he identifies as the king of the Underworld (perhaps suggested to him by the sulphurous fire). Nonetheless, he makes it clear that they are involved in some kind of martial action involving their darts and targets and, regardless of the details, the point remains that the use of a king of Moors and retainers in some kind of choreographed combat is taken directly from European guild processions and, in all probability, derives ultimately from Moros y Cristianos displays. Thus it is not unthinkable that the processional morris derived from the same source, although it was a much earlier arrival. The king of the Moors and his train appeared for the first time in 1521, but the Drapers' company had a morris dance as early as 1477, so that even if both evolved from Moros y Cristianos dance/dramas they could, nonetheless, have appeared quite distinct and not even be equated in the minds of contemporary performers and audiences because of the fifty-year period between the importation of the two.

It cannot be ruled out, though, that the processional urban morris was an indigenous English dance that until the late fifteenth century went by a different name or was unrecorded. No hard evidence in the form of primary documents for or against such a hypothesis exists at present. It does, however, seem highly implausible that there could exist simultaneously in the early-sixteenth-century continental morescas accompanying midsummer guild processions and English morrises accompanying midsummer guild processions, and that, despite the coincidence of contexts and the parallelism of cognate names, the dance types were entirely unrelated. Tentatively, then, we may conclude that the London processional morris was martial and exotic.

Further conclusions on the dance's form may be drawn based on the physical nature of processions. A procession is a special form of dramatic spectacle because it is made of units strung out linearly that parade past a static audience, so that the average audience member sees each unit only for a brief span of time. From the other vantage point, people in the procession are constantly presented with a new audience. This fact places severe constraints on what the participants may accomplish in the way of narrative or sequenced action. They cannot carry out any acts that take longer to comprehend than the time it takes to pass a point along the way. Great emphasis must, therefore, be placed on displays that can be taken in all at once, such as a company of halbadiers in glittering armour, or a pageant tableau where the narrative is either implicit in a frozen moment or played out in a series of simple, repeated acts, such as throwing (fake) rocks in defence of a castle. A morris dance that is part of a procession must, therefore, place little, if any, stress on choreography that takes time to develop a comprehensible pattern, and place more on simple repeatable motions, such as rhythmic leaping, stepping, or the clashing of weapons. It must also allow for forward progress, travelling on average at the same pace as marching soldiers. They may stop or backtrack periodically, but they must do so for brief spells only, because they are being followed closely and inexorably by the next unit in the procession.

Mountgomery's description of the hobby horse dance in 1585 provides an analogy, which is perhaps especially apt if, as several historians including myself have asserted, morris and matachin have cross fertilized (see Forrest 1984):

ITEM, 12 propper boyes, on hobbye horses fynely covered with some prettye coloured thinge … which saide boyes to have everie one a little sworde, (I meane foyles of iron to be verie lighte and bright) that after praunsing, mountinge, and fetchinge upp their horses alofte on all fower, they maie at divers tymes in the watche make combatt all together, to wete, all 12 to fighte at one instant, to saie 6 against 6, in true form and order of a matachina; which if they be trulye taughte, one shall not hurte another, but allwaies strike uppon the sworde.
                                             (BL Harl. MS 3741, Mountgomery 1585, 9:395)

This ensemble, then, mostly moves forward with a horsey, dancing gait but periodically halts the forward action for a brief engagement before continuing. I speculate that the morris was similar in conception. In this regard it should also be noted that Mountgomery has a rough idea of how much space a morris dance should take up in the procession because he has a detailed account concerning the number of cresset lights needed to illuminate the whole based, in part, on his computation of the length of the entire procession (Mountgomery 1585, 9:393). In his overall calculations he counts a single line of soldiers abreast as his unit of forward length, viz., one rank. Thus a drum, fife, and ensign abreast count one rank, as does every horseman. A pageant, however, counts as two ranks. It is difficult to give an idiosyncratic unit such as the rank a fixed measurement but six to eight feet would seem generous. Thus his allotment of two ranks for a morris dance would amount to roughly fifteen feet. Given that the group was commonly made up of eight dancers (see below) this does not seem a great space to operate within, and suggests that they were *not* drawn up in the double column formation familiar in more modern processional morrises. If this were their formation they would require four ranks. They must, therefore, have used two ranks of four or some other configuration – such as the square – which would be more compact than columns. Whatever the case, their main action would have been simple, repetitious, and mobile.

From the audience member's point of view, the narrative element of the processions consists in the *succession* of units, rather than in the individual meanings of the units. As such it might be styled a protocinematic event in that it is a patterned sequence of frames that, seen in order, creates the drama (the analogy heightened in this case

because the parade takes place in a darkened environment and is brilliantly illumin-
ated by flickering lamps).[5] Thus the order of the units in the procession is by no means
trivial; it is a critical value for conveying the narrative meaning of the whole, and
attributing significance to the parts.

Three separate sources exist concerning the overall sequence of the Midsummer
Watch; two are sets of instructions and the third, an eyewitness account. The rough
minutes of the Drapers for 1525–6 contain an abbreviated order of the watch that
is clearly incomplete, especially in respect to the participants in the sheriffs' watches
(see London Drapers' Minute Book 140a, 1525, f.8b cited in Johnson 1914–15,
11). It is incomplete because the Drapers were interested in what they had to supply only – as sponsors of the mayor, who was a draper – and were not giving a complete inventory of the procession. Later the same manuscript records the order of the
junior sheriff's watch for the following year (1526), which is much like the mayor's
watch although smaller in scale. The Minute Book also contains the following direct-
ive for the sheriffs' watches in 1525:

A morysdance at bothe ther charges servyng the chef Shiref the first nyght and the other
Shiref the ij[d] nyght to fetch them severally at ther severall houses & going bifore them to
the place wher ther severall watches assembldy & so fforth, etc. The eldest Shireffes harnest
men with a mynstrell & ii sergeantes bifore. Than a mynstrell & ii sergeantes before the
harnest men of the ii[d] Shirif ...
(Minute Book 140a, 1525, f.9a, cited in Johnson 1914–15, 2:12)

These directives indicate that the morris dance had a kind of heralding function,
and this function extended beyond the procession proper. The morris dancers actually went to the sheriffs' houses and escorted them to the place where the official
procession began, creating what might be thought of as tributary processions feeding into the main event. In the actual procession the morris dancers led a section
that consisted of the mayor's and the sheriffs' private companies.

The Drapers' rudimentary outline of the procession suggests that the linear sequence consisted of a dramatic opening – a drummer, a giant, gunners, and the
Drapers' banner – followed by six companies of men in armour (all but the last com-
prised of eighty men) each led by a taborer.[6] Then came the mayor's entourage –
constables, waits, sergeants, and sword-bearers – led by morris dancers. Then followed
the sheriffs' companies, the morris dancers leading the senior sheriff's on St John
the Baptist's Eve and the junior's on St Peter's Eve.

Spinelli's eyewitness account focuses on the pageantry and misses much detail. It
also clearly mistakes the order of some of the elements, or is obscure in reporting them.
He appears to indicate that the mayor and sheriffs are together in the procession,
for example, and this is clearly an error, either of memory or of transcription.

Because the description of the procession in the Drapers' minutes is incomplete and Spinelli's is unreliable in its details, it is useful to look at Mountgomery's instructions for 1585 to get a sense of the structure of the whole show and how exactly the morris dancers fit in (see Mountgomery 1585, 9:403–7, for complete details). He divides the procession into five units – the first battalion, the lord mayor and his company, the first sheriff and his company, the second sheriff and his company, and the second battalion – each separated from the next by a distance of eight paces so that the onlookers will get a sense of discrete blocks. Each of these units has its own inner structure and integrity.

The two battalions frame the event at start and finish and consist entirely of soldiers in companies led by fife and drum. The mayor and his company is as follows:

Firste 2 cressetts light.
One companye of morris dauncers.
Then 12 hobbye horses, 3 in a rancke.
Then 2 sworde players with longe swords to make rome.
Two cressets light.
Two drommes, a fyfe, and an ensigne.
The 48 constables and their pages, 3 in a rancke, and in the middest of them 2 drommes,
     a fyfe, and an ensigne.
Then one sworde player.
Then 2 cressetts for the pagent, to wete, one in the front and one on the side.
Then a pageant.
Then one sworde player.
Then the 24 grave personages, three in a rancke.
Then 1 sounde of trumpetts contayninge 4.
Then the waytes or musicke of the cittye.
Then the sworde bearer mounted uppon a great courser.
Then the Lord Maior mounted uppon a faier courser, with his 2 spare horses, footmen, and
     staffe-torche-bearers.
Then the 2 henchmen mounted uppon greate stirringe coursers, with their 4 spare horses,
     footmen, and staffe-torche-bearers.
Two sworde players.
Then one dromme, a fyfe, and an ensigne.
Then the Lord Maior his garde, 30 men in light armor, everie man his partesan, which is
     10 ranckes, and in the middest of them a dromme, fyfe, and ensigne.
                                        (BL Harl. MS 3741, Mountgomery 1585, 9:404–5)

The two sheriffs' companies are similar but on a smaller scale.

What seems evident from this and the other accounts is that the procession's linear sequence involves a degree of what in traditional ballad scholarship is called 'incremental repetition plus variation.' Certain discrete units or formulae repeat at periodic intervals, sometimes unchanged, sometimes modified slightly as the narrative unfolds. In this procession the repetition of units takes place on several levels. At the most elementary level, bands of guards, footmen, pikemen, and the like consist of identically dressed men repeated a number of times. In the mayor's company, for example, one band – his guard – consists of thirty men,

whose apparaille to be jerkins with sleves of male, hansome hatts, or red capps, partesans, swordes, daggers, scarfes, and clenlye hose. (BL Harl. MS 3741, Mountgomery 1585, 9:395)

There are several such bands in his company: the twelve hobby horses, the forty-eight constables, the twenty-four grave personages, and so forth. Such basic repetition has the primary affective meaning of abundance, of overwhelming the audience with quantity. This is especially true of the first battalion where some bands contain as many as one hundred and eighty armed men in sixty ranks of three abreast. Consideration of the sheer time alone it would take for sixty ranks of identically dressed men to pass any point reinforces the notion that plain repetition of individual elements was a key ingredient in the procession.

These large bands are punctuated by small repeating units. In the Drapers' rough minutes the various companies of 'lxxx harnest men' are each separated by 'a taberet of fote.' In the description from 1585 there are several of these punctuating small units, such as 'two sworde players,' or 'one dromme, a fyfe, and an ensigne,' or 'two cressets light.'

Repetition of a higher order also takes place. These bands and punctuating units (along with special items) make up the mayor's company, for example. But when the senior sheriff's company comes along it is almost an exact repeat of the order of the mayor's except on a slightly less grand scale, and the junior sheriff's likewise. So there is repetition built upon repetition. At this level, the incremental repetition plus variation indicates that the sheriffs are on a par with one another and of a similar, though less august, rank as the mayor. There are also yet higher orders of repetition, because the parade marches from west to east, turns around, and retraces its steps to the starting point, thus repeating the *whole*. Then too the watch is repeated year after year, and so on.

The morris dancers have a special role in all of this repetition. They are not a large band – where numbers are indicated, the group consists of six to eight men. Neither are they small punctuating units – they appear at *one* point only in each company, and form more than one rank. They stand somewhere between the two types – a special unit that heralds the entourage of each dignitary.

In many other respects the morris is a special entity. Whereas the livery companies oversaw the detailed construction of many of the displays in the watches, the morris dancers were always hired as a bloc – generally through an individual leader. When the Drapers had a king of Moors and entourage there are pages of accounts for costumes and props, actors' fees, scenic equipment, and so forth. The payments for the morris dancers are, by comparison, at most a few lines indicating that they are to be hired as a single entity for a flat fee. The accounts for 1522,

It' to Willm' Burnet for a morysdaûnce of viij & ij mynstrelles riding in ou^r apparelles. ij hattes &. xviij^s (Robertson and Gordon 1954, 12)

and 1525,

It' to Walter ffount & his company that is to say viij persones w^t there mynstrell for a morisdance bothe nyghtes for the Mair' all goyng on fote bifore the côstables Sm^a xv^s
                                                    (Robertson and Gordon 1954, 17)

give the general idea. The dancers are a private group for hire that comes as a team, not an entity put together purely for the watch. As such they are possibly a unique element in the procession.

Analysis of the cost of hiring the team provides some additional information concerning the dancers, particularly their social status. It is difficult to determine the costs of the dance alone because their fee is usually parcelled in with other costs. Table 2 breaks down all the costs for morris dances at Midsummer Watches in the livery company records and indicates what items are parcelled with the morris fee.

The references before 1521 are of little help because so much is parcelled in with them. However, after that date the picture is relatively clear. Fees range from a high of 26s 8d (1532) to a low of 8s (1526, 1539), but there is not a continuous range over these two extremes. They are usually paid either around 15s or around 25s. The 8s fees are an anomaly that I believe can be explained. In 1526 the Drapers' records say:

It' for ou^r. Shireffes parte M' Askue for a morisdaunce for bothe nyghtes onely for the ij Shireffes. seruing them. equally. Sm^a viij^s (Robertson and Gordon 1954, 18)

That is, the dance that year is to serve for both sheriffs, but only one, Christopher Askue, was a draper. The other, John Caunton, whose company is now unknown, is unlikely to have been the benefactor of a free gift of dancers from the Drapers. Presumably his company paid half the fee for half their services, but these accounts are now lost. Thus the dancers would have received a total of 16s, in line with the fees in other years. This is confirmed by the other 8s fee from 1539. In this year the watch

TABLE 2
Guild morris costs

Date	Cost	Parcelled with
1477	28s 9d	9 worthies
1512	£12 17s 9d	3 pageants
1515	£14 19s 4d	80 harnessed men, gunners, minstrels
1521	14s 0d	2 minstrels (both nights), 2 hats
1522	18s 0d	2 minstrels, 2 hats
1525	15s 0d	1 minstrel (both nights)
1526	8s 0d	(both nights, sheriffs' morris)
1529	14s 4d	(both nights)
1530	15s 0d	1 minstrel (both nights)
1532	26s 8d	none
1535	25s 0d	(both nights)
1536	15s 8d	(both nights)
1539	8s 0d	porters (one night)
1541	23s 4d	1 minstrel, costumes, (both nights)

Based on Robertson and Gordon 1954, 1–34

was cancelled by royal command because of the special muster. But the Grocers had already built pageants for their sheriff Nicholas Gibson and had marched them from Leaden Hall, where they were made, to Grocers' Hall in preparation for the watch. This prewatch parade included a morris dance:

Itm̄ paid to porters for bringing them [2 pageants] from leden hall to the Grocers hall wᵗ a Morrys Dawnce viij s   (Robertson and Gordon 1954, 31)

The 8s is thus payment for *one* day's performance, and thus is in line with the other fees (i.e., two nights = 16s).

However, the disparity between the two sets of fees requires further investigation. In 1541 there are two interesting records. The first is a complaint about escalating costs:

The seyd Mʳ Wardeyns as concernyng the charges of this hows for my lord mayre in his Wetche, dyd recyte befor the sayd Assystens & thod' that they for euyry grot' in tyme past, ar now ffayne to gyve v. and that in dyu's thinges as shall appere in the hyryng of Drumes mynstrelles flag dragers two hand swerd pleyrs, morysdaunc's & berers of the Gyaunte Whiche hath rysyne by a wanton and superfluows p'cydence begon by mayres and Shereffes of the m'cery And after the same so recyted The seyd Assistens sayd what remedy but go through wyth all   (Robertson and Gordon 1954, 32)

This is not so much a complaint about inflation as an indication that the magnificence, hence the cost, of the spectacle was beginning to get out of hand. Furthermore, the Drapers claim, the Mercers started it! In fact, it was this extravagant, outdoing-your-brother kind of display that was responsible in the end for the termination of the watches around this time (coupled with crippling inflation through the 1540s). As it happens a great deal of the spectacle – the pageantry, for example – was transferred to the Lord Mayor's Show which celebrated the inauguration of a new mayor. But the morris dance did not make the transition, perhaps adding circumstantial support to the hypothesis that it was a martial dance suited to a watch, but not to a nonmilitary parade. Having carped about their mounting expenses the Drapers agreed to hire morris dancers to accompany Sir William Roche, their mayor, and expressly recorded that the fee was meant in part to dress them richly:

payd to John lymyr, bow string maker dwelling in St Johns strete, for hym & hys compeny vij morys-dauncers & their minstrell for bothe the nyghts so that they be well trimmyd after the gorgious fashion xxiij^s iiij^d (Johnson 1914–15, 2:276)

Comparable fees were paid in 1532 and 1535; in the other years they average around 15s. It seems reasonable to assert, therefore, that this higher fee, stated or unstated, includes a sum for the purchase of new costumes, and that this is part of the escalating costs that the Drapers are complaining about. Earlier they simply hired the morris dancers, who appeared in their own costumes. Now they have to dress them 'after the gorgious fashion' as well as pay for their dancing. If, therefore, the basic fee for two nights' dancing was around 15s, the next question is, among how many people was it divided, and was it divided evenly?

When numbers of dancers are mentioned in the accounts there are customarily eight, as well as one or two minstrels (see Robertson and Gordon 1954, 11–20). Minstrels and dancers were paid a lump sum as a fixed contract, so the problem is to decide what each took from the total. One simple solution is to surmise that they all took equal shares, that is, 15s divided by 9 (for one minstrel) or by 10 (for two minstrels), which would be either 1s 8d or 1s 6d each for both nights (i.e., 10d or 9d per night per man). These figures are reasonably in keeping with wages paid to comparable minstrels hired directly by the guilds, although there are enormous, and frequently inexplicable, variations in these sums. In 1521 a tabor and a kit player were paid a total of 2s 8d (i.e., 1s 4d each) for both nights (Robertson and Gordon 1954, 10). In 1534 a harper and luter were likewise paid 2s 8d for both nights, and another similar pair received 2s 4d (Robertson and Gordon 1954, 23).

By 1541, however, there are intimations that inflation was having an effect on minstrels' fees. Harpers and shawm players received 2s 8d *each* for both nights (i.e., twice the 1521 fee) and a drummer received 20d for one night (Johnson 1914–15,

2:277). But these general increases are not reflected in a rise in average sums paid to morris dancers. Curiously, though, there are fewer dancers and minstrels mentioned in the later years, and this reduction may have kept incomes more in line with rising wages. In 1536, for example, seven dancers and one minstrel were paid 15s 8d for both nights, which, divided evenly amounts to 23½d each (Robertson and Gordon 1954, 27).

Whatever the precise details, it is evident that the morris dancers were commanding wages akin to those of professional musicians, and this conclusion is not simply an artefact of the method of computing wages by dividing evenly. For the dancers to have earned significantly less than their minstrels, their minstrels would have had to have earned substantially more than the average for their class, and there is no reason why this should be the case.[7] Even taking the lowest estimate, 9d per night per man, this is still a generous sum of money for an evening's performance, and puts them in a professional class.

Several comparisons can be made to indicate what this sort of wage meant in social terms. On a general level, such a wage places them with or above the better craftsmen. In the first quarter of the sixteenth century a building labourer earned 4d per ten-hour work day and a master craftsman 6d (Darby 1973, 198), and even by the mid-1540s, when inflation was starting to hit hard, a craftsman tailor and a craftsman joiner earned around 8d per day (Feuillerat 1914, 3–6). Dancers' wages were, therefore, good even in comparison with these highly trained guild artisans. It should be remembered also that the dancers' fee was not for a full day's work. Spinelli records that the entire watch lasted from 11 pm to 2 am (Spinelli 1521, 96), and even given several hours' preparation and the leading of the mayor and sheriffs from their houses, this still only amounts to five or six hours' work. And, on top of these wages, they received compensation for breakfast and ale.

Dancers' wages also put them well above the level of the nonskilled participants in the processions. In 1521 actors on the pageants received 8d each for both nights (i.e., 4d per night), and the Moors, 4d each for both nights. Even those with a certain level of skill, the two-handed staff and sword players, received only 8d each for both nights (Robertson and Gordon 1954, 7–8). Dancers' wages are more than double this level.

Financial indicators, therefore, point to a company of trained dancers with considerable social standing. Other circumstantial evidence points in the same direction. From 1521 to 1541 five different men are recorded in the guild accounts as agents for teams of dancers: Robert Greves (1521), William Burnet (1522), Walter Fount (1525, 1529, 1535, 1536), William Darrell (1530), and John Lymyr (1541). Lymyr is recorded as being a bowstring-maker as well as leader of the morris, and Darrell was a leather-seller. Both are respectable guild crafts. Admittedly they are not of the twelve great companies, but they are liverymen nonetheless.

That there were at least five companies of dancers active in the relatively short time span between 1521 and 1541 means several things. First, it suggests a degree of ephemerality, with only Fount's team showing any ability to persist in time. Second, it is an index of the relative popularity of urban morris in this era. Each watch required a minimum of two companies – one for the mayor and one shared by the sheriffs – and could have used three. But two nights' work for a few shillings would not have been adequate incentive to train, costume, and market a band of eight dancers. There must have been other occasions throughout the year for turning a profit. Two calendar festivals noted below, the Christmas revels and May games, may have been such times. It is also possible that the isolated references to morris dancers at court in the very early sixteenth century mentioned in the previous chapter (that is, those that are distinct from the morisks and morrises associated with disguisings) represent appearances there by similar companies. If so, this implies that two distinct morrises played in the courts of the early Tudors – the aristocratic disguising variety, and the urban professional type.

Regardless of the monetary rewards there were still not enough events in the year to make dancing more than a money-making sideline. In this respect morris dancing was quite unlike contemporary minstrelsy, even though the fees for services rendered per person per event were comparable. The most important consideration here is that the dancers (unlike minstrels) had to perform in companies that were hired as a unit, at prices that only wealthy people or groups could afford for special circumstances. The dancers were thus men with other full-time employment who trained in their off hours. Perhaps, like dancers in later centuries, they got involved as young active men – as apprentices, maybe – and dropped out as other responsibilities crowded in. This would account for the high turnover of companies, and be consistent with other data. Whatever the case, this could not be what Mike Heaney calls a 'plebeian' morris (Heaney 1989). The dance they performed was an expensive honour to mark the entourages of the highest officials in the nation's capital, and they were compensated appropriately. All indications point to them coming from the petite bourgeoisie, or class of minor liverymen.

LORD OF MISRULE PROCESSIONS

Midwinter carries with it many of the attributes of midsummer, as well as some polar opposites. It is not surprising, therefore, that urban morris dancing should have been associated with this festival also. Midwinter, like midsummer, marks the solstice, the turning of the year, the moment when the days cease to get shorter and nights cease to lengthen. For reasons already alluded to (see also Eliade 1949), these festivals mark periods in which control of the social order is especially important (in part because festivity can easily lead to *dis*order). The most important difference, though, is that Midsummer tends to emphasize the maintenance of order, whereas midwinter is a season that focuses on customs that revel in the breakdown of order. Midwinter and Midsummer are, therefore, in that respect mirror image festivals.

E.K. Chambers in *The Mediaeval Stage* (1903, 1:228–419) provides ample evidence that across Europe in the late Middle Ages the midwinter season (represented by the various holy days of Christmastide) was the opportunity for the celebration of festivals of inversion, that is, ceremonies that mocked the normal order of things. One such was the *festum fatuorum* or *festum stultorum* (feast of fools), best known from French accounts of the fourteenth and fifteenth centuries. A letter of 1445 from Eustace de Mesnil, representing the Faculty of Theology at the University of Paris, to the bishops and chapters of France gives the general idea:

Quis, quaeso, Christianorum sensatus non diceret malos illos sacerdotes et clericos, quos divini officii tempore videret larvatos, monstruosis vultibus, aut in vestibus mulierum, aut lenonum, vel histrionum choreas ducere in choro, cantilenas inhonestas cantare, offas pingues supra cornu altaris iuxta celebrantem missam comedere, ludum taxillorum ibidem exercere, thurificare de fumo fetido ex corio veterum sotularium, et per totam ecclesiam currere, turpitudinem suam non erubescere, ac deinde per villam et theatra in curribus et vehiculis sordidis duci ad infamia spectacula, pro risu astantium et concurrentium turpes gesticulationes sui corporis faciendo, et verba impudicissima ac scurrilia proferendo?

[What intelligent Christian, I ask, would not call wicked those priests and clerks seen masked in monstrous visages at the time of divine office, dancing in the choir dressed as women, panders, or actors, singing wanton songs, eating greasy sausages at the horn of the altar while the celebrant says mass, and playing dice there, censing with stinking fumes from the soles of old shoes, and running and leaping through the church not blushing at their disgrace; then driving through the town and theatres in shabby carts and carriages and rousing the laughter of their companions and bystanders in infamous performances with indecent gestures and unchaste and scurrilous verses?]   (cited in Chambers 1903, 1:294).

A like custom, much more commonly noted in English cathedrals, involved the election of a choir boy as mock bishop for one or more of the holy days (such as Holy Innocents). The secular equivalent of these ecclesiastical customs of inversion of order was the annual reign of the Lord of Misrule of whom Stow says:

... in the feast of Christmas, there was in the king's house, wheresoever he was lodged, a lord of misrule, or master of merry disports, and the like had ye in the house of every nobleman of honour or good worship, were he spiritual or temporal. Amongst the which the mayor of London, and either of the sheriffs, had their several lords of misrule, ever contending, without quarrel or offence, who should make the rarest pastimes to delight the beholders. (Stow 1908, 89)

The important point to note is that these are feasts glorying in the inversion of social order that are not only condoned by the authorities, but actively supported by them and employing their own people in carrying out the acts of sacrilege and abuse. These are not, therefore, rituals of rebellion against authority by outsiders, but acts of cathartic parody from those within the system, albeit those in subordinate roles. Consequently they can be seen as acts stemming from a foundation of institutional security. When the church came under genuine threat from reformers it quickly made efforts to eradicate any appearance of impiety, by banning the *festa fatuorum* and Boy Bishops. Lords of Misrule were, likewise, members of the ruling class in the employ of the nobility, and they enjoyed considerable vogue in the royal courts of Henry VII and VIII.

The first Lord of Misrule on record appears in Henry VII's accounts for Christmas 1491 (Anglo 1960, 27), and similar entries appear annually under both Henrys from that date until around 1520. Little documentary evidence exists to indicate what exactly these lords did, but in the last two years of the reign of Edward VI the records become much richer. In the Christmas season of 1551/2 the duke of Northumberland planned an especially lavish celebration orchestrated by Sir George Ferrers as Lord of Misrule, to distract the young king from the imminent execution of the duke of Somerset, his mother's brother. The event was so successful that it was repeated the following year. Ferrers's letter stating his plans for the festivities of Christmas 1552/3 is extant and provides a general overview of the activities of the Lord of Misrule:

Sir wheras you required me to write, for that *your* busynes is great/ I haue in as few wordes as I maie signefied to you such thing*es* as I thinke moste necessarie for my purpose/
ffirst as towching my Introduction where the last yeare my devise was to cum oute of the mone/ this yeare I Imagin to cum oute of a place caulled *vastum vacuum* .I. the great waste/ asmoche to saie as a place voyde or emptie *with*oute the worlde where is neither fier ayre water nor earth/ and that I haue bene remayning there sins the Last yeare And bicause of Certaine devisis whiche I haue towching this matter/ I wolde yf it were possyble haue all myne apparrell blewe the first daie that I present my self to the king*es* Maie*s*tie and even as I shewe my self that daie, so my mynd is in like order & in like sue*tes* to shew my self at my com*m*yng into London after the halowed daies/
Againe how I shall cum into the courte whether vnder a Canepie as the last yeare, or in a chare trivmphall, or vppon some straunge beast that I reserve to you/ But the serpente with sevin heddes cauled hidra is the chief beast of myne armes./ and the wholie bushe is the devise of my Crest/ my worde is *semper ferians* .I. alwaies feasting or keping holie daie/
Vppon Christmas daie I send a solempe ambassade to the king*es* Maie*s*tie by an herrald trumpet an orator speaking in a straunge language an// Interpreter or a truchman with hym, to which per*s*ons thre were requisit to haue convenient furnyture which I referre to you/

I haue provided one to plaie vppon a kettell drom with his boye and a nother drome with a
fyffe whiche must be apparelled like turkes garment*es* according to the patornes I send you her-
with on St Stephens daie/ I wolde yf it were possyble be with the king*es* mai*es*tie before dyn-
ner M^r windham being my admyrall as appointed to receive me beneth the bridge withe the
king*es* Brigandyne and other vessell*es* apointed for the same purpose/ his desire is to haue the
poope of his vessell covered with white and blew like as I signefie to you by a nother *lettre*/
Sir george howard being my M*aster* of the horsis receiveth me at my Landing at grenwiche
with a spare horse and iiij pag*es* of hono*ur* one carieng my hedpece a nother my Shelde/ the
thirde my sword and the fourth my axe/ As for their furniture I know nothing as yet provided
either for my pag*es* or other wise save a hedpece that I caused to be made/
My counsailo*urs* with suche other necessarie p*er*sons y^t attend vppon me that daie must also
be consydered/ There maie be no fewer than sixe counsailo*urs* at the least/ I must also have a
divine a philosopher an astronom*er* a poet a phisician/ a potecarie/ a M^r of request*es* a sivilian/
a disard/ two gentlmen vshers besides Iuglers/ tomblers/ fooles/ friers and suche other/
The residue of the wholie daies I will spend other devises/ as one daie in feat*es* of armes &
then wolde I haue a challeng p*er*formed with hobbie horsis where I purpose to be in p*er*son
a nother daie in honting & hawking/ the residue of the tyme Shalbe spent in other devisis
whiche I will declare to you by mouth to haue yo*ur* ayde and advice therin/

(Feuillerat 1914, 89–90)

In essence, the Lord of Misrule acts as a mock king, surrounded by all the trappings
of a royal court and arrayed in the most elaborate of costumes (he is to have a newly
made suit of the finest materials for each day of the revels). Each event replicates the
usual kingly pastimes, but in mock form – a tournament, but with riders on hobby
horses, for example. The aspect of these revels that most concerns us here, however,
is a visit to London briefly and uninformatively alluded to in Ferrers's letter. It is
evident from entries in other sections of the accounts that this tour of the city is meant
to be a parody of the Midsummer Watches. In 1551/2 one item reads,

Item agaynst tomorow nyghte for a Midsomer nyghte as many Counterfett harnesses &
weapons as ye may spare and hoby horsses   (Feuillerat 1914, 27)

and in the following year,

Item vj hobby horses for mydsom*er* watch   (Feuillerat 1914, 92)

Hence the notion that the themes of midwinter celebrations mirror (or invert) those
of midsummer is explicitly confirmed. Eyewitness accounts of these 'watches' indicate
that they parodied the implementation of social order. Machyn's eyewitness account
of the Christmas procession held in January 1552, for example, clearly indicates

that the main public spectacle associated with the mock watch took place on a specially built scaffold in Cheapside, one of the widest thoroughfares and market-
places in the centre of the city. Here the Lord of Misrule set up mock versions of
the pillory, stocks, and gibbet, presumably for comic trials and punishments:

The iiij day of Januarii was mad a grett skaffold [in Ch]epe hard by the crosse, agaynst the
kynges lord of myss[rule] cumyng from Grenwych; and landyd at Towre warff [and with]
hym yonge knyghts and gentyllmen a gret nombur on [horseb]ake sum in gownes and cotes
and chynes abowt ther nekes, every man havyng a balderyke of yelow and grene abowt ther
nekes, and on the Towre hyll ther they [went in] order, furst a standard of yelow and grene
sylke with Sant Gorge, and then gonnes and skuybes, and trompets and bagespypes, and
drousselars and flutes, and then a gret compeny all in yelow and gren, and docturs declaryng
my lord grett, and then the mores danse dansyng with a tabret, and afor xx of ys consell on
horsbake in gownes of chanabulle lynyd with blue taffata and capes of the sam, lyke sage
(men); then cam my lord with a gowne of gold furyd with fur of the goodlyest collers as ever
youe saw, and then ys [...] and after cam alff a hundred in red and whyt, tallmen [of] the
gard, with hods of the sam coler, and cam in to the cete; and after cam a carte, the whyche
cared the pelere, the a [...] [the] jubett, the stokes, and at the crose in Chepe a gret brod
s[kaffold] for to go up ...   (Machyn 1848, 13–14)

Machyn's text is corrupt at the point where he describes the equipment for punishment carried in procession by the Lord of Misrule, but the accounts make it
appear as if a mock beheading was part of the spectacle, which would indeed have
been a black joke given Somerset's looming fate (Feuillerat 1914, 72).

   Beheading was a form of capital punishment reserved for the nobility, so there
is a strong element of the upper class parodying its own forms of social control, as
well as satire on the punishments for the lesser ranks – hanging, the stocks, and the
pillory. Some account books also contain payments for a portable gaol cell as well
as manacles for prisoners and keys for the gaolers, so that the whole focus of the
drama at Cheapside cross must have been general caricature of crime and punishment.

   The burlesque of social control as a key aspect of the day's events is even clearer in
Machyn's account of the procession from the following year:

The sam day a-ffor non landyd at the Towre wh[arf] the Kynges lord of myssrulle, and ther
mett with hym the [Shreyffes] lord of myssrulle with ys men ...
... and a-for hym gret horses and in cottes and clokes of [...] in-brodered with gold and with
balderykes a-bowt ther nekes, whytt and blue sarsenets, and chynes of gold, and the rest of
ys servands in bluw gardyd with whytt, and next a-for ys consell in bluw taffata and ther
capes of whytt [...] ys trumpeters, taburs, drumes, and flutes and fulles and ys mores dansse,
gunes, mores-pykes, bagpypes; and ys mass [...] and ys gayllers with pelere, stokes, and ys

axe, gyffes, and boltes, sum fast by the leges and sum by the nekes, and so rod thrugh Marke lane, and so thrugh Grasyus strett and Cornhylle ...   (Machyn 1848, 28–9)

What is evident here is that, although the royal Lord of Misrule is satirizing the pride of the city – the watches of the mayor and sheriffs – these dignitaries happily include themselves in the revelry, sheriff John Maynard hiring his own Lord of Misrule to caricature his office (concerned fundamentally with law and order). The joke is taken one step further by having the king's lord 'knight' the sheriff's lord as a reward for services rendered.

It is hard to establish the precise role of the morris dance in this seasonal buffoonery. Most likely it was included to add to the procession the general flavour of the Midsummer Watch, of which it was a key element. But were the dancers a regular company hired to be part of the parade, or members of the nobility dressed as morris dancers in imitation of the real thing? There is really no way to tell because of lack of documentary evidence on either side. There are no payments in the accounts for a company of dancers, neither are there any for costumes or other morris paraphernalia. There are, at best, circumstantial hints that these were regular companies. One is the fact that John Maynard had a company in his entourage and they would certainly not have been nobles. During the Lenten season Maynard held a Jack-a-Lent procession, akin in some respects to the Lord of Misrule parade, and here too he had a company of morris dancers (Machyn 1848, 33). The morris dance may thus have been considered a generally festive element, not something that could or should be parodied. That is, it was a processional dance that, although martial in character, could be transferred from one kind of parade to another provided there was a military element for it to attach to (all of the above mentioned were concerned to one degree or other with civil and military power expressed through bands of armed men); it did not have the kind of narrative or symbolic meaning that would tie it rigidly to specific events or times of the year.

It is interesting to note in this regard, that the morris dance was not an automatic inclusion in Lord of Misrule processions. Machyn, for example, notes such parades in London in the Christmas seasons of 1556/7 (Machyn 1848, 125) and 1561/2 (Machyn 1848, 273–4), and neither had a morris dance. This again is only a circumstantial hint, but it seems to indicate that the processions designed by Ferrers were special inasmuch as they were conscious parodies of the Midsummer Watch, and that was the reason the morris dance was included.

Other processions in which the morris is included are clearly as military as the watches, or have significant military elements. John Maynard's Lenten procession combined several military (and other) aspects of the Midsummer and Midwinter processions. Likewise a Lenten muster involving a procession and organized sports ordered by Queen Elizabeth to honour her household officers in 1559 had a morris dance as part of its general spectacle:

The xxj of Marche the quen('s) master cokes and odur her offesers, and at Mylle-end ther they dynyd, [with] all maner of mett and drynke; and ther was all maner of artelere, as drumes, flutes, trumpetes, gones, mores pykes, halbardes, to the nomber of vC.; the gonners in shurtes of maylle and [...] pykes in bryght harnes, and mony swardes and v grett pesses of gones and shot in [...] the wyche dyd myche hurt unto glass wy[ndows;] and cam a grett gyant danssyng, and after [that a] mores dansse dansyng, and gones and mor[es pikes]; and after cam a cart with a grett wyth and ij [bears?] with-in the cartt, and be-syd whent a gret [...] of grett mastes; and then cam the master cokes rydyng in cottes in brodere, and chynes of gold, and mony of the quen('s) servandes in ther levery, to the cowrt, and ther they shott ther pesses, and with-in the parke was ij C. chamburs gret and smalle shot, and the Quen's grace standyn in the galere; and so evere man whent in-to the parke, showhyng them in batell ray, shutyng and playhyng at bowt the parke; and a-for the quen was on of bayres was bated, and after the mores dansers whent in-to the cowrt, dansyng in mony offeses.   (Machyn 1848, 191)

This event is also noteworthy in that it brings together for the first time the two dance locations so far discussed – urban streets and the royal court. The dancers processed with the muster around the town, but also entered the court and danced in the 'mony offeses,' that is, the offices, such as the kitchen, that were being honoured. This suggests that the dance as it was performed at the time could be both processional and static, unless the dancers simply paraded through the rooms without stopping. More likely, as suggested earlier, the dance was akin to the hobby horse dance described by Mountgomery in that it was basically processional, but could pause for short periods for some static action, such as a mock fight or fancy sword play.

This union of processional dance around the city and a court visit was repeated later in the year as part of a May game, which in London also had a strong martial component, and for a while the urban morris attached itself to May festivities (see below). What this implies is that with the demise of the London watches in the 1540s some of the elements of the procession – such as the morris dance – attached themselves to other parades, such as Lenten musters and May games, because they needed a well-funded event to support them. It also suggests that such elements had a 'parade quality,' that is, they were simple in themselves, and acquired meaning by being part of a procession; they could not sustain themselves as individual events. Parade elements such as giants, the nine worthies, companies of armed men, *and the urban morris dance* were thus not self-sustaining spectacles; they needed each other and the parade itself to have sufficient justification for their presentation. It is also interesting to speculate that around the 1550s the processional dance was beginning to evolve into a more static form because of the need to adjust to new venues in place of the old. Before considering the rise of the morris at May games in detail, however, we reach a fork in the road, and I shall first consider the guild processional morris as it continued in cities other than London.

GUILD PROCESSIONS OUTSIDE LONDON

Apart from the occasional attempt at revival, the London Midsummer Watches were defunct by the 1540s and much of their pageantry was transferred to the Lord Mayor's Show marking the election of a new mayor in October. Cities other than London continued Midsummer Watches beyond this period, however, and sometimes included morris dancers. Borough accounts from Chester, for example, are remarkably similar to those from the London guilds. The first that includes morris dancing is dated 1569:

Itam paid the mores dansares at mydsomer   vj s. viij d.
Itam paid the mynstrells which plaid before them   xvj d.
(Chester CCA: TAR/1/13, mb 4, in Clopper 1979, 87)

Like entries show up in the treasurers' accounts until 1593, the sum of 6s 8d remaining constant throughout. Two entries in this period mention Thomas Gillam as the leader/agent for the dancers (Clopper 1979, 120 and 151), and given that they are eleven years apart (1577 and 1588) they suggest a degree of continuity in the company. The similarity to the London watches is further confirmed by longer entries that give some descriptive detail, such as this one from 1589:

Itam the xxvth of Ivne to the morres dauncers ffor daunsynge at the Watche
before the Shereffes is some   vj s. viij d.
(Chester CCA: TAR/1/18, mb 6, in Clopper 1979, 155)

From the end of the sixteenth century until the time of the Restoration the morris dance does not appear in the accounts, possibly because of mounting Puritan sentiment and church opposition to various forms of dancing and licence, although the Midsummer Show itself continued sporadically until the Commonwealth. I shall discuss the role of the church in supporting and opposing morris dancing in due course. For the moment I will simply note that visitation articles for Chester diocese published in 1581 and renewed in 1604, 1617, 1634, and 1637 specifically condemn morris dancing:

Whether ... your said church, chapel or churchyard be abused or profaned by any unlawful or unseemly act, game, or exercise, as by Lords of Misrule, Summer lords or ladies, pipers, rushbearers, Morris dancers, pedlars, bearwards, and such like; then through whose default, and what be the names of the offenders in that behalf?
(Visitation Articles Chester 1581 in Kennedy 1924, 2:110)

At the Restoration of Charles II, however, the city made efforts to revive the Midsummer Show. A series of manuscripts in the Harleian collection record some of the sentiments of the times, as for example this general letter from the city assembly to the city guilds:

Wheras there hath byn an auntient and laudable Custome in this Citty Comonly called midsomer show or wach ∧[caused to besett forth &] approued of by our ∧[Ancestors the] Maiestrates [thetofore] for the great [vtility of that citty by] drawing in of Strangers by ther great Comerse and trafick for the benifite of the sayd citty & Cittizens which by late obstruc-tiue tymes hath byn much hindred it is thought meet ∧[at the last generall assembly] [for the tranquility therof] and taken into Consideration the sayd show may be agayne reuiued for the publick benifite of this Citty and for the [your] good approbation and furtherance therin in respect diuers thinges of Consernment ∧[therin] are wantinge, to know [what] what will-ingly your Company is pleased to contribute to ward the sayd charge that it may not be retarded and to be subscribed here vnder the hands of your Aldermen or [&] Stewards to se whether the some ∧[in generall gathared] will equilize the Charge of expences, it beinge a particular profite to eich one & honor to the Citty to preserue theis auntient Customs
(BL Harl. MS 2150 f 201v, in Clopper 1979, 478)

The power of the purse apparently meant more than the power of the pulpit in the changed political climate. The city and guilds thus saw the Midsummer Show as a financial investment: make it grand and people will flock to see it and spend money in the city. In 1661 the council estimated that it would cost 45 li 9s 8d to make all new pageant materials (because all the old stock had been broken up), and to hire the necessary performers. Included in this calculation was a payment for,

the ∧[6] morris dancers & Tabrett & pipe   xx s.
(BL Harl. MS 2150 f 203, in Clopper 1979, 481)

The city's enthusiasm was short-lived, however, and, after intermittent revivals, the Midsummer Show was abolished in 1678. There is no firm evidence that morris dancers performed at any of these shows, the 1661 line item being an estimate, not an actual cost. Nonetheless, there are other indications that there was at least one company of morris dancers active in Chester at the time. A manuscript from 1660 also concerning the costs for the revival of the Midsummer Show states:

the morris dancers ∧[had x s from citt but now] haue no fee but the Curtesye after the show at eich house what the please   (BL Harl. MS 2150 f 201, in Clopper 1979, 478)

This suggests that although morris dancers' fees are not mentioned in the accounts of Midsummer Shows after 1594 they may have continued dancing from time to time, despite church opposition (which may have been the cause of the cessation of official sponsorship) for what they could earn by begging. Whatever the case, they are not heard of again after the 1661 revival.

A much more complex picture is in evidence in Salisbury, although many details repeat those from Chester.[8] Morris dancing was supported, starting in the 1560s, by the Salisbury Tailors' Company, whose patron saint was John the Baptist. In honour of their patron they held a number of commemorative events including processions carrying lights to chantries sponsored by the company on the eve of the feast of John the Baptist. Company ledgers indicate that these celebrations were regular events by 1444. The city of Salisbury also initiated Midsummer Watches on the eves of the feasts of John the Baptist and SS. Peter and Paul in 1440, as in London. Thus, for a time the Tailors' annual processions and the first of the watches coincided, although presumably the timing of the various events on the day would have prevented scheduling conflicts. The processions particular to the tailors were during the morning, afternoon, and early evening hours, and the watch was at night (see Douglas 1989, 36). That the tailors did participate in the watches, including those on the eve of St John the Baptist, rather than avoiding them in favour of celebrating their feast privately, is attested by city and guild accounts of 1481. However by 1503 the Midsummer Watches were defunct, leaving the tailors' processions as the sole public markers of Midsummer.[9]

With the dissolution of many religious foundations, including chantries, under Henry VIII and various reformers' attempts to remove superstitious elements from the church, such as bearing commemorative lights to church, the processions to the chantries had disappeared by the late 1540s. There was a brief return to traditional practice under Mary, but by the beginning of Elizabeth's reign what was left of the old patronal feast and procession had been heavily secularized, and contained elements much more reminiscent of the old Midsummer Watches: pageants, giants, hobby horses, and morris dancers. One might speculate that these elements had at one time been part of the now defunct city watches (although morris dancers are not in evidence in city accounts), and were adopted by the tailors to replace the forbidden religious components, the translation made possible by the temporal coincidence in the past of the city and company processions.

The first record of morris dancers in the Tailors' ledgers comes from 1564:

At thys assembly was receyued for the puttynge owt of the Morrys Cots iii s. iv d. and yt ys agreyd that Gregory Clerke shall have the kepynge of the ffyve morrys-cots, with xxti dosyn of Myllan-bells, for the space of xii yeres, yf he so longe lyve, payeng yerely to the occupacon iii s. iv d., and also the said Gregory do stand bound to the occupacon in the some of ffive pounds of lawfull money of England, to delyver the same ffyve morys cots and xx doysen of Myllan-bells, at thend of the said xii yeres, or at the oure of death of the said Gregory if he

dye before, in as good case as he receyved it, and further the said Gregory byndyth hymself
by these presents to delyver the said Cotts and bells at all tymes to the said occupacion yf
they wyll haue them to the use of the occupacion, and yt ys agreyd that the said Gregory
shalbe bound to the Wardens of the occupacion, by wrytyng, obligatory in the some of ffyve
poundes.   (Haskins 1912, 171–2)

This reference is significant for several reasons. Above all it indicates that morris
costumes for guild processions were exorbitantly expensive items. Gregory Clerk,
according to this account, agreed to pay the tailors a total of 40s over a twelve-year
period, and to be bound to pay 5 li should the costumes be damaged or lost. These
are substantial sums of money in an era when a skilled tailor's monthly wage might
not amount to 20s. In effect the agreement is claiming that the replacement cost of
the coats and bells is 5 li, and given that there are five coats, this works out at 1 li
(i.e., 20s) per costume (including a set of 4 dozen bells per dancer).

Clerk was relying on making a profit on an annual expenditure of 3s 4d, so it is
reasonable to presume that there were a number of events in and around Salisbury at
the time that called for the hire of morris dancers (who in turn hired their costumes,
because they were not wealthy enough to be able to afford their own). The logic is
straightforward. Apart from the Tailors' procession, there must have been at least one
other event at which morris dancers performed; otherwise Clerk would have had no
motive for his contract. But if there were just one other event it would scarcely be
in his interest to act as a middleman, and all he would have been doing was adding
his costs to the costs of hiring the costumes directly from the Tailors' Company, thus
potentially discouraging the dancers, leaving him with a rental fee to pay the Tailors
and no takers. Even two events per annum runs the same sort of risks. He must have
imagined multiple occasions on which dancers would be coming to him throughout the year (one company and one event at a time, given that he had but one set of
costumes). Furthermore, he confidently expected these events to continue on a regular basis for twelve years.

That the bargain was financially sound is argued also by the fact that in 1584
Thomas Barker made a similar one for all the morris gear and other costumes (which
had grown to include a Maid Marian's costume, a hobby horse, and a few more
bells),[10] only this time the contract was for ten years and the annual rental was considerably reduced to 2s 6d, with no bond for loss or damage. It is possible to interpret this as a sign of diminished interest in morris dancing, possibly reflecting the
rise of church opposition, as in Chester. Visitation articles opposing morris were
published in the diocese in 1581 and, as discussed below, were eventually vigorously
acted upon. But these cannot have had an immediate effect because Barker made
his contract three years after they were enacted. Rather, I suspect that the price was
low, and no bond required, because the costumes were getting worn and in need of

replacement. This conjecture is supported by the Tailors' accounts which record a decision in 1591 to make a new set of morris coats for that year's patronal feast (Trowbridge, Wilts RO G23/1/252 f.83r). The old coats were simply a source of a little extra revenue for the company, and if they were damaged no great loss would be incurred (between Clerk's and Barker's contracts the Tailors had recouped 65 per cent of their initial outlay on the costumes – assuming 5 li is a reasonable estimate – and had had thirty years' use from them as well). If this surmise is correct, it also suggests that the bond posted by Clerk in 1564 is an index of the coats being new (or nearly so) in that year.

It is not surprising that a guild of tailors should make their own morris costumes and lend them to dancers in their processions, as well as hire them out for other occasions: that was their occupation. But this fact may have other social implications. It is certainly the case that the Salisbury morris dancers were not as independent as their London counterparts, who, owning all the necessary equipment, could hire themselves out as autonomous companies, charging what the market would bear and performing at will. This also, incidentally, indicates that the London companies had a considerable investment tied up in their gear, perhaps through the entrepreneurship of people such as Walter Fount. Dancers in Salisbury were beholden to the tailors or their agent for their gear and, therefore, could not perform at will, or for flexible fees: they had to be guaranteed their rental costs. And since there was but one set of coats there could be only one company active at a time. All of this bespeaks a lowering of the social status of the dancers, maybe in conjunction with the belt-tightening effects of rampant inflation and only slowly rising wages.

From the 1560s onward there are sporadic indications that the Tailors employed morris dancers in connection with their annual feast, which from Elizabethan times was only loosely tied to Midsummer, a Sunday a week or two hence being the favoured choice. There are no indications of a typical wage, to know whether it was lower than for groups in other cities who provided their own gear. In the minutes of 1569, however, there is a note to the effect that meat and drink works out at 1s per person; wages were paid out over and above this amount. Agreements to hire morris dancers for the feast appear in the Tailors' records for 1568, 1569, 1579, 1580, 1591, 1592, and 1610, suggesting a regular performance through this period. Then in 1611 we learn rather more about the morris than from the terse records in the Tailors' accounts, because their appearance led to the imprisonment of the wardens of the company.

In 1611 the Tailors decided to hold their annual patronal feast, including the usual procession from church with morris dancers, on St John the Baptist's eve. As had been the custom for several decades the feast day was a Sunday. The mayor of Salisbury, Bartholomew Tookey, took exception to this proposal and wrote to the wardens on the afternoon of the feast day:

fforasmuch as heretofore the Lordes Sabbaoth Day hath bene prophaned by some ydell and evill dysposed persones with the Morrys Dauncers and dromers from the churches and in tyme of prayers, yt is thought fitt the same shold ende and be forborne These are therefore nowe to entreate and also to require youe that youe forbeare further to prophane the sabbaoth day as heretofore youe haue donne eyther with dromes or Morris Dauncers other then in your owne private howse, as youe and the Actors therein offendynge shall answere the contrarye Sa[llisbu]ry the xxiijth of June 1611 Barth. Tokye maior.   (PRO SP/14/64/f.89)

The wardens respectfully replied:

so soddenlye they cold not stay the goinge forth of the dauncers for that the elders and the company were dispersed and departed, affirming that if they had had but a Dayes warninge of his pleasure before herein, they wold have conformed thereof, with their company and stayed yt well enoughe. And althoughe they had so short warninge: yet they willed their messingers to tell him that the Morris dauncers shold not showe them selves that Day before that eveninge prayer shold be donne & ended in all churches   (PRO SP/14/64/ff.90–1)

Contemporary accounts by the wardens indicate that they acted as indicated in their letter, and accuse the mayor of sending an agent provocateur to incite punishable offences, especially among the apprentices (PRO SP/14/64/ff.89–91). Notwithstanding, the wardens were summoned to answer charges of sabbath violations and contempt before the mayor, and on arrival were ordered to put up bail against the next quarter sessions or go to prison. Not being able to post securities on the spot they were placed in custody, but were released after two days. The manuscript account of the affair is headed with the single word 'repealed,' suggesting that either they were acquitted at the sessions, or the matter was dropped before it went to trial.

It is difficult to assess what laws were being broken here. Strictly, sabbath profanation came under ecclesiastical rather than civil law and, therefore, was not within the mayor's jurisdiction (as the wardens noted in their defence). Furthermore, the appropriate laws applied primarily to performances on church property during times of worship (see Visitation Articles Diocese of Salisbury, 1581, sig. B4). To parade from the church they must have danced initially on church grounds, but the tailors were careful to wait until all services in the city were over before beginning the procession, thus abiding by the letter of the ecclesiastical law.

The sole bone of contention between Tookey and the tailors seems to be the public performance of the morris and the accompanying drumming. He apparently did not object to the procession from church in general nor to feasting on the sabbath. Neither did he oppose morris dancing as long as it was performed exclusively within the tailors' hall. Thus there was something especially vile, in his eyes, about morris dancing in the streets in particular. The point seems to have been that morris dancing by its 'wanton' and 'ribald' nature was apt to stir up trouble among the populace. At the very least it was loud and disruptive, potentially distracting to people attending divine worship. The tailors, by waiting until all services were ended, implicitly agreed that the dance could be noisy and a potential disturbance, but they disagreed with the mayor concerning its effects. In their defence they claimed,

that which they did was not mislyked but lyked of by the best in the cittye and what they had donne, was donne for tyme out of mynde of man and alwayes approved by the best of the cittye. to which Mr Maior sayed And who are the best   (PRO SP/14/64/f.90)

The mayor's sending of a mischief-maker may also be tacit agreement on his part that the dance was not inevitably liable to cause trouble. Nonetheless, he was not acting arbitrarily nor from personal motives alone; his actions were in accord with the spirit of the applicable ecclesiastical laws, even if he was acting outside of his jurisdiction. It is also worth noting for later consideration that the wardens were not, as far as records show, called to answer for their misdeeds before the diocesan visitor. The urban bourgeoisie largely escaped prosecution under these laws.

One can speculate from all of this that the processional morris dance of the time was especially wild and raucous, with significant martial elements to stir the blood and perhaps incite rambunctiousness in its spectators. A useful comparison might be made with a contemporary dance from Wells, discussed in detail below under May games, that also fell foul of municipal authorities, and for which much more detailed accounts exist.

Although the Salisbury tailors can be said to have made their point (and did not exactly lose their case), the incident appears to have dampened their support for morris dancing. Their annual feast continued regularly through the seventeenth century, but it was not until 1632 that their accounts again indicate the hiring of morris dancers for their procession, and this is an isolated record. Subsequently – starting over a century later – the company hired morris dancers for borough celebrations rather than for its own processions. Such events occurred from the mid-eighteenth century onwards, and so mostly fall outside our period (see Cawte 1978, 29–35 for details). The only one that does fall within our scope is typical of later events, and is described in a contemporary newspaper:

The Thanksgiving day was observed here, with the greatest loyalty and decorum. At dawn, its approach was proclaimed by the firing of cannon. Between ten and eleven, the various companies of the city, headed by their several officers and a great number of youths, with white wands and scarlet cockades, met in the Market Place, where they were drawn up behind their respective gay banners. They afterwards walked in procession (the cannon firing) to the Cathedral, through vast crowds of spectators ... To divert the populace, the 'Giant' (a colossal figure, near 25 feet high) with Hobnob, his renowned 'squire, encircled with morris dancers, went up and down the town.   (*Salisbury and Winchester Journal* 13–10–1746)

This account cannot be taken as indicative of the seventeenth-century morris because it comes after such a long break in the tradition. It could just as easily represent a new era of dance style. By analogy one may compare the state of affairs in Salisbury in the twentieth century. In 1911 the morris dancers of Salisbury performed in procession with the giant, and their costumes and other paraphernalia are consistent with those shown in photographs from the nineteenth century (see Haskins 1912, plate opp. 396 and Cawte 1978, 34). But when the giant was paraded again in 1953 the dancers performed in costumes modelled on those from nineteenth-century Oxfordshire (and danced in a manner common to Oxfordshire), because at that time the morris of the south Midlands had diffused rapidly over southern England due to the efforts of the morris revival begun by Cecil Sharp and coworkers. This radical change occurred after a break of only forty years.

From 1746 onwards it is also clear from the records that there is a close association between the giant, hob-nob (the hobby horse), and the morris dancers, but this cannot have been the case in the sixteenth and seventeenth centuries, since for much of that time the giant was too great an expense for the Tailors to keep operative. In 1579 the Tailors' accounts include:

At this assemblie it is agreed yt the accustomed ffeast of this companie shalbe kept vppon sondaye beinge the vth daye of Iuly next comminge. And yt is lukewise agreed that the gyaunt shalbe lett downe and goe nomore by cause of the charge whiche he causeth yearely to this companie. And yt is lukewise agreed that the Stewerds shall fynde the morris dauncers and their companie theire sufficient meate and drynke, the mitigation therof to be at the wardens discretion yffe theie see cause, the wages of the sayed morris dauncers and others to be at the only charge of the chamber of this companie. (Trowbridge, Wilts RO G23/1/252 f.21r)

So at this time it was quite possible for the morris dancers to perform without the giant. It is not until the isolated record of 1632 that we read in the accounts:

It is thought fitt by the Maior parte of this Corporacion beinge here present that the Gyant and morris daunce shall go at the ffeast as in tymes past. (Trowbridge, Wilts RO G23/1/254 f.6)

All of this suggests that the dance of 1746 was unconnected with that of the sixteenth and early seventeenth centuries.

Although the Tailors stopped their active patronage of morris dancers after the events of 1611, they continued to rent out the costumes. Accounts for 1663, 1665, and 1667 include receipts for hire of the coats, in the first case the renters being specifically identified as men from Downton, a village about six miles south of Salisbury. Thus the Restoration may have seen a brief revival of interest in morris, but perhaps more in the countryside than the city.

Besides Chester and Salisbury there are no other provincial cities known to have patronized morris at Midsummer on a regular basis. There are, however, isolated hints that other traditions may have existed. The borough records for Edinburgh for June 1554, for example, contain the following:

The prouest baillies and counsale ordanis the thesauror Robert Grahame to pay the werkmen, merchandis, carteris, paynteris, and vtheris that furneist the grayth to the convoy of the moris to the Abbay and of the play maid that samyn day the tent day of Junii instant the sowm of xxxvij li xvj s ij d as the compt producit be Sir William Makdougall maister of werk thairupoun proportit, prouiding alwayis that the said Sir Williame deliuer to the dene of gyld the handscenye and canves specifit in the said tikkit to be kepit to the behuif of the town. Item, the day of the playing of the play at the trone, with the convoy of the moris: payit for graithing of the Quenes luging foiranent the samyn, for flours, beirks, and rocheis, and beiring of furmes and trestis thairto, xvj s.   (Cited in Mill 1927, 180)

Likewise, the town accounts from Wells include the general order of companies and their pageantry for a public show in August 1613. Three of the companies include morris dancers:

The ffirst companie.
The Hammermen which were the Carpenters Ioyners Cowpers Mazons Tylers & Blackesmethes. And they presented. A Streamer with their armes and Noath buildinge the arke. Vulcan Worckinge at the fforge. Venus carried in a Charriott & [Cui] Cupid sitting in her lapp with his bowe bent. A morrice daunce. The dragon which devoured the virgins...
The ffowerth companie.
The Cordyners who presented St Crispian & *(blank)* both of them sonnes to a kinge and the youngest a shoemaker who married his Masters daughter they allsoe presented a morrice daunce and a Streamer with their armes...
The sixth companie.
The Mercers who presented a Streamer. A Morrice daunce of Younge children The Giant and the Giantesse. Kinge Ptolomeus with his Queene & daughter which was to bee devoured of the dragon. St George with his knightes who slew the dragon and rescued the virgin. Diana & her nymphes carried in a Charriott who turned Acteon to a Harte.
               (Wells Corporation Act Book 3, 1553–1623, f.376 in Stokes 1996, 1:372)

Finally, the Staffordshire Quarter Session rolls for 1652 include the following indictment:

The names of the morris dancers that danced in Wolverhampton on the 1st day of July 1652 in contempt of several ministers that were arbitrating a difference between two gentlemen in the house of Mr. Richard Francis.

Dancers
1. William Taylor the Tailor
2. Edward Meakin the Tailor
3. William Bill the Tailor
4. Walter Ensworth the Tailor
5. John Brailes the Tailor
6. Mark Brailes the Tailor
7. Richard Southwicke the Tailor
8. Richard Ingram the Tailor
9. Nicholas Creswell the Tailor
10. Edward Wilkes the Tailor
11. Samuel Wikes Tabbrer.

Two of the said William Taylor's journeymen, the one sword-bearer (12) the other the fool (13). Thomas Westley (14), Thomas Burne (15) and William Campbell (16) did accommodate the sword-bearer being all tailors and Herculus Hoult (17) carried the flag. I took Nicholas Creswell lying drunk in the minister's porch that he could not stand nor go and the rest were but little better

(Staffs Quarter Sessions Rolls, 1652, Transl.6, ch.2, cited in Marriott 1957, 106–7)

This source is noteworthy because it demonstrates that in some towns guildsmen themselves were the performers, as is only hinted at by the London records. There is also an indication here of a much bigger retinue of dancers and other characters than in the records of other cities. Besides ten dancers and a musician (the only person not in the Tailors' guild) there are a sword-bearer plus attendants, a flag-bearer, and a fool (a character absent in all other urban processional morrises). The whole affair seems to be a self-contained procession rather than an element in a larger parade, and may suggest a kinship with the Tailors' processions in Salisbury where the processional was a public component of a private feast or celebration.

These are all isolated records, however, and merely provide a suspicion that the guild processional morris, originating in London, diffused out to the provinces in the later sixteenth and early seventeenth centuries, having died out or been transformed at its source. We are probably not looking at a common urban provincial tradition, however, but rather a practice that took hold in certain cities (for reasons that are unclear), and not in others. REED editors in their search for evidence of dramatic activities have combed the records of cities like Newcastle, Norwich, Coventry, and York (as well as smaller towns such as Shrewsbury), where there are abundant documents, and have found no trace of civic morris. The pattern and mode of diffusion is, thus, enigmatic and perhaps now impossible to reconstruct.

Furthermore, by the time urban morris traditions had begun to take hold in specific provincial cities, puritanical attitudes leading to prosecutions made it difficult for the customs to maintain a permanent hold. Thus, by the mid-seventeenth century the guild-sponsored processional morris was, for all intents and purposes, a thing of the past.[11]

MAY GAMES

Midsummer and midwinter are critical annual festivals because they mark turning points in the year. The year has other turning points, however; or one might say that the year can be measured in different ways, each of which will produce different axial times. Midsummer and midwinter are junctures in the year when it is measured as an *astronomical* phenomenon: they are determined by the passage of the sun between the tropics. There is a strict, mathematically precise orderliness to the recurrence of the solstices. They fall on or near the same day every year, and their timing can be predicted accurately, and infinitely into the future, with relatively elementary knowledge – even false theories – of the motion of the sun. Hence their celebration concerns order (and disorder).

The year may also be seen as an *organic* phenomenon, marked by biological events such as the appearance of buds and new shoots, the flowering of plants, the ripening of fruits, the fall of leaves. These markers proceed in predictable cycles also and are tied to the passage of the solar year, but they are not rigidly determined by it. Flowers may blossom earlier or later depending on whether the spring has been wet or dry, hot or cold, and generally they will appear sooner in more southerly latitudes, at lower altitudes, or where local effects, such as ocean currents, warm the land. The markers in the organic year are sequential (crocuses bloom before daffodils) but not calendrically predictable (we cannot predict with any accuracy what day the first violets will bloom in Chester in the year 2020, but we can calculate exactly when the winter solstice will fall).

The agricultural year follows the markers of the organic year rather more than those of the astronomical year, because the farmer must be sensitive to the vagaries of the growing season to maximize effort and yields. You make hay when the sun shines (and when the grasses are tall enough to mow), not when haymaking day arrives on the calendar; you turn the cows out to pasture when the pasture is ready for them. True, there are some calendar days that once marked the beginning of certain agricultural activities – Plough Monday, for example, which is the first Monday after Epiphany, and traditionally marked the beginning of the ploughing season. But you cannot plough sodden or frozen fields, Plough Monday or no.

The organic year can be said to have multiple turning points, but there are two that have held critical importance throughout Europe: the celebration of the first fruits of spring (around late April/early May) and of the last fruits of autumn (around late October/early November). There are specific calendric holidays associated with these times – May Eve/May Day and Halloween/All Saints – but historically the celebrations of the seasons could easily be moved to coincide with developments in the organic world. A late spring meant holding off May revels until there were some first fruits to celebrate.

'Bringing in' May and autumn are certainly old customs in England. Robert Grosseteste, bishop of Lincoln, writing to his archdeacons in 1244, ordered them to suppress games that included 'Inductio Maii sive Autumni' (see Chambers 1903, 1:91n). In the sixteenth century there are several full accounts of the order of these games. Phillip Stubbes's account of bringing home the maypole is well known, and despite its adversarial and polemical tone is rich in detail (Stubbes 1583, M3v–4r; see also Stone 1912, 183).

The main elements of the urban May game from these accounts are a procession from town to the woods, the gathering of greenery, a procession back to the town, decorating of the town with the greenery, and dancing in the streets. It is possible that the preponderance of descriptions of urban May games in this period reflects nothing more than the literacy and interest of city dwellers in what was a universal celebration. It is also possible that the specifically urban May game had a special enduring significance.

The astronomical year is as much in evidence to the urbanite as the rustic: days are the same length for both, and both can experience directly the passage between the solstices in terms of changing amounts of light and darkness. This is not true for the organic year. Those who live in the bricked, gravelled, and carpentered world of the city cannot appreciate the first buds of spring, or the turning of the leaves in autumn without leaving their artefactual environment and venturing into the countryside. In Tudor England such an enterprise did not involve travelling any great distance – fields and woods began right beyond the city walls, usually an easy walk from any quarter – but you had to make the effort. Bringing in May was an acknowledgment of the ecological opposition of town and country. Going out into the countryside allowed townspeople to encounter the organic world firsthand. Stow notes:

In the month of May, namely, on May-day in the morning, every man, except impediment, would walk into the sweet meadows and green woods, there to rejoice their spirits with the beauty and savour of sweet flowers, and with the harmony of birds, praising God in their kind ...

(Stow 1908, 90)

Townspeople brought back from the countryside ephemeral tokens of the turning of the organic year to adorn the fronts of houses, briefly mixing up the two worlds of town and country. Such tokens symbolized the growth and fruitfulness of the organic world, and in general the axial moments of the organic year were marked by the celebration of natural fecundity in material form – green boughs, flowers, fresh fruit.

Other aspects of May revelling apparently complemented the spirit of fertility prevalent in the festivals. Stubbes notes as part of his tirade against May games:

I haue heard it credibly reported (and that, *viua voce*) by men of great grauitie and reputa- tion, that of fortie, threescore, or a hundred maides going to the wood ouer night, there haue scaresly the third part of them returned home againe undefiled   (Stubbes 1583, M4r)

This does not imply, as ritual theorists of old would have it, that May games are the descendants of pagan fertility rites, but only that the season has a natural connection with bud, blossom, and birth.

The association of morris dancing with specifically urban May games does not begin in primary sources until the middle of the sixteenth century.[12] The first refer- ence comes from Machyn's diary for 1552:

The xxvj day of May came in to Fa[nchurch] parryche a goodly May-polle as youe h[ave seen. It was] pentyd whyt and gren, and ther the men and [women did] wher a-bowt ther neke baldrykes [of white and] gren, the gyant, the mores-danse, and the [...] had a castylle in the myd with pensels, and [...] plasys of sylke and gylded; and the sam [day the] lord mayre by conselle causyd yt to be [taken] done and broken, for I have not sene [...]
                                                         (Machyn 1848, 20)

The reference is, unfortunately, corrupt but the general outline is reasonably clear, and reinforced by later entries. In 1557, for example, he reports another May game in Fenchurch street:

The xxx day of May was a goly May-gam in Fanch-chyrche-strett with drumes and gunes and pykes, and ix wordes dyd ryd; and thay had speches evere man, and the morris dansse and the sauden, and a elevant with the castyll, and the sauden and yonge morens with tar- gattes and darttes, and the lord and the lade of the Maye.   (Machyn 1848, 137)

This description seems more reminiscent of the Midsummer Watches than of the May games described in other parts of the country: drums, guns, pikemen, the nine wor- thies, pageants, armed Moors are all elements that appear regularly in the guild ac- counts for Midsummer. Stow's general account of May games appears to support this view:

I find also that in the moneth of May, the Citizens of London of all estates, lightly in euery

Parish, or sometimes two or three parishes ioyning togither, had their seuerall mayings, and did fetch in Maypoles, with diuerse warlike shewes, with good Archers, Morice dauncers, and other deuices for pastime all the day long, and towards the Euening they had stage playes, and Bonefiers in the streetes ...   (Stow 1908, 90)

Apart from the maypole the main elements mentioned are 'warlike shewes' and 'good Archers' (as well as the morris dance). Only Machyn's account of a May game in the parish of St John Zachary in 1559 contains any of the characters conventionally associated with May revels, that is, Robin Hood and his men (Machyn 1848, 201). But even here these characters are only a part of a procession that includes a number of watchlike martial elements.

May games with morris dancing appear in references from other cities (Gloucester and Plymouth primarily) around the same time, but they are mostly fragments from account books, and therefore do not contain enough details to determine whether the London events were idiosyncratic for that period. By the end of the century, however, the May procession with guns, drums, and other military paraphernalia, along with the morris dance appears to be common in provincial cities, combined sometimes with characters more typically associated with the May games described at the outset of this section. For example in Oxford in 1599:

The inhabitants assembled on the two Sundays before Ascension Day, and on that day, with drum and shot and other weapons, and men attired in women's apparel, brought into the town a woman bedecked with garlands and flowers named by them the Queen of the May. They also had Morrishe dancers and other disordered and unseemly sports, and intended the next Sunday to continue the same abuses.   (Salisbury 1899, 201)

Similar processions are reported in Leicester in 1599 and 1603 (Kelly 1865, 100–1, 230–2, 237–43) and Wells in 1607 (PRO STAC 8/161/1 John Hole vs Edmund White et al. in Stokes 1996, 1:261–357).

I speculate, based on the chronology of events, that the martial (and pageant) elements were once part of the Midsummer Watches only, but in those cities, such as London, where the watches were abandoned mid-century, popular components survived by being reattached to the nearest convenient processional celebration, even though the association was not wholly appropriate (nor utterly inappropriate). Both May games and Midsummer Watches mark the advent of the summer season, the one as represented by the organic cycle, the other, the astronomical. So, at a very general level they are similar festivals, even though their specific meanings are in many ways distinct. Furthermore, there was a rough temporal coincidence of the two. Despite the name, May games were not exclusively associated with any particular date (such as May Day), nor even with the month of May. They were often celebrated around Whitsuntide, which frequently falls in June. Machyn saw a May game in Westminster on Whit Monday 1555, which was in June (Machyn 1848, 162), and the one he saw at St John Zachary was actually on Midsummer's Day itself.

The martial elements from the watches could not have attached themselves to May processions, however, unless there was a component of the latter that gave some relevance to them, that provided a linkage point. That nexus may well have been Robin Hood and associated characters who were renowned as archers, and who had been represented at May games since at least the beginning of the sixteenth century. (Robin Hood, as will be explored more fully in the next chapter, is a natural character to be bound up with May celebrations because of his greenwood habitation.) Hall's *Chronicle* tells of a famous May game in 1515:

The king [Henry VIII] & the quene accompanyed with many lordes and ladies roade to the high ground of shoters hil to take the open ayre, and as they passed by the way, they espied a company of tall yeomen, clothed all in grene with grene whodes & bowes & arrowes, to the number of iiC. Then one of them, which called him selfe Robyn hood, came to the kyng, desyring him to se his men shoote, & the kyng was content. Then he whisteled, & all the. iiC. archers shot & losed at once, & then he whisteled agayne, and they likewyse shot agayne, their arrowes whisteled by crafte of the head, so that the noyes was straunge and great, & muche pleased the kynge the quene and all the company.   (Hall 1809, 582)

It is possible, therefore, that the archers and display of archery connected with Robin Hood (and also other feats of arms commonly associated with the tales of Robin Hood), provided the 'warlike' element to which the martial units from the watches could attach.

Thus, at one point the symbolic and affective meanings of watches and May celebrations were distinct – with some points of contact – but as the practice of the former declined, the two sets of values became merged in the latter, which survived for a while longer. If this speculation concerning the history of urban May games is correct, it has implications for the evolutionary history of morris because it suggests that the association of morris dancing with urban May games was originally partially happenstance, and that when it first attached to that festival it had no particular relevance for it (any more than the pikemen and musketeers did), although it may have, over time, developed bonds.

I should make it clear that this argument applies primarily to London (and a few provincial cities, such as Wells) and solely concerns *urban* morris and *urban* May games. There were May games and morrises together in more rural areas as early as the beginning of the sixteenth century (in Kingston on Thames principally), and, no doubt, the rural connection of the two helped in their urban marriage. But in line with the basic methodology of this whole work, I am not assuming that the morris associated with one kind of venue and geographic location was *at the outset* at all like that associated with another (in this case an urban street secular event versus a village churchyard ale): just the opposite, I am predisposed to think of them as unlike. I am taking it as more logical to imagine that the London May games of the later sixteenth century adopted London street morris dances, rather than that they somehow coopted a style of dancing from Kingston (or some other more rural location) because it suited May games better than the local version. I am asserting a degree of local continuity of dance style even in the face of changing contexts – although over time the contexts had their effects on performance.

The most significant, and most basic, contextual change that occurred in the transition from watch to May games concerns the nature of the venue itself. The watch was a procession and nothing else, so the dances that were part of it had to be purely processional. The May games, on the other hand, while they had a significant processional element, also involved stationary events. When the procession arrived in the city it might stop at key locations – conduits, market crosses – for the delivery of comic speeches (as Machyn notes several times in the characteristic phrase 'thay had spechys rond a-bowt London'), and it had an ultimate destination and purpose: to set up a maypole (or bower or other decorated area) to be the scene of feasting and dancing. The morris dance must have, therefore, either limited itself to the procession (which may have happened at first), or evolved to be performable as a nonprocessional dance.

There is some ambiguous evidence that the morris associated with urban May games in the late sixteenth and early seventeenth centuries used the maypole as a focus for the dance, which would indicate a major change in the dance from a processional form (perhaps through slow infusion of ideas from rural contexts, where static events were the mainstay of May games and church ales). But none of the evidence is direct, and may not refer to urban morris at all. One of the tracts issued during the Marprelate controversy contains the following:

If Menippus, or the Man in the Moone, be so quick-sighted, that he beholds, these bitter sweet Jests, these railing outcries: this shouing at Prelats, to cast them downe, and heauing at Martin to hang him vp for Martilmas biefe: what would he imagine otherwise, then as that stranger, which seeing a Quintessence (beside the foole & the Maid Marian) of all the picked youth, straind out of an whole Endship, footing the Morris about a May pole.

(Harvey 1590, 8)

For this comic allusion to make sense to an urban audience one might presuppose that the author expected them to know that morris dancers danced around maypoles; but this is supposition only, and could well apply to rural sports with which they were familiar. Other contemporary texts, such as this excerpt from a London play of 1607, exhibit similar difficulties:

Mendatio: ... How now Hunger? How do'st thou my fine may-pole, ha?
Appetitus: I may well be calld a may-pole, for the senses do nothing but dance a morrice
about mee.   (Anon 1607, sig.K3r)

By the Restoration, however, it is well documented that the maypole was the focus
for urban morris dance. Two separate eyewitnesses to the raising of a maypole in the
Strand by sailors in April 1661 attest that the morris dancers danced round the pole:

Ap[ril]. 1661. A May pole in the Strond set up ... Under the new May pole in the Strand,
41 yards high, in the balconie that was made about on storie high, were wine, musick, and
under it a knot of morris dancers, the worst that ever were.   (Rugg 1961, 175)

... after that came a Morice Dance finely deckt, with purple Scarfs, in their half-shirts, with
a Taber and Pipe the antient Musick, and Danced round about the Maypole, after that
Danced the rounds of their Liberty.   (Anon 1661, 4)

It is difficult to assess how, if at all, these dances are related to the morrises associated
with London May games from earlier in the century. There is a considerable hiatus
to account for – no street morris is recorded in London between 1606 and 1661 –
so that it would be overpresumptuous to suggest a direct evolutionary line from sixteenth-century May morrises to those of the Restoration. It is quite plausible, for
example, that types of dancing from other locations influenced the revived London
dances. Although there is no documented street tradition in London through most
of the first half of the seventeenth century, there were stage plays performed in the
city that included morris dances. As is discussed in chapter 6, these dances synthesized elements from a number of disparate sources and may, in turn, have fed back
into the street tradition. In addition there are a few records starting as early as 1589
of country dancers travelling to cities to perform as part of general May festivities.
In that year, for example, dancers from the village of Herne toured the environs of
Canterbury, finishing up in the city, where they were prosecuted for disturbing the
peace (Canterbury Cathedral Lib. JQ 1589, cited in part in Clark 1983, 129–30).

   Thus the urban dance of the mid-seventeenth century could have developed under
the influence of multiple traditions, and the revival might well have owed as much
to outside sources as to a continuation of a single urban style. What this (as well as the
venue seriations) hints at is the possibility of shifting centres of gravity for creative
development of the dances. By 1660, because of a variety of factors (legal, economic,
social, religious), the centre had moved from cities to the countryside and, within
cities, from the streets to indoor locations.

   It is also significant that there is no direct evidence of morris dances performed
around maypoles in other urban centres in the sixteenth and seventeenth centuries
(and little from rural locations). The use of the maypole as the focus of the dance ap-

pears to have been a quite limited phenomenon: an evolutionary dead end for urban morris. After the joyous revivals of the Restoration the London morris disappeared, and apart from the tenacious, irregular survivors mentioned earlier, the urban morris ceased to exist after the mid-seventeenth century.

The demise of the urban morris might be attributed to several factors. The half-century gap in performances in London (if absence of records is a genuine index of absence of performances) is a quite sufficient time span for knowledge of the choreography of the dances to pass from living memory. Thomas Rugg's comment that the 1661 dancers were 'the worst that ever were' is suggestive in this regard (although he may have had an axe to grind). It is also possible that the old urban processional dances from the watches were not able to adapt sufficiently, in the long run, to the new context of the May games; in particular maybe they were not able to convert to a static form. Again it should be noted in this regard that the morris of 1661 'Danced round about the Maypole, after that Danced the rounds of their Liberty,' indicating either a continued strong processional element that prevented the dance from being fully assimilated into the static parts of the May games, or else that the dance simply could not assimilate.

Perhaps the maypole morris was little more than the processional (martial) dance converted from a linear to a circular track. If so there would not be much in the way of choreographic interest to sustain it. The whole point of a processional dance form is that it is simple, and is one component in a much larger whole; it is there one minute and gone the next, replaced by another spectacle. To convert to a static dance it would have had to have become more complex. But what little evidence there is points to its continuance as a processional form, which ultimately paid the price of inflexibility.

Clearly the May games of the sixteenth century had a major processional component and are reminiscent in some respects of the Lord of Misrule events. The people paraded out into the country and back (another possible nexus for the introduction of country dance styles), and then toured around the city delivering set speeches at major gathering places. For this type of revel the processional morris would be appropriate, it being a way of linking the various sites of speech-making with a continuous performance.

An example of the kind of speech delivered is provided for us in Beaumont and Fletcher's *Knight of the Burning Pestle*, and also gives an account of some of the substance of the early-seventeenth century London May game and attendant morris:

Enter Raph.
RAFE. London, to thee I do present the merry Month o May,
Let each true Subject be content to heare me what I say:

For from the top of Conduit head, as plainely may appeare,
I will both tell my name to you and wherefore I came heere.
My name is Raph, by due discent, though not ignoble I,
Yet far inferior to the Flocke of gratious Grocery.
And by the Common-councell, of my fellowes in the Strand,
With guilded Staffe, and crossed Skarfe, the May-lord here I stand.
Rejoyce, o English hearts, rejoyce, rejoyce o Lovers deere,
Rejoyce o citty, towne, and Country, rejoyce eke every Shire;
For now the fragrant Flowers do spring and sprout in seemely sort,
The little Birds do sit and sing, the Lambes do make fine sport.
And now the Burchin Tree doth bud that maks the Schoole boy cry,
The morrice rings while Hobby-horse doth foote it feateously:
The Lords and Ladies now abroad for their disport and play,
Do kisse sometimes upon the Grasse, and sometimes in the Hey …
With bels on legs, and napkins cleane unto your shoulders tide,
With Scarfes and Garters as you please, and Hey for our Town cri'd …

(Beaumont and Fletcher 1613, 76–7)

This account is not entirely reliable for several reasons. Most important, it is an artefact from a play, not a report of an actual speech. This objection does not entirely rule it out of court, however. Poets and playwrights were routinely hired in this era to write festival speeches of this sort. Furthermore, the speech would have to pass muster with a London audience – the same people who were audience and participants in May games. So even if the speech parodied such events (and it does not seem to), it would have to do so in a way that did not strike a false note with the original.

The speech reaffirms the primacy of the natural world in the celebration of May games; the great bulk of the speech is devoted to the natural events of spring and early summer and their effects on townspeople. It also gives us the only indication we have, outside of account books, of urban morris costume – 'With bels on legs, and napkins cleane unto your shoulders tide,/ With Scarfes and Garters as you please.' This is still not a lot to go on, but it can help to flesh things out. Generally the accounts of the guilds mention special coats and bells as their inventory of morris goods, which implies that the dancers supplied the rest; these were the unique (that is, definitive) and expensive components of their costumes.

The fact that the coats are identified in many sources by the special combination 'morris coats,' that they were specially made, and that they were kept by guilds and hired out all points to them having attributes that mark them apart from everyday clothes. Rafe's speech provides an indication as to the nature of the coats, as does the famous woodcut of Will Kemp and Tom Slye of 1600 (figure 19), and the following quotation from Samuel Rowlands:

Figure 19: Etching from the title page of *Kemps Nine Daies Wonder* (Kemp 1840)

How bad I and my fellow Dimond goes,
We never yet had Garter to our Hose,
Nor any shooe to put upon our feete,
With such base cloaths, tis e'en a shame to see't:
My Sleeves are like some Morris-dancing fellow,
My stockings Ideot-like, red, greene and yealow.   (Rowlands 1880, B1b)

It is the sleeves that are special. On Kemp's outfit they appear to be made in two parts: there is a normal jacket sleeve covering his arms down to the wrists, and then there is a separate length of material that flows down from the shoulders (possibly loosely attached to the elbows). This material is long enough to reach near the ground when the dancer is standing still with arms to his sides – otherwise it floats about his arms as he gestures – and is jagged at the ends. This is commonly called a 'dagged' sleeve and was, in the sixteenth century, a morisco fashion used in masquerades and processions throughout Europe. Usually the sleeve in the sixteenth century was heavily slashed, and this would explain the Rowlands quotation: the narrator is saying, in despair, that his coat is so ragged that the sleeves remind him of a morris dagged sleeve.

Thus the coat style would visually and explicitly (in the eyes of a contemporary audience) identify the dancers with moriscos.

Such coats would have to be specially made, but one might also create a close substitute by pinning material to the sleeves or shoulders – hence Rafe's description of the dancer with 'napkins cleane unto your shoulders tide.' I am also given to speculate whether this is not the origin of the later practice of carrying handkerchiefs found in certain regions. That is, coats with dagged sleeves were expensive to make and could not be used for everyday wear, but they were important for emphasizing arm motions. As an economy, dancers (perhaps poorer rural dancers) first substituted pinned material on their ordinary coats, then they held the material in their hands. The transition time, if this surmise is correct, would be around the end of the sixteenth century, when the morisco fashion had fallen from favour (and when inflation was creating serious problems). By this time too the connection of the urban processional morris with European morescas might well be forgotten or unimportant, the dance having been an active part of street tradition for well over a century. Rafe also suggests that scarves and garters are additional decorative elements for the dancers. He himself wears 'crossed Skarfe,' meaning one over each shoulder, tied at the waist, and crossed over his breast.

It is not at all clear who were the sponsors of urban May games, but the guilds were certainly involved at one level or another. For example, in 1562 Machyn notes:

The sam day [25–05–1562] was sett up at the cuckold haven a grett May-polle by bochers and fysher-men, fulle of hornes ...   (Machyn 1848, 283)

In Leicester in 1603 the dancers included a tailor, a baker, a whittawer (saddler), a shoemaker, a smith, and a glover, and in several plays the May games are presented as under the aegis of certain guilds, notably grocers and shoemakers. But the picture is murky. In the Wells May game of 1607 (PRO STAC 8/161/1 in Stokes 1996, 261–74) the participants are from a variety of occupations – some guild trades, some not (and include a number of gentry) – but the plaintiffs (that is, its opponents) are primarily guildsmen. Furthermore, the defendants (that is, the people who supported the games) are specifically charged with mocking a variety of guild trades. Yet for the summer pageant in Wells in 1613 it was the guilds that hired morris companies (Stokes 1986, 342–3). This ambiguity is reminiscent of the prosecution of the Salisbury tailors where guildsmen stood on both sides of the fence, some stoutly upholding tradition, others going along with the rising tide of puritanism.

It is conceivable that the union of urban morris and May games created this ambiguous situation and eventually sealed the fate of both from a legal standpoint. As is discussed in greater depth in the next and later chapters, the Puritan voices against May games and morris dancing were strong by the 1590s, but according to

my seriation of sources (see p.34) the first spate of lawsuits was not in the ecclesiastical but civil courts, and it may have been the addition of martial elements – guns,
drums, and morris – to the May games that first made civil authorities sympathetic
with the Puritan cause.

The Puritans attacked May games primarily on ideological grounds. They objected, for example, to their 'heathen' content, Stubbes's comments about the maypole
being typical:[13]

And then fall they to daunce about it like as the heathen people did at the dedication of the
Idols, whereof this is a perfect pattern, or rather the thing it self   (Stubbes 1583, M3v–4r)

Although the civil authorities in prosecuting May games use some of this kind of
puritanical language, their primary concern appears to be the potential danger to
civil order created by hordes of (drunken) men parading the town with guns, swords,
and other weapons, as the bill of complaint from Wells in 1607 makes clear:

In all humblenes complayninge sheweth & informeth your most excellent *Maiestie your*
highnes dutifull & loyall subiect Iohn Hole of the Citty of Welles in *your* highnes County
of So*m*ersett, Clothier, … that one Edmond White [and others] … did in the Moneths of Maye
and Iune last … riotouslie & vnlawfully assemble themselues togeather in the Citty of Welles
then armed with vnlawfull weapons and drumes & then & there acted not only many disordered Maygames Morice Daunces longe Daunces men in weamens apparall, new deuised
lordes and ladyes, and Churchales, but further acted very p*ro*phane & vnseemely showes &
pastymes whereby many vnruly & dangerous assemblyes were then & there gathered
togeather …   (PRO STAC 8/161/1 f.219, in Stokes 1996, 261–2)

Although the civil authorities got the ball rolling it was the ecclesiastical courts that
launched the most significant campaign against May games and morris dancing
throughout the country. For complex reasons, explored in later chapters, morris dancing became symbolic of many things to many people and took centre stage in the
ideological struggles between Puritans and loyalists that led to the Civil War. For
both sides it became a symbol of rebellion, and gained power for its oppositional
role. It also became a rallying point for royalist sympathizers, hence its enormous
popularity immediately upon the restoration of Charles II. It also seems that once
robbed of this symbolic and oppositional position its power and popularity declined.
Anthony Wood notes in 1660:

This Holy Thursday [31–05–1660] the people of Oxon were soe violent for Maypoles in
opposition to the Puritans that there was numbred 12 Maypoles besides 3 or 4 morrises, etc.
But no opposition appearing afterwards, the rabble flaged in their zeal; and seldom after above
1 or 2 in a year.   (Wood 1891, 1:317)

Understanding the Puritans' outlook and the general opposition of the official church to morris requires a detailed exploration of the place of morris dancing in the ecclesiastical realm. The seeming paradox that must be interpreted is that at one time, before the rise of Puritanism, the church was one of the most significant *sponsors* of morris dancing, and a prime mover in the rapid diffusion of the dance through England. This investigation takes us back to the beginning of the sixteenth century when church sponsorship of morris dancing began.

6

Church Property

Church sponsorship of morris dancing is unique in that it has a clear terminus in the 1630s following its heyday around 1540 to 1570 (whereas dance events at all other venues continue, sometimes sporadically, sometimes regularly, to the end of our period once they have appeared). This state of affairs is due to a complete reversal of church policy towards morris dancing from active encouragement to vigorous prosecution of both the dance and of the events of which it formed a part. Paradoxically, therefore, the church was largely responsible both for the great diffusion of morris dancing into the countryside, and for its precipitous decline in the same areas. A glance back at the distribution maps makes the point graphically evident. Figure 7 (p 39) shows the explosive diffusion of church-sponsored morris events out into the countryside in southern England in the mid-sixteenth century, and figure 9 (p 41) indicates the sudden burst of church actions against dancing at the beginning of the seventeenth century, leaving a sparse representation of events in later periods. A careful study of the church's changing relationship to morris dancing reveals the intimate connection between the dance and a broad range of economic, social, political, and theological values in Tudor and Stuart England.

Church sponsorship of the morris is closely tied to the economics of rural parishes in the late fifteenth and early sixteenth centuries because the dance was used, starting in that period, as a special attraction at church ales, that is, revels whose primary economic purpose was to provide the parish with a cash surplus. There are different kinds of church ales recorded in primary sources (see Blair 1940) – May ales, king ales, bid ales etcetera – but the bewildering array of rubrics should not distract us from the underlying similarity of structure of all types. All ales had three basic components: entertainment, food, and ale (or beer).[1] Differences in the form of these components, notably the entertainment, account for most of the differences in the types of ale.

Stubbes can, as usual, be relied on to provide a rudimentary outline of the kernel of church ales, the production of the eponymous liquor:

The manner of them is thus. In certain Townes where drunken *Bachus* beares all the sway, against a Christmas, an Easter, Whitsonday, or some other time, the Church-wardens (for so they call them) of euery parish, with the consent of the whole Parish, prouide half a score or twenty quarters of mault, whereof some they buy of the Church-stock, and some is giuen them of the Parishioners them selues, euery one conferring somewhat, according to his abilitie, which mault being made into very strongale or beere, it is set to sale, either in the Church or some other place assigned to that purpose.   (Stubbes 1583, sig. M4 verso)

His description is confirmed in a general way by churchwardens' accounts, although his estimate of the amount of malt made into ale and beer at one event seems characteristically exaggerated. It is much commoner to find entries for purchases or gifts of a half a quarter or a quarter of malt, but there is a considerable range.[2]

It is impossible to know with any accuracy how much beer or ale a quarter of malt produced at that time because the amount would have altered significantly according to the strength of the brew desired, method of malting, length of fermentation, and so forth. However, some general parameters may be specified based on old recipes and statutes. Gervase Markham in the section of *The English Housewife* on brewing states:

Touching ordinary beer, which is that wherewith either nobleman, gentleman, yeoman, or husbandman shall maintain his family the whole year; it is meet first that our English housewife respect the proportion or allowance of malt due to the same, which amongst the best husbands is thought most convenient, and it is held that to draw from one quarter of good malt three hogsheads of beer is the best ordinary proportion that can be allowed ...

Now for the brewing of the best March beer you shall allow to a hogshead thereof a quarter of the best malt well ground ...   (Markham 1986, 204–7)

The hogshead was not a uniform liquid measure at that time, but assuming it was sixty gallons (which was a reasonably widespread standard), then a quarter of malt could produce anywhere from sixty gallons of a beer with an alcohol content by volume of perhaps 9 per cent or better, to 180 gallons of beer of roughly 3.5 per cent alcohol. This is but a rough guess, but it is possible to get some kind of comparative perspective on the volume of beer produced for ales, and perhaps, thereby, the relative size of the events.

What appears immediately obvious is the mighty compass from the spare to the prodigal. At the upper end of the scale there are towns such as Yatton in Somerset whose brewing equipment inventoried by the wardens in 1492 included five fermentation vats of a tun capacity apiece, or enough to brew 1200 gallons at a time (Blair

1940, 44), and for a play ale in 1511, Bassingbourn parish in Cambridgeshire received gifts of malt for brewing totalling over eleven quarters, or enough to make around 1980 gallons of beer (Cox 1913, 270–1).[3] Much commoner, though, are accounts of the brewing of between one and two quarters, as for example, at the parish of St Laurence, Reading, in 1503 where they brewed ten bushels, or at St Michael's Bishop's Stortford, Hertfordshire, when a brewer was paid 16d in the account year 1485–6 to brew sixteen bushels for the Hock ale (Blair 1940, 38).

There is some indication that the scale of the brewings diminished as the sixteenth century progressed (and as the effects of Puritan attacks were felt) but, even so, the general average for this period is on the order of 200–300 gallons of beer for a day's event.

The churchwardens accounts of the play ale held in Bassingbourn in 1511 are particularly detailed and reveal that the large amount of malt contributed was intended to serve visitors from a wide area attending the performance of a special St George play:

Memorandum Receyved atte the playe had on seynte margarye daye anno domini. M^l. v^C. & xj^{mo}. and the iij ^{de} yereoff the Reign off kyng harrye the viijth. had in bassingburne off the holy martire seynt george. att that tyme Chirchewardeyns Iohn ayworthe & Iohn good than the elder in bassingbourne in the westend. by theym receyved than as affter folowith –

ffirst receyved off the Townshyppe off Royston summa –	xij s.
Item receyved off the townshyppe off Tharffeld summa –	vj s. viij d.
Item receyved off Melbourne. v s. iiij d. off Lyttyllyngton	
v s. ij d. ob summa –	x s. vj d. ob.
Item receyved off whaddon iiij s. iiij d. ob. off Stepulmordon.	
iiij s. j d. summa –	viij s. v d. ob.
Item receyved off Berly. iiij s. j d. off asshewell. iiij s. summa –	viij s. j d.
Item receyved off abyngton iij s. iiij d. off Orwell iij s. summa –	vj s. iiij d.
Item receyved off wendey. ij s. ix d. Off wyndpole. ij s. vij d summa –	v s. iiij d.
Item receyved off meldreth. ij s. iiij d. off arryngton. ij s. iiij d summa –	iiij s. viij d.
Item receyved off shepreth. ij s. iiij d. off kelsey. ij s. v d. summa –	iiij s. ix d.
Item receyved off wyllyngham. xxij d. off ffulmar. xx d. summa –	iij s. vj d.
Item receyved off gyldynmordon. xvj d. off Taddelowe. xij d. summa –	ij s. iiij d.
Item receyved off Crawdeyn. xvj d. off hattely. x d. summa –	ij s. ij d.
Item receyved off wrastlyngworthe. ix d. off hasselyngffeld ix d. summa –	xviij d.
Item receyved off Barkwey. viij d. off ffoxtun iiij d. summa –	xij d.
Item receyved off kneseworthe with vj d. of hekys gefft ther summa –	ij s. vj d.

(Brannen 1992, 197–8; see also Cox 1913, 270)

This portion of the accounts bears further scrutiny because of the light it sheds on the general organization of church ales. The long list of contributing towns indicates that representatives from Bassingbourn visited every settlement, no matter how small, within a radius of about 4.5 miles of their home, soliciting contributions towards the costs of the ale. The line items, which are generally arranged in descending order of amount collected per village, show that even though none of these villages is of any great size, many produced relatively large sums. The size of the collection does not appear to correlate with the size of the village (although as to be expected the ancient market town of Royston heads the list), but rather with distance from Bassingbourn. Foxton, for example, is nearly six miles away and contributed a mere 4d, whereas Whaddon, although smaller, is barely two miles away (by footpath) and contributed 4s 4d, thirteen times as much.

The major effort put in here to cover a wide area and the relative size of the contributions suggests that this ale was extraordinary in its proportions, and aimed at major capital improvement (part of the profits – 33s ½d – went to pay off a debt owing for the purchase of an image of St George). In the 1497–8 account year the parish held ten ales at regular intervals in order to buy and transport a new treble bell from London, and made free and clear *from all ten* £5 10s 5½d (Cox 1913, 290), whereas here the contributions from neighbouring villages prior to the event alone for a *single* ale (only thirteen years later, and before inflation showed much effect) amount to £3 19s 10d. So it remains to be considered why so much cash had to be collected before the event – rivalling the profits of a whole year's moneymaking – especially since the raw ingredients for the ale and other provender were contributed by the parishioners. To answer requires examining the different kinds of ales that were held in the period and their economic (and social) functions.[4]

The simplest ales were no more than communal suppers, as the following description from the Plymouth Corporation Book in Henry VIII's reign indicates:

For the honour of God and for thencreasing of the benefittes of the Chirche of seynt Androwe of plymouthe It is agreed … that in the ffeast of corporis *christi* eu*e*ry warde of the said Burghe shall fro hensforthe this x[th] day of Iune make an hale yn the *p*arisshe churche yarde of seynt Androwe aforesaid And eu*e*ry *p*erson of the said warde to bring with theym except Brede and drinke such vytayle as the like Best And haue there suche And asmany *p*ersons estraungers as they think Beste of theyr ffrendes And aquaynted men and Women for thencressing of the said Ile paing for brede And ale As it co*m*meth therto in rekening for their dyners And sopers the same day &c.   (Wasson 1986, 225–6)

The main features of these relatively plain ales are that the two men who are chosen as churchwardens for the year seek in kind contributions from the parishioners, primarily of malt and wheat to be turned into ale and bread, and which, in turn, the parishioners buy back at a communal supper, each family also contributing victuals to the general stock. There is, therefore, a guaranteed profit for the church, because the raw materials for the feast have been contributed by the very people who buy them back in their metamorphosed state. There is little or no capital outlay, except possibly for the services of a brewer, or for the hire of brewing and baking equipment if the church house does not possess them, or for other small incidental expenses not readily covered by in kind contributions.

The other point to notice is that these ales are a time for social visiting between parishes ('estraungers' [strangers] being the technical term for members of other parishes). Through much of the sixteenth century it was difficult for people to visit between parishes because they were required to attend services at their local churches on Sundays, with the threat of excommunication for recusancy. Thus an officially sanctioned opportunity for interparish visiting would attract a large number of people – the ulterior motive for this relaxation of regulations by the church being to swell the coffers with extra purchases of ale, partly through the increased numbers and partly on account of the sociability of the occasion.

Such an ale would be a relatively small financial burden on the parishioners because it entailed in kind contributions in proportion with one's holdings, and the voluntary purchase of normal adjuncts to dinner, bread and beer. But it must be realized that some burden was involved given that households normally did their own baking and brewing, and attendance at the ales was often mandatory for the locals. The alternative though, some form of taxation, would have been equally burdensome and by no means as socially engaging.

The Bassingbourn accounts of funds gathered from surrounding villages represent a considerable expansion of the form and function of the ale from this rather plain type. Clearly the underlying idea and justification are the same – the gathering of neighbouring people to feast together – but the need for cash in hand before the event from the strangers indicates a different sort of affair.

It might be supposed that the Bassingbourn ale was simply a much grander affair and, therefore, more initial outlay was needed. But no matter how large the feast planned, the raw materials could still have been acquired through in kind contribution. The point is that the staging of the play of St George itself required considerable materials and labour that could not be obtained except through cash purchase. Cash expenditures associated with the production of the play amount to well over two pounds (see Brannen 1992 and Cox 1913, 272), a sum equal to, or exceeding, the entire profit of many ales of the period. The wardens had to be sure before they committed themselves to extravagant expenditures that they would recoup enough in income to assure a profit. The most obvious way to do this was to sell admissions to the play before the day itself, which would provide an immediate injection of capital and also provide a good estimate of numbers for gauging amounts of food and drink to supply. Emissaries or the wardens themselves went to the neighbouring villages to solicit contributions, making a special effort in Royston. It appears from the accounts that some minstrels accompanied the delegation to Royston (presumably on market day), and perhaps to other villages, their duty being to tease the crowds into wanting more, and parting with their money in the expectation of a good entertainment.

A general survey of the profits of various types of ales indicates that those that laid out hard cash on professional sports and amusements reaped larger profits in the long run. The concomitant onus on the organizers was that they had to get out into the surrounding villages and sell the event vigorously. It was into this milieu at the beginning of the sixteenth century that the morris dance made its appearance, that is, as a paid adjunct to other professional diversions, with the express purpose of promoting the events of which they were part, and thereby attracting larger crowds.

Chief among the methods of selling entrances to ales was the election of mock officials, who, acting as delegates of the church and wardens, toured the neighbourhood with a band of deputies to wrest contributions from all and sundry through a mixture of cajolery, mockery, and tomfoolery. Stubbes in his classic description calls the leader the Lord of Misrule, but there were often two corulers – one male, one female – known variously as the Summer Lord and Lady, the May Lord and Lady, or King and Queen of the May:

First, all the wilde-heds of the Parish, conuenting together, chuse them a Graund-Captain (of all mischeefe) whome they innoble with the title of my Lord of Mis-rule, and him they crowne with great solemnitie, and adopt for their king. This king anointed, chuseth forth twentie, fortie, threescore or a hundred lustie Guttes like to him self to waighte vppon his lordly Maiestie, and to guarde his noble person. Then euerie one of these his men, he inuesteth with his liueries, of green, yellow or some other light wanton colour. (Stubbes 1583, sig. M2)

He makes the affair sound as if the election is itself a mockery but, though it may have been accompanied by some badinage, it was not usually a jest conducted solely by the parish hooligans, but more of an honour or a duty conferred by *all* the village, as can be seen from this memorandum from Wing in Buckinghamshire, 1565:

Memorandum that S. Wylliam Dormer knyght, ffrauncᵉ darrell and John a more gentlemen, with the consent of the church wardens thʳ beyng, and the rest of the parryshe have agreed and taken an order that all suche yonge men as shall hereafter by order of the hole parryshe be chosen for to be lorde at Whyts-ontyde for the behafe of the churche, and refuse so to be, shall forfeyt and pay for the use of the churche iij s. iiij d. to be levyed vppon the sayde yonge men and theyr fathers and maysters wherere the just default can be founde. and every mayde refusyng to be lady for the sayd purpose to forfet vnto the sayde vse xx d. to be levyed in lyke order as is before expressed. (Cox 1913, 285)

This statute clearly indicates that the election was actively supported by the village quality, and was seen as a duty to the church.

The election of the mock Lord began a whole process of the inauguration of a mock court that toured the local villages and then established itself in a festive setting in the church, church house, or churchyard on the day of the ale.[5] As Stubbes indicates, the first step after the election was the creation of mock courtiers to wait on the Lord and Lady. As in a real court of the day, these servants were granted the wearing of special liveries known as the 'great liveries,' which are not clearly described in the accounts but which were probably partial costumes – tunics, perhaps, or baldrics – of some cheap material painted with the Lord's insignia. There were also considerably more *small* liveries made, which were the badges or favours that the Lord and Lady and their deputies went round the nearby villages to sell to individuals as tickets of admission to the ale (see Stubbes 1583, sig. M2v–M3).

It is not clear from the accounts whether a fixed contribution was expected or whether the Lord and Lady's deputies tried to solicit/extort whatever they could. The sums collected at Bassingbourn, for example, are not clearly divisible by any integer and so, unless the standard donations were a halfpenny, they must have varied according to the means and generosity of the donors.

Some of the social implications of the reign of the Summer Lord and Lady are equivalent to those for the Lord of Misrule discussed in the previous chapter. Stubbes ironically takes note of the inversion of common values when he states that he who drinks the most ale is counted the 'godliest' of the crowd. But he also shows that there is not absolute social equality at the ale inasmuch as the Lord's livery bought admission to the general entertainment and feast only; the ale or beer itself was an added expense (Stubbes 1583, sig. M4v).

Detailed descriptions of the proceedings are hard to come by, but there seems general agreement that it was common for the Lord and Lady to set themselves up in a bower in the churchyard where they presided over the general feast, and were waited upon by their liverymen (see, for example, Stubbes 1583, sig. M2–M3). The scene was one ripe for impromtu fooling and horseplay based on the temporary suspension of social norms, and like its urban counterpart, may have been the locus for set speeches and play action. This was a natural environment for the cooption of the greatest of English folk heros, famous for upsetting the status quo, Robin Hood. The mock court was also a suitable setting for the importation of morris, given the popularity of the dance among the nobility in the Tudor court, the morris of the summer bower perhaps parodying the courtiers' fad. Thus at some stage in the process of church ales adopting popular customs, Robin Hood and the morris became entangled in a way that makes it now difficult to separate out the threads.[6]

It would be impossible to rehearse the whole catalogue of research concerning the development of Robin Hood games and plays in the late Middle Ages and early

Renaissance, but some of the ground must be turned over one more time to dispel some old and enduring mistakes about the relationship between the characters involved in Robin Hood games and morris dancing. To begin, it is important to acknowledge that it is the rare primary text that unambiguously states that Robin Hood games directly involved morris dancing, although there is solid evidence that plays of Robin Hood and morris dancing were featured at the same general event. Any attempt to reconstruct how they might have been related is, therefore, largely guesswork. That the two were connected in more ways than simply being performed on the same day in the same place is made plausible by the fact that through the sixteenth century, characters that are now routinely associated with Robin Hood – notably Maid Marian, but to a lesser extent Friar Tuck – played roles in the morris. The unsolved problem is whether these characters came to the morris via the Robin Hood games or vice versa.

Both David Wiles (1981) and Malcolm Nelson (1973) hypothesize that Robin Hood first appeared at church ales as a Summer Lord, and that he took on all the requisite functions – creating liverymen, gathering money, holding court, play acting – with no difficulty because of the nature of the legend at the time.[7] The early ballads portray Robin as having a large company (sometimes dressed alike in green), who demanded money from wayfarers (or fought them for it in classic duels if they refused), and then feasted the night away in greenwood bowers. Electing someone as the local Robin Hood instead of Whitsun Lord could, therefore, have been a relatively simple transformation effected some time in the mid-fifteenth century. In fact an order of 1508 from Aberdeen appears to indicate that this kind of transformation was quite explicit:

Robert Huyid and Litile Johne, quhilk was callit in yers bipast, Abbat and Prior of Bonacord.
(Cited in Chambers 1903, 1:174)

But there is also some reason to question the simple equation of Summer Lords and Robin Hood. Wiles's speculations on this point are based in part on a faulty transcription from a primary document (see Johnston 1994, 44) and on an unrepresentative sample of church accounts. More recent studies by REED editors Alexandra Johnston and Sally-Beth MacLean on a wider range of primary documents suggest that the picture was more complex and may well have varied considerably from region to region (see Johnston 1998, and Johnston and MacLean 1997).[8]

In light of these investigations it is possible to suggest two modifications to Wiles's hypothesis. First, we must be open to the possibility that the role of Robin Hood in ales was quite variable over time and space. Second, the accounts at Kingston (see below) and elsewhere in the Thames Valley seem to indicate that Robin Hood appeared in conjunction with Summer Lords (or Kings), not in place of them. If anything, therefore, Robin Hood played the part of a suitable adjunct to the Summer Lord. That is, just as the Summer Lord was a burlesque of a true noble, so Robin Hood was a parody of a chivalric knight in his court. However he got there, though, once Robin Hood found a place at church ales he began to develop as a theatrical character, and this evolution, in turn, fed back into the development of the ballad figure, as well as other strands of the legend.

There is only the most circumstantial evidence of dramatic activity associated with Summer Lords and May games in general in this period, but at some venues Robin Hood brought with him a strong dramatic element. General consensus, beginning with Francis James Child (Child 1965, 3:42), now supports the view that Robin Hood was a creature of narrative ballads and minstrelsy, but in the fifteenth century he had found his way into other vehicles. The well-known confession speech of Sloth the secular priest from *Piers Plowman*,

> I can noȝt parfitly my Paternoster as þe preest it syngeþ,
> But I kan rymes of Robyn hood and Randolf Erl of Chestre,
> Ac neiþer of oure lord ne of oure lady þe leeste þat euere was maked.
> (Langland 1975, 331. Passus V, ll.394–6)

has for a long time set the earliest reference to Robin Hood ballads at 1377, and in the process adds support to the general thesis that Robin Hood was in his earliest incarnations associated with balladry.[9] It also appears to make the ambivalent association of the church with Robin Hood as venerable as the legend itself.[10]

Walter Bower, writing around 1447 in *Scotichronicon*, speaks of

> Robertus Hode et Litill-Johanne, cum eorum complicibus, de quibus stolidum vulgus hianter in comoediis et in tragoediis prurienter festum faciunt, et prae ceteris romanciis mimos et bardanos cantitare delectantur.

> [Robert Hood and Little John, with their accomplices, of whom the ignorant rabble eagerly and lewdly make merry in comedies and tragedies [*in comoediis et in tragoediis*], and of whom, in preference to other tales, actor and bard are delighted to sing again and again.]
> (Child 1965, 3:41n)

suggesting that by the mid-fifteenth century Robin Hood was to be found in a variety of narrative forms, dramatic as well as musical. Despite Child's assertion (following Ritson's opinion, based on a faulty translation of the Latin) that the 'comedies' and 'tragedies' described here were ballads, I take the implication of the text at face value, namely, that minstrels sang the ballads of Robin Hood, while the common people made up folk plays for their holiday feasts on the same themes. Primary materials appear to confirm this observation in general fashion.

There are three play texts concerning Robin Hood extant from the fifteenth and sixteenth centuries, each of which has certain narrative similarities with a particular Robin Hood ballad (Child # 118: 'Robin Hood and Guy of Gisborne,' Child # 121: 'Robin Hood and the Potter,' and Child # 123: 'Robin Hood and the Curtal Friar'). However, in no case is there a complete match of events or general narrative structure, so that it would be inappropriate to presuppose – as does Child – that the ballads were the sole sources of the play texts, and that the evolution of the dramatic form was a simple linear process of debasement of the (high art) ballad into (folk) drama. It could be, as Wiles suggests, that the process was symbiotic; ballads suggested themes for plays but, in turn, plays provided seed material for later ballads. Or it could be that both play and ballad drew on a common stock of ideas circulating in the oral tradition, each developing in ways unique to the medium, but also influencing the other.

Play texts and ballads are by no means equivalent in their treatment of Robin Hood; the two media have rather different audiences and limitations on narrative form. But certain broad elements are common to both and give a general idea of the nature of the hero in the Tudor mind (quite different from his modern descendant). It is particularly important to note that in his literary context he can be understood by considering what he is *not*, as much as by a rehearsal of what he *is*. In particular, he is not, in the earliest narratives, a genuine chivalric knight (fallen or otherwise, as later ballads and plays suggest). Rather he is a broad parody of the Arthurian archetype: his acts are most easily comprehended as a comic foil to romantic knighthood.

Both ballads and plays have echoes of Arthurian themes, but these generally turn into broad comedy or approval of the overthrow of the symbols of feudal hierarchical society on which knighthood relied. For example, the 'Gest of Robin Hood,' a romancelike compilation of several tales interwoven into one, opens with a vow from Robin Hood that he will not dine until a rich stranger can be found to pay for the meal:

Than bespake Lytell John*n*
All vntoo Robyn Hode:
Maister, and ye wolde dyne betyme
It wolde doo you moche gode.

Tha*n* bespake hy*m* gode Robyn:
To dyne haue I noo lust,
Till that I haue *som* bolde baro*n*,
Or som vnkouth gest

[missing]
That may pay for the best,
Or som knyght or [som] squyer,
That dwelleth here bi west   (Child 1965, 3:56, stanzas 5–7)

This echoes and gently mocks the kind of sentiments that set the stage for several Arthurian tales, such as in the opening of *Sir Gawayne and the Grene Knight*, where it is said that it was Arthur's custom not to dine on high feast days until he had heard of a marvel.

Likewise Robin is devoted, in knightly fashion, to the church and in particular is dedicated to the Virgin. Nor will he harm a woman or her company:

A gode maner than had Robyn;
In londe where that he were,
Euery day or he wolde dyne
Thre messis wolde he here.

The one in the worship of the Fader,
And another of the Holy Gost,
The thirde of Our derë Lady,
That he loued allther moste.

Robyn loued Oure derë Lady;
For dout of dydly synne,
Wolde he neuer do compani harme
That any woman was in.   (Child 1965, 3:57, stanzas 8–10)

This aspect of Robin's character may explain why he became popular for a time at church ales, but the official attitude of the church hierarchy was at best ambiguous and often hostile. Even as early as the reign of Edward VI – well before general Puritan condemnation of May games – Hugh Latimer preached a now well-known sermon attacking Robin Hood customs (see Nelson 1973, 67). The problem was that Robin was a pious Christian but no respecter of fat clerics: he was authentic in his religion, not a blind follower of ecclesiastical authority. Under a secure universal church his antics could be dismissed as cathartic fun – in much the same way as those of the Abbot of Unreason or the Boy Bishop were – but as soon as the Reformation had gathered momentum his character took on dark political undertones. Bishop Latimer accused him of being a simple traitor and a thief (Nelson 1973, 67), but Hood's antiepiscopal, antiauthoritarian stand was almost certainly more deeply troubling. In one ballad he lays out orders to his men as to whom to capture and rob:

These bisshopp*es* and these archebishopp*es*,
Ye shall them bete and bynde;
The hyë sherif of Notyingham,
Hym holde ye in your mynde.   (Child 1965, 3:57, stanza 15)

This passage reminds us that the centrepiece of all early Robin Hood ballads and plays was a challenge to a classic duel, seemingly placing the narratives within the knightly tournamenting tradition – a sort of *Pas D'Armes* of yeomanry. But the general personnel and other treatments of the subject matter show that the outward tourney form was simply the instrument for farce. True, Robin Hood is skilled with bow and sword – proverbially so – but his adversaries more often than not come from the lower orders (a potter, butcher, or tanner are typical) and he invariably ends up getting a sound thrashing at their hands, even though he uses sword and buckler against their quarterstaff. When his opponents come from the genuine knightly class, however, Robin is usually victorious. The whole chivalric tradition is thus stood on its head with Robin Hood himself acting as the litmus test of true valour and skill at arms versus the evidence of superficial characteristics – shining armour as opposed to homespun, or a handsome pedigree over against a craftsman's rude title. If you can defeat Robin Hood you are a true knight.

The only Robin Hood play that exists in reasonably complete form is a version of a story found also in the ballad 'Robin Hood and the Curtal Friar.' The play was first printed *c* 1560 under the title *the playe of Robyn Hoode, verye proper to be played in Maye games* (Wiles 1981, 72–6), but the text is actually a collation of two distinct folk plays and appears to be older than the date of publication. Investigation of the text gives some clues as to the possible relationship between the dramatics of the church ales and the morris dance.

The structure of the play is simple and, using fragments of other plays and ballad narratives for comparison, may be conjectured as of a type. Robin Hood and the friar in turn introduce themselves in long speeches and issue challenges to the other. Then they meet and hurl insults one to the other, followed by some buffoonery involving carrying each other across a river. This clowning results in the friar throwing Robin in the water which precipitates a fight in earnest. Robin summons his men and the friar does likewise. The resultant donnybrook ends with Robin inviting the friar to join his crew, and presenting him with a 'Lady free.' The whole is concluded with the friar suggesting a general dance (see Wiles 1981, 76).

The structure of this play is highly reminiscent of the tournament form outlined in chapter 4 – formal challenge of adversaries, single combat, general mêlée resulting in a single victor, prize-giving, and general dance. Given this overt congruence, it is possible to speculate concerning the role of the morris dance in the general spectacle.

Some scholars have suggested that the dance which the friar mentions is itself the morris dance, with the friar and the lady (often equated with Maid Marian) as the main characters, but also perhaps including Robin Hood and his men (see, for example, Simeone 1951 and Nelson 1973, 54–6). This interpretation has certain strengths but also runs into a number of problems. There is no doubt that in considerably later texts a friar (often specified as Friar Tuck) and Maid Marian are conventionally associated as dance partners, sometimes expressly in a morris dance. Often cited in this regard is this passage from Ben Jonson's *Gypsies Metamorphosed*, first performed in 1621:

Dance. 3.
During wch enter ye Clownes
Cockrell. Clod. Towneshead Puppy.

...

CLOD. They should be Morris dancers by theire gingle but they haue no Napkins.
COC. No nor a Hobby horse.
CLOD. O he is often forgotten, that's no rule; but there is no Maidmarrian nor ffrier
amongst them, wch is the surer marke.   (Jonson 1621, 589)

In Thomas Ravenscroft's *Pammelia*, a compilation of rounds and catches published in 1609, there is a tune entitled 'A Round of three Country Dances in One,' which is a variant of a melody found in the sixteenth century associated with Robin Hood. This same tune appears in an untitled medley by William Cobbold of *c* 1612 (BL Add. MS 18936 fol. 60) with the words:

Robin hood Robin hood and little John,
they leand them to a tree a tree,
Frier Tuck and Maid Marrian,
soe turn ye about all three,
frier Tuck and mayd Marrian,
soe turne ye about all three,
        about all three.   (Cited in Bronson 1966, 3:14)

It is reasonable, therefore, to say that *at some point* Friar Tuck and Maid Marian were well-known dancing partners. But these texts all come from the seventeenth century, and are none of them strictly satisfactory as accounts of rural morris. They are texts composed by urban playwrights and musicians to create a desired dramatic effect, not straightforward reportage. However, there is some indirect confirmation that the morris was linked specifically to these characters in the Kingston churchwardens' accounts. The records headed 'ffor ye Maye game and Robartte Hode' for 1519 include the line item:

Item payett for viij payer of schewes for ye mores dansserers ye freer & made maryen at viij d.
ye payer v s. iiij d.   (Surrey CRO KG 2/2/1, f. 97)

Here the friar and Maid Marian are parcelled together with the morris dancers —
and distinct from the rest of Robin Hood's company — seeming to imply a link be-
ween them, and apparently confirming the later identification of the two with the
morris. But the open question is whether the friar and Maid Marian were old morris characters that were grafted on to the Robin Hood legend or vice versa. The former
is most often asserted by modern Robin Hood scholars (see Nelson, 1973 54–79
for a summary), but their largely similar and well-worn arguments are based on slim
or faulty evidence.

One major piece of 'evidence' frequently used to buttress their cases is the Betley
window (figure 20), which is also by far the most commonly reproduced image of 'old'
morris dancing. Commonly, contemporary scholars follow E.J. Nicol's assertion —
based on George Tollett's published 'Opinion concerning the Morris Dancers upon
his window' (Tollett 1793) — that the window dates from *c* 1500 and, therefore, provides direct pictorial evidence for the nature of the morris dance and May games at
the beginning of the sixteenth century (Nicol 1953). What they basically say is that
the window depicts morris dancers, a hobby horse, a pipe and taborer, and maypole
(superscribed 'A Mery May'), with, in addition, a friar and a lady whom they infer
to be Maid Marian. This representation, they argue, confirms the notion that the latter two characters were key components in the morris dance performed at May games
at the start of the sixteenth century, when Robin Hood plays were just building in
popularity at the same venue. Furthermore Robin Hood and his men are absent from
the window. *Ergo*, the friar and Maid Marian originated with the morris and were
transferred to the Robin Hood legend.

However, both Tollett and Nicol use costume evidence alone to date the window,
which is a highly suspect method. The bulk of the figures on the window are direct
copies of an Israel van Meckenem engraving — see figure 16 (p 80) — (which fact
neither Tollett nor Nicol directly acknowledges). Therefore it is not surprising that
the dancers seem to be dressed à la mode for *c* 1500, but this says nothing of the
dating of the window, only of the van Meckenem originals. In fact, the Victoria and
Albert Museum now dates the window as early *seventeenth* century, based on the
nature of the materials employed and the style of the work; as the part of Betley
Hall where the window was originally situated was built in 1621 (according to a dated
stone), it is a reasonable conjecture to date the window in or around that year. Thus,
the best that the window can do is support the literary evidence, already cited, of the
same period.

Before moving to other forms of evidence, however, we can glean a little more information from the Betley window about morris in the early seventeenth century because
it is not an exact copy of the van Meckenem engraving, and hence the differences

Figure 20: Reproduction of the Betley window

should bear some significance. That is, if there were no differences between the window and the engraving except expected stylistic or aesthetic variations, then there would be no reason to trust the former as any kind of document of English customs. But because there are substantive additions in the depictions in the window, it can reasonably be inferred that these differences represent an attempt on the artist's part to bring the figures of the engraving in line with local custom.

The most obvious difference is that all of the dancers on the window copied from the engraving are wearing garter bands of bells under their knees or on their ankles, and sometimes at their wrists, where the originals have none. In general the costumes show obvious congruences, but there are notable differences, particularly in those of the identifiable characters. The fools' outfits, for example, are made on completely different lines: van Meckenem's fool wearing a belled cap with asses' ears, knee-length tunic coat with long pendant sleeves, and calf boots – characteristic of continental models of the time – whereas the Betley fool has more of the look of the English court jester with hooded jester's coxcomb cap, short doublet, and hose. It is also worthy of note that the Betley fool is clearly gesticulating with his free hand, the thumb and first two fingers standing out straight and the third and fourth curled into the palm. This is a deliberate addition by the window's artist, the original engraving showing the fool grasping his marotte in one hand and a branch in the other – and is the only clear intimation of chironomy in either depiction, the other dancers using simple open hand gestures.

The lady in the engraving wears a high steeple headdress and long dress with tight bodice and amply flowing skirts; in her hand she holds out an apple. The lady on the window wears a golden crown, a floor-length sleeved robe and surcoat with stomacher, while in her hand she holds a flower. The crown is often taken as indicative that she is supposed to represent the Queen of the May, as opposed to a simple 'lady.' Two of the dancers in the engraving have ribbony morisco sleeves that twine and flow with, and to some extent are lost in, the decorative branch work. Their analogues in the window have dagged sleeves that are much more prominent, representing a flowing outer sleeve slashed at the elbow.

There are, in addition, two characters, the hobby horse and the friar, on the window – as well as the maypole – which are not represented in the engraving. The hobby horse is interesting in that the rider's cheeks appear to be pierced with daggers, prompting scholars (see Cawte 1979, 58) to see this character as a legerdemain artist along the lines of the description of the hobby horse rider in Jonson's *Every Man Out of His Humor*:

I have danc't in it my selfe too ... there's ne're a gentleman i' the countrey has the like humours for the hobby-horse, as I have; I have the method for the threeding of the needle and all ... I, the leigeritie for that, and the wigh-hie, and the daggers in the

nose, and the travels of the egge from finger to finger, all the humours incident to the
quality.   (Jonson 1599, 460–1, II.ii.40–68)

The Betley friar's posture is identical with that of the dancer above him on the window, apparently indicating that he is dancing also. He is dressed in a habit of russet,
denoting him as a member of the Franciscan order, which accords with the Kingston
accounts of the church ale morris in 1519:

Item payett for iij brode yerdes of rosett to make ye freers cott iij s. vj d.
                                                  (Surrey CRO KG 2/2/1, f.97)

The curtal friar from the ballad, however, is a Cistercian (from Fountains Abbey), and
the Kingston accounts of 1509 – when there was no morris – call for white material
for the friar's coat (Surrey CRO KG 2/2/1, f.66), casting him as a Carmelite. So it
would seem that either his precise ecclesiastical affiliation was less important than
his being a friar – that is, a mendicant with a mission to the world at large, rather
than a cloistered monk – or that the friar was not a single fixed character (that is,
was not specifically Friar Tuck). Primary sources appear to indicate that the drunk-
en, lecherous, brawling, dancing friar had multiple manifestions in folk dance and
drama and was only loosely affiliated with Robin Hood and the morris dance. This
thought leads us back to the early sixteenth century when the friar first appears as
a character in *both*.

Given the nature of the primary data it seems virtually beyond question that the
friar first made an appearance in the Robin Hood plays associated with church ales,
and then became attached to the morris dance (for a limited period). Robin Hood plays
are recorded as vital elements of church ales in a steady stream of references through
the latter half of the fifteenth century (see Wiles 1981, 64–6), and the friar was an
established figure in the plays at that time. In a manuscript fragment of *c* 1475
there is the following couplet that is probably a character's self introductory phrase:

Be holde wele ffrere tuke howe he dothe his bowe pluke   (Wiles 1981, 71)

These lines follow what appears to be the beginning of a scene in which some of
Robin's men are gathering to rescue Robin and another part of his band who have
been imprisoned by the sheriff. Two lines later one of the characters indicates that
the action (not specified in the dialogue) has culminated with Tuck being imprisoned
along with Robin and his men. So it would seem that at this point a friar (specifically Friar Tuck) was an integral part of the folk legend of Robin Hood and his band.
And this is fully a generation before the morris dance is found in relation to Robin
Hood and May games – the first instance being 1507 in Kingston upon Thames.

How the character Maid Marian became associated with Tuck and the morris dance (and with Robin Hood's band) is more elusive. She first shows up in the Kingston upon Thames churchwardens' accounts as part of the Robin Hood games in 1509, two years after the morris had appeared there for the first time, and thereafter she is found in close association with morris dancing – in Kingston and elsewhere. In fact she becomes a definitive figure of the rural dance from then until the end of the period covered by this study.

Graphic seriation of the early morris database concerning the appearance of Robin Hood, Little John, the friar, and Maid Marian (figure 21) in relation to morris dancing presents a curious picture. The curves for the first three are roughly similar, that is, slender curves that peak early and taper off gradually through the sixteenth and early seventeenth centuries. Maid Marian's curve is the complete inverse, tapering out slowly to the end of the sixteenth century and then holding steady to the end of our period. Treated as a simple binary pair (that is Robin Hood, Little John, and the friar as one versus Maid Marian as the other) these curves show the classic signs of the rise and fall of *competing* fashions.

The morris dance was, therefore, the nexus for Tuck and Marian to come together for a brief interval, the dance itself being a vehicle for Tuck to detach from the Robin Hood legend and for Marian to attach to it. One might see the Robin Hood plays on the one hand, and the morris dance on the other, as fluid concatenations of characters loosely bound to certain dramatic or choreographic ideas, but able to shift from one to the other when the two came together. But to make this scenario plausible the two forms must have had more in common than simple coincidence at the same general event; they must have been drawn together by some kind of conceptual unity or similarity.

This idea leads back to the point I made at the outset, that the Robin Hood plays of the church ales have an underlying structure that parodies the tournament form. It is reasonable to conjecture, therefore, that because the courtly morris dance was an essential component of the latter day dramatic evolution of the knightly tournament, at the end of the satire of such a tournament there should be a satire of the courtly morris dance. This would certainly not be a necessary ingredient in the folk plays, and the primary evidence seems to indicate that they managed successfully without the dance throughout the fifteenth century. But then the morris was not a significant fashion at court until the 1510–40 period, and this is precisely when it starts up at church ales as well (see figures 2 and 3, pp 29 and 32).

That *some* of the church ale morrises were like the morisks of the courts may be confirmed by indirect evidence from the primary sources.[11] The morris associated with the Robin Hood games in Kingston upon Thames 1507, for example, seems to have been made up of between four and six dancers in bells and sparkling costumes, and a lady. The accounts for that year include the following:

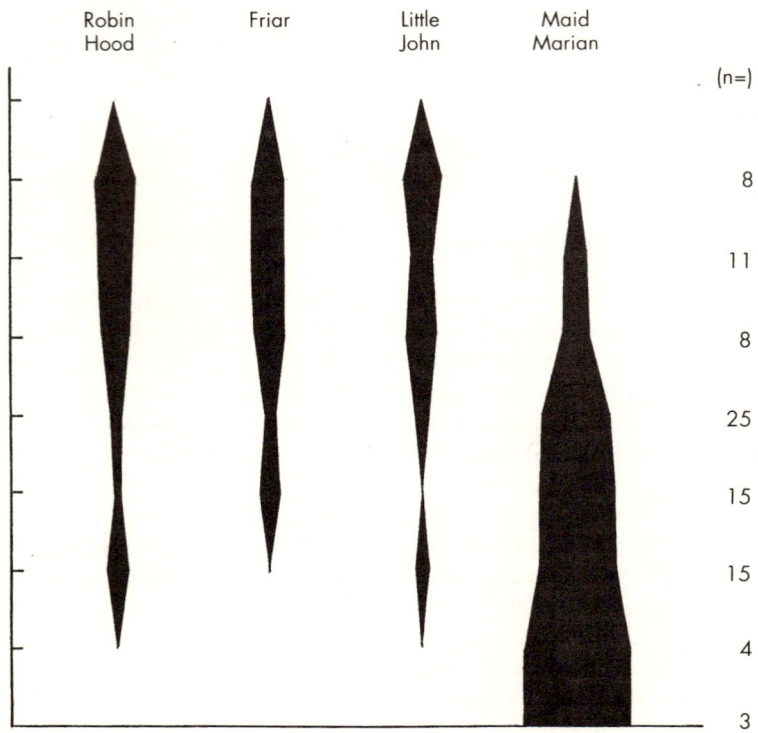

Figure 21: Seriation of Robin Hood, Little John, Friar, and Maid Marian

Item for garterynge of iiij dosen bellys iij d.

...

Item for payntyng of ye mores garmentes and for sarten gret leveres ij s. iiij d.

...

Item for iiij plytes and a quartar of laun for ye mores garmentes ij s. xj d.

Item for orseden for ye same x d.

Item for a goun for ye lady viij d.

Item for ye makynge of ye mores garmentes & for yer met & for fetteng of ye ger at London ix s. iiij d.

Item for bells for ye daunsars xij d.

...

Item to Robard Felere for chone for ye daunsars iiij s. iiij d. (Surrey CRO KG 2/2/1, ff.53–4)

These items are difficult to interpret as to the specifics but the general idea seems clear.

The morris dancers wore lawn shirts or tunics that were painted (perhaps to represent Robin Hood's livery, since the painter who painted them also painted the great liveries) and ornamented with glittering orsedy – much like the Moorish-style courtly morisk coats. Most indicators point to there being four dancers – there are four hats mentioned in among other costs associated with the morris and four dozen bells gartered (which at a dozen apiece – or six per garter – is a reasonable number). A 'plight' was a measure unique to lawn, now unknown, and possibly quite variable, but an account book of 1502 indicates that a plight was enough for a small but fancy shirt:

A plyte of lawnde for a shirte for the childe of grace at Reding   (Nicolas 1830, 50)

So four-and-one-quarter plights could reasonably be enough for four relatively plain garments. The cost of shoes, however, seems to indicate six or more dancers. If there were but four dancers then the shoes would have cost 1s 1d per pair, which is too expensive. Even in 1536, after inflation had begun to have an effect on the cost of clothing, double-soled shoes for Kingston performers cost only 9d per pair (Surrey CRO KG 2/2/1, f.178). Six pairs of shoes would be a reasonable number as far as general cost per pair is concerned (around 8½d), but this raises the question of who the other dancers were. One surmise – which is really no more than a guess – is that they were the lady herself, and Robin Hood (or some other character) acting the part of the fool, the dance being a parody of symbolic courtship for a wife.

The Kingston churchwardens' inventory at the end of their account book (for the account year 1538–9) includes morris gear that seems to correspond even more closely than the earlier costumes to inventories (such as Gibson's) of royal morisk equipment:

Md. Lefte in the kyping of the wardens nowe being a fryeres Cote of Russett & a Kyrtell of wostedde weltyd wt Redd cloth a mowrens Cote of Bvckrame & iiij morres Dawnseres Cotes of whitte fustyan spangelyd & ij gryne saten Cotes and a [Disardes] Dysarddes Cote of Cotten and vj payre of garderes wt Belles   (Surrey CRO KG 2/2/1, f.185)

Specifically, the morris coats are 'spangelyd,' and there are also costumes for a lady ('Kyrtell') and a fool ('Dysarddes Cote'), as well as other characters associated with both Robin Hood and the morris, namely, the friar and the Moor ('mowrens cote'), and two green coats, possibly Robin Hood's livery of green.

A great deal more concerning the history of church ale morris can be inferred from the Kingston accounts, but before investigating them in detail it is useful to look at records from other towns to demonstrate that the Kingston materials are not unique or idiosyncratic (although they are, in general, the most detailed). For example, in 1529 St Lawrence parish, Reading, paid out,

Item for belles for the Morece dauncers iij s. vj d.
Item for iij hattes for the Morece dauncers vj d.
Item for ffyve elles of Canves for A cote for made Maryon at iij d. ob thell xvij d. ob
Item for iij yerdes of bockerham for the morec dauncers xij d.
> (Berkshire Record Office D/P 97/5/2, pp 177–8,
> in Kerry 1883, 226, and Johnston forthcoming)

This seems to indicate that there were three dancers plus a Maid Marian as the lady. Even as late as 1623, when church morris was in serious decline, the churchwardens of Bray recorded as part of their inventory of permanent goods:

The goodes belongeinge tothe church delyuerd by Thomas Laurence & Richard markyn iiij[th] of maye 1623 to the then churchwardens ... fower coates for morrice daunsers and for the mayd maryan & a payre of breeches and dooblet for the foole & a cupp.
> (Berkshire Record Office D/P 23/5/1, f.17 recto,
> in Kerry 1861, 30, and Johnston forthcoming).

This again seems to indicate a morisk-like dance of a lady, fool, and four morris dancers.

Many towns record payments for painting of the morris coats – usually in conjunction with the liveries for the church ale. In 1541 in St Lawrence, Reading:

Payd for lyverys & payntyng the mores cotes xj d.   (Kerry 1883, 226)

and in 1556 their neighbor parish of St Mary's records:

Item payed for the morrysdaunsers and the mynstrelles mete and Drink at whitsontyde iij s. iiij d.
payed to them the Sonday after mayday xx d.
payed to the painter for paynting of ther Cottes ij s. viij d.
payed to the painter for ij C dimidium of Lyveryes xx d.
> (Garry and Garry 1893, 28–9, and Johnston forthcoming)

Likewise in the churchwardens' acounts of Thatcham, Berkshire, for 1566 there is the entry:

Item payd for payntyng of the morrys daunssers coyttes ij s.
> (Berkshire CRO D/P 130 5/1A f.4 verso,
> in Barfield 1901, 2:93 and in Johnston forthcoming)

Given the high figures for painting recorded here, the morris coats must have been elaborately embellished. At St Mary's Reading, for example, the painter was paid 20d for 250 liveries (small, no doubt) and 2s 8d, or more than half as much again, for the coats alone. If for the sake of comparison we assume that the painter charged 8d per (twelve-hour) day for his work, then he was painting 100 liveries per day, and the coats took him four days (or one day each if there were four).

There are also intimations from these references that the Thames valley was one of the principal avenues of diffusion of dance ideas, starting at Kingston upon Thames and moving along the river corridor. The full scope of this diffusion can be seen in figure 7 (p 39).

Finally, church records generally indicate that a morris dancer's costume consisted at minimum of a special coat and a pair of garters of bells, and, where the numbers are explicit, four dancers is the clear norm (with six being a minor alternative). Four to six dancers was also the norm for the courtly morisks.

Having determined, therefore, that the Kingston accounts, while more detailed, are generally in accord with other church records, we may return to them with a view to discovering more about the nature of church ale morris. What seems most obvious at the outset is that the dance went through a number of changes from its first record in 1507 to the final inventory in 1538–9.[12]

It seems likely that 1507 was the first year in which morris appeared at the Kingston church ale; everything was made new in that year (including the garters of bells) and some materials had to be carried from London. The overall expenses were not small given the profits for the event (around 22s laid out for morris gear and around 39s profit), but in comparison with later years they are conservative. Presumably the costumes were expected to last for several years, so that the initial investment would be recouped over time. Thus, in the following year the only entries relating directly to morris dancers are these:

Item payd for [the mores] mete & drynke for the mores daunsars on the fayre day xiiij d.
Item payd for ij peyre of shone for ye moreys daunsers xiiij d.
(Surrey CRO KG 2/2/1, f.62)

The profit from the whole event was four marks (53s 4d).

It is also likely that Maid Marian appeared in the dance for the first time this year, although she is not mentioned in the accounts until 1509 when a special costume was made for her and she was paid for her work (this is the first recorded appearance of the character anywhere in English):

Item paid to mayde marion for hir labor for ij yere ij s.　　(Surrey CRO KG 2/2/1, f.66)

This implies that she performed in 1508, possibly wearing the 'lady's' costume from 1507.

In 1510 the morris gear underwent a slight refurbishment and there is mention for the first time of a fool:

Item payd for ye foles cote xiiij d.

...

Item payd syluer paper for the mores daunce vij d.

...

Item for vj payre of shone for ye mores daunsers iiij s.   (Surrey CRO KG 2/2/1, ff.17–19)

The silver paper would presumably have been used to dress up the tinselled areas of the costumes, dulled and cracked after several years' use and storage. The need for six pairs of shoes is interesting also, because there is no mention of additional coats. I take this to mean, therefore, that the Maid Marian and the fool are included in the calculations (although it may indicate an increase in the number of dancers). Up until this point the only payment that the dancers received was food and drink, suggesting that they were local men, satisfied to perform for a free feast, certainly not professionals and not brought in from elsewhere.

From 1510 to 1515 there are no performances of morris reported in the accounts (although there is a gap of two years in the record book).[14] Then in 1515, although there are no new costumes provided, every dancer received a new pair of shoes. The itemized list of recipients of shoes is interesting for several reasons:

Chones for mores davnsars *& Roben Hod and his compenye*
ferst to Jhon at benes A peyer of chone viij d.
tomas Kendauall A peyer chone viij d.
tomas batteng A peyer chone viij d.
leycroftes man A peyer viij d.
brenkerstes man A peyer viij d.
Harry godman A peyer viij d.
Robard uell A peyer viij d.
Rycharde Kneyte A peyer viij d.
Jhon Homleye viij d.
Item for rebaud for ther choes j d. ob.
Item for Roben Hod A peyer of chone viij d.
Item for Jhon ffoull A per of chone viij d.
Item for paulmares man A peyer of chone viij d.
Item for Robard Webe viij d.   (Surrey CRO KG 2/2/1, f.84)[15]

The original list was simply headed 'Chones for mores davnsars' but somebody at a later date added '& Roben Hod and his compenye,' presumably to clarify that these thirteen men were not all morris dancers. But it is not at all clear who belonged to which group, even though some commentators have taken the line item 'rebaud for ther choes' as a caesura dividing the morris dancers from Robin Hood's company (Heaney 1989, 91, Wiles 1981, 23). But this is not a fully acceptable conclusion. Churchwardens' accounts are not typically so rationally organized, and it is common to have a list of related items broken by one seemingly out of place. What is more, in all the other account years at Kingston where morris is mentioned, the most gener-ous interpretation of the data cannot make the number of morris dancers more than six, but here there would be nine if all those above the caesura were morris men.

Rather, what this list suggests is that by this time the morris dance had become much more integrated into the Robin Hood play, with perhaps the dancers particip-ating more in the action and some of the Robin Hood players getting involved in the dancing (hence the confusion about the heading). One item in the accounts,

Item for makeng of a croun for ye mores daunsers ij d.   (Surrey CRO KG 2/2/1, f.84)

seems to confirm this view, hinting that one of the dancers had a specific role that involved him in the action. And the provision of shoes for Robin Hood's men is prima facie evidence that they were engaged in dancing of some sort. But not all of Hood's men were dancers. Even if we subtract the lowest possible number of morris dancers, that is four, from the list, that still leaves only nine other dancers, and according to the accounts there were sixteen great liveries made that year for Robin Hood's com-pany. So the dancers were Robin Hood and a select group from his company, along with the morris dancers.

Even though the action may have become more integrated, the morris dancers were still definitely subordinate to Robin Hood and his men. The accounts continue with payments for the various performers:

Item for met & drenk for ye mores daunsars vpon feyer daye ix d.
Item to Roben Hod for hes labor xij d.
Item to leytell Jhon for hes labor x d.
Item to ffreer tuk viij d.
Item in money Amongest Roben Hodes men at nythe viij d.
Item for Ataberare apon may daye viij d.
Item in mony to young men that tok Apon them to pleye the mores dauns vj d.
                                                                 (Surrey CRO KG 2/2/1, f.84)

As usual the morris dancers were remunerated through food and drink primarily, but there is also a curious entry for 6d to be given specifically to the 'young men' who danced. This item is interesting for a number of reasons. It is the only recorded payment at Kingston to morris dancers in cash money. Yet the main Robin Hood players routinely received some kind of reward, usually (as here) equivalent to a day's wage or more. The relative importance of Robin Hood, Little John, and Friar Tuck can be seen reflected in their respective incomes. The men of Robin Hood's company, on the other hand, got a mere 8d to share between them, or ½d apiece, so their compensation in cash was no more than a petty gratuity, an evening's drinking money in return for relatively limited service. And it appears that the morris dancers received something equivalent. That is, their performance, as expressed in financial terms, was on a par with the rank and file in Robin Hood's company, and not with the chief players.

That the young men were paid *at all* bears further scrutiny because there are few payments in the accounts of church ales to individual participants (that is, to people engaged in the day's entertainments rather than to suppliers of food or equipment). Given that the ale was a money-making venture sponsored by the parishioners, it would not be appropriate for participants to require a fee unless their labours were in some sense extraordinary as were, for example, Robin Hood's; he had to travel around the district over several market days drumming up business. This means that the morris dancers were parishioners themselves, working for the profit of the church and generally content with a full belly as sufficient reward for time devoted to dance practices. But four or six young men can eat and drink a goodly amount, particularly after strenuous exercise. In 1510, for example, the parish paid out at least 2s on one occasion for the dancers' fare. So, rather than being an extra reward, this cash sum may represent an attempt to limit the expenses the church would incur in limitless free ale to them, by requiring the morris dancers to buy their own and paying them something towards its cost.

The list also tells us something of the social status of the performers in the community. Most of the performers are identified by name but three are designated as someone's 'man,' meaning they were either servants or apprentices. Therefore, some of the performers, at least, were young (as is also indicated by the appellation 'young men') and of relatively low standing. This conclusion would also explain why the dancers received such a low compensation.

In 1519 the morris reappeared, again with intimations of a close association with the Robin Hood play but still in a subordinate role (see Surrey CRO KG 2/2/1, f.97). Robin Hood and his men had elaborate new costumes made for them, but the regular morris dancers simply got new shoes (as did the friar and Maid Marian) and some extra bells. The line entries clearly indicate that now there were six dancers ('Item payett for viij payer of schewes for ye mores dansserers ye freer & made maryen'), and that, for this year, the integration with the Robin Hood plays involved the friar, who had a special russet coat made which was distinct from the other costumes, and suggests that he had a significant new role that year.

In 1522 the morris dancers had new costumes made (or remade) and this may signal yet another metamorphosis in the role of the dance. The accounts call for:

Item paid for viij yerdes of ffustyan for ye Mores daunsers cotes iiij s.
Item paid for xij dosyn of belles iij s.
Item paid for a dosyn of gold skynnes for ye mores x d.   (Surrey CRO KG 2/2/1, f.112)

There is some question as to whether these materials are enough to reclothe the dancers (Heaney 1989, 92), and certainly if the fustian were the main body of their coats, seven yards would by no means be sufficient. One alternative is to imagine that the 'gold skynnes' (i.e., gilded leather) are literally whole skins – as the term is generally interpreted in accounts of the period – and that, therefore, the bodies of the costumes are leather trimmed with fustian. But 10d seems rather too little to pay for such a quantity of leather. Another possibility is that the leather was a smaller amount, and was used to make spangles to be sewn on the old costumes to dress them up, (along with the fustian for trimming). The coats in the inventory of 1538–9 are described as 'spangelyd,' so this is a reasonable possibility. And, even though the coats were remade once again in 1536, there are no line items in the accounts for spangles in that year, so it is possible that they were reused from the 1522 costumes. The costumes also required a significant increase in the number of bells, meaning either that the dancers' garters were enlarged considerably or, like their courtly analogues, the costumes had bells sewn directly on them among the spangles.

The 1522 accounts also provide some costume details of the other characters for that year:

Item paid for iiij yardes of bokeram for ye morenys Cote xvj d.
Item paid for iiij Estrygge ffethers for Robyn Hode xx d.
Item paid for ij peyre of shone for Robyn Hode & lytell john xxj d.
Item paid for makyng of ye Mores cote v d.   (Surrey CRO KG 2/2/1, f.112)

Robin Hood and Little John have new shoes, but otherwise their costumes are the same as for 1519 (the four ostrich feathers replacing those damaged or lost from the previous occasion – there being no plays in the intervening years). There is also, for the first time, mention of a Moor's costume ('ye morenys Cote'). His costume costs are grouped with Robin Hood's and separated from the morris dancers' so his primary role may have been in the Robin Hood play. But the use of gold skins on the morris dancers' costumes (coupled with the great increase in the use of bells) seems to signal a deliberate effort to emphasize their (purported) Moorishness, so there might well have been a Moorish theme to the whole event – perhaps with a play 'Robin Hood and the Moor' – making the morris dance especially pertinent.

After 1522 there is another hiatus until 1536 when all items of the costumes for the morris dancers, the friar, the fool, and Maid Marian were completely renewed (see Surrey CRO KG 2/2/1, ff.175–8). This time the coats were made of fustian (perhaps stiffened at points with buckram), and the dancers had new hats, shoes, and purses, the latter again suggesting that the dancers had a dramatic role of some kind. What is confusing is the number of dancers involved, since there are accounts for four purses, five hats, and six pairs of shoes.[16] My surmise is that there were four dancers, mainly on the grounds that there were only four morris coats in the church's keeping two years later (although it is always possible that two were lost or irreparably damaged). Thus, there were four purses for the morris dancers, the five hats were for the morris dancers plus one of the supernumerary characters, and the six pairs of shoes were for the morris dancers plus Maid Marian and the friar (just as they were parcelled together in 1519).

In 1537 there was no church-sponsored dance but the coats were hired out for 2s (Surrey CRO KG 2/2/1, f.179), and then in the 1538–9 fiscal year there is the general inventory of goods held by the church. So 1536 is the last year in which a church sponsored morris is recorded in Kingston. For subsequent years the relevant accounts are not extant, but the records from 1507 to 1536 give a good overall impression of the development of morris dancing at Kingston, so that some themes of interest emerge.

The records in this period are detailed and complete enough – although not extant for every year between 1507 and 1536 – to indicate that 1507 was the first year for morris at Kingston church and that from that date it appeared sporadically (1508, 1510, 1515, 1519, 1522, 1536) not as an annual or even as a regular, expectable component of festivities.[17] Thus periods of abeyance followed by revival were the norm, with the former growing longer over time. At the beginning it appears that the revivals were modest affairs; a few cheap materials were provided to dress up the costumes at most. Later, the renovations were much more elaborate, the costumes changing quite considerably in character. These changes could be due to a number of (not necessarily mutually exclusive) factors. It may simply have been that prolonged storage in the later part of the period caused serious damage to the costumes, requiring their complete replacement, or it could have been that the dance's function (or form) changed over time, requiring different costumes to signal this. The small information on props and additional characters seems to support the latter point of view, but the data are completely circumstantial. Whatever the cause, the information at our disposal indicates that some components of the dance evolved from 1507 to 1536.

Thus, the dance may well have begun in 1507 as a straightforward parody of the contemporary courtly morisk, but such a form – based on satire and currentness – would not be able to sustain itself, without change, indefinitely. That is, the performances in 1508 and 1510 might have been simple repetitions of an original idea that proved popular, mounted with very little additional outlay after the first year. By 1522, however, not only the costumes, but also the general idea had become worn and in need of updating. The morisk was no longer popular in the courts, so the element of parody would have lost its force. Nor was this morris the kind of dance that patrons of the ale were expecting to see as an annual custom, repeated along traditionally accepted lines, and so they would not be upset to see it in a new guise. The number of dancers, extra characters, integration in play action, and costumes all varied over time.

It is also true that the courtly morisks were not a single dance but rather a series of quite different dances based on a general set of choreographic ideas that could be elaborated on. The two basic themes of the courtly dance – competition (or combat) and symbolic wooing – could be improvised in numerous ways, and the dance could be subject to choreographic influences from other sources. That the courtly dance manifested considerable variety during its heyday meant that a rural satire could and, perhaps should, change with the times also, and would develop and evolve under analogous influences.

It seems reasonable, for example, given subsequent developments (discussed more fully in later chapters), that the rural dance adopted figures from country dancing.[18] There is no clear evidence concerning how the first adoption of figures by rural morrises came about – whether by copying courtly dances, by independent invention, by synthesis with country dances, or whether they were present at the outset – but certainly through the sixteenth century the rural dances were drawing ideas from country dancing.

The accounts from Kingston for 1515 are suggestive concerning the adoption of new dance ideas but, as usual, the data are elusive and circumstantial. This is the year in which a number of men from Robin Hood's company along with the morris dancers were bought shoes, an outlay apparently reserved for dancers only in other account years. These accounts are also notable in that there appears to be some confusion concerning who performed the morris and who was in Robin Hood's company. Given the other evidence from the accounts of the evolving integration of the morris into the other dramatic events of the ales, and the general hypothesis that the course of the performance events at ales was loosely patterned on the model of courtly disguisings, then the morris would naturally be followed by a general dance of all present, but initiated by the main protagonists of the drama – that is, Robin and his men, and the morris dancers. Thus, the morris, although quite distinct from the general dance (which in the rural areas was presumably a country dance), would be juxtaposed with it and would lead quite smoothly into it.

How the morris and figures from the general dances might have converged choreographically can be speculated on by examining some meager evidence of figures that appeared in the rural morris in the late sixteenth century. The polemical pamphlet *A Treatise of Daunses, Wherein it is Shewed, that they are Accessories to Whoredome*, contains the following description:

When the lusty and fyne man should holde a young damosel, or a woman by the hand, and keeping his measures he shal remoue himselfe, whirle about, & shake his legges aloft (which the daunsers call crosse capring) for pleasure, doth not she in ye meane while make a good threede, playing at the Moris on her behalfe ...?   (Anon 1581, sig. B7–B7v)

The figure called 'threede' here is probably a variant of what is later called 'thread-needle' or 'thread the needle,' a weaving around the man (or men). The following passage from Stephen Gosson's *School of Abuse* is cryptic (and is an indirect allusion to the biblical figure of the camel and the needle's eye), but could conceivably support the idea that a form of the thread the needle was used in rural dance:

If you enquire howe manie such Poetes and Pipers wee haue in our Age, I am perswaded that euerie one of them may creepe through a ring, or daunce the wilde Morice in a Needles eye.
                                                        (Gosson 1579, 27)[19]

The image that occurs is of the morris dancers capering and gesturing in a circle while the Maid Marian weaves between them, in a kind of hey.[20] If this is close to correct then it suggests that the figure of the central lady changed from a static and passive role to a more active one. This surmise is supported by the fact that Maid Marian was not issued shoes in Kingston when she first appeared, but was later. The sexual connotations of this figure are also patent, so that its use in the rural morris would be a legitimate extension of the symbolic wooing inherent in the morisk. But if this is true the woman may have had a more active role in several senses; thread the needle allows her to be flirtatious and responsive to the men's actions. The parody of the ring morisk is also blatant in that the woman herself (rather than the symbolic apple) is the prize for the winner – possibly Friar Tuck, who ought not to be competing for her at all.

The sexual comedy may in some places have been further heightened by the fact that the Maid Marian was often, although not always, played by a boy or a man. The records are sometimes unclear in this regard, but there are many instances, especially later in the century, where the performer is obviously male. There are, in addition, other data – particularly from literary sources – which confirm that Maid Marian was stereotypically male. In Shakespeare's *Henry IV Part 1*, for example, there is this famous exchange between the hostess of the Blue Boar, Mistress Quickly, and Falstaff:

HOSTESS. There's neither faith, truth, nor womanhood in me else.

FALSTAFF. There's no more faith in thee than in a stewed prune, nor no more truth in thee than in a drawn fox – and for womanhood, Maid Marian may be the deputy's wife of the ward to thee. (1 Henry IV, III.iii.114–19)

That is, Maid Marian was neither a woman nor a symbol of womanly virtues. Contemporary literary accounts of the morris confirm that in Elizabethan times Maid Marian was commonly a man whose sexuality and gender caused ribald humour. In Robert Greene's satire *A Qvip for an Vpstart Courtier* Cloth-breeches says of the courtier:

... queasie maister veluet breeches ... must if the lest spot of morphue come on his face, haue his oyle of Tartar, his *Lac virginis*, his camphire dissolved in veriuice, to make the foole as faire forsooth, as if he were to playe Maidmarian in a May game or Moris-daunce ...
(Greene 1592, 248–9)

And Thomas Nashe in *The Return of Pasquill* uses the general form of the morris and its stock characters to mock the political actions of Elizabethan churchmen in the midst of the Marprelate controversy:

... *The May-game of Martinisme* ... *Penry* the welchman is the foregallant of the Morrice, with the treble belles, shot through the wit with a Woodcocks bill ... *Martin* him-selfe is the Mayd-marian, trimlie drest vppe in a cast Gowne, and a Kercher of Dame *Lawsons*, his face handsomlie muffled with a Diaper-napkin to couer his beard, and a great Nosegay in his hande, of the principalest flowers I could gather out of all hys works. *Wiggenton* daunces round about him in a Cotten-coate, to court him with a Leatherne pudding, and a woodden Ladle.
(Nashe 1589, 83)

The use of the morris to ridicule certain kinds of churchmen is discussed below. For present purposes this shows, not only the sexual ambiguity of Maid Marian (and her role as a flirt and dissembler), but also confirms that the general form of the dance is as hypothesized – that is, a courtship of Maid Marian involving suggestive motions (especially by the fool with his leather bauble and ladle) while dancing around her.

The account books from the very beginning of the sixteenth century, however, could indicate that the Maid Marian was at that time a woman, although evidence in this direction is quite ambiguous. In 1509 in relation to Maid Marian they speak of 'hir labor for ij yere' which probably establishes the gender of the person playing the part (although it is within the bounds of possibility that the pronoun refers to the character only). These data too, then, hint at the evolution of the dance through the development of one of its characters. At first the central lady of the dance was an anonymous figure who, having gained a specific name and role in the Robin Hood games, turned from a woman who was simply the subject of courtship, to a ribald she-male who gave as good as 'she' got. Having developed a well established and well-liked personality, Maid Marian remained a fixture in the rural morris long after the dance separated from the church and from Robin Hood games.

There is a curious footnote to this passage in the evolution of the morris provided by Robert Langham[21] in his well-known letter describing a series of entertainments given before Queen Elizabeth at Kenilworth Castle in 1575. One of the pieces he records is a lampoon of a country bride ale. A principal part of the proceedings is a general procession which involved in the groom's train,

... a liuely morisdauns, according too the auncient manner, six daunserz, Mawdmarion, and the fool.   (Laneham 1968, 28)

The 'auncient manner' here almost certainly means simply 'old fashioned'; thus some of the humour rested on the notion that rustics were hopelessly out of fashion in comparison with the sophisticates of the court. There is also the implication that the wedding of peasants, deliberately represented by Langham as unlovely, was as grotesque as the choreographed courtship of a shemale by a fool, from the point of view of the urbane. More important for present purposes, the description indicates that the cycle of parody and imitation had by this time come full circle. The rural dance that began as a satire of the manners of the court had, in turn, been satirized within the court, indicating that the flow of dance ideas in the evolution of forms was not simply linear nor uni-directional, but partly cyclic and two-way. And meaning becomes piled on meaning: the new (courtly) Maid Marian, for example, is a burlesque of a parody – a boy playing a woman imitating the lewd bawdiness of a country dancer who is mocking the virginal damosel of the tournaments.

The figure of the friar was not able to undergo the same kind of transformations in the dance as Maid Marian. Certainly he was free-floating enough to be able to break away from Robin Hood plays and become part of the morris, but his involvement there was short-lived. A glance back at the seriation of characters (figure 21, p.158) shows that his popularity rose and fell in roughly the same era as Robin Hood's. While the morris was part of the Robin Hood plays the friar could dance in it, playing the part of the fool (or perhaps sometimes vying with the fool) in his courtship of the lady, and thus providing, through his character, a strong link between the play and the dance. When the dance and play separated, the link was no longer necessary, so the friar's character metamorphosed back into that of the fool, who had a more general basis for humour, and perhaps more universal appeal.

There is no question that, apart from general entertainment associated with May games and Robin Hood plays, the morris dance's function at rural church ales was economic, and in such a way that made it quite different from its courtly and urban counterparts. Both courtly and urban morris in the sixteenth century were spectacles, sometimes extraordinarily lavish, that cost their sponsors considerable money and generated no revenues, because they were parts of events that were concerned solely with display. For the courts, the financial burden of producing the dance was less of a problem than for the guilds who, as inflation began to bite in the 1530s and 1540s, grumbled about increased costs, then found small ways to generate income (such as hiring out the costumes), and finally scaled down or abandoned their sponsorship altogether. But in the countryside the morris was a major drawing card at income-producing events, and so exactly the opposite economic forces from those of urban settings were called into play over the course of the sixteenth century. That is, as inflation worsened there was increasing need for parishes to make money, so there were more ales, providing more opportunities for dancing.

Simply put, the economic ills of the mid-sixteenth century simultaneously killed urban guild morris and promoted rural church morris. Thus, the shift of focus of morris activity from cities to the countryside was not simply a matter of shifting economic and social values (although these played a part) but, more specifically, a function of the way the dances were tied to their contexts. This also begins to explain why the dance evolved so rapidly in this era in the countryside. For the dance to serve its function of attracting paying customers to ales, it had, *a fortiori*, to be attractive, that is, not stale and hackneyed but new and vital.

There are a number of related reasons why ales gained such prominence in the countryside in the sixteenth century – all ultimately stemming from national economic policies – which, in turn, led to such popularity of morris dancing. But as the century progressed, the increase in ales and dancing brought them to the notice of high-ranking clerics, and, as puritanism gained power, set the stage for a clash of ideologies with dancing serving as a symbol for both sides.

All ales raised money, but certain types were distinguished from one another by what the money was being raised for. A clerk ale was held to provide the annual stipend for the church clerk, a help ale gathered emergency funds for those with special needs, and a bride ale gave the newly-weds an economic boost. But by far the commonest purpose for the generic church ale (often named for the holiday on which it was celebrated – Whitsun ale, Hock ale, Christmas ale) was the upkeep of the church fabric and its contents.

Church ales, as such, are not recorded before the fifteenth century because there are no churchwardens' accounts extant from that period. They first appear in church accounts in the early fifteenth century and then dramatically increase in popularity until bishops begin moving against them in the 1570s.[22] Figure 22 gives a rough indication of the trends through the fifteenth and sixteenth centuries based on extant accounts, which, though sparse and uneven, provide a sufficient sample to quantify. From the beginning of the fifteenth century to the beginning of the sixteenth there was a

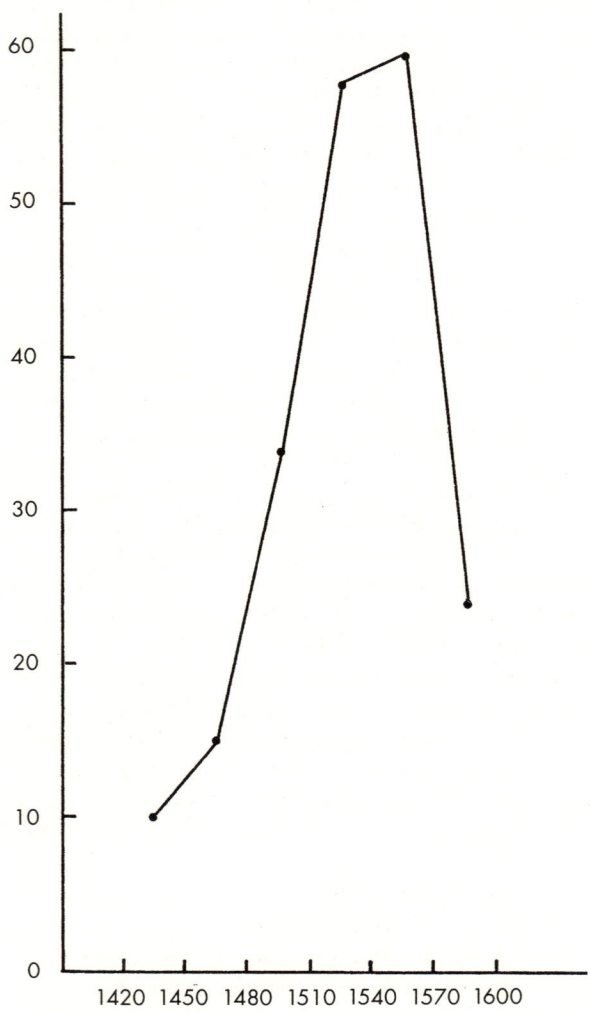

Figure 22: Graph of occurrence of ales

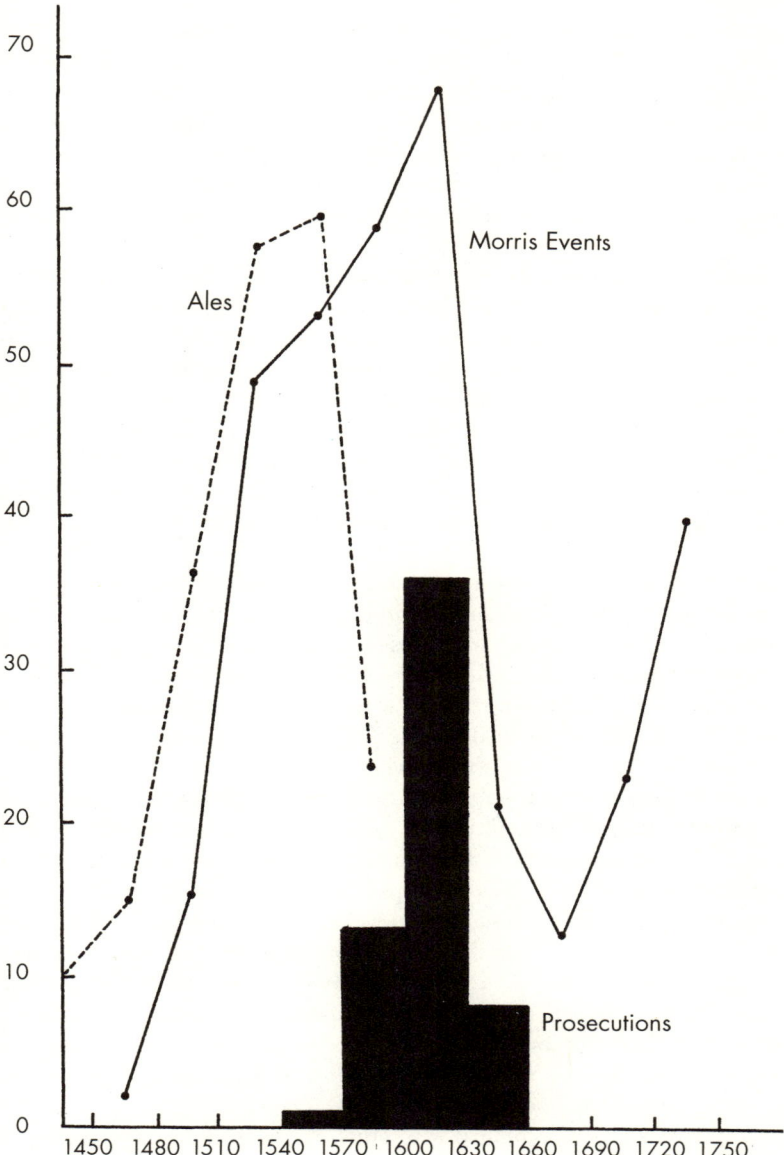

Figure 23: Graph of absolute number of ales and morris events linked to the rise of prosecutions

steep increase in the number of ales, with strong interest maintained through the third quarter of that century, followed by a precipitous decline. Comparison of this graph with figure 23, indicating the absolute number of morris events in the period, shows a certain congruence in shape but a difference in timing. The number of morris events increases steeply, holds steady, then sharply declines, but the main increase starts at the beginning of the sixteenth century when the occurrence of church ales was peaking, and the peak of morris events coincides with the virtual demise of church ales.

That ales should rise in popularity before morris dancing makes sense in that the context must precede the content; also morris dancing was a significant expense that could not be justified until the economics of ales was clear empirically to the church-wardens. That ales should decline before morris dancing is also understandable in that, while both were odious to church reformers, the former were more easily curtailed than the latter because they were a function of the church itself and could be suppressed by decree, whereas morris dancers could hive off and find other performance contexts (which, as the graph shows, is what they did). Because of this free-floating, independent nature, it took both decree and aggressive prosecution to curb the morris.

The great increase in the popularity of church ales may be attributed to three factors: first, changes in field systems and agricultural methods, which resulted in lost revenues to the churches; second, the ravages of inflation; and, third, extraordinary expenses incurred because of the Reformation and Counter-Reformation. Some of these issues, particularly the first, are taken up in more detail in later chapters, but they are mentioned here, in brief, to set the context for discussion of the economic and social effects of Puritan reforms in the church.

Enclosure (and engrossing) coupled with rural depopulation in the fifteenth and sixteenth centuries, caused a significant loss of tithes in country parishes.[23] As land was enclosed many incumbents lost the great tithe, which was often partly (but not completely) compensated for by increases in glebe lands. As these inroads were made into church income, ales and other sources of revenue became increasingly important. But there is no straightforward correlation between rate of enclosure and incidence of ales, so this is not a monolithic factor by any means. Between 1455 and 1607 the highest rates of enclosure were in the country's midsection (Berkshire, Oxfordshire, Buckinghamshire, Bedfordshire, Middlesex, Northamptonshire, and Leicestershire) but there are no more ales recorded in these counties at that time than in the surrounding areas of the south and midlands.

Enclosure, however, was combined with other factors – such as the leasing of demesne lands – to produce a steadily growing rural class of rentier farmers and wage labourers who had the disposable income necessary to patronize ales. Consequently, while ales were quite widespread, those that involved large cash sums to provide lavish entertainments and feasting (as opposed to those that depended more on in kind contributions, and tended to be smaller), do seem to be concentrated in the very section where enclosure and leasehold were expanding most rapidly. It was this kind of ale that typically sponsored morris dancing, because of the reliance of the dance on a significant cash flow to pay for costumes and equipment. Thus, church-sponsored morris dance is also grouped largely in the country's midsection. (see figures 24–32 at the end of this chapter).

It is also interesting to note that as official church sentiment turned against dancing on church property, and morris dancers sought other venues, there was a sustained outburst against them, because they took their revenues with them, thus depriving the church further and, perhaps in turn, hastening the pace of episcopal opposition and prosecution. The following is taken from a polemical poem by Henry Farley written at the height of church persecution of morris:

> To see a strange out-landish Fowle,
> A quaint Baboon, an Ape, an Owle,
> …
> A morris-dance, a Puppit play,
> Mad Tom to sing a Roundelay,
> …
> A Rimers Iests, a Iuglers cheats,
> A Tumbler shewing cunning feats,
> Or Players acting on the Stage,
> There goes the Bounty of our Age:
> But vnto any pious motion,
> There's little coine, and lesse deuotion.   (Farley 1621, sig. E4–E4v)

The implication here is that people with disposable cash are spending it on morris dancers (and other impious recreations) and not on the church. If the morris is stopped then the church might well get some of this disposable cash back in donations, as it did when it sponsored the morris.

There is no need to become embroiled in arguments concerning the causes and precise nature of inflation in the mid-sixteenth century. That prices rose precipitously, and wages lagged further and further behind them, is universally acknowledged. Rural parish economies that were marginal at the best of times could ill afford even modest inflation, and had to look to all means at their disposal to stay solvent.

Aside from the costs of general maintenance, the Reformation and Counter-Reformation brought unusual expenses on local parishes. Churchwardens' accounts indicate that the parishes had to bear the burden of reorganizing their interiors according to Protestant dogma under Edward VI, of returning them to proper Catholic form under Mary, and then of restoring their Protestant furnishings under Elizabeth – all within the space of ten years or so (roughly between 1548 and 1558). This was especially true further south where visitations were more frequent (the same region where ales were frequent in this period).

All the while that parishes were able to mount ales and other fund-raisers it was theoretically possible for them to stay solvent despite these extraordinary expenses. However, there was not an unlimited supply of cash available to be exploited, and inflation cut into the buying power of what there was. Therefore, through the 1540s to the 1560s the incidence of ales reached its peak. But the accession of Elizabeth also saw a number of clergymen, exiled under Mary, return with a new puritan zeal, having been schooled in Europe in the ways of Luther, Calvin, and Zwingli. To them these ales, although employed as a way to fund the changes they desired, were an abomination to be exterminated. The stage was set for a battle on several fronts: between the episcopacy and the Presbyterians, between the political interests of the monarchy and those of the church, between the secular and ecclesiastical polities, and between the economics of local churches and the ideology of the church. Sandwiched in the middle of all these confrontations was morris dancing, which, like so many customs, became symbolic of all that was good or ill in the realm, depending on where you stood.

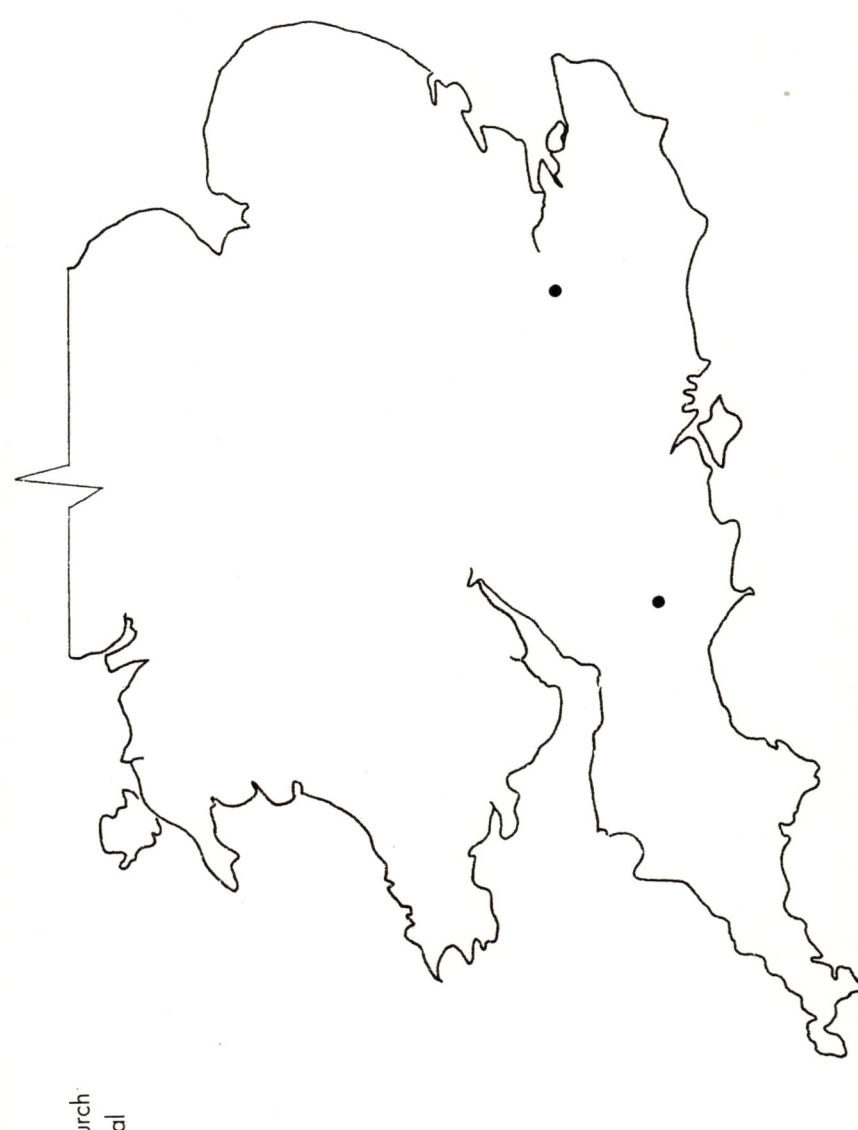

Figure 24: Distribution of morris events (church and rural), 1466–1510

Church
Rural

●
◄

Figure 25: Distribution of morris events (church and rural), 1511–40

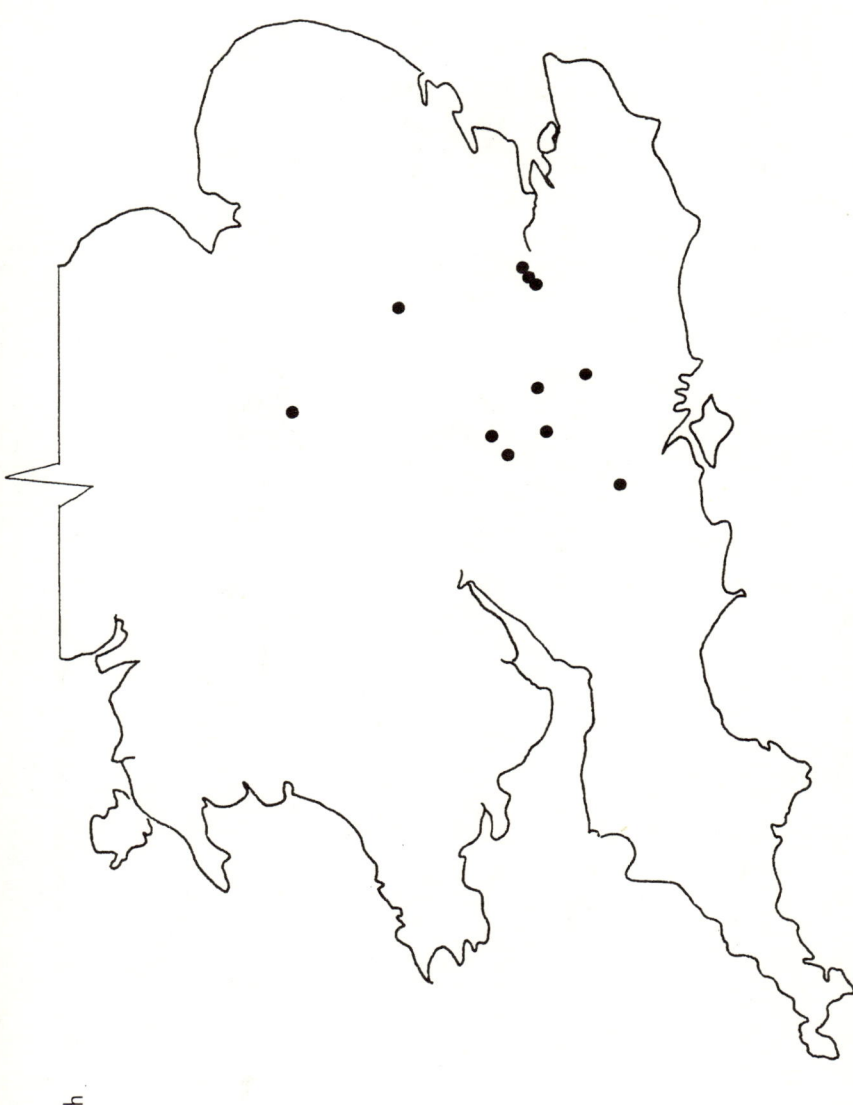

● Church
▲ Rural

Figure 26: Distribution of morris events (church and rural), 1541–70

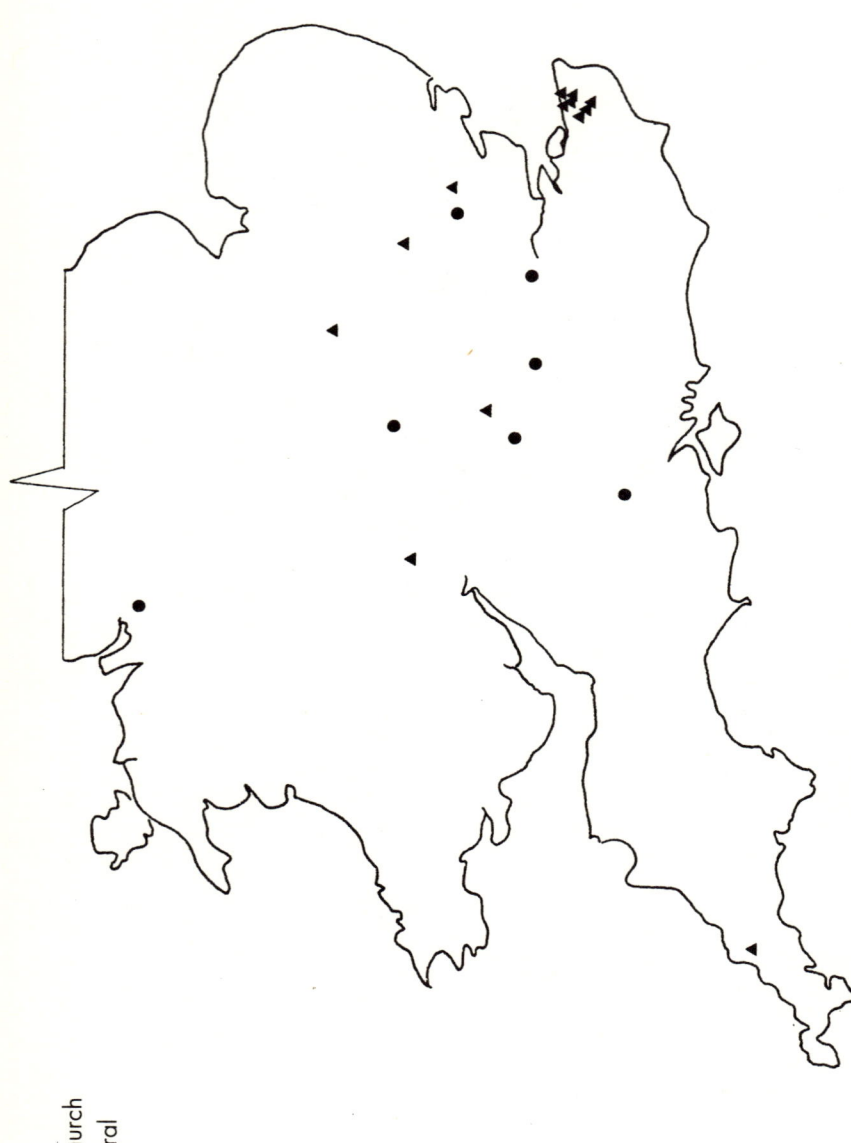

Figure 27: Distribution of morris events (church and rural), 1571–1600

Church
Rural

● Church
◀ Rural

● Church
▲ Rural

Figure 28: Distribution of morris events (church and rural), 1601–30

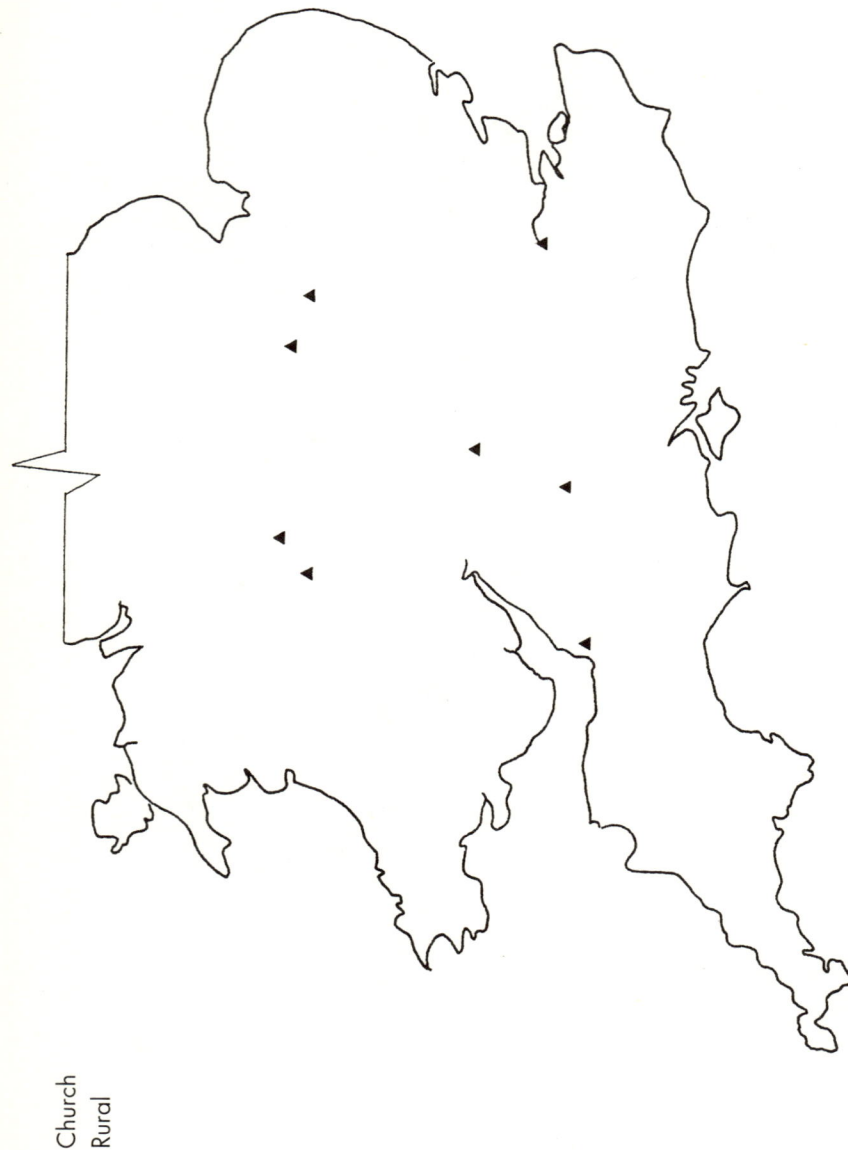

Church ●
Rural ▲

Figure 29: Distribution of morris events (church and rural), 1631–60

Church
Rural

●
▲

Figure 30: Distribution of morris events (church and rural), 1661–90

Church
Rural

● Church
◄ Rural

Figure 31: Distribution of morris events (church and rural), 1691–1720

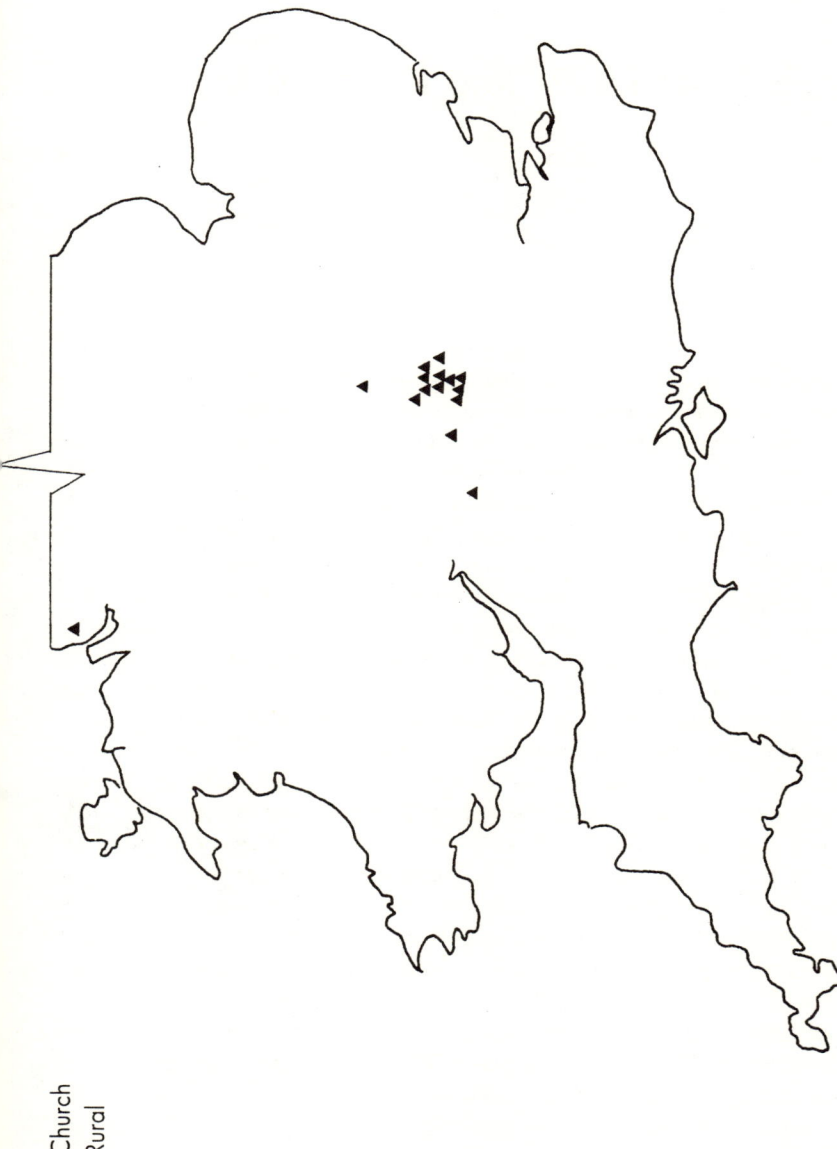

● Church
▲ Rural

Figure 32: Distribution of morris events (church and rural), 1721–50

7

Church Proscription and Prosecution

The church's reversal of policy towards morris dancing from active support to rigorous prosecution marked a significant turning point in the evolution and diffusion of the dance. Nothing could be more dramatic than the evidence presented in figure 23 (p 173), which documents the absolute number of morris events over our period, superimposed with statistics concerning church prosecutions. The key point to notice is that in the 1601–30 period church prosecutions reached their zenith, and in the following period (1631–60) there was a calamitous decline in dance events.

Although the turnabout seems almost instantaneous and dramatic, the theological and legal preliminaries were, in fact, long and complex (and not readily represented by a simple graphing of overt actions). First, it is important to understand that although opposition to morris dancing came from a number of directions, the most decisive was from the episcopacy, which, in this stance, was directly at odds with the needs and values of local parishes. The clash was more a matter of centralized ideology versus parochial customs than of new versus old doctrines. There was certainly nothing novel, nor especially puritanical, in the bishops being opposed to potentially sacrilegious folk traditions of the church, as Robert Grosseteste's thirteenth-century injunctions against various ludi attest. But the widespread vitriolic condemnation of the dance and its virulent persecution in the sixteenth and early seventeenth centuries owes a great deal to the political and social circumstances of Queen Elizabeth's Protestant settlement, with which morris dancing became unwittingly, but inextricably, entangled.[1]

Church opposition to morris dancing manifested itself in three ways that are to some extent separable for analytic purposes. Beginning around 1540 sermons and polemical writings directly or indirectly moralized about the dance and dancers. Then in 1571 specific episcopal injunctions against morris dancing appeared for the first time, and rapidly became standard in visitation articles. Henceforth ecclesiastical courts prosecuted dancers: most actively in the early seventeenth century. It might seem that the second two modes of opposition were effectively the same but, while it is true that prosecution could not have occurred without the relevant laws in place, the realms of legal *fact* and legal *practice* are distinguishable. There were, for example, many dioceses that banned morris dancing but never prosecuted anyone for dancing. Furthermore, laws opposing morris dancing existed on the books long after active prosecutions had ceased. Conversely, there are a few instances of dancers being prosecuted under general statutes when no specific ordinance against morris dancing existed. Although all three modes operated simultaneously for many decades, there were times when one voice was louder than the others, and times of clashes between them. Because these activities in relation to morris dancing were occurring against a background of religious and sociopolitical turmoil I shall dissect them into several parts based on major political periods – the reign of Elizabeth, the reigns of James I and VI and Charles I taken as a unit, the Interregnum, and the Restoration.

THE ELIZABETHAN ERA (1558–1603)

Prior to Elizabeth I's reign there was the occasional gibe aimed sideways by reforming clerics at morris dancing in their attacks on popish practices. For example, Hugh Latimer in a sermon preached in 1552 says:

Here were a good place to speak against our clergymen which go so gallantly now-a-days. I hear say that some of them wear velvet shoes and velvet slippers. Such fellows are more meet to dance the morrice-dance than to be admitted to preach.   (Latimer 1845, 83)

Latimer here is using a mildly derisory tone towards morris dancing but dancers are not the main target of his invective. Rather, he is ridiculing Catholic clergy and their over-lavish vestments by comparing them to morris dancers who dress well, but are figures of fun. Even such references are scarce, however, although this casual association made between morris and old popish customs was to prove a hardy notion.

In some ways the opposition of the Puritans to morris is easy to understand because of their general antagonism towards all dancing and 'frivolous' pastimes, but it is a great mistake to assume that it was their attitudes that led directly to the prosecution of dancers. Although their polemical writings stirred up enormous controversy, they did not, for the most part, occupy the kinds of positions in the ecclesiastical hierarchy that would allow them to legislate and litigate on such matters. Instead, it was the more moderate bishops – who did have the power – who undertook the bulk of the actions against morris, and who ultimately must bear the responsibility for its subsequent decline. But they did not do so because they supported the Puritans in this area – quite the contrary. It was the constant mutual enmity between Puritans and moderates that created the context within which morris became a helpless shuttlecock.

Precisely because the Puritans did not have the power to condemn morris through their actions, they were forced to proclaim their views through voluminous philippics, and even though these were subject to official censorship, a great deal of their point of view found its way into print. Probably their best-known assertion is that dancing is by its physical nature a powerful inducement to lustful sexual activity (which is inherently sinful because its primary purpose is pleasure rather than procreation). Stubbes provides us with a substantial dissertation on the topic, which is unquestionably typical of many other writers of the period since a great deal of it is cribbed (see, for example, Stubbes 1583, sig. N1).

Stubbes's arguments range far and wide, but for present purposes the main points are that dancing involves gestures, such as hugging and touching, that induce lust, and others that are directly imitative of sexual activity, which likewise act as powerful provocations. He is, therefore, particularly contemptuous of mixed dancing. During his tirade on the ills of dancing he refers directly to morris only fleetingly and does not refer to its sexual nature specifically, but his general points apply nonetheless, since the sexual themes in the church-sponsored morris of the time were so blatant.

Other commentators (from whom Stubbes borrows materials) make the link between sexuality and the morris quite plain, however. Christopher Fetherston in *A Dialogue against Light, Lewde and Lascivious Dancing*, for example, deals at length with the sexual aspects of morris dancing and May games:

For the abuses whiche are comitted in your maygaymes are infinite. The first wherof is this, that you doe vse to attyre men in womans apparell, whom you doe most commenly call may-marrions, whereby you infringe that straight commaundement which is giuen in Deut. 22.5. That men must not put on womens apparrell for feare of enormities. Nay, I myself haue seene in a maygaime a troupe, the greater part wherof hath been men, and yet haue they been attyred so like vnto women, that theyr faces being hidde (as they were indeede) a man coulde not discerne them from women. What an horrible abuse was this? what abhominable sinnes might haue herevpon ensued? The seconde abuse, which of all other is the greatest, is this, that it hath been toulde that your morice dauncers haue daunced naked in nettes: what greater entisement vnto naughtines, could haue been deuised? The thirde abuse, is, that you (because you will loose no tyme) doe vse commonly to runne into woodes in the night time, amongst maidens, to fet bowes, in so muche, as I haue hearde of tenne maidens which went to fet May, and nine of them came home with childe.   (Fetherston 1582, sigs. D7–D8)

Although the exact meaning of the reference to morris dancing here is obscure, and nowhere else is the image of morris dancers dancing 'naked in nettes' corroborated, nonetheless the general implication that morris dancing is expressly sexual is apparent, even though the evidence is hearsay and perhaps deliberately hyperbolic. To the essential lustful sexuality of the dance Fetherstone adds two factors that further aggravate its condemnation in his eyes. In the first place, the dance involves the character Maid Marian played by a man dressed as a woman, which practice is not only opposed by Mosaic law as it stands, but is also an inducement to homosexuality. In the second place, the dance is an enticement to fornication, and the clergy who assent to such dances are equally susceptible to their consequences.

Although the notion that morris dancing is directly and indirectly sexual is the most prominent strain in Puritan polemics, several other themes, perhaps linked to the dominant one, occur with reasonable regularity. In particular the dances are spoken of as devilish and heathen. Generally the implication that morris dancing is devilish has no special meaning other than that it is sinful and is to be catalogued with a host of other traditional customs, as in the mockingly ironic poem 'The Practice of the Divell' by Laurence Ramsey (Ramsey 1577, sig. Cij). But Christopher Fetherston, in his diatribe against May games and morris, provides a more specific reason for the devilish appellation:

But are these all the abuses whiche doe followe your maygames? nay, nay, there be many more than these. What mere madnes is this, that a man whome God hath endued with witt & reason, shoulde put on a noddies coate, and feigne him selfe to bee a foole, and to be destitute of both these most precious giftes? doeth hee not thinke that if the Lorde shoulde deale with him in Justice, that hee doeth deserue to be made a foole against his will, which playeth the foole so willingly? What a shame, nay what a sinne is it for him, who wilbe angrie with that man which shall not call him a Christian: to play the part of a diuel, who is an vtter enemie to Christ and al Christians?   (Fetherston 1582, sig. D8)

These sentiments help to explain and pull together many of the foregoing issues. Featherston is following a standard Elizabethan Protestant philosophy in arguing that all beings have a God-given place in the world which it is their duty, their vocation, to cherish and nurture. To oppose one's natural being is clearly the work of the devil. The devil opposes God in all things, and all things that oppose God spawn ultimately from him. So the lucid person who plays the fool, the sensible man who drinks himself witless, the man who dresses as a woman, the man who seduces another man (in the guise of a woman) – viz., morris dancers – threaten not only their own souls, but the harmony of the world.

Humans are uniquely capable of threatening the world order in this manner because of their median position in the chain of creation. Within them are united the carnal nature of animals and the spiritual nature of angels, and theirs is the power, via free will, to hold the middle ground, or move away from it towards either pole. Narcissistic adornment of the body and the choreographed representation of sexual appetite automatically serve to drag the morris dancer in the direction of the carnal.

But it is also important to understand that Elizabethans saw all humans as occupying a position in a hierarchy that was a microcosm of the greater cosmic order, with kings and nobles closer to the angels and the peasantry closer to the beasts. The lower orders were already dangerously near the carnal by their very natures, so that morris dancing and other lecherous pleasures could readily cause their further descent, and upset the stability of the entire system.

As noted in chapter 1, some Elizabethan Puritans also wrote of the folk customs of their age as sinful because in their carnality they replicated the exercises of 'pagans' or 'heathens' whose unsaved natures condemned them to bodily excesses and to ultimate damnation. Thus Stubbes writes of the maypole:

And then fall they to daunce about it [the maypole] like as the heathen people did at the dedication of the Idols, whereof this is a perfect pattern, or rather the thing it self.

(Stubbes 1583, sig. M4)

The visitation book of Winchester in like manner condemns a range of folk customs including the morris, and links the customs of heathens directly to devil worship (see p. 4).

As well as simply finding reasons to assail certain customs, the Puritan polemicists were also trying to find a way to bridge their concerns and those of the episcopacy, from whom they were so widely separated on key ethical and political issues and, if possible, to shift moderates to a more radical position by force of argument. As it happens, the accusation that morris dancing was heathen proved to be just such a nexus because 'pagan' was equatable with 'devilish superstition,' as was 'popery'; and all sides readily agreed that popery was the common enemy (see, for example, Moresinus 1594). The actual link in the Elizabethan mind between paganism and popery, going back to Polydor Vergil, was the city of Rome. Elizabethan Puritans, when they spoke of paganism, did not mean any pre-Christian culture (and certainly not pre-Christian Britain), but were specifically referring to ancient Rome, pagan capital of the classical world. According to a well-known Reformation argument, the Catholic church, because its capital was Rome, had become heir to the paganism of that city, and, thus, a great many traditions of the Roman church (including traditional sports and recreations) were seen as descendants of pagan customs.

The following extract from Samuel Harsnet's *A Declaration of Egregious Popish Impostures* is one of the first clear statements of what was to become a standard slander under the first Stuarts, namely that morris dancing is popish and, as such, is the work of devils incarnate. Sara is a mad woman (possessed by devils) who in this piece acts as the central lady round whom four other devils cavort accompanied by their liverymen, signifying how the morris corrupts not only its practitioners, but all who follow it:

Frateretto, Fliberdigibbet, Hoberdidance, Tocobatto were foure devils of the round, or Morrice, whom Sara in her fits, tuned together, in measure and sweet cadence. And least you should conceive, that the devils had no musicke in hell, especially that they would goe a maying without theyr musicke, the Fidler comes in with his Taber, & Pipe, and a whole Morice after him, with motley visards for theyr better grace. These four had forty assistants under them, as themselves doe confesse.   (Harsnet 1603, 49)

The idea that the morris was heathenish, devilish, and popish did indeed have an impact on the episcopacy, although such accusations were not the sole cause of the dance's official condemnation.

The proscription of morris dancing by the episcopacy began in 1571 coincident with two major events in English ecclesiastical history – the adoption of the Thirty-Nine Articles of canon law, and the appointment of Edmund Grindal to the archdiocese of York. Both were to a great extent responses to a Catholic crisis that had been engulfing Elizabeth, represented by such events as the papal bull excommunicating the queen, and the Catholic rebellion of the northern earls. The articles sought to solidify the Elizabethan religious settlement and place the nature of conformity beyond dispute. Grindal was sent to York, articles in hand, to root out Catholicism and recusant practices at the local level in order to eliminate the base of support for future rebellions. Thus, immediately on his assumption of the position, he issued a series of injuctions to the clergy and laity of the province and in May of 1571 began a visitation of all parishes based on these articles.

As one might expect, Grindal's injunctions and articles for enquiry set out Elizabethan orthodoxy very clearly, and established the means for educating the laity in it, and the penalties for negligence. But they are also shot through with direct and indirect references to papists and popery. Prior to the visitation he wrote that the province was

not well affected to godly religion: among the people there are many remnants of the old. They keep Holy days and fasts abrogated: they offer money, eggs, etc., at the burial of their dead: they pray on beads etc.; so it seemeth to be, as it were, another church, rather than a member of the rest.   (Grindal to Cecil 29 August 1570, in Frere 1910, 3:253)

His special task was to eliminate all such superstitious customs. Morris dancing might well have come under this rubric – certainly by the Puritans' lights – but its attachment to Catholicism was much more indirect than, say, praying in Latin or using a rosary. Certainly morris dancing was connected with the old religion, but it was not a direct outgrowth of its theology. But nor was it merely a profane abuse, such as adultery or drunkenness, to be condemned as sinful regardless of the circumstances. Grindal's injuctions deal forcefully with such matters, but in a completely separate section of articles. Rather, morris dancing was a profane activity that became an abuse

when directly supported by the church or when it interfered with the orderly functioning of the church as a Christian institution (as it had done in Catholic times). Its
proscription, therefore, fit the standard Reformation mission – on which moderates
and radicals agreed – of returning the church to its central Christian purpose.

Article 44 of Grindal's injunctions states:

Item that the minister and churchewardens shall not suffer anye lordes of misrule or sommerr
Lordes or ladyes or anye disguised persons or others in christmasse or at may gammes or anye
minstrels morice dauncers or others at Ryshebearinges or at any other tymes to come vnrever-
entlye into anye churche or chappell or churchyeard and there daunce or playe anye vnseemelye
partes with scoffes ieastes wanton gestures or rybaulde talke namely in the tyme of divine service
or of anye sermon.   (Frere 1910, 3:291)

This is the first record of morris dancing being officially banned, and the specific
language and associations are worth close examination as a means of understanding
what Grindal was really concerned about. First, though, it must be understood that
these articles and injunctions were not made up from whole cloth. All such documents
of the period are patchworks of scraps taken from canon law and earlier sets of
injunctions and articles. Examination of John Parkhurst's injunctions for Norwich,
1569, shows that the spine of Grindal's article was taken directly from them, or
from Parkhurst's model, now lost:

Item, that no person or persons calling themselves the Lords of Misrule in the Christmas time,
or other irreverent persons at any other time, presume to come into the church unreverently,
playing their lewd parts with scoffing, jesting or ribaldry talk, and if any such have already
offended herein, to present them and their names to the Ordinary.   (Frere 1910, 3:209)

Grindal's additions to this basic framework are significant, and reveal a great deal
about his attitude towards morris dancing. Parkhurst's article is relatively clear cut and
simple: it bans the type of performance that could go under the general heading of
'Lords of Misrule,' and gives an epitome of the kind of performance that is intended
(i.e., ones that involve 'playing their lewd parts with scoffing, jesting or ribaldry talk').
Summer Lords, morris dancing, mummers, masked players, and so forth could well
be prosecuted under such an article – particularly since the phrase 'or other irreverent persons' gathers them all in – but the basic wording makes it appear that Parkhurst's primary concern was Christmas Lords of Misrule, and the more generalized
language seems to be added as a catchall afterthought whose vagueness could work
for or against a zealous prosecutor.

Grindal's language tightens the article considerably, giving many more specific
references to the kinds of practices that he sees as akin to lords of Misrule (while still

leaving the convenient catchalls in place). Thus he sees Summer Lords and Ladies, May games (which might include Robin Hood and his entourage), disguised performers, minstrels, morris dancers, and rush-bearing ceremonies as sharing a common ground with Lords of Misrule. What seems to be at issue here in Grindal's mind is the maintenance of social order; these practices both explicitly and implicitly challenge that order in ways already rehearsed in chapter 5. The point is that he was not just trying to eradicate Catholicism and thereby create a healthy uniformity of worship which would act as a check on rebellion; he was also seeking to promote a strong sense of obedience to the secular and ecclesiastical hierarchy as everyone's God-ordained duty. Thus his 1571 injunctions also contain the following:

Item, you shall exhort your parishioners to obedience towards their Prince, and all other that be in authority ... and if ye cannot preach, ye shall teach children to read, to write, and to know their duties towards God, their Prince, parents and all others ...   (Frere 1910, 3:281)

Lords of Misrule and their kind preached just the opposite. May games were especially problematic because Robin Hood was notoriously antiepiscopal, and his mocking tone, acceptable in quieter times, had become dangerously politicized. And Friar Tuck, the major link between morris dancing and May games, was triply objectionable. In the first place, he was lecherous and drunken, and so cast the church in a bad moral light. Second, he was a Catholic, so that revelling in his antics could be construed as tacit support for the old ways. Third, he was a friar, a member of a class of mendicants who had historically been a thorn in the side of the bishops, because they were exempt from local episcopal jurisdiction, and answerable only to the pope directly. The essence of the Elizabethan settlement – which Grindal was vigorously enforcing – was that the queen was the head of the church, and there were to be no ecclesiastical authorities to turn to above her or beyond the bounds of her realm. Both Catholics and Puritans bridled at this fusion of church and state; Friar Tuck, although neither the most appealing nor the most direct symbol of transnational religious institutions, served as an emblem of their position. Indeed, Friar Tuck persisted as a popular folk character because so many friars were proverbial in their worldliness, and were so largely because their excesses could not be curbed by local or state authority.

Grindal's additions not only target morris dancing specifically in the list of banned activities, but also reinforce the prohibition via special wording at intervals throughout the text. For example, he adds the prohibition 'and there daunce' to the general ban on coming irreverently into the church, and includes 'wanton gestures' in the list of offensive actions. The general tone of the whole article is not puritanical, so much as a call for general decorum as a means to social harmony, but these phrases do have puritan tones, indicating that Grindal did have some leanings in that direction (or perhaps a greater tolerance for Puritan than for Catholic doctrine), as his later political life was to show.

However, it would not be fair to stress possible puritanical motivations for the ban on morris dancing and other profane activities. The widening of the list of banned activities was to some extent ameliorated by the restrictions on *where* and *when* these activities were unlawful, which, in turn, set up a decades-long controversy. The Puritans saw certain profane activities, such as morris dancing, as offensive and sinful *in principle*, but Grindal's injunctions are careful to specify place and time, leaving open the implication that he was morally neutral to the dance elsewhere and elsewhen. His main concern was the dance *vis-à-vis* the church, not the dance as an absolute moral entity; neither was he apparently interested in policing all aspects of public morality.

Grindal also closed a possible loophole in Parkhurst's injunctions by prohibiting the use, not just of the church but of the churchyard and other ecclesiastical property for morris dancing. Despite Stubbes's assertions, there are few indications that morris dancers made a habit of dancing in the church itself, but the churchyard was a routine venue. Thus, if there had been no widening of the spatial scope of the original prohibition, local churches could have stuck by the letter of the law and still sponsored morris. The new language effectively prevented church patronage. Once the church itself could no longer be in the business of promoting profane activites (which was easily secured by a few suits), the force of prosecution could shift away from the ministers and churchwardens to the dancers themselves. This also meant shifting the emphasis from where they danced to when.

Parkhurst's article does not put any temporal limits on the prohibition of irreverent performances, but Grindal's specifies that the ban applies 'in the tyme of divine service or of anye sermon.' This might seem a superfluous statement inasmuch as parishioners were required, by other articles, to attend divine service on pain of fines or excommunication. If they were attending service as they ought, then they could not be dancing. But attendance laws were notoriously difficult to enforce. In some parishes the churches were too small to accommodate all the villagers were they to show up en masse (and for this reason weddings, which did draw large crowds, were customarily held out of doors). The articles were also rather loose in their wording and allowed a range of excuses for periodic, although not chronic, nonattendance. Thus one could stay within the limits of tolerance of attendance laws and still dance during service time. But it is also important to note that by specifying the temporal limits of the law Grindal was remaining tacitly (and legally) neutral to morris at other times.

The establishment of these spatial and temporal limits on the prohibition of morris dancing had significant class implications. Guildsmen, nobles, and other wealthy patrons of the morris could easily avoid trouble with ecclesiastical authorities by holding their revels on their own premises, and on days other than Sundays. But the poorer classes had fewer options since they had little free time apart from Sundays and other church-mandated holidays, and few places to dance. There was also the more general problem that without church patronage they had to find other sources of revenue for the purchase of costumes, food, and drink. Soliciting contributions from public audiences, without official church sanction, ran them the risk of prosecution for vagabondage or beggary, which carried harsh civil penalties.

It is informative to note in this regard that during Grindal's tenure at York (1570–6) the guild morris in Chester – a major city in his jurisdiction – was active, and continued unfettered by his injunctions. It is also curious to consider that this is the only morris documented within his bailiwick. Morris dancing was simply not a common northern practice at this time. Thus Grindal's injunctions were a token of his attitudes towards certain customs that he knew of from the south of the country, and not a measure of their popularity or diffusion. Also, until he was appointed archbishop of Canterbury in 1576, his were the only articles prohibiting morris.

In 1577 Grindal ordered a visitation of the province of Canterbury and used his articles from York as a model for the new Canterbury articles. The section on Lords of Misrule and so forth was more or less the same:

Whether the Minister & Churchwardens have suffered any Lords of Misrule, or summer Lords, or Ladies, or any disguised persons, or other in Christmas, or at May games, or any Morrice dauncers, or at any other times, to come unreverently into the church or churchyard & there to daunce, or play any unseemely parts, with scoffes, jeastes, wanton gestures, or ribald talke, namely in the time of common prayer. And what they be that committ such disorder, or accompanie or maintayne them.

(Visitation Articles Province Canterbury 1577, sig. Cii, *STC* 10155.3)

But there is one noteworthy omission. He took out the phrase 'or others at Ryshe-bearinges' after 'Morrice dauncers,' presumably on the grounds that rush-bearing was primarily a northern custom, but in so doing he made the sentence ungrammatical.[2] From the historian's point of view, this is a fortuitous circumstance because it allows us extra insights into how Grindal's articles were used as models by other bishops.

First, because the two are slightly different, we know that it was not his York articles that were used as the template for other bishops, but those from Canterbury; and throughout Elizabeth's reign it was almost exclusively bishops from Canterbury province who followed Grindal's lead in banning morris. William Chaderton of Chester was the principal exception and he, like Grindal, had a special mission to root out Catholicism in the north. Chaderton did not use Grindal's article as an exemplar, but created new text which he subsequently took with him when he was translated from Chester to Lincoln. Otherwise all articles issued in the reign of Elizabeth were patterned on Grindal's.

Second, Grindal's language, including the grammatical error, was copied wholesale into five sets of visitation articles issued outside of Canterbury between 1579 and 1584.[3] This fact raises the question of the degree of concern that these bishops had for the prohibited customs included therein. Certainly they were concerned enough to include the article in the first place, but there is also an intimation of a less-than-painstaking care for the legal particulars, suggesting that these customs were by no means their first interest. The key to understanding episcopal attitudes, therefore, is not the simple existence of certain laws, but the record of prosecution, which, incomplete though it may be, supports the general assertion that the proscription of traditional customs was of relatively minor interest to Elizabethan bishops. In addition, other local records seem to indicate a degree of ambivalence towards morris dancing on the part of the authorities, sacred and secular.

Table 3 shows who issued visitation articles against morris dancing in the Elizabethan era and when, and figure 33 indicates the geographic extent of the dioceses in question. There are, no doubt, a great many data missing, but what exist are a reasonable sample, and help elucidate a number of points. Most significant, the period covered is thirty-two years and in that time there were twenty-four metropolitical or diocesan visitations that specifically banned morris dancing. Yet in all that time there are only eleven prosecutions known. Missing data or no, this can hardly be considered a ruthless extermination of the custom, and is mild in comparison with what was to come in later reigns.

Of the eleven prosecutions five are of incumbents or wardens for directly or indirectly supporting morris dancing on church property; the other six involve parishioners for dancing in service time (and usually for absenting themselves from the parish in addition). After Elizabeth's reign the former became an absolute rarity and the latter commonplace. The suggestion is, therefore, that the bishops' overarching concern at this point was to clean house, and then to begin policing the laity once the church as an institution had been purged of offensive practices. This surmise is supported by the chronology of known prosecutions, in that four of the five prosecutions of church officers occurred in the years 1576–85 (and during that time there are no prosecutions of the laity). Prosecutions of the laity did not start until 1590, nearly twenty years after Grindal's first injunctions.

The evidence is sketchy but it appears as if the church officers knuckled under without much of a fight – incumbents, after all, stood to lose their livings, and wardens were subject to serious fines. But the laity were not always so easily cowed, and in some cases fought back as best they could, occasionally taking advantage of the fact that the bishops were not united on this issue. In the face of a persistent prosecutor, however, the common people could not hold out indefinitely because they could be excommunicated which, if the matter were not resolved through penance, could lead to loss of livelihood.

Table 3
Visitation articles banning morris under Elizabeth I

Date	Diocese (or province)	Bishop
1571	York (Province)	Edmund Grindal
1577	Canterbury (Province)	Edmund Grindal
1577	London	John Aylmer
1577	York (Province)	Edwin Sandys
1579	Exeter	John Woolton
1580	Lincoln	Thomas Cooper
1580	Canterbury	Edmund Grindal
1581	Chester	William Chaderton
1581	Salisbury	John Piers
1582	Canterbury	Edmund Grindal
1583	London	John Aylmer
1584	Winchester	Thomas Cooper
1584	Coventry & Lichfield	William Overton
1585	Lincoln	William Wickham
1586	London	John Aylmer
1589	London	John Aylmer
1594	Gloucester & Bristol	John Bullingham
1597	Winchester	William Day
1598	Lincoln	William Chaderton
1598	London	Richard Bancroft
1601	Lincoln	William Chaderton
1601	London	Richard Bancroft
1603	Winchester	Thomas Bilson
1603	Bristol	John Thornborough

Thus, for example, in 1602 Miles Conney of Tedstone Delamere in Herefordshire, was brought before James Bailie LLD, in Hereford Cathedral consistory, to answer for having danced the morris during divine service.[4] He immediately confessed and was ordered to do penance and supply the names of those who had danced with him, which he did. Most of those whom he implicated (including his brother and sister it seems) appeared at the next court day and, after penance, were dismissed. But several appear to have put up at least a passive fight. Richard Brooke of Avenbury was impeached and ordered to appear before the court. When he failed to appear he was excommunicated, and by the beginning of the following year the court recorded that he still had not appeared and the excommunication stood. Henry Boyce, also of Avenbury, was similarly ordered to appear and did so, confessing and offering to do penance. However, when next ordered to appear he could not certify having done penance, and had to be ordered to appear again. It is also worth noting that a Tedstone Delamere

Figure 33: Boundaries of dioceses in Tudor England and Wales

parishioner was back at the same court two years after this case was resolved on a similar charge.

Thus the common people could, at best, passively resist the church through inactivity, delaying, and recidivism. But citizens of higher standing sometimes took more active measures. For example, on 20 May 1589 the constable of Banbury hundred, supposedly in support of ecclesiastical law, sent out several edicts akin to the following to civil officers within his jurisdiction:[5]

Precept from Richard Wheatlye, Constable of the Hundred of Banbury, to Wm. Long, Constable of Nethorp and Cothorp, to take down all May-poles within his district and to repress and put down all Whitsun-ales, May-games, and Morris-dances, and utterly to forbid any wakes or fairs to be kept.   (Lemor 1865, 601)

But in this he ran afoul of John Danvers, sheriff of Oxfordshire who, two days later, wrote to the lord chancellor that he had,

... been obliged to acquaint the Archbishop of Canterbury with the bad proceedings of Anthony Cope and others of the town of Banbury, who under the plea of religion were practising to abolish most pastimes used in the country, as May-poles, Morris-dances, Whitsun-ales, and others to the great discontentment of Her Majesty's loving subjects. Desires that the matter may be considered by the Council.   (Lemor 1865, 601)

Which means that some of 'Her Majesty's loving subjects' had promptly taken it upon themselves to complain directly to Danvers, who, in turn, supported them against this outburst of Puritan zeal, which he accused the radical Presbyterian Anthony Cope of fomenting. Cope, at least, was quick to reply to the charge in a letter of 25 May 1589 (perhaps recalling a spell in the Tower for having proposed Puritan reforms to the church in parliament):

Anthony Cope to the Council. Defends himself from the malice of Mr Danvers, the sheriff, and prays to be heard at the Council table. Protests that he never had any suspicious meetings about religion. Has never restrained Whitsun-ales and Morris-dances.   (Lemor 1865, 602)

Danvers directed part of his attack via appeal to the archbishop of Canterbury because Banbury was a peculiar and therefore not subject to normal diocesan jurisdiction. But it is interesting to note that the see was occupied at the time by John Whitgift, harrier of Puritans. He had taken the position on Grindal's death in 1583, at a time when Grindal was only barely surviving Elizabeth's wrath for certain puritan sympathies, and Whitgift was storming from one anti-Puritan crusade to another, having set his star high in the queen's eye with his merciless attacks on Thomas Cartwright.

Whitgift's surviving Visitation articles from Worcester and Canterbury are notable in that they do *not* contain prohibitions of ales and morris dances, and this must have been deliberate policy on his part, given how widespread the ban that followed the Grindal text was, and how simple and common it was to cut and paste articles. His apparent tolerance for traditional customs may have created the tone that prevented overzealous prosecutions in the Elizabethan era, despite the efforts made by the likes of Grindal and Chaderton to codify doctrine. Danvers's appeal to him seems to confirm this point of view, and establishes the notion that bishops prosecuted morris dancers less because these bishops had puritanical inclinations and more because morris and like sports represented the old (lax) ways of Rome.

Whitgift's fervour in consolidating the Elizabethan settlement was also the prime catalyst for the battle of pro- and antiepiscopal pamphlets that became known as the Marprelate controversy, and in which morris dancing played a symbolic role on both sides. The Martinist, antiepiscopal pamphleteers used the dance as a symbol of what they conceived to be the papist sympathies of the bishops; that is, they – especially Whitgift and his ilk – supported sinful sports as did Catholics of old. In the following excerpt from the tract 'Hay any worke for Cooper,' for example, John Aylmer, bishop of London ('John of London') is specifically targeted (and in the preamble John Whitgift and Thomas Cooper are also cited):

Alas good priests that their diginitie is like to fall to the ground. It is pitie it should be so/ for they are such notable pulpit men. There is a neighbour of ours/ an honest priest/ who was sometimes (symple as he now standes) a vice in a playe for want of a better/ his name is Gliberie of Hawsteade in Essex/ he goes much to the pulpit. On a time/ I think it was the last Maie/ he went up with a full resolution/ to do his businesse with great commendations. But see the fortune of it. A boy in the Church/ hearing either the sommer Lord with his Maie game/ or Robin Hood with his Morrice daunce going by the church/ out goes the boye. Good Gliberie/ though he were in the pulpit/ yet had a minde to his olde companions abroad (a company of merrie grigs you must think them to be/ as merry as a vice on a stage) seeing ỳ boy going out/ finished his matter presently with John of Londons Amen, saying/ ha/ ye faith boie/ are they there/ then, ha ẁ thee. & so came down and among them hee goes. Were it not then pittie/ that the dignitie of such a priest should decay?   (Marprelate 1589b, 3–4)

The proepiscopal hirelings, such as Thomas Nashe, who were given the task of replying to the Martinists, used the morris as a simple figure of fun or mockery – not something to be taken terribly seriously – and cast the Martinists as characters in the dance (as in *The Return of Pasquill*, Nashe 1589) to suggest that neither the dances nor the Martinists should be taken in earnest.

Thus, all sides in Elizabethan England were complexly pro- or antimorris: it was damnable sin or harmless jape, lawful or unlawful, lawful only at certain times and places or unlawful all the time. Basically the period was more a time of polarization and debate than of concrete action. Morris dancers were not generally prosecuted, and they had as many defenders as adversaries. But the most prominent sponsors of the rural morris, namely, local parishes, were forcibly removed from that role by the episcopacy, which weakened the dance tradition without having to go after the dancers themselves. Furthermore, the battle lines had been drawn and trenches dug deep so that on the death of Elizabeth a bitter struggle was unavoidable.

THE FIRST STUARTS (1603–49)

When James VI of Scotland ascended the English throne as James I in 1603, all sides saw a chance to consolidate their positions. The Puritans nursed hopes that he would support their cause, given the successes of Presbyterianism in his native land; Catholics expected sympathy, given the faith and martyrdom of his mother; and moderate Anglicans believed that his temporal aspirations would accord well with the Elizabethan settlement. But James's unique blend of belief in Calvinism and in the divine right of kings set him on a collision course with all constituencies, and inaugurated a battle royal for the moral and political high ground.

As the forces of Puritanism gained power and momentum in the reigns of James VI and I and Charles I, prosecutions of morris dancers increased significantly, but the volume of rhetoric opposing the dance remained relatively small, and might have been virtually insignificant were it not for specific actions taken by James, and reinforced by his son. Polemics opposing morris dancing ceased around the time of the execution of the Martinist conspirators and did not pick up in number until well into James's reign, becoming a distinct voice mostly under Charles. However, under the Stuarts, unlike in Elizabeth's reign, they were almost exactly counterbalanced (perhaps even provoked) by strong words in favour of the dance. Much of the debate centred on a proclamation in 1618 by James, 'The King's Majesties Declaration to his Subjects concerning Lawfull Sports to be Used,' now more commonly known as the *Book of Sports*, which contained the following:

Our pleasure likewise is, That after the end of Diuine Seruice, Our good people be not disturbed, letted, or discouraged from any lawfull Recreation; Such as dauncing, either men or women, Archerie for men, leaping, vaulting, or any other such harmelesse Recreation, nor from hauing May-Games, Whitson Ales, and Morris-dances, and the setting vp of May-poles and other sports therwith vsed, so as the same be had in due and conuenient time, without impediment or neglect of diuine Seruice: And that women shall haue leaue to carry rushes to the Church for the decoring of it, according to their old custom.   (James VI and I 1982, 107)

In 1633 Charles reissued the proclamation framed with a strongly supportive text (see

James VI and I 1982, 238). The position of both kings on morris dancing, therefore, was moderate, antipuritan, and in the letter (if perhaps not in the spirit), fully in accord with Elizabethan canon law as expressed in visitation articles. The proclamation defined the morris as a 'harmelesse Recreation' provided its practitioners go to church *first*, which did not sit well with Puritan dogma on lewd dances, but which meshed well enough with the sentiments expressed in articles modelled on Grindal's injunctions. Such a stance was designed to provide a base of popular (largely rural) support for the Stuarts, and to encourage honest, public gatherings instead of sedition. In 1632 bishop William Pierce, having surveyed his see of Bath and Wells for the occurrence of church ales at the behest of William Laud, wrote back that they were practically defunct, but that some of the recreations licensed by the *Book of Sports* were still popular. In his opinion,

... if the people should not have their honest and lawful Recreations upon Sundays after evening Prayer, they would go either into tippling houses, talk of matters of the Church or State, or else into Conventicles.   (Cited in Solt 1990, 184)

Under James there were relatively few polemics produced for or against the morris (although there was extensive legal action in which popular sentiment found ample expression). Under Charles the pace picked up considerably with the renewed *Book of Sports* acting as a rallying point for both sides. Moderates supported James and Charles by arguing that traditional sports and recreations were in themselves harmless or of little consequence; what was important for salvation or perdition was the *inner* self, which could not be judged by such outward acts. Motivation was the key, not overt action; morris dancing was not by nature sinful, but only when abused by people acting on sinful impulses. This sentiment is tersely expressed in a sermon by Samuel Burton in 1619:

I would therefore wish that those paineful and zealous Preachers, whiche seeme so dearely to tender the instruction of the people, would for a time forbeare these May-poles and morrice-dances, and other such trifles, vpon which they spend too much of their strength; and would press this point of Obedience more closely to the Consciences of the people. (Burton 1620, 13)

It was greatly expanded upon in such works as Gilbert Ironside's *Seven Questions of the Sabbath Briefly Disputed, after the Manner of the Schooles* (Ironside 1637, 271–2).

James had initially required that his 'Declaration' be published by all bishops in parishes under their control, but many Puritan ministers refused to read it, and James prudently withdrew the order. Charles, in line with his more intractable political nature, renewed the order and stuck with it, causing some Puritans to be deprived of their livings when they refused, and fanning the flames of opposition – hence the greater exchange of pamphlets under Charles, and the greater tolerance for prosecutions (in parishes well away from London) under James.

Apart from an active campaign of prosecution for dancing during service time, as was allowed them by the *Book of Sports*, the Puritans had several responses to the actions of the moderates. Some, such as William Prynne, continued an all-out attack as in this passage from *Histrio-Mastix*, published in response to the *Book of Sports*:

The way to Heaven is too steepe, too narrow for men to dance in, and keepe revell rout: No way is large or smooth enough for capering Roisters, for iumping, skipping, dancing Dames, but that broad beaten pleasant road that leads to Hell. The gate of Heaven is to strait, the way to blisse to narrow, for whole roundes, whole troopes of Dancers to march in together: Men never went as yet by multitudes, much less by Morrice-dancing troopes to Heaven: Alas there are but few who finde that narrow way; they scarce goe two together.   (Prynne 1633, 244)

But this was a dangerous stance to take at a time when Laud ran Star Chamber. On a flimsy pretext Prynne was arrested and convicted of seditious libel, for which offence he had his ears cut off and was imprisoned in the Tower.

Another possibility was to call on the testimony of divine revelation, as did Prynne's collaborator Henry Burton in *A Divine Tragedie Lately Acted*:

At Woolston in the same countrey, where the said Ministers father had been Minister fourty yeers, and by Gods blessing upon his labours, had reformed things very well, yet upon the publication of this book in print [*Book of Sports*], many of the inhabitants the Spring following, were imboldned to set up Maypoles, Morice daunce, and a Whitson ale, continuing their rude revelling a week together, with many affronts to their ancient and reverend Pastor: but it pleased God, not long after, a spark from a Smiths shop, caught in that roome where the ale was brewed, and though means were ready at hand, yet it could not be quenched, but set the house on fire, and presently flew to the barn in which their disorder was, and burnt the same with thirteen dwelling houses more, most of whose Inhabitants were actors or abetters in the same: This is testified by many.   (Burton 1641, 7–8)

This was scarcely any better, for the general Puritan implication here that *jure divino* authority belonged to God alone and could not be superceded by the courts of bishops and kings strongly offended Charles and Laud (who both argued that they governed by divine right). Thus Burton was also convicted of seditious libel, fined £5,000, and sentenced to lose his ears and be imprisoned for life. Prynne was tried as complicit at the same time, likewise fined £5,000, and sentenced to have the stumps of his ears removed, to have his cheeks branded SL ('Seditious Libeler'), and to be imprisoned for life.

A third position, which had slightly better success was to stress the allegation of an association between rural sports and popery. Both James and Charles were notable in their anti-Catholic attitudes, so there was a slim chance for the Puritans to wreak some damage on this course. Burton laid out the issue several years before his conviction in *A Tryall of Private Devotions*:

[John Cosin] saith, they [Puritans] offend ... that condemn the ioyfull festiuitie of this high holy-day, which the Church allowes ... iollity, and iouialty, such as he termes necessary recreations: for example, Rush-bearings, Whitson Ales, Morice-dances, setting vp of May-poles, hearing of a play, or seeing of a Maske, or Dicing and Carding, or bouling or bowsing, or whatsoeuer other Glosse the carnall vulgar may make of this vnlimited ioyful Festiuity or necessary recreation. But, he saith, that this ioyfull Festiuity the Church allowes. What Church? surely none other ... but his holy mother Church of Rome. Indeed that Church allowes a most licentious vnlimited latitude of all such ioyfull Festiuity.   (Burton 1628, sig. F3v)

Their aim, thus, was to accuse individuals, such as Cosin, of backsliding towards Rome and to use these individuals' tolerance of morris dancing, and the like, as an index of their recusant tendencies.

Under James there was a steady stream of visitation articles issued against morris dancing over a wide area – most issued before the *Book of Sports* – and with a geographic preponderance in the north (see table 4). Before the *Book of Sports* was published the articles frequently followed Grindal's wording, but afterwards those following Chaderton's predominate (see appendix B). Chaderton confined himself in the phrasing of his articles to the prophanation of church property itself, and his became the common model in the Stuart period:

First, whether your Church, Chappell, or Chancell, be well and sufficiently repaired, & cleanely kept ... and your Churchyard well fenced, and cleanely kept? And if any default be made in the premisses: or your said Church, Chappel, or Churchyard, be abused or prophaned by any unlawful, or unseemely act, game, or exercise; as by lords of misrule, sommer lords, or ladies, pipers, rushbearers, morice-dancers, pedlers, bowlers, beare-wards, and such like. Then through whose default, and what be the names of the offenders in that behalfe.

(Visitation Articles Diocese of Lincoln [*STC* 10236.5] 1604, sig. A3)

By the reign of Charles the issuance of articles prohibiting morris had tailed off and was mostly confined to the north (see table 5).

The incidence of lawsuits against dancers follows the same general trend as the issuance of visitation articles – vigorous in the early years of James's reign and dwindling to a trickle under Charles. Two contradictory forces may be at work here. The most obvious is the increase in tolerance brought about by the publication and republication of the *Book of Sports*, and by Laud's general stance on local customs. But it is also

Table 4

Visitation articles banning morris under James VI and I

Date	Diocese (or province)	Bishop
1604	London	Richard Bancroft
1604	Lincoln	William Chaderton
1604	Chester	Richard Vaughan
1607	York (Province)	Tobias Matthew
1607	Lincoln	William Chadderton
1610	Lichfield & Coventry	Richard Neile
1610	York	Tobias Matthew
1617	Chester	Thomas Morton
1618	Lincoln	George Montaigne
1618	York	Tobias Matthew
1619	Oxford	John Howson
1622	Oxford	John Howson
1622	Lincoln	John Williams
1623	York (Province)	Tobias Matthew

Table 5

Visitation articles banning morris under Charles I

Date	Diocese (or province)	Bishop
1628	Winchester	Richard Neile
1629	York Metrop.	Samuel Harsnet
1629	Carlisle	Barnaby Potter
1629	Oxford	Richard Corbet
1632	Carlisle	Barnaby Potter
1633	York Metrop.	Richard Neile
1634	Chester	John Bridgeman
1636	York	Richard Neile
1637	Chester	John Bridgeman
1638	Rochester	John Warner
1638	Norwich	Richard Montagu
1640	York Metrop.	Richard Neile

clear that by the midpoint of Charles's reign morris dance events had fallen off dramatically as a result of earlier prosecutions (see figure 23, p.173), so there were fewer performers left to prosecute.

The transcripts of the trials of dancers in this period provide details concerning the motivations of the prosecutors, and the responses of the defendants. It is patent that these trials represent part of the visible trace of a major battle for political and social control of the country, and that the dancers made every effort to fight back, without avail.

A trial of guildsmen in Leicester for disorderly conduct in the early part of James's reign shows that there was some popular sentiment that laws had unfairly tightened on the death of Elizabeth, but this was not the king's doing. Rather it was local authorities taking the opportunity of a new reign to clamp down on the people. The discussion excerpted here from the testimony of two disputants concerning a morris dance and the setting up of a maypole focuses on the pole, but the trial was specifically of morris dancers:

The said Examinate [William Saunderson] sayth comynge towards Symon Yngs dore in Leicester, found dyvers women sitting theire vppon Sayturdaye nighte the last of Aprill last past, Symon Ynge then rageinge at the setting vpp of the Maye pole standinge neire to his howse in the Sowthe gate; and sayde that they (meyninge the Maye Poles) weare suffered in noe towne but here in Leic. Wherevnto this Examinate said, that yf the King did allow of them, then wee ought not to gaine saye itt. The Kinge, sayd he (the said Symon Ynge), I will obey Queene Elizabeth her lawes. Then sayde this Examinate the Queene is dead, and that her lawes were nowe the Kings lawes. Then the said Symon Ynge answered againe & said that the Kinge had noe lawes ...

And the said Examinate said he dyd thinke the King, as yet, had made no newe lawes, but those that were in the Queenes Majesties tyme ...   (Kelly 1865, 238–42)

Saunderson is essentially claiming that Inge is disguising a personal (Puritan) prejudice under the thin veil of a spurious law, and that such local customs were generally tolerated in Elizabeth's time, and should continue so under a new king who himself expressed tolerance. Nonetheless Inge won the day and the dancers were punished. The arguments and results of this trial might well serve as a token for the events of the reign.

As the Puritan grip tightened morris dancing seems to have become more than just a popular local custom – now existing under a cloud – but a definite (if somewhat spontaneous) form of active rebellion against church repression. For example in 1619 the Windsor archdeacon's visitation presentments contain the following complaint:

That the said Thomas Hall vpon the feast day of the Ascension last past, when one of the morrice dauncers had leaped & daunced in the face of the minister standing in his owne doore, did before a great number of people, revile & abuse the minister with these reprothfull speaches sc. that the morrice dauncers should dance before his doore, & before his face in spite of him & in spite of his teeth, & that they should ridd the towne of him; asking him disdainfullie what he was, with many other threatning speeches.

(Peyton 1928, xix, and Johnston forthcoming).

In Shropshire in 1619 there is an even more blatant and general case of morris dancers defying the church through sacrilege, in that they 'borrowed' the communion cloth from the parish church of Abdon and used it as a flag in their general perambulation of villages in the neighborhood of Clee St Margaret on Whit Monday and Tuesday of that year (see Somerset 1994, 40–50). Only two dancers were charged in actually devising the plan and taking the cloth, but fourteen others admitted, on being indicted, that though they were not privy to the plan, they had been informed subsequently that the flag was the Abdon communion cloth, and had danced before it regardless. The whole smacks of a huge country prank perpetrated by a few but enjoyed by many, until their actions (inevitably) came to the notice of church authorities.

The timing of all the preceding cases is most interesting, inasmuch as they all occurred soon after the publication of the *Book of Sports* by James, and there is a definite swelling of the number of lawsuits brought in this period. The king's declaration seems to have spurred both sides to action, giving the supporters of local customs endorsement of their sports, and galvanizing opponents into resistance. The paradox is, therefore, that James's deliberate support of rural morris dancing may have significantly contributed to its rapid demise in the early seventeenth century. By the time Charles reiterated his father's message of tolerance there was little left to support except pockets of stubborn resistance in isolated places that were subject to occasional suppression.

THE INTERREGNUM (1649–60)

During the Interregnum the episcopacy was abolished, and thus there was a clear break in the trends in ecclesiastical law that this chapter has been following. There were no diocesan visitation articles issued and no prosecutions for morris dancing under canon law. Instead, secular courts took over large areas of what had formerly been church prerogatives, and new ordinances were issued to replace diocesan injunctions. 'An Ordinance for Ejecting Scandalous, Ignorant and Insufficient Ministers and Schoolmasters,' of 1654 contains the following:

... such Ministers and Schoolmasters shall be deemed and accompted scandalous in their Lives and Conversations, as shall be proved guilty of ... or do incourage and countenance by word or practice any Whitson-Ales, Wakes, Morris-dances, May-poles, Stage-plays, or suchlike Licentious practices, by which men are encouraged in a loose and prophane Conversation.   (Firth and Rait 1911, 2:977)

This ordinance disposed of support of morris dancing by the church on a national level. Local ordinances further removed support for the dance, as in this declaration from the Warwickshire Quarter Sessions in May 1655:

Whereas the court was informed that vsually heretofore there haue beeneatt Henley in Arden in this County severall vnlawfull meeteings of idle & vain persons about this time of yeare for erectinge of MayPoles and mayBushes and for vseinge of Morris dances and other heatheanish and vnlawfull Customs the observac*i*on whereof tendeth to draw together agreat concourse of loose people and consequently to ye hazard of the publique peace besides other evill consequences ffor the pr*e*venc*i*on whereof for the future this court doth recommend it to the diligent care of the Bayliffe [⟨B...⟩] constable & other officers of the said Towne of Henley to pr*e*vent or otherwise suppresse the said meetings for any the aforesaid purposes And they are hereby required to cause publique notice to bee given to the Inh*a*bitants of the said Towne that they are hereby Com*m*aunded to forbeare to meete about the setting up of any May-Poles or May-Bush or about thaforesaid morricdances or other vnlawfull Sports and incase any person or persons shall offend herein the aforesaid are required to haue them before the next Justice of ye Peace for this County whoe is desired to bind them over to the next Sessions of the Peace to beeholden for this county that they may receiue condigne Punishm*ent*: accordinge to law And the said Bayliffe and burgesses are likewise to take care for ye due observac*i*on of the Lord's day and to pr*e*sent all offenders in y*a* case at the next Sessions after their offence committed To the end that due and legall punishment may bee alsoe inflicted vpon them And hereof they and every of them are not to fayle/

(Warws RO QS 40/1 f. 202v; see also Ratcliff and Johnson 1937, 275–6)

Although moral issues are raised in both these ordinances, the political implications are evident, namely, that large assemblies of (probably drunken) people can easily convert to riot and rebellion. These regulations are thus, perhaps fittingly, driven by motives equal and opposite to those of James and Charles in their publication of the *Book of Sports*, who saw public sports as an antidote to sedition.

Prosecutions for morris dancing in the Interregnum were infrequent, and usually involved indictments for a combination of sabbath breaking as well as some significant disruption of the peace as in this famous case from Shropshire:

August 9th 1652.

To the Wor'full the Bayliffe and Justices of the Towne and lybertyes of Much Wenlock certifying

That all wee whose names are subscribed Inhabitants of the Pshe of Astley Abbotts doe certify that upon Munday in Whitsunday week being the 7th of June last past there came a Morrice daunce forth of the Pish of Broseley, with six sword bearers and a rude companye of followers throwe ye whole bodie of this our saide Pish being uninvited or desired by any one within the said Pish that wee doe know of ...

The most abusive were Thomas Lee sword bearer who formerly and also in ye last service att Worcester bore armes agt ye Pliaent. John Eavans badger of flanen a revolted Pliaent souldier as hee confeseth and sayes hee will now continue a cavelleire as long as he lives ... (S 1885)

Here the issues are more complex than the mere fact that morris dancers came uninvited to Astley Abbots. They threatened and abused the local population, stole ale, and disturbed the peace. But, equally important, they served in the civil wars against Cromwell and declared publicly their hostility to his government, precisely confirming the opinions expressed in the ordinances above. Although this is the only suit in which such issues are so clear cut, all others of the period share the same political flavour.

Nonetheless, prosecutions are still rare in comparison with the number under James VI and I, contrary to what one would expect of a puritan government, and suggesting two, not necessarily mutually exclusive, possibilities. The first, and most obvious, is that the earlier suits had so weakened the rural tradition that there was little left to prosecute (coupled with the demise of the church ale that had left the dancers without sponsors). Second, the prosecution of morris dancers was not normally vigorously pursued unless the dancers threatened the social or political stability in other more direct ways, as at Astley Abbots. Probably a combination of these two circumstances is closest the mark.

Not surprisingly there are no polemics from the Interregnum railing against morris dancing, and, for this brief period, its supporters were also judiciously silent. The most important point to note here is that the Interregnum was not a time of abrupt change in official attitudes towards morris dancing. Rather, there was an ongoing three-way struggle between traditionalists/recusants, moderate Anglicans, and Puritans for control of local parishes, with public sentiment constantly shifting between them. The pendulum had swung to its puritan apogee under Cromwell, but attacks on morris dancing began in Elizabeth's reign (or even earlier). Furthermore, when the monarchy was restored there was not an immediate renaissance of morris, as if the Interregnum had created a short and brutally enforced hiatus in a spirited tradition. The dance had been crippled by the Jacobean purges and took fully a century to recover its vitality.

THE RESTORATION

Charles II entered London as king on his thirtieth birthday, 29th May 1660. Part of the procession to the capital is described by an eyewitness:

On Tuesday, May the 29th (which happily fell out to be the anniversary of his Majesty's birthday) he set forth from Rochester in his coach; but afterwards took horse on the farther side of Blackheath: on which spacious plain he found divers great and eminent troops of horse, in a most splendid and glorious equipage; and a kind of rural triumph, expressed by the country swains, in a morrice dance with the old music of taber and pipe; which was performed with all agility and cheerfulness imaginable.   (Firth 1903, 428)

The picture is certainly merry and romantic but ultimately misleading. True, the Restoration inaugurated a season of rejoicing with ales, maypoles, and morris dances, but these were hothouse flowers, forced into bloom by the radiance of the renewed monarchy, and destined to an equally rapid decay. It is almost as if they were a sentimental memory of earlier times, brought out, like bunting from an attic trunk, to cheer in the new era, and then tucked away again. After 1660, the picture is not so very different from that before (and during) the Interregnum.

With the Puritans once more out of power, polemics against morris dancing appeared with renewed vigour though not with much originality, Thomas Hall's classic *Funebria Florae, the Downfall of May-games* being a fair sample of the genre (Hall 1661, 13). On the other side of the coin, Charles was encouraged to adopt a policy towards traditional customs close to that of his father and grandfather. In 1660 William Cavendish wrote *A Treatise on Government* directed towards the new king. Part of his advice is:

For the countreye recreations: Maye Games, Moris Danses, the Lords off the Maye & Ladye off the Maye, the foole, – & the Hobye Horse muste nott bee forgotten. – Also the Whitson Lorde, & Ladye, – Thrashinge off Hens at Shrovetite [&c] … The Countereye People with their fresher Lasses to tripp on the Toune Greene aboute the Maye pole, to the Louder Baggpipe ther to bee refreshte with their Ale & Cakes … The devirtisments will amuse the peoples thoughts, & keepe them In harmles action which will free your Majestie from faction & Rebellion.   (Cavendish 1660, 227)

The Act of Uniformity of 1662 that sealed the Restoration religious settlement required a new set of diocesan visitation articles to ensure its publication and enforcement. Most of these articles are taken from a single blueprint and contain the following phrase:

Do you permit no Minstrels, no Moris-dancers, no Doggs, Hawks, or Hounds to be brought or come into your Church, to the disturbance of the Congregation?
                              (House of Commons 1867–8, 619)

As a prohibition this wording has none of the moral or theological force of earlier articles, and seems nothing more than a grab bag. In fact this prohibition is normally collected under one article with the ban on leaning against or placing one's hat on

Table 6
Visitation articles banning morris under Charles II and James II

Date	Diocese (or province)	Bishop
1662	Chichester	Henry King
1662	Llandaff	Hugh Lloyd
1662	Exeter	Seth Ward
1662	St David's	William Lucy
1662	Oxford	Robert Skinner
1662	Hereford	Herbert Croft
1662	Winchester	George Morley
1662	Durham	John Cosin
1662	Peterborough	Benjamin Laney
1662	Lincoln	Robert Sanderson
1662	Bath and Wells	William Peirs
1664	Peterborough	Joseph Henshaw
1666	Lincoln	Benjamin Laney
1666	Oxford	Walter Blandford
1668	Winchester	George Morley
1671	St David's	William Lucy
1671	Lincoln	William Fuller
1673	Peterborough	Joseph Henshaw
1674	Exeter	Anthony Sparrow
1674	Salisbury	Seth Ward
1674	Winchester	George Morley
1677	Exeter	Thomas Lamplugh
1677	Salisbury	Seth Ward
1680	Peterborough	William Lloyd
1682	Canterbury	William Sancroft
1683	Peterborough	William Lloyd
1686	Lincoln	[Sancroft]
1686	Norwich	William Lloyd

the communion table, that is, acts that are acceptable in the secular world, but become offensive in the sacred. So, there is nothing *intrinsically* wrong with hawks, or hounds, or minstrels, or morris dancers. They *become* sacrilegious only when introduced into a house of worship.

Table 6 shows the general distribution of visitation articles containing this wording. The great preponderance of virtually identically worded articles issued in 1662 is evident, and this relatively unthinking replication is clearly responsible for the widespread distribution of the prohibition – even in remote places such as St David's in the west of Wales, where morris dancing was unheard of. These 1662 articles account for nearly half of all the articles prohibiting morris in Charles II's reign.

Due to a combination of factors – the general decline in morris dancing, the more tolerant political climate, and the limitation of the ban to actually dancing in the church – there are no prosecutions recorded in this period. The article banning morris was gradually dropped, often when a new bishop arrived and took the opportunity to revise and update the articles, removing obsolete material. Bath and Wells, for example, used the wording in 1662 but dropped it in 1676; likewise articles for Oxford appeared without the ban in 1672. By the 1680s the great majority of sees had purged their articles of the language, so that those few bishops who kept the prohibition into the reign of James II were simply suffering from a lack of editorial energy rather than holding steadfastly to an ideology that had any contemporary merit.

CODA

Morris dancing was a casualty of church policy in the late sixteenth and early seventeenth century because it was caught in a number of struggles, and this chapter should serve to show that the forces at work were multiple and complex. Popular notions, including the idea that a rising tide of Puritanism swept dancing and merriment aside, are not merely simplistic, but false. It is quite possible that even without the existence of the Puritan movement, local customs would have come under severe attack by an episcopacy seeking national conformity of worship and a semblance of piety, although such moves were obviously given greater urgency because of the threat to their polity from the Puritans.

Whosoever railed against morris dancing, it was the episcopacy that rooted it out of the countryside. The essential irony of the situation is that the bishops (and perhaps also the Puritans) saw morris dancing as disruptive of social order, but their actions were ultimately more disruptive of the traditional order, and it is intriguing to speculate whether this was a deliberate goal. To see how this happened requires reexamining the nature of the church ales that sponsored morris.

For the countryside the parish church served many of the same kinds of functions for the local population as urban organizations (such as guilds) did for city dwellers – including the sponsoring of morris dancing. The church not only provided a convenient and central place to meet for festival activities, it also had the fiscal basis (and equipment) to mount large-scale ventures. So even in the simplest terms, by shutting down the church as a locus for parish festivity, the episcopacy effectively ended such events, because there was no other local institution capable of providing a similar structure within which to operate. The church in its spiritual mission, already existed as a gathering place and as a financial entity, with a body of officers to handle its general operation. Moreover, within its spiritual purview it supported festive events associated with rites of passage such as marriage and baptism. The addition of other types of ales, wakes, and feasts was therefore no great matter because the infrastructure was already in place. No social entity existed in the secular world to carry on where the church was forced to leave off. But the issue is yet deeper.

The earliest ales, described at the beginning of the last chapter, were complex social events even though one of their main objectives was to make money for the parish. After all, the parish officers had a variety of means at their disposal to make money, the principal being to tithe the parishioners, to charge fees for services rendered, and to run profit-making ventures. The decision that many rural parishes took to rely on ales to balance the books, however, was really not much of a choice. Many were in financial trouble because of the continual erosion of tithes through enclosure, engrossing, and the simple refusal to pay them (coupled with poor management of glebe terriers), so increasing tithes was not possible. Raising fees might have been a temporary stopgap, but there were only limited occasions on which to charge parishioners, and inflation in the latter part of the sixteenth century easily ate up increases. Ales and their like were therefore the only option short of straightforward solicitation of funds (which was also practised).

Empirical experience may well have shown that a fund-raising event was likely to generate more income than overt solicitation, because the event itself was fun and socially engaging. Church ales are what I have called elsewhere 'aesthetic/incorporative' events (Forrest 1988a): that is, they involve the raising of funds, but they are fundamentally *aesthetic* events, and the making of money is not geared to a strict transactional reciprocity – people contribute to the event through money and in kind goods (food, malt) and services (brewing, dancing) according to their abilities, and then buy or barter for what they desire in food and drink. The event thus brings everyone in the community together (i.e., *incorporates* them) in a spirit of conviviality.

The social opposite of the aesthetic/incorporative is the material/transactional, which has the spirit of a legal contract and operates according to strict reciprocity. Thus, passing through a toll gate involves the passenger paying a fixed and established fee to the gatekeeper, for which fee the gate is opened and the passenger allowed access to the toll road for a number of miles. The *transactional* relationship between passenger and gatekeeper is based on the *material* worth of what is traded between them and is fleeting; it lasts only as long as the transaction lasts. Paying tithes or fees has this material/transactional quality.

Thus, when the episcopacy banned ales and their kin they were implicitly forcing rural parishes to move from an aesthetic/incorporative to a material/transactional mode of money-making and, as such, potentially diminishing the socially incorporative role of the church. There are several ironies here. Doctrinally it could be argued that the reformed church in England, certainly under Elizabeth, was attempting to move from a transactional to an incorporative practice, in that the stereotypical Catholic cycle of sin and penance was the model of reciprocal transactionality, whereas the

Protestant dogma of the church as the body of Christ is prototypically incorporative. Therefore, while church creeds moved in one direction, fiscal and social policy
moved entirely counter to them, thus suggesting that ideologically the reformed
church in England, even as designed by moderate bishops, was far from homogeneous
in its practices and therefore inherently unstable. With the benefit of hindsight it
is easy to 'predict' that the position of someone like Edmund Grindal would have to
weaken either in allowing some transactionality in worship or some incorporativeness
in social activity, to stablize the situation; this, of course, was the case in the Stuart
era.

The greater irony is that ales were banned because the bishops (and Puritans) saw
their constituent components – Lords of Misrule, Robin Hood plays, morris dancing –
as anti-social. By prohibiting ales, what they actually did was destroy a significant
opportunity for social cohesion in the countryside; as is now well established in
anthropological theory, rites of inversion of the social order serve as powerful agents
for the maintenance of the status quo. Repression of these rites causes tension to
erupt in other spheres. The Stuart kings understood this lesson well, but they could
not force the policy on bishops who had little or no experience of rural life.

The result of banning ales was not the complete demise of its components (although some, such as Robin Hood plays, did disappear). Rather, they became free-
floating performances without a sponsor. What happened to Summer Lords and so
forth is for other historians to pursue. What happened to morris dancers is our subject.
Having been outlawed by the same church that had nurtured them in times past, they
clearly became at first resentful of the church, and danced regardless of the law;
they became a vehicle for social protest against an ecclesiastical hierarchy that was
insensitive to the needs of rural communities. So, although the dancers were at one
point a force for social cohesion, having been branded as antisocial they became so –
disturbing the peace and breaking the law. Consequently their actions brought them
up against civil as well as church authority, leading to further persecution, and in
many cases, extinction. Nonetheless, there were pockets of continued resistance in
the more isolated parts of the countryside, where morris, now radically altered in its
social character survived and ultimately found new sponsors.

8

The Public Stage

Morris dances appeared in plays performed on the public stage from the late Elizabethan era to the Restoration, with a high point of popularity around the time that
the dance was being rigorously prosecuted in the countryside. In fact, one might even
speculate that the interest of urban playwrights in the dance heightened Puritan
animosity to it by linking it to another activity with a sulfurous reek. Certainly, a
number of the plays including morris contain strong polemical, anti-Puritan sentiments. However, it would be an overstatement to imagine that the public stage as
a 'venue' had anywhere near the importance of the others for the general developmental history of the dances – although it was not entirely inconsequential either.

Table 7 indicates all plays known to have actual morris dances written into them
(as opposed to those that simply mention morris dancing or those that have morris
dancers as characters but who do not dance onstage).[1] From this table it can be seen
that the fashion for including the dance in plays had a vogue of only about thirty-
five years, from 1589 to 1623 (with several gaps). To be sure, this time span represents
a whole generation, but this was an extraordinarily fecund period for playwriting –
with hundreds of plays being produced for quick consumption – and yet only eleven
have a morris dance in them (and there are only fourteen overall). Furthermore,
these plays are, for the most part, not among the evergreens, and most are quite obscure. Only *Shoemakers' Holiday* and *Witch of Edmonton* can be said to be anything
like popular favourites, and even their importance is relatively minor. Mostly these
plays were light comedies run off quickly as potboilers and crowd pleasers, with a
bit of country sport added as an extra fillip. The dances in the plays are, as far as
internal evidence indicates, quite diverse and seem to form a watershed of choreographic ideas from courtly, urban, and rural sources, allowing us a glimpse into one
form of developmental synthesis. Also, not to be taken lightly, stage morris begat the
most celebrated morris event of all time, Will Kemp's dance from London to Norwich
in 1600.

Table 7

Plays containing directions for a morris dance.

Date	Play	Author(s)	Initial Company
1589	John a Kent and John a Cumber	Munday	[Admiral's]
1592	Summers Last Will and Testament	Nashe	Whitgift's Servants [plus Paul's Boys]
1599	Shoemakers' Holiday	Dekker	Admiral's
1599	Histrio-Mastix	Marston	Paul's Boys
1600	Iacke Drums Entertainment	Marston	Paul's Boys
1613	Two Noble Kinsmen	Fletcher & Shakespeare	King's
1617	ΤΕΧΝΟΓΑΜΙΑ	Holyday	Christchurch College, Oxon
1619	Women Pleas'd	Fletcher	King's
1621	Witch of Edmonton	Rowley, Dekker, & Ford	Prince's
1623	The Sun's Darling	Dekker & Ford	King's/Prince's
1623	Fucus; sive Histriomastix	Ward	Queen's College, Cantab
1632	Amyntas	Randolph	Children of the Revels
1655	Acteon and Diana	Cox	[Red Bull]
1664	The Rivals	D'Avenant	Duke of York's

Before dealing with the specific issues of the sources of dance ideas in stage morris, however, there is a practical issue to confront. Stage plays are unlike any other 'venue' for morris dancing in that every play (and hence every dance within a play) exists in at least two distinguishable contexts, namely, the world constructed by the play narrative, and the world of the theatre and its audience. Thus, the morris dance in Dekker's *Shoemakers' Holiday* takes place, within the play world, at Stratford Bow performed by shoemakers, but within the theatre world, it was originally performed in a London theatre by professional actors. For convenience I shall subsequently call the inner world of the play the 'dramatic' context, and the world of the theatre the 'theatric' context. Both contexts exist simultaneously, and this duality was essential to much of the playwriting of the period, because it gave the opportunity to separate, bridge, or confuse the two worlds. The common convention of the *aside*, for example, briefly blurs the two contexts by either moving the play character out of the dramatic into the theatric world, or drawing the audience from the theatric into the dramatic. The ability of these two contexts to unite and separate allowed the Elizabethan and Stuart theatre to hybridize a number of morris dance forms and contexts.

The complexities of the simultaneous existence of dramatic and theatric contexts will be explored in due course, but a few general observations will help to anchor the discussion. Most important is the notion that a dance, whether viewed in dramatic or theatric context is always a dance – change of context changes interpretation, but does not change certain fundamentals of form. By contrast a sword fight to the death on stage is two quite different entities when viewed through the two contexts: dramatically it is a violent act, but theatrically it is a stylized choreography. An audience member can flip contexts in order to view the event as something shocking (dramatically), or a fine piece of technical stage play to be admired (theatrically), or hold both in mind simultaneously. When professional actors perform a rural morris dance on stage it may be viewed as a piece of crude rustic horseplay (dramatically) or as a sophisticated parody (theatrically) – but in both contexts the audience is seeing the events as *dances* (however complexly conceived or layered cognitively). An enactment of a dance is still a dance (whereas an enactment of a fight is not a fight outside the dramatic context).

Elizabethan and Jacobean playwrights incorporated morris dances in their plays in large measure because they brought with them an authentic rustic air, and because different classes in the audience could view them differently (dramatically and theatrically), yet equally derive pleasure from them. The lower classes might find them directly appealing for what they were meant to represent (i.e., view them more in dramatic context), whereas the more educated might treat them more as an amusing replica (i.e. view them more in a theatric context). It is also worth noting that by the late sixteenth and early seventeenth centuries morris dancing was predominantly a rural sport, but the professional theatre allowed urban masses to enjoy it too, by introducing it into plays with rural settings – where it was at the same time tied to its conventional country context (i.e., rural May games) dramatically, yet liberated from it theatrically inasmuch as the plays could be performed in any season and in any locale. For a short period, therefore, morris dancing could be enjoyed just about anywhere at any time without it losing its character as a dance emanating from a particular social mileu.

Morris dancing seems to have arrived at the public stage via several avenues, the result of which was a considerable diversity of dance forms found in plays. The two broadest influences seem to be urban May games, and courtly masques and entertainments.

The rise of the popular public Elizabethan theatre is roughly coincident with the renewed interest in urbanized versions of country sports in London in the mid-sixteenth century. May games of various stripes had had a long heritage in London, but after the early years of Henry VIII's reign they had fallen into disfavour and were in general decline. They returned to cities in new guise and with new vigour in the 1550s because several historical trends coalesced to create the right environment. Rural May games, Whitsun ales, and the like began to peak in popularity mid-century and evidently attracted the interest of the urban quality. Wealthy urbanites maintained country residences and, as is evident from the play texts and other primary sources, were key audience members for rural games because of the largesse they had to distribute. Soto in John Fletcher's *Women Pleas'd* remarks, for example,

Theres ne're a Duke in Christendome but loves a May-game.   (Fletcher 1619, 498)

and in several plays a major part of the stage business involves a local dignitary giving beer, victuals, and cash to the morris dancers. In fact, in the great majority of the plays, the morris dancers perform for a noble or rich gentleman with land holdings in the country where the morris dancers reside, confirming the basic fact that rural sports, though chiefly provided by the lower classes, were enjoyed by all ranks – seemingly without especial condescension from the upper crust, if the plays are to be trusted as pseudo-eyewitnesses. Thus there was a class of people who lived in both country and city who could be expected to sponsor the (re)importing of May games into an urban context.

It should be remembered, however, that the London May games of the 1550s and later were not simply replicas of rural events. True, they took elements from country games, such as the characters of Robin Hood and his men, but this was also the era when Midsummer Watches were in serious decline. The demise of the watches left a gap in seasonal celebration that the urban May games were able to fill, and the latter co-opted many components of the watches that were adaptable enough to make the transition.

At the same time, either as a catalyst or as a result of urban interest in May games, the major themes of the Robin Hood tradition appeared in print in substantial literary pieces, beginning a long-standing tradition of counterpoise between rural and urban visions of the folk hero. Chief of these is William Copland's edition of *A Mery Geste of Robyn Hode*, published *c* 1560, and including with it a play of Robin Hood to be used at May games (see Child 1965, 3:39–89). This seems to be the start of a tradition of professional writers providing material for urban May games (as they had for other street spectacles such as triumphs and royal entries), although in this case Copland has done little more than cobble together a text from folk plays that had somehow come into his possession.

The revived custom of elaborate London May games appears not to have lasted longer than a few decades, if that, but professional writers kept the surge of public interest in rural sports alive by adapting to the professional stage the subjects they were familiar with or had written about for street theatre.[2] Archetypical is George Peele's chronicle play *King Edward the First* (Peele 1911), in which, for an interlude, Lluellen, rebellious Prince of Wales, suggests that he and his followers (including his friar/chaplain) amuse themselves with some country games:

weele get the next daie from *Brecknocke* the booke of *Robin Hood*, the Frier he shal instruct vs in his cause and weele euen here fair and well since the king hath put vs amongst the discarding cardes, and as it were turned vs with deuces and traies out of the decke ... and wander like irregulers vp and down the wildernesse, ile be maister of misrule, ile be *Robin Hood* that once, cousin *Kice* thou shalt be little *Iohn*, and hers Frier *Dauid* as fit as a die for Frier *Tucke*, now my sweet *Nel* if you wil make vp the messe with a good heart for Maide marian and doe well with *Lluellen* vnder the greene wood trees, with as good a wil as in the good townes, why *plena est curia*.   (Peele 1911, sig. E4 recto)

Subsequently Lluellen and his band act out classic scenes from Robin Hood plays, thus enlivening with popular diversions an otherwise insipid play.[3] There is no sense here that the May games are being patronized; they are a beloved entertainment, fit for exploitation, and the adaptation is without condescension.

Anthony Munday, noted for his attempts at ennobling the Robin Hood of the May game plays in *The Downfall of Robert, Earl of Huntingdon* and *The Death of Robert, Earl of Huntingdon*, was apparently the first playwright to use a rustic morris in a play – *John a Kent and John a Cumber* – and he set a very clear pattern that was generally followed. The stage morris was typically performed by a rural troupe (often played by the company's clowns) as part of a May game or other spring festival, forming an interlude in the main drama for the amusement of the main characters in the play. The dancers were usually supernumerary characters with little or no connection to the plot, and if they had any dialogue at all, it was conventionally a comic preliminary to the dance, reminiscent of the banter of May plays. The fad for importing images specifically from May games into stage plays peaked around 1600 and again around 1620, but by the 1630s was passé.

Of rather less importance, but significant nonetheless, is the path of morris dances from courtly masques and entertainments to the public stage, although here too, the vogue of May games may have been a considerable influence; indeed the royal spectacles were perhaps a detour that the morris of May games took before entering the plays of the public stage, rather than being an utterly independent vehicle. There was also a great deal of cross-fertilization between masques and plays (and there are also some dramatic forms that do not fit neatly into either category), so that a single direct line from the one to the other is impossible to justify.

It is tempting to create a lineage of courtly and noble morris starting with the dances of the disguisings, interludes, and masques of the earliest Tudor period, leading down to the dramatically complex and sophisticated dances of the entertainments and antimasques of the Jacobean age, but the primary texts that would support this lineage are problematic. Oft cited as an early version of a 'masque' containing a morris is the disguising of 'governance ruled by dissipation and negligence' played at Gray's Inn in 1527 before Cardinal Wolsey:

This Christmas was a goodly disguisyng plaied at Greis-inne, which was compiled for the moste part, by master Ihon Roo ... the effecte of the plaie was that lord gouernance was ruled by dissipacion and negligence. This plaie was so set furth with riche and costlie apparel, with straunge diuises of Maskes & Morrishes that it was highly praised of all menne ...

(Hall 1809, 719)

But then there is a hiatus in the record until the entertainment at Kenilworth in 1575. In 1579 there is reference to a 'Morris Mask' now lost (Harbage 1964, 48–9), and then there is another gap until 1603 when Ben Jonson produced his 'Entertainment at Althorpe' for Queen Elizabeth (Jonson 1603). Jonson suggests in the text of the clown/usher that the morris is a rustic species of masque, and this part of the entertainment has an antimasque quality, although it was the sole production of the final day of the entertainment (that is, there is no masque following it).

> *Munday ... after dinner ... there was a speech sodainly thought on, to induce a morris of the clownes thereabout, who most officiously presented themselves, but by reason of the throng of the countrey that came in, their speaker could not be heard, who was in the person of* No-body, *to deliuer this following speech, and attyred in a paire of breeches which were made to come vp to his neck, with his armes out at his pockets, and a cap drowning his face ...*
> We are the Huisher to a Morise
> (A kind of Masque) whereof good store is
> In the countrey hereabout ...   (Jonson 1603, 128)

The whole has a (ludicrous) May game quality to it (the rustic fool/lord heralding the dance), but it may just as easily have been directly influenced by contemporary stage plays in which morrises of rustic clowns were standard fare. And this is the only unequivocal reference to a morris in a seventeenth-century courtly masque/entertainment. So the idea of a continuous tradition of morrises related to Tudor and Stuart royal spectacles is not firmly rooted in contemporary sources. Rather it seems that the use of morris in royal interludes and the like was a matter of occasional fashion dictated by outside influences (renewed interest in May games, popularity in public theatres, etc.), so that it is perhaps more reasonable to see the later courtly spectacles as synthetic, pulling themes from popular as well as older courtly tradition.

There is only indirect evidence from No-body's speech (Jonson 1603, 128–30) concerning the form of this morris, but it is a reasonable conjecture that it is a form of the wooing ring dance, like its earlier counterpart at the entertainment at Kenilworth. First, No-body says that the dance is a species of rustic masque, indicating that it had mimetic qualities of some kind rather than being pure figures or steps without any narrative references. Second, it is clear that the dance is meant to involve wooing and courtship by virtue of No-body's negative assertion that the clown/rustic dancers will not appeal sexually to the ladies (although the much more coarsely blatant fool may be attractive to a servingwoman). Again, as at Kenilworth, there are complex sexual and class issues layered together here. The dancers were presumably young courtiers acting the rustic buffoon, and parodying a rural dance that was, at one time, a parody of the refinements of a courtly dance.

Morrises in other masques and entertainments of the seventeenth century are hard to come by, and what few references there are, are to moriscos, with little or no further information concerning their form barring the name itself. For example, in Aurelian Townshend's masque *Albion's Triumph*, performed by Charles I and his courtiers in 1631, the antimasque is described:

The Anti-Maskes enter.
First, Fooles__6
Secondly, Saltators or Tumblers__7
Thirdly, Pugili or Buffeters__3
Fourthly, Satyrs, like Daunncers__2
Fiftly, One Giant, and Pigmies__5
Sixtly, Gladiators or Fencers__4
Seventhly, Mimicks or Morescoes__7   (Townshend 1631, 68)

Thus, the lineage of morris ideas within courtly spectacle would appear to be frail and fragmented, and, hence, its possible influence on more popular vehicles, such as stage plays, relatively insignificant. But there is one curious example of a morris dance that did make the transition from masque to public stage, which bears examination for the light it sheds on the hybridizing of dramatic ideas in the period.

The dance first appears as the second antimasque in Francis Beaumont's *Masque of the Inner Temple and Gray's Inn* performed on 20 February 1613 before James VI & I (Beaumont 1613) to mark the marriage of the princess Elizabeth to Frederick, elector palatine, and later, king of Bohemia. The masque has a classical theme: Jupiter and Juno, to celebrate the marriage of the Thames and the Rhine, send down Mercury and Iris to contend in honouring the couple. The stage scene was a pageant mountain reminiscent of those used in Tudor disguisings except that it was stationary and curtained off (Beaumont 1613, 128).

Mercury begins the contest with an antimasque of Naiads and Hyades, which Iris scoffs at as lacking life because it consists of dancers of one sex only. Mercury then calls forth cupids to dance with the nymphs, and after that gives 'Artificiall life' to statues who dance solemnly before the king. This artificiality Iris disdains too:

Then *Iris* for her part in scorne of this high flying devise, and in token that the Match shall likewise be blessed with the love of the Common People, calles to *Flora* her confederate ...

to bring in a May-daunce or Rurall daunce, consisting likewise not of any suted persons, but of a confusion, or commixture of all such persons as are naturall and proper for Countrey sports. This is the second Anti-masque.   (Beaumont 1613, 127)

This May dance is described:

IRIS. … Send hither all the Rurall company,
Which decke the May-games with their Countrey sports;
Juno will have it so.
The second Anti-masque rush in, daunce their Measure, and
as rudely depart, consisting of a Pedant

May Lord,	May Lady.
Servingman,	Chambermaide.
A Countrey Clowne, or Shepheard,	Countrey Wench.
An Host,	Hostesse.
A Hee Baboone,	Shee Baboone.
A Hee Foole,	Shee Foole.

ushering them in.

All these persons apparelled to the life, the Men issuing out of one side of the Boscage [thicket], and the Woemen from the other: the Musicke was extremely well fitted, having such a spirit of Countrey jolitie, as can hardly be imagined, but the perpetuall laughter and applause was above the Musicke.

The dance likewise was of the same strain, and the Dancers, or rather Actors, expressed every one their part so naturally, and aptly, as when a Mans eye was caught with the one, and then past on to the other, hee could not satisfie himselfe which did best.
                                              (Beaumont 1613, 133–4)

Without additional direct information it is difficult to say much about the form of this dance, although there is enough to make a few basic assertions. It is immediately evident from the cast of characters that the dance is quite different from the forms of morris so far discussed, and its appearance at this juncture perhaps signals a new direction in the evolution of the country morris (see the next chapter for further details). The performers are *partnered*, male and female, and each partnership has a distinct social identity. The identically clad nymphs and cupids, according to Iris, represent bland and sterile repetition (who, if they could reproduce would simply replicate their own featureless selves), whereas the May dance represents the variety inherent in human social order – a symbolic miniature of robust and fertile diversity (reproducing endless diversity through sexual appetite). It is over this world that the newly-wed couple will rule and to which their own sexuality will contribute life.

Some of the dance characters need to be explained in order for us to understand how the hierarchy of the dance is put together. The May Lord and Lady, of course represent the rulers of the rustic company, while the servingman and chambermaid symbolize the retainer/servant class. The use of the word 'clown' here is curious in that at that time it had two uses. Originally a clown was simply a farm labourer – stereotypically cloddish (clown = clod etymologically). But rustics/clowns had become stock characters on the Elizabethan stage, played by the great comic actors such as Richard Tarleton and William Kemp, and had, thus, become the stage equivalent of court fools. The clown here is, therefore, partly symbolic of the farm labourer class (bulwarks of May games) in straightforward fashion, and partly a stock stage parody of that type. The host and hostess are the concupiscent entrepreneurs, supplying all the company's needs – at a price. The baboon is something of a mystery if by the term is meant a species of monkey, since they were hardly typical country revellers. But the word also meant at this time a grotesque gargoyle or other architectural ornament (from the French *baboue*, a grimace) and may have been applied by extension to people who were grotesque, such as the simpleton or natural. Or, the baboon may have been a stock May game character – a species of tumbler – dressed as a stereotyped baboon and perhaps combining gymnastics with foolish antics, as is suggested by this description of the part of the Bavian (a variant of 'baboon') in the analogue morris dance in *The Two Noble Kinsmen*:

SCHOOLEMASTER. ... wher's the *Bavian?*
My friend, carry your taile without offence
Or scandall to the Ladies; and be sure
You tumble with audacity and manhood,
And when you barke, doe it with judgment.
BAVIAN.   Yes, sir.   (Fletcher and Shakespeare 1613, 214)

The Bavian/baboon may have been a natural, but the fool, by contrast, was only playing the simpleton and was, thus, capable of turning the whole order upside down, the wittiest playing the witless, and leading the company from the rear.

The dance company was, it seems, a collection of *types* who combined to form a whole – a microcosm of the social macrocosm. Again there are complex issues of class displayed here, because these are all characters played by actors, either skilled dancers from the Inns of Court or professionals. The gentry and nobility were representing the range of social ranks via parody, and within the context of the overarching social philosophy that a promiscuous commixture of rustic types was somehow more 'real' or 'authentic' – certainly more alive – than collections of gods or nymphs. There is a commonly repeated theme in the history of art here, namely, that periodically elite arts have a tendency to become rarefied and self absorbed, and artists feel the need for inspiration from outside to break down the incestuousness. This is the express subtext in this piece, and seems to represent something of the spirit of the age. The dance thus (dramatically) represents a social hierarchy, but (theatrically) in its mode of presentation and inspiration it challenges a basic premise of hierarchies, that is, that the top is superior to, and leads, the bottom in all affairs.

The fact that the dancers are in couples is the key to understanding the basic meaning of this dance, and the dance clearly needs every social type to exist in a couple to function. In most other descriptions of morris, the fool exists as a unique individual – even when other dancers are paired off. So the slightly cumbersome device of having both a he-fool and a she-fool indicates that Beaumont wanted a fool in the dance (because morris dances have fools) but had to duplicate the role to keep everyone partnered. Thus, the dance is somewhat of a fanciful creation of the masquewright and perhaps only indirectly or loosely related to rural prototypes.

The heavy emphasis on partners, in fact, suggests that the dance performed here was a kind of country dance, a dance vogue which had entered elite circles towards the end of Elizabeth's reign. There are several kinds of country dance that might fit the bill, but the most obvious for six couples at this time would be a circular, progressive dance. The longways formation (i.e., two lines) was known at the time, but was not particularly popular until the Restoration and later; round dances were much more common in the early seventeenth century.[4] Furthermore, the old country morris probably used a circular formation (although with a central focus), so this could be a point of continuity with it.

A circular, *progressive* dance is one in which a sequence of figures is followed by a change of partners (typically each man, or woman, moving around one place in the circle to pick up a new partner) and then repeated. In this dance, it would take six such changes for the original partners to be back together again, creating a dance that starts in order, devolves into a chaotic intermingling of types – allowing for much byplay and humour – and then returns to order. Such a dance would fit the description of it as a 'confusion, or commixture of all such persons as are naturall and proper for Countrey sports' and may also help to interpret the expression, 'the Dancers, or rather Actors, expressed every one their part so naturally, and aptly, as when a Mans eye was caught with the one, and then past on to the other,' although this could equally apply to an audience member watching.

Whatever the formal circumstances of the dance, there is no question that its underlying theme was love and courtship, given the use of stereotyped partners, as well as the dramatic and theatric contexts, both of which were the celebration of marriage. The contexts also involved playful contention (between Mercury and Iris, between the couples, and between the partners possibly), so that, while the form of the morris had changed substantially from the ring morisk, certain themes had been retained. There are still faint echoes of the older disguisings based on the tournament tradition (including the use of the Pedant as a kind of herald), even though much of the substance has changed.[5]

Because of its popularity at court, Beaumont's partner John Fletcher imported the dance wholesale into his joint effort with Shakespeare *The Two Noble Kinsmen*, a play based on Chaucer's *Knight's Tale*. The transposition into a completely different vehicle required some modifications – in particular the addition of dialogue for some of the characters – but it retained its basic form. The transfer was made possible, in part, by the fact that the play, although quite different in conception and specifics, shares certain themes with the masque (e.g., contention in love), making the dance appropriate to both.

The main narrative of the play concerns Arcite and Palamon (Theban prisoners of Theseus, duke of Athens) who both, while in captivity, fall in love with Emilia, the duke's sister-in-law, and vow to fight to the death for her. However, before they get the chance, Arcite is serendipitously released into exile, and Palamon escapes with the aid of the jailer's daughter, who is in love with him. Palamon arranges a meeting with her in a wood outside Athens to remove his shackles, but meanwhile stumbles into Arcite, who has not gone into exile but remained in Athens secretly to attempt to court Emilia. This so inflames Palamon that they arrange for a mortal duel. The jailer's daughter, meanwhile, wanders through the wood seeking Palamon and eventually goes mad. At length she comes upon a rustic crew rehearsing a morris to be presented to Theseus while he is out hunting. The morris is led by a schoolmaster (i.e., pedant) Gerrold, who is in the process of explaining how the morris should be presented when she comes by:

> ... here stand I; here the Duke comes; there are you close in the Thicket; the Duke appears, I meete him and unto him I utter learned things, and many figures, he hears, and nods, and hums, and then cries rare, and I goe forward, at length I fling my Cap up; marke there; then do you as once did *Meleager*, and the Bore break comly out before him: like true lovers, cast your selves in a Body decently, and sweetly, by a figure trace, and turne, Boyes.
> (Fletcher and Shakespeare 1613, 213)

It is thus evident that the scene and stage business from the play almost exactly replicate those of the masque dance – that is, a pedant introduces the dancers who rush from a thicket and present their figures.

Having established their manner of entry, the dancers couple up to make sure that everyone is present, discovering, thereby, that one woman is missing.[6] The dancers are desperate for a replacement and, on seeing the jailer's daughter, immediately recruit her. There is an implication in the text that being mad, rather than being a disqualification, is an advantage for morris dancing (specifically in terms of wild movements), and also punning on the common literary metaphor 'mad morris.' She partners the second countryman who, if their order of enumeration represents their places in the dance, plays the servingman, and, therefore, her part is that of the chambermaid. This device helps integrate the morris dance into the narrative of the play, even though it is clearly an interruption to the main narrative, and the whole conceit rather artificially grafted in. It also brings the play more in line with others that include a morris dance inasmuch as it is common to involve one or two of the main characters in the dance.

When the duke and his train pass through on their stag hunt Gerrold halts them and delivers an introductory speech, reminiscent of No-body's, thus blending the style of the court spectacle and the stage play:

> SCHOOLEMASTER. If you but favor, our Country pastime made is;
> We are a few of those collected here
> That ruder Tongues distinguish villager;
> And to say veritie, and not to fable,
> We are a merry rout, or else a rable
> Or company, or, by a figure, *Choris,*
> That 'fore thy dignitie will dance a Morris ...   (Fletcher and Shakespeare 1613, 216–17)

The villagers rush in and dance. Towards the end of the dance (judging from the words), they sing the following lyric, which was not part of the masque dance:

> *Ladies, if we have beene merry*
> *And have pleasd ye with a derry,*
> *And a derry, and a downe,*
> *Say the Schoolemaster's no Clowne:*
> *Duke, if we have pleasd thee too*
> *And have done as good Boyes should doe,*
> *Give us but a tree or twaine*
> *For a Maypole, and againe*
> *Ere another yeare run out,*
> *Wee'l make thee laugh and all this rout.*   (Fletcher and Shakespeare 1613, 217)

Some confusion among scholars about the morris of the masque and the play being a maypole dance derives from this song, which some have interpreted as meaning that the dancers were actually using a maypole here (see Sabol 1978, 577–8). But it is evident from the lyric that they are asking for permission to cut a tree for a maypole for *future* performances. Furthermore, nothing in the text prior to the dance indicates that they have set up a maypole – which would be an incongruous thing to do in the woods anyway. Customarily the maypole was drawn home *from* the woods and set up in town, so it would be appropriate for the villagers to seek permission to cut a tree for that purpose – for future dances – while in the woods (and illegal to have done so without the duke's authorization). After the dance the duke rewards the dancers:

> THESEUS. Schoolemaster, I thanke you; One see 'em rewarded.
> PIRITHOUS. And heer's something to paint your Pole withall.
>
> (Fletcher and Shakespeare 1613, 218)

Although Pirithous's statement is a double entendre, the implication here is also that the making of the maypole is a future event.

The transition of the dance from masque to play was, thus, relatively straightforward, the changes (mostly narrative, such as the schoolmaster's introduction) reflecting the greater reliance of plays on dialogue versus the emphasis on action and mime in masques; this case study also indicates that masques and other private spectacles could act as direct sources for stage morris. But curiously the track does not end there because William D'Avenant rewrote the whole play for the Restoration theatre under the title *The Rivals* and also included an interlude with morris dancing in it. This was the last play to include a morris and is also the only Restoration play to do so. What is particularly interesting about D'Avenant's morris is that its dramatic context is much the same as Fletcher's in broad outline, but the rustic interlude in the woods that it forms part of is almost a representation of a full-blown masque (the morris being the antimasque). So, in an involuted fashion, the morris has returned to the masque context (in this case a masque within a play). It is also curious that D'Avenant should be intent on including a morris in the masque, since internal evidence in the play suggests that he was not sure how to go about staging it, presumably because by this time morris (off stage and on) was a rarity. Further details concerning this play and its morris may be found later in the chapter.

The morris of stage plays thus derived from several sources, and may represent a hybrid of influences. And of course once the vogue was established, plays influenced each other, producing more complex hybrid forms. Nonetheless, certain basic strains emerge from the texts. Before examining the texts themselves, though, one methodological point needs to be re-emphasized. In the past, commentators on play texts have generally sidestepped internal textual evidence to discover what the morris in the plays was like, in favour of using external (usually anachronistic and often irrelevant) data. In my examination of the texts here I start from a thoroughly agnostic position – making no assumptions concerning what the dances were like (and not even assuming that stage morrises resembled each other) – and use only internal evidence to develop hypotheses concerning form, *subsequently* noting congruences with other morrises on and off stage.

ELIZABETHAN PLAYS

Anthony Munday's *John a Kent and John a Cumber* appears to be the first stage play to incorporate a morris dance. Modern scholarship places the date of composition of the play in the late 1580s with a *terminus ad quem* of 1589 (see Pennell 1980, 43–5, for details). This means that there was roughly a ten year gap (until 1599) before the production of the next publicly staged play with a morris as part of the action.[7] So it cannot reasonably be maintained that Munday's idea immediately started a fashion. Indeed, it is quite conceivable that his effort passed without notice, and that the interest in morris on stage that blossomed around 1599/1600 – in the midst of which Kemp performed his celebrated jig – was an independent invention.

The whole question of the influence of *John a Kent and John a Cumber* on later plays really hinges on the importance of the play in its day, and this is a matter of considerable uncertainty given that there is no written evidence of production of the play under that name at all. One line of argument – the most parsimonious – would be that, since the play text exists in a unique and fragmented prompt book manuscript, since there is no record of its production among the major companies, and since the play can at best be described as mediocre, it had an extremely limited life on the stage.

Some scholars have, however, tried to give the play a longer life by equating it with the title *The Wise Man of West Chester*, which appears frequently in the Admiral's company records, but for which no text exists. The case for the identity of the two rests on the fact that the action of *John a Kent and John a Cumber* takes place in West Chester, and that the lead character, John a Kent, may be described as a 'wise man' (see Pennell 1980, 53). Tenuous though the argument may be, if we accept that *John a Kent and John a Cumber* is *The Wise Man of West Chester*, then the tables are completely turned, because this latter was enormously successful. Alfred Harbage calculates that the play was performed at least thirty-two times between 1594 and 1597 to a total audience in excess of 42,000 (Harbage 1941, 43), and would, therefore, have been a model well worth emulating. The main reason to doubt this analysis is that the text as it exists has little literary or dramatic merit, and so would have had to rely heavily on stage business (especially play with disguises) to sustain itself. It is consonant with the scant sources to suppose that Munday's stage morris was an early experiment whose time had not yet come.

John a Kent and John a Cumber, although not an especially worthy play when taken strictly on its dramatic merits is, nonetheless, of historic interest, not just in connection with the development of stage morris. Most important for present purposes, Munday is apparently the first playwright to integrate clowns into the plot structure of the play instead of using them merely as comic interludes that interrupt it. As such he was able to draw on folk practices (such as morris dancing), via the clowns, for inspiration and as a way of appealing to the groundlings.

John a Kent and John a Cumber has a simple plot structure possibly derivative of a basic folk theme. The magicians named in the title compete on Midsummer's eve to see which of the two can be successful, using disguise, cunning, and illusion, in getting his patrons betrothed to the two principal women, Sydanen and Marian. Cumber is initially successful but he is ultimately defeated by Kent, who is clearly the master occultist beside Cumber's stumbling efforts. Cumber's allies include the play's clowns, Turnop, Hugh the sexton, Thomas the Taberer, Spurling, Robert, and Will the boy.

At the end of one of Cumber's defeats, while he is disguised as Kent, his own clowns, led by Kent disguised as Cumber, find him sitting in contemplation and, thinking him their master's rival, seek to mock him by making him the fool in their morris:

> HUGH. Good Lord looke how Iohn a Kent sits in a browne study as it were, who[s ...] begin now? come lets knowe that.
>
> TURNOP. who shall begin? what a question is that? let mayde Marian haue the f[...] flurt at him, to set an edge on our stomacks, and let me alone in faith [...] to ierke it after her ...
>
> TURNOP. Heare ye Sir, you Sir, as one would say, good man you Sir, because breuitie is best in such queazie action, it is concluded or conditioned among vs that haus some authoritie in this case that because our Morris lacks a foole, and we knowe none fitter for it then you Mr. Iohn heeres a coat spick and span new, it neuer came on any mans back since it was made, therfore for your further credit, we will giue you hanse[...] of it, and where we took ye for a wise man before, we are contented to account of ye as our foole for euer heerafter.
>
> (Pennell 1980, 138–9)

The basic form of this morris seems reasonably clear; it involved a pipe and taborer (Thomas), four dancers (Turnop, Hugh, Spurling, and Robert), Maid Marian (Will the boy), and a fool (Cumber), and inasmuch as personnel is an index of the dance itself, it would seem to be the kind of country wooing morisk/morris popular at ales in the 1580s described in the previous chapter. Munday's purpose is, therefore, simply to import the country morris wholesale, because its clownish nature was precisely what he needed for plot purposes, that is, a dance that would undignify Cumber and set a seal on his defeat.

But there is more to Kent's revenge than certifying Cumber a clodhopper. In a previous bout Cumber had outwitted Kent by a cunningly orchestrated dance with song. It was Cumber's task to get his patrons into a locked castle where the two women resided under Kent's watchful eye. Cumber succeeds by first disguising as Kent, then outfitting his men to resemble their rivals, and then further dressing them as 'antics.'[8] In this masquerade they enter one by one, dance and sing before Kent's patrons, and enter the castle. Although the parallel is not exact, there is nonetheless a fair correspondence between this dance and the morris – four antics woo the ladies and in the process make Kent the fool in the first case, and in the second, four clowns woo Maid Marian and make Cumber the fool.

The comparison also entails clear issues of class. Cumber's antic is performed by nobles playing the part of grotesques and wooing genuinely beautiful women by using exotically contorted movements and carefully crafted song, whereas the morris involves clowns who, though attempting to be gracious, are by nature grotesque, and are seeking the love of a woman who is merely a boy in disguise. Munday's morris is thus deeply enmeshed in the dramatic and aesthetic structure of the entire play and is not simply tacked on for rustic effect. Perhaps for this reason his experiment remained unique for over a decade.

The stage history of the play, as already indicated, is unknown, but if the script were originally devised for the Strange/Admiral's company, as most critics suggest, the clowns could have been chosen from the celebrated trio of Thomas Pope, George Bryan, and William Kemp (see Pennell 1980, 43–54, for details). The one piece of circumstantial evidence to support this view is that Munday has Will the boy sing in Welsh, and the apprentice Robert Gough (or Goffe) was well known for Welsh parts; he often sang and improvised comic lines in Welsh. As an apprentice he was routinely paired with his 'running mate' William Eccleston. Gough's master was Pope, and Eccleston's was Kemp. If Kemp were Turnop he would be the leader of the morris, and thus his connection with the dance would have been established early. But these must remain exceedingly tenuous speculations.

It is not until 1599 that plays written for the general public include morris dances, but there is one text published in 1600 that may have been performed privately as early as 1592 – Thomas Nashe's *Summers Last Will and Testament.* Chambers conjectures, on the basis of internal textual evidence, that the play was performed privately by members of Archbishop Whitgift's household – possibly eked out by some of Paul's Boys – when the plague had closed public theatres (Chambers 1928, 3:451–3). The play certainly bears the stamp of an academic chamber piece rather than a popular comedy, with its bucolic setting and frequent learned classical allusions.

The play, Nashe's first, is based on an extended play on words. The lead character is (the ghost of) Will Summers, Henry VIII's celebrated fool, and the whole is a tribute to him. The ostensible theme is the passage of the seasons beginning with Spring and progressing through Summer, Autumn, and Winter – each season ushering in his train and presenting his best to the audience, the whole orchestrated by Vertumnus, god of the seasons. But of course there is a continuous deliberate confusion between Summer (the god) and Summers (the fool).

Spring opens the play proper by introducing sports suitable to his season to Will Summers:

Ver goes in, and fetcheth out the Hobby-horse & the morris daunce, who daunce about.

SUMMER. How now? is this the reckoning we shall have?

WINTER. My Lord he doth abuse you brooke it not.

AUTUMNE. *Summa totalis*, I feare, will proue him but a foole.

VER. About, about, liuely, put your horse to it, reyne him harder, ierke him with your wand, sit fast, sit fast, man; foole hold vp your bable there.

WILL SUMMER. O braue hall! O, well sayd, butcher. Now for the credit of Wostershire. The finest set of Morris-dauncers that is betweene this and Stretham: mary, me thinks there is one of them daunceth like a Clothyers horse, with a wool-pack on his backe. You, friend with the hobby-horse, goe not too fast, for feare of wearing out my Lords tylestones with your hob-nayles.

VER. So, so, so; trot the ring twise ouer, and away. May it please my lord, this is the grand capitall summe; but there are certayne parcels behind as you shall see.

SUMMER. Nay, nay, no more; for this is all too much.

VER. Content your selfe, we'le haue variety.

Here enter 3. Clownes, & 3. maids, singing this song, daunsing.

Trip and goe ...   (Nashe 1600, 239–40)

This is the sum of the morris's involvement in the play; there is no deeper connection to the plot (such as it is), so that the dance is really no more than an interlude. There is little direct evidence therefore concerning the form of the dance, but there are certain clues. Perhaps most important, the hobby horse appears in this dance and is clearly a paramount character, drawing forth considerable comment from Summers and Vertumnus concerning his proper dance style. This is the first use of a hobby horse in a stage morris and one of the earliest references to the morris hobby in any context. Nashe, thus, is most likely capitalizing on a new rural morris fad; the hobby horse gets most of the attention as is appropriate for a new celebrity.

It also seems evident that the hobby's antics are rather separate from the rest of the dance (the character is apparently a supernumerary attraction – he is told to 'trot the ring twise ouer, and *away*'), suggesting that he had been grafted on to the dance from a distinct source and still maintained some separate identity and status. This issue is taken up more fully in the next chapter; suffice it here to say that the hobby horse had been a well-known dance and folk character in England for several hundred years, but its association with the morris was not established until the 1590s, that is, around the time of the rise of rural (non-church sponsored) morris, when morris dance ideas appear to have been in considerable ferment.[9]

Although Nashe gives no indication of the dance form there are several inferences to be made from this text and his other works, although the overall picture is confusing. In the passage from *The Return of Pasquill* cited earlier (p. 169) he clearly identifies the morris with the ring morisk, but in his preface to Sir Philip Sidney's *Astrophel & Stella* he says:

Indeede, to say the truth, my stile is somewhat heauie gated, and cannot daunce trip and goe
so liuely, with oh my loue, ah my loue, all my loues gone, as other Sheepheards that haue beene
fooles in the Morris time out of minde ...   (Nashe 1591, 332)

This seems to suggest that he thinks 'Trip and Go' is a rural morris dance (although
it is just possible to read the passage to mean that shepherds dance 'Trip and Go' *and*
the morris). But 'Trip and Go' was a well-known partner dance for men and women,
and Nashe clearly knew this, because he introduces a version for three men and
women *after* the morris in *Summers Last Will and Testament*, specifically for 'variety.'
So it would make sense to interpret Nashe's intention as to have a morris of the ring
morisk type, followed by a partner country dance. But this leaves the role of the hobby
horse obscure; it would have no part to play in the wooing of the lady, although it
could simply be a general supernumerary with no specific function – especially since
his part seems to be limited to a particular act.

What this discussion may ultimately suggest is that literary minds, such as Nashe's,
were not entirely clear what a morris dance entailed, and may have confused morris
and other dances from May games (such as partner dances), because the difference was
of little interest to them. Or, it may be that at this time the morris dance was pick-
ing up ideas from other dances (at some point morris did adopt ideas from partner
dances), and Nashe's confusion derives from a certain confusion in the original. It
is at the very least plausible to assume that innovation in the rural dance at this time
made it newly (if ephemerally) attractive to literati and the urbane, and hence its
appearance in stage plays. Still further, it is possible that the melting pot of ideas
presented on stage may have cycled back through the audience into the tradition
(particularly on provincial tours) fueling greater synthesis and innovation, although
the obscurity of most of these plays makes this process, at best, a minor source for
creative change.

The clustering of plays with morrises in them around 1599/1600 derives from an
attraction for the dance on the part of an anonymous playwright (almost certainly John
Marston) and interest in the morris stirred up by Kemp's famous tour. The play
Histrio-Mastix Or, The Player Whipt was given in revival by Paul's Boys in 1599, but it
may be a rewritten version of an earlier play. Marston may therefore not be responsible for the entire piece and, further, it is possible that he did not initiate the use
of morris in it. However, the original, if it ever existed, is now lost, so we must focus
on the extant text (see Chambers 1923, 4:17–19, for consideration of the play's
predecessor).

Histrio-Mastix as the title suggests is a comic attack on professional acting companies contained within a rather academic framework (the 'original' academic play
is arguably the protoplay, perhaps performed at a college, the Inns of Court, or in
a private household). The basic narrative thread is the supposed cyclic course of the

state through Peace, Plenty, Envy, War, Poverty, and back to Peace, examined in microcosm by following the progression of a company of actors, who wax and wane in their fortunes like a state in miniature. Their leading poet, Posthaste, is a parody of Anthony Munday, and many of his devices (including the morris) are the subject of lampoon. In fact, the play, like Munday's, constantly introduces folk figures who perform a thematic song or dance to add variety to the dialogue. The morris is introduced as one such interlude at a time when the company is growing fat in Plenty:

> PORTER. A Morrice-daunce of neighbours craue admittance.
> CLAR. Porter, let them in man.
> *Enter Morrice-dancers.*
> Butler, make them drinke their skinnes full.
> OMNES MOR. DAN. God blesse the founder.   (Marston 1610, sig C2v)

There is no clear indication here that the dancers actually perform, although it can be taken as implied on their entrance (the drink is a reward for the show), and the general message is that in times of plenty everyone can afford to be generous, and those who have to dance the morris to get a skinful can be satisfied. Otherwise there is no internal evidence concerning the nature of the dance intended.

This notion of the morris dance flourishing at the generosity of the well-to-do is strongly echoed in Marston's *Iacke Drums Entertainment*, first performed by Paul's Boys in 1600. The morris dance forms part of the opening moments of the play (Marston 1601, sig. A2v–A3), and although the dance is not really integrated into the plot, neither is it merely an interlude. The social milieu of the dance, especially the remuneration of the dancers in cash and drink, is used as a context for exploring the characters of two of the leads, Sir Edward, a rich man with two eligible daughters, and M. Mamon, a userer who is vying for one of them in marriage.

The dramatic device here is expressly one of contrasts. M. Mamon tries to be ingratiating by asking about the royal court, and Sir Edward turns away the flattery by suggesting that talking about Kemp's morris would be *less* foolish than what the courtiers spend their time discussing. This discussion signals the arrival of what is apparently more than just Holloway morris, but an entire May game with May Lord and maypole.

> *The Taber and Pipe strike up a morrice.*
> *A shoute within.*
> *A Lord, a Lord, a Lord, who!*
> ED. Oh a Morice is come, observe our country sport,
> Tis Whitson-tyde, and we must frolick it.
> *Enter the Morrice.*

The Song.
Skip it, & trip it, nimbly, nimbly, tickle it, tickle it lustily,
Strike up the Taber, for the wenches favor, tickle it, tickle it lustily:
Let us be seene, on Hygate Greene, to daunce for the honour of Holloway.
Since we are come hither, lets spare for no leather,
To daunce for the honour of Holloway.   (Marston 1601, sig. A2v–A3)

Subsequently Sir Edward explicity states that the court of the May Lord is more alive than the royal court (echoed later in other texts such as Beaumont's *Masque of the Inner Temple and Gray's Inn*), and that he would rather wear the May Lord's livery than that of any other court. The general theme, therefore, is that the morris dance is emblematic of honest recreation and pleasure, and that the rustic life that spawns it is genuine or authentic (not artificial like the court).

The subsequent dialogue of the fool with Mamon confirms this interpretation and adds another dimension, namely, that the existence of the court and nobility, although artificial, is extremely costly, and beggars the honest working class ('a fewe great make a many small'). Mamon is content with this state of affairs (because he aspires to the court), but Sir Edward values noblesse oblige, and sets to a lengthy argument with Mamon on the subject, that stands as a symbol of the battle between the old values of the landed gentry and the new values of the self-made capitalists. Mamon thus does not oppose morris dancing because he is a Puritan (although he bears some of the marks), but because the dancers demand more money than they have 'earned' as members of a free market economy (hence he gives only a small contribution to the fool). The whole discussion, therefore, records in miniature the socioeconomic cleavage tearing at the foundations of the English state, and morris dancing, once again, typifies old values. In the final analysis the dance and the results of largesse are to Sir Edward a source of amusement and are not measureable in financial terms, and his attitude towards appropriate holiday demeanour is distinctly anti-Puritan.

There is little to conjecture concerning the actual form of the morris because of the sparseness of the internal evidence. About the only hard data are that they had a fool as one character (whose role included bantering with and collecting from the audience), the dancers sang as they danced, and, apparently, they danced as they progressed from Holloway along with the general May game procession. They may have used a maypole in the dance or (more likely from the dialogue) it may have been part of the general scene of the May game, perhaps not even visible on-stage.

The only other play in the Elizabethan era to show anything like Munday's attempt to integrate the morris dance into the plot structure is Thomas Dekker's *The Shoemakers' Holiday*, performed first at court by the Admiral's company on New Year's Day 1600. The dancers are main characters, not extras brought in for effect.

Rowland Lacy (nephew to the earl of Lincoln) loves the mayor of London's daughter (Rose) much to his uncle's dismay. To end the suit, Lincoln sends Lacy off to war, but Lacy endeavours to stay in London disguised as a Dutch shoemaker and seeks employment with Simon Eyre. When Eyre is elected sheriff of London his journeymen (including Lacy) meet him at Old Ford (the mayor's country house) and celebrate his election with a morris. The dance is also an opportunity for Lacy to do some secret courting:

> *A noyse within of a Taber and a Pipe.*
> L.MA. What noyse is this?
> EYRE. O my Lord Maior, a crue of good fellowes that for loue to your honour, are come hither with a morrisdance, come in my Mesopotamians cheerely.
> *Enter* Hodge. [Lacie *as*] Hans, Ralphe, Firke, *and other shooe-makers in a morris: after a little dauncing the* Lord Maior *speakes.*
> L.MA. Maister *Eyre*, are al these shoe-makers
> EYRE. Al Cordwainers my good Lord Maior.
> ROSE. How like my *Lacie* lookes yond shooe-maker   [*Aside*]
> LACIE. O that I durst but speake vnto my loue   [*Aside*]
> L.MA. *Sibil*, go fetch some wine to make these drinke, You are al welcome.
> ALL. We thanke your Lordship.
> …
> L.MA. Wel, vrgent busines cals me backe to *London*:
> Good fellowes, first go in and taste our cheare,
> And to make merrie as you homeward go,
> Spend these two angels in beere at *Stratford Boe*.
> EYRE. To these two my madde lads *Sim Eyre* adds another, then cheerely Firke, tickle it Haunce, and al for the honour of shoe-makers.
> *All goe dauncing out.*   (Dekker 1600, 56–7)

This reference is something of an oddity in that it purportedly represents guild morris, yet guild support of, and participation in, morris dancing was at a low ebb at this point (it had completely died out in London and survived only in small provincial cities), so it is doubtful that Dekker was trying to represent an active urban tradition. However, leaving aside the nature of the personnel, in all other circumstantial and contextual respects the dance resembles a rural morris, so it seems likely that Dekker was being syncretic (and perhaps anachronistic) for the sake of a useful plot device. That is, he grafted a contemporary rural morris idea on to a plot involving members of a London craft guild, knowing that London guildsmen at one time (just about within living memory) danced the morris, but not having any other models to draw on besides the popular rural version of the day.

In many respects this passage and the morris passage in *Iacke Drums Entertainment* resemble each other – the dancers process to a country setting to entertain a rich man and his eligible daughter, subsequently to be rewarded with drink and money, which act spawns a plot development – and there are also some slight similarities of language – 'tickle it lustily:/ Let us be seene, on Hygate Greene, to daunce for the honour of *Holloway*,' versus 'then cheerely Firke, tickle it Haunce, and al for the honour of shoe-makers.' So there is possibly some borrowing between the two (Marston would be copying Dekker, because the reference to Kemp in *Iacke Drums Entertainment* places the first performance of the play after Lent 1600, and *Shoemakers' Holiday* was played at the start of that year).

Dekker's dance involves four main characters, plus extras, but there are no indications as to the form of the dance. If it were a rural ring morisk it would be appropriate for the plot, but nothing in the text necessitates this interpretation, and it could just as easily be a simple processional. It does not seem to have much variety to it if the stage direction '*after a little dauncing the* Lord Maior *speakes*' is to be taken literally. It seems to indicate that the dance is relatively simple and, thus, can be stopped at an arbitrary point.

Although it is not clear in all cases which companies these plays in the Elizabethan era were originally written for, the Admiral's Company and Paul's Boys (who were occasionally associated with each other) are the dominant forces. This suggests that the drive to include morris in plays came as much from the personnel of these companies as from the creativity of the playwrights, or, rather that, as in the creation of certain characters, there was an artistic interdependence between company and playwright. At any event, this apparent exclusivity of dance and company did not extend beyond Elizabeth's reign.

KEMP'S MORRIS

Strictly speaking William Kemp's morris dance from London to Norwich in 1600 was not a stage performance, but it was so intimately connected with the theatrical milieu of the late Elizabethan period that it is best understood in that context. In turn, analysis of the dance sheds light on the stage performance of the time.

Little is known about Kemp, and perhaps even less would be known were it not for his dancing feat, which produced a great deal of publicity for him (positive and negative), prompting him to publish his own account of the journey – whose full title hints at the notoriety he had achieved in a few short days:

Kemps nine daies wonder. Performed in a daunce from London to Norwich. Containing the plaeasure, paines and kinde entertainment *of* William Kemp *between* London *and that Citty in his late Morrice. Wherein is somewhat set downe worth note; to reprooue the slaunders spred of him: many things merry, nothing hurtfull.* Written by himselfe to satisfie his friends.

Several points about his life prior to the morris are reasonably well attested, how-ever. He was an adventurer, he was one of the best stage clowns of his day, and he was well known for his stage jigs (see Chambers 1923, 2:325–7, for a summary of sources). Kemp first appears in 1585 as a member of a breakaway group of Leices-ter's men who toured Denmark in that year and the next, and then moved on to Saxony before returning to England in 1587. On the earl of Leicester's death in 1588, the company disbanded and several of its principal actors (including Kemp) joined the Strange company which, after many metamorphoses, became the Cham-berlain's company, with which he performed with Shakespeare and Burbage (see MacLean 1988, 487–93, for details).

In the 1590s he was clearly the preeminent stage clown in England. Thomas Nashe dedicated the anti-Martinist tract *An Almond for a Parrat* to him in glowing words (Nashe 1590, 342), and it is clear that his reputation was tremendous at the time, and continued to grow. Through the 1590s he published four jigs (no longer extant) which were short comic postludes – made up of verse, song, and dance – tacked on to the main drama of the day as a bonus (see Baskervill 1929). Although there is no clear connection between the music and Kemp's pieces, there are several tunes entitled 'Kemp's Jig' that were popular for dance melodies in the seventeenth century. One, for example, appears in the first edition of John Playford's *English Dancing Master*. Whether directly associated or not, they attest his popularity as a dancer and jig-maker. Likewise, the expression 'Kemp's Jig' was a byword in the late sixteenth century for buffoonery.

Early in 1599 Kemp sold his share in the Chamberlain's company for reasons unknown. Nor is it known what he did for the next year. There is little question, though, that the idea to dance the morris from London to Norwich was calculated to both raise money and gain him publicity – perhaps more the former than the latter, although the result was quite the reverse. The journey was conducted as part of a wager in which all comers pledged three-to-one that Kemp could not dance from London to Norwich in nine days. The exact terms of the wager are no longer available, but it appears that there was a great deal of cavilling after the event, and Kemp did not raise all that he had hoped. He records at the end of *Nine Daies Wonder*:

It resteth now that in a word I shew what profit I haue made by my Morrice. True it is I put out some money to haue threefold gaine at my return: some that loue me, regard my paines, and respect their promise, haue sent home the treble worth; some other at the first sight haue paide me, if I came to seek them; others I cannot see, nor wil they willingly be found, and these are the greater number.   (Kemp 1600, 19)

Part of the point (the main point perhaps) of writing *Nine Daies Wonder* appears to have been to establish that he did indeed accomplish the task as set – contrary to rumours running around London – and to warn his debtors that they were in default. He even threatens to publish a list of their names unless they pay up. The curious thing about the narrative is, however, that it by no means demonstrates that he danced from London to Norwich in nine days, if this truly was the kernel of the wager. The journey took close to a month if one reckons strictly by calendar time, although this may not have been a critical issue. The point according to Kemp was how many days he was actually dancing, which he claims to have been nine. Even if we allow that the final entry into Norwich (which was delayed several days to allow the city notables a chance to prepare a proper welcome) not be counted in the total, he still took *eleven* days of dancing for the full journey, although some dubious sophistry creeps into his narrative to reduce the number to nine. Basically two days, marked in the itinerary below as 'half' days, were only short stints of a few miles that Kemp did not count, but tacked on to the next 'full' day.

According to the account in *Nine Daies Wonder* Kemp's tour was as follows:

DAY 1	11–02–1600	London to Romford
DAY 2	14–02–1600	Romford to Ingatestone
DAY 3	15–02–1600	Ingatestone to Chelmsford
(DAY 3.5	16–02–1600	3 miles out of Chelmsford)
DAY 4	18–02–1600	Chelmsford to Braintree
(DAY 4.5	19–02–1600	3 miles out of Braintree)
DAY 5	20–02–1600	Braintree to Melford
DAY 6	23–02–1600	Melford to Bury St Edmunds
DAY 7	29–02–1600	Bury to Thetford
DAY 8	03–03–1600	Thetford to Hingham
DAY 9	04–03–1600[10]	Hingham to Norwich
	08–03–1600	Norwich entry.
	11–03–1600	(Repeat of Norwich entry)

The details of the journey can easily be read in the original, but there are several issues concerning the nature of the morris which we may consider here. The text itself says very little concerning the form of the dance, implying that a literate audience would not need such information. Instead, he concentrates on the events surrounding the journey: people met, unusual happenings, kindnesses bestowed. Even so, in the course of these descriptions hints about the dance are dropped, and certain choreographic ideas are implicit.

Perhaps too obvious to be noted, Kemp's (and his followers') notion of a morris was something that could be done solo. That is, the essence of the dance lay not in figured choreography or other business (although these may have occurred in dances for greater numbers), but in the actions of individuals – recalling once again the ring morisk whose performers vied for the love of the central lady by each leaping and cavorting in his own manner. Certainly Kemp's morris involved vigorous leaping and capering; he occasionally refers to his dances as 'leaps' or 'jumps' and many of his anecdotes – particularly towards the end when he set up a punishing pace – concern leaving his would-be companions panting in the dust (or mud). The most famous of these (inspiration of more than one poem) concerns a Sudbury butcher:

> In this towne of Sudbury there came a lusty, tall fellow, a butcher by his profession, that would in a Morrice keepe mee company to Bury: I being glad of his friendly offer, gaue him thankes, and forward wee did set; but ere euer wee had measur'd halfe a mile of our way, he gaue me ouer in the plain field, protesting that if he might get 100 pound, he would not hold out with me; for indeed my pace in dauncing is not ordinary.
>
> As he and I were parting, a lusty Country lasse being among the people, cal'd him faint hearted lout, saying, 'If I had begun to daunce, I would haue held out one myle though it had cost me my life.' At which wordes many laughed. 'Nay,' saith she, 'if the Dauncer will lend me a leash of his belles, Ile venter to treade one mile with him my selfe.' I lookt vpon her, saw mirth in her eies, heard boldnes in her words, and beheld her ready to tucke vp her russet petticoate; I fitted her with bels, which [s]he merrily taking, garnisht her thicke short legs, and with a smooth brow bad the Tabrer begin. The Drum strucke; forward marcht I with my merry Maydemarian, who shooke her fat sides, and footed it merrily to Melfoord, being a long myle. There parting with her, I gaue her (besides her skinfull of drinke) an English crowne to buy more drinke; for good wench, she was in a pittious heate: my kindnes she requited with dropping some dozen of short courtsies, and bidding God blesse the Dauncer. I bad her adieu; and to giue her her due, she had a good eare, daunst truely, and wee parted friendly.   (Kemp 1840, 9–10)

This account raises several other issues, notably that women could and did dance at this time, and that apparently the morris was reasonably well known by country people along his route.

That women were able dancers is corroborated by another incident earlier in his journey:

> At Chelmsford, a Mayde not passing fourteene yeares of age, dwelling with one Sudley, my kinde friend, made request to her Master and Dame that she might dance the Morrice with me in a great large roome. They being intreated, I was soone wonne to fit her with bels; besides she would haue the olde fashion, with napking on her armes; and to our jumps we fell. A whole houre she held out; but then being ready to lye downe I left her off; but thus much in her praise, I would haue challenged the strongest man in Chelmsford, and amongst many I thinke few would haue done so much.   (Kemp 1840, 7)

Kemp seems not to find the idea of women dancing the morris peculiar, although these citations are among the first references to women performing in the dance. Admittedly he uses the term 'Maid Marian' for them – placing them in a standard morris role – but this was normally a boy's part. What these incidents may signal is the changing of rural fashions of dance, with women taking an increasingly active role, in the process assisting the transformation of the rural dance.

These two accounts together also yield further insights into the nature of the dance itself. It could be performed stationary or as a processional, yet in both cases was enormously vigorous. Neither does the dance have any obvious beginning or end. The woman at Chelmsford danced for an hour (presumably without respite), at which point Kemp quit; but the implication is that, in principle, either could have danced longer, or left off sooner. It is also implicit that the dances Kemp and his companions were performing were roughly equivalent, although they might have varied somewhat in style. The dance in Chelmsford would not have had much justification if the two were performing completely different dances (and they could not have performed to the same music), although some individual variation would not only have been normal, but, presumably, part of the point of the dance. Furthermore Kemp compliments the Sudbury women by saying she 'daunst truely,' again suggesting that there was a standard (however flexible) against which one might be judged. In turn, then, it follows that if Kemp and the country people were performing roughly the same dance, that the stage morris of Kemp's time was drawn from rural models.

Somewhat more about the dance may also be gleaned from the woodcut on the title page (figure 19, p.136). The image is quite basic, with much detail missing and little attempt to be more than minimally representational. Tom Slye the taborer is wearing what appear to be simple street clothes – a jerkin and knee breeches, with a wide-brimmed, high crowned hat. His pipe – played in the left hand – if drawn to scale is around thirty inches long, which would make it a rather deep instrument, and the drum is around the size of a small side-drum.

Kemp has on his head a high-crowned narrow-brimmed hat decorated on the right side with a showy (possibly ostrich) feather. His long hair (typical of actors and much railed at by Puritans) flows out from under the brim down to his long full beard. He is also wearing a vine-patterned waist-length jacket with long dagged points attached to the upper arms and flowing out free from the elbows. With hands by his sides these points would reach the ground, but in dancing with arms raised and jerked upwards they flow and swirl around the dancer. To move them would require vigorous motions of the whole arm from the shoulder (and whole body movements). Kemp notes that the maid from Chelmsford 'would haue the olde fashion, with napking on her armes' suggesting that napkins could be used as an alternative to the 'morris' sleeve, which corroborates the description in Ralph's speech in Beaumont and Fletcher's *The Knight of the Burning Pestle* – 'and napkins cleane unto your shoulders tide.' But there is no primary material to support Kemp's assertion that this was the 'old' style in comparison with his – quite the contrary. It is only the second reference in the primary literature to the use of napkins in the dance, the earlier being roughly contemporary (1591). But, as reported in previous chapters, special coats (probably with dagged sleeves) are as old as the morris in England. Either way, the use of flowing material at the arms was a key component in the dance. It is also possible that Kemp is gesticulating with his fingers since every other aspect of his body is drawn in a stylized manner, but the finger attitudes are quite marked.

His knee breeches are cut very full and balloon out conspicuously from the waist to the knee. Below the knees, covering most of his calves, he has on pads of crotal bells. Eight or nine are showing, so he may have on as many as a dozen per leg. His shoes – described as 'buskins' (i.e., half boots) in the text – are too stylized to make out, but seem to come up his calf to the bottoms of his bell pads. He was heavily shod, no doubt, to combat the perilous state of disrepair the roads were in; this is his almost constant comment.

On its completion, the dance and Kemp were the talk of the nation, and remained so for many years. At least two stage plays featured Kemp as a character *in propria persona* – *The Return from Parnassus* and *The Travailes of the Three English Brothers* – and there are numerous references to him in popular texts.

There are also vague hints in the primary texts that he replicated his dance in France or Italy around 1601 or 1602, although there may also be some hyperbole in them. Subsequently, he seems to have gone back to acting, this time with Worcester's men. Not long thereafter (probably before 1608) he died; yet even in death his morris remained his most clebrated feat:

Welcome from Norwich, Kempe! all joy to see
Thy safe return moriscoed lustily.
But out, alas, how soone's thy morice done
When Pipe and Taber, all thy friends be gone
And leaue thee now to dance the second part
With feeble nature, not with nimble art;
Then all thy triumphs fraught with strains of mirth,
Shall be cag'd vp within a chest of earth:
Shall be? they are: th'ast danc'd thee out of breath
And now must make thy parting dance with death.   (Brathwait 1618, sig F5)

JACOBEAN AND CAROLINE PLAYS

Kemp's journey may have stirred up interest in the morris on stage around the turn of the seventeenth century, but the fame mainly seems to have accrued to the dancer and not to the dance. It is nearly two decades later that a fresh vogue for the dance in plays occurs, although the slate is not entirely blank in the intervening years. Fletcher and Shakespeare's *Two Noble Kinsmen* appeared in 1613, and the context of the dance, as rehearsed above, is akin to those of Elizabethan stage morrises – rustics entertain a local noble with a morris as part of their May festivities in return for drinking money. However, the dance was not derived directly from rural morris, but adapted from Beaumont's masque, and appeared in the play because of the success of the masque dance at the Inns, not because rural morris per se was fashionable or especially popular at the time.

The new trend for including morrises in plays begins with an obscure work, *TEXNOΓAMIA: or the Marriages of the Arts*, by Barten Holyday (Holyday 1618). Holyday was a scholar and the piece was written to be performed by the students of his college, Christchurch, Oxford. It was performed once in 1617 by the students in their college hall where it was received indifferently, and once in 1621 before King James at Woodstock. The king found the work so tedious that he tried several times to leave in the middle, but was prevailed upon to stay by his companions so as not to discourage the players. Nonetheless the incident spawned numerous jest verses at Holyday's expense, so that the play and playwright became a universal laughing stock (see Cavanaugh 1942, xxix–xlii). Subsequently *TEXNOΓAMIA* disappeared. It can hardly be said, therefore, that the play was the motive for the new trend to include morrises in plays, Holyday's example not being one to emulate. But what he had a bent to do was clearly in line with the creative energies and minds of his day.

The main characters in *TEXNOΓAMIA* are personifications of the liberal arts who, abetted by their servants the humours, are courting one another in a web of amorous entanglements (each love affair having a symbolic, academic meaning). The morris dance has no connection to the central plot, but is simply an interlude, rather clumsily introduced (as one of several song and dance pieces).

MELAN. Prethee, *Musica*, tell mee, what thou hast in thy packe?

MUSIC. Why, because you speake kindly now, and intreat me, Ile shew you.

MELAN. Hay, braue! what's here?

SANG. Morrice-bels?

PHLEG. And waste-coates, and napkins?

CHOLER. Why, how com'st thou by them?

MUSIC. Why, thus: my Mistris had beene ill a good while, and because I tended her very carefully; shee gaue mee leaue to recreate my selfe to day; and i'faith I light on merry companie, where they vs'd these jinglers: and when they had done, they pray'd mee to carrie them home with this bottle of drinke.

SANG. Faith, and there were enow, wee'd dance.

MUSIC. Enow? now I thinke on't, there's iust enow, there's six paire.

SANG. Faith wee'll to it then, but what wouldst thou doe, *Musica?*

MUSIC. Why, Ile play the maid *Marian.*

SANG. A match, a match: dresse, dresse, wee'll haue braue jingling.

They dresse themselues.

MELAN. I can't dance.

MUSIC. Nay, prethee be not sullen, good *Melancholico.*

MELAN. If I doe, Ile weare no bels.

MUSIC. Why then lay one paire aside.

MELAN. But I woun't dance now.

MUSIC. Why, *Melancholico?*

MELAN. I woun't dance, vnlesse I haue one of the wrought waste-coates.

MUSIC. Why, now they haue put them on.

MELAN. I care not, I woun't dance else.

MUSIC. Come prethee, *Cheiromantes,* slip off thine againe and change with him; *Melancholico* must haue his sullen humours. So, now vve want nothing but the Tabor wee talk't of: but 'tis no matter, since hee does not come, wee'll sing, and so make musike to our selues. Who can tune the Morrice best?

Enter an hobby horse dancing the Morrice and a Tabourer.

Oh, here they are both, here they are both.

The hobby-horse rushes on them, and throwes them all downe.

CHEIRO. O my arme, my arme

SANG. O my shinne

CHOLER. Ah, murren on him; who the deuill's this?

PHLEG. I haue hurt my brest.

PHYSIOG. O the side of my face

MELAN. A rope on you, must you throw me quite downe?

MUSIC. Prethee dance the morrice quietly with vs: vp, vp, ho, and wee'll dance.*

* *They dance three times, the hobby-horse ouer throwes them all againe, kisses* Musica *and runnes away with the Tabourer.*   (Holyday 1618, sig. L1 recto & verso)

This description contains a great deal of detail about the form of the dance, although it must be treated with caution given the labyrinthine metaphors woven into the scene. The dancers all belong to a servant class and the equipment they are using comes from a local company, presumably of rustics (the gift of the costumes to Musica being an awkward and incongruous contrivance). There are six costumes for the main dancers (the four humours – Melancholico, Sanguis, Phlegmatico, and Choler – and two gypsy fortune-tellers – Physiognomus and Cheiromantes), consisting of bell pads, napkins, and waistcoats, some of which are 'wrought' and some not. It is tempting to suppose that the wrought waistcoats denote a function for the wearer in the dance, such as indicating the lead dancers or marking one of two columns. There were several of them, however, so they were not simply the emblem of a single foreman or foregallant.

It is clear that they need all six men for a dance. This strongly suggests that the dance was choreographed in figures, and possibly partnered (that is, any *even* number could perform – four or six being standard. If one sat out, another would have to sit out as well to balance the couples). Given the metaphoric quality of the play I would argue, however, that four men could not perform the morris that Holyday had in mind because, if they could he would have had just the four humours performing, and would not have called on the services of two gypsies to fill out the set. The image that Holyday is trying to create is of the humours grouping and regrouping in their courtship of the lively and spirited Musica, and two fortune-tellers are somewhat out of place (although it could be argued that face and palm are registers of the balance or imbalance of the humours in the body). It is useful, also, to note that Maid Marian does not wear bells, which means that she is either stationary – the partners performing in a ring around her – or her motions are much less vigorous than the men's.

The hobby horse, played by Phantastes in disguise, also plays a symbolic role, but one that presumably replicates the horse's actions in morrises of the day. He takes something of the role of the fool/trickster, causing general choas with his antics. As such he is not an intrinsic part of the formal choreography, but a supernumerary with a largely ex tempore function. His allegorical function here is to demonstrate that when he works in league with Musica (i.e., when fantasy and music unite in a fantasia) they discommode the humours. The hobby horse also seems to echo the role of the fool in the old ring morisk in that, not only is he a prankster, but he is ultimately successful in wooing the lady (he is the one who gets to kiss Musica).

Another point to note in the allegory is that melancholy (Melancholico) is temperamentally unsuited to the dance and, in fact, chooses not to dance with bells on even when he gets his way concerning the fancy waistcoats. The bells by their sound banish melancholy.

Music is supplied by pipe and tabor, from a musician who has no other role in the play; he is simply a companion to Phantastes. But before he arrives with the hobby horse, Musica, fearing he may not appear, proposes to do without him and sing the morris tune instead, using language that implies that sung music was common enough (as earlier play texts seem to corroborate). She also seems to imply that the melody is generally well known.

By contrast to *TEXNOΓAMIA*, the bulk of the plays in the 1620s that employed morris were successful pieces by popular playwrights, and their common theme is the battle brewing between the forces of tradition and puritanism – morris dancing being the ideal proving ground for their conflict. The most explicit staged version of the crisis of creeds occurs in Fletcher's *Women Pleas'd*, and the crisis occupies most of the time that the morris dancers are on stage.

The whole morris episode in *Women Pleas'd* is grafted into the play rather gratuitously. Silvio, a suitor to the beautiful heiress of Florence, Belvidere, has been exiled for a year with a riddle to solve in order to gain her hand. Meanwhile, Belvidere disappears and the duke of Siena, another suitor, declares war on Florence. Silvio hires on with a rich farmer, father to the clown/servant Soto, at harvest time when they are preparing harvest games that include a morris dance (with Soto as Lord of the Harvest/ May Lord). When Silvio appears before Soto in regular garb he is admonished in mock court style for not wearing his livery:

> SOTO. What a Devill ayles this fellow? this foolish fellow,
> Being admitted to be one of us too,
> That are the masters of the Sports proceeding,
> Thus to appeare, before me too, unmorriss'd?
> Do you know me friend?
> SILVIO.   You are my Masters Son, Sir.
> SOTO. And do you know what sports are now in season?
> SILVIO. I heare there are some a foot.
> SOTO.   Where are your Bells then?
> Your Rings, your Ribanes, and your clean Napkins?
> Your nosegay in your hat, pinn'd up? am not I here,
> My fathers eldest Son, and at this time, Sir,
> I would have ye know it, though ye be ten times his servant,
> A better man then my father far, Lord of this Harvest, sir,
> And shall a man of my place want attendance?
> SILVIO. 'Twas want of knowledge, Sir, not duty, bred this,
> I would have made suit else for your Lordships service   (Fletcher 1619, 495–6)

The morris dancers enter with Bomby the cobbler as the hobby horse, but before the dancing can commence alarums of war reach the countryside and a captain insists on enlisting Soto for the ensuing battle with Siena. Silvio offers to go in his place so that the festivities can continue, and so that he will not be exposed. All seems set for the dance, but there arises a new problem in that Bomby has been converted to Puritanism and will no longer play the hobby horse. There ensues a long comic argument between Bomby and the rest of the company (see Fletcher 1619, 499–501). In this dialogue the tone of Bomby's speeches replicates well the polemics of the Puritans – casting the morris as Popish, pagan, devilish and so on – but what is especially interesting about this interchange is that it gives a graphic account of the kinds of tensions that were pulling communities apart at the time. Bomby is drawn in one direction by his wife and preachers, and in another by his fellows. The latter cozen and then threaten him with loss of livelihood, violence, confinement, and legal proceedings before he reluctantly consents to dance. He, thus, stands for many of his contemporary countryfolk, torn between tradition and conscience. Of course the whole is cast in the form of punning banter, but the underlying issues must have been well known and keenly felt by the audience of the day for such an extended passage, not directly connected to the main plot, to sustain itself dramatically.

The Witch of Edmonton is probably the best known of all the plays that contain a morris, and certainly the most popular in its day (including a performance at court in its long run). The theme is Faustian, though the characters and plot are some-what more earthbound than their counterparts in Marlowe. Several threads weave through the narrative, and, as usual it is the comic interest of the clowns and country-men that involves the morris.

Mother Sawyer, to avenge herself on the people of Edmonton for labelling her a witch, makes a pact with the devil (who appears in the shape of a black dog) to act as her familiar in return for her soul. Cuddy Banks, clown and morris dancer, is in love with Katherine, a rich yeoman's daughter, and tries to enlist mother Sawyer (and the dog) to aid in his courtship. However, the two combine to make him foolish. Thus the serious and ultimately deadly pact of mother Sawyer is paralleled by the comic one of Cuddy Banks. All of Cuddy's preparations for a morris dance are en-twined in his connivances with mother Sawyer and the dog.

The first appearance of the dancers is typical; they are generally preparing for their performance, discussing repairs and additions to their equipment, and deciding on places to visit. The initial part of this dialogue has routinely been taken as an indication that morris dancers wore bells of different sizes to tune their jangling:

Enter Young [Cuddy] Banks [*the Clown*],
and three or four more.

CLOW. A new head for the Tabor, and silver tipping for the Pipe. Remember that, and forget not five leash of new Bells.

1. Double Bells: *Crooked Lane*, ye shall have 'em straight in *Crooked Lane*: double Bells all, if it be possible.

CLOW. Double Bells? double Coxcombs; Trebles: buy me Trebles, all Trebles: for our purpose is to be in the Altitudes.

2. All Trebles? not a Mean?

CLOW. Not one: The Morrice is so cast, we'll have neither Mean nor Base in our compa-ny, Fellow *Rowland.*

3. What? nor a Counter?

CLOW. By no means, no hunting Counter; leave that to *Envile Chase-*Men: all Trebles, all in the Altitudes. Now for the disposing of parts in the Morrice, little or no labour will serve.

(Dekker et al. 1621, 507)

However, it should be clear that this is no more than the typical clown's punningly befuddling speech, and has little bearing on actual costumes. Some, perhaps most, of the punning idioms are drawn from bell-ringing terminology (and this is echoed later when the dance actually takes place), so that the dialogue concerns any sort of bells, not strictly morris bells. In fact, the centre of the double talk concerns an imaginary quartet of bells covering the standard voices – treble, counter, mean, and bass – and plays on ambiguity and homophony in these names (e.g., mean/middle versus mean/miserly). So, for example, when Cuddy says 'we'll have neither Mean nor Base in our company' he is not making a literal statement about bells; he is not saying anything about bells at all. Yet it is surprising how many commentators want to see this as a simple, explicit command, and use it as evidence that the morris of the time used tuned bells of different sizes (see, for example, Cawte 1978, 55).

Thus, there is no contradiction when the musician Sawgut later counts off the men:

> FIDL. Come, will you set your selves in Morrice-ray? the fore-Bell, second Bell, Tenor and great Bell; Maid-marion for the same Bell. But where's the Weather-cock now? the Hobby-horse? (Dekker et al. 1621, 533)

He, like Cuddy, is using bell-ringing terminology to mark off the men (i.e., fore-bell = foregallant, and so forth), and, indeed, he may be indicating that the four are arranged in a circle (as are bells in a bell-tower) – with Maid Marian also in the circle, and the hobby horse either in the centre, or else curveting and careering around (the weather-cock of the tower).

It is abundantly clear from references in this play that the role of the hobby horse is blatantly sexual (and therefore the especial target of Puritan ire as indicated by Bomby's speeches in the previous reference). For example, Cuddy is determined to play the hobby horse because he thinks it will help in his courtship of Katherine, and it is his determination to play the hobby horse that clues his mates to the fact that he wishes to court her (see Dekker et al. 1621, 520). And a little later the dog/devil tricks him by making a spirit appear in Katherine's form before him:

> *Enter Spirit in shape of* Katherine ...
> CLOW. ... What? dost thou trip from me? Oh that I were upon my Hobby-horse, I would mount after thee so nimble. (Dekker et al. 1621, 522)

There are also a number of comic allusions in the play to the notion that the morris is governed by the devil (see Dekker et al. 1621, 534). It is the devil who plays the fiddle for the morris best (no doubt a play on the Puritans' motif of the 'devil's morris'), but it is equally clear that no real harm to anyone is done thereby. In other parts of the play the devil's handiwork is truly damning – causing lust, jealousy, adultery, murder – but here all is in jest, and the simple message is that country pleasures are harmless – too innocent to be the stuff of real devilry.

Two years later Dekker and Ford collaborated on a play *The Sun's Darling: A Moral Masque* that also features a morris, but here the dance is simply an interlude akin to those in plays of the Elizabethan era. The whole, in fact, is most reminiscent of *Summers Last Will and Testament*, although as the subtitle suggests it is something of a hybrid form with much of the spectacle and pageantry of a masque (fleshed out with dance and song), but with more dialogue and some pretense at a plot. The play was popular in its day, being active for at least fifteen years, probably attracting audiences because of its major use of music and dance rather than for its literary qualities.

The basic story recalls a masque: Raybright, a youthful beauty and child of the sun (perhaps symbolic of prince Charles and his father, King James), comes to earth to experience the four seasons. A rural morris is presented to him as part of the light-hearted festivities in the court of Spring (see Dekker and Ford 1623, 28–9).

In the same year as the first production of *The Sun's Darling*, Robert Ward wrote an academic piece, *Fucus; sive Histriomastix* (The Hypocrite, or the Scourge of Players), to be performed by the students of Queens' College, Cambridge, as a protest against the increasing force of the Puritan outcry over stage plays. It was written in Latin and so was not in any sense a public play. It was, like the similarly academic *TEXNOΓAMIA*, performed for King James and, also like its Oxford counterpart, is an allegory of love between characters named for the arts – Poetry, Comedy, and so forth.

The main character, Fucus, is a tutor appointed to oversee the work of Cornelius, a freshman. While openly seeming to approve sports and plays, Fucus works to turn his protégé against them, and in the process lays out the standard Puritan arguments against plays. Cornelius quickly discovers his tutor's disingenuousness, however, and the bulk of the play turns on the battle between Fucus and the arts personified. The morris dance, typically, is part of a subplot involving rustics whose rural games Fucus tries to suppress. The leader of the dancers is Villanus, who with other countrymen and musicians, provides a variety of rural songs and dances throughout the play, much to Fucus's disgust. Villanus and Fucus have a comic wrangle that at one point turns into a kind of maypole dance, with Villanus and his friends using Fucus as the pole.

The stage directions for the dances are not explicit enough to determine what they entail (frequently no more than *saltant* [they dance]), but there are some indications that the morris is a wooing dance, inasmuch as it comes in a courtship scene between Villanus and Ballada, who is carried away by the dance (see Ward 1909, 33). The character list at the beginning of the scene names *Choraules. Hirsutus. Ballada. Villanus. 4 Comites saltantes. Mimus*, so we may reasonably conjecture that the dance involved four morris men (the 'saltantes'), possibly Villanus and Hirsutus as well, and the music was provided by a pipe and taborer. The musician is here simply called 'Choraules,' which is literally a flute player for the chorus in the Greek drama, but later in the play, when the morris dancers are in mock lament, there is the following stage direction as part of a mime:

Vtricularius tibijs in vtre a tergo suspensis, ad eundem modum Choraules tympano et fistula a tergo suspensis et brachijs complicatis, capite demisso ambulant.

[The bagpiper, his bagpipes slung on his back, and, in the same manner, a piper (Choraules), pipe and tabor slung on his back and arms folded, walk with lowered heads.] (Ward 1909, 77)

It is clear that 'Choraules' is the best that Ward could come up with as a Latin version of pipe and taborer.

Fucus; sive Histriomastix was the last play containing a morris performed before King James, and there was only one other such play, Thomas Randolph's *Amyntas, or The Impossible Dowry*, produced in the reign of Charles I (performed at court in 1632). The story is set as a pastoral of nymphs, fairies, and shepherds with many entanglements of love crossing the worlds of all three (perhaps borrowed from Shakespeare's *Midsummer Night's Dream*). The morris takes place in a topsy-turvy context, in that it is led by Jocastus – a fairy knight disguised as a shepherd – playing Maid Marian, and performed in a mock fairy court, with a knavish boy, Dorylas, playing Oberon, king of the fairies. The whole is, therefore, a complex play on the mock courts of May games, which themselves deliberately overturn the social order.

There are few hints concerning the nature of the dance, although there may have been an element of wooing in it. The chief source of humour in the dialogue is that Jocastus (a stirling knight) has taken the part of a woman in the dance, and Oberon/Dorylas pretends to court him/her as more beautiful than Queen Mab. Bromius, Jocastus's man, takes the part of the clown/fool, but there are no other dancers or musicians mentioned to determine the overall structure of the piece. However, earlier in the play when Jocastus is preparing his revels there occurs the following dialogue:

THES. What are you studying of, Jocastus, ha?
JOC. A rare device, a masque to entertain
His grace of fairy with.
THES.   A masque! what is't?
JOC. An anti-masque of fleas, which I have taught
To dance corantoes on a spider's thread.
MOP. An anti-masque of fleas? brother, methinks
A masque of birds were better, that could dance

> The morrice in the air, wrens and robin-redbreasts,
> Linnets and titmice.   (Randolph 1632, 280)

This offers little extra help because of the ironic tone, but suggests that the morris dancers flit and twist, and that the dance has masque qualities (as would befit this subject matter). Jocastus's speech concerning the dance appears to confirm this general conjecture:

> JOC. I did not thinke there had been such delight
> In any mortall Morrice, they doe caper
> Like quarter Fairies, at the least: by my Knighthood,
> And by this sweet Mellisonant Tingle tangle,
> The ensigne of my glory, you shall bee
> Of Oberon's Revels.   (Randolph 1632, 363–4)

Randolph's morris is something of a curiosity in that it is a burlesque of the typical rustic dance but, nonetheless, the setting and the personel, as far as they can be known, seem to draw the dance (via parody) within the general norm for stage morrises.

As explored in the previous chapter, it is one of the seeming paradoxes of social history that Charles I actively supported May games and morris dances, yet they suffered a momentous decline in his reign, from which they did not recover for a century and more. The decline in the countryside was paralleled on the stage as urban tastes sought fresh inspiration elsewhere, and as the dance became less well known in town and country. Thus, well before the general prohibition of public plays, the stage morris had dwindled away.

INTERREGNUM

The popular conception that the Puritans closed the playhouses during the Interregnum, and that the theatre (like music and dancing) had to closet itself away in private houses to await a warmer climate, is an oversimplification that needs considerable qualification. It is true that – especially in Cromwell's early years – many playwrights and dramatists kept themselves in business through private patronage, but some so-called private stagings of new plays were really small-scale versions of public shows, and towards the end of the Interregnum it became easier for some individuals to obtain limited licences for full-scale public theatre. Thus Robert Cox's *Acteon and Diana*, a publicly staged play in which a morris appears, is not some anomaly, but part of a trickle of public performances linking the great streams of dramatic productions in early Stuart and Restoration London.

The performance history of the play is largely unknown, although it appears to have been produced first around 1655. There are two editions of the text, the first undated (presumably *c* 1655) and the second dated 1656. The latter contains on the cover page the notice 'Acted at the *Red Bull* with great applause' such a self-advertisement perhaps being confirmed by the existence of two editions published in relatively close order. This statement, however, may also be an attempt to bring intimations of public sentiment to bear against would-be Puritan detractors. The preface to the second edition, entitled 'To all the Worthy-minded Gentry,' abets this conclusion in that he states plainly that the piece has no intentions (seditious or otherwise) but to be light comedy, and that the best judge of his 'hopes or merits' is the general public (i.e., not Puritan officials).

The work is hard to categorize, being something of a play, entertainment, masque, proto-ballet, and proto-opera rolled into one. It is loosely cast in the form of four episodes, all concerned with love, the principals in each corresponding to the four humours. Two of these episodes, the stories of Bumpkin the huntsmen and Hobbinal the shepherd, have comic overtones but are set in a classical framework that has serious underpinnings – the first being the story of Actaeon and Diana itself (Bumpkin is one of the huntsmen), the second being a conceit of the nymph Oenone and several shepherds in love with her. The other two, the stories of Singing Simpkin the clown and John Swabber the seaman, are broad farces of cuckoldry with no serious components. The two types are alternated thus: Bumpkin (melancholic), Simpkin (phlegmatic), Hobbinal (sanguine), and Swabber (choleric).

The two classical episodes have rural settings and are heavily larded with country customs. The tale of Bumpkin, for example, contains the famous maypole song 'Come you youngmen' as an entrance piece for a chorus of huntsmen and country lasses, and a general country dance, along with other presumably more conventional stage pieces, including a huntsmen's dance and a dance of nymphs. Incidentally, the maypole song was set to the tune 'Stanes Morris' (see chapter 9) by William Chappell in the nineteenth century on the grounds that the two fit so well together, and for no other reason (Chappell 1859, 125–6). Yet, since Chappell's serendipitous experiment, almost universally, secondary sources have uncritically taken the match to be historically legitimate (see for example Dean-Smith 1957, 73, for a discussion), thus asserting a spurious equation between morris and maypoles. There is no evidence that the words and music were ever performed together before the nineteenth century.

The morris occurs in the tale of Hobbinal which is somewhat kin, although only in rudimentary fashion, to Randolph's *Amyntas*. The central theme of the episode is that it is Oenone's birthday, and Hobbinal (the archetypical rustic) has somehow conceived that the nymph loves him, and is in the process of preparing to court her – to the amusement of four other shepherds (two of whom, Amyntas and Dorilas, are also in love with her). Oenone is deeply grieved because of her loss of Paris, and the shepherds attempt to comfort and amuse her. Dorilas leads her in a dance (refusing Hobbinal's hand), after a few turns of which Hobbinal remarks:

> HOB. ... Pshaw waw, this dancing is like my mothers Mares trot, *Sport*, shal I shew thee a dance of my own fashion?
>
> OENONE. It cannot but content.
>
> HOB. Nay, I know that, hark hither, Lads. *Ex. Hob. Str.*   (Cox 1656, 24)

There follows a short soliloquy by Oenone after which, '*Hobbinall and the Shepherds dance a Morris*' (Cox 1656, 25). There must be some theatric reason why the shepherds leave briefly before the dance, the simplest hypothesis being that they need to (quickly) strap on bells. The dance seems to follow a common stage formula, namely, four main dancers and a fool (Hobbinal) woo a lady (Oenone), much as the morris in *Amyntas*, on which it may well be based.

Dramatically the dance serves as a foil to two others, Dorilas's attempt at a refined courtly (and courting) dance, and a dance of satyrs serving Pan (god of flocks and shepherds) that concludes the episode (and that does meet Oenone's approval). The morris therefore has a complex symbolic position. That is, Dorilas tries to be refined and fails, Hobbinal attempts to do what rustics do best (rather than emulate the courtly manners of the elite) and does manage to amuse Oenone although not win her love, and, finally, Pan and the satyrs succeed in seducing her.

It is hardly to be wondered at, given the blatant delight in sexual themes of questionable virtue in the play, that Cox had to appeal to the gentry to support him in case of attacks by the Puritan establishment. In fact, it is surprising that he was granted a licence at all. But again, these facts go more to suggest that a monolithic view of the Interregnum as a period of relentless repression of sex, dance, drama, and the like needs qualification, and that there are threads that act as slender lines of continuity from the early Stuart stage to the Restoration.

RESTORATION PLAYS

Sir William D'Avenant was one of the key figures in reviving the public stage after the Interregnum. He had kept it alive under the Puritan ban, skirting the edges of the law, by staging semiprivate shows, and had even managed to get a licence from the puritan government to produce a limited number of public performances. When Charles II removed the ban on theatres D'Avenant was of singular importance in recreating the stage in its former glory. His stock in trade was 'adaptating' classics of the Elizabethan and Jacobean stage – which in many cases (his version of Shakespeare's *Macbeth*, for example) involved more straight copying than rewriting. Often his goal in revising texts seems to have been to pick up the pace (and shorten the whole) by cutting long discursive sections and thereby raising the level of action.

D'Avenant's version of Fletcher and Shakespeare's *Two Noble Kinsmen*, entitled *The Rivals*, is, however, a genuine adaptation in that he has retained the structure of the original (somewhat condensed), but the dialogue, setting, and characters are mostly new. It is, therefore, something of a surprise that the section of *The Rivals* in which the morris dance appears directly plagiarizes much of Fletcher's language.[11] The following parallel transcription of a section of D'Avenant's adaptation gives a good idea of his mode of working; it also sheds light on the morris dance he created.[12]

D'Avenant	Fletcher
1. COUN. Draw up the Company! Where's the Taberer?	2. Draw up the Company; Where's the Taborour?
Ent. Taberer	
	3. Why *Timothy.*
TAB. Here, Boyes, here.	TABORER. Here, my mad boys; have at ye.
1. COUN. You all know how to make your honours.	
ALL. Yes, Yes. [*All make honours*]	
1. COUN. Sr. Reverence! You make an honour, you sh–	
Cast your selves decently into a Body	{cast your selves in a Body decently,
By a Trace, and turn Boyes thus. [turns]	and sweetly, by a figure trace, and turne, Boyes.
2. COUN. And sweetly we will do't, Neighbours.	1. And sweetly we will doe it Master *Gerrold.*}
	SCHOOLEMASTER. But I say where's their women?
	4. Here's *Friz* and *Maudline.*
	2. And little *Luce* with the white legs, and bouncing *Barbery.*
	1. And freckled *Nel*; that never fail'd her master.
1. COUN. Where are your Ribbands Maids?	SCHOOLEMASTER. Wher be your Ribands, maids?
Swim with your Bodies.	swym with your Bodies,
	And carry it sweetly, and deliverly,
	And now and then a favour, and a friske.
	NEL. Let us alone Sir.
	SCHOOLEMASTER. Wher's the rest o'th Musicke.
	3. Dispersd as you commanded.
3. COUN. That they may do, they are light enough.	

1. COUN. Couple then and see what's wanting.

Friend, pray carry your tail without offence
Or scandal to the Ladies; and be sure

You dance with confidence, without being mov'd:
And when you stand still, do it with Judgment.
3. COUN. I'le warrant you Is'e not stand a step amiss.

SCHOOLEMASTER. Couple then,
And see what's wanting; wher's the *Bavian*?
My friend, carry your taile without offence
Or scandall to the Ladies; and be sure
You tumble with audacity and manhood,

And when you barke, doe it with judgment.

BAVIAN. Yes, sir.

Several differences are easily noted. D'Avenant has cut out the dialogue involving the listing of the women dancers' names and their attributes, partly to quicken the pace, but mostly because he has cut the business of finding a woman missing and substituting the jailer's daughter (here called Celania) for her. Instead when Celania interrupts the morris practice with her mad ramblings, her father's man (Cunopes) and the countrymen come to blows, forcing the latter to find another site to rehearse. The following dialogue occurs as part of the preliminaries to the knockabout:

1. COUN. Woman avoid: if it be your vocation to be mad
Pray be mad in some more fitting place,
This is no place for Mad-folks.
CUNOP. But 'tis for Fools.
1. COUN. For though we have Bells here; yet we have no Whips.
Tho' we are about a Morrice, 'tis no mad Morrice.   (D'Avenant 1668, 33)

D'Avenant, therefore, avoids making the association between mad caperings and the morris, and instead uses the occasion to make a mild pun, 'mad morris' being a dead metaphor at the time for a general confusion of things, as well as a common epithet for morris in general earlier in the century (hence all the mad/made puns in *The Two Noble Kinsmen*). Note also that D'Avenant's taborer does not call the dancers 'mad boys,' again to keep the distinction between intentional buffoonery and the unwitting foolishness of the insane.

Because D'Avenant does not incorporate Celania in the dance the expression 'Couple then and see what's wanting,' taken directly from Fletcher, has no obvious purpose, unless he means by it 'get into couples and let us see what we still need to rehearse,' which makes grammatical sense but clearly misinterprets the original. In fact, this statement starts a whole section that D'Avenant apparently does not understand and so has modified to make some contemporary sense. He has cut out the next question 'wher's the *Bavian?*' either because he does not know what a bavian is, or because he has chosen not to use Fletcher's characters at all (or possibly the two agendas are related). He has kept the pedant's instructions to the bavian with some modifications (for example, changing 'barke' to 'stand still') so that they are suitable for a general dancer, but he has also retained a highly particular phrase 'carry your tail without offence/ Or scandal to the Ladies,' without any further textual edification to explain why a dancer should have a tail. Probably the third countryman plays the hobby horse, but that surmise is by no means clear at this point in the text; D'Avenant does not, for example, use the expression 'where's the hobby?' and there is no indication that the third countryman is wearing a special costume at this point in the play (whereas later the hobby horse is identified explicitly).

There is, therefore, little question that D'Avenant did not understand Fletcher's morris at all, and so had to modify the dialogue to suit what he was capable of producing. But the fact that he retained so much of Fletcher's language (without complete comprehension) in the rehearsal scene, where throughout the rest of the play he has provided completely new text, seems to indicate that he did not have a firm idea of what to replace the dance with either, and so used as much of Fletcher's framework as he could retain to give an air of authenticity. Morris was, thus, becoming something of a learned archaism – in this case being treated as an antimasque in a small attempt to recreate a Stuart masque within the play.

This argument leads to the general supposition that D'Avenant's morris dance was a nonce affair created as a pastiche of elements from other plays that D'Avenant knew from his work of adaptation (and not drawn from contemporary country morris either). Thus, he retained the idea of a speech to introduce the dance, but could not copy Fletcher's pedant's speech because of its multiple references to characters ultimately deriving from Beaumont's masque. Instead he doubles one of the dancers as a Master of Revels and gives him a new speech to introduce stock characters:

Enter first Country-man as Master of the Revels.
ARCON. This seems to be the Country Poet. What
Represent you first?
I. COUN. We represent a Morrice for the first thing,
Whose Coutrements hang heavy on my purse-string,
Tho' lightly on the hobby-horse and dancers,
He learns to Wighy, and the rest to prance-Sirs.
They are all so Skittish, that when you behold 'em,
You may e'en swear the hobby-horse has foald 'em.
ARCON. Are they ready?
I. COUN. Th'are entering and (to shew I do not bob ye)
The Horse comes first here which is call'd the Hobby.
Enter Hobby-Horse

Some with long Spoons (quoth Proverb stale and addle)
Eate with the Devil; this Sir has a Ladle.
Enter Tab.
Next comes the man with Taber, which by some
Among the Pygmies is yclep'd a Drum.
Enter all.
Then with the rest comes in that ugly Carrion
Which Countrey Batchelours do call Maid-Marrion.
They dance the Morrice here.   (D'Avenant 1668, 35–6)

This combination of hobby horse, Maid Marian, and couple dance of men and women is unique in the annals of morris, and suggests that D'Avenant was drawing on multiple (literary) sources to create an aesthetically pleasing (and unprecedented) agglomeration. The idea of using a couple dance comes directly from *The Two Noble Kinsmen,* and the Maid Marian/hobby horse duo was common in other pre-Restoration plays. In the introductory speech, Fletcher's characters give way to Maid Marian and the hobby horse, presumably because if the audience knew any morris characters at all they would be these rather than the odd collection put together by Beaumont for his masque and copied by Fletcher (and not found elsewhere). Maid Marian enters with the other dancers, so presumably she takes a woman's part in the main dance (most likely a popular country dance), while the hobby acts as a supernumerary, dancing around the outside of the main set and interacting directly with the (dramatic) audience.

This 'antimasque' is followed by a 'masque' of a hunt represented in music and narrated in song by two foresters and a huntress, all of which is original to this play and owes nothing to Fletcher, whose idea was merely to introduce a rustic interlude as a break in the action. Here the interlude has become a full-blown masque within a play, with the morris occupying its traditional role as antimasque.

Contemporary critics aver that this interlude was immensely popular (see D'Avenant 1872–4, 5:216); however, the use of morris in stage plays was not emulated by later Restoration playwrights, undoubtedly because the vogue had passed. D'Avenant's inspiration comes directly from Fletcher and, therefore, was the result of a particular circumstance, and was not symptomatic of a renewed interest in the morris on stage or elsewhere.

It must be admitted that there were a few obscure and abortive attempts to resurrect stage morris during the Restoration, but for all intents and purposes D'Avenant is the end of the line. For example, around 1671 John Aubrey sketched in a notebook an entertainment, *The Country Revel* – somewhat along the lines of *Acteon and Diana* – with the following notation:

enter country fellowes & countrey wenches & the Melancholy shepherd & shepherdess,
then the Gypsies and Ld & Lady of the Maypole. Fortunes. Dance.
A Morisco-dance.   (Bodleian MS Aubrey 21 1671, f.18)

But the piece never got further than this planning stage. Other references to stage morris are even vaguer, indicating that the great decline of the dance in the countryside
had sealed its fate on stage.

CONCLUSIONS

The stage, although by no means a major venue for morris was nonetheless a watershed in the developmental history of the dance, bringing together strands from court,
urban, and rural dance, elite and popular culture, professional and amateur performance. Despite the many differences in particulars, though, it is easy to articulate
a prototypical stage performance, which shows that the dance had a basic fixed form
and meaning for playwrights in the early seventeenth century.

   The morris is performed by rustics (between four and six), with a clown/wit as
their leader. The dancers meet to discuss arrangements for an upcoming dance, in
the Maying season, for a local notable, from whom they expect a reward for their
services. The preparations involve a deal of banter and word play as well as providing scope for comic business. Where the dance involves a hobby horse, there may
be some contention over this prized role, or at least an indication that it is highly
regarded. The dance is greeted with genuine enthusiasm from the notable, although
members of his entourage may be disdainful of country sports. Either before or (more
typically) after performing, the dancers are rewarded with drink and a purse.

   On the one hand, the stage morris is an excuse for bringing on the clowns to
provide their buffoonery in relief of more weighty dramatic matter, but, on the other,
the dance has an important part to play in locating the narrative in place and time.
The morris is a breath of authentic rusticity; it roots the play in the countryside in
the spring. In its dramatic context the morris is *always* approved of by its local audience, but it is difficult to determine what its reception was theatrically. Did the urban
audience enjoy it at face value (identifying with the dramatic audience), for example,
or did they laugh at it for its artlessness? To a great degree these questions cannot
be answered, because so much depends on how the parts were played. But it seems
clear from the use of stage morris as a tool in the battle against the Puritans, that the
audience was expected to be sympathetic, and there is a sense that the dance in the
Stuart era was less an object of fun than in Elizabethan times.

   The morris is also clearly a class marker when presented on stage; the performers
are typically countrymen, and when someone not of their class gets involved in the

dance it is an event of some dramatic significance. Yet the dance is not treated strictly as a low-class entertainment, but is often presented as a species of masque or antimasque (as it often was in the court). So there is a division between elite and popular culture expressed, but the division is not qualitatively absolute – that is, kings and peasants had their own kinds of masques and entertainments, but each could (in principal) appreciate the other because they were of the same kind, if on very different scales. Not only were antimasques and masques involving morrises a continuing practice in the Tudor and Stuart courts, but there were morrises in the stage plays that were presented to royalty (sometimes as antimasques within the plays). Thus, plays became the heirs of courtly masques and other spectacles as vehicles for the morris *at court*, as well as for the general public, which means that even though morris dancing was becoming increasingly confined to the rural lower classes, it still had an outlet in the early seventeenth century to all classes, urban and rural, via the stage. Apart from anything else, this meant that the dance as anti-Puritan propaganda had a voice in high places. Once the morris was no longer popular on the stage, it became an almost exclusively country pastime, treated by the urbane as distinct from sophisticated arts and of only passing interest.

What should be clear, though, is that the morris in stage plays is a rustic pleasure, although seen through the eyes of townsmen whose association with the dance, no matter how sympathetic, may have been fleeting at best. So, there are some uniformities in the dance on stage which certainly reflect choreographic realities at some level of precision. For a clearer image of the rural dance it is necessary to turn to more direct primary sources, and to other kinds of eyewitnesses.

9

Rural Locations

Examination of the seriation graph of venue (figure 2, p. 29) and the distribution maps of dance events (especially figures 5–8, pp. 37–40) might well give the impression that the 'rural' morris began in the late sixteenth century as a new breed of dance, but it is more accurate to think of it as a continuation of, and development from, the church-sponsored morris. As chapter 6 shows, it was local churches that first encouraged the spread of morris dancing into the countryside and, subsequently, it was the centralized church hierarchy that banned the dance and the events that had provided it with a context. Countrypeople, however, did not everywhere see the loss of church support (or its active opposition) as the death blow to their cherished festivities, although some ingenuity was required on their part to find ways to keep up their sports without running athwart ecclesiastical authority. Essentially, the end of church support for morris entailed three things: the loss of a *sponsor*, the loss of a *place* to dance, and the loss of an *occasion* for dancing. Replacing each of these proved difficult in many villages so that in them the dance lapsed. In others the dance survived but had to change to suit the new circumstances. Thus our subject in this chapter mostly concerns how the secularization of the dance context influenced the dance itself, rather than how the rural dance arose *ex nihilo*.

Before dealing with substantive issues though, a short note on primary sources for descriptions of the rural morris is in order. The simple fact is that reliable sources for this style of dancing are virtually impossible to come by. Part of the problem lies in the fact that for most of the seventeenth century the dance was in decline, so there was little to record. The dance was also in bad odour with many local authorities and therefore not routinely made the subject of lengthy descriptive tributes. And the performers were almost all illiterate and thus not able to record their own feelings first-hand. This is not to say that there are no eyewitness accounts, but they are all limited in their trustworthiness. The main source of eyewitness information comes from the transcripts of ecclesiastical and secular trials, in which certain basic, incontrovertible facts are usually clear, but in which the adversarial nature of the proceedings tends to obscure the truth as each side turns the interpretation of events to its best advantage, and in which morris dancing itself is almost always cast as villainous. General fiction and literary works (including plays) form the other significant block of sources, most of which are comic pieces or segments that use images of country life as figures of fun. Such references provide snatches and clues as to the dance's character, because the authors had to be minimally truthful to the original in order for their caricatures to make sense. But there were certainly no rigid constraints on their detailed veracity, nor was there any need to be more that allusively descriptive, so that the information contained therein is scanty at best. Piecing together a picture of the rural dance is therefore a highly speculative enterprise.

Even if the loss of church sponsorship had not been accompanied by dogged persecution in some regions, the dance would have been in a dire situation and in need of radical alteration. Working under the patronage of the church meant several things: the dancers did not have out-of-pocket expenses for costumes and equipment, and they were assured in advance of a reward in food and drink, or cash, or both. Local churches not only had the credit and resources to make up elaborate costumes, they also had the capacity to store them for re-use and for rental, so that they could recoup their costs over several years. Private individuals from the countryside could not realistically emulate the church in this regard. All the time the church supported morris, individuals could hire the costumes at a reasonable rate for their own purposes, but once church involvement was forbidden, the costumes would have been sold or destroyed (deliberately or through neglect), and once this source was depleted there was no like institution to carry on where the church left off.

The Marlow churchwardens' account book for 1593–1674, for example, gives intimations that at the turn of the sixteenth century there was a flourishing church ale tradition in the surrounding Thames valley region. There are two entries concerning loans of their morris gear to dancers in Maidenhead in 1595 (f.5v) and in Bisham in 1612 (f. 25), at a rent of about 4d per costume. Then from 1615 to 1617 there are terse entries recording the morris gear as part of the church goods passed on to the next year's churchwardens (with no other indications that they were used):

Item, fower paire of morris bells
fower morris Coates and a fooles Coate
ffower ffeathers   (Buckinghamshire Record Office, PR 140/5/1 f. 32)

But in 1621 similar entries have the marginal comment 'in the handes of Edward Wooden' appended, suggesting that the church was no longer able to use the gear and so had let it out (while still retaining nominal possession) to an agent who could put it to use. After 1629 all references to the morris gear cease with no record that it was sold or destroyed. One may reasonably presume, based on the accounts from Kingston and elsewhere, that the equipment had run its life's course. In general, therefore, even if the alienation of those church goods that were abominable to reformers provided a windfall for some enterprising agent in the short term, the costumes would eventually have worn out, and could not have been replaced easily because of their high cost.

One solution that suggests itself to this problem was to simplify the costumes, while yet retaining critical elements. In *Greene's Farewell to Folly*, for example, Robert Greene presents a description of a late-sixteenth-century rural morris dancer's costume that makes it seem that it was little more than customary holiday gear, with little to identify it as specifically for a morris:

… he was a tall slender youth, cleane made with a good indifferent face, hauing on his head a strawne hat steeple wise, bound about with a band of blue buckram: he had on his fathers best tawnye worsted iacket: for that this daies exploit stood vpon his credit: he was in a pair of hose of red kersies close trust with a point afore, his mother had lent him a newe muffler for a napkin, & that was tied to his girdle for loosing: he had a paire of haruest gloues on his hands as shewing good husbandry, & a pen and inckhorn at his backe: for the young man was a little bookish, his pompes were a little too heauie, being trimmed start-vps made of a paire of boote-legges, tied before with two white leather thongs …   (Greene 1591, 265–6)

Green's description is meant to be amusing to an urbane audience, but the humour would lie, in no small part, in the description's verisimilitude. What he is presenting is the image of the rustic youth attempting to play the dandy, but appearing quaintly clumsy to sophisticates – his dancing 'pumps,' for example, are heavy work boots, and his jacket and 'napkin' are borrowed. Nonetheless, the main point, that Sunday best was perfectly suitable for the morris dance in the countryside in this period, stands. Greene makes mention of a muffler to be used for a napkin, but does not include bells in his description, perhaps because the youth was on his way, and so would not be wearing them while travelling.

This case can be thought of as marking the extreme of 'costumeless' attire for the dance: all of the elements of the outfit could be used for other occasions; none are unique to the dance. As such, the dancer's outlay on costume was virtually nothing. By contrast, the costumes of the Tudor court represent the other extreme: the outfits employed there were uniquely designed for the dance itself and had no other function. From the church inventories of the sixteenth century it would seem that the morris common at church ales stood somewhere in the middle in this regard – some elements of the outfits (coats, bells, and hats in particular) were unique to the dance, and other elements (hose or breeches, for example) were common items of everyday apparel. Judging from the bulk of sources, it seems that the rural morris was, for the most part, not as extreme in its lack of distinct costume as Greene's account, but contained fewer (and cheaper) specifically 'costume' elements than the church ale morris had.

The painting 'The Thames at Richmond,' executed by a member of Vincken-boom's school around 1620, shows what is in all likelihood a team of rural morris dancers although, of course, the painting does not identify them as such. However, all the features of the performance match contemporary verbal descriptions of the dance – it appears to be a dance of three men, Maid Marian, a hobby horse, and a fool, with music supplied by pipe and tabor. The basics of the men's costumes – shirt, breeches, and hose – are not costume elements, but standard working wear. The hose and full-cut breeches, for example, are very similar to those worn by the boatman on the riverside to the right of the dancers. What transforms their everyday (or perhaps best) wear into dance costumes are ribbons, bells, and feathers.

The men have 'points' of ribbon – bands fastened with rosettes – below their elbows and knees, with streamers of ribbon trailing from the rosettes, long at the elbows, rather shorter at the knees. The elbow ribbons undoubtedly served the same function as the trailing 'morisco' sleeves of the old-fashioned morris coats, accentuating and elaborating any full arm motions. The main difference between the two styles was an enormous difference in price, even given that ribbons were not cheap household items in the early seventeenth century. The dancers are also wearing leather leggings from which hang four rows of three bells (i.e., a dozen) on each leg, and each has a feather in his hat.

It is hard to estimate the combined cost of these costume items, but a figure of around 2s 6d to 3s per man is within reasonable bounds. Morris bells, which were imported in large quantities from Europe in the sixteenth and seventeenth centuries stayed stable in price for some time. Import and merchandizing rate records from 1582 (Willan 1962, 8) to 1657 (Anon 1657, 6) indicate that the standard price for bells was 5s per gross or 5d per dozen. So two dozen bells plus some leather for the gaiters would cost around 11d. Feathers for the morris dancers' hats in Kingston in 1519 cost 4d apiece, so allowing for threefold inflation over the course of the century, they would be around 1s by 1600. The cost of ribbons in this period covers an enormous gamut depending on their quality and provenance, but roughly 6d to 1s per man is a fair estimate. Certainly this is still a good deal of money to spend on a costume at a time when the standard daily wage for a laborer was 1s (Darby 1973, 198), but the gear was compact and so could be stored easily and used for many years with no significant costs for refurbishment. And, even if the amount seems high, it was considerably lower than the 1 li or more that the guilds were paying for morris coats in this period, which would have placed them completely out of the reach of labourers.

Probably for like reasons, the basic costume idea of regular shirt and trousers tricked out with ribbons, bell pads at the knees, and a decorated hat remained the classic pattern for rural morris dancers in a broad swathe of central England, extending from the Welsh borders to East Anglia, down to the nineteenth century, although the variations on the theme were legion.

The loss of the church as a sponsor could to some extent be mitigated by reducing costume costs, but there was no getting around the fact that the dancers had to find someone else to support them or go out of business. The main problem here was that local people, rich and poor, supported church ales (sometimes after semiserious cajolery from the May Lord's liverymen) knowing that the proceeds were destined for a project, such as repair of the church fabric, that benefited the whole community, even if (as endless prosecutions for failure to pay tithes indicate) local landowners were not favourably disposed to funding local churches (see Hill 1956). And, even if a few morris dancers got a few drinks into the bargain, one could still (begrudgingly perhaps) accept the outlay in terms of the ends justifying the means. Once the episcopacy ruled that the means must be spiritually consonant with the ends and therefore public drunkenness could not logically lead to the church's well-being, the morris men had to find their financing elsewhere. But finding new public sources of income ran two risks – one social, the other legal.

The model that most obviously presented itself to the dancers was to collect from the general public as the May Lords had done, but now on their own behalf instead of as agents for the parish. But this was socially precarious because such collecting was clearly a self-interested enterprise (with converting the proceeds to alcohol as a significant publicly perceived motive), and so was dangerously close to begging. Charity was well established as a means of eking out a living for religious mendicants and the permanently disabled, but not as a source of indulgence for patently hale and sturdy youths. Justices of the peace in the early to mid-seventeenth century began explicitly asserting that rural morris dancing was illegal because the collecting element infringed upon laws against sturdy beggars. Michael Dalton in 1618, for example, asks:

Quaere of dauncings of the Morrisse, or other open dauncings, Beare-baytings, common playes and Fencings: all these seeme to be prohibited by Statute, 39.Eliz.4. (Dalton 1618, 48–9)

The act in question was 'an Act for Punishing Rogues Vagabonds and Sturdy Beggars.' Thus, the dance had to be (nominally) skilled enough to appear to warrant a payment as a kind of fee for services. As the play texts cited in chapter 8 indicate, there was some debate on this issue among potential patrons of the morris in the countryside, some seeing the dance as worthy of support as a curious and amusing traditional custom that provided a nominal pretext for largesse, others opposing it as thinly disguised begging for a worthless enterprise. Those who supported the dance appear to be (from literary texts) those landowners who benefited most from the status quo, and who saw the dance as an affirmation of traditional values, and those who opposed it were those who had most to gain by social change and upheaval, and therefore saw the dance as symbolic of the corruption of the old ways. In both cases the dance was labelled as 'old' or 'customary' even though there is strong evidence that it was in a state of dramatic change. Apparently the actual form of the dance was less important than its perceived social status.

The association of the rural morris with the old customary ways is confirmed not only in fiction but in fact, as the following anecdote concerning a roisterous band of cavaliers (at the height of the Civil War, and only a year before the fall of Oxford) indicates:

Witney is a towne neere Oxford whither divers Courtiers and Officers of Oxford Garison went to the Wakes to bee merry, where they sung and drank themselves out of all their sences ...

These Gallants being arrived at Witney; early in the morning, (with their traine from Oxford) where they had appointed certaine morris-Dancers to meete them at the Wakes, as also severall Musitians, with various sorts of Musicke, viz., the Country Fidler, a Taberer; a payre of bagge-Pipes, and a Harper, and being come to their quarters where they were resolved to be merry, they first began to drink hard, but the morris-Dancers, and the Musick being ready to attend them, first of all began the morris-Dancers to caper before them, with one who gave the Lords favour to divers Gentlemen that gave him some a shilling, some 6; some more, some lesse for the common stocke of the company. There were some 6. or 7. Country fellowes with Napkins, and Scarfes, and Ribons tyed about them, and bells at their knees, according to the manner of that sport, and with them a Mayd-Marian, and two fooles, who fell a dansing and capering before the Oxford blades, and made them sport a good while.   (Loyd 1646, 4)

The piece goes on in much the same vein, describing the Oxford rakes as they participate in a variety of country sports, all the while descending into incapacitating drunkenness, the core issue of the whole scenario being that scions of the ancien régime found pleasure in simple, 'old-fashioned' country revels and were happy to pay generously for their *inclusion* in them. Getting drunk with the peasants was an aggressively anti-Puritan act, uniting members of widely different economic classes in a common social goal. But besides the specific political issues involved here, there are also rather deeper and more general social matters at stake.

The nobles of the cavalier party and the rustics stood in what is sometimes called a 'complementary' relationship, and this fact has profound implications for the ultimate social meaning of this event. There are a great number of social roles that derive their meaning and value from the fact that they exist in *relation* to other roles. One cannot fill the role of parent, for example, all by oneself: one must have an offspring. 'Parent' and 'offspring' are mutually defining and mutually dependent social roles. All kinship terms are of this order, but non-kin relationships may also be similarly mutually interdependent, such as, landlord/tenant, lord/vassal, performer/audience, or patron/

client. Gregory Bateson has divided these dyadic relationships into two types, symmetric and complementary (see Bateson 1972 for complete details). Symmetric relationships are those in which the participants respond to each other in ways that are socially *equivalent*. Thus, for example, siblings compete with one another by trying to excel at the same kinds of activities. Their behaviours mirror each other. Complementary relationships, such as lord/vassal, involve the participants in behaviours that are *opposite* in a social sense. Dominant/submissive, active/passive, extroverted/introverted are typical social opposites that are embodied in a number of complementary relationships.

Bateson argues that often when complementary relationships are established they are not especially onerous because they are entered into with a spirit of the possibility of benefit for all parties, and because the complementary roles are not absolute. But over time, and especially when the relationships are stressed by external factors, the parties increasingly fall back on their typical status behaviours, which leads to radical polarization of the constituent roles; in economic hard times, for example, a dominant landlord becomes increasingly domineering, which results in increasing submission from powerless tenants as a form of self protection, which only serves to reinforce the dominance of the landlord. This cyclic feedback process he calls 'schismogenesis,' and he sees it as lying at the heart of a great number of troubled social relations. The problem that schismogenesis creates is that it mercilessly represses the complex desires of all the parties involved. Tenants may have a leaning towards submission, but they also have a desire (however rudimentary) to dominate that must be constantly suppressed, while landlords have no room to indulge any submissive leanings they may have. Thus, left unchecked, schismogenesis must lead to some kind of breakdown in the system as roles become increasingly rigid and endlessly repressed feelings boil over.

Lords of Misrule, May Lords and other festivals of inversion are one antidote to schismogenesis in that they allow those in subordinate positions a brief period of dominance; this takes the pressure off their repressed desires long enough to keep the system in balance. Another solution, represented by the anecdote above, is to periodically transform a complementary relationship into a symmetric one. The day's festivities started out with everyone sober, and with their complementary roles in place. The cavaliers acted as paying patrons and the rustics as hireling performers. But as the cavaliers got drunker they ceased to play the role of audience, and began to participate *equally* in the proceedings. They danced country dances with the local women (presumably with other country couples in the sets), and ended up singing catches. In the process everyone got equally incapable.

Festivals that briefly make complementary relationships symmetric are quite different from festivals of inversion, even if they achieve the same social ends. It is quite clearly not the case that the cavaliers became more submissive during the day, or that the rustics became more dominant: both sides dissolved their social differences in alcohol downed communally. High and low momentarily ceased to have meaning at all. It is perhaps misleading (and potentially blasphemous) to call such a drunken revel a 'secular sacrament,' but the idea has some merit, nonetheless. The day was one of complete social *communion* achieved through common drinking. And the bond thus created was not achieved through intellectual or abstract means, but through a shared *physical* experience.

Such outcomes (and methods) were obviously anathema to the Puritans as a general rule, but they were especially emotionally charged immediately before and during the Civil War when the royal party derived a great deal of its support from the countryside, and the Puritans were attempting to cut it off. But they probably were not fully aware of how damaging their methods were. What, in effect, they were doing by opposing morris dancing and its attendant festivals was removing the safety valves from a seriously schismogenic system, which act, of course, resulted in disorder on a national scale. What they replaced the old with during the Interregnum, however, was equally unstable in that it had almost all of the complementary social relationships of the old order – a few heads had rolled but the government of church and state was still fundamentally hierarchical – and there were no new safety valves to avoid the ills of schismogenesis. In fact, that whole Puritan ethos denied the need for safety valves and preached worldly asceticism in its stead. However pious and honourable the motives, such a social experiment was likely to fail.

This analysis may also explain why the rural morris persisted during the Interregnum (albeit in weakened form) and why it took on a distinctly socio-political character. That is, countrypeople (consciously or unconsciously) knew the value of their safety valves and were prepared to have them by right even if such an assertion required force of might to defend it. The following is taken from the Wiltshire Quarter Sessions of 1652:

The Testimony and Examinacon of William Farmoe and Joane his Wife of Woodborough taken at Pewsey ... the twentieth Day of May ... 1652. Who say that Edward Smyth and Edward Hawking of Woodburrow did upon the last Lords Day being the 16th of this Instat May after diner time Travaile and goe to a place called Allcanings and there did invite severall people of Cannings aforesayd to the number of twelve persons or neer there aboute who upon the Munday morning following came armed with musketts powder match and bandaleares which they brought with them to Woodborough and that Robert Golfe also of Woodboroughe went unto Marlburroughe upon the sayd Lords Day to get a drummer to head the sd leude company and aboute one a clocke that same Sunday night came away out of Marlburghe with the sd drummer to Woodburrough. And they further say that Thomas Beasant of Woodburroughe labourer did upon the sayd Lords day goe into a place called Ram Ally in the pishe of Easton and there invited and procured a fidler who came to Woodburroughe upon Munday morning following and by the instigacon of the before named partie three hundred persons or there aboutes were assembled and gathered together in a Riotous Routous Warlicke and very disorderly manner with Musketts pistolls bills swords drawne and other unlawful weapons, who upon Munday the said 17th of May did march together to the pishe of Pewsey and there very disorderly daunced the Morrice daunce and committing severall other misdemeanors there as drinkeing and Tipling in the Inn and Alehouse till many of them were drunke.

(Cunnington 1932, 221)

There is a clear sense here and in the well-known case brought in Much Wenlock, Shropshire, in the same year (cited in chapter 7) that the dancers were part of a general body whose explicit aim was to intimidate all who stood in their way of celebrating in the traditional manner, legal or not.

This case, therefore, represents yet a third way of expressing repressed emotions engendered by complementary schismogenesis – that is, temporarily reversing the normal social order *by show of force* – and was by far the most socially dangerous from the point of view of the ruling classes, because there were potentially fewer constraints or limits on behaviour, and because those in subordinate positions were seizing a moment of power without the consent (tacit or otherwise) of the rest of society. Lord of Misrule festivals inverted the social order with the express consent of all involved, and even though sometimes events got out of hand, there were customary boundaries of desirable behaviour. But the context of the kind of 'Riotous Routous Warlicke and very disorderly' assemblies described above was very different from other 'customary' festivals.

Enclosure, and other forms of agricultural revolution that gained great headway in the sixteenth and seventeenth centuries, had caused great hardship for many of the poorer farmers and labourers, leading in some regions to mass, armed demonstrations, the tearing down of enclosing hedgerows, and sometimes to open rebellion. The sociological implications of such protests have been dealt with at length elsewhere and should not greatly concern us here (see, for example, Rudé 1964 and Underdown 1985). What is relevant is that in this period, what are ostensibly holiday amusements took somewhat the form of riot and rebellion (even if only semiseriously), and used the general uncertainty of the outcome of the assembly to force sponsorship of the revels out of reluctant or hapless bystanders. This spirit of intimidation (although not by any means universal) appears to have continued as one of the methods of obtaining sponsorship for the morris, into the eighteenth century and beyond. Lady Fermanagh in a letter dated 2–5–1716, for example, writes:

We have whisen ayls all about us, which brings such A Bundance of rabble & the worst sort of Company round us that I wish noe mischifes Happens. Old Oliffe alarmed all the town a Sunday night crying out Thieves, and all the neighbours went to his assistance upon his letting off 2 guns; his daughter was come home to him without clothes, he sent her back again for them, and tis thought some of the Kings Companions did it to fright the old man. I can't help giving the Morrises monny when they come, for they tell me everybody doing it is the best way to send them going – there is one at Steeple Claydon, one at hoggshaw, one at Buckingham and one att Stratton Audley.   (Verney 1930, 2:41)

These texts also remind us that the loss of church sponsorship involved the loss of an occasion and a venue for dancing, so that the morris had either to attach itself to other events or create occasions and venues of its own. Certainly Whit ales, bridales, wakes, and the like continued as secular events, and the morris dance easily attached to them much as they had done to their ecclesiastical counterparts. The minister at Lapley in Staffordshire in 1655, for example, complained that despite the law, secular ales were in abundance in the county (see Johnson and Vaisey 1964, 38–9). And this complaint followed a suit brought by him against two groups of morris dancers who performed at a secular ale in Lapley, and against some of the local authorities for not stopping them (see below). But beginning around the time of the demise of church ales, morris dancers also began to work independently of occasions of which they were merely a part, and sought to make the dance the occasion itself. Thus began the idea of the rural morris tour.

The first rural morris tour on record comes from Kent in 1589, and concerns a team from the Herne area who undertook a perambulation of the region in the general neighbourhood of Herne and Canterbury in early May. All went well until the dancers performed in Canterbury itself. There, when they danced before the mayor's house they were summoned to appear before him for performing without a licence. The following description of the tour is excerpted from the testimony of N. Saynt, one of the dancers:

… says that on May day last they were dancing at Herne with the company & on Sunday last they also danced there in the afternoon & a little in the forenoon & says that on Assension day they danced at Reculver in the forenoon & in the afternoone at [Hothe ?] & says that the company of them went from Hothe up into east Kent & yesterday being Friday they came to Bridge to the alehouse & there lay; & from thence came to Canterbury to the sign of the George at St Georges in Cant. & says they were going to St Stephens to Mr Peter Manwood & that Mr Manwood did not request to his knowledge but went of their own minds. And that they began at St. George's gate to daunce & so ensued till they came into the high street & there against Mr Mayor's door & daunced once or twice about till by the officer the serjt. the musician was called before Mr Mayor & then the rest of the company and says that when they came against Mr Mayor's door there was one said Here, here & thereupon they stayed & daunced about once or twice as before.

(Canterbury Cathedral Lib. JQ 1589; see also Clark 1983, 129–30)

The testimony of the others adds a few more details. The team consisted of a twelve-year-old boy who played Maid Marian, a vice, a fiddler, and four dancers, all aged around twenty. So the dance was probably of the ring morisk type, or its descendant, as was current at church ales at the time, supporting the original supposition that the rural dance was, *at first*, simply a translation of the church ale dance into a new setting. Changes came later as the new settting affected the dance form.

There are also strong indications that the tour was a serious money-maker. J. Turfrey, the vice, indicates in his testimony that they had requested the fiddler to be available to them throughout May and June and offered him a fee of 4s per day (four times the going rate for a labourer in that era). The musician was, thus, not a member of the team but a well-paid hired adjunct, and this was to be the norm throughout our period (and beyond) for rural tours. The incomes of the other dancers are not indicated, presumably because they worked for shares of the total collected. However, the sums gathered must have been substantial in order to guarantee the musician's fee and other costs (costumes, food, drink), plus a profit.

It is also interesting, in relation to the profits made, to note that all the original dancers on the tour (with the exception of the boy/Maid Marian) were nineteen or twenty years old, a tightly associated age group. When one of the dancers fell ill before the team arrived in Canterbury, an older man from Herne was recruited to replace him. Possibly, therefore, tours were undertaken by small groups of young, unmarried age-graded peer groups, who toured for several years and then passed on the tradition to a younger peer group to take over. Certainly if the morris were a significant income-producer in slack agricultural times, knowledge of its manner of performance would be information to be kept within a small coterie. Later in the seventeenth and eighteenth centuries, extended families became the repositories of such information, but at the beginning point of touring, there are no intimations of kin ties between the dancers (all the Herne dancers had different surnames and, where indicated, worked for different masters).

The need for exactly four dancers also implies that the dance entailed some kind of figures (as would also be expected given the hypothesized evolution of the church ale dance of the period from a competitive/individual ring dance of the courtly model to a circular, figured dance). If the dance were not choreographed for certain set patterns, they would presumably have been able to get by with three men.

Conflating all of the dancers' accounts produces a clear picture of the overall scope of the tour. They performed in Herne on May Day (a Thursday) and again on the following Sunday (the 4th). Then on Ascension Day (Thursday the 8th) they visited Reculver, Chislet, and Hoath, and on the next day (Friday the 9th) they performed in Bridge, staying over in 'Borne' (which could be any one of several – Patrixbourne, Bekesbourne, Littlebourne – in the Bridge vicinity). Thence they went to Canterbury (Saturday the 10th) and apparently had plans to continue performing on Sunday south of the city. The tour proper (that is, the time spent dancing away from Herne), therefore, occupied four days, the two ends of which were holidays, and encompassed a radius of six or seven miles.

This kind of tour was novel in some respects but it was built on an old model, namely, the tour of local villages by the May Lord and his liverymen (and occasionally morris dancers and musicians) prior to a church ale, to raise funds to meet costs. The morris tour took over this form, but altered its function in that the dancers were not the preamble to an event but the event itself. Church ales of the sixteenth century might be described as centripetal events: the great majority that engaged morris dancers in that era were held in market towns to which people were normally drawn from all directions as a natural function of weekly, monthly, or annual life. The tour of the May Lord simply built on this convergent role of the market town, magnifying it for a special occasion. Hence the morris dance at the ale provided a central focus (among other entertainments) for those people drawn together from diverse segments of the market's hinterland. The event was thus large scale, unifying, and centralizing.

The morris tour, by contrast, was decentralizing in that the dance went out to individual villages and hamlets in the hinterland and did not draw the inhabitants away to a central place. Although they sometimes still performed in market towns (as in Canterbury, for example) this was merely one stop among many on a long itinerary, and was by no means a necessity. It may well be that there were pragmatic reasons for touring the villages of the hinterland and avoiding large centres, as the Herne dancers discovered. There were fewer officials to run afoul of in the countryside, and those who might prove troublesome could be skirted. What is more, in the days of poor communications and severe local isolation, an annual tour of a few men around a handful of small villages could easily escape the notice of authorities located but a few miles away. Indeed, it may have been the mounting risk of prosecution in the early-sixteenth century that accounts for the paucity of records concerning rural morris, in that those who chose to continue dancing became increasingly discreet.

Also, by touring a number of locations, stopping briefly in each, the dancers were able to set their own timetable, and did not have to wait for a major church festival or local holiday, because their performance in any one location was more of a momentary distraction than a serious impediment to the daily routine. Naturally they concentrated on Sundays and other slack times in the agricultural routine, both to ensure a good audience and because they needed time away from their own work in order to dance. But all indications are that teams got together whenever they were able and not just on major feast days – sometimes for many weeks in succession (primarily in May and June).

Decentralizing the dance occasions and touring the dance around the countryside produced a number of concomitant changes in the morris over time, continuing the process of evolution and diversification begun while the dance was under the church's patronage. It is clear, for example, that by the turn of the seventeenth century morris-dance teams were perceived as representing specific villages. Frequently literary references to rural morris in this period use the expression 'for our town' as a standard audience cheer in response to the dancing – which may or may not be wholly realistic in itself, but which undoubtedly reflects a genuine sense of communal esteem invested in the performers by local audiences.

We may also infer from a number of these references (see, for example, Weelkes 1597, 282) that the development of teams representing particular villages or localities spawned intergroup competition. Of course, such rivalry required that there be several groups within easy reach of one another, and the primary material seems to support the notion that wherever one finds a rural morris team, another is likely to exist nearby (and, conversely there were some areas that remained barren of the tradition). As already mentioned above, at Lapley in Staffordshire, for example, the minister complained that wakes and morris dancing were common in the region. He also brought particular dancers up on charges for an ale in Lapley:

Articles of misdemeanour committed at Lapley in the county of Stafford especially on May 6th, 1655, presented at Stafford Assizes, August 7th, 1655.

1. The wakes were kept especially by Walter Brindley, Nicholas Bridgin, Thomas Floyd and Silvanus Garfield all at Lapley and their family wither resorted great company day and night as witnesseth John Jackson and John Anson.

2. Two companies of Maurice-dancers: The names of the one company were these viz.: Edmund, John and Matthew the sons of Walter Brindley, husbandman and Papist. Ellen Perry (alias Perryn) servant to the said Walter, spinster. Edward, Robert, Richard, Hugh and Francis, sons of Sibley Floyd of Lapley, Papist widow. Ann Perry (or Perryn) spinster; ibid Thomas Preston, servant to John Collins, Papist husbandman, ibid Katherine Blake, servant to Thomas Petre of Lapley Esq. Papist. Frances Anslem, daughter of Robert Anslem of Lapley, Papist and yet third-borough.

All of which men and women danced promiscuously and Francis Floyd, apprentice to Thomas Floyd, danced in Women's apparel.

All which recusants are presented for absence from the church the four last Sabbaths.

John Low of Church-eaton parish for being their musician.

The other company of Maurice-dancers were about 16 that came from Stretton in Penkridge parish and danced in Lapley, viz.: Joseph Patrick, servant to Richard Congreve, Esq., Edward Poole, tailor, Francis Poole, husbandman, etc., as witnesseth John Anson.

3. Richard Floyd aforesaid also for acting the foll's part, and profanely cursing others with the plague twice as witnesseth John Anson.

4. Thomas Floyd and Sibley Floyd of Lapley recusants for absence from the church, selling ale without licence and harbouring tiplers in their houses by day and by night as witnesseth John Anson.

5. Robert Anslem aforesaid, third-borough for apprehending neither the musicians nor any other strangers.

6. John Eccles and Margaret his wife for tippling with many others as witnesseth John Anson. And for being married contrary to law formerly and so living as witnesseth John Anson of Mitton. Sworn to the truth hereof in court, John Jackson, John Anson. 7th August, 1655.

(Johnson and Vaisey 1964, 39–40)

A great many points emerge from this case, but for present purposes the most obvious issue is that Lapley and Stretton are barely two miles apart (along a Roman road, the best kind of throughfare in that era), yet each could sport a team of morris dancers consisting of a dozen or more performers. In general, therefore, it seems that where one team could find financial support from the countryside, another could develop to try to reap some of the economic benefits (thus bringing into play classic market forces associated with competition for disposable income). It is also interesting to note that the Lapley dancers almost all came from two farming families (and as far as the information goes there seem to be kin ties among the Stretton dancers), indicating that one of the ways to try and keep the supply of a profitable entity, such as morris dancing, from exceeding demand was to try to keep ownership of its mysteries within one or two local families, passing on its use (like land) to the next generation.

It is not clear from this and like texts from the seventeenth century, what degree of formal rivalry existed between neighbouring teams, but by the early eighteenth century morris dancing was recognized as a competitive rural sport for which prizes could be awarded at annual festivals. The following notice appeared in Epsom, Surrey, some time around 1702:

At Epsom Old Wells ... on Whitson Tuesday will be Moris Dancing Set against Set, for Lac'd Hats, at 10 a Clock, with other Diversions.   (Ashton 1904, 244)

And the following appeared in the *Gloucester Journal* in 1744:

NOTICE is hereby given

That on Whitsun-monday next, at the Sign of the Swan, In Cown-allins, near Fairford, Gloucestershire, will be given a HAT of a Guinea Price, to be play'd for at Backsword, by five or seven Men of a side, and that Side that can break the most Heads shall be entitled to the Hat, each side to appear on the Stage by One o'Clock.

Likewise, on the Morrow, there will be six exceeding good KNOTS to be Morrice-danc'd for, Free Gift, and Six Pair of Gloves to be Bowl'd for at Nine-Pins. (*Gloucester Journal* 1 May 1744, 4)

So formal rivalry did eventually develop out of what was most likely an informally competitive (and not necessarily always friendly) situation.

There are many possible effects of intervillage competition on dance form, but because of the slimness of the primary materials few can be confirmed. Clearly local teams needed to distinguish themselves from one another in some way – possibly through costume elements, the development of unique dance movements, or styles of performing common movements, and the like. In such a way, local competition would act as a spur on dance evolution; the greater the density of teams in the area, the greater the variety of differences within that area. Yet simultaneously there were factors that retarded runaway evolution. Although we have no details concerning the way that formal competitions were conducted, for example, whatever rules existed must have served to keep dance forms in any particular region within certain bounds; otherwise they would not have been comparable enough to be judged for a winner. There would also be economic constraints: what worked last year to fill the collecting box could not be jettisoned simply for the sake of change. Thus, what may have happened in highly competitive situations is that each team evolved a style of performing that fit a common core of ideas and yet was distinctive, and then preserved the style for some time. However, all such hypothesizing must remain purely conjectural in the absence of specific data – although it is clear that the rural morris took on numerous faces in the seventeenth century, so some such forces must have been at work.

Another key to the evolution of the rural dance was the nature of local touring practices. Ales and the like provided a complex context for the dance, and provided multiple amusements for the crowd – mock courts, plays, musicians, and so forth. Under that aegis the dance did not have to find an audience, or work it up into a state of generosity, or prepare it in any special way. People at the ales were in holiday spirit, were eating and drinking cheerfully and, therefore, were primed for a show. But a touring morris arrived in a small village largely unannounced where people were dispersed as they went about their business, and sober. So they had to gather an audience together and present a *total* performance. It would not have been enough to walk into a central place, dance, and pass the hat. It would take people time to gather, and they had to be warmed up for the central act – they had to have a sense of anticipation developed in them followed by a sense of gratitude for the performance, all of which required that the dance event employ certain standard forms. Collating texts produces the following as a prototypic village dance event, serving to expand even a single dance into a total event:

- processional into town
- comic speech by the foreman/vice/fool
- dance
- collection
- processional away

Different teams may have adapted this prototype to their own needs but there is strong circumstantial evidence from literary sources to confirm the basic form. Review of the play texts concerning rural morris in chapter 7 is sufficient to justify this notion of the overall shape of the morris event, and other texts may be brought into the picture to elucidate the role of each individual element.

The first task of the performers was to enter the village with as much noise and ceremony as possible to draw a crowd together and herald the main event. A madrigal by Thomas Morley contains the following graphic depiction of the dramatic entry of the dancers:

Ho! Who comes here all along with bagpiping and drumming?
O 'tis the Morris-dance I see a-coming,
Come ladies, out, come quickly!
And see how trim they dance and trickly.
Hey! there again! how the bells they shake it!
Hey ho! now for our town! and take it!
Soft awhile, not away so fast! They melt them.
Piper! be hanged, knave, see'st thou not the dancers how they swelt them?
Stand out awhile! you come too far, I say, in.
There give the hobby-horse more room to play in!   (Morley 1594, 143)

In an era when there were few loud sounds in the English countryside the tumult of pipes, drums, and bells would instantly draw attention and be recognizable immediately for what it was. From a purely dramatic point of view such a procession would be most effective for a small group of four to six dancers if they performed in single file, because such a formation expands the profile of the group to its maximum, and because it encourages people to follow along. That such a procession was typical of the morris of the period is confirmed by the following metaphorical account of the passage of a year:

Behold them [six months] therefore at hand, how they come frisking in single file one after another, like so many Morrice-Dancers, (my selfe being the Hobby-horse) and euery Month wearing in his Cap, instead of a Feather, Foure vnhansome wholesome Rimes; conformable to the fashion of our Neotericke Prognosticators. And thus heere the Foreman of the Morice deliuers his speech.   (Spelman 1622, 49)

The entry of the dancers in single file was normal for the performers of the ring morisk, so that this idea may have been drawn from the older dance. Presumably the dance itself was a rudimentary series of steps and leaps ('frisking') suitable for covering the ground while making a show (presumably it was this style of morris that Will Kemp

performed from London to Norwich). Whatever its provenance, the idea of a processional into the dance space in single file (regardless of the form of the stationary
dance) was long lived, surviving well into the nineteenth century, and clearly demonstrating its effectiveness for drumming up a crowd.

As the Spelman citation above indicates, the next order of business was a comic
speech delivered either by the foreman or the fool. This feature seems to have been
usurped from the May Lords, and served several functions: it amused the audience,
gave the dancers a break from their processional, and developed a sense of anticipation for the dance. It also helped create a rapport between foreman/fool and audience in preparation for later collecting. There are some indications from literary
texts that these speeches were set pieces composed by the performer – a mixture of
crude puns and lewd references – but obviously none survive and all that we have
to reckon them with are their literary equivalents (see, for example, Jonson 1603, 128,
and Beaumont and Fletcher 1613, 76–7).

The nature of the dance itself, that followed the speech, is considered in detail
below. However, in thinking of the dance as a total event, a general point can be
made. Judging from a variety of texts it seems that the performers can be divided
into two species based on their relationship to the audience during the dance. These
may be labelled 'introverted' and 'extroverted,' using the terms not in their usual
psychological senses, but in their more literal senses of 'turned inward' and 'turned
outward.' The general dancers are essentially introverted; their concern is to relate to
each other as a group and even though their activities may contain elements of outward display, they are still required by the nature of the choreography of group performance to be responsive to each other and act cohesively. Their focus is centripetal
– the central dance itself. The hobby horse, by contrast, does not seem to have had
a fixed role in the central dance, but was free at times to react directly with the audience via tricks and impromptu tomfoolery, that is, he was extroverted. His focus
was centrifugal, touring the periphery of the dance space and even entering the audience to relate directly with individuals.[1]

Maid Marian, by all accounts, was generally an introverted character, participating in the general choreography and not becoming involved in direct engagement
with the audience. The fool's role, however, is difficult to judge, and may have varied
or evolved over time. In the ring morisk, the fool was almost certainly introverted,
as was the entire dance, but some descriptions of the rural morris contain fools who
have all the appearance of extroverted characters, akin to the hobby horse, tum-
bling and playing tricks with their baubles (see, for example, Rablet 1614, sig. D3
recto-verso). It is quite possible that the fool's role changed from an introverted to
an extroverted one as the nature of the central dance changed from one in which
his role was central (that is, the ring morisk) to a type, or types (such as those based
on figured set formations like country dances), in which he had less direct involve-

ment with the main choreography, and so had to carve out a new niche for himself.

'The Thames at Richmond' is a good illustration of the introverted and extroverted roles of the various dancers – the general dancers and Maid Marian are working together at the centre while the hobby horse and the fool are turned outward toward the audience – and also demonstrates part of the point of the latter role. By developing a strong rapport with the audience (through comic speeches, tricks, and the like) it was easier for the fool – or other extroverted characters – to make the transition to collecting as a natural extension of his general extroverted functions (and, one assumes, harder for audience members to refuse him, having become directly connected to him). Extroverted roles were thus vital to the rural morris in a way that they never had been before, because sponsorship via direct collecting from the audience during and after the dance was new and required the dance to adapt to these circumstances if it was to be profitable. A dance that was totally introverted would be less likely to be able to draw audience members into participating with their purses than one with extroverted elements, because it would not have drawn them into any kind of participatory relationship beforehand. Their role up to that point would be largely passive and alienated. Thus, there may have been evolutionary principles of selection at work – those teams that made the transition to accommodating extroverted characters had a greater chance of surviving economically than those that did not.

In regard to economics and evolution of the dance form, two points which are evaluated later in the chapter may be mentioned here. It is clear that the hobby horse was grafted on to the rural morris around the time that touring began, so his inclusion in the team may have been a direct attempt to add an extroverted element to the total event. It may also be that regional and local material and economic variables were the prime movers in determining the fortunes of touring teams. Those areas where a significant percentage of the rural population had money to spare for the morris box were those where the dance had a chance of surviving the rigours of prosecution.

It would be too prudish to suggest that the dancers having gathered what coins they could, bade the audience a sad farewell and danced in procession out of the village and on to the next venue. All evidence points to the next step being a visit to the alehouse, sometimes of considerable duration, before moving on.

A processional out of town after the collection box had passed around may seem gratuitous, and of all the stages of the total event outlined above, the one most easily dispensed with. But many literary texts, already cited, refer explicitly to the dancers dancing away from the performance site as a seemingly normal occurrence. The most obvious reason for so doing on a tour (apart from mellow benevolence) was to draw the crowd along with them to the next village, perhaps to curry another coin, but certainly to increase the festive atmosphere of the event. Kemp refers to the crowds that followed him along the way, and many lawsuits against dancers specifically refer to the 'rabble' that followed them on their tours.

The basic structure of the rural morris tour changed very little, even down to the nineteenth century, presumably because it worked. But there is strong evidence that the dances at the center of the event underwent continuous, occasionally rapid, change, leading eventually to considerable diversity across the country. The most parsimonious hypothesis concerning the direction of evolution is that the rural morris continued to build on changes begun during the sixteenth century (when the dance was under church patronage), there was a general move from individual, competitive movements (from the morisk) to group, figured action. This change to set figures opened the door for a number of new directions for evolution of the dance – all of which were pursued in one region of the country or another – such as, the syncretic use of figures from other figured dances (notably country dances), which in turn could lead to the inclusion of figures using couples (single sex or mixed), and so on. Country dances specifically identified as 'morris' are considered at length in chapter 10. What is of interest here is the possibility that the general style of country dances as a whole was a major influence on morris dances from the end of the Elizabethan era onwards.

A great deal of the popularity of country dances at this time was due to the interest of the queen herself. For example, Sir Philip Sidney in 1600 notes:

Her majestie is in very good health, and comes much abroad these holidayes; for almost every night she is in the presence to see the ladies daunce the old and new Country dances, with the taber and pipe   (Cited in Chambers 1923, 4:115)

What precisely was meant by 'country dance' at this time is not completely clear because the term was first used around 1580, more or less in contrastive fashion, rather than as an absolute category. Country dances were those that were commonly performed by English country people as opposed to those dances popular at court, or abroad. 'Country dance,' therefore, refers as much to a way of comporting oneself as to any unique choreography, at that time. However, Melusine Wood (Wood 1937) makes a case for the proposition that the dances of the countryside circa 1580 were mostly circular formation couple dances, but by 1600 a synthesis with Italian *contrapassi* was beginning – due to the strong Italianate influences on the arts in Elizabeth's court – and this radically altered the direction of evolution of English country dances, including the increased use of the longways set, and the establishment of formal sequences of figures for each dance.

Wood's argument is, in essence, that Elizabeth's regard for country dances sparked an explosive interest in them at court and among the nobility in general. Such interest caused the dances of the people to come to the attention of dancing masters, whose business it was to keep the nobility supplied with new dances conforming to the fashions of the times. These dancing masters would have been familiar with *contrapassi* – Italian figured couple dances predominantly in longways formation – either from manuals such as Fabritio Caroso's *Il Ballarino* (Caroso 1581) or from personal training in them; and because the overall style, form, and comportment of these dances (they were perhaps ultimately derived from Italian rustic dances themselves) were not dissimilar from those of English country dances, it was a simple act to blend ideas from both to create a new style of 'country' dancing that suited English courtiers.[2] Thus, what developed by the early seventeenth century was a two-tiered system of *courtly* country dances (created by professionals), on the one hand, and *rustic* country dances (evolved by countrypeople), on the other – and this class divide continued right through the seventeenth and early eighteenth centuries.

The two-tiered system was by no means rigidly stratified and segregated, however. There is some evidence that the dancing masters of the seventeenth century used folk ideas in their choreography, and that there was ample opportunity for countrypeople to copy the fads of the town, so that a two-way influence was always possible. The first edition of John Playford's *English Dancing Master* (Playford 1651), for example, contains dances that are likely drawn directly from contemporary folk tradition. And, contrariwise, there are indications that in country dances a promiscuous mixing of classes was not only appropriate, but in some ways aesthetically appealing (see Nichols 1823, 3:95). Furthermore, John Selden in *Table Talk* says that country dances were routinely performed after the more formal court dances:

… all the Company Dance, Lord and Groom, Lady and Kitchen-Maid, no distinction.

(Cited in Emmerson 1972, 265)

It would be ludicrous to suggest, based on these citations, that prince and pauper danced their way merrily together through Tudor and Stuart England, yet it is evident that there were more than occasional points of contact in country dances between the classes in this era. Indeed, it may have been such commingling that lay beneath the Puritans' attacks on mixed dancing – not only did it promote lust, which was bad enough, but it threatened the general social fabric by setting at nought social status in favour of the egalitarian nature of the dance. In fact, the hallmark of country dances was not so much any particular set formation (longways or otherwise), nor even any particular choreographic style or stepping, but the fact that everyone danced together, rather than in the isolated *solitude à deux* couples of the courtly dances.

Out of the ferment of courtly and rustic, foreign and domestic choreographic ideas in the late Elizabethan and early Jacobean periods came, eventually, an almost monolithic use in England of the longways set formation in country dances; but the transition from other formations, notably rounds, took time. Playford's first edition stands somewhere in the middle of the transition period, with a majority of longways dances included but also with a great number of rounds and other set formations. By the time *The Dancing Master* reached its eighteenth edition (*c* 1728), however, virtually all the dances contained therein were longways, the other set formations having largely disappeared.

Circumstantial evidence suggests that morris dances in the late-sixteenth and early-seventeenth centuries adopted ideas from the 'new' country dances. It is even likely that in some regions (particularly the Welsh border counties of Herefordshire and Shropshire) morris became transformed completely into 'country dance' style dances, with only certain incidental items (such as ribbons and bells) distinguishing and identifying the performance as 'morris.'

The most compelling evidence for the infiltration of country dance ideas into morris are the repeated references (in literary sources first, but followed soon after by eyewitness accounts) of mixed couples performing morris dances, starting at the tail end of the sixteenth century. The first comes from a book of 1593 entitled *The Passionate Morrice*:

To the Gentlemen and others of England ... But seeing my desire to bee possessed of the better cordiall, makes me hart-strong to suppe of that potion which is likest to lengthen my welfare, the same being an assured confidence of your continuall carefulnes, in shrowding with your affection the slender substance of my humorous Morrice.
[Contents page:]
Eight couples of lovers.

The first couple of Morris-dancers: a passionate ass and a peevish wench;
The second couple: a lusty widower and a gallant wench;
The third couple: a bachelor and a covetous widow;
The fourth couple: a miserly churl and a rich widow;
The fifth couple: a discreet young gentleman and an immodest damsel;
The sixth couple: a coy dame and her suitors;
The seventh couple: a prentice and a girl wearied of a long engagement to him;
The eighth couple: a seducer and his victim.   (A 1593, 47–9)

Obviously the text is metaphorical but the author expects his readership to accept, without question or confusion, the basic symbolic framework of an eight couple mixed set of morris dancers. Other roughly contemporary texts make it clear that by the Jacobean period mixed couple dancing was normal for morris (see, for example, Anon *c* 1600, 361). And lawsuits beginning in the early seventeenth century, especially in the Welsh borders, routinely implicate men and women for dancing together in the morris. For example, Miles Conney of Tedstone Delamere in Herefordshire was brought before the Hereford Cathedral consistory to answer for sabbath breaking – especially dancing the morris – on 8 August 1602:

milo Cunny/
ffor prophaininge the Saboathe day and daunsinge and revelinge with morrice daunces tempore divinorum, and namely 8° Augusti vlt*imo* beinge Sonday, and would not desist albeit he was admonished therof by mr Grenewiche   (Klausner 1990, 169)

He was ordered to confess his crime in penitential garb in his local church, and to name the morris dancers who performed with him. He implicated a large body of men *and women* from Tedstone Delamere and nearby Avenbury. This case is followed by similar ones in the west Midlands in the early part of the seventeenth century – prosecutions of relatively large groups of dancers (sixteen and upwards), male and female. Such listings of personnel are completely inconsistent with those from church ale account books of the sixteenth century, and seem to confirm the hypothesis of a radical new direction of evolution of the morris, namely, the importation of figured movements in the country dance style (although such a new style need not have been in any sense universal, nor need the new dances have of necessity involved mixed couples).

Thus, the couple dance in *Two Noble Kinsmen*, which at first sight (and compared with morris dances in other plays of the era) appears to be an oddity – imported from a popular courtly masque whose need to be realistically representational was minimal – turns out to be indicative of new trends in morris dancing in the early seventeenth century and, in that sense, not an oddity at all. Yet it should also be noted that at that time and later, stage morrises did not involve mixed couples: the dance was by those lights, therefore, idiosyncratic. What this fact most likely bespeaks is that the mixed couple rural morris was a short-lived fashion (and possibly rather confined geographically), and was a natural outgrowth of the rampant spread of 'new' country dance ideas in rural dances in general. Subsequent to the early-seventeenth-century fashion, country dances styled 'morris' continued only in country dance halls and assemblies (which is the subject of chapter 10).

As already suggested in chapter 6, the church ale morris was likely to have involved set figures in some locations as the sixteenth century dance evolved, and it is equally likely that some of the courtly morisks that were the progenitors and precursors of the church ale morris used set figures as well. So, it would not be legitimate to say that the use of set figures in rural morris came about because of borrowing from popular country dances. Rather, the synthesis of the early-sixteenth-century morris with country dances was made possible, or facilitated, because the morris of the time already had a form (in particular, it employed some set figures) that allowed for the exchange of ideas. Dances need some basic common ground for borrowing betweeen them to be feasible. What I am suggesting, though, is that the tremendous creative energy that was poured into the invention and development of Elizabethan and Jacobean country dances spilled over into the morris dance, indirectly causing rapid change there as well.

Undoubtedly changes proceeded at different paces and in different directions in different regions, creating a kind of 'speciation' of forms of the morris, as well as allowing for the possibility of variants of the dance in the same region. Thus, for example, the use of large mixed couple sets seems to have been common for a time in the Welsh border counties but rare elsewhere.

The 'new' country dances offered morris at least two areas for evolution. First, the general shift, over time, from rounds to longways formation (and the experimentation with other set formations) in the country dance may well have been emulated by the morris, as a corollary form. Second, the great increase in the stock of set figures in the country dance, which allowed for the invention (eventually) of literally thousands of new dances, gave the same opportunity to morris dances. A village team could, for example, experiment with a stock of figures so as to create different sequences, which could be thought of as variations of the *same* dance, or as *different* dances, depending on how they chose to treat them. Again, the nature of touring may well be the key here.

Judging from Saynt's testimony in Canterbury (see above) an enthusiastic audience response encouraged the performers to keep dancing, and there would certainly be financial incentives to continue performing (up to a point) for a responsive crowd. Having a large inventory of figures to choose from would give considerable flexibility to the dancers in this regard – the dance could be as long or short, simple or complex as the foreman chose. Or they could have a repertoire of several different dances, made up of different sequences of figures, to draw from as circumstances dictated.

While it seems reasonable to suggest that morris dances picked up figures and other formal qualities from country dances, this does not imply that rural morris dances thereby became like country dances; these dance forms are defined as much by context as by choreography. Rural morris was primarily a *spectacular* dance designed as a showpiece for audience members who were quite separate from the dancers. The characters, accoutrements, and style of the dance, exemplified above, were all central to the purpose of the dance – to create a showy, noisy, amusing, exciting, entertaining spectacle. The core of the dance was the spectacle of leaping, jingling, flirting, shimmering dancers; the floor patterns that they mapped out in their motions were the 'peripherals.'

A country dance, by comparison, was primarily a *social* dance, which, although it may well have had an audience, was designed for the entertainment of the dancers themselves (and members of the audience could, at times, become dancers and vice versa). For the dancers, the floor patterns made by the figures were the core of the dance, because it was through them that the dancers met and parted from other dancers in a complex series of briefly made and unmade human contacts. Thus, by this analysis, a rural morris dance could completely change its stock of figured movements and still be perceived by a local audience as the same, as long as the *core* attributes remained stable. This analysis also suggests that from an anthropological perspective we cannot classify any one set of attributes of a dance (floor patterns, or gestures, or body attitudes) as absolutely 'core' or absolutely 'peripheral' when defining the nature of the dance. All such judgments must be seen relative to the dance context, so that what may appear to a neutral observer as the same movements in two dances may actually be markedly different in that they are central to the one and peripheral to the other.

If anything, the advent of new choreographic ideas in the seventeenth century would have helped to solidify the 'classic' features of the morris – such as bells, napkins, and Maid Marian – because these were the stable defining elements amid major changes in choreography. Jonson's observations in this well-known section of *Gypsies Metamorphosed*, thus, becomes especially apposite:

> *Dance. 3.*
> *During wch enter ye Clownes*
> *Cockrell. Clod. Towneshead Puppy.*
>
> ...
>
> CLOD. They should be Morris dancers by theire gingle but they haue no Napkins.
> COC. No nor a Hobby horse.
> CLOD. O he is often forgotten thats no rule but there is no Maidmarrian nor ffrier amongst them wch is the surer marke.
> COC. Nor a foole that I see.
> COC. vnles they be all fooles.
> (Jonson 1621, 589)

Jonson is *not* saying, as is sometimes inferred from this piece, that bells alone define a performance as 'morris'; clearly this is not true, because the dance in the antimasque that the clowns are commenting on does indeed employ bells, yet is not a morris. What he is saying, rather, is that bells are one of several diagnostic features of the morris – napkins, Maid Marian, the friar, and the fool being others of equal importance. The characters and the accoutrements define the *total performance* as 'morris' because it is these features taken together that give the dance event its special personality and distinguishes it from, say, a country dance.

Taken alone this citation might be cause for asserting that the hobby horse was not an essential feature of the morris of the period, but the matter is somewhat complex and requires a moment's detour into the merging of morris and hobby horse traditions in the late sixteenth century.[3] The hobby horse shows up in primary documents associated with the rural morris around 1590, and continued to be a well-known feature of the dance (though intermittent in actual appearance) until the beginning of the eighteenth century. Yet, at the time of the hobby horse's initial association with the morris, there seems to have arisen a catch phrase, joke, or other sort of stock remark – 'For oh! For oh! The hobby horse is forgot' – perhaps originally from a song lyric but whose meaning and connotations are now unknown. The first reference on record of the expression is from Shakespeare's *Love's Labour's Lost* (1595), in an exchange between Don Adriano de Armado and his page Moth concerning the nature of love:

ARMADO. How hast thou purchased this experience?
MOTH. By my penny of observation.
ARMADO. But O, but O,
MOTH. The hobby-horse is forgot.   (III.i.27–30)

It is evident from the context that Armado is merely stumbling for words and that Moth mischievously completes the sentence with the catch phrase. Shakespeare also uses the like expression in *Hamlet* (III.ii.138–40). This idea that the hobby horse was the prototypic ephemeral gewgaw, whose absence (especially from the morris) was worthy of comic lament, caught the fancy of the literati in the early seventeenth century, so that the catch phrase ended up being a well-worn joke.[4] Thus Jonson's use of the phrase is no more than a piece of popular humour imported into the text for a quick laugh, and not necessarily pertinent to the actual history of the morris hobby horse.

This knotty side issue notwithstanding, the hobby horse was not by any means universally employed in the rural morris, though apparently well liked whenever it appeared. The reasons for its irregular appearance in connection with the rural morris, and its relatively brief vogue, are matters for conjecture, although the answers are reasonable enough when the synthesis of hobby horse and morris traditions is investigated.

The primary references are scant, but it seems that in the sixteenth century some churches used a hobby horse entertainment to collect money for candles, and later, when candles were less in use because of liturgical reforms, for general repairs (see Cawte 1978, 17–18). The custom (which may never have been terribly widespread) was beginning to die out by the middle of the sixteenth century because of official church opposition – the collecting function where necessary being replaced by rates. So, by the end of the sixteenth century, both the morris and the hobby horse – until that point quite separate traditions – were deprived of their former patron. One can envisage numerous scenarios in which a union of these two newly sponsorless customs was effected. An enterprising agent might have bought or rented a parcel of obsolete church goods that included morris and hobby horse costumes. Or a team of dancers may have been able to pick up a hobby horse cheaply from a sale of alienated church goods. It was certainly not in the rural morris dancers' financial interests at the time that they were looking for new sponsors to increase their outlay substantially by making a hobby horse from scratch. Nor was it particularly handy to carry such paraphernalia around on a walking tour of villages. But if the equipment were available ready-made at a favourable price there were good reasons to snag it.

First, the hobby horse would add variety to the total performance of the morris – as seems clear from references already cited, the hobby horse had a repertoire of dances and other tricks all his own which could alternate with the morris dances or work in conjunction with them. Second, the hobby horse was a well-known extroverted figure, who could fill some of the role of the fool (either in place of or in conjunction with him), and whose function as a crowd pleaser cum money collector was well established and well understood.

The potentially negative qualities of the hobby horse are also clear. Many references speak of making room for the horse, the frame being large and unwieldy, and requiring ample space for manoeuvring. So, unlike other characters, extroverted or not, the morris hobby horse was destined to a role completely outside the evolutions of the figured dance, and therefore always to occupy a marginal and hence dispensible choreographic position.[5] The upkeep of the costume was also high and, despite the fortuitous cheapness of the initial outlay, eventually the whole affair would have to be renewed at considerable cost (and at a time when the rural morris was under increasing attack from the authorities).

This reasoning suggests why the hobby horse was unlikely to become a common or permanent character in the rural morris. Yet in play texts that represent morris in the countryside the hobby horse is a virtual fixture, and generally a role eagerly sought after because of its extroverted potential, as in the following interchange in William Sampson's *Vow Breaker*:

MILES. ... still give me the hobby-Horse.

BAL. But who shall play the hobby-Horse? Master *Major*?

MI. I hope, I looke as like a hobby-Horse as Master *Major*; I have not liv'd to these yeares, but a man woo'd thinke I should be old enough, and wise enough, to play the hobby-Horse, as well as ever a *Major* on'em all;

BAL. Not so, cholericke *Miles*.

MI. Let the *Major* play the hobby-Horse among his brethren, and he will; I hope our Towne Ladds cannot want a hobby-horse; have I practic'd my Reines, my Caree'res, my Pranckers, my Ambles, my false Trotts, my smooth Ambles, and *Canterbury* Paces, and shall Master *Major* put me besides the hobby-Horse?   (Sampson 1625, 68)

In this text and other plays the extroverted nature of the hobby horse emphasizes overt courtship of women in the audience (and possibly also Maid Marian). This text also suggests that in dressing the horse – which was an elaborate affair – there was a degree of beg-borrow-and-steal, and that Miles takes on the job of finding the necessary adornments in order to strengthen his claim to the role in the dance. And in many plays the playing of the hobby horse is a source for much humourous dialogue. So either the hobby horse was more common in the country morris in the seventeenth century than direct primary texts allow, or stage play texts overrepresent the hobby's appearance. The latter view is slightly more compelling only because the direct references are so few. It is also true that stage companies would have had relatively little trouble adding a hobby horse to their morrises because the equipment would have been a standard part of their properties (hobby horses conventionally being used in plays to represent real horses). Given that the hobby horse was an easy source of scripted and impromptu fun with the groundlings – and cost virtually nothing to provide – there would be every reason to include it with the morris; hence it would become more of a stock character on-stage than off. It is also conceivable that the stage hobby helped foster the vogue in rural morrises. Certainly the fortunes of the two were linked: they arose at the same time, and with the disappearance of the stage morris hobby horse, the rural hobby declined also.

Issues of chronology and the direction of causation aside, primary evidence suggests that the hobby horse was a useful addition to the rural morris when the local dance custom was active enough to support the cost and inconvenience of equipping the character, but was never a particularly common addition to the company. With the general decline of the morris in the countryside in the post–Civil War era, the hobby horse appeared more infrequently and did not survive into the eighteenth century.

What is hardest of all to uncover from vague and indifferent primary sources are the steps and gestures of the rural dance, which may have had as much to do with defining the dance as 'morris' in the audience's mind as characters or accoutrements. After all, it is conceivable that seventeenth-century country dances and morris dances shared a considerable inventory of figures but differed widely in their modes of stepping through the floor patterns. Judging from the standard gear of napkins for arms or shoulders and bells for legs, rural morris dancers executed figures with rhythmic stepping, and coordinated or exaggerated arm gestures. Otherwise there are virtually no indications of the manner of arm motions and only general hints as to stepping and leg motions in the primary record. Not surprisingly, though, all clues point to vigorous leaping and capering interspersed with skipping and stepping, that is energetic enough to exhaust muscles and joints, as in the following:

Strike it up, tabor
And pipe us a favour
Thou shalt be well paid for thy labour.

I mean to spend my shoe sole
To dance about the maypole
I will be blithe and brisk,
Leap and skip;
Hop and trip,
Turn about
In the rout,
Until weary joints can scarce fisk.

Lusty Dick Hopkin,
Lay on with thy napkin,
The stitching cost me but a dodkin.
The morris were half undone
Were't not for Martin of Compton.
O well said, jigging Alice
Pretty Jill
Stand you still
Dapper Jack
Means to smack.
How now? fie! fie! you dance false.   (Weelkes 1608, 301)

Furthermore, in addition to the sense of the spectacular created by leaping and gesturing, the dance must have presented a certain mien to the public via the interplay between its characters and main dancers – perhaps a general element of burlesque and foolery, sometimes introverted, sometimes extroverted. Nicholas Breton, for example, seems to indicate that the fool and Maid Marian could form a couple and participate in an improvised way with the rest of the set during their figures:

A letter to a proud Mistresse ... your haire is none of your owne, and for your steeple-tire, it is like the gaud of a Maid-Marion, so that had you a foole by the hand, you might walke where you would in a Moris-dance ...   (Breton 1605, 33)

This coupling of specific characters, both broad caricatures with well-established symbolic personae, immediately suggests an element of parody of country dance manners and style and, indeed, the existence of these characters *at all* supports the more general notion.

There is also the possibility that the rural morris was defined by special music, but the evidence is equivocal and, as always, indirect. John Ward (Ward 1986) has gathered together all the sixteenth- and seventeenth-century tunes labelled 'morris' and hypothesized that a number of them can be fitted together into a single family tree (the others being unrelated). From this testimony he makes the audacious leap to the conclusion that this tune family represents the branching out regionally and historically of the old 'ritual' country morris tune via the process of traditional oral transmission (the other tunes being associated with 'non-ritual' morris). He further asserts that the existence of the tune family is prima facie evidence for the existence of a single rural dance tradition. The full-blown thesis rests on a frangible base but its central tenets may be salvageable.[6]

The first problem is that Ward relies exclusively on elite sources for his music; he provides no direct evidence that the tunes he reproduces were ever played in country villages. Certainly all hypotheses concerning rural morris have to rely to some extent on literary and other indirect sources, but there are always a few direct eyewitness accounts (no matter how fragmentary) to provide a minimal skeleton on which to build. Ward offers no such direct evidence. Second, he virtually ignores the bulk of the primary (verbal) record from the sixteenth and seventeenth centuries in favour of the musical record, as if somehow the latter provides its own incontrovertible witness to the truth. Third, there is abundant evidence in the musical record alone – which Ward cites – that the tune family was by no means exclusively, or even primarily, associated with the morris (nor even with England in general). Therefore it cannot be argued that the ubiquity of the tune bespeaks the ubiquity and (hence) antiquity of the dance.

If we are to rely on literary evidence at all, then we must reach the determination that rural morris dances used not one, but a number of different tunes. Nashe mentions 'Trip and Go' for the morris (Nashe 1591, 332), and the fiddler in *The Witch of Edmonton* apparently used 'The Flowers in May' as a morris tune (Dekker et al. 1621, 522). Furthermore the rustic morris dancers in a number of plays sing songs while they are dancing that vary in line length and metre, suggesting the use of different melodies. So there is no easy correspondence between melody and dance. Certainly as the dance speciated under the influence of country dance there would be call for a greater variety of tunes (the two mentioned above are country dance tunes) to suit the variety of figured movements. There may also have been a need in the sixteenth and seventeenth centuries, as there was later, to work with the repertoire of the musicians available, whose stock in trade would have been social dance tunes. Primary data already cited also makes it clear that the musicians were hired per diem by the dancers and were not otherwise affiliated with the team, and hence had no prior or necessary commitment to a specifically 'morris' repertoire.

For figured movement what matters are phrase length and strong beats in the bar, and for stepping and leaping patterns certain metres may be preferable to others, but a specific tune is rarely essential – especially a tune with so little character as the supposedly prototypic morris tune (see figure 34). This reasoning cuts both ways, however. On the one hand, the featurelessness of the morris tune means that it could

Figure 34: Melody from *Ayers or Phantasticke Spirites for Three Voices* by Thomas Weelkes

be replaced with no difficulty (and certainly was), but on the other, its persistence as a morris tune despite its blandness indicates its potentially firm ties to the dance (although its empirical connection to the rural dance is entirely unknown in this period).

All of these caveats noted, there does seem to be a case to be made that in the late sixteenth and seventeenth centuries there was a recognizable morris tune – associated with the dance in many people's minds. Weelkes, for example, uses the tune for a section of a madrigal devoted to Will Kemp (Weelkes 1608, 302), and the tune occurs in a number of other literary contexts associated with morris dancing (see Ward 1986 for details).

At the core of the original tune are two four-bar phrases in duple time that can be repeated and alternated in a number of patterns as needed. This basic musical framework may also indicate the evolution of the dance from the ring morisk style to the more figured country dance style. The classic morris dance tune shows up in the record around the time that country dance was having an influence on morris in the countryside, and is perhaps best suited to a dance that relies on stepping through figures for its choreography – rather than exaggerated and grotesque leaping accompanying chironomic pantomime. In this regard, we may also note that the tune is plain, even sedate – most useful for the hopping, skipping, tripping steps of travelling processionwise or executing figured floor patterns.

In the nineteenth century, descendants of the old morris tune were used for processional dances, and teams used other melodies for stationary dances. Perhaps something similar occurred in the seventeenth century as the dance types were speciating. Perhaps the old tune remained a standard part of the musicians' and dancers' repertoires, alongside newer forms. Fads came and went but the old tune managed to hold a place as a sort of traditional signature of the morris in a number of locations. But without contemporary empirical support, such assertions remain pure conjecture.

We may, then, identify three forces at work on the rural morris through the seventeenth into the eighteenth century: first, the creation of a core of 'classic' features; second, the speciation of choreographic forms under the influence of country dance; and, third, the precipitous decline in dance occasions and events. These forces molded the dance that emerged in the countryside around the end of our period.

The classic features already discussed were certainly not universal – Maid Marian could be 'forgot' as well as the hobby horse – but most of them appeared most of the time. In Ludwig Wittgenstein's terminology, morris in this era was not a rigidly definable category of dances but an 'open concept' definable only in terms of 'family resemblances' (i.e., the classic features).[7] The mixing and remixing of these features could produce considerable variety by itself, but added to that process was the adoption of new choreographic forms. Under this rubric there are numerous possibilities, some already articulated:

- use of partners (single sex or mixed)
- use of a maypole for the focus of circular dances
- use of multiple set formations (single file, longways, rounds)
- use of the whole inventory of country dance figures

Combining and recombining these forms also produces a huge array of formal variations, clearly reflected in the primary record. Not least, there is the possibility that active teams developed variations of their main dance or a repertoire of several different dances. The simplest means of varying a dance might have been to allow the foreman to call figures at will – certain sequences inevitably crystallizing over time.

But rapid speciation at the beginning of the seventeenth century was countered by the aggressive onslaught of church and civil authorities, causing total extinction of the dance in many areas, and leaving only small and isolated pockets of activity, primarily in remote areas (see figures 9–11, pp. 41–3). The results of these contradictory forces were, no doubt, akin to the process of natural selection among biologically related species under extremely adverse environmental conditions so that what developed were regionally distinct dance forms specifically suited to local conditions, the common identity of the whole group of dances (across the country) and their relation to common ancestors being hidden because of the extinction of intermediate forms. Two key areas of survival of distinct forms were the south Midlands and the Welsh borders. Subsequently, when adverse conditions lifted the dance prospered again, diffusing out from these isolated pockets of resistance but now with a distinct regional character.

What is difficult to determine is what represented favourable circumstances for the morris to survive in during the purges of the seventeenth century. The immediate issue of the presence or absence of hostile authorities does not begin to address the problem because, as described in chapter 7, there were some regions of the country where attacks against the morris were ardent, but teams continued to perform nonetheless, whereas in others teams vanished at the first signs of legal confrontation. It would seem, therefore, that there were deeper issues involved – possibly basic material factors, for example – that determined the success or failure of local teams. Yet, what such factors might be is elusive.

The spatial patterns of diffusion of church and then rural morris are reasonably clear (see figures 26–34, pp. 179–85, 198, 288). From around 1500 to 1570 church ale morris diffused out from the London environs to the Thames valley, the south Midlands, and parts of the central south. From 1571 to 1600 there was a general thinning out of church-related events in the central zone and the (isolated) establishment of rural morris events on the periphery of the region dominated by church morris. From 1601 to 1630 church events thin out to extinction, and rural events become firmly established in the peripheral region – notably the Welsh borders and west Midland counties, and East Anglia. From 1630 to 1720 there is a rapid decline of rural events followed by a long period of sparse performance anywhere in the country. From 1720 to 1750 there is a resurgence of rural events especially in the central and south Midlands.

From a purely spatial standpoint such a pattern of diffusion appears unremarkable. Like ripples in a pond, the wave of interest in the morris spread outward from the London environs, carried first by church patronage and then by secular support. As church sponsorship ended, the activity in the centre of the diffusion pattern collapsed, followed by a thinning of all events as times became unfavourable. As the tide turned once more, growth at the centre renewed, ready to expand outward again. But such an analysis takes no account of the geographic, or sociopolitical, or economic aspects of the terrain over which the dance was diffusing, and could only make straightforward sense if the landscape were uniform. But it was not. The dance diffused out across the 'grain' of the Midlands to uplands, downlands, and vales; to areas of clay, chalk, and sandstone; to regions specializing in wood pasture, open pasture, and mixed arable; to points inside and outside the projected limits of the 'Midland' field system; to regions with advanced and tardy rates of enclosure; to strongholds of royalism and of Puritanism.

One cannot point to a monolithic material or social variable that correlates precisely with the diffusion pattern. Were it true that dance diffusion is unrelated to material or social variables this would have immense significance for dance history, because it would suggest that the adoption of certain aesthetic forms is not dependent on other variables but is, rather, an independent variable that can override material circumstances. This finding may be a result of incompleteness of the underlying data, however, and there are some identifiable trends within the diffusion pattern. It is true, for example, that the south Midland counties were relatively slow to enclose, but there were certain pockets of early enclosure within the region – particularly in the Cotswold and Chiltern uplands.[8] Thus, it is conceivable that the morris diffused primarily to villages with advanced enclosure even though many of them were in regions where the overall rate of enclosure was slow. Unfortunately data for such fine-grained correlation analysis do not exist as yet.

But even given the limits presented by incompleteness of data, it is possible to draw several tentative conclusions from the diffusion pattern. First, the centre of gravity of dance events shifted sharply north and west over the course of the period 1570 to 1630 (see figure 14, p. 46). As Puritanism expanded in importance, the dance spread more into the regions of England that were to become the areas of greatest royalist sympathy. It must be remembered, however, that this is only a trend, not an absolute correlation; the rural dance also diffused into parts of the south and east that were to become proparliament, as well as into portions of East Anglia. This historic/geographic tendency is supported by the primary evidence, presented earlier, that links morris dancing with the cavalier spirit and old customary ways.

Second, there is a rather more complex trend associated with rates of enclosure. When the morris was church sponsored there was a concentration of events in areas of the Midlands associated with low rates of enclosure, but by the time the dance was banned by the church the periphery of the area of diffusion had reached counties with high rates of enclosure (such as the Welsh borders where some regions were 70 per cent enclosed by 1600). Dancing prospered briefly in the periphery under private sponsorship while it was dying in the central zone under the church. Then in the early to mid-eighteenth centuries when enclosure began in earnest in the south Midlands (and with puritanical legal codes a thing of the past) the dance flourished anew in the central zone. Such a trend, again, merely confirms ideas presented earlier based on primary materials, viz., that in areas of low enclosure the church represented a central institution with the financial resources to buy costumes and hire dancers. In these areas with the church barred from participation there were few other sponsors to turn to. But in areas of greater enclosure wealthy farmers provided patronage, while sons (and daughters) of the lesser landholders performed the dances, as they had the private resources necessary to costume themselves, albeit on a smaller scale than when the church funded the events. The increasing financial reliance on wealthy rural landholders in the eighteenth century (especially in the south Midlands) is also affirmed by the seriation curves of venue and sponsorship (see figures 2 and 3, pp. 29, 32).

These trends, though theoretically tantalizing and empirically justifiable to a degree, must be viewed with caution, however. It cannot be argued fruitfully that the spread or demise of the morris was caused or driven by political or socioeconomic factors. At best it can be said that social factors and material circumstances presented impediments or encouragement to the development of the dance in certain regions, but having a willing sponsor could not make villagers dance, and not having one did not prevent them. Aesthetic, affective, and emotional values could, and did, override the purely material.

Thus the rural morris reached its first peak of popularity in a distinctly oppositional climate – a climate that was to forge its symbolic identity in perpetuity. The dance represented the simple, unsophisticated, but wholesome pleasures of the country people in contrast to the rarefied and extravagant tastes of the urbanite and courtier, the old ways as opposed to the new, the cavalier over against the roundhead. And it was its fate to suffer a long decline and slow rebirth because of this identity – imposed as much by its detractors as supporters in polemics of vilification and songs of praise.

10

Assemblies and the Country Dance Hall

To those whose main experience of morris dancing has been through the contemporary folk dance revival, it may seem odd to see a chapter concerning country dance halls included in a work devoted to the morris. It is an axiom of this revival that spectacular dances (typified by morris) and social dances (typified by country dances) are categorically distinct in every way possible. This position derives ultimately from Cecil Sharp himself, who makes it crystal clear in his introduction to *The Country Dance Book* that as far as he is concerned the two types have virtually no points of contact (Sharp 1909–22, 1:10).

In summary, morris was, according to Sharp, ceremonial, spectacular, formal, skilled, vigorous, male only, and asexual, whereas the country dance was unceremonial, social, informal, unskilled, relaxed, mixed, and sexual. There is no question that the analytic distinction between *spectacular* and *social* dances is a useful one: it marks the broad contrast between dances which are displayed for an audience versus those whose primary purpose is participation, and for which an audience is irrelevant or unnecessary (and some of the merits of this distinction are outlined in the previous chapter). It is, however, a fundamental mistake to assume that all (or any) dances belong uniquely to one category or the other by virtue of some inner essential qualities (as Sharp is suggesting). Indeed in his own day Sharp and his coworkers used country dances for display purposes, thus transmuting them from the social to the spectacular realms. No doubt Sharp would have argued that he was perverting the essence of these dances for educational purposes only, but there are deeper issues involved that he could not see because of his narrowly focused perspective.

Sharp's attitude towards morris and country dances is understandable given the type of methods he was employing to collect and reconstruct them. He gathered the great bulk of his information on morris dances from living informants (many being aged and sole surviving members of nineteenth-century teams), and he had only scant historical sources at his disposal to supplement these contemporary data. His knowledge of country dances derived in small part from very limited field experience with living practitioners (the subject of the first part of *The Country Dance Book*), and in greater part from his attempts at reconstructing the notations found in the various editions of John Playford's *Dancing Master* – these, in turn, influenced heavily by his knowledge of contemporary country dances. Thus his perception of the two 'types' was based on a small (and idiosyncratically determined) subset of the historical possibilities for these dances, and strongly determined by conditions as they existed at the turn of the twentieth century.

In one respect, therefore, Sharp's point of view came about via the fallacy of presentism; that is, he projected contemporary conditions (with country and morris as distinct types) endlessly into the past, and then chose to examine only those historical examples of the two dance 'types' that corroborated the contemporary distinction as he saw it. However, a more catholic and inclusive use of historical sources – as presented in previous chapters of this work – fatally weakens the presentist's position. The morris drew syncretically on country dances for ideas in the late sixteenth and early seventeenth centuries, and vice versa. Furthermore, there were country dances that were indubitably social in character (and fitting all of Sharp's criteria for country dances) that were termed 'morris.' Indeed it is these dances that are the topic of this chapter.

Revivalists following Sharp's lead, might argue that the name 'morris' when applied to country dances is somehow a false attribution, but to make such a claim is to make a premise from something that is far from axiomatic or self evident. It seems much more reasonable to start from the assumption that names matter and that they meant something particular to the people who originally used them. Therefore, the premise here is that country dances that are styled 'morris' are so named because (no matter how minimally) they share qualities with other dances also termed 'morris.' And such a premise is made the more justifiable by the clear historical links between morris and country dances in the sixteenth and seventeenth centuries. Starting from this point of view, we arrive at the quite sensible position that 'morris' is not some absolute and eternal dance essence – as Sharp maintained – defined by rigid markers, but a fluid agglomeration of ideas that could transcend even the boundary between spectacular and social dances, although it must be admitted that the evolution of the dance on the social side of the line was, at best, rudimentary, and ultimately a dead end.[1]

Before dealing with specific data it is also worth stressing that this chapter, like the preceding, is concerned with *venue* and not dance type. It is, therefore, not directed toward morris dances that were country dances but, rather, toward dances called 'morris' that were performed at public assemblies and country dance halls. This may seem like a semantic quibble but the distinction is not only necessary in order to preserve the overall logic of this work; it is also of genuine substantive interest. It is likely *not* the case – as previous chapters have elucidated – that dances styled 'morris' and using basically a country dance format (i.e., mixed couples performing figures in longways or round formations) were performed only in country dance halls; they appeared on the public stage and in rural settings at least. Certainly these dances were for display (i.e., spectacular) rather than being social and, therefore, must have differed significantly from the social dances of formal assemblies. But the point must be granted that set formation, figured, mixed couple morrises were found in a number of distinct venues. And, indeed, it is a basic hypothesis of this chapter that the hybridizing of morris and country dance forms allowed for morris as a dance 'type' to cross from the figured dances of the countryside to the elegant setting of the assembly room, albeit in drastically changed form. Our topic here, therefore, is only those dances called 'morris' that were performed in formal assemblies.

Data for these dances are at once detailed and meager. On the one hand there exist choreographic records for several of them. These consist mostly of shorthand sequences of figures only (although complete Feuillet notation exists for one); as they are the only choreographic details in the entire archive for the period under consideration, their form is of great historical importance. However, the venue 'assembly rooms' does not appear in the seriations discussed in chapter 3 because there is not a single primary source that specifically indicates when and where these morris dances were performed. All the contextual information – normally so rich in the archive – must be inferred from the nature of the source materials and from descriptions of analogous dances.

As indicated in the previous chapter, the elite interest in what became styled 'country' dances received considerable impetus in the later years of the reign of Elizabeth, and by the turn of the seventeenth century dancing masters were collecting and inventing dances in the 'country' style to suit this new bourgeois taste. Very little of substance is known concerning the nature of the genuinely rural country dances of the time or of the changes wrought on them by dancing masters. There are a few literary references that give leads to titles of dances/tunes, as in the following from Nashe's *Have with you to Saffron-Walden*:

... or doo as *Dick Haruey* did ... that hauing preacht and beat downe three pulpits in inueighing against dauncing, one Sunday euening, when hys Wench or Friskin was footing it aloft on the Greene, with foote out and foote in, and as busie as might be at *Rogero, Basilino, Turkelony, All the flowers of the broom, Pepper is black, Greene Sleeues, Peggie Ramsey,* he came sneaking behinde a tree, and lookt on ...   (Nashe 1596, 122)

However, the choreography of these dances is virtually unknown. The titles show up in later dance manuals; 'Pepper's Black,' for example, appears in the first edition of *The English Dancing Master*. But even though Playford's dance is based on a progressive circular set for as many as will, which, as the previous chapter indicates, is conjectured to be the 'old' style of country dancing, there is no solid evidence that the dance he described in 1651 is the same or similar to that named in 1596. In fact, there is good reason to suppose that country dances evolved as much as morris dances, and under similar principles. Take, for example, the dance called 'Trenchmore.' This is mentioned frequently in late-sixteenth-century literary sources as a popular country dance – almost proverbially so. The name may derive from the gaelic *rinnce mor* (big circle), which, if true, would make the original an 'old' style dance. Yet when Playford published a version of it in the second edition of *The Dancing Master* (1652), he described it as a longways for as many as will, that is, as a 'new' style dance. It is quite unlikely, therefore, that Playford's dance represents the one alluded to by sixteenth-century authors.

By the time that John Playford published the first edition of *The English Dancing Master*, the country dance was still very much of a grab bag of choreographic ideas and, although developed in style for refined tastes, still showed clearly its rustic origins. Indeed, it seems that the appeal of these dances lay in their supposed simplicity and innocence, providing a respite for the upper classes from the strenuous precision of the courtly dances of the day.

Although Playford's clientele was elite, and although the elite interest in country dances had been a fact of life for fifty years or more in England, the links between the country dances as found in manuals (and as taught by professional dancing masters) and as performed in the countryside were still strong. What is more, there was still apparently a direct interface (or tension) between courtly and lower class practitioners. Edward Phillips in *The Mysteries of Love and Eloquence* (Phillips 1658b) presents the following conjectured dialogue between a dancing master and a serving maid in a section titled 'The Mode of Balls':

The Dancing Master

Come stir yourselves, Maidens, 'twill bring a fresh colour into your cheeks, rub hard, and let the Ladies see their faces in the boards, you may lose nothing by't, if you be ready to light'm out of doors your selves.

And by the Mass that will I do, and make 'um such fine dops and curtsies in my best Wastecoat, that they shall not chuse but take notice of me; and *Sarah* shall dance a North countrey Jigg before 'um too; I warrant it will please the Ladies better than all your French whisks and frisks; I had rather see one freak of jolly Milkmaids, then all the story that will be here tonight.

That's your ignorance *Bess*.   (Phillips 1658b, 9–10)

Obviously this piece is intensely satirical, but certain social circumstances alluded to are, of necessity, realistic; otherwise the satire would have no force. Both Bess and the dancing master are servants of the upper class, but of a rather different order. Bess is a representative of the lower classes, whose only mode of interaction with the nobility is through outright acts of subservience – 'dops and curtsies' – even when it is clear that she means to use such courtesies aggressively so as to be noticed. She also represents her class in loudly approving the dances of milkmaids over the Frenchified performances of the upper classes. The dancing master has to disagree, because his patronage comes from teaching such dances – yet he is also caught in the middle, because in this period the dances of the lower classes appealed to the nobility and, as is evident from this interchange (and other sources), they were perfomed alongside the more 'artful' dances with great success. Bess suggests, to the dancing master's displeasure, that Sarah's 'North countrey Jigg' will win the day, for example.

The appeal of the country dance to the aristocracy in Playford's time seems to have lain in two separable (although analytically related) spheres. In the first edition of *The English Dancing Master* there are a few dances that are, to some extent, mimetic or playful. 'New Boe peep,' for example, contains the following directions:[2]

We. goe all to the wall and stand, men go up to your owne We. and peepe foure times on each side behinde them, fall to your places all and turn S. ⌐ Then men goe to the wall and stand, We. go up to your backs and peepe foure times, then fall to your places and turne S. ⸴

(Playford 1651, 83)

The playfulness here contains a strong element of class consciousness – the women, for example, are playing at being the proverbially cute shepherdess, Little Bo Peep – and part of the point of the dance (at least from the upper class's point of view) is that shepherds and shepherdesses flirt and sport freely without concern for the typical bourgeois worries about making a fitting marriage, comporting oneself in public with decorum, and so forth. The amorous designs of rustics are, supposedly, rather more direct and basic. In this respect these dances are closely linked to certain dances in Stuart masques and plays – the morris in the second antimasque in Francis Beaumont's *Masque of the Inner Temple and Gray's Inn*, for example, where the rustic couples represent the natural and instinctive union of man and woman, in contradistinction to the effete, and ultimately sterile, posturings of the gentry (symbolized by gods and nymphs).

The power of the sexuality in these dances, therefore, lay in the fact that the actions had a dual, or liminal, nature – they could be seen as directly indicative of the desires of the participants, or, conversely as 'mere' play acting. They also embodied a degree of sexual equality not to be found in the culture at large. In 'New Boe peep,' for example, following the principle of symmetric figured action that is the commonplace of these dances, the men first flirt with the women, then their roles are reversed. To complete the symmetry, following another figure, the flirting figure is repeated with the women going first.

These playful, mimetic, do-as-the-rustics-do qualities of the country dances of the élite continued as a minor theme through the eighteenth century, but, as is explored later in this chapter, there was a constant tension between the desire of some people to romp, peasantlike, through the dances, and the aesthetic sensibilities of certain dancing masters who wished to preserve a degree of decorum in motion. To some extent this tension was characterized as the difference between English and French manners. Margaret Dean-Smith, in her annotated edition of *The English Dancing Master*, for example, argues that the title of the work itself is meant to draw attention to the notion that the dances contained therein were specifically *not* French, and it is certainly true that Playford was passionately anti-French in his general writings on dance (Dean-Smith 1957, xv).

Country dances also appealed to the gentry because of their form. The progressive longways set in particular, which quickly became the dominant type, allows for everyone to dance with everyone, so that the dances are completely social – allowing (eventually, and if choreographed appropriately) for direct physical contact between all the men and all the women dancing. Thus, the Master of Ceremonies at Phillips's ball, under the rubric 'At their going to dance Countrey Dances' announces:

Ladies, will you be pleased to dance a Countrey Dance or two, for 'tis that which makes you truly sociable, and us truly happy; being like the Chorus of a Song, where all the parts sing together.   (Phillips 1658b, 12)

The reference here is clearly contrastive; Phillips is saying that unlike the minuet, for example, where couples dance by themselves, country dancing takes place in set formations where, of necessity the couples must interact 'like the Chorus of a Song.' However, certain set formations were more sociable than others in that they involved large numbers of couples (such as the 'longways for as many as will,' which could, in principle, accommodate as many couples as could comfortably fit into the assembly room or hall), or they involved progressions of couples, meaning that at the end of each sequence of figures, sets of couples split up and reformed the set in new combinations of couples, began the sequence of figures again, and so on. This meant that there was a wide spectrum of sociability in country dancing from the most intimate sets, consisting of two couples, to the most gregarious, namely the longways for as many as will with elaborate progressions. Over the course of the seventeenth century there was a rapid decline, recorded in the manuals, of the former type and an enormous collateral increase in the popularity of the latter, suggesting that it was precisely the gregariousness of the longways that was the chief appeal of the country dance in England. It also appears, though, that even in the mid-seventeenth century, when country dancing had been in vogue for a generation or two, set formations, modes of progression, and other fundamental choreographic principles were still in considerable flux.

The actual forms of progressive longways set dances in the mid-seventeenth century are, in addition, difficult to determine because the choreographic record is scanty in this respect. Certainly, there were quirks peculiar to some dances, and it is impossible to avoid the intrusion of anachronistic interpretations based on later country dances whose record is more complete. This latter problem exists, in large part, because the main thrust of analysis of the seventeenth-century dance record in the past has been reconstruction, for the purposes of contemporary (i.e., twentieth century) performance, and to a lesser extent because of hindsight fallacies (it is easy, for example, knowing that the progressive longways for as many as will achieved a certain classic form by the turn of the eighteenth century, to interpret earlier notations of longways dances as conforming to that classic form when the record is silent or obscure in that regard). In neither case can reconstruction tolerate obscurity; choreographers must make concrete decisions even when these rest on flimsy or absent data. But scholarship can afford to let uninterpretable primary data stand.

Thus it is necessary to aver that a number (perhaps even a majority) of notations in Playford's manuals, and elsewhere, are not clear enough, taken literally, to produce uncontroversial reconstructions. Sometimes the strain of music seems too long or short for the figures described, sometimes the figures themselves are insufficiently documented, sometimes the mode of progression is not apparent, and so forth. From a strictly scholarly point of view, therefore, there is no alternative but to examine each document in turn, noting its oddities and obscurities, and trying not to be too quick to fit the dance into a few generalized templates or models. Having noted these caveats, however, several overarching points may be made about country dance set formations before examining particular sources in detail.

A version of the longways set that became extremely popular by the end of the seventeenth century (essentially a variety of the classic form), and the simplest to understand, is what is now called – following Sharp's terminology – the 'duple minor' formation. As far as is possible to discern from Playford's notations, this form was used in the mid-seventeenth century, but it was one among many and had only minority representation in his earlier works. It is also the commonest set formation for country dances styled 'morris.'

As in all longways formations, the men stand in one long file and the women in another, to the right of the men. For certain figures, mostly of a preliminary nature, these two files act as a single unit, but for most figures the larger set can be broken into smaller (i.e., minor) units of two couples (i.e., duples) as shown in figure 35.

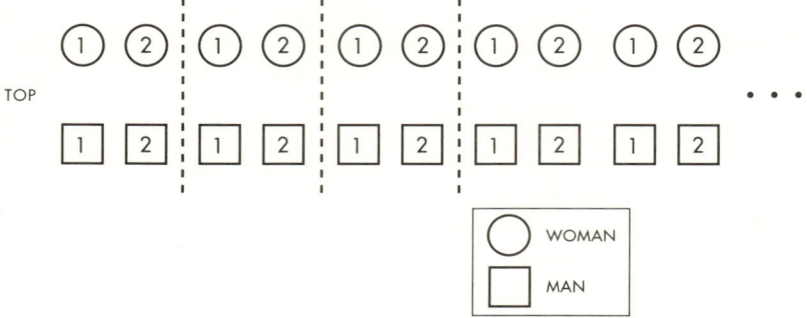

Figure 35: Duple minor sets in the longways formation

The couple in each duple minor unit closest the top of the long set are designated the 'first' couple, and the couple farthest from the top, the 'second.' For one pass through the sequence of figures that defines the dance, each duple minor set down the longways set acts as a separate, contained unit responding to and interacting with the couples within it, and not to individuals outside of it. A highly simplified and idealized such sequence – using no technical language – might be as follows (graphically represented in figures 36–9):

First man turn second woman a full turn and kiss her.
Second man turn first woman a full turn and kiss her.
All four take hands in a circle and go clockwise halfway round.
Men turn their partners a half turn and kiss them.

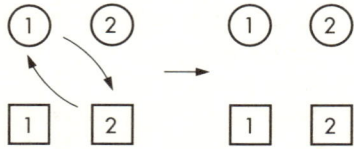

Figure 36: Idealized duple minor sequence

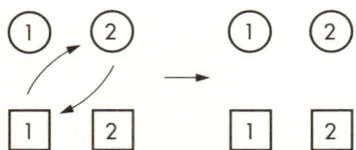

Figure 37: Idealized duple minor sequence

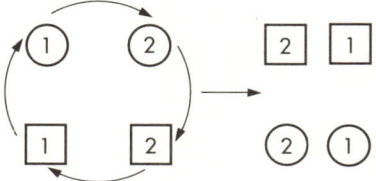

Figure 38: Idealized duple minor sequence

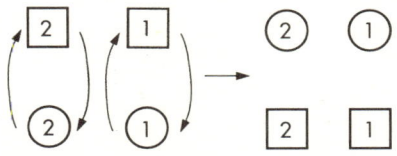

Figure 39: Idealized duple minor sequence

The last two figures here combine to form the actual longways progression. What has happened is that the first couple of each duple minor set has moved down the longways set one place, and the second couples have each moved up one, forming new duple minor sets (figure 40). The sequence can now begin again in these new sets. At every other turn, one second couple will be stranded at the top of the set with no first couple to meet, and, likewise, one first couple will end up by itself at the bottom. This is a problem that may not have been fully resolved in the mid-seventeenth century, which may be why the duple minor longways set was relatively uncommon. If the dance keeps going through sequences with a couple landing unoccupied at every turn, the dance would soon end with all the second couples at the top and all the firsts at the bottom. This state of affairs may have been quite reasonable for seventeenth-century dancers: some dance notations do seem to indicate that there were dances in which large numbers of couples were idle either at the beginnings or ends of the dances. But there is a simple solution in the case of the duple minor, namely, the end couples can stand idle for one turn, and then reenter the set, transformed into their opposites (that is, seconds can become firsts and vice versa). Thus, for example, the seconds transformed into firsts meet a second couple progressing up to the top of the set, and they (the new firsts) can now begin the progression down the set (figure 41). This folding back in of the end couples makes the dance theoretically infinite in duration.

The progression is crucial to this form of the longways because it allows for end-less recombining of duple minor sets and, most important, by the time a couple is back in the place in the longways formation in which they started they have danced in duple minor sets with every other couple in the longways set twice (once as a first couple and once as a second). Feeding this knowledge back into the idealized figure sequence, it is easy to see that such a progression allows every man and every woman in the dance to interact with one another (in this case by kissing – proverbially common

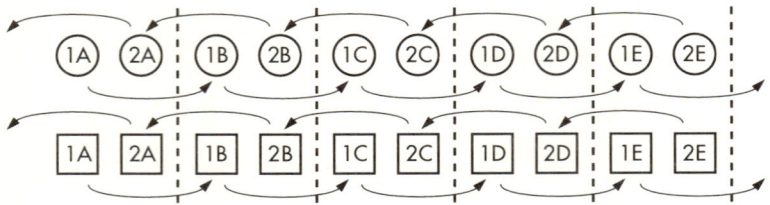

Figure 40: Longways progression

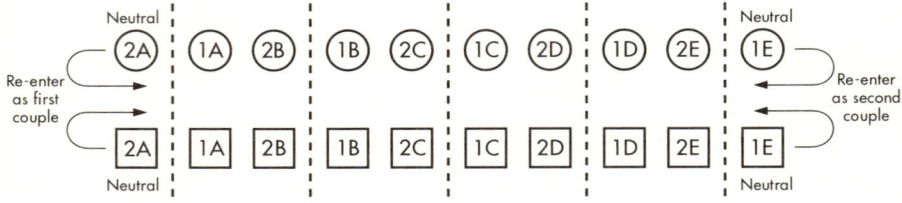

Figure 41: Neutral couples in the longways set, about to re-enter

in English country dances), hence the notion that these dances were 'truly sociable' with 'all the parts' performing together.

It is no surprise, therefore, that such dances proved endlessly popular down to the latter part of the nineteenth century, when isolated couple dances (such as the waltz) regained the ascendancy. Progressive longways dances had a direct physical and sexual appeal, combined with a gregarious social component, which made them for a time quintessentially (almost jingoistically) English. French dancing masters disdained their directness and vulgarity. Yet the dance form spread to the European continent regardless, and a great deal of insight into the battle between English and French styles, as discussed at greater length below, comes from French country dance manuals (see, for example, Feuillet 1706a).

All told, there are extant notations for seven country dances with the word 'morris' in their titles dating from c 1650 to 1735, five of which come from various editions of Playford's *Dancing Master*. Given that John Playford and his heirs published many hundreds of dances, it is clear that the morris strain in bourgeois country dance is minimal. Furthermore, the dance notations were published over an eighty-year period, making on average for the appearance of less than one every decade – again a sign that such dances were extreme rarities. For purposes of analysis, though, it is reasonable to group these dances into those of the mid- to late seventeenth century (1650, 1651, 1686) and those of around the second quarter of the eighteenth century (four published between 1721 and 1735), so that one might say that there were slight clusters of popularity for these generally uncommon dances.

THE SEVENTEENTH CENTURY

Possibly the first reference to a morris country dance comes from a seventeenth-century manuscript, although its date of composition is obscure:

The Maurice daunce.
Lead all ye Mates round ye Roome.
1 ffig: The 1& 2d Man meete the 1 & 2d woaman & passe through them to ye contrary sides & soe faces about then ye 1 & 2d Cu: take hands & meete each other then let goe hands & turne round all 4 single; then ye 1 man takes ye 2d man by ye right hand, & soe also ye 1 woaman & ye 2d woa: & turne yeir places & so caper, then doe ye same each with his mate & caper againe. Doe this all along.

2d ffig: The 1 Cu: cast off & goe downe into ye 2d place, whilest ye 2d Cu: lead up bewteen them into ye 1 place & there change places one with another still holding hands; then ye 2d Cu: being in ye 1 place cast of & goe downe as ye first Cu: did before whilst ye 1 Cu: doe as ye 2d Cu: did before then ye 1 & 2d man take right hands & change places as in ye first fig: ye 1 & 2d woemen ye same at ye same time; then each change with his mate as in ye first fig: Doe this all along.

3 ffig: The 1 & 2d men take hands, ye 1 & 2d woemen ye same; & fall back from each other, then meete & change places each with his mate; then ye 1 Cu: cast of & goe downe into ye 2d place whilst ye 2d Cu: goe up into ye first place betweene them, then ye 1 & 2d men ioyne both hands, & soe ye 1 & 2d woemen & meete each other slipping one foote before ye other; then slip apart againe ye men from ye woemen still holding hands, & soe Caper, then take hands each man with his mate, & change places with them then caper. Doe this all along.

(BL Add. MS 41996 f. 18)

Choreographically the dance seems relatively straightforward, with little to distinguish the basic formations from other longways dances of the period, but the mode of progression is possibly a little more complicated than most. The dance is divided into three 'figures,' each of which is apparently to be performed in a complete longways progression before the next begins.[3] As such, the whole is akin to three miniature (and separable) longways dances. Indeed there are whole dances in the Playford corpus that are no more complex than one of these figures. Yet even though the figures appear as if they are independent dances, there are elements that hold them together; basically the three figures are part of what could be an endless series of variations on a theme. Comparing the first two figures gets the general gist of things.

By good fortune this notation – being rather more detailed than that found in most published works – can be transformed into something resembling a reconstructed dance in a matter of minutes by anyone generally familiar with seventeenth-century country dance. The progression of the first figure is easily understood (see figure 42). The men cross over into the women's places and there perform an evolution that does not alter anyone's place in the set. Then the men change places while simultaneously the women change places. And finally partners change places. This effects the longways progression. 'Doe this all along' seems to indicate, as discussed below, that the progression is worked all the way through the longways set before the second figure commences.

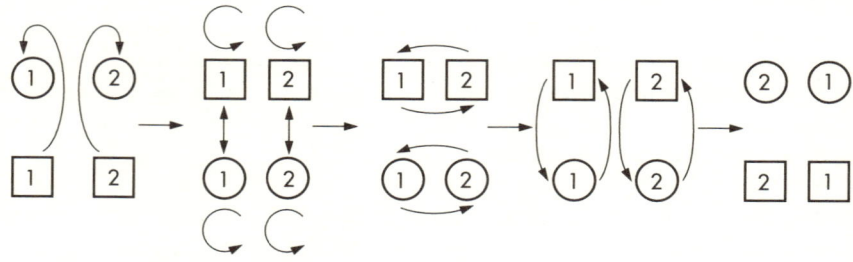

Figure 42: Illustration of 1 ffig. from 1650 Maurice daunce

The second figure is a simple variation on the first, in that it takes two evolutions instead of one to get the men on the women's side (see figure 43). The first couple cast down to the second place, and the second couple move up crossing over as they go, thus putting the second man on the women's side. A repeat of this evolution gets the first couple back to their original place with the first man now also on the women's side. From there the rest of the progression works as in the first figure.

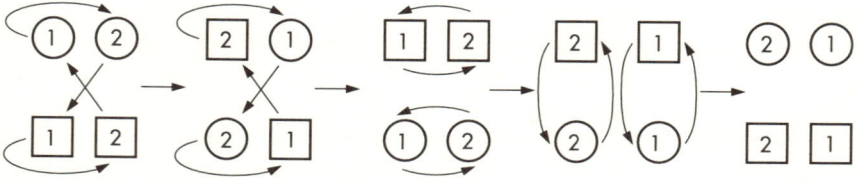

Figure 43: Illustration of 2 ffig. from 1650 Maurice daunce

It is a simple step to move from these specific evolutions to a general principle that guides the figures notated – and others that could be added. The flow of the formations (howsoever effected) is:

- Men cross to the women's side.
- Men change places while women change places.
- Partners change places.

Each figure represents a different way to accomplish these formations and each is

'decorated' in different ways (i.e., there are evolutions that do not alter the set formation, such as slipping forward and back with your partner), but the underlying
'idea' of the dance is what in modern parlance would be called 'three changes of the
circular hey.' In other words, each figure is simply a variation on a basic theme, so
that there could be more or fewer included as the dancers saw fit or had the ingenuity to produce. In that sense the whole dance is not three little dances strung together but, rather, three versions of one idea.

There are two obvious possibilities for interpreting the command 'Doe this all
along.' The first is that this is simply a shorthand to indicate the duple minor progression oulined above, that is, have every couple in the longways set designated as
first or second, and have each duple minor 'Doe this' to start the progression off 'all
along.' But there is another possibility consonant with descriptions of contemporary
and later dances. In these descriptions the longways set begins with a first, second,
third, fourth, fifth ... nth couple, which could be translated into a first couple plus n
second couples. The dance begins with the first couple dancing with the second, while
the rest stand idle. At the end of the first progression the first couple move down to
dance with the third couple (who act as a new second couple), then on to the fourth
(also dancing as a second couple) and so on down the set. This long string of second
couples as they reach the top of the set stand idle for a turn and then progress down as
first couples (the same as in the regular duple minor), the effect thus being of the
original first couple 'activating' the dance by starting each couple in turn. The dance
ends, like other duple minors, when the original first couple is back at the top. In the
case of this notation the arrival of the first couple at the top would signal the beginning
of the next figure, whose progression would be likewise, until the end of the third figure.

The whole effect of a figure plus variations being pursued inexorably through all
its longways progressions may, thus, be thought of as having a kind of inevitable
mathematical beauty to it; and this may help explain why longways country dances
particularly intrigued aestheticians in the Enlightenment. That is, the progressions
of the duple minor set appealed not only to the physical sensibilities of the dancers,
but also to their mental sense of order as the foundation of social values – no matter
what confusion the dancers appeared to twist themselves into in the course of a
dance, and no matter who partnered whom in the interim, the outcome was always
the restoration of the original set.

It must be remembered that the foregoing discussion of the sequences of per-
mutations of the duple minor set deals with the *floor plan* of the dances only; such
analyses tend to dominate academic discussion of historic country dances because
that is what the older notations focus on. But there is a great deal more to country
dancing than the trace of bodies across a plane surface. Unfortunately little is to be
gleaned from primary texts concerning stepping, body attitude, energy, pace, and
the like, and most of the evidence is indirect. Nicholas Breton, for example, gives a
satirical picture of country dance at the beginning of the seventeenth century, which

seems to indicate that there was more variety than uniformity in general dance style:

But to behold the graces of each dame
How some would dance as though they did but walk;
And some would trip as though one leg were lame,
And some would mince it like a sparrow hawk;
And some would dance upright as any bolt;
And some would leap and skip like a young colt

And some would fidge, as though she had the itch;
And some would bow half crooked in the joints;
And some would have a trick, and some a twitch;
Some shook their arms, as they had hung up points ... (Quoted in Emmerson 1972, 286)

This description of the general confusion of styles in the country dance is echoed through the seventeenth century, so that from the second quarter of the eighteenth century onwards manuals, mostly originating in France, began appearing and their express purpose was to formalize and regularize the dance style, and to urge greater grace and poise. However, their continued urgings in this direction points to their lack of success and suggests that a rough and ready manner of dancing served as the norm.

Breton's remarks do, nonetheless, give a few clues as to some standards of practice in the midst of diversity. He seems to indicate, for example, that a walking step (which has become common practice in modern reconstructions) was not usual; 'some would dance as though they did but walk' taken literally means that dance steps were distinct from ordinary walking steps. Instead, the dances were apparently composed of skipping, tripping, and leaping. Whether such steps were left to the discretion or creativity of individual dancers, or whether certain styles had periodic vogues is unclear, although it is possible to speculate that different dances could employ different kinds of steps. Playford occasionally specifies a particular step to be employed, and the notation currently under consideration does so in parts of each figure.

Given the general proclivity of dancing masters to exclude stepping information, its inclusion in any notation must be taken as a sign that such steps are a mandatory (or, at least, very important) component of the overall choreography. Thus, Playford's commonest references to stepping call for a 'slip' step, denoting that for a particular figure the dancer's motion should be sideways. That is, the difference between the directions: 'first couple *go* down between the second couple and, first couple *slip* down between the second couple' is that in the first case, the first couple face down and dance forwards, and in the second they face each other and dance sideways down the set (probably with a sliding step). Such a difference was clearly important enough to be noted routinely, whereas other kinds of steps did not have the same degree of significance. Following this reasoning we must presuppose that the stepping directions in the notation under consideration are vital to the choreography.

There are two distinct stepping instructions, the first common to all the figures, and the second found in the third figure only. In all figures when the men and women change places, and then when partners change places to complete the duple minor progression, they are directed to caper at the end of each change. The term 'caper' has undergone a number of changes of meaning as dance styles have changed, but the basic concept is not so different from the balletic *entrechat*, of which it is a forerunner. The dancer leaps in the air while, as dexterously as possible, crossing or shaking the feet, timing the leap so as to land on the beat, and thus continue into the next part of the dance (see Arbeau 1596, 47–8, for the French analog 'capriole'). This is obviously a skilled manoeuver requiring considerable practice and yet it is called for repeatedly in this dance – almost as a kind of chorus or flourish to end each progression.

Capers were an intrinsic component of many galliards, and other elite, skilled dances of the sixteenth and seventeenth centuries and may have entered the country dance via this kind of source. After all, dancing masters taught all manner of dances, and in choreographing country dances they were often ready to import steps and gestures from other sources. This would be particularly so for those dancing masters who wished to knock the crude rustic edges off the country dance. Dances in later-seventeenth-century editions of *The Dancing Master*, for example, frequently call for movements taken directly from the minuet. Even so, it is possible to speculate that the caper, while deriving from an elite tradition, was meant to imitate the energetic leaping of the rustic morris (albeit in refined form), and that, therefore, this dance (and perhaps other country dance morrises) is one of many links in the general trading of dance ideas – through imitation and parody – between classes that is the backbone of the developmental history of the morris. That is, the dance itself was probably the product of a bourgeois dancing master following a standard country dance format for the figures, but its style of performance (including specific steps and gestures) could well have been influenced not just by rustic country dancing in general, but by rural morrises in particular – and this may have been a principle observed in other country dances identified as morris.

These speculations, based as they are on a single document, may be tempered by investigation of the first published country dance morris – Stanes Morris.[4] The dance notation first appeared in 1651 (Playford 1651, 87) and was included in the first three editions of *The Dancing Master* (i.e., 1651, 1652, and 1665), but with the major reorganization of the collection for the fourth edition in 1670, Playford dropped it. The popularity of the tune itself, independent of dance notation, however, spanned a much longer period (see Ward 1986, 299, 303–5). It may first be found in two manuscript lute books of the late Elizabethan era (*c* 1595–1600), The Trumbull

Lute Book (Berkshire Record Office MS D/ED C1 f.9v), and William Ballet's Lute Book (Trinity College, Dublin MS D.1.21/1.f.91), and last shows up in our period of record in two versions in Daniel Wright's *An Extraordinary Collection of Pleasant & Merry Humours, Never Before Published* (Wright *c* 1713, Nos. 3 and 13), whence it leaves popular tradition until the morris revivals of the late nineteenth century.

During the 120-year span of the tune's popularity it may be found scored for lute, cittern, keyboard, and treble viol, and was used both as a plain melody and as an accompaniment for part song and for dancing.[5] John Ward (Ward 1986), as part of his general thesis that there was a single tune – with many variants – for the rural English morris in the sixteenth and seventeenth centuries, argues that the Stanes morris group of variants forms a branch off from the main family tree of morris tunes. Caveats concerning his reasoning have already been noted (see chapter 9), and a few more may be added here. He draws a parallel between what he calls the 'old version' of the morris tune represented by a melody in Weelkes's *Ayres or Phantasticke Spirites for Three Voices* (Weelkes 1608, No. 20) and two versions of Stanes morris – one scored for cittern (Cambridge University Library MS Dd.4.23 f.19) and another for solo melody instrument such as the treble viol (Wright *c* 1713, No.3) (see figure 44). His description of the way in which the Stanes 'branch' differs from the 'trunk' representing the old, basic tune group is as follows:

> It retains the general shape of the [basic morris] tune but includes several notable changes in pitch content, i.e., the leap up to *c'* in bar 1 (a small variant, but striking enough to identify the Staines branch); the descent to *g* in bar 2 (the whole of bar 2 is a mirror version of the corresponding bar of the basic morris tune); the altering and transposing of bars 5–6 down a tone; the four bar varied repeat of bars 5–6 in bars 7–8, which alters the overall form from *abcb* to *abcc*; and the tonal ambivalence created by the close alternation of *b*-natural/*b*-flat and, in two of the versions, *e*-natural/*e*-flat. (Ward 1986, 303)

Ward's analysis suffers two serious problems. First, one could just as easily use his description of the two tunes to argue that they are *unrelated*. The leap to *c'* in bar 1 of Stanes morris, while only a difference of one note from the Weelkes tune, creates a radically different feel to the shape of the bar (especially when the tonal ambivalence of the final *b*-natural is engendered by the *b*-flat in the next bar). Likewise, the shape of bar 2 of Stanes morris could better be described as a modal descent from *c'* to *a* whereas the same bar in the Weelkes tune hovers constantly around *c'* – that is, the contours of the bars are quite different. Bar 4 of both is a descent to the tonic – unremarkable in a major scale folk tune – but the Weelkes tune descends *e* to *c*, and Stanes descends *d* to *c*. The likeness of the A parts of the two tunes, thus rests on bar 3 alone. If anything, bars 5–8 of the two tunes are even more unlike, in both contour and tonality.

The second problem is one of chronology. Ward claims that the Stanes 'branch'

Figure 44: Weelkes air and Stanes morris (2 versions) compared

diverted from the main tune family at some point, yet his prototype of the main tune was published in 1608 and, therefore, is *later* than several of the oldest versions of Stanes morris, including one that he uses as a model. Thus, all other criteria being equal, Stanes morris could be the old tune and Weelkes's version (and its relatives) the younger branch. Or, as likely, both could be elite reworkings of an older traditional tune that has not been recorded.

Whatever the results of internal tune analysis show, there are other external reasons for supposing that the *tune* Stanes morris has traditional antecedents. The first is a probabilistic argument, namely that the first edition of *The English Dancing Master* is known to have called on traditional tunes and dances for much of its inspiration, and that in the mid-sixteenth century it was precisely the closeness of elite country dances to folk models (albeit with a veneer of refinement) that was their charm to the nobility. As Playford's collection included more consciously composed dances (and melodies) with fewer roots in traditional practice, Stanes morris was dropped. Thus it may have been conceived of as a rustic-style tune. Second, the name itself, appearing at a time when the rural morris was in the ascendency (and elite forms in decline), suggests an association with traditional roots.

But the known history of the tune also cautions against making overbold assertions about links between rural morris and country dance morrises bearing the same name. By the time Playford used the tune for his choreography it had been used in settings quite divorced from dance, or not associated with any particular dance, for over sixty years. His version of the tune also represents a significant reworking of its structure in many respects (figure 45). Although still ambiguously modal (especially in the first part), Playford's tune has an overall minor cast to it (made stronger if the use of a flattened sixth – i.e., drawing the tune away from a dorian mode – is assumed in the second and third parts of the melody, as Jeremy Barlow (Barlow 1985, 36) suggests based on contemporary performance practice). Also Playford has added a third part made up of two new bars cobbled to the last two bars of the first part, in order to make the tune fit his choreography. There is every reason to suppose, therefore, that even if the original tune derived from a rural morris, it had been separated from it for several generations, and had eventually been completely recast to suit elite musical tastes and a new choreography.

In other words a tune with 'morris' in its title (although at one time used for a rustic morris) could become separated from its original choreography and, after many transformations, reused in an utterly different context, even though the name still adhered to indicate its source. Such is likely the case with Stanes morris, which, incidentally, lost its 'morris' name on occasions when it was used outside a dance context. The cittern version in figure 44, for example, is untitled and a vocal version (Brett 1967, 168) is simply embedded in a quodlibet without verbal reference to the original. *Specific* associations between the country dance called 'Stanes morris' and any particular rural morris, therefore, are likely remote. Rather, the links are of a general kind; that is, beside using a common tune, they drew on a common stock of figured set movements and, as articulated for the previous notation, elite 'morris' country dances of the seventeenth century may have used some steps or gestures reminiscent of the rural morris in deference to the tunes' origins. But by the eighteenth century even this tenuous link was broken.

Playford's Stanes morris is a kissing dance, with an uncommon form of longways progression that lost favour in the later seventeenth century. The notation is divided into figures by ruled lines across the page, and the evolutions for each part of the music (A to C) are listed under the relevant section of music. In the following transcription the relationship between figures and music is noted in brackets:

Figure 45: John Playford's Stanes morris (showing the added flats from later editions)

Longwayes for as many as will

[First figure]

[A music]
Lead up all a D. forward and back ⁙ That again ⁙

[B music]
All a D. to the left hand ⁙ Back againe ⁙

[C music]
Set and turn S. ⁙ That againe ⁙

[Second figure]

[A music]
First man go downe between the rest to the last Wo. ⁙

Sides once with her ⁙

[B music]
Take her by one hand ⁙ Then by the other ⁙

[C music]
Turne her halfe about, holding both hands and salute her, as much the other way ⁙ Bring her up ⁙

[First figure repeated]

[A music]
Lead up as at the first ⁙

[B music]
As at the 1 time ⁙

[C music]
As at the first time ⁙

[Second figure repeated]

[A music]
This as the 2. time ⦂

[B music]
As the 2. time ⦂

[C music]
As the 2. time ⦂

Do thus till you have fetcht up all the We.   (Playford 1651, 87)

Basically the two figures, repeated as many times as there are couples in the set (which brings the original first couple back together again), divide the dance into two distinct parts. The first figure is performed by the whole longways set simultaneously, and the second only by the first man and the woman occupying the last place. So it can be thought of as a dance alternating between whole set figures and solo couple evolutions.

The first figure is extremely simple and could be peformed by anyone with the most minimal knowledge of country dance style. The first evolution, for example – 'Lead up all a D. forward and back' – is no more than four steps forward bringing the feet together at the end, followed by four like steps backwards. The other evolutions in the figure are equally straightforward and would be well known to anyone with knowledge of basse dances or bransles. The couples in the whole set thus move en masse, forward and back, then side to side, then all turn on the spot.

For the second figure, all dancers stand still except the first man (who remains the same throughout the dance) and the last woman (who changes at each progression). After two preliminary evolutions – which have a flirtatious quality – the first man kisses the last woman twice and then leads her up to the top of the set, the other women moving down one place. The progression is thus one-sided: the men retain their original positions, and the women move down one place each time. Each man partners each woman in turn so that all have danced with all by the end of the dance. But there is no breaking into minor sets and only the first man – with a succession of women partners – performs the second figure, leaving everyone else standing idle for half the dance.

Judging by the steps prescribed and the metric qualities of the music, the dance was relatively sedate and graceful with more of the feel of the old basse dances of court than of a rustic romp. Nonetheless, the continual exchange of partners, the simultaneous figured action of whole sets, and the centrality of kissing and flirtatious physical contact place the dance firmly within the orbit of country dance style action, despite the veneer of courtly grace.

Stanes morris is, in several respects, an atypical dance within Playford's first edition, although its general form fits a standard model. While it is true to say that the dances of the first edition are a mixed bag – as is to be expected of a manual issued

when both elite and rural country dances were undergoing fundamental changes –
a little probing below the surface variety reveals a number of common features, which
may give insight into the folk models that provided their inspiration. Comparison
of two different dance notations helps emphasis the common features:

Blew Cap   *Longwayes for six*

[A music]
Lead up a D. forwards and back ⌐
That againe ⸪

[B music]
First man set to his owne, the last man set to his owne, the 2. man salute his owne and
turne her ⌐ That againe, the last man beginning ⸪

[A music]
Sides all ⌐ That againe ⸪

[B music]
First man set to his Wo. the 2. as much, third man salute his owne and turn her ⌐
That againe last man beginning ⸪

[A music]
Armes all ⌐ That againe ⸪

[B music]
First man and last Wo. change places, first Wo. and last man change, middle man salute,
and turne his owne ⌐ All this againe to your places ⸪   (Playford 1651, 2)

The Night-Peece   *Longwayes for six*

[A music]
Lead up a D. forwards and back ⌐
That againe ⸪

[B music]
The middle Cu fall back and slip up, while the first and last Cu. change places. That
againe. That againe ⸪

[A music]
Sides all ⌐ That againe ⸪

[B music]
First Cu. crosse over, fall into the 2. place, crosse againe, fall into the last, the next Cu. as
much, the next Cu. as much ⸪

[A music]

Armes all ⌣ That againe ⦂

[B music]

First man change places with the 2. Wo. first Wo. change with the 2 man, while the last changes with his owne: Then change with the last Wo. your Wo. change with the last man, while the other changes with his owne: Set all and turne single. ⦂   (Playford 1651, 3)

The particulars of these two dances are not important for current purposes; what is worth noting, though, is that the two are cut from the same general template. That is, the evolutions to the A music for both are identical,

• Lead up a double and back
• Sides all
• Arms all

The evolutions for the B music for each are different, but *within* each dance they form a series of variations on a theme. In fact, in the first edition there are twenty dances that are based on a longways for six formation that have virtually identical figures to the A music and unique variations on a theme for the B music. So, we may postulate that this is a standard model, perhaps derived ultimately from rural country dance, upon which dancing masters could improvise endlessly. This is only a small part of the story, however. Compare the following notation of a round dance with those above:

The Fine Companion   *Round for eight*

[A music]

Hands all and meet a D. backe again set and turne S. ⌣

That againe ⦂

[B music]

Men meet and go back againe, We. as much, men meet hands and goe round ⌣ We. meet and goe back, men as much, We. hands and go round ⦂

[A music]

Sides all. Set and turne S. ⌣ That againe ⦂

[B music]

The two Cu. against each other meet and back, the other foure as much. The first foure hands and goe round ⌣ That againe, the last foure beginning.

[A music]

Armes all. Set and turne S. ⌣ That againe ⦂

[B music]
Men meet, turne back to back, the We. go round about, the men to their places ⌐ We.
meet, turne back to back, men go about the We. ∴   (Playford 1651, 33)

Again the specifics of the choreography are not as important as the overall pattern
of the dance, which it is easy to see is generally the same as that for the longways
dances – the only difference being that the first A music figure is a lead inwards and
outwards (rather than up and back), as befits a round dance. Otherwise the pattern
of a fixed sequence of figures to the A music – lead up and back, sides all, arms all –
and variations on a theme to the B music obtains, suggesting that this basic model
is of major significance.

Examination of the entire corpus of dances in Playford's first edition reveals that
this template was used for dances of almost all the set formations used in the work,
as follows:

longways for 6	20
longways for 8	12
longways for as many as will	19
rounds (all types)	8
two couples	5
square 8	1
TOTAL	65

There are 104 dances in the book, so those based on this model represent almost two-
thirds of the corpus. By the publication of the ninth edition of *The Dancing Master*
in 1695, however, all of these dances, with the exception of a handful of the longways for as many as will dances (essentially those employing duple and triple minor
progressions) were dropped. In other words, this basic model, so fecund a source for
new dances in the mid-seventeenth century, was considered old-fashioned a generation later. When John Playford's nephew, Henry Playford, took over publication of
the work, beginning with the eighth edition in 1690 he made it clear that he was
starting a major editing process of weeding out the 'old' dances of his uncle's days,
and compensating his fashion-conscious readership with twice as many newly composed ones (Dean-Smith 1951, xxv). This process was presumably a successful selling point because it continued with greater vigour in the ninth edition, where a cluster
of the new maggots appear for the first time as well as a number of dances composed
by the newly popular Mr Beveridge.

There is some evidence on which to build the speculation that the old style basic
sequence of figures from the early editions of *The Dancing Master* entered elite English

country dance from Italy.[6] Courtly Italian dancing masters at the turn of the seventeenth century, notably Fabritio Caroso (Caroso 1581, 1600) and Carlo Negri (Negri 1604), appear to have introduced the idea of regularizing the choreography of country dances by creating a limited and set sequence of figures alternated with a 'chorus' of variations. In fact Caroso may be credited with inventing a form of the lead up and back, siding, arming sequence that had become so entrenched by Playford's time.

Analysis of the proportion of the various set formations that used this model also suggests a possible line of evolution once the template was adopted in England. The basic pattern is distributed in the first edition as shown in table 8. What this table appears to show – provided that the sample is representative of mid-seventeenth-century dance styles – is that the basic model is especially suited to, even diagnostic of, the longways for 6 or 8 (80 per cent and 75 per cent respectively of the dances of this formation use the basic model), and rather less so for the other formations. So, regardless of the origins of the basic model, it had an affinity for a particular set formation which had a well defined currency – that is, the one from the middle decades of the seventeenth century. At this time, when dancing masters began composing rounds and longways for as many as will, they found the form rather less useful, particularly so with the latter. Once the idea of duple and triple minor sets in longways formations had caught hold, there was a greater tendency to build choreographies based on these minor sets with a strong focus on the progression, and to avoid figures that involved the whole set at once, either because they were unwieldy, or uninteresting, or because focus on the whole set interrupted the general sense of progression. The longways dances for 6 or 8, by contrast, tended to be nonprogressive, so that a focus on the whole set was perfectly appropriate. Thus the general evolution of country dances in England from nonprogressive small sets (for 6 or 8) to progressive large sets (for as many as will) ended the popularity of the basic template and it passed out of elite usage.

The model did persist in other quarters, however, and could still be seen in the morris dances of the South Midland counties around Oxfordshire and Gloucestershire at the turn of the twentieth century when Cecil Sharp and his coworkers began salvaging the remaining shards of a once vital rural tradition. These dances are outside the scope of this work, and their choreography has been considered at great length by scholars throughout this century, but a brief analysis of their form is germane to the topic at hand.[7]

Although there is not general agreement that nineteenth-century South Midland morris dances *always* followed one of a limited set of templates (see Forrest 1985a and Abbott and Forrest 1986 for details), there were unquestionably some villages where the model of fixed sequence of whole set figures alternating with a chorus was the norm. Take Bampton in Oxfordshire, for example, where a team was still active at the time that Sharp was collecting (and is still the locus of a thriving tradition). There, as in the entire South Midland region, the usual set formation was a longways for six

Table 8
Dances from the first edition of *The English Dancing Master* exhibiting the model figure sequence.

Formation	Total no.	No. showing basic pattern	Percentage of total
longways for 6	25	20	80%
longways for 8	16	12	75
longways for as many as will	37	19	51
rounds (all types)	14	8	57
two couples	8	5	62
square 8	3	1	33

men, rather than for mixed couples,[8] yet arranged like the couple sets in two columns of three, so that each man had a partner with whom to perform certain figures. The almost invariant sequence of figures at Bampton was:[9]

foot up (similar in track to lead up and back)
half hands (equivalent to sides all)
gipsy (following the track of arms all, but without the actual physical link)
rounds (dancers all move round in a ring and back)

Virtually all Bampton dances use this sequence, and they differ only in the tune employed and the chorus movements that alternate with the basic figures. So it is an easy step to assert that dances of this ilk owe their foundational figure structure to seventeenth-century country dance style. That said, though, it must be noted that there are a great many differences between the two practices: hand gestures, stepping patterns, dance accoutrements, costumes, and the like, mark the two traditions off from one another.

The point here is not that nineteenth-century morris is a relic or rudiment of seventeenth-century country dance but, rather, that certain formal principles of choreography passed from elite to rural dance in the seventeenth century. The arguments presented in chapter 9 support the general notion that rural morris picked up ideas from (all manner of) country dances in the sixteenth and seventeenth centuries. What is important here is that it is possible to argue that *particular* ideas made the transition, and it is possible to give rough dates when the transition might have taken place. That is, longways dances for 6 and 8 reached their peak of popularity in the mid-seventeenth century and began to wane by the 1680s. They may have hung on in country circles longer than at the court, but rural fashions in country dances eventually followed the lead of the elite in favouring the longways for as many as will. Thus, it is a fair assumption that rural morrises around the late seventeenth century were adopting the general style of the longways for 6 or 8 that was so popular in Playford's first edition.

It is noteworthy that this choreographic form should last so long in rural morris – over two hundred years – and yet be so short-lived in elite country dancing. The reason for this phenomenon undoubtedly lies in the differing needs of the two dances' contexts. Country dancing was primarily used as a vehicle for social visiting, flirting, and general contact *within* the dance. Thus, the duple minor longways progression was the ideal form to suit the function. Small, nonprogressive sets limited the social contact available to each dancer, so were less popular and soon disappeared from the assembly hall. For spectacular dances such as rural morris, however, rather different values were important.

Rural morrises did not need to employ large sets or progressive figures, because their primary function was not visiting within the set; rather, the dance set *as a whole* acted as the unit that toured around, visiting neighbouring villages. In a sense, it was the whole set that 'progressed' from place to place. Furthermore a small set was functional in that it limited the number of dancers who shared in the money collected on tour (which would be more or less fixed by the disposable funds available to the audience). Six dancers was a handy number to form a set also, in that they could perform a wide inventory of figures, including complex forms such as reels and heys – many more than could, say, four dancers who would have a greater share of the income than six, but who would be severely limited in their choreographic abilities (and, therefore, not so attractive to a potentially paying audience).

I have also argued elsewhere that the basic form of dancing a sequence of stock figures to the A music alternated with a variable chorus to the B music was a highly effective strategy for rural morris on a number of levels (Forrest 1988b). It was an easy system for dancers to learn and remember, particularly important for labourers with little time for practice before major events. Once they had a sense of the stock figures, which they may also have been familiar with from country dancing, learning new dances involved learning the new choruses only. By the same argument, *creating* new dances was relatively easy. This line of reasoning, therefore, also complements arguments in chapter 9 that with the adoption of a basic dance template from country dance, rural morris teams were able to expand their repertoires from one or two dances to as many as the leader cared to create using the basic form. Such creativity could take several forms, namely, keeping the stock of figures constant and changing choruses, or playing with the sequences of figures, or both.

The alternation of verse and chorus also created a complex aesthetic event with the affective focus shifting to different parts of the total performance. Once the audience members had a sense of the stock figures, their attention might wander during, say, the half hands figure in the third dance of the set, from the central dancers to the fool – who could take the opportunity of a quiet moment in the dance to make some fun – or to the musician, who might play variations on the main melody. During the variations in the chorus, though, attention would shift back to the central dance, fixing on energetic leaping or complex figures. All these factors taken together made the six person nonprogressive set alternating figures and chorus an ideal form for rural spectacular morris, and ensured its continuance long after it had fallen out of favour in other circles.

Stanes morris does not fit this basic pattern of mid-seventeenth-century country dance, and so cannot be said unambiguously to lie on any main or direct evolutionary line in the developmental history of morris. Yet it is not entirely unrelated either. It is technically a longways dance for as many as will, but it is not particularly suited to that form. If the set were to become too long the progression would take forever, and the chorus action of the first man meeting the last woman and leading her up to the top would require ungainly steps and hurried motions. Clearly it would work best with a small set – so the dance can be seen as a transitional form between the longways for 6 (or 8) and the longways for as many as will – a kind of 'longways for a many as will, as long as this is not too many.' As such, it might be an adaptation by a dancing master of a (rural) dance originally performed by a smaller set.

Stanes morris does not fit the pattern of the verse and chorus alternation of A and B musics, but neither is it utterly distinct. It does employ an alternation of whole set figures and chorus, but the sequence of figures happens all at once, instead of being interspersed with choruses. This format is necessitated by the longways progression. If the dance were performed by a three couple set it could follow the standard model, thus:

lead up a double and back
chorus (bring # 3 woman up)
lead sideways a double and back
chorus (bring # 2 woman up)
set and turn single
chorus (bring # 1 woman up)

And the progression would work. As soon as more than three couples enter the set, one must either insist on multiples of three to complete the progression using this formula or run all the figures together and alternate the total agglomeration with the chorus (as it is notated in Playford). This argument would explain why Playford had to create a third part to the music (to accommodate the running together of the three figures).

It is, therefore, possible to conceive of Stanes morris as an adaptation by dancing masters of a rural dance idea that was only partially successful, and so quickly dropped from the repertoire. Below the form as we now have it may be the rudiments of a kind of rural morris that was intermediate between the old and new styles that eventually crystallized into fixed forms by the end of the seventeenth century.

There is only one other notation for a country dance style morris in the seventeenth century, the 'Maids Morris,' which first appeared in the third supplement to the seventh edition of *The Dancing Master* (1689), thence in the eighth edition, and reprinted, with slight variations, in all but the sixteenth. The dance is a standard duple minor longways for as many as will:

Longways for as many as will
The two men take hands and fall back, then meet ther Partners and turn S. the two we. doing the like afterwards.
All four take hands and go half round and turn S. then half round and back again, then the double Figure, and the 1. cu. lead down the middle.   (Playford 1689, 1)

Here the basic form of the dances of the mid-seventeenth century has been completely replaced with figures that are confined to the duple minor set; that is, there are no whole set figures. And there is no clear alternation of verse and chorus between the A music and the B music; instead both parts of the melody accompany evolutions within the minor set.

Perhaps Maids Morris was a kind of replacement for the (now) old-fashioned country dance morrises of the Stanes morris type, or it may simply be a composed country dance in the new style to a popular air. Certainly there is nothing in the notation to suggest that the dance has any choreographic connection to rural morrises, and its general style is completely consonant with other contemporary elite country dances. If there is any link at all with other morrises, it may reside in the tune, whose title is not strictly appropriate to the dance notated, and is reminiscent of statements in earlier primary sources, such as, for example, Gilpin's ironic gibe at popish priests:

why he trippes sometime to the one ende of the Altar, and sometime to the other side of the Altar, as though he were daunsing the Maides Morice.   (Gilpin 1580, f. 218)

There may have been a specific dance, the Maid's Morris, which had a well-known melody, a version of which was appropriated by Playford for a new style choreography. Otherwise, the dance is entirely an index of the triumph of the elite, new style dances over the rural based old style dances in country dance halls.

THE EIGHTEENTH CENTURY

New country dances called 'morris' did not appear in dance manuals for a generation after the first publication of Maid's Morris, but then they enjoyed a brief vogue in the 1720s. The timing is of some interest in that it was in 1728 that John Gay first produced *The Beggar's Opera*. The enormous success of this opera may have been an index of popular feeling in England concerning what many considered the high-flown effeteness and unnaturalness of elite arts (attributed to the tastes of foreigners, chiefly French and Italian), and the wholesome and earthy flavour of the home-grown traditional product. Gay eschewed the 'artificial' forms of Italian opera, such as the recitative. And while, admittedly, some members of the London public lionized the Italianate forms, others were equally voluble against them (see, for example, Bond 1965, 1:119–20).

Gay's use of popular and traditional melodies for his airs proved immensely successful with all classes and so-called ballad operas became the rage in the ensuing decade. Nor was it simply Gay's use of popular music that appealed to the general public. His setting was the urban underworld and his characters were all drawn from the lower classes. He was thus drawing battle lines between high and low tastes in mass arts. A similar tussle was developing in the dance world between practitioners who wished to keep country dance close to its rustic roots and those who wished to 'elevate' it.

The call to improve and dignify dance in England derived from dancing masters strongly influenced by the French tradition. In this vein it is instructive to note that French technical dance manuals, which multiplied in the early eighteenth century, were speedily translated into English – an enterprise thoroughly endorsed by dancing masters throughout the British Isles. The translation by John Weaver of Raoul Feuillet's ground-breaking *Orchesography* (Feuillet 1706b), for example, was subscribed to by thirty-nine dancing masters whose names read like a who's who of early-eighteenth-century choreographers. This was quickly followed by John Essex's translation in 1710 of Feuillet's *Recueil de Contredances* (Feuillet 1706a) under the title *For the Further Improvement of Dancing, A Treatise of Chorography or ye Art of Dancing Country Dances after a New Character*, and in 1728 of Pierre Rameau's classic survey of correct dance style, *Le Maître à Danser*.

The French dancing masters' influence on country dance style was profound in that they called for the use of steps and gestures drawn directly from elite dance, and roundly condemned any motion smacking of rusticity. Thus in Essex's translation of *Recueil de Contredances* there is the seemingly democratic statement:

Tho my designe is not to mark any steps in Country Dances being willing to leave the Dancers ye liberty of composing the same as they please; there are some motions with ye Feet, Hands & Armes which I can't omitt incerting here.   (Feuillet 1706b, 7)

This seems to imply that the essence of country dance is its informal and improvisatory manner. But farther on, the advice turns rather more dogmatic:

Advice concerning ye steps that best sute with Country Dances.

The most ordinary steps in Country Dances (those excepted that are upon Minuet Airs) are steps of Gavot, drive sideways Bouree step and some small Iumps forward of either Foot in a hopping manner ...

In all figures that goe forwards, and backward, or backwards, and forwards, you must always make Gavott steps. In all figures that goe sideways you must always drive sideways.

(Feuillet 1706b, 15–16)

In other words, the liberty that the dancers had lay within narrowly defined limits. Nonetheless, Rameau lamented several years later:

All the perfection of these Country Dances, is by distorting of the body in turning about, and stamping with their feet as if they had wooden shoes on, and putting themselves in several ridiculous postures ...   (Rameau 1725 cited in Emmerson 1972, 287)

There was obviously a continuing interest on the part of some dancers in treating country dances as antidotes to formality. The extent of this ongoing tension between empirical practice and stated ideal cannot now be discovered because the extant works – consisting almost exclusively of dance manuals – lean, quite naturally, towards the latter end of the scale.

It may be, therefore, that the reappearance in the late 1720s of country dances styled 'morris' represents some aspect of the battle for territory between the two camps – elite and popular – concerning what country dancing was really all about. At the very least it might be suggested that the vogue peaking in 1727 had some of the qualities of *Beggar's Opera*, namely, that dancing masters consciously took well-known country morris tunes for their latest creations as a way of reidentifying with its roots what was becoming an increasingly mannered practice. One tune, 'the French Morris,' for example, spawned at least two attempts by dancing masters to super-impose elite choreography on a simple melody.[10]

The first effort, in 1716, by the renowned Mr Isaac may possibly provide some insight into the steps and gestures of early-eighteenth-century elite 'morris,' because Feuillet notation for the dance is extant. However, the dance must be treated with some care because it is not a country dance but rather a *danse à deux* in the style of those made fashionable first in the court of Louis XIV, and now generally known as the French noble style.[11] The dance form is very much in the mold of other single couple dances that Isaac composed to popular melodies in the first decades of the eighteenth century. It represents an effort of the French-influenced dancing masters of England to apply courtly modes of dancing to popular tunes – something of a compromise position between the need for formal dance rules and the desire to incorporate some flavour of the rustic.

An extract of the notation (page 2) is as follows:

The track passes to the right of the woman and heads off diagonally to the corner of the room
17: Bend on right, turn 1/4 left to face partner, step sideways with left, and rise.
   Step into second with right
   Turn 1/4 more to left to jeté backwards along the track
18: A turning pas de bourrée. Step backward with right
   Turn 1/4 left to step into second with left
   Turn another 1/4 left to step forward along the track with right foot
19: Step forward left, close into third behind with right
   Jeté forward onto left
20: Step forward with quick right and left.
   Jeté around with a 1/2 turn to the right to end in first facing back the way you came.[12]

The figured or floor pattern elements of the dance are minor in comparison with the complex and highly technical stepping patterns that require a precision of execution only long study could produce. As such, it is most likely that this piece is unique (or virtually so), and cannot fairly be used to generalize about the rural/urban morris nexus in the eighteenth century. However, it may have an identifiable place in the developmental history.

In August 1712 notices for plays at the Drury Lane Theatre appear somewhat as follows:

The Feign'd Innocence …
Also The Stage Coach
The last new Morrice Dance by Prince and others.   (Avery 1960, 2:280)

It was common for public stage plays from the Elizabethan period onwards to end with dances and other entertainments (prior to the development of ballet as a separate staged genre). The jigs that Kemp was renowned for are part of this overall tradition. Moreover, it seems that in the early eighteenth century specially choreographed dances styled 'morris' had a brief vogue on the stage in this epilogue role, and these may well have been formal dances in the style of Isaac's morris. If so, Isaac's morris is illustrative of a brief nexus point between courtly style, the public stage, and the rural tradition (chiefly represented by the tune).

The French Morris tune was popular enough to be used again in 1727 for a standard longways country dance (see Young c 1727, 195). There is nothing out of the ordinary about this dance to suggest that there is anything idiomatically 'morris' about the choreography; it appears to be a set of time-worn ideas fitted to a popular tune. However, it is worthy of note that in a short period (roughly 1728–30) numerous tunes and dances labelled as 'morris' appeared in print under the imprimatur of celebrated dancing masters such as Playford and Walsh. One other, the 'Scotch Morris' came out in the same volume as the 'French Morris,' and Walsh printed three – 'Carpenter's Morris,' 'The Running Morris,' and 'New Wild Morris' – in his compendium *The Third Book of the Most Celebrated Jiggs, Lancashire Hornpipes, Scotch and Highland Lilts, Northern Frisks, Morris's and Cheshire Rounds, with Hornpipes the Bagpipe Manner* (Walsh c 1730, ff.8v–9, 18v–19, 22v–3), with a fourth 'The Welsh Morris' in the third volume of his collection of country dances (Walsh 1735, 103). These tunes all purport to be of traditional or rustic origin (as Walsh's title suggests), although some appear slightly dressed up for urban fashion, and this fact supports the general hypothesis that in this period there was a deliberate and sustained effort to root elite practice in a traditional rural heritage no matter how tenuous was the link with the latter.

Otherwise there is little to single out as common in the tunes or dances labelled 'morris' of the late 1720s. Some of the tunes are in duple, some triple (simple and compound) metres, some of the dances are for duple minor, some for triple minor progressions, and all employ stock figures of the period, making the dances more akin to other country dances than a separable and identifiable genre. Certainly one might be inclined to argue that this attempted return to the traditional roots of country dancing presages well-known arguments concerning the beauty of simplicity over the complex and high-flown classical forms of the elite (see, for example, Hogarth 1753). This was Gay's point and it seems to have pervaded many of the performing arts of the period. Thus, the pendulum swung back yet again towards the lauding of traditional practices as fertile and authentic – and thereby grist for the elite practitioners' ruthlessly exploitive mills.

But, as always, the flow of ideas could move in both directions. Tunes adapted or composed for elite country dancing throughout the seventeenth and eighteenth centuries became the stock in trade of amateur and professional musicians employed by all classes for country dancing. These same musicians were hired by rural morris teams who were often forced, or chose, to take these musicians' country dance melody repertoires as the basis for creating their dances – certain of these tunes, such as Constant Billy, Lumps of Plum Pudding, Bobby and Joan, becoming wide-spread classics (see Forrest 1985b and Chandler 1993a, 173–88 for details).

Thus, the country dances of the seventeenth and eighteenth centuries, while seeming at first to be but a small side branch in the general evolution of morris dancing prove to be rather more significant, acting as yet another node in a complex interchange of ideas between eras, regions, and classes.

11

Private Premises

It is patent from the seriation curves that with the termination of financial support for morris dances by the church, patronage from private individuals (and, sporadically, from a few private groups) came into its own and, no doubt, prevented the complete demise of dancing in the countryside. This chapter concerns the contributions made to the upkeep of morris dancing by the private sector, focusing especially on the role of private individuals. As always, the prime concern is *venue* rather than strictly patronage per se, but in the case of performances at the country estates of rich individuals, venue and patronage are virtually synonymous. Before dealing with the more extensive data on private individuals, and because of their chronological priority in the seriations, however, it is convenient to deal with the venue of special groups' premises first.

To some extent the part played by special groups has been covered in previous chapters and need not be repeated. The trade guilds, for example, occasionally hired dancers to perform in their guildhalls. To a great extent the ability of special groups to hire local morris sides to perform on special occasions was circumscribed by the social and political climate, so their involvement mirrors trends already rehearsed. The legal battles that the tailors of Salisbury fought concerning dancing in the streets and in their hall, may be recalled. A brief overview of the use of special groups' premises for morris dancing via a case study – morris dancing at Oxford colleges – should therefore serve to delineate this venue.

Morris dancing at Oxford colleges occurred in a variety of contexts, but it seems to have been most popular in early Stuart times as a direct response to the issuance of the *Book of Sports* under James VI and I. Barten Holyday's play *TEXNOΓAMIA*, with its simulacrum of a rustic morris, for example, was written expressly to be performed before King James at Christchurch, and at least one other morris was danced before him in 1605 in a play context as indicated by the following record from the university archives:

x 6. Suites for morrice dancers all lyke with garters of bels ...
For the Playes at ye Kinges comminge. 1605.   (Boas 1909, 252)

But there were also dancers performing at colleges to mark general festivities. For example, the Christmas prince at St John's College (a kind of prince of revels or Lord of Misrule) was honoured by a local morris in 1607:

St Steevens day was past over in silence, and so had St. John's day also; butt that some of the Princes honest neighbours of St. Giles's presented him with a maske or morris, wch though it were but rudely performed, yet itt being so freely & lovingly profered, it could not but bee as lovingly received.   (Boas 1922, 55)

Anthony Wood, antiquarian, records that such activities were stopped by Puritan factions within the university:

They [Presbyterians and Independents] were great enimies to May-games and would never suffer anything therof to be done in the Universitie or city, as May-poles, morrices, Whitson ales; nay, scarce wakes.   (Clark 1891, 317)

Upon the Restoration they were renewed with their former vigour (for a time at least):

It now remaines that I should say something (1) of what was done by the persons restor'd to make themselves and their doctrine acceptable to the people, and how by some dispised, and of their learning; (2) of what was done by some of the old scholars that had weathered out the times from 1648 to this year ...

Their suffering may-games, morrises, revells, etc., on purpose to vex the precise party, stage-playes as well by Academicians as common actors, drunkenness, swearing, wenching, etc.
                              (Clark 1891, 357–60)

Despite Wood's assertion, no more is recorded in the public record of morris at the university, and it is to be presumed that such sponsorship disappeared once the initial glow of success of the royalist party evanesced. This is typical of sponsorship by special groups – always swayed by the political climate, and never more than a minor patron (not in any obvious way responsible for the success or failure of local teams). Sponsorship by private individuals was quite a different matter, however, given that they were less beholden to public policy, and could thwart general social and political trends if they were so inclined, mainly because in the England of the seventeenth and eighteenth century a great deal of power was wielded in local regions by large landholders regardless of national political conditions.

The indirect record suggests that dancing by rural morris teams at the houses of the country gentry was well established in late Tudor times. The visit of the dancers to a country house is, for example, a common device in Elizabethan and Jacobean plays for introducing an interlude of music and dance (see chapter 8), and there is nothing obviously forced or contrived about the invention. Direct evidence is rather more sparse, and takes the form almost entirely of entries in domestic account books for payments to groups of dancers. Because of this fact, virtually the entire record of dancers' performances at country estates may be tabulated according to a few variables – date, place of performance, provenance of the dance team, and size of remuneration by the landowner (see table 9).

Certain trends are immediately manifest from such a tabulation, although the nature of the data themselves suggests some caution in interpretation. Domestic account books are not equivalent to public documents, such as borough and church-wardens' accounts, in that there was less of a legal or moral burden on landholders to preserve them for posterity. What has survived of such accounts, therefore, is largely a matter of serendipity, and their completeness (or lack of it) is determined entirely by the thoroughness of the individuals doing the record keeping. Thus, for example, the accounts kept by Joshua Burton on behalf of Sir Thomas Cartwright of Aynho House between the years 1691 and 1735 almost always indicate the proven-ance of the morris dancers remunerated, whereas most other domestic accounts simply record a sum paid to 'morris dancers' with no indication of their home village. Furthermore, it is unclear how many such account books exist in private hands or obscure locations, that have yet to be culled for data on morris teams. On the posi-tive side, however, it may also be noted that continued investigation of such accounts as they become available, seems to reinforce the trends discussed below.[1]

As noted in chapter 9, there is a definite shift in the centre of gravity of locations of performance from East Anglia (in the pre–Civil War era), to the south Midlands (from the Restoration into the eighteenth century). This may reflect a significant rise in the prosperity and importance of the south Midlands region, not only because of the accelerated pace of enclosure and agricultural improvement there during the Restoration and beyond, but also because of a dramatic increase in the building of country seats there for members of parliament because they wished to be within reasonable commuting distance of London (and to whom power and influence con-tinued to accrue throughout the late seventeenth and eighteenth centuries as the monarchy increasingly lost it; see Barley 1985, 600–19).

Many of the most magnificent estates and parks in all of England, such as Blenheim Palace, were created in this region in the first decades of the eighteenth century, bringing money and patronage with them. Morris dancing was, as usual, symbolic of the sports of local people, so that the general principles of noblesse oblige for the rural gentry entailed supporting local teams as a way of keeping everyone happy.

Table 9
Payment for morris by private individuals grouped by 30-year periods.
(County boundaries as of 1750)

Year	Dance venue	Dancers' provenance	Payment
1562	Grimsthorpe, LINCS	Little Bytham, LINCS	2s
1562	London		3s 4d
1576	Kirtling, CAMBS		2s
1576	Kirtling, CAMBS		1s 4d
1578	Kirtling, CAMBS		2s 2d
1583	Hengrave Hall, SUFFOLK		2s
1603	Felbrigg, NORFOLK		3s 4d
1606	Hardwick Hall, DERBYS		2s 6d
1620	Warwick, WARW		[5s][a]
1624	Arbury, WARW	Nuneaton, WARW	2s
1627	Hengrave Hall, SUFFOLK		1s
1629	Arbury, WARW	Nuneaton, WARW	1s 6d
1633	East Harling, NORFOLK		2s
1633	East Harling, NORFOLK		1s 6d
1635	Stiffkey, NORFOLK		1s
1636	Hatfield Broad Oak, ESSX		[5s]
1655	(Little Wolford, WARW)		1s
1658	Moor Hall, Coughton WARW		6s
1660	London		6d
1664	Belvoir, LEICS		2s 6d
1674	Frampton-on-Severn, GLOS		1s
1680	Stowe, BUCKS		£1
1680	BUCKS		£1
1680	Little Wolford, WARW	Shipston-on-Stour, WARW	2s 6d
1681	BUCKS		£1
1696	Aynho House, NTHNTS		2s 6d
1701	Weston Underwood, BUCKS		2s 6d
1701	Weston Underwood, BUCKS		2s 8d
1704	Aynho House, NTHNTS		15s
1705	Weston Underwood, BUCKS	Stony Stratford, BUCKS	1s
1711	Sherborne, GLOS		1s
1711	Sherborne, GLOS		1s
1713	Aynho House, NTHNTS		[£1 8s]
1714	Wells, SOMERSET		1s
1721	Churchill, OXON		6s

Table 9 (concluded)

Year	Dance venue	Dancers' provenance	Payment
1722	Aylesbury?, BUCKS		5s
1723	Aynho House, NTHNTS	Aynho, NTHNTS	5s
1723	Aynho House, NTHNTS	King's Sutton, NTHNTS	5s
1723	Aynho House, NTHNTS	Chesterton, OXON	5s
1724	Revesby, LINCS		6d
1724	Revesby, LINCS		1s
1725	Aynho House, NTHNTS	Brackley, NTHNTS	10s 6d
1725	Aynho House, NTHNTS	Syresham, NTHNTS	10s 6d
1726	Aynho House, NTHNTS	Hethe, OXON	5s
1727	Aynho House, NTHNTS	Chesterton, OXON	5s
1731	Aynho House, NTHNTS	Croughton, OXON	2s 6d
1731	Aynho House, NTHNTS	Croughton, OXON	2s 6d
1731	Aynho House, NTHNTS	Aynho, NTHNTS	2s 6d
1731	Aynho House, NTHNTS	Brackley, NTHNTS	10s 6d
1731	Aynho House, NTHNTS	Middleton Cheney, OXON	2s 6d
1731	Sherborne, GLOS	Northleach, GLOS	5s
1732	Aynho House, NTHNTS	Somerton, OXON	2s 6d
1732	Kirtlington, OXON	Kirtlington, OXON	5s
1735	Shalstone Manor, BUCKS		1s 6d
1735	Shalstone Manor, BUCKS		1s
1735	Shalstone Manor, BUCKS	Turweston, BUCKS	2s 6d
1737	Stowe House?, BUCKS		[£6 15s]
1739	Stowe House?, BUCKS		7s 6d
1739	Stowe House, BUCKS		5s
1739	Stowe House, BUCKS		10s 6d
1742	Shalstone Manor, BUCKS	Shalstone, BUCKS	3s 6d
1742	Shalstone Manor, BUCKS	Shalstone, BUCKS	2s 6d
1742	London?	Brill, BUCKS	5s
1742	Stowe House?, BUCKS		10s 6d
1743	DERBYSHIRE?		£1 11s 6d
1744	Shalstone Manor, BUCKS	Buckingham, BUCKS	3s
1746	Stowe House?, BUCKS		8s
1748	Stowe House?, BUCKS		£1 0s 6d
1748	Shalstone Manor, BUCKS	Shalstone, BUCKS	—
1750	Stowe House?, BUCKS	Buckingham, BUCKS	10s 6d

[a] Parcelled payments are indicated in square brackets.
Note: The dancers from Little Wolford (1655) were paid not to perform, and the payments made at Aynho House in 1704 and Stowe House in 1748 were each to be shared among three teams

Thus, at the laying of the foundation stone for Blenheim Palace in 1705 there was a general merrymaking for the locals, involving a variety of morrises:

There were several sorts of musick, three morris dances; one of young fellowes, one of maidens, and one of old beldames. There were about a hundred buckets, bowls, and pans, filled with wine, punch, cakes, and ale.   (Green 1951, 50)

Elections of the MPs to parliament were also opportunities for lavish expenditures in which morris dancers might share generously. The duke of Marlborough's accounts from Blenheim in 1727, for example, contain the following:

Paid at the Election at Woodstock Aug: 23, 1727

...

moris dancers 01–1–0   (BL Add. MS 61468 Blenheim papers vol. 368 f.183)

For the elections of 1741, when Richard Grenville was elected member for Bucking-hamshire and his brother, George was elected to the family's pocket borough, Buck-ingham (temporarily vacated by Richard), they sponsored no less than eleven morris events covering a wide sector of north Buckinghamshire at a total cost of £5 16s 6d (Huntington Library MS STG Elections box 1 folder 4). It is also worth noting that Richard Grenville eventually inherited Stowe House through his mother, Hester Temple, and both were consistent sponsors of morris there, as indicated in table 9 (as were later generations beyond our period). Furthermore, Richard's grandfather (Hester's father), Sir Richard Temple, Bart, had sponsored dances at Stowe, and was known to be sympathetic to and supportive of rural customs in general. Thus in the period around 1680, when many villagers in the region were attempting to regain ground lost during the Interregnum, Sir Richard's tenants – 'ye Inhabitants of Stowe' – sent him a petition:

That whereas the youth of ye parish of Stowe, having now ingaged themselves in reveiving ye antient Custome, of kepping a whisson Ale this year for ye divertissement of themselves, and this side of the Countrey, and are in good hope to performe it to their credit as well as some other their neighbour Townes have done it, with ye vsuall countenance and assistance of the Gentlemen here about: some whereof have alredy granted them May Poles, with other favours.
                (Huntington Library Stowe MSS STTM, box 3, folder 26 [1] in Chandler 1993a, 64)

This makes it clear that a degree of patronage for local customs by the gentry was expected, and primary evidence suggests that the revival of Whitsun Ales in the late seventeenth and early eighteenth centuries was due almost entirely to such financial contributions. Local family accounts from Churchill, Oxfordshire, for example, con-tain the following records for payments to musicians, dancers, performers and so forth in connection with a Whitsun ale in 1721:

The morris x 0–6–0

[five maids x 0–12–6]
The Lady x 0–2–6
The Lord and Lady gave to ye foole x 0–1–6
...
The Lord's & Lady's earnest 1–1–6
paid to ye Squier 1–00–00
the foole 1–0–0
the ffidler 0–10–6 (Oxford University Museum Smith MS 'The Whitsun Ale Accounts for 1721')

Thus, what had once been a money-making enterprise for the church became a secular vehicle for largesse from the gentry and, in turn, became an important venue for morris dancing, although mostly later in the eighteenth century, beyond the period covered by this work (see Chandler 1993a, 57–76, for details).

One of the curiosities of the tabulation of remuneration of morris dancers by the gentry is that there are no clear trends nor any consistency across the period. It is true that until the late seventeenth century rewards tended to be modest (that is, in the range of a few shillings), but from then on a team might receive anything from a shilling to half a guinea, with no obvious rationale for the size of the payments and no sense of them trending with inflation or other general economic factors.

There do seem to be certain local consistencies, however. The Temples and Grenvilles of Stowe, for example, seem to have been consistently generous, giving half a guinea or more as a usual contribution to visiting teams, whereas the Cartwrights of Aynho (no doubt in line with their more modest circumstances) tended to give in the range of half a crown to a crown. In fact, the latter almost seem to have budgeted their contributions to various teams: each year their total outlay on morris is around a guinea – so the more teams visiting, the smaller the payment to each. Thus in 1731 of the five teams visiting most received half a crown, whereas in 1723 the three visiting teams each received a crown, and in 1725 when only two showed up they received half a guinea apiece. Market forces were clearly at work here, operating to keep the number of local teams within the bounds set by available cash from the gentry, but also causing, or contributing to, intermittent peaks and valleys in dance activity.

Apart from the highest payments, which may represent special circumstances, the bulk of the patronage appears to be in the range of beer money. Table 10 gives an idea of beer and ale prices from the Restoration onwards, when support by the gentry gradually increased. These data are extracted from records kept by the lord steward's department and provide year-by-year sequences that cover our entire period. They should not be taken as absolute figures, however, because they represent fractions of bulk commodities. Nonetheless, they do suggest the relative range of costs and are some indication of retail values. The two series represented are for relatively weak barrelled beer sold by the tun (240 gallons), and a rather stronger bottled ale sold by the dozen quarts.

Table 10
Prices of beer and ale per decade 1660–1750

Year	Small Beer (per 10 gals)		Lambeth Ale (per doz qts)	
1660	2s	6d	4s	
1670	2s	3½d	3s	6d
1680	2s	7¼d	3s	3d
1690	2s	9d	3s	
1700	2s	8½d	4s	
1710	3s	2d	4s	3d
1720	3s	4d	5s	
1730	3s	4d	5s	
1740	3s	4d	5s	
1750	3s	4d	5s	

Source: Beveridge 1939, 428–9, 434–5

The general stability of prices indicated here, particularly in the eighteenth century when there was a long-term depression in agricultural prices, explains in part why contributions to the treasury of morris teams should be consistent at the local level. Assuming the entire morris entourage was somewhere between eight and ten men (i.e., roughly six dancers, a fool, a musician, plus other supernumeraries), a contribution of half a crown to a crown would go a long way to providing beer of reasonable strength for a day. But the team would not be able to rely on such contributions alone. The visit to the 'big house' would be the buttress of the treasury, but the additional farthings and halfpennies from humbler onlookers would also be vital to the financial success of the annual outing. So the rural tour described in chapter 9 would still be standard fare for most rural teams; there would not be sufficient financial incentive in most locales (given the cost of necessary equipment, and the need for some practice time away from general labour) to raise a team without the reasonable expectation of some financial rewards from the general community. Yet, on the other hand, without the support of the gentry few, if any, teams in the first half of the eighteenth century could have survived either. Support from *all* classes was essential and should not be overshadowed entirely in analysis by the (obviously important) contributions of the rich, who happen to have kept good financial records, and whose largesse can otherwise take on monolithic significance.

It cannot be denied either that there was a significant increase in the absolute number of morris dance events and of teams in the first half of the eighteenth century. It is difficult not to correlate these facts with the seemingly easy, and occasionally generous, contributions made by the gentry for dancing at their country houses. In fact,

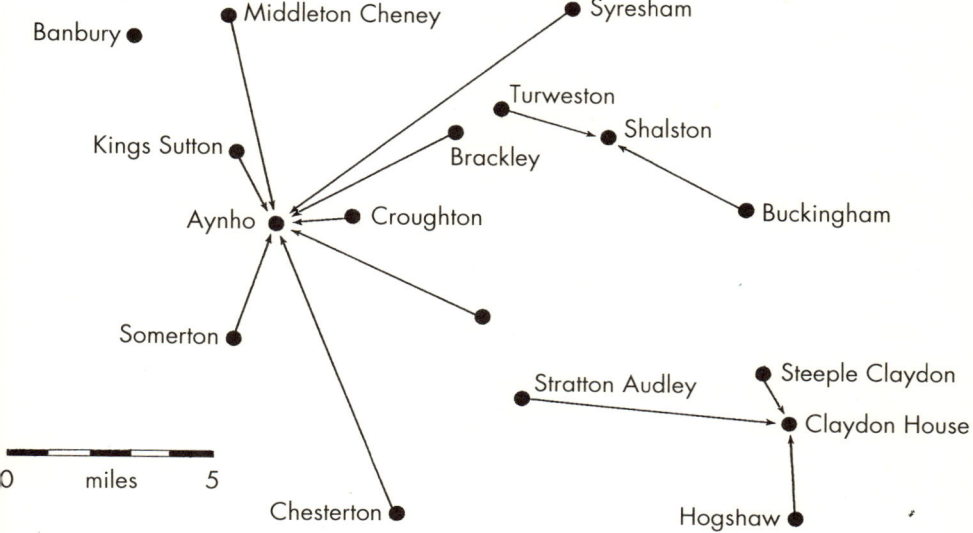

Figure 46: Trips to country houses in the border region of Oxfordshire, Buckinghamshire, and Northamptonshire

mapping the home villages of dance teams, the locations of country houses favourably disposed to dancing, and the tours of teams to these houses in the region of Oxford-shire, Northamptonshire, and Buckinghamshire where morris teams were found in the first half of the eighteenth century (figure 46), shows that country estates acted as centres of gravity, attracting teams to them from all points of the compass. The great-est density of teams was, therefore, in the vicinity of such estates, and outside the ambit of such ready sources of income they are much more sparsely represented.

Unfortunately domestic account books are erratic as primary sources for data on morris dancing beyond the size of payments made, but the records from Aynho House are slightly better than others. Therefore, it is useful to take this example for a more extended case study which may reasonably be generalized to similar estates in the vicinity. In order to make the case study fully intelligible, it is necessary to lay out a certain amount of background information on the village's historical geography.[2]

The village of Aynho lies to the east of the Cherwell on the margin of gentle uplands, about 6 miles southeast of Banbury on the Oxfordshire–Northamptonshire border. Until parliamentary enclosure in 1792 all the dwellings of the village sat in the middle of the farmland of the manor, a slightly butterfly-shaped oblong stretch-ing east from the Cherwell, approximately 2¼ miles by 1 to 1½ miles. Soils to the west and south of the village are in the Wickham series – fine loam over clay that may be seasonally waterlogged, and therefore more suitable for meadow and pasture than for arable – leading to heavy clay alluvium in the river valley. Soils to the east and north of the village, into the uplands, are in the Aberford and Banbury series – fine to coarse loams over limestone or ironstone – well drained and suitable for arable. The centre of the village forms a crossroads on major thoroughfares leading to markets in Buckingham, Bicester, Banbury, and Chipping Norton, thence farther afield to Oxford and London.

Aynho is mentioned in the Domesday Book, and the manor had a succession of noble owners through the Middle Ages into Tudor times, but in 1540 Rowland Shakerley, a London mercer, took over the estate to settle up debts incurred by its owner William FitzAlan (the eleventh earl of Arundel), and in 1552 bought it outright. Thence it passed from aristocratic (absentee) hands into those of the rising mercantile middle class, who took a greater interest in local affairs and in governing the village for efficient profit.

Shakerley's main impact on the village at the outset of his tenure seems to have been the strict enforcement of all his seigneurial rights, many of which had lapsed under the Arundel stewards. But the chiefest commotion he caused was to undertake an enclosure of a portion of the land in the manor in 1561. The details are sketchy but it seems that he consolidated much of his demesne lands (until then scattered in strips in the open fields) into a single parcel to the south of the village, making it much more efficient to work.

We might not have any historical record of this enclosure were it not for the formal protests of the villagers led by Nicholas Hanslope. The fact of this grievance brings to light an important point about the socio-economic structure of Tudor Aynho, namely, that it was not a one-lord closed village: far from it. Tax rolls of 1544–5 show four substantial freeholders, as well as copyholders and leaseholders with significant property (Cooper 1984, 293). It is true that the freeholders held minor amounts of land in comparison with the lord of the manor, so that protests against enclosure were liable to fail, but they were, to some extent, independent yeomen and able to exert a degree of self-directed and autonomous action. Over the next half-century this class increased significantly because of the financial difficulties encountered by successive owners of the manor.

The complex economic problems engendered by the fact that Rowland Shakerley divided his estate unequally among six female heirs need not be detailed here. His son-in-law, Thomas Marmion, tried to rectify the problems of divided ownership by buying out his sisters-in-law, and succeeded in consolidating two-thirds of the estate. But he left his son, Shakerley Marmion, £1500 in debt on his death, who, himself, continued the family's tradition of personal impoverishment to the point where in 1611 his best course of action for raising funds was to sell freeholds to eleven copyholders. The sale of lands dramatically increased the number of independent yeomen in the village. All of these new freeholders had by virtue of their land ownership, rights to a voice in the political economy of the manor, even though they owed certain nominal allegiances to the squire.

Despite such desperate expedients for raising cash, Marmion was forced to sell his part of the manor in 1615 to Richard Cartwright, a rich London lawyer, who next year bought out the remaining heirs, to become sole owner and to achieve what the Shakerley/Marmions could not, the establishment of a permanent county seat for his descendants for centuries to come. Like Rowland Shakerley before him, one of Cartwright's first acts was to attempt the enclosure of part of the manor – this time to provide separate pasture for his livestock to insulate them from the diseases of the common herd. But the sale of so much freehold by Marmion meant that he had a tougher battle to get his enclosure accomplished than his predecessor, although he did eventually succeed at great expense of time and money.

Some idea of the relative power in agricultural affairs of the squire versus the freeholders can be gleaned by looking at the distribution of land ownership at the time of Cartwright's arrival. Then, approximately 2080 acres were being farmed, of which 807 lay in the lord's demesne, 803 were held by freeholders or tenants of landowners other than the squire, and the rest (470 acres) was rented by copyholders and tenants of the squire. Cartwright definitely held the balance of power, but it was far from absolute, and a consolidated action by the yeomen could cause him considerable trouble.

The result of the enclosure, effected in 1619, was roughly to partition the manor into two halves – west and east. The common arable land west of the village was divided into closes (small enclosed pastures) for the freeholders, the common pasture in the west mostly became enclosed pasture for the squire's livestock, and the rest remained common pasture and meadow. All common arable now lay in open fields to the east of the village (see figure 47). This disposition of the land of the manor remained in effect until the full parliamentary enclosures undertaken in 1792.

Thus, from the turn of the eighteenth century to the end of the period covered by this work, when morris dancing was a regular event in Aynho, one cannot strictly call the village unenclosed, nor enclosed either (and Aynho was by no means unique in this arrangement). By the standards of a full-blown parliamentary enclosure, the manor was definitely unenclosed in that there were still common arable fields farmed in strips, and some common pasture. But something like a third of all acreage in the manor was under permanent enclosure in the hands of the squire or freeholders. Such facts indicate that it is necessary to look deeper into the farming practices of the community than a simple binary assertion (enclosed vs unenclosed) can achieve to understand correlations between the rise of morris dancing in the village and social circumstances therein. One cannot speak monolithically of 'enclosure' as if complete enclosure is all that matters historically, and is the only significant event –

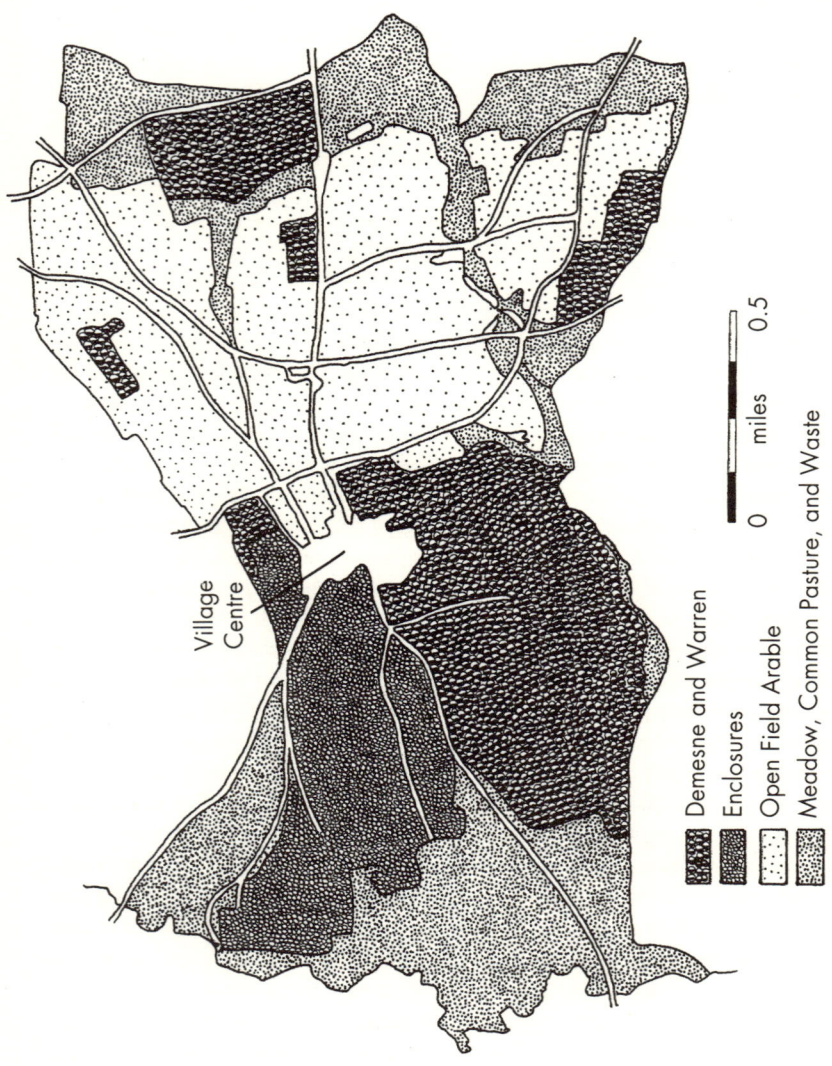

Village
Centre

■ Demesne and Warren
■ Enclosures
· Open Field Arable
▒ Meadow, Common Pasture, and Waste

0   miles   0.5

Figure 47: Map of Aynho following enclosure (after Cooper 1984, 100)

in all or nothing terms – when attempting to correlate farming practices with other social factors.

Of great importance in Aynho are the slow changes in the balance of power that took place in the village over the course of the seventeenth century. They were less dramatic than national political events (which had their impact), but potentially more far-reaching in their long-term consequences. Richard Cartwright died in 1637 leaving his son John the legacy of a pitched battle with the king's agents over the payment of ship money, and which ultimately led him to the side of parliament during the Civil War.

In 1676 John Cartwright died and as there were no living sons, his grandson Thomas inherited the estate at age five, with his mother, Ursula (John's daughter-in-law), acting on his behalf until his majority. It was Thomas Cartwright who sponsored morris dancing at the manor house from 1696 until the 1730s. The property he inherited was, in many respects, similarly ordered as when his great grandfather Richard had run it, and Thomas had no great schemes for further enclosure or radical improvement. But the day of the independent yeoman farmer was waning, so that the new squire stepped into a situation where, without any great force of will on his part, his holdings, power, and influence rose in the village over time (and in the larger world as well). Indeed it is ironic that his forebears – Richard and John – were forceful personalities who spent much energy and money alternately battling and cozening the freeholders in order to have their way, and Thomas rose to almost absolute power in the village with scarcely a raised voice. Many factors, global and local, contributed to this shift in the balance of power.

One quirk of fate was that an unusually high proportion of the yeomen farmers died leaving only daughters as heirs (who customarily split the patrimony, whereas a single male heir would have inherited the entire parcel). Many of these 'heiresses' married outside the village, selling their shares in land to the squire, or else they let their portions (often of little use by themselves for having been subdivided from already relatively small holdings) to village farmers until such time as they needed cash when, again, they mortgaged or sold the land to the squire.

In other cases smallholders sold out because farming was becoming unprofitable on the small scale. Prices at the turn of the eighteenth century were stable or falling because of a severe agricultural depression (as can be seen reflected in beer prices in table 10), but costs were rising. There was a land tax of 4s in the pound, and a spiralling poor rate. The latter was to run almost out of control for compounding reasons. Most significant was the dramatic rise in population in the seventeenth and eighteenth centuries. In 1620 there were fifty-six households in Aynho and a total population of around 275, but in 1740 there were 124 households and a population of 567; in about a century the population had doubled yet there was not double the work to accommodate the increase (see Cooper 1984, 119). Therefore, increasing numbers fell on poor relief, creating a greater tax burden on the freeholders who eventually had to sell out when their costs exceeded their profits (their own downward social mobility increasing the pressure on poor relief).

A few simple statistics indicate the trends that operated throughout the seventeenth century and into the eighteenth. In 1618, thirty-two of the total of fifty-six households in the village were engaged in some kind of farming, with the mean farm size being around 45 acres. Of these farmers thirteen were freeholders and their lands totalled around 700 acres (see Cooper 1984, 296–7).[3] By 1740/44 only twenty of 124 households were engaged in farming an acre or more, and the mean farm size was about seventy acres. Only five freeholders remained, and their lands totalled little more than 160 acres (see Cooper 1984, 299).[4] These statistics are broken down in figure 48. From these figures, the shifts towards smaller numbers of larger farms and from freehold to tenancy are clear, although it is of interest to note that the absolute numbers of the smallest holdings – representing sidelines for craftsmen and tradesmen primarily – stayed the same. The social consequences of these shifts are of major importance to village life at all levels.

Essentially the transition of agriculture from a yeoman to a rentier economy helped solidify and rigidify the village class structure. Although the wealthiest freeholders of the seventeenth century had holdings well short of those held by the lord of the manor, and although they were in certain legal senses subordinate to him, it is clear from the many wrangles between yeoman and squire over commons rights, enclosure, and the like, noted in manor court records, that the former considered themselves 'equal' enough to the squire to be able to stand up to him, and certainly to make life difficult for him, having the strength of their freeholds to buttress them. Tenants were in no such position. Even in Richard Cartwright's day, when battle lines were drawn over his proposed enclosures, all his tenants sided with him in public (whatever their private views). So as tenancies increased and freeholds decreased in the village the squire's status and power rose in the direction of the absolute.

The farmer's change in status was not all downward, however. Concomitant with the move to a rentier economy was a decrease in the number of farms, and a dramatic increase in their average size, meaning that those who were able to stay in business became relatively well off financially (often better than freeholders of old). Those smallholders who sold their land or were dispossessed of their copyholds either moved the family business into trades and crafts, or (more commonly) became wage labourers under the employ of the tenant farmers. Such labourers, once semi-autonomous in that they worked land that they had some ancestral claim to (even if only by copyhold), were now totally subservient to a wage-paying master. Although it would be overstating the case to suggest that at the beginning of the seventeenth century the field system was democratic, land holdings were more evenly spread across the households in the village than in the eighteenth century, and even

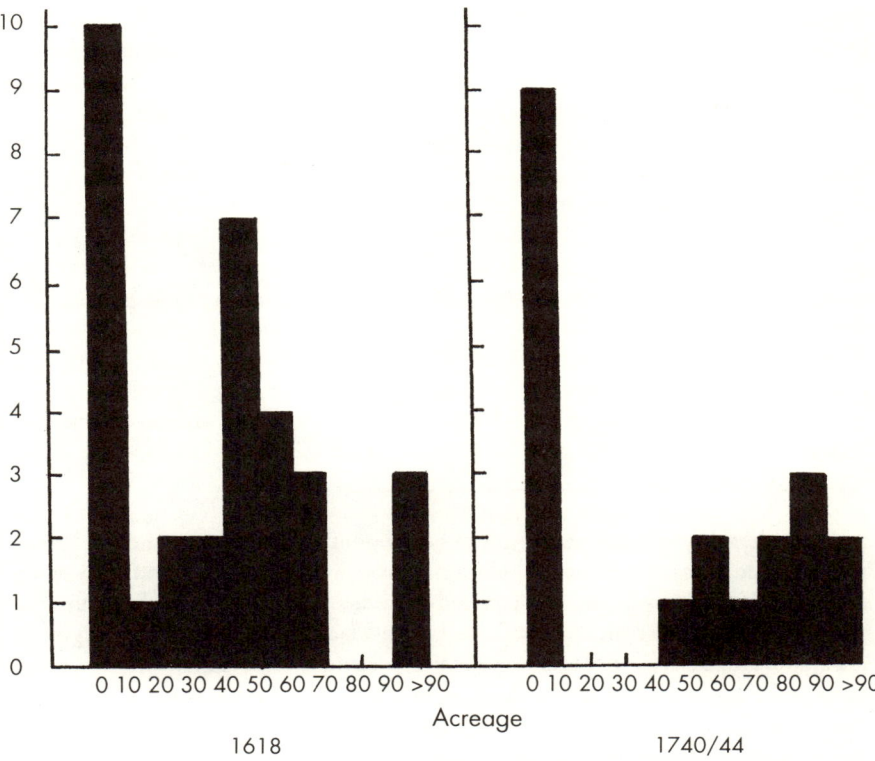

Figure 48: Graph of farm sizes in Aynho in 1618 and 1740/44

the smallest farmer had the right to voice his concerns in the manor court. By the mid-eighteenth century the farm structure was almost entirely vertically hierarchical – squire over the tenants over the labourers.

The old farming system had also been somewhat fluid; tenants could buy free-holds under certain conditions (thereby raising their status), and smallholders could incrementally increase their acreage over time by hard work, cunning, and oppor-tunism. Thus there was always the possibility (albeit slender) for upward mobility. But a rentier economy was much more rigid; if one tenant failed another could be found (usually from outside the village), so that the status quo was preserved regard-less of the individuals occupying the tenancies. It was unlikely in the extreme that a labourer would ever be able to accrue sufficient capital to become a tenant, and because all the farms had already been consolidated into large units, he could not acquire property piecemeal or incrementally to raise his status by degrees. Tenancy was an all-or-nothing endeavour. Note in table 11 that in the 1740/44 period there

Table 11
Farm sizes in 1618 and 1740/44.

| Acreage | All holdings | | Freeholds | |
	1618	1740/44	1618	1740
< 10	10	9	0	3
11–20	1	0	1	0
21–30	2	0	1	0
31–40	2	0	2	0
41–50	7	1	2	0
51–60	4	2	3	1
61–70	3	1	1	0
71–80	0	2	0	0
81–90	0	3	0	1
> 90	3	2	3	0
Totals	32	20	13	5

is a considerable gap between the minor holdings of a few acres and the smallest of the full-scale farms. There are no holdings at that time between ten and forty acres, for example, whereas in the 1618 period holdings are more evenly distributed at the lower end of the scale. As a corollary to this fact there was a certain degree of geographic mobility at the tenant level; tenants came to farms in Aynho from other parts of the country where before vacancies had been filled from within. In that sense, there was also an additional burden of alienation of labour added to the rigidity of the hierarchy – wage labourers were as likely as not to work for a 'stranger' tenant whose motive in farming was profit, not an old established association with the land and its people.

As indicated, the older families remained in the village although now in a variety of subordinate positions. Some went into service in the manor house, which also had its own rigid hierarchy, or performed outservice functions for the manor for a contracted fee. Others worked in trades and crafts – smithing, masonry, milling, baking – partly dependent on the manor and partly on the farmers and villagers for a livelihood. To round out the village hierarchy, therefore, we may place the various artisans in a class immediately below the richest of the tenant farmers, and on a par with the smaller.

It should also be noted that the overall social changes described above can also be seen as a general move to a cash economy. The old style smallholder who grew wheat and barley to be ground or malted for his bread and beer, and kept a cow or two for milk and meat, now earned a wage with which to purchase these commodities from a third party. The rector had most of his tithes commuted from in kind contributions to cash equivalents, saving himself the innumerable headaches of collecting his fair share of the farm produce but, in turn, distancing him from the daily affairs of the community.

The alienation of the worker locked into a rigid class structure in a cash economy, whose worth is measured in pounds, shillings and pence, has been examined at length by political economists and need not be repeated here. But there are a few specific points about the conversion to farming for profit in Aynho that are of relevance to the larger topic. In particular, the intangible worth of the knowledge of old heads who had lived in the village all their lives, and whose families had lived there before them for centuries lost its currency, and with it its possessors lost their value to the village hierarchy. Such a loss happened over time and on many planes.

On a general level, the oldest farmers had the longest experience (and the collected experience of their forebears) dealing with the particular arable conditions that obtained in Aynho, so that they would know well when was the best time, say, to plough the southern fields after hard frosts and a sodden spring. But these were times of great agricultural changes across the country and these tides affected Aynho and its traditional knowledge base. Farming for cash profit meant trying the most modern methods and the latest crops. Thus at various times in the first part of the eighteenth century the squire and farmers experimented with sanfoin, turnip greens for fodder, undersowing the wheat with clover, and similar 'improvements' over the basic three-course rotation – wheat, barley, fallow – that had been in operation since 1639. But these new methods alienated traditional knowledge. It was no use asking an oldster when to turn the beasts onto the turnips in a dry year; he didn't know. Information from *outside* experts, therefore, became more useful than *local* knowledge.

The need for another kind of traditional local knowledge residing behind grey beards, that concerning rights and legalities, also passed away in the eighteenth century. The following memorandum is recorded in the proceedings of the manor court at the time that Richard Cartwright took over the lordship and concerns his inquiries into the disposition of certain lands:

Memorandum that Thomas Baker being of the age of iiii score years old dwelt in the tenement that Thomas Baker his son dwelleth in now: showeth him that Wainmore Hook lay to the Lord's tenements as the other meads do

John Grene being of the same age showed Henry Leche that the same hook lay to his house as the other meadows do

And also that the lays at Spichwell lie to the tenants as the other lands do & hath been in the time of their grandfathers and in their fathers' time that dwelt in the same tenements.

(Cited in Cooper 1984, 36)

Here the testimony of two octogenarians as to the rights of certain tenants on speci-fied grazing lands based on their memories of practices going back to their grand-fathers' times was taken as legally binding. But with the consolidation of lands in the squire's hands, the end of ancient copyholds (replaced with newly defined ten-ancies), and the amalgamation of numerous smallholdings into a few substantial farms, much of this oral lore became irrelevant.

Old families must, therefore, have felt a weakening in their sense of identity in relation to the village and to the community, which in turn would place a great symbolic value on those local customs that had managed to survive the onslaught of progress. Local place names are clearly of this order: they identify certain closes, or meads, or the like, as having once belonged to an old village family, and both the family and the place are immortalized in the name. For example, as late as 1960 one pasture just to the northwest of the village was known as Burberow's Close (Cooper 1984, 308–11). The same location had been named Tim Burberow's Close around 1700 (Cooper 1984, 304–7), and there had been a substantial Burberow freeholder (Richard Burberye) in Aynho as early as 1544; yet Burberows had not farmed in the village since soon after the parliamentary enclosure of 1792. Like-wise, morris dancing was a local custom with a clear village identity that had the capacity (given a little push in the right direction) to help maintain a sense of local community among the old families in the face of massive social changes.

Such details as there are of morris performances at Aynho manor house, recorded by Thomas Cartwright's steward, Joshua Burton, in his account books are summar-ized in table 12. Whether or not teams visited the manor before or after the starting and ending dates listed here is hard to say because adequate records do not survive. This time span is covered by two account books kept by Burton over the periods 1691–1722 (Northamptonshire Record Office ML 1306) and 1722–35 (Northamp-tonshire Record Office ML 1307). The first book is rather less detailed than the sec-ond; Burton does not record the provenance of the teams until the second, and tends to parcel payments together in the first. Nonetheless, there seems to be a marked increase in dance events from the period of the first to that of the second book. In the first book there are reports of payments to five teams in three different years covering a total span of seventeen years. So visits then were few and far between. But starting in 1723, teams came almost annually for ten years, there being a total of thirteen events in that time.

Even though the 1720s and early 1730s were boom years for morris, certain years were more popular than others, and this unevenness seems to be related to local affairs, as much as it is possible to ascertain. In 1724, for example, there were no

Table 12
Morris teams patronized at Aynho House, Northants.

Date	Dancers' provenance	Distance (miles)	Payment	
1696–07			2s	6d
1704–06 [W]	3 teams		15s	
1713–05 [W]			[£1	8s]
1723–06 [W]	Aynho, NTHNTS	0	5s	
1723–06 [W]	Chesterton, OXON	8	5s	
1723–06 [W]	King's Sutton, NTHNTS	2	5s	
1725–05 [W]	Brackley, NTHNTS	5	10s	6d
1725–05 [W]	Syresham, NTHNTS	9	10s	6d
1726–05 [W]	Hethe, OXON	5.5	5s	
1727–06	Chesterton, OXON	8	5s	
1731–06 [W]	Aynho, NTHNTS	0	2s	6d
1731–06 [W]	Brackley, NTHNTS	5	10s	6d
1731–06 [W]	Croughton, OXON	2	2s	6d
1731–06 [W]	Croughton, OXON	2	2s	6d
1731–06 [W]	Middleton Cheney, OXON	5	2s	6d
1732–06 [W]	Somerton, OXON	3	2s	6d

Note: [W] indicates a month in which all or part of Whit week falls.

dances because there was a smallpox epidemic raging in the village, but it is difficult to surmise why three or more teams showed up in 1704, 1723, and 1731. It is
noteworthy, however, that in these years, where the provenance of the teams is known,
a team from Aynho itself is included, and in all other years the teams are from outside the village. This might suggest that in these years it was general knowledge in
the vicinity that the squire would be favourably disposed to visits by dancers, so a
team was got up to benefit from his generosity.

One conjecture for 1731 is that this was the year in which his only son, William,
turned twenty-one. His birth date is not recorded so we may not be certain on this
issue, but the coming to majority of the squire's heir was commonly a cause for major
celebrations in the village. At Stowe in the later eighteenth and nineteenth centuries,
for example, the Grenville-Temple family routinely hired morris teams to help celebrate the coming of age of the eldest son, and even provided the wherewithall for
kit and equipment (Chandler 1993a, 199–200). It is even possible that the Aynho
morris consisted of younger servants in the manor house, although one might expect
the account book to make note of this instead of calling the team 'Aynho morrice'
as if it were any other village team.

A diary kept by Anne Tracy in the early eighteenth century concerning manor
house life in Stanway, Gloucestershire, contains the following series for April and

May 1724, which provides analagous material to supplement the Aynho records, and suggests another line of approach for understanding the peaks and valleys in visits by teams:

April 3rd Looked on a set of morrice dancers
...
May 25th Vast preparation among the servant that our Morrice might out-do all the rest at the Whitsun Ale.
...
May 28th Almost distracted with ye perpetual noise of morrice in ye morn.
...
May 30th Almost stunned with Morrice Dancing.   (Winkless 1987, 206)

The dates here represent Good Friday, and the Monday, Thursday, and Saturday of Whit week, and there is a clear implication that this particular Whitsun ale was an extraordinary occasion, drawing teams from a wide area, the local team being (in some way) sponsored by the manor house as representatives of local village pride. Other descriptions of Whitsun ales somewhat later in the eighteenth century, but still pertinent to the current analysis, make it clear that these secular events were quite similar to their immediate ancestor, the church ale:

On the Coteswolds is a customary annual meeting at Whitsuntide, vulgarly called an Ale, or Whitsun-ale ... Two persons are chosen, previous to the meeting, to be lord and lady ... who dress as suitably as they can to the characters they assume. A large empty barn, or some such building, is provided for the lord's hall, and fitted up with seats to accommodate the company. Here they assemble to dance and to regale in the best manner their circumstances and the place will afford, and each young fellow treats his girl with a ribband, or favour. The lord and lady honour the hall with their presence, attended by the steward, sword-bearer, purse-bearer, and mace-bearer, with their several badges or ensigns of office. They have likewise a page, or train bearer, and a jester, drest in a party coloured jacket, whose ribaldry and gesticulation contribute not a little to the entertainment of some part of the company.
                              (Rudder 1779, 24; see also Anon 1886, 198–200)

Several points may be drawn from such descriptions for current purposes. One marked difference between secular Whitsun ales and church ales was that the latter were designed as money-making enterprises (even if sometimes they did not actually make a profit), but the former could lose money and still be deemed a success because economic gain was not necessarily their fundamental purpose. Secular ales were entertainments, pure and simple, and because they were expensive to run, had to be underwritten by the wealthier end of the spectrum in the village. This point has already been made with respect to the Temples in Stowe in the seventeenth century, and apparently the situation was much the same a century later. As such, secular ales were not likely to be annual events, by any means, but more likely to be planned to coincide with other celebrations of import in the local area.

Keith Chandler has culled primary sources for occurrences of secular Whitsun ales in the South Midland counties after the Restoration, and the picture he presents of the late seventeenth and early eighteenth centuries is one of sporadic events scattered throughout the region, not of fixed annual traditions in specific villages (Chandler 1993a, 227). By the nineteenth century, certainly there were well-established sites of annual events, so we may view the eighteenth century as a transitional time when ales were being held infrequently across the region. A few proved to be some combination of successful, economically viable, entertaining, and socially cohesive and thus became regular; the bulk, on the other hand, were flashes in the pan, leaving little trace.

These occasional events would draw teams from a wide radius around the villages holding them, but representation by specific village teams would, in part, be determined by the locus of the ale itself, and by the state of local teams at the time. So, for example, King's Sutton had a Whit ale in 1735, and Shalstone, Bucks, held one in 1743. There is no record of the morris teams that attended these ales (if any), but one would conjecture that the Brackley morris could have visited both because their village lies about equidistant between the other two. If teams were active at the time in Turweston and Buckingham, they would have travelled to Shalstone but not to King's Sutton. Conversely the Middleton Cheney team would likely visit King's Sutton but not Shalstone.

As much probably depended on the status of local teams at the time of the ale as on distance to events, however. If the Aynho records show anything, it is the lack of consistency in the appearance of teams from any one locale. Even the Brackley team, which survived for over two hundred years and which had a strong reputation in the region in the eighteenth century, appeared only twice in the ten-year period when teams were visiting Aynho manor regularly. This probably means that the team had spells of relative activity punctuated by moribund phases. Certainly this would be consistent with data from later in the century and into the nineteenth century, when teams in the region routinely lost critical mass and had to be revived periodically (usually in conjunction with a major local event).

It may well have been that the early announcement (i.e., around or before Easter) of a Whit ale was one kind of necessary incentive to raise or revive a local team. Thus the two times that an Aynho morris appears in the accounts may represent years when there were nearby ales. There seems little doubt that the visits to Aynho by morris teams were in Whit week even though the accounts do not specify exact dates. The best that Burton did was to indicate the month of payment, which was either May or June, but in the great majority of cases (see table 12) the month of payment is for the month in which Whit week fell that year. This is too much of a coincidence to be the result of pure chance: the visits must have been in and around Whit week.

It is purely a matter of speculation, but Whit ales at King's Sutton in 1723 and Croughton in 1731 would account for the data in table 12. It is not likely that there were ales in Aynho itself in those years because there would almost certainly be some record in Burton's accounts of payments made directly to the supervisors of these ales, as there is for the King's Sutton ale in 1735. Croughton is a strong candidate for an ale (or like event) in 1731 because Burton's accounts indicate that two distinct teams from that village visited Aynho, and such a small location could not have supported two teams unless both had a realistic expectation of reward. Both King's Sutton and Croughton are an easy walk from Aynho (around two miles), so raising a side to visit them would not be presented with an undue obstacle. Surely some such extra incentive as a nearby ale was necessary to raise a team in Aynho, because in other years when outsiders were coming in for sure profit (notably 1725, when both teams received half a guinea), it would seem to make logical sense for locals to attempt to cash in if all that was necessary was a dusting off of kit and a few practices. That is, the reward at the manor house (although certain in these years) was not enough by itself to raise a local team.

It may have been, also, that there was a Whit ale in or near Brackley in 1725. This would go some way to explaining why a team from Syresham, fully nine miles from Aynho, made the trip and why they did it just once. They would have had to pass through Brackley to get to Aynho, so one possible scenario is that they journeyed to Brackley, joined up with the Brackley men there, and then went on to Aynho. Brackley is the only team to receive half a guinea as a regular payment, and Syresham the only other to receive that much, and so it would seem likely that Syresham and Brackley were at the manor together – and therefore in fairness had to receive the same reward. In 1731 Brackley received half a guinea and all the other teams, half a crown, intimating that in that year the team danced independently of the others (although some of the others – the two Croughton teams, for example, whose payments are recorded adjacently – may have danced together).

One may go farther in speculating why Brackley received such a high reward in relation to the other teams. The situation for morris teams at the beginning of the eighteenth century seems to have been similar to that for Whit ales and other traditional customs. Having been under a cloud for so long, and having been the subjects of rigorous ecclesiastical and secular repression, such customs, although able to survive (barely) through the seventeenth century, could not simply reconstitute themselves in the more favourable climate of the eighteenth century without substantial patronage, and without other social conditions being congenial to their revival. So, there were a great many attempts at revival, but various principles of selection – economic, social, legal, political, demographic – acted on these revivals to ensure the survival of only the stronger of them.

Out of all the teams that visited Aynho, only King's Sutton and Brackley showed any longevity (both down to the latter part of the nineteenth century). One can imagine numerous possibilities for explaining this state of affairs. Some local areas must have had richer pickings than others, some families who acted as repositories of morris knowledge had more sons who stayed in the village than others, some local squires were strongly supportive of local traditions while others were not, and so on. No doubt a number of such factors played their parts, but beyond these social issues is the basic fact that some teams (maybe a small number) were better than the majority in terms of entertainment value and general aesthetic interest. In some ways there would be a self-stoking cycle involved here. The longer a team was able to stay in business, the easier it would be for it to maintain a decent level of performance. Given that practice time was meagre, it would be easier to refresh a seasoned team (with maybe one or two newcomers) to a reasonable performance level than to start a whole new team from scratch (see Chandler 1993a, 119–43, for a lengthier analysis of later data).

There is, therefore, a necessary symbiosis between aesthetic and social factors involved here. A team that had certain social advantages (for example, availability of cash rewards) could survive long enough to reach a fair level of performance, which, in turn could strengthen the social advantages (for example, encourage greater economic rewards), and so on. But some crucial variables might be beyond the control of individuals. There is no doubt that teams survived longest where one family, or a group of related families could, generation after generation, field the bulk of the village side, for example. This is certainly true in Brackley where four generations of Howards carried the tradition from the eighteenth into the twentieth century (see Chandler 1993a, 135). Fathers and sons have more time together – especially at odd moments – to pass traditions along, and perhaps more incentive as well. A generation without sons could cause an irreparable break in tradition.

Whatever the specific variables involved, there is strong indirect evidence that Brackley had a reputation over a wide area for good dancing. In particular, the team was hired in 1766 to accompany the Whit Lord at an ale in Oxford (*Jackson's Oxford Journal*, 31 May 1766, 3), even though it is twenty-five miles from Brackley to Oxford, and there were almost certainly other teams closer to Oxford that could have been employed. So it is quite within the realms of possibility that Brackley received such a disproportionately high reward at Aynho because they were a celebrated team, and because they provided a rousing exhibition well above the standards of their local rivals. If this is true, then the economics of patronage at manor houses contributed significantly to the long-term survival or demise of teams;

this does not entail thereby any kind of simple economic determinism but, rather, a complex of interrelated variables.

In thinking about patronage it is also important to dispel any romantic and over-simple images of the system that may linger from the scenes painted in the plays of the turn of the seventeenth century. In them there was a clear message that support of the morris was an aspect of old-fashioned *incorporative* community values. The morris dancers performed directly for the lord of the manor, who looked on approvingly before regaling the revellers with wine, beer, and a purse to be going on with. Although the Aynho accounts are bald and limited, they present a completely different picture from that of the plays. First, there is no reason to believe that Thomas Cartwright was ever present at Aynho when the morris teams arrived, although he must have approved of the payments to them. As suggested already, there appears to be a certain budgeting for the teams (which implies a knowledge ahead of time of the number of teams likely to appear in a season), which might well have been worked out between Cartwright and his steward in advance. In these, as in all financial dealings, it was the steward Burton who acted as the financial agent for the Cartwrights; he would reward the dancers as he would pay masons or carpenters working on the manor house. And in at least one case the dancers also had what appears to be an agent. In 1723 when teams from Aynho, Chesterton, and King's Sutton came to the manor the accounts contain the following for the Chesterton men:

pd mr Acam and he gave Chesterton morrice – 5 –

(Northamptonshire Record Office ML 1307)

whereas the other entries (which are typical of most years) read:

gave Aynho morrice – 5 –
...
gave Sutton Morrice – 5 –   (Northamptonshire Record Office ML 1307)

Agents for tours were not unknown in this period, and given that the Chesterton morris had to travel eight miles to Aynho, their tour might have had to have some kind of advanced planning by an entrepreneur to ensure its profitability. If this is so, then the whole transaction becomes much more akin to a standard contracting arrangement, even though the acts of dancing and rewarding were supposedly benevolent. Such an outlook is made more plausible if the notion is accepted that some teams were paid more than others because they put on a better show. Simply put, by the eighteenth century, as part of the changing times, morris performances were shifting from the *incorporative* to the *transactional.* Dance teams were becoming like wage labourers, remunerated by the steward at the end of their 'work' according to their worth, and to what the market would bear that year.

Such a transformation of morris to the ethos of wage labour may reflect the general social transformations occurring in the village, as outlined above, which, in turn, raises the issue of the social status of the dancers themselves. There are no records of the names of the dancers who performed at Aynho, nor of their employment, but some extrapolation from other data is possible. On the rare occasions when rural morris dancers' employment is mentioned in general primary texts, they are either in trades and crafts (mason, potter, butcher), or identified as so-and-so's 'servant,' which could mean literally 'house servant,' or wage labourer in general (including agricultural labourer).

When census records become stable, and morris dancers can be identified by name in them (that is, from 1841 onwards), the breakdown of status is much the same as in the seventeenth century, namely, a strong showing of people in trades and crafts, but also a large percentage of general agricultural wage labourers. The relative balance of the two varied from village to village, but in teams that survived long enough in the Aynho region to have their members appear in the census, that is, Brackley and Adderbury (near King's Sutton, and with whom they shared dancers and musicians), there tends to be a slight preponderance of tradesmen over labourers in most years (see Chandler 1993b, 106–10 and 125–7). It is precisely these workers who represent the oldest families of the villages – one-time yeomen and small-holders who had been forced by circumstances to sell out and move into trades and wage labour. But this group also represented the largest repository of local lore (much more than the relatively transient, or absent, squires and tenants). As discussed above, a great deal of this lore had been made irrelevant by changing times and technology, making the remnant – such as knowledge of local morris dances – that much more important as a symbol of family stature in the community.

Assuming a degree of continuity from the earliest records in the seventeenth century to the latest in the eighteenth to fill the gap in the record for the period under discussion, it may be speculated that the dancers at Aynho were from the middle to lower rungs of the village hierarchy, and were engaged exclusively in the cash economy by letting their services out for hire to the lord of the manor or his tenants. The pleasures of Whit were, therefore, an extension of these everyday relationships. This is a far cry from the description of the cavalier soldiers getting royally drunk with the peasants at Witney on the eve of the Civil War, in which all social differences were dissolved in abundant alcohol. Now the dance continued to confirm the existence of the village hierarchy, and the dancers benefited by fitting into the hierarchy in prescribed ways. Their 'labor' done, they took their 'wages' *elsewhere* to spend them (perhaps to one of the inns in the village – both of which were owned by the squire), rather than drinking directly with the squire and his retinue.

And, in truth, the rewards for their labor – also reflecting larger social values – were paltry given the squire's wealth. This is less a matter of noblesse oblige, and more of hard-headed economic realism: a few coins at Whit kept the people (whose former holdings the squire now owned and rented to strangers) quiet.

Put perhaps in somewhat more partisan tones, the rise of the middle class country gentry – of the order of the Cartwrights – bred in them a middle-class notion of bounty towards 'their' villagers – a token wage for a token performance, perhaps not begrudgingly given, but scarcely worth the effort at times. It may, therefore, be no wonder that as the years went by Thomas Cartwright's charity diminished. Although five teams came by in 1731, only one danced in 1732, and they received the standard half a crown of the year before. Thenceforth, apparently, the game was not worth the candle, or perhaps the people were quiet enough without largesse (they survived the cut from a crown apiece to half a crown), so why encourage scrounging.

But economics cannot have been the only issue for those teams that survived in times of diminishing rewards. For some – such as Brackley and Adderbury – morris may have become increasingly important because of the values that it preserved. The Howards of Brackley and the Waltons of Adderbury (both engaged in the morris for four generations or more) had a stake in keeping their village traditions going in that the dances confirmed their personal bona fides as village labouring aristocracy, even if their stature as people in the larger world was small. Being involved in morris dancing became a way of humanizing on the local level an increasingly alienated world, governed by strangers with profit in their eyes. As much as they could, morris dancers exploited this alienated world to keep their teams going, but cash was not their only reward nor their primary motivation.

As the industrial capitalist economy began the inexorable grind towards measuring a person's worth in monetary terms, rural morris dancers found other, contrary, values to succour them. For another century the treasures of the morris enriched and ennobled their keepers as long as they stayed rooted to their ancestral village homes. Once the traditional performers left the places that gave the dances meaning, however, as many were forced to under severe economic pressures, the game was quickly lost. Dance, performer, and place were, by then, so inexorably tied together that the one could not exist without the others. Dancers who joined the crowds migrating to cities lost their distinctiveness in the urban multitudes, and the dances they left behind died for want of vital bodies. City and country were equally impoverished by the transition. The merest flicker of the tradition survived into the twentieth century to be 'discovered' once more by the urban middle class in their cyclically insatiable quest for the authentic life as an antidote to their self-inflicted ennui.

12

Endings

In attempting to build an evolutionary or developmental model to suit morris dance data, it is clear from the wealth of data in previous chapters that a simple *linear*, or *replacement*, model is wholly inadequate. It would clearly not be correct to say, for example, that royal court morris was superceded by urban morris, which in turn was replaced by church-sponsored morris. Although chronological seriation may give that initial impression – each having its heyday – the substantive details of the histories of the three types show a great degree of interplay between them, as well as a degree of discreteness. Also it is easy to see that while each had a heyday, some of the types – urban, for example – continued to find popular favour in isolated regions at the same time that others were coming and going. Principles of symbiosis and coevolution are, therefore, more likely to apply than simple replacement models.

However, it is worth examining the basic theory of replacement models as they derive from art history, in order to understand the effects they have had in the past on theories of folklore. Although the day is past when one might speak in plain terms of the transition from the Middle Ages to the Renaissance and from the Renaissance to the Baroque without a series of qualifying remarks and addenda, it is still a commonplace of cultural history and art history to talk in terms of stylistic periods such as these. The basic idea is a remnant of nineteenth-century German social philosophy that viewed historical periods as having a *zeitgeist*, a spirit of the age, that pervaded all aspects of social life.

The passage of history and the development of the arts in these periods, therefore, was much like the evolution of science as outlined by Thomas Kuhn in *The Structure of Scientific Revolutions* (Kuhn 1962). The *zeitgeist* is a kind of cultural paradigm that serves well enough to direct people's affairs in all spheres – aesthetic, political, economic, personal, religious – for long periods. But as people work through the cultural paradigm to solve their problems, weaknesses and paradoxes appear, and they assume larger and larger importance until they are too destabilizing for the old paradigm to cope with. At that point the whole culture shifts to a new paradigm that resolves these paradoxes. It then continues along working through this new paradigm until its own weaknesses emerge.

The general notion of paradigm shifts in history has come under increasing criticism in the twentieth century, but despite the academic wrangling over the ontological nature of historically marked eras, the terminology of discrete phases in history replacing one another in linear fashion is trenchantly persistent in art history. Part of the reason for this is that in the various branches of the arts there have been signal events that have launched new styles almost overnight. In music, for example, the establishment of the well-tempered scale solved myriad problems of tuning, orchestration, and modulation that had deviled composers and performers, and ushered in the so-called classical period, an incredibly fertile era for composers because of the freedom this new musical paradigm gave them.

What rarely gets acknowledged, except implicitly, is that such revolutions in the arts, in religion, in economics occur first at the elite level, creating a general impression that cultures change because of discoveries and inventions by elite artists, scientists, politicians, or theologians. The term 'art history' masquerades as a neutral term, for example, whereas the bulk of its researches should bear the label 'elite art history.' The fact that the usual title is an unmarked case indicates the implicit assumption that elite art is normative, and the marked cases, such as popular art, folk art, and domestic art are in some sense derivative or secondary. Or we may put together collocations of eras and statuses to see how the former terms apply strictly to elites only. Renaissance king, Baroque composer, and Enlightenment politician all seem unremarkable, but Baroque ploughman, Enlightenment peasant, or Neo-classical swineherd either ring false as oxymorons, or else seem like labels for images in elite art.

Furthermore, one of the corollaries of the doctrine of survivals, particularly as employed by the likes of Frazer, Tylor, and Chambers in their reconstructions of the evolution of social institutions, is the notion that cultural ideas evolve among elites and then sift *downward* from there to the lower classes, where they remain (sometimes in transmuted or rudimentary form), as if the lowest social stratum was a kind of sedimentary bed for discarded ideas. The whole study of Popular Antiquities (the antiquarian precursor of academic folklore) grew up on this premise. Compendia such as John Brand's *Observations on the Popular Antiquities of Great Britain Chiefly Illustrating the Origin of our Vulgar and Provincial Customs, Ceremonies, and Superstitions* (Brand 1849) attempted to show through encyclopedic collation of sources that a wide variety of lower-class customs originated in normative elite practices of bygone eras. The logical extension of such thinking was that to reconstruct the elite practices of the past one need only look at the peasantry of today. This is the essential method used by E.K. Chambers, for example, in his reconstructions of early European dramatic traditions (see especially Chambers 1903).

It scarcely needs be said that such an elitist standpoint – not surprisingly the product of the elite intellectual world – misunderstands the nature of peasant and other lower-class cultures. It views them largely as uncreative, unreflective, illogical, and entirely derivative. What the substantive accounts of data in this work, as well as the mass of contemporary ethnography, make plain is that all levels of complex societies have the capacity to be creative, reflective, and logical, and routinely contribute ideas to each other. So, while we may allow (in qualified fashion) the legitimacy of the historian's view of European elites as passing through a number of identifiable periods, we must also allow that other classes have passed through periods of their own, and that these phases are not always directly responsive to, or derivative of, transitions at the elite level. That is, we must admit of the possibility of multiple paradigms existing simultaneously at different levels of society, of the ability of all these paradigms – high and low – to evolve, and of the capacity of these paradigms to interact symbiotically one with another creating changes at both levels.[1] Morris dance primary sources, as laid out in previous chapters, strongly support such suppositions.

Data on the church-sponsored morris and its successor, the rural morris, show that throughout the sixteenth and seventeenth centuries dance forms (and their contexts) were in a constant state of evolution – deriving dance ideas from a variety of sources – elite and peasant. On occasion these morrises drew inspiration directly from elite sources, imitating ideas wholesale; at other times the dances parodied elite models transforming the forms into caricatures. But the flow of ideas – and the methods of borrowing – was entirely bidirectional. Elite choreographers, masquewrights, playwrights, and dancing masters sometimes copied lower class dance forms directly, and sometimes lampooned them. The dances were then free to evolve at this level before being copied again at the lower level ... and so the cycle continued, evolution occurring at all social levels more or less continually, and borrowing between them taking place intermittently.

At the elite level there is explicit confirmation in the primary sources that direct borrowing from the lower classes was an antidote to aesthetic decadence. Elite aesthetic genres (according to elite analysts) have a tendency to rise in the hands of a few capable practitioners to soaring heights, but then this period of brilliance is followed by a period of increasingly derivative, overblown, forced, and overwrought works by lesser hands. This period of decadence is usually the signal for a paradigm shift, but for an immediate injection of fresh life, elite practitioners look to lower-class forms which they characterize as 'vital' or 'authentic.' Periods of heavy direct borrowing (as well as parody) of lower-class dance ideas noted in the primary sources in previous chapters include the mid-sixteenth century (the rise of the urban May-game), the turn of the seventeenth century (morris in the public theatres), the mid-seventeenth century (the advent of bourgeois country dancing), and the early eighteenth century (the aftermath of Gay's *Beggar's Opera*).

It is also interesting to note in this regard that much of the academic folklore discussed in chapter 1 was born at the turn of the twentieth century when classical tonality seemed worn out and many composers turned folklorist/collector, going into remote rural spots to record songs and melodies to be incorporated into elite compositions. Cecil Sharp himself was a minor figure in this regard, but of greater weight were Béla Bartók, Zoltán Kodály, Ralph Vaughan-Williams, and Percy Grainger – the latter especially famous in his day for his settings of morris tunes (including the longstanding favourite 'Country Gardens'). This so-called primitivist movement had analogues in dance (Nijinsky's choreography of *Le Sacre du Printemps*, for example, represents the theory of ritual origins of folk dance in a Russian balletic setting) and in the plastic arts (Pablo Picasso being the examplar); the whole movement served as a bridge into the 'modernist' paradigm.

What caused the borrowing of elite ideas by lower-class dancers, and when were the critical periods, are more difficult questions to answer because of the lack of self-reflective primary sources. But indirect evidence seems to point to at least the early-sixteenth century (the rise of the church sponsored morris), and at some point in the early seventeenth century (the adoption by rural morris of 'Italian' figured dance sequences). Perhaps their reasons for searching outside existing forms for new ideas are cognate with those of the upper classes, that is, the old forms had become stale and overworked and in need of an infusion of novelty. At least imitation of the elite via parody is better understood, and the relationship between such trends and the defusing of complementary schismogenesis has been well reviewed in previous chapters, as has the sources of the periodic (occasionally draconian) proscription of lower-class customs that mock elites.

But, obviously, satire is a weapon for both sides, although in the hands of the elite it is a force in direct support of the complementary status quo (as is lower-class satire in an indirect way; by acting as a safety valve for the excesses of complementarity, it helps preserve it). There is also an implicit sense in which parody acknowledges the power of the aesthetic vehicles of the other camp: satire has no force if it seeks to mock only the insignificant or irrelevant. And this fact, in turn, supports the original proposition that aesthetic vitality resides in different classes (or different paradigms) in different historic periods, thus creating the basis for constant reciprocal borrowing of ideas.

But many other processes besides direct borrowing between classes are in operation in the evolution of aesthetic forms. The overworked example of the many kinds of changes created by the traditional passing on of materials from generation to generation *within the same class* can easily act as a foil to such a simplistic notion that a lower/upper-class symbiotic exchange of ideas is the only process involved in creative change. Indeed, it may be more profitable to speak of the processes of development rather than of any single process (however complex). For analytic purposes these processes may be drawn together under the rubric of dialectics – by which I mean, generally speaking, the creative tension emerging from the interaction of like or opposing social entities (such as classes, generations, or individual performers) – and, thereby, certain necessary connections between different dialectical systems may be exposed.

The dialectical model that I choose to start with is not the familiar Hegelian system of entities that generate their opposites on the road to a mediating synthesis – nor the many Marxist variations on this theme – although there is something of a family resemblance. Rather I prefer to think of a series of dialectical processes that coexist, occasionally intersecting in their actions, and nested in analytically discrete levels. These dialectical processes occur between two entities of the same social order but which perceive themselves to be different from one another in critical ways (although not necessarily opposite). The process may occur, for example, between teams from nearby villages in competition with each other for economic resources, and who, therefore, attempt to outdo each other in various components of their display which, in turn, contributes to certain kinds of elaboration. Or, as discussed above, representatives of different social classes may borrow or parody each other's styles using them as the basis for further elaboration.

What we may speak of, therefore, rather than of a dialectic of opposition leading to synthesis or mediation (following Hegel) is a dialectic of (perceived) *difference* leading to *elaboration* or change. At first glance, the examples given above of this dialectic of difference in action may seem to fit Bateson's typology of systems of schismogenesis, the village-to-village dialectic being symmetric and the high-to-low class dialectic being complementary. But the situation is more complex than Bateson's model will allow. As discussed in previous chapters, there have been times in English history when peasant customs have been the instrument for the dissolution of complementary systems between the classes (e.g., on the eve of the Civil War), and other times when they have resolutely supported them (e.g., at the turn of the eighteenth century). What is more, systems that seem obviously symmetric, as in the case of intervillage competition may, due to circumstances, become complementary.

Classic examples of symmetric schismogenesis, such as sibling rivalry, involve the two parties outdoing one another in the *same* spheres (that is, direct and endless conflict in the same arenas over the same rewards). But intervillage rivalry (which ought to be symmetric) may result in one team deciding that it cannot compete effectively by, say, attempting to caper even higher than its rivals, and so, instead, it may evolve complex patterns of figures or stick-clashing rhythms, turning the would-be symmetric system into a kind of complementary one, where further elaboration in one sphere by one team involves elaboration in a *different* sphere by its rival. Put more simply, Bateson saw complementary systems as forces for (oppositional) heterogeneity and symmetric ones for homogeneity, whereas within the dialectical processes I propose, both hetero- and homogenizing forces may operate within classic complementary and symmetric systems, depending on other historically particular social forces at work at the time.

A segment of my model of the nested levels of dialectical process is represented in figure 49.

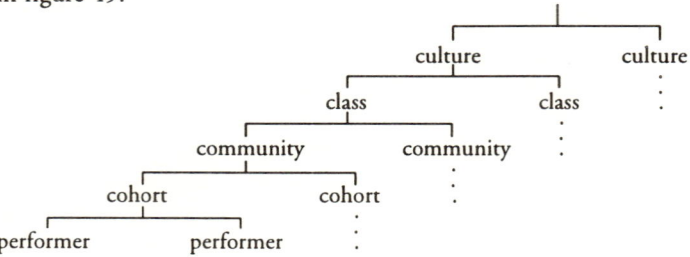

Figure 49: Nested levels of the dialectic of difference

The simplest way to understand this model is to look briefly at the levels in turn – relating them back to examples in previous chapters and, then exploring some of the ways in which the levels intersect and interact. The most general dialectical process that operates at all levels is one of *imitation* coupled with *variation*, which itself implies that in all cases there is a critically perceived difference between the two entities or poles of the dialectic, such that information flows from one to the other.

At the broadest end of the spectrum there are culture areas (sometimes nations) that act as generative centres for new aesthetic ideas, but these centres can quickly shift or become more like nodes in the reciprocal flow of information. Italy in Elizabethan times, for example, was the fount for many elite dance ideas, including set and figure formations in country dances. England readily absorbed these ideas and, having created a bourgeois country dance form of its own in the seventeenth century, became the generative centre for dancing masters in France (and Italy) to emulate. Subsequently, in the early eighteenth century, French dancing masters became arbiters of country dance style, readily copied in England.

The dialectic of high and low class has been alluded to at length in the substantive chapters, but a new dimension can be added to this process by investigating some of the ways in which it intersects with the culture-to-culture dialectic. Previous chapters have shown that, in the main, the flow of dance ideas from culture to culture in our period took place at the elite level, but the influx of ideas into England was sporadic, depending on a variety of social and political circumstances at the international/elite level. Having entered English culture at the elite level, they were copied by lower classes, and then recopied by the elite. Thus, for example, English bourgeois country dances of the seventeenth century were a synthesis of ideas flowing between elite dancing masters (who derived some of their ideas from other cultures) and lower-class dancers (who derived some of their ideas from other dances in their local sphere). Yet the same process was also occurring in Italy – elite dancing masters borrowed ideas from peasants ... and so forth.

So it is possible to imagine a particular choreographic idea moving from the Italian peasantry to the Italian elite, thence from the Italian elite to the English elite, and thence from the English elite to the English peasantry. Generations later the elite forms may be obsolete, but the peasant forms may persist, leading a fieldworker to posit (falsely) the need for direct contact between the two lower-class groups to 'explain' the consonance – hence the endless speculation in the nineteenth century concerning English common soldiers bringing dance ideas back from their continental excursions to explain choreographic congruences in widely diverse cultural regions.

In a general sense, therefore, the flow of ideas from high to low class, among other things is potentially a move from internationalism to localism. Ideas may be elaborated at both poles (high and low), but it is most often at the elite level that they flow between cultures, and more likely at the lower level that they diffuse on the local scale. This model of intersecting dialectical processes thus avoids the basic fallacy that the dances have always been the exclusive property of the lower classes and that, therefore, they can only disseminate within those classes (which thinking can only set up absurd models of historic/spatial diffusion).

A sublevel of the class-to-class dialectic is the community-to-community dialectic. Here the term 'community' strictly means 'community of performers' rather than simply village, town, or local region. Obviously the social context of many morris teams is a village or town or some like entity, and the term 'community' is meant to embrace these contexts too; but the locus of the term is the team itself, and only secondarily as representative of the larger social context that it comes out of. Thus, for example, Brackley morris was a community of performers that represented the village of Brackley – but not all the members came from Brackley and not all of Brackley concerned itself with the morris team. Neither does the term 'community' here simply refer to the currently active dancers. Again, these form the core of the community, but they are influenced in their actions and decisions by former dancers, and by the general heritage of their village tradition. Community thus means a team considered as an entity at the center of social, historic, and geographic contexts.

The most obvious form of community-to-community dialectic involves various forms of competition. On the one hand, there were the straightforward intervillage competitions for prizes, whose existence necessarily prompted extra practices to promote uniformity of team style as well as a sense of distinctiveness to distinguish 'our' team from the rest. On the other hand, the general competition for cash (and other) rewards during tours would produce results similar to formal competitive events, even if the rivalry were not face-to-face or head-to-head.

But, such competition also led to the general dissemination of new dance ideas between villages, and formal competition in particular acted to keep differences between teams within certain bounds (otherwise judging would have been impossible). Thus team-to-team competition worked simultaneously as a force for intercommunity heterogeneity and homogeneity – supporting the drive to create individual team styles of performance, but keeping those styles contained within general limits.

It is also possible to subsume under the community-to-community dialectic the rather more abstract notion of a dance-to-dance dialectic where one dance is the prerogative of one team and a second (contrasting dance) of another. 'Our' team may see another performing a dance in its own village style with a new and unusual chorus, take the chorus idea home with them, and fit it into their distinctive style of steps and figures. The exchange has taken place on the level of individual dances, although the vehicles for the exchange are the individual communities. More generally, then, the idea of community as a pole of a dialectical exchange entails not simply a group of performers but also the stock of dance ideas that makes them a community and not just an aggregate of people.

A community of performers that survives for any length of time contains within it one or more cohorts (or generations). Thus, the passing on of dance ideas from older to younger dancers forms a cohort-to-cohort dialectic. The functioning of such a dialectic is largely determined by the degree of year-to-year continuity within each community. A team whose members routinely practice each year, introducing new dancers as the need arises, is likely to maintain a high degree of homogeneity from cohort to cohort, because the experienced dancers (i.e., the senior cohort) will tend to form a majority style that is simplest for neophytes to copy; it is also true that a longstanding team could well develop individual performer styles within it (particularly in the absence of external competition), due to the performer-to-performer dialectic discussed below.

Data from the primary sources indicate that year-to-year continuity was far from the norm, however. More likely teams went into abeyance for several years or more, to be revived by one or two senior dancers when a likely crop of youths (maybe their sons) came of age in the community. In this case the cohort-to-cohort dialectic could result in a constant narrowing (hence shifting) of dance style. A team may have a range of dance styles represented within it during its active life, but when a single dancer from that cohort teaches a new team he will teach his style *only* (he will not say, for example, 'When my brother danced in that position he always hitched his leg like so when he capered,' but will teach his mode of performing to all his pupils). Over time, such narrowing of styles can lead to 'drift' in overall style.

Such drift may also occur because of a differing mental sense from cohort to cohort of what are the essentials of any particular dance style, and what are unimportant variations. In anthropological terms we may speak of a shift in the emics of the dance, that is, a change over time in the dancers' sense of what differences in performance style are truly different moves (i.e., potentially *wrong* or *right*) versus those that are different to an outsider's eye but essentially the same from the dancers' point of view (even though they may acknowledge that differences exist).[2] Some teachers may have a narrow sense of what is right and wrong emically, while others may take a broader view, the former resulting in greater observable homogeneity within a team's style, the latter giving greater freedom for observable heterogeneity; narrowing and broadening of the emic perspective may change from cohort to cohort.

Teams that have significant breaks between revivals may also have a definite sense of 'our' cohort versus some other, in much the same way that intervillage rivalry may produce differences of style ('our fathers did it that way, but we do it this way'). There is abundant evidence of such forces at work in nineteenth-century data (see Abbott and Forrest 1986), which may be historically particular or, more likely, a continuation of former practice.

At the most individual level there is the performer-to-performer dialectic. Again, both homogenizing and heterogenizing forces are at work here. In some instances dancers may try to compete with each other to see who can caper higher or step more lightly, thus reinforcing in each other a sense of symmetric uniformity (even though they may be of unequal ability). In others, individuals may seek to develop a style of dancing that makes them stand out as unique from their fellows (although there may be external limits on the extent to which individuals in a cohort may differentiate themselves, such as the need to present a uniform team style in competition). There may also be certain gestures that would be considered 'wrong' by other performers in the cohort, with the possibility of concomitant pressure to eradicate such moves – the degree of success of individuals introducing such idiosyncratic innovations being determined largely by the interpersonal dynamics of the team (as well as the success of such moves in public performance).

The musician (and other characters besides the set dancers) should also be included in the performer-to-performer dialectic because there must be a degree of co-adaptability between musician and set dancers who tend to operate in different, though intersecting spheres. Professional musicians have to play for more than a few days' morris dancing to make a living, steadier profits coming from being able to play for country and other social dances that know no special season. So their repertoire would have been generally skewed in the direction of popular social dances rather than in favour of the specialized needs of morris dancers. But the flow was not all one way; musicians had to make concessions of tempi, metre, phrase pattern, and so forth to meet certain choreographic needs of the morris. Subsumed under this example, therefore, is the more abstract music to dance dialectic (see Forrest 1988b and 1996 for examples of this dialectic in operation).

Several refinements and comments should be added to this bald description of the general model. First, and of great importance, it should be understood that there are other dialectical systems besides this complex hierarchical dialectic of difference in operation (which also intersect with levels of the model). The performer-to-audience dialectic, for example, is of great significance in the general evolution of ideas, and its power has been touched upon in previous chapters. To an extent the results of this dialectic are covered by the community-to-community dialectic inasmuch as all teams try their best (in competition with one another) to exact as much money as they can from their audiences. That is, the community-to-community dialectic may play itself out in the context of performer/audience relations, but even when no rivalry between teams exists, there must still be a performer/audience dynamic – being more profitable the more skillfully it is manipulated.

Second, not all levels of the model are equally active at any given time. Historically, the locus of dialectical tension has shifted due to a variety of social circumstances, as has the ability for different levels to intersect. There have been times of social and political isolation, for example, when the international flow of dance ideas has slowed to a trickle, and likewise there have been periods when the elite view was cast away from lower-class practices, and vice versa, eliminating the functioning of the class dialectic. Lack of regional competition eliminates the community dialectic, and so on.

Conversely, the vitality of one level of the dialectical model may enliven or permute another level. As noted, the existence of community-to-community competition must have an effect on the performer to performer dialectic; with competition there is a greater need for homogeneity within the team – which in turn will narrow the range of possibilities for the cohort to cohort dialectic. Without competition the performer-to-performer dialectic may tend towards greater heterogeneity, broadening the possibilities for drift via the cohort-to-cohort dialectic.

Third, it must be understood that what I have described here is really one abstract thread or dimension of a much more complex reality. The lines of dots in figure 49 indicate areas of the model that should be extrapolated to create a fully multidimensional picture. The segments I have elucidated here simply serve to configure the bulk of the data presented in previous chapters. But equally a community-to-community, or cohort-to-cohort dialectic exists in the elite sphere, and so on.

Acknowledgment of the existence of such dialectical processes helps exorcise some longstanding demons in folklore theory. To begin at our starting point, it shows up the inherent logical problems in the search for monolithic origins of customs, and in any remaining interest in theories of the linear evolution of aesthetic forms. A dialectical approach assumes that all social entities are the products of multiple sources, each of which, in turn, is the product of other dialectical processes; so the search for chimerical discrete origins can be replaced with the identification of critical points in the dialectical process – points, for example, when particular levels of the model were highly energized, creating a rapid flow of information and fueling creative growth. A dialectical approach also asserts the multiplex nature of the evolution of social forms. Intersecting levels of the dialectical model take input from diverse quarters and spawn diverse offspring.

On a more general level, though, the dialectical model questions the very theoretical and empirical bases of folklore (at least as it was originally conceived, and as it still manifests itself in some quarters). Not having the kind of time depth presented in this book, nineteenth-century folklorists could easily define their disciplinary boundaries in class and regional terms. Folklore for them was the study of the customs, habits, and traditions of the rural peasantry – pure and simple. This was the result of a 'snapshot' effect, perhaps peculiar to the nineteenth century, that made it appear that a highly distinctive set of customs was the unique prerogative of the rural lower classes (and that these customs were rapidly dying out and in need of preservation). Although the aims of these folklorists were laudatory, there is no question that by setting up the category 'folklore' they helped further solidify the marginal status of 'folk' peoples whom they were trying to raise from their humble position. Even today one need only examine such collocations as 'folk art' in popular parlance to see that the term 'folk' has marginal (occasionally perjorative) overtones: folk art is, by definition, not mainstream, not part of the canon.

The field of folklore quickly gained a more theoretical underpinning when its practitioners recognized that the hallmark of peasant culture was the *oral* transmission of forms, and that 'oral culture' had certain qualities that marked it off from 'literate culture.' Thus, over the course of the twentieth century, the discipline expanded to accommodate oral cultures wherever they might be found – urban street corners, gatherer/hunter campfires, and so on – and interest centred on ways in which oral cultures were unique. It has also been generally accepted that oral cultures (including the traditional peasant varieties) do not necessarily create de novo all (or any) of their tales, ballads, and dances but, rather, draw syncretically on outside traditions, including the literate.

But the idea of orality as a central marker of folk culture, and the prime concern of folklore, has not been without difficulties. One problem is that oral culture can be found everywhere. The principal forms of ballet, for example, are transmitted entirely orally, yet most folklorists would be reluctant to designate the Royal Ballet as a community of folk dancers. Clearly the term 'folk' retains a sense of non-elite status, even when the theoretical emphasis has shifted to the oral transmission of forms. Likewise there are some performers who meet most people's intuitive definition of 'folk' who happily embrace the literate. The Copper family of Rottingdean in Sussex, for example, are without doubt traditional folk singers, yet for four generations they have sung in public from a manuscript book of lyrics set down by 'Brasser' Copper in the nineteenth century to preserve the family's songs (and Brasser's grandson, Bob, actively collected songs from traditional performers using wire recorders and tape recorders, transcribing them for publication).

To overcome these difficulties some folklorists (see, for example, Dundes 1965) have fallen back on classic dichotomies from social science, such as *Gemeinschaft* and *Gesellschaft*, or Great Tradition and Little Tradition, arguing that the oral is less important than the notion that folk cultures are by nature small, intimate, localized, kin-based, and the like. Again, problems with such oppositions have been well discussed in the anthropological literature and need not be repeated here (see Harris 1968). What we can say instead is that all these vexations to draw boundaries around the field are made irrelevant by a processual and dialectical approach to performance forms. There is no part or level of the dialectical model – culture, class, community, cohort, individual – that can be usefully isolated as a discrete entity capable of analysis without reference to other parts of the model. To be sure, levels have been isolated historically (that is what creates the 'snapshot' effect), but those are the accidents of history that we must rise above, and delve below. This work is, therefore, dedicated to a new vision of the 'folk' in the hope that by *not* drawing boundaries around them, they may one day cease to exist as a marginal (or any other kind of) category defined by Western elites.

Methodological Issues: The Early Morris Database and Archive

SOURCES

In building a database of primary sources on morris dancing in Britain, the initial problem is to decide what to include and what to exclude. Here, for the first of many times, anachronism can rear its seductive, but ultimately traitorous, head. The following exquisite sketch, excerpted from Phillip Stubbes's *Anatomie of Abuses* (1583) has often been taken as a major source for morris dancing in the sixteenth century:

First, all the wilde-heds of the Parish, conuenting together, chuse them a Graund-Captain (of all mischeefe) whome they innoble with the title of my Lord of Mis-rule, and him they crowne with great solemnitie, and adopt for their king. This king anointed, chuseth forth twentie, fortie, threescore or a hundred lustie Guttes like to him self to waighte vppon his lordly Maiestie, and to guarde his noble person. Then euerie one of these his men, he inuesteth with his liueries, of green, yellow or some other light wanton colour. And as though that were not (baudie) gaudie enough I should say, they bedecke them selues with scarfs, ribons & laces hanged all ouer ẁgolde rings, precious stones & other iewels: this doon, they tye about either leg xx. or xl bels, with rich handkercheifs in their hands, and sometimes laid a crosse ouer their shoulders & necks, borrowed for the most parte of their pretie Mopsies & loouing Besses, for bussing them in ẏ dark. Thus all things set in order, then haue they their Hobby-horses, dragons & other Antiques, together with their baudie Pipers and thundering Drummers to strike vp the devils daunce withall, then marche these heathen company towards the Church and Church-yard, their pipers pipeing, their drummers thundring, their stumps dauncing, their bels iyngling, their handkerchefs swinging about their heds like madmen, their hobbie horses and other monsters skirmishing amongst the route: in this sorte they go to the Church (I say) & into the Church (though the Minister be at praier or preaching) dancing & swinging [t]heir handkercheifs ouer their heds, in the Church, like devils incarnate ẁsuch a confuse noise, ẏ no man can hear his own voice. Then the foolish people, they looke, they stare, they laugh, they fleer, & mount vpon fourmes and pewes to see these goodly pageants solemned in this sort. Then after this, about the Church they goe againe and again. & so foorth into ỹ church-yard, where they haue commonly their Sommer-haules, their bowers, arbors, & banqueting houses set up, wherin they feast banquet & daunce al that day, & (peradventure) all the night too.   (Stubbes 1583, sig. M2 recto and verso)

This is a superb description of local customs – one of the best. Despite the outbursts of puritanical rage there is almost a delight in recording details accurately, much to the benefit of historians. This could well be a portrait of morris dancing but nowhere does Stubbes *say* that it is. The decision to include the reference in the morris canon is based more on twentieth-century images of morris dancing than on comparisons with other late sixteenth-century sources. Carelessness of this sort can easily lead to circular reasoning when attempting to build a developmental history. That is, the analyst casts around primary sources for morris dance material, finds a description (such as Stubbes's) that 'looks like morris,' then asserts that the dance has not changed significantly in 400 years. This is purely circular, because the step of finding a dance that 'looks like' morris already assumes that the dance has *not* changed.

It is conceivable that the sixteenth-century dance that 'looks like' (twentieth-century) morris but is not called by that name is not morris dancing at all. Maybe morris dancing in this era was completely different, and Stubbes's type of dancing (which for the present has a description but no name) was a new fad on the scene, parts of which got co-opted by morris dancers because they were appealing – hence the latter day similarities. Or maybe Stubbes's dancers really are morris dancers after all. Nothing can be assumed; all must be argued for and justified using as rigorous a method as possible given the limitations of the source material.

An obvious starting point is to gather together *all* – and *only* – those references that specifically use the name 'morris' dancing; being named 'morris' is both a necessary and sufficient condition for the inclusion of a source. As it stands this sounds like an entirely rigorous procedure, because it relies exclusively on internal evidence from the sources themselves to determine what morris dancing is in each era, and avoids all anachronistic judgments. Unfortunately things are not quite so simple.

To begin, there is the problem of old orthographies prior to standardization. This in itself is relatively minor but indicates a larger, more important issue. The modern spelling – morris – is comparatively rare prior to the eighteenth century, and in earlier times no single spelling was preferred. 'Moreys,' 'morisse,' 'mores,' 'morice,' 'moris,' 'morys,' 'moryce,' and all manner of recombinations thereof turn up. Confusing though this alphabet soup of names may appear it is easy enough to see that the forms listed are all trying to capture the same underlying phonetic idea. Even so, one cannot simply build a list of possible spellings and use that as a mechanical arbiter for deciding whether a primary source contains a reference to morris dancing.

To illustrate the problem, consider the following reference taken from early-six-teenth-century (1527) churchwardens' accounts in Great Dunmow, Essex:

Item payd for a blakk morres coott xij d.   (Essex CRO D/P 11/5/1)

This could be transcribed into modern spelling as:

Item paid for a black morris coat 12 old pence

meaning that the churchwardens paid twelve pence for a morris coat coloured black. This would certainly be in keeping with other sixteenth-century church accounts and is the interpretation given by one investigator (see Smith 1973, 9). Morris coats are a standard costume item mentioned in church account books throughout the century. For example, the churchwardens of Kingston on Thames in 1522 record:

Item paid for viij yerdes of ffustyan for ye Mores daunsers cotes iiij s.
                                                    (Surrey CRO KG 2/2/1, f.112)

So, by analogy, the Essex text might suggest the presence of a church related morris dancing custom in and around Great Dunmow in the earlier sixteenth century, and would merit inclusion in the database. But the general context of the Essex account, and a little knowledge of old lexical conventions, makes it much more likely that the text should be transliterated:

Item paid for a black(-a-)moor's coat 12 old pence.

The compound black + moor was the usual form in the sixteenth and seventeenth centuries, gradually replaced by the composite blackamoor (see *Oxford English Dictionary* 'blackamoor'). In addition it is not at all common to find the *colour* of a morris coat mentioned in account books (although it is rather more so to find colours listed where the accounts record the *material* for making up the coats). So, the reference really concerns a costume item for a player taking the part of a Moor.

Thus, every potential reference must be viewed carefully to determine whether the key word is truly a variant of 'morris,' or a red herring. Even so, there are bound to be some borderline examples, which must be held in a separate file for later examination. For strict analysis it is paramount that the core database of sources be made up of unequivocal references. Then if the doubtful cases seem to fit in, they can be used, with caution, to supplement the descriptions in the trustworthy material.

The problem of word variation does not cease with orthography, however. Confusion over the derivation of the word morris, and confusion over what the word was thought to be, led some writers (primarily in the seventeenth century) to concoct a number of variant titles for the dance. Examine, for example, the definition of 'Morisco' in Edward Phillips' *The New World of English Words*:

Morisco, (Span.) a moor, also a kind of Dance which seemeth to be the same as that which the Greeks call Pyrrhica, we vulgarly call it the Morris Dance, as it were the Moorish Dance.
(Phillips 1658a, sig. Cc4)

This reference seems to suggest that, in some people's minds, the words 'morris,' 'morisco,' and 'Moorish' were interchangeable. This most emphatically does *not* imply that the three words were always used in English to refer to the same dances, but it does mean that for some people, some of the time, one term was as good as another. Later in the same century we come across this definition in the *Gazophylacium Anglicanum*:

Morrice-dance, from the Ital. A la Moresca, or the Fr. Moresque; q.d. a Dance after the fashion of the Moors, a Moorish-dance.   (Anon 1689)

In the next century in an anonymous pamphlet, *An Agreeable Companion*, appears:

On May-Day, and at Whitsuntide, was wont to be Morisk, commonly called Morrice, but properly Morish-Dancing, that is Dancing after the manner of the Moors, from whome the Name is derived.   (Anon 1742)

I am not concerned whether the word 'morris' is actually derived from 'Moorish' or 'moresque' but only with the fact that they were historically *perceived* to be related, or variant forms of one another. It is possible, in fact, to isolate five distinct word sounds found in English language texts (and subject to all the idiosyncrasies of old spelling) that had a degree of interchangeability. They can be represented graphically thus:

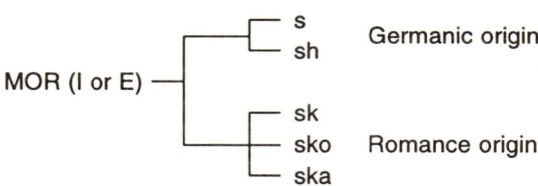

That is, the words' sounds differ primarily because of their endings – morris (ending in an /s/), mo(o)rish (ending in an aspirated /sh/); and the related morisk (ending in /sk/ with no subsequent vowel), and morisco/moresca (ending in /sk/ plus a distinct vowel sound). Basically the distinct sounds represent different languages of origin.

The texts above clearly indicate that each of these word sounds was used on some occasions to designate a morris dance, and in many cases the context makes it clear that such is the case. All the quotations above, for example, use the word 'morris' and one of the variants in addition, so there is no doubt that they are references to morris dance. Problems arise only where a variant word other than 'morris' is found by itself, because each of these words has one or more other meanings. A morisco, for example, may be a morris dance (or dancer), or a Moor (or a person playing a Moor); a Moorish dance may be a morris dance or a dance performed by Moors. Thus a reference to a Shrovetide banquet for Henry VIII in 1510 at which the torch-bearers

were appareyled in crymosen satyne and grene lyke Moreskoes, their faces blacke ...

(Hall 1809, 513)

is ambiguous because they could be dressed as morris dancers or as Moors (or possibly both). But further on in the description of the banquet it is stated that among the guests were

Two ladyes ... in kyrtels of Crymosyne ... and ouer their garmentes were rochettes of pleasantes [a gauzy material] ... their heades rouled in pleasaunts and typpets lyke the Egipcians, enbroudered with golde. Their faces, neckes, armes & handes couered with fyne pleasaunce blacke: Some call it Lumberdynes, which is marueylous thine, so that the same ladies seemed to be nygrost or blacke Mores.

(Hall 1809, 514)

So it would be reasonable to deduce that in 1510 among the nobility it was fashionable to dress as Moors and, therefore, the 'Moreskoes' are more likely Moors than morris dancers.

It must also be borne in mind that the morisco and moresque were well known and distinctive performance types in Spain and France respectively that may or may not have been related to English morris dances. Thus, mention of Spaniards or Frenchmen (or other foreigners) performing morisks, or the like, must be kept in a category of references separate from those that are clearly about English dances and dancers. And even where the context is clearly English but the dance is referred to as a morisk only, the citation must be examined with care and used only as an adjunct to other, unequivocal, references. It could be that European morisks influenced morris dancing, or even that the first morris dances in England were imported, as has frequently been asserted. But these are all parts of the developmental history that must be established through documentation, not built into the principles for creating the database. Otherwise all argument from the database is circular.

It is also bad historical method to choose one's sources simply to support a hypothesis, and to ignore all those that do not fit preconceptions, but it happens – sometimes unwittingly – especially when data are scarce. It is all too easy to develop an idea and then hunt and peck one's way through the primary sources, blazing a narrow, winding trail that others can follow blindly, provided the rest of the world is hidden from their view. In the days before sophisticated methods of data storage and retrieval this mode of writing history was, if not completely forgivable, at least understandable. Faced with hundreds, perhaps thousands, of sources, it is virtually impossible to see patterns without some assistance and, therefore, easy to 'find' whatever patterns one is looking for. Now, using electronic database management, it is relatively easy to determine the degree to which a particular source matches others from the same era, provided the sources are systematized in such a way as to make comparison possible.

Consider the following three references. In 1576 the parson of Huntley, Gloucestershire, was presented to diocesan authorities:

for suffringe the may lorde and the morice daunces [to] come into the churche.
(Price 1938, 11)

In the same year the rector of Cranoe, Leicestershire was brought up on a similar charge:

Against the rector of Cranehoo ... Richard Hackney, ... who confessed that he suffred poppettes to plaie in the Churche ... & howse of praier to be prophanely abused with Poppet plaies ... And he is discharged, and in no wise hereafter shall suffer any such order eyther by morrys daunce or otherwise to be in his Churche but shall beforehand complaine unto the Justices thereof.
(Foster 1912, 137–8)

And a year later, in 1577, morris dancers made an appearance in church in Liverpool:

And on wednesdaye his honor [the Earl of Derby] came to churche to morning Prayer ... There was manye thinges done & pastymes made as A morres daunce over & besides the premisses which were all so orderlye & trymlie handled as was to the great lykinge & pleasure of the said right honorable erle The lyke wherof was never sene or knowen to be done in this said towne of Liuerpole ...
(George 1991, 43; see also Twemlow 1935)

Do these sources basically support one another or not? And do they suggest that Stubbes's account fits a typical pattern? All three give some indication that at that time morris dancing was performed on church property, but there are numerous differences as well. In Huntley and Cranoe the church superiors took legal action against the dance, whereas in Liverpool it was performed expressly with the approval of one of the most senior nobles in the land. At Cranoe there is no absolute statement that morris dancers actually danced on the occasion that caused the indictment. The charge involves allowing puppet plays; it is the conditions of discharge that mention morris dancing. At Liverpool it is not entirely clear whether the dance actually entered church property, or was performed in streets nearby. The Huntley reference mentions a May Lord accompanying the dance and the others do not. Then there is the fact that the references come from three distinct regions of the country. Taken altogether then, these references are arguably as distinct as they are similar.

To solve this problem I devised a method for comparing dance sources on a point-by-point basis. The essence of the approach was that references could be fractionally distilled into separate parts, and these parts could be recorded under a series of separate general headings (Setting, Group Structure, Music, etc) each with a number of subheadings for greater specificity. I presented this system in *Morris and Matachin: A Study in Comparative Choreography* (1984), using a limited set of data to show its value.

As my archive of early morris sources grew, it was clear that the original system was inadequate for the kind and range of data accumulating. So I constructed a new system that had the old one at heart but was considerably expanded. Then began my collaboration with Heaney, which resulted in further refinements and elaborations on his suggestion. What resulted became the core of our indexing system for the early morris database, published as *Annals of Early Morris* (Heaney and Forrest 1991). For a detailed analysis of this indexing system, the reader should consult the original work. However I present its outline here – each of the subheadings is more or less self-explanatory – to demonstrate some of its research potential:

Header
a. date of source
b. date of dance
c. place of dance
d. home of performers

A. Nomenclature
a. morris, b. Moorish, c. morisk, d. morisco, e. other, f. unnamed

B. Setting
a. royal/noble patronage, b. guild sponsored, c. borough sponsored, d. mayor present, e. part of pageant, f. part of procession, g. annual feast/festival, h. special feast/festival, i. stage play/performance, j. church sponsored/church ale, k. non-church/Whitsun ale, l. maypole present

C. Dance Types
a. round dance w/o central focus, b. dance round central lady, c. dance around maypole, d. processional, e. double file, f. single file, g. male and female couples, h. combative, i. solo jig, j. other

D. Elements of the dance
a. figures indicated, b. postures indicated, c. arm/hand movements indicated, d. foot/leg movements indicated, e. other movements indicated

E. Accompaniment
a. pipe and tabor, b. fiddle, c. drum, d. bagpipes, e. other instruments

F. Appurtenances
a. coats/jackets, b. shirts, c. hats, d. shoes, e. bells, f. baldrics, g. sashes/scarves, h. belts, i. ribbons, j. handkerchiefs/napkins, k. feathers, l. sticks, m. swords/weapons, n. lady's costume, o. fool's costume p. hobby horse costume, q. other costume elements (specified), r. other costume elements (unspecified)

G. Characters of the Performance
a. morris dancers, b. fool/vice/squire, c. lady, d. collector, e. sword-bearer, f. flag-bearer, g. whiffler, h. musician, i. hobby horse, j. Robin Hood, k. Maid Marian, l. Little John, m. Friar Tuck, n. Moor, o. giant, p. Lord of Misrule/May Lord/Abbot of Unreason, q. Queen of the May/May Lady, r. other nondancing supernumeraries, s. other dancers

H. Identity of the Performers
a. named persons, b. person identified by status, c. dancers identified as women

I. Type of Venue
a. court/noble's estate, b. guildhall/special group's premises, c. church property, d. urban streets, e. public house, f. out of doors in village, g. hilltop/open country, h. private house, i. unlocalized.

J. Type of Date
a. single dated performance, b. month and/or year stated, c. movable feast, d. season, e. repeated event, f. undated event, g. not a datable event

K. Form of Source
a. iconic, b. music notation, c. dance notation, d. an entertainment, e. interlude/masque, f. play, g. ballad/song, h. poem, i. prose fiction, [j. - n. = polemic/sermon], j. attacks on, k. defences of, l. complaints, m. approval of, n. neutral, o. nonfiction work, [p.- y. = records], p. state, q. local, r. legal, s. prohibitions, t. licence, u. lawsuits, v. ecclesiastical, w. commercial, x. domestic, y. personal/diary, z. proposal/prospectus/advertisement.

L. Relation of source to data
a. direct eyewitness account, b. indirect account of actual performance, c. generalized account of several actual performances, d. general purportedly factual descriptions, e. figurative or comparative usage, f. translation, g. account of payment made or commercial transaction, h. account of property owned.

Each primary source can be combed for data and then coded according to whether individual items appear. Thus the Liverpool reference above can be coded as follows:

1577	(date of source)
1577–04–24	(date of dancing)
Liverpool, LANCASHIRE	(place of dance)
(not stated)	(home of dancers)

Aa (word 'morris' used)
Ba (nobility present)
Bc (borough sponsored)
Bg (annual festival)
Ic (dancing on church property)
Id (dancing on urban streets)
Ja (single dated event)
Kq (source from local records)
La (direct eyewitness account)

As such it is indexed for a wide variety of data, and can be compared with other sources. The other two sources can be coded (without all the explanatory parentheses) as follows:

1576
1576
Huntley, GLOUCESTERSHIRE
–

Aa Bj Gap Ic Jf Kuv Lb

1576
1576–07(or 08)
(Cranoe, LEICESTERSHIRE)
–

Aa Ic Jb Ksv

And Stubbes would be coded:

1583

—

—

—

Af Ecd Fegijq Gaipr Hb Ic Kj Lc

This system makes it much more straightforward to compare these sources (and all the others in the database) to decide whether they corroborate each other and, *for individual points*, whether they represent the database as a whole in this era. Concerning dancing on church property, for example, I examined all the sources in the archive covering a period fifteen years before and fifteen years after Stubbes (a total of 139 individual references). Of these, forty-two mention a specific venue, and these may be broken down as follows:

Ia. court/noble's estate	2
Ib. guildhall/special group's premises	0
Ic. church property	7
Id. urban streets	9
Ie. public house	2
If. out of doors in village	16
Ig. hilltop/open country	2
Ih. private house	4

This is not an atypical spread, showing diverse locations, with three (church property, urban streets, and village) making up the bulk of the references. I explore the problem of quantifying these data in more detail in chapter 2. Here it is sufficient to note that seven of the forty-two (or approximately 16.7 per cent) refer to dancing on church property; thus Stubbes represents a significant minority. Taking several other of Stubbes's statements I discovered that thirty-five of the references in the period mention costume items and, of these, twenty-five (71.4 per cent) refer to bells explicitly, and none refer to handkerchiefs. So in some areas he is highly representative, and in others, hardly at all.

A significant problem with quantifying representativeness using percentages, however, is that it assumes the underlying archive is exhaustive or, at least, is a fair sample of the references to morris dancing. Unfortunately there is no way to know whether this is true, although the larger the body of sources, the more likely it is to be so. And there are reasons to suppose the opposite, that is, that it is skewed in some ways. Without scanning every piece of writing in English it is impossible to assert that any archive is complete. The only reason that the earliest reference to morris in England is 1458 is that no one has found an earlier; but it could exist. The problem is knowing where to look.

Borough account books are a good source in the sixteenth century but they are long, often highly detailed, and written in a script that is difficult to read with any speed. And there were a lot of boroughs. No single researcher could work through them all in a lifetime. Instead, primary research often concentrates on 'likely' boroughs at 'likely' times of the year. But this involves a fallacy, labelled *presentism* by one historian (Fischer 1970, 135–40). Likely boroughs are those in an area where morris dancing has been performed in more recent years, and likely times of year are those that are still popular. So the diligent worker goes to Oxford, say, or Gloucester (centres of a well-established modern morris tradition) and combs records covering Whitsun (their usual time of appearance). This search turns up either something – which suggests that the tradition is long-standing and stable – or nothing – which gives the imagination much more scope. In either case, the past is being controlled by the view from the present. While there was nothing happening in Oxford there might have been a thriving tradition in Reading, and though Gloucester may have been bereft of dancers at Whitsun they might have been thick underfoot at Christmas.

Fortunately morris references are turned up in many other ways. Most commonly they appear while researchers are exploring other topics, such as, civil and canon law, agrarian reform, or the theatre. Although these investigators may each have their own forms of historical tunnel-vision they are not limited by those of the morris dance researcher, and so could well discover the references in Reading or at Christmas.[1] Even so, the methods can still be hit-or-miss, and it is not beyond the bounds of possibility that whole realms of morris history lie undiscovered. The only riposte that can be made to such an accusation is a plea of sheer volume. The current early morris archive has close to 800 references covering 1458 to 1750 (see Heaney and Forrest 1991). As such, some claim can be made for its overall representativeness, even though it is undoubtedly far from exhaustive.

SERIATION

The original technique of seriation on which mine is based was invented by James Ford (Ford 1962) and further tested and exploited by James Deetz (Deetz 1967). Its purpose was to solve a common archaeological problem, namely, how to give relative dates to assemblages of artefacts when the stratigraphy is confused, and when other forms of dating are inapplicable. The basic premise of the method is that an innovation does not abruptly supersede an old habit; rather, the one replaces the other slowly. The succession of innovations can be given graphic form using a kind of horizontal bar graph, where the bars represent not absolute numbers of items but percentages of the total assemblage for a particular time period. Figure 50 is reproduced from the experimental work of Edwin Dethlefsen and James Deetz (Dethlefsen and Deetz 1966) and demonstrates the graphing process, in this case used to illustrate a straightforward example of the succession of styles of gravestones.

There are three columns, representing three patterns of incising on gravestones from a cemetery in Stoneham, Massachusetts: Death's Head, Cherub, and Urn and Willow. The vertical axis is a time line broken up into ten-year units. Each ten year period is represented by one or more horizontal bars, the combined width of which is always the same (i.e., representing 100 per cent), but may be broken up in different proportions. Absolute numbers are *not* represented. So, at the start of the sequence (1720–9) Death's Head is the only style that shows up and, therefore, is represented as the only horizontal bar on the graph. In the next period (1730–9) Death's Head is still the only style in the sample, and so is represented by a bar *of the same width*, it is still 100 per cent of the sample even though there may have actually been twenty gravestones in the first sample and sixty in the second. Death's Head remains the only style until the 1760–9 period, when a few Cherub stones show up. Now the two horizontal bars show the relative proportions of the two styles. Cherub rises to a peak width in 1780–9 and then dwindles to nothing as Urn and Willow takes over.

This graph was developed by Dethlefsen and Deetz as a test case to show an ideal example of the succession of innovations. What it demonstrates in archetypical form is the so-called battleship curve (traced with a dotted line on the Cherub column) – the slow acceptance of an innovation which eventually reaches a peak value followed by a decline as another innovation supersedes it.[2] Here, of course, there are no problems of stratigraphy, and absolute dates are assured – they are carved right on the stones themselves! This is simply an experimental case illustrating the known so that the unknown may be extrapolated from it.

The early morris database presents a different kind of seriation question for which my use of graphic methods provides one solution. Absolute dates are available, and the relative proportions of variables (such as type of venue) can easily be computed for suitable units of time. What is not known is whether a particular variable represents a sequence of innovations over time or constantly simultaneous alternatives – that is, graphs must be drawn to see if battleship curves (or any other kind of curves with bulges in them) show up *at all*. In this way it can be discovered whether morris in royal courts, say, was popular around the same time as dancing in urban streets, or whether one supplanted the other as an innovation. There is no a priori reason for supposing that either is, of necessity, the case. And if one did succeed the other, some grasp of the time spans involved in the increase, peak, and decrease of popularity can be gained through these graphic methods.

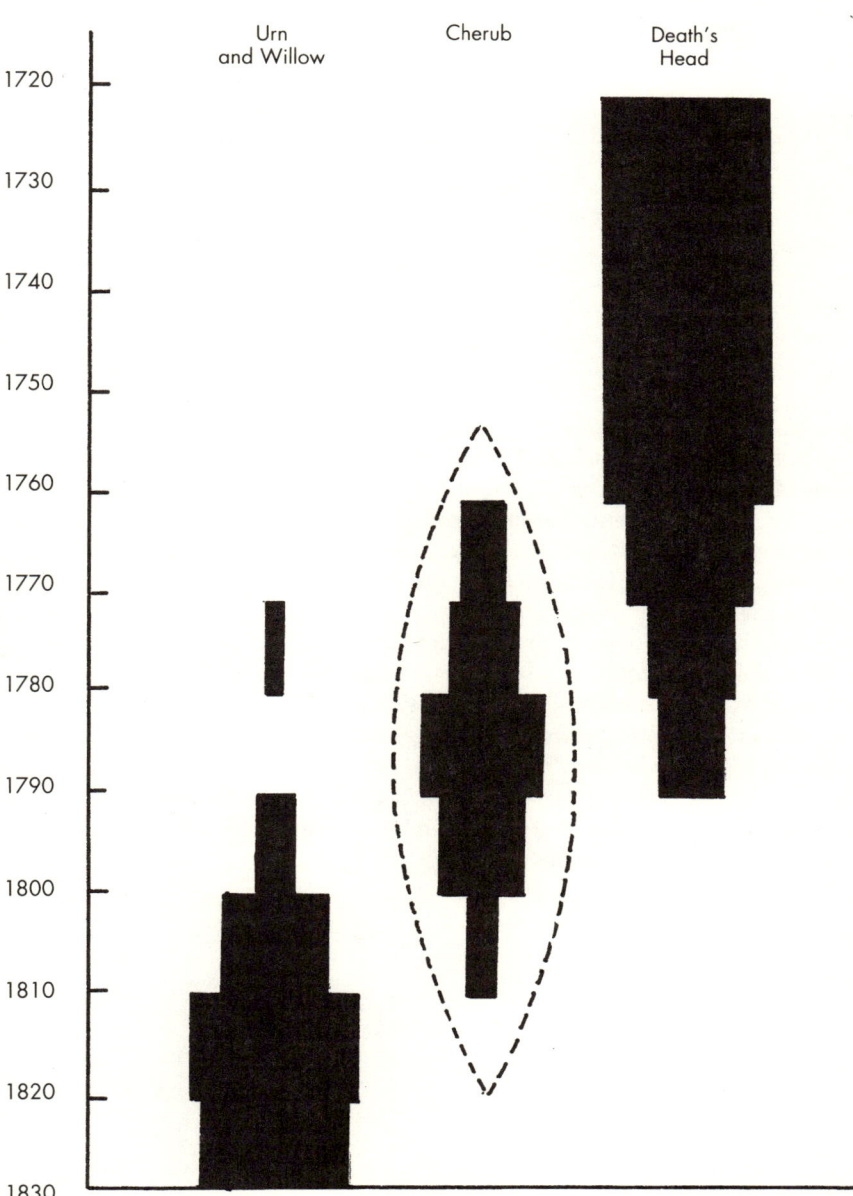

Figure 50: New England graves seriation

Visitation Articles Banning Morris

As noted in chapter 7, visitation articles in the sixteenth and seventeenth centuries copied freely from one another. The following tabulation traces this copying to give some idea of the process, and to sound a caution concerning how visitation articles should be used as evidence for the existence of morris dancing in a region. Articles that have been copied numerous times over a wide region (as, for example, the Restoration model) are less likely to indicate the presence of an active tradition than new, newly edited, or unique articles.

I have built a typology of these articles that reflects the pattern of copying and editing. Each type represents a brand new wording for the prohibition. Type 1, for example, was the text originally created by Edmund Grindal for York Province. The tree diagram shows the progress of editing over the years. Each text has a numeral code that represents its place in the tree diagram. Thus 1 is the original text of type 1; 1.1 is the first variant of 1, and 1.2 is the second; 1.1.1 is the first variant of type 1.1, and so on. Following the tree diagrams are examples of each text, with explanations concerning variations.

TYPE 1 TEXT

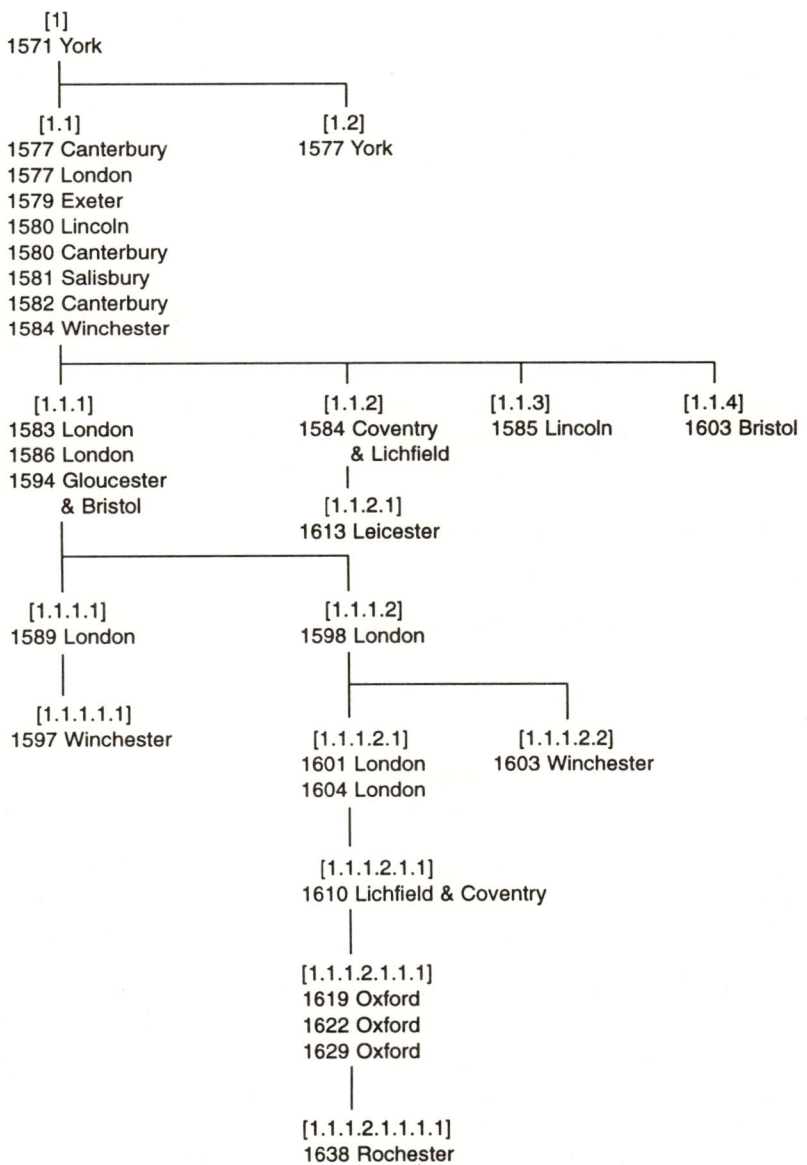

[1]
1571 York

[1.1]
1577 Canterbury
1577 London
1579 Exeter
1580 Lincoln
1580 Canterbury
1581 Salisbury
1582 Canterbury
1584 Winchester

[1.2]
1577 York

[1.1.1]
1583 London
1586 London
1594 Gloucester
& Bristol

[1.1.2]
1584 Coventry
& Lichfield

[1.1.2.1]
1613 Leicester

[1.1.3]
1585 Lincoln

[1.1.4]
1603 Bristol

[1.1.1.1]
1589 London

[1.1.1.2]
1598 London

[1.1.1.1.1]
1597 Winchester

[1.1.1.2.1]
1601 London
1604 London

[1.1.1.2.2]
1603 Winchester

[1.1.1.2.1.1]
1610 Lichfield & Coventry

[1.1.1.2.1.1.1]
1619 Oxford
1622 Oxford
1629 Oxford

[1.1.1.2.1.1.1.1]
1638 Rochester

TYPE 1 Text first created by Edmund Grindal.
[1571 York]
Whether the minister and churchwardens have suffered any Lords of Misrule, or
Summer Lords or ladies, or any disguised persons, or others, in Christmas, or at May
games, or any Morris-dancers or others at rush bearings, or at any other times, to
come unreverently into the Church or churchyard, and there to dance, or play any
unseemly parts with scoffs, jests, wanton gestures or ribald talk, namely in the time
of Common Prayer. And what they be that commit such disorder, or accompany
or maintain them?

TYPE 1.1 Omission of 'or others at rush bearings' making the text ungrammatical.
[1577 Canterbury]
Whether the Minister & Churchwardens have suffered any Lords of Misrule, or
summer Lords, or Ladies, or any disguised persons, or others in Christmas, or at May
games, or any Morrice dauncers, or at any other times, to come unreverently into
the church or churchyard & there to daunce, or play any unseemely parts, with scoffes,
jeastes, wanton gestures, or ribald talke, namely in the time of common prayer. And
what they be that committ such disorder, or accompanie or maintayne them.

TYPE 1.2 Drastic abbreviation of TYPE 1 [unique]
[1577 York Province]
Whether any morice-dauncers, rishe bearers, or any others have come unreuerntly
into the church or churchyard, and there daunced, or played any unseemely [part...].

TYPE 1.1.1 Correction of the grammatical error by a shift of phrases and shift of the
last two verbs into past tense.
[1583 London]
Whether the minister & churchwardens have suffered any Lords of misrule: or sommer Lords or Ladies, or any disguised persons, or others, or maygames, or any Morice
dauncers at Christmas, or at any other tymes to come vnreverently into the church
or churchyard, & there to daunce, or play any vnseemely parts, with scoffes, ieastes,
wanton ieastures, or ribaulde talke, especially in the time of common prayer, and
what they be that commit suche disorder, or accompanied or mayntayned them.

TYPE 1.1.2 Not derived from 1.1.1 but directly from 1.1
[1584 Coventry & Lichfield]
Whether the minister or churchwardens have suffered any Lords of Misrule, or
Summer Lords or Ladies, or any disguised persons, or Morris-dancers or others at
Christmas, or any time in Summer, to come unreverently piping, dancing or play-
ing in church or churchyard, with unseemly scoffs, jests, ribaldry, or at any other

place and time, namely in time of Divine Service or sermons; and what they be that commit such disorders, or accompany or maintain them?

TYPE 1.1.2.1 Several omissions from TYPE 1.1.2 – note especially the corruption of the last phrase, perhaps through viva voce dictation.
[1613 Archdeaconry of Leicester]
Whether the Minister or Church-wardens have suffered any Lords of Misrule, or Summer Lords or Ladies, or any disguised persons, as morris-dancers, to come unreverently piping, dancing or playing in the Church, or Church-yard, with unseemely scoffes, jests, or ribaulderie, in time of Divine Service or Sermons, and what they bee that commit such disorders, and the company that maintaineth them.

TYPE 1.1.3 Missing 'or others' after 'disguised person'
[1585 Lincoln]
Whether your Minister and Church-wardens haue suffred any Lords of misrule, or sommer Lords, or Ladies or any disguised person in Christmas, or at maigames, or morris dancers or at any other time, to come vnreuerently into the Churchyard, and there to daunce or play any vnsemely part with scoffs, iestes, wanton gestures, or ribald talk, namely in time of common praier: and what they bee that commit such disorder, or accompany or maintaine them.

TYPE 1.1.4 Series of omissions from TYPE 1.1
[1603 Bristol]
Whether the Minister and Church-wardens, have suffered any Lords of Mis-rule, or Summer-Lords, or Ladies, or any disguised persons, to may-games morishdances, or the like, to come unreverently into the church, or churchyard, & there to dance, or play any unseemely parts, wt scofes, jestes, wanton gestures, or ribauld talke, especially in the time of common praier? ...

TYPE 1.1.1.1 Omission of numerous phrases from the London text of 1583/86
[1589 London]
Whether the Minister and Churchwardens have suffered any Lords of misrule, or Summer Lords, or Ladies, or anie disguised persons, or May games, or anie morrice dancers at anie times to come unreverentlie into the Church or Churchyard and there to dance or play, especially in the time of common praier: and what they be that commit such disorder: or that accompanied or mainteined them.

TYPE 1.1.1.1.1 Further omissions from 1.1.1.1 at the end.
[1597 Winchester]
Item, Whether your Minister and church-wardens haue suffered anie Lord of misrule or Summer Lord or Ladies, or anie disguised persons, or May-games, or anie Morice

dancers at any time to come vnreuerently into the church or churchyard and there to dance or play, especially in the time of common praier, seruice, or sermon.

TYPE 1.1.1.2 Seems to be derived by omissions (except the last phrase) from TYPE 1.1.1
[1598 London]
Whether the minister and churchwardens have suffered anie lord of mis-rule, or summer lord or ladies, or any disguised persons, any players, or maie-games, or any moris dauncers, at any time to come vnreuerently into the church or churchyarde, and there to daunce or play any vnseemely partes, or shew themselues disguised in the time of common prayer, and what they be that commit such disorder, or that accompanied or maintained them, or any playes to be played in the church.

TYPE 1.1.1.2.1 Phrase 'any unseemly parts' omitted
[1601 London]
Whether the minister and churchwardens have suffered anye lords of mis-rule, or summer lord or ladies, or any disguised persons, any players, or maie-games, or any moris-dauncers, at any time to come unreverently into the church or churchyard, and there to daunce or play, or shew themselves dssguised [sic] in the time of common prayer, & what they be that commit such disorder, or accompanied or maintained them, or any playes to be played in the church.

TYPE 1.1.1.2.2 Several omissions from TYPE 1.1.1.2
[1603 Winchester]
Item, whether your Minister and Church-wardens have suffered any lord of misrule or summer Lords or ladies, or any disguised persons, or May-games, or morice dancers, at any time to come unreverently into the church or churchyard, and there to daunce or play, in the time of common Praier, Service, or Sermon uppon the Saboath day?

TYPE 1.1.1.2.1.1 'Feastes &c' added to the preamble of 1.1.1.2.1
[1610 Lichfield & Coventry]
Whether the Minsters and Church-wardens haue suffered any Feastes, Banquets, Churchales, or Drinkinges in the Church, or any Lords of Misrule, or Summer Lord or Lady, or any disguised persons: any Players, or May-games, or any Moris dauncers at any time to come vnreuerently into the Church or Church-yarde, and there to daunce or play, or shew themselues disguised in the time of common prayer, and what they be that commit such disorder, or that accompanied or maintayned them, or any Playes to be played in the Church?

TYPE 1.1.1.2.1.1.1 Two changes to TYPE 1.1.1.2.1.1 from which it derives: the syntactic change 'players of May games,' and omission of 'in the time of common prayer'

[1619 Oxford]
Whether the Minister & Churchwardens have suffered any Feastes, Banquets, Churchales, or Drinkings in the Church, or any Lords of Misrule, or Sommer Lord or Lady, or any disguised persons; and players of May games, or any Moris-dancers, at any time to come unreverently into the Church or Church-yard, and there to dance or play, or shew themselves disguised, and what they be that commit such disorder, or that accompanied or maintained them: or any Plaies to be plaied in the Church?

TYPE 1.1.1.2.1.1.1.1 Last line changed from TYPE 1.1.1.2.1.1.1 and some slight additions
[1638 Rochester]
Whether the Minister and Churchwardens have suffered any Fea[...] banquet church-ale or drinking [.....] [s]ummer Lord or Ladie or any disguised persons, & players of May-games [or a]ny Morrisdancers, at any time to come irrevently into the Church or [Chu]rch-yeard, and there to dance or play, or shew themselves disguised, and [wh]at they be that commit such disorder, or that accompanied or maintained [the]m, or any Playes disorders or prophanations to be commited in th [Chu]rch?

TYPE 2 TEXT

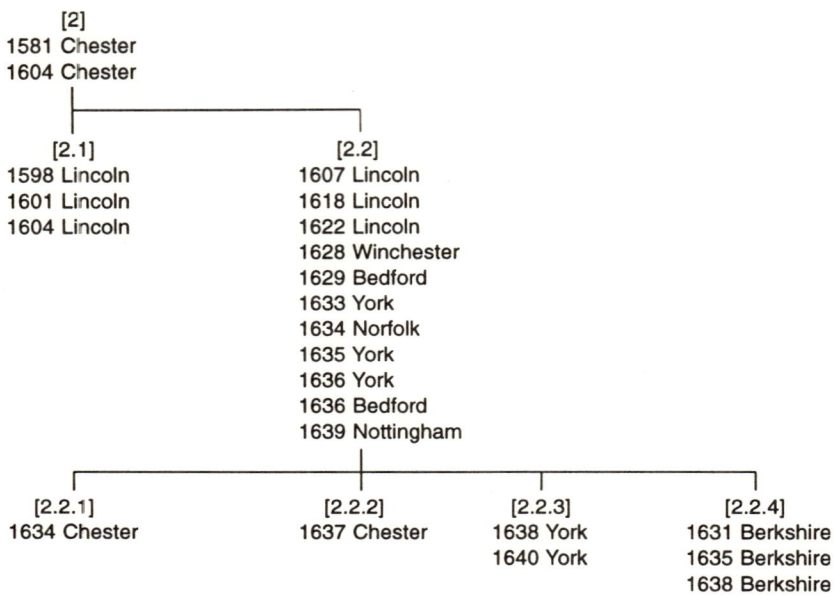

```
              [2]
          1581 Chester
          1604 Chester
               |
      _____
     |                           |
   [2.1]                       [2.2]
1598 Lincoln               1607 Lincoln
1601 Lincoln               1618 Lincoln
1604 Lincoln               1622 Lincoln
                           1628 Winchester
                           1629 Bedford
                           1633 York
                           1634 Norfolk
                           1635 York
                           1636 York
                           1636 Bedford
                           1639 Nottingham
```

```
  _____
 |                    |                |               |
[2.2.1]             [2.2.2]          [2.2.3]         [2.2.4]
1634 Chester        1637 Chester     1638 York       1631 Berkshire
                                     1640 York       1635 Berkshire
                                                     1638 Berkshire
```

TYPE 2 Text first created by William Chaderton
[1581 Chester]
Whether … your said church, chapel or churchyard be abused or profaned by any un-lawful or unseemly act, game, or exercise, as by Lords of Misrule, Summer lords or ladies, pipers, rushbearers, Morris dancers, pedlars, bearwards, and such like; then through whose default, and what be the names of the offenders in that behalf?

TYPE 2.1 Addition of 'bowlers' to the list
[1598 Lincoln]
First, whether … your said Church, Chappell, or Churchyard, be abused or pro-phaned by any vnlawful or vnseemly act, game, or exercise, as by lords of misrule, sommer lords, or ladies, pipers, rush-bearers, morrice-dancers, pedlers, bowlers, bearewards, and such like. Then thorough whose default and what be the names of the offenders in that behalfe.

TYPE 2.2 Based directly on TYPE 2, and still written by Chaderton, but with signi-ficant additions to the list suggesting actual abuses? The summer lady has been dropped.

[1607 Lincoln]
Whether hath your Church or churchyard bin abused and prophaned by any fighting, chiding, brawling or quarrelling, any playes, lords of misrule, sommer Lords, Morrisse dauncers, pedlers, bowlers, berewards, butchers, feastes, scooles, temporall courts, or Leetes, lay Iuries, musters, or other prophane vsage in your Church or Churchyard, any bells superstitiously rong on holy daies, or their Eues, or at any other time without good cause, allowed by the minister, and churchwardens; haue any trees been felled in your churchyard, and by whome?

TYPE 2.2.1 Slight additions to 2.2
[1634 Chester]
Item, whether hath your Church or Chappel, Church-yard, or Chappel-yard beene abused or profaned by any fighting, quarelling, chiding, brawling, or by any Plaies, Lords of mis-rule, Summer Lords, Morris-dancers, Pedlers, Bowlers, Beare-wards, Feasts, Schooles, Temporall Courts, or Leets, Laie-Juries, Musters, or any other profane usage whatsoever?

TYPE 2.2.2 Some omissions from 2.2 and reordering of the list
[1637 Chester]
Hath your church or churchyard been defiled by … fighting, quarrelling, chiding, brawling, Beare-baiting, or by any playes, Lords of misrule, Morice-dancers, Pedlers, Bowlers, or of any feasts Schooles, Temporall Courts, Mustars, Faires, or Markets been kept therin … ?

TYPE 2.2.3 Change: 'and plays' instead of 'any plays'
[1638 York]
Whether hath your Church or Church-yarde beene abused and prophaned by any fighting, chiding, brawling or quarrelling and plays, Lords of misrule, summer Lords, morris-dancers, pedlers, bowlers, bearewards, butchers, feastes, schooles, temporall courts, or Leets, Lay Juries musters, or other prophane vsage in your Church or Church-yard … ?

TYPE 2.2.4 Some additions and omissions to the list in 2.2
[1631 Archdeaconry of Berkshire]
Whether have your Church, Church porch or Church yeard beene prophaned by any plaies, feasts, banquets, church-ales, Maygames, Morricedancings, drinkings, temporall courts or Leets, Layjuries, Musters, Fayres, Markets, selling of wares, or any unlawfull Games, as Bowling, tennis, or the like?

TYPE 3 TEXT

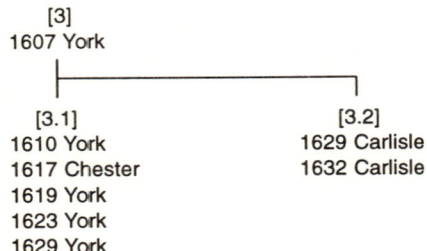

        [3]
1607 York

        [3.1]   [3.2]
1610 York   1629 Carlisle
1617 Chester   1632 Carlisle
1619 York
1623 York
1629 York

TYPE 3 Text first created by Tobias Matthew
[1607 Metropolitanate of York]
Item, Whether are there within your saide parish or Chappellry any Rush bearings,
Bull-baytings, Beare-baitings, May-games, Morrice-dances, Ailes, or any such like
prophane pastimes or other godly exercises.

TYPE 3.1 Additions to the final phrase in 3
[1610 York]
Item. Whether are there within your said Parish or Chappelry any Rush bearings,
Bull-baytings, Beare-baytings, May-gaimes, Morice-dances, Ales, or any such like
prophane pastimes or assemblies on the Sabboth, to the hindrance of Prayers, Sermons, or other godly exercises.

TYPE 3.2 Addition of 'marriage offerings'
[1629 Carlisle]
Whether are there within your said Parish or Chappelrie, any rush-bearing, bull-
baitings, beare baitings, may-games, morice-dances, marriage offerings, ales, or any
such like prophane pastimes or assemblies on the Sabboth.

TYPE 4 (unique)
[1638 Norwich]
Concerning the Church-yard ... [not to be used for trade] Much lesse is it to be
unhallowed with dancings, morises, meetings at Easter, drinkings, Whitsun-ales,
Midsummer-merrymakes, or the like, nor by stool-ball, foot-ball, wrastlings, wasters,
or boyes sports. If such abuse hath been comitted, say by whom, whose procure-
ment, countenance or abetting.

TYPE 5 All Restoration forms

Do you permit no Minstrels, no Moris-dancers, no Doggs, Hawks, or Hounds to be brought or come into your Church, to the disturbance of the Congregation?

APPENDIX C

Mr Isaac's Morris 1716

Transcription from Feuillet notation (Isaac 1716) by Allan Terry

The following transcribes the man's part. The woman's part generally mirrors the man's except where shown. The man and woman start facing front (the Presence), man on the left of the woman. Both start in fourth position with inside foot pointed back (man's right, woman's left).

Performers would have been expected to decide on their own arm movements within the confines of the period's style. Arms are usually specified only to the extent of taking and dropping of hands. This dance is unusual in the 'arms A Kimbo' section which provides an explicit 'folk' flavour. Terry's notes appear within [   ].

1. Turn quarter to face partner and take both hands. Bend/step to second right and immediately slide left across in front. Step right to second again and immediately slide left behind right. A kind of grapevine.
   Timing: & [turn, take both hands]; 1&, –, 3&, –

2. Bend/step right to second. Bend/step left to second, going through first. Turn quarter left [to face up] and step right into fourth behind left. A kind of pas de bourrée. [Note he shows you the final foot position just before you drop hands.]
   Timing: 1, 2, 3, –
   [It is written that you drop outside hands in the next bar, but it would be better do it before the last step in the last bar.]

3. Contretemps ballonné onto left. Timing: 1, –, 3, –

4. Ballonné onto right.

5. Like bar 1.
   Turn quarter to face partner. Bend/step left to second and immediately slide right in front.

Take outside hands [so you now are holding both again].
Step left to side, immediately slide right behind.

6. Step left to second [note probably typo in man's part, no bend/place written].
Step right to second on other side, going through first.
Bring left foot into fourth with left behind.
Drop outside hands [man's right].

7. Hop on left while turning a quarter turn to right and bringing right foot around to nice open position. Leave right in air.
Jeté onto right. [A ballonné with an initial turn.]

8. Moving forward [but away from Presence] take two steps of pas de bourrée.
Drop hands.
Jump half around to the left [left shoulder back] to land in first facing up.

9. Bend/step right to second, close left behind in third.
Jeté right into 2nd

10. Bend/step left, close right behind into third, step left again.

11. Hop on right and step as in contretemps de gavotte, starting to go around a curve to the left. Jeté with left, by this point directly away from partner.

12. Jeté into first, partly continuing the track and partly doing quarter turn to left, so end facing partner. Pause [a rest is notated].

13. Pas de bourrée with first step away from partner to third behind, and the other two steps forward. The last step ends with the right heel on the ground and the toe pointed up.

14. Hop on left bringing right back in the air.
Two quick steps forward with bend/place on the first.

15. Cut right under left like a chassé but end with left in the air and a bit to the side.
Bend on right, place left in third behind right, rise, and quickly step forward on right.

16. Same as 15 but start with simple step forward on left ending heel down and toe up. |
The man's track passes to his right of the woman and heads off diagonally to the corner of the room

17. Bend on right, turn quarter right to face partner right shoulder to right, step sideways with left, and rise.
Step into second with right.
Turn quarter more to left to jeté backwards along the track away from the partner.

18. A turning pas de bourrée. Bend/step backward with right.
Turn quarter left to step into second with left.
Turn another quarter left to step forward along the track with right foot.

19. Bend/step forward left, close into third behind with right.
Jeté forward onto left.

20. Bend/step forward with quick right and left.
    Jeté around with a half turn to the right to end in first position facing back the way you came.
21. Continue another half turn to the right as you step with left into coupé; lift right to side in air.
22. Pas de bourrée around a track that turns half around to right.
23. A simple bend/step forward.
24. Coupé into assemblé. Right forward, then close with left.
25. [Should be face to face with partner.] Take both hands. Pas de rigaudon together.
26. [the bend, spring, pause of the rigodoun end].
27. Drop hands.
    Bend and rise, extending left to second in air.
    Bend and step left back.
28. Bend and rise, extending right to second in air.
    Bend and step right back. |
29. Couples are facing and at a slight offset from up and down the room.
    Half pirouette to the right, on the toes and remaining there
30. Step out of this position with a quarter turn to the right [which ends up in front] into a pas de bourrée that is starting around a clockwise circular track.
31. Ballonné onto left.
32. Pas de bourrée [partners have now switched places].
33. Jeté into fourth with left in front. There is a quarter turn to the right [clockwise] before landing and an implicit extra quarter turn from the direction of the track. Land in plié. The partners are now facing.
    Hop on left with half turn outward to right. Land back to partner with right foot raised in second. [The woman's part is written differently from the man's (has left foot raised behind) and may be a typo. The man's part makes more physical sense.]
34. Turn a quarter right into pas de bourrée along the track: right to the side, cross left in front, right to second again.
35. Contretemps de gavotte to the side. Hopping from second, extend to second then cross left in front of right for the step.
36. Contretemps de gavotte again.
37. Plié, turn a quarter to the right to face along the track, bend/step immediately behind the right foot with the left. [This might not be one of the five standard positions due to the turn.] Step forward right and then left.
38. Another one of those odd bourrées. Step behind left with right. [Note that the notated foot position is turned slightly inward. It seems to be a way to turn/redirect slightly in place.] Step along track left and right.
39. Turning contretemps de gavotte. Hop on right, then do half turn as you step left

with your back to the track. Step right out of the circle and close left to right in first. You are facing down the hall.

Woman: closes into third, not first.

40. At this point, the man has done about a one and a quarter turn around the centre of the hall and is at the left side [seen from facing the Presence].

Both: turn quarter left and bend/step back with right foot.

Jeté backwards into assemblé, with a bit of a gesture with the left foot. |

41. Turn quarter right while stepping into second with left foot and immediately slide right across left in front.

Step into second with left again and immediately slide right behind.

42. Jeté [basically in place] onto left in first position, still facing down the hall. Pause. 'Set the Arms A Kimbo' [fists on waist, palms facing back?].

43. Plié, spring up and turn half to left. Pause.

44. Start around a track mostly to the right. Bend/step diagonally forward onto right into second. Slide left across in front.

45. Take hands in an allemande-like hold. Stand side by side, facing in opposite directions, with the woman on the man's right. The man's left takes the woman's right behind his back while his right extends to his right side to take her left behind her back.

46. Ballonné onto left but continuing clockwise turn with partner.

47. Release arms.

Pas de bourrée continuing around circle.

48. Turn quarter right to face up the hall on the next step. While doing this, leave the right foot in a raised second.

Jeté onto right backward with nice round gesture into assemblé. |

49. You are now three quarters around the hall from the start of the last page [measure 41] and basically do the same thing around the other way as the last page.

Turn quarter left to step into second with the right and immediately slide left in front.

Step right into second again while sliding left behind.

50. Put arms akimbo.

Jeté with right around into assemblé, still facing side of hall. Pause

51. Plié, spring, turn half right, land, pause.

52. Now start around a counterclockwise track. Turn quarter to right so back is to centre and step into second with left.

Slide left across right in front.

53. Take arms as above but facing the other way.

Ballonné onto left.

54. Balonné onto right.

55. Continue counterclockwise turn around partner with pas de bourrée. Drop arms [note in last page he dropped them before the bourrée].

56. Turn quarter left and step into second [facing down], leaving the left foot in a raised second.
Jeté backward onto left into assemblé facing partner. |

57. Take hands.
Pas de bourrée starting right along a slightly clockwise track.

58. Drop hands.
Contretemps de gavotte hop and step. There is quarter turn to the right after the hop and the step follows a track that continues turning another quarter. Step right into second. Close left to behind right in third with the left toe only on the ground.

59. Take hands again.
Pas de bourrée starting left in a slight counterclockwise track.

60. Drop hands.
Contretemps de gavotte hop and step, turning half left by the end.
Step left and slightly back into second. Close right behind left into fifth. Weight is on both feet.
[These four measures seem like a kind of gypsy or siding]

61. Bend, bring left around to behind right into fifth on point.
Pirouette half to right remaining on the toes.

62. From new orientation, bring right around to behind left in fifth on point. Pirouette half to left again.

63. Turn quarter right and bend/step sideways right [man steps up hall crossing right over left]. Turn another quarter right and take the next step. Continues same track.
Jeté backwards [still along same direction] onto right.

64. Pas de bourrée starting with bend/step backward with left. Turn quarter right with next two steps to end facing along the track. |

65. Contretemps de gavotte hop right into second and step. Third step crosses left behind right and starts around a clockwise-turning track.

66. Pas de bourrée that follows a track that turns over quarter to right.
First step turns quarter right, from there follow the track.

67. Contretemps de gavotte hop, turn quarter right, and step sideways onto left.
Next step sideways crosses left behind right

68. Turn quarter left and step with left.
Complete a half turn to left by jeté around with right into assemblé facing the recent track. |

69. Pas de bourrée starting towards partner but veering left at the end.
Take inside hands [man's right, woman's left] on the second step.

70. Pas de bourrée both going up the hall. Drop hands during third step.

71. Pas de sissonne with left in front then raising right [trailing foot].
You should be facing away from partner.
72. Turn quarter to right, jeté sideways into another pas de sissonne facing up the hall.
Right is in front of left, raise left.
73. [Does not show a quarter turn to right but you obviously must].
Pas de bourrée towards partner but veering right with last step.
Take new inside hands [man's left, woman's right] on second step.
74. Pas de bourrée, both going down the hall.
Drop hands.
75. Jump into pas de sissonne with half turn to left [to right for woman]. Left is behind right, left lifts.
76. Bend, turn half to left [away from partner] both step down the hall.
Turn quarter toward partner by extending right to second touching toe to floor.
77. Take both hands for a clockwise circle.
Jeté onto right. Bend and take two quick steps
78. Complete a turn with another jeté and two quick steps.
79. Bend/step towards partner with right and immediately close left behind in third.
Drop outside hands
Bend, turn quarter left to open out, short jeté sideways away from partner onto right foot immediately extending left into second raised. Both face forwards.
80. Drop remaining hands.
Accomplish a three quarters turn away from partner in half a measure with a pas de bourrée. Turn quarter away [left for man] and follow quickly with two steps around curving track. End facing.
Man: turn quarter left and bend/step towards partner into second. Slide left behind right into fourth.
Woman: Turn quarter right and bend/step towards partner into second. Slide right to left into assemblé.
Finis

Extant Churchwardens' Accounts

It is a perennial problem of scholarship in the early modern period to determine whether trends that appear in the existing data are a true representation of historical fact or simply an artefact of the presence or absence of pertinent documents. It is a legitimate question to ask whether the apparent rise and fall of interest in church ales and morris dancing from the late fifteenth century to the seventeenth century are genuine social trends, or merely a function of the existence of churchwardens' accounts documenting such events. The simplest way to address such a question is to chart the general existence of churchwardens' accounts. To do this I used data provided by Ronald Hutton in *The Rise and Fall of Merry England* (Hutton 1994) where he records the existence of all extant churchwardens' accounts by decade for our period.

Figure 51 graphs all of Hutton's data, and shows one clear trend. There is a steady rise in the number of account books available from the mid-fifteenth century onward. Therefore, any claim that a particular custom or event sponsored by the church steadily increased in popularity over this period must be treated with great caution. Such a trend may, indeed, be an artefact of the existence of suitable records. But a claim that a custom declined in popularity over this period must be treated seriously, and cannot simply be explained by the presence or absence of pertinent data.

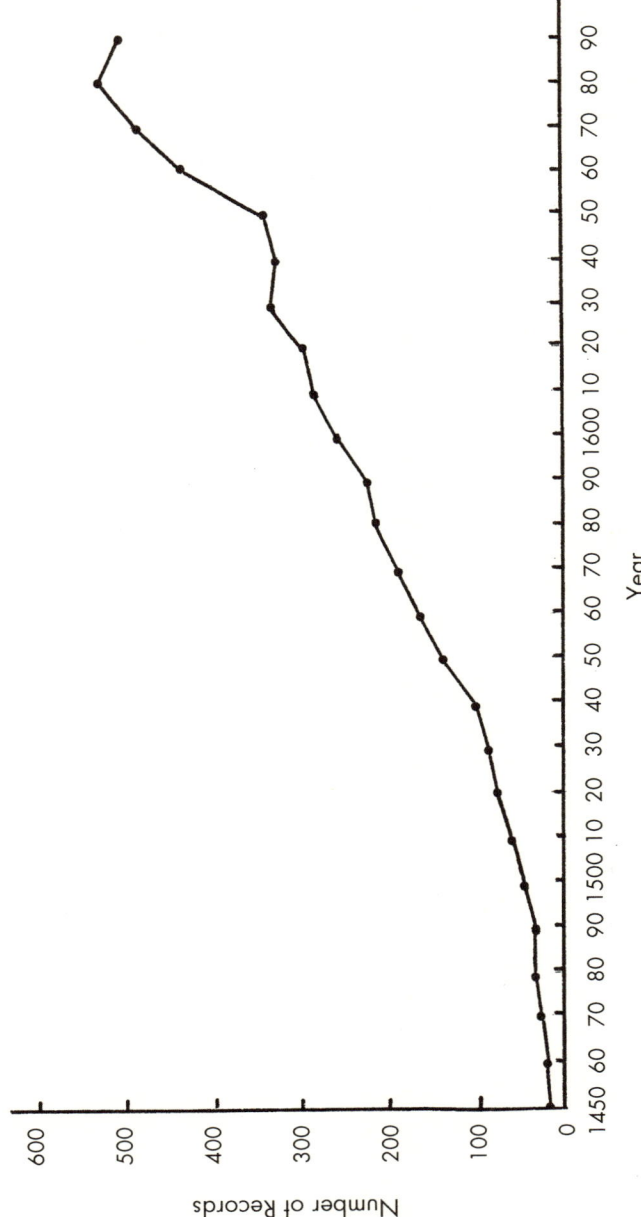

Figure 51: Number of extant churchwardens' accounts in the period of record (source Hutton 1994)

Notes

1 THEORIES OF ORIGIN

1 These arguments are ultimately based on the writings of Polydor Vergil, notably *De Rerum Inventoribus*, first published in 1502 and reprinted in various editions for over 100 years.

2 The orthography of primary texts is as close to the originals as modern standard type faces will allow, while also remaining clearly readable. I have generally omitted certain common manuscript characters (such as the 'es' mark, abbreviations for 'er,' and the like) and replaced them with their modern equivalents. Likewise I have sometimes replaced the characters thorn with 'th,' and yogh with 'gh,' 'y,' or 'w' as appropriate. In many cases I have had to rely on printed editions of manuscripts because of the loss or unavailability to me of the originals. Here I have generally followed the orthographic conventions of the editors, even though some inconsistency between texts has resulted. Quotations from REED volumes follow REED conventions: italics indicate editorial expansions and [ ] appear around cancellations in the original.

3 Ronald Hutton's *The Stations of the Sun* (Hutton 1996) is a refreshing antidote to these popular misunderstandings, and provides a solid compendium of the scholarship that is slowly turning the tide against romantic images of popular culture and tradition in England.

4 The clash of the Genesis and evolutionary models at the turn of the century cannot be underestimated in its cultural significance. Even today the battle between evolutionary biologists and evangelical Christians is far from over, with both sides understanding the immense power of theoretical paradigms.

2 THE CONTEXTS

1 Much of the basic analysis presented in this chapter appeared first in Forrest and Heaney 1991, although it is put to somewhat different use here. Regardless of usage, however,

the methodological ideas, particularly with regard to the 30 year maps, owe a debt to my collaboration with Heaney.

2 See chapter 8 for details.

3 EARLIEST REFERENCES

1 Unless expressly noted, the translations of foreign language originals are my own, and deliberately tend towards the literal. The translations include the original spellings of morisk and cognates in italics.

2 The word 'morisk' is a European cognate of 'morris.' As explored later (p 68–9) and in appendix A, morris and morisk may describe different kinds of performance but were frequently used with a degree of interchangeability.

3 All dates in the text are given in English style which is day-month-year. This usage avoids inconsistency between citations from primary documents and my text.

4 ROYAL COURT

1 There was a disguising in 1494 at Christmastide directed by Walter Alwyn (see record below), but the fact that the payment for the morris was made on 02–01–1494, and for the disguising on 15–02–1494 points to them being separate events under the direction of different men. If Alwyn had incorporated the morris into his disguising, it would have been more usual accounting practice of John Heron to have all of the costs parcelled together. However, it must at least be considered a possibility that the morris was part of the disguising, in which case this record would have to be removed from its present category.

2 Some care must be taken in the interpretation of this text because it is actually a reprint by John Stow of an earlier document whose date is not precisely known. The use of the term 'mumming' could, therefore, be an anachronism. On the other hand, there are well documented examples of courtly mumming less than sixty years later, so it is possible to accept the source, provisionally, as legitimate.

3 The full text may be found in Harleian MS 247, and is also cited in Welsford 1927, 38–9.

4 See Forrest 1984 for an extended analysis of the relationship between these two dances.

5 Atteláni, *men that with fowle mouthes, vnseemely speeches, disfigured faces, minike gestures and strange actions professe to procure laughter* (Florio 1611, 46) and Morésca, *a Morice, or Antique dance* (Florio 1611, 322).

6 See Lowe 1957, 81–2, for a partial list of iconic references throughout Europe.

7 See Tietze-Conrat 1957, 94–6, for a discussion of borrowing in images of European morisks.

8 See Mugnier 1887, 163, and Pansier 1919, 15–22, 49–51, for a longer discussion.

9 See Prunières 1914 for an examination of the contribution of the European morisk to early ballet.

10 It should also be noted that the morisk evolved in continental Europe into a number of diverse folk traditions that are beyond of the scope of this work.

5 URBAN STREETS

1 Stow attributes the MS to Mountgomery but the extant copy is unsigned.

2 For a somewhat different interpretation see Heaney 1989, 94.

3 The castle was perhaps the most popular image in Midsummer recorded in the guild records, in 1523 when he was sheriff and again in 1529 when he was mayor, Sir John Rudstone was provided by the drapers with a pageant of Saint Ursula in a castle; in 1535 the ironmongers provided their sheriff, William Denham, with a pageant of Denham castle; and in 1536 the drapers had a pageant of Monmouth castle for their sheriff, Humfrey Monmouth (see Robertson and Gordon 1954, 1–36).

4 The dance/drama was also taken by Spanish imperialists to new colonies in the sixteenth century where it became a fixture from Mexico to the Philippines.

5 This analogy was suggested to me by film historian Tom Gunning.

6 I surmise that the distinction between a drummer and taborer represents more than the size of their respective percussive instruments – although I have no doubt that a 'drum' was substantially larger than a 'tabor.' I believe, though, that the taborer was actually what is now called a 'pipe and taborer,' that is, a musician playing a three-holed pipe with the left hand and beating the tabor (slung over the left elbow) with the right. Documentary evidence is difficult to come by to support this surmise, but it should be noted that Will Kemp calls his musician, Thomas Slye, his 'taborer' (Kemp 1600, 3) and the accompanying woodcut indicates he plays the pipe and tabor (see figure 19, p 136).

7 For example, if eight dancers earned only 6d per night per man, their minstrel would garner the remainder of 15s, that is 7s, which is absurdly high (even for two minstrels).

8 The following discussion draws heavily from Audrey Douglas 'Midsummer in Salisbury: The Tailors' Guild and Confraternity' (1989), which should be consulted for a deeper analysis of the tailors' celebrations. Several of the citations are from Douglas's forthcoming volume on Salisbury in the REED series, and were kindly supplied to the early morris archive in advance of publication by the author.

9 A special watch peculiar to Salisbury, that on the eve of the translation of St Osmund (15 July) – builder of the first cathedral in Old Sarum – lasted several decades longer.

10 It is not clear whether the Maid Marian and hobby horse costumes were part of the morris gear or separate items. In 1572 they are mentioned in the tailors' accounts as distinct from the morris equipment:

At the audit holden at the Taylors Hall the xxv of Februarie

...

in the xiv yeare of the raigne of o'r Soveraigne ladie Elizabethe, the Quenes Maiestie that nowe is, before the Wardens and masters of the Company at the audit, Thomas Barker dyd bringe in one Hobby-Horse, and one mayde Marrians Coate, with a kertell, and a gyrdell of red crimson sarcenet, and a cloke and a vellet cappe … (Haskins 1912, 172–3).

Whether they were meant to supplement the morris gear as new additions or were simply additions to the general pageant equiment cannot now be ascertained.

11 It is tempting to argue that the contemporary processional urban-based morrises of the northwest are descendants of the guild-sponsored processionals, but there are too many gaps in the records (and virtually no choreographic evidence) to make this assertion with any confidence.

12 See the next chapter for earlier May games sponsored by the church.

13 It is curious to note that many twentieth-century revivalists and investigators have taken these thoughts at face value and used them as their justification for *supporting* folk customs.

6 CHURCH PROPERTY

1 Although there is an important distinction to be made between beverages labelled ale and beer, in this period the terms were frequently used interchangeably.

2 For the sake of convenience the following capacities table should be consulted for the details in the ensuing paragraphs, although it must be remembered that these measures varied somewhat from region to region at this time.

Dry measure
1 quarter = 8 bushels
1 bushel = 4 pecks
1 peck = 2 gallons

Fluid Measure
1 tun = 240 gallons
1 hogshead = 60 gallons
1 barrel = 36 gallons of beer or 32 of ale
1 kilderkin = ½ barrel
1 firkin = ¼ barrel

3 For a complete account of this ale and the St George play see Brannen 1992.

4 The following discussion may seem to suggest a linear evolution of ale types from the simple, homespun to the elaborate and professional, but this is not my intention nor would such a conclusion be warranted by the data. Even what I recount here indicates that a wide variety of ales existed side by side through the sixteenth century. However, certain kinds of entertainment at ales definitely did have a vogue, and their rise and fall can be clearly documented as a strand in an evolutionary web.

5 Greater detail on these affairs may be found in the relevant sections of Hutton 1994 and 1996.

6 Good recent texts to consult for further details concerning Robin Hood games and plays, and their relationship to church ales are David Wiles, *The Early Plays of Robin Hood* (Wiles 1981) and Malcolm Nelson, *The Robin Hood Tradition in the English Renaissance* (Nelson 1973), but both contain serious errors of interpretation of morris history, and some errors in interpreting primary data. Although dated, Francis James Child's discussion of the Robin Hood tradition in oral and written texts – as well as the compilation of the texts themselves – in *The English and Scottish Popular Ballads* is still useful (Child 1965, 3:39–233), as is Joseph Ritson's partisan polemic in the classic *Robin Hood* (Ritson 1832). The Robin Hood of the primary records is discussed in some detail in Johnston 1998, Johnston 1994, Johnston and MacLean 1997, and MacLean 1987.

7 In this they are followed by more recent scholars such as Ronald Hutton (see Hutton 1996).

8 Note also that the citation from the Marprelate tract 'Hay any worke for Cooper' in the next chapter (p 200), seems to indicate that Robin Hood and his company are distinct from the Summer Lord and his.

9 There is one earlier reference in 1262 describing an outlaw as 'Robehod' suggesting that this was a generic term at the time (see Richmond 1993).

10 Several lines on, Sloth indicates a predeliction for balladry and summer games over clerical matters:

I haue leuere here an harlotrye or a Somer game of Souters,

Or lesynge[s] to lauȝen [of] and bilye my neȝebores,

Than al þat euere Marc made, Mathew, Iohan, and Lucas. (Langland 1975, 332. Passus V, ll.406–8)

11 Some of the ideas presented here concerning the Kingston morris build on insights developed by Michael Heaney (see especially Heaney 1989).

12 It is important to note that the accounts for Kingston are extant only from 1503 to 1539, and that for the period 1503–6 they exist as summaries rather than complete records. Therefore the starting and ending points of customs cannot be determined with certainty.

13 There is also an entry for a friar's coat for 3s (just before the entry for the morris) which would have to be added to the bill if he were part of the morris.

14 There is also a record of the purchase of three dozen bells in the 1513–14 fiscal year, which might have been for a morris, again reminding us that, as with the royal accounts discussed earlier, absence of a payment does not mean absence of the morris.

15 The text between the asterisks is in a different hand.

16 The accounts indicate payments for six pairs of double-soled shoes, presumably for dancers, and six pairs of single-soled shoes, presumably for other participants.

17 By contrast Robin Hood appeared virtually every year in this period (see MacLean 1987).

18 A 'figure' is a concerted action by a group of dancers whose main interest and purpose lies in the floor track that the dancers weave – such as a hey or figure 8 – rather than in elaborate stepping or body movements. Thus a 'figure dance' is one whose main action consists of figures, as do the English country dances of the period.

19 This same image is repeated by Stubbes (Stubbes 1583, 171).

20 From the Jonson quote cited on p. 155 it appears that the hobby horse might well have performed similar evolutions.

21 Old texts refer to him as Robert Laneham, but his surname is now known to be Langham.

22 Part of this increase is undoubtedly a product of the increase in the number of extant account books from the period. However, this is not the only cause of the increase. Figure 51 in appendix D plots the number of extant account books by decade for the period of this book. It is clear that the increase in ales is much steeper than the increase in numbers of account books over the fifteenth century.

23 Basic data used here are derived from Darby 1973. See chapter 8 for greater detail.

24 For a representative sample see the accounts for Ludlow for this period (Wright 1869, 33–164).

7 CHURCH PROSCRIPTION AND PROSECUTION

1 A broader view of the relationship between the church and traditional customs may be found in Hutton 1994 and Cressy 1989. Historical studies of the general sweep of the Reformation in England and of the respective roles of the puritans and the episcopacy, which provide useful background, include Collinson 1967 and 1988, Haigh 1975 and 1982, and Duffy 1992.

2 Michael Heaney first pointed this out in an as yet unpublished article on visitation articles.

3 A genealogy of copied texts of articles banning morris may be found in appendix B. This gives a more detailed account of who was following whom among the bishops.

4 Complete trial transcripts may be found in Klausner 1990, 168–72.

5 This case is discussed at greater length in Blankenfeld 1985, 154–64. In particular Blakenfeld argues that this was a case of the more urbanized officials of Banbury, where puritanism had a strong hold, attempting to impose their will on the surrounding rural areas where traditional values were more lasting.

8 THE PUBLIC STAGE

1 This table does not include masques, interludes, and other entertainments meant primarily for single, private performance.

2 We might also recognize here the general tendency for public sports and pastimes, such as processions and May games, to give way to audience-based recreations, such as public

plays, in the late sixteenth century that Ian Archer describes (Archer 1991). In the last quarter of the sixteenth century and the first quarter of the seventeenth there are virtually no references to morris in London outside of the public stage.

3 See Nelson (1973, 87–97) for a full survey of the relationship between May games and Peele's play.

4 See chapters 9 and 10 for details of country dance formations and the evolution of dance styles.

5 See Sabol 1978, 577–8, for a fanciful alternative hypothesis concerning the nature of the dance.

6 There has been a certain amount of confusion among drama historians concerning the number of male dancers involved because of seeming inconsistencies between stage directions and text. According to the text there are six men (including the Bavian/baboon), but the stage directions indicate only four men plus the Bavian. It is likely that the stage directions are in error, because the text is clear – in two separate places – on the number of men, and they may well refer to men with speaking parts; only four of the dancers have dialogue.

7 Nashe's *Summer's Last Will and Testament* may have been produced as early as 1592, but this is a speculation based on slim internal evidence. What is more, it was performed privately at the time and was not popularized until its publication in 1600 (see Chambers 1923, 3:451–53).

8 Exactly what an antic (or antique) might be is not fully clear, but generally the term referred to a grotesque of some sort, and on stage frequently meant a clown or mountebank.

9 Hobby horses appeared in urban processions alongside morris in the sixteenth century, but there is no indication that the two were choreographically associated. For a full history of the urban hobby horse see E.C. Cawte's *Ritual Animal Disguise* (Cawte 1978).

10 This date is an inference from the text itself because the heading for the day is clearly in error.

11 It is generally agreed that Fletcher wrote the parts in which the morris is contained (see Bowers 1989, 156).

12 The lines in braces in the Fletcher transcription are out of order from the original; they come from earlier in the dialogue.

9 RURAL LOCATIONS

1 To a degree this distinction parallels the dramatic/theatric distinction made in chapter 7, the dramatic having introverted qualities and the theatric, extroverted. But the terms are not completely isomorphic.

2 This does not necessarily imply that the English longways set formation for country dances is Italian in origin; there could well have been 'old' English country dances based

on the longways set (although there is no primary evidence one way or the other). The point is, rather, that the influence of Italian *contrapassi* on English dances dramatically increased the popularity of the longways set over rounds, which had previously held the vogue.

3 This discussion is based largely on material from E.C. Cawte's *Ritual Animal Disguise* (Cawte 1978), which should be consulted for greater detail.

4 Cawte (1978, 49) cites twelve examples from works published between 1595 and 1624.

5 The most obvious exception to the general principle here is the Abbots Bromley Horn Dance, where the hobby horse is an integral part of the figured set. But this is not a morris dance.

6 Ward's thesis, though never explicitly stated by the author for obvious reasons, is clearly a valiant effort to puff a last breath of life into a Frazerian pre-Christian ritual theory of origins. It cannot succeed ultimately because the earliest data available to him come from elite sources of the late sixteenth century.

7 Members of a biological family are recognizable as such, not because they all look the same, but because they bear between them a stock of traits; yet no single individual in the family need have all the traits to 'look like' the others. This is the central principle of the family resemblances approach to definition (see Wittgenstein 1953 for details).

8 Data on the historical geography of agrarian England are drawn form *The Agrarian History of England and Wales*, vol. 4 (Finberg 1967) and vol. 5 (Thirsk 1984–5).

10 ASSEMBLIES AND THE COUNTY DANCE HALL

1 It must also be recognized (as articulated in the previous chapter) that certain features emerged as markers of 'morris' at certain historical periods. Such markers are not the same as Sharp's notion of an inner perpetual essence, however.

2 In this notation Playford uses the following abbreviations:
S. Single
Cu. Couple
We. Women
⌣ Once through the strain of music
⌣ Twice through the strain

3 This use of the expression 'figure' (i.e., ffig) to mean a *series* of evolutions that form a single progressive unit, is much commoner in nineteenth-century country dance terminology.

4 The title is variously spelled Staynes, Stains, and Staines. The latter has become a common spelling as if signifying that the dance or tune originated in Staines. There are no data to support this assumption, nor Margaret Dean-Smith's conjecture that it is a personal name (Dean-Smith 1951, 73 n.3). Therefore, I prefer the spelling found in the first edition of Playford and in the first recorded source of the tune The Trumbull Lute Book (f.9v).

5 As discussed in chapter 7, its perhaps best-known association – with the maypole song 'Come, ye young men' from *Acteon and Diana* – is spurious.

6 I am indebted to Mary Railing for these insights.

7 See Bacon 1974 for the most comprehensive listing of dance notations including those by Sharp. See Chandler 1993a and 1993b for a detailed social history and documentation of primary historical material focusing on the eighteenth and nineteenth centuries.

8 Occasionally sets of all women were noted in the region.

9 Specific practice (and names of figures) have been subject to some change over time, but the general principles – which are all that are relevant here – obtain regardless of this.

10 This tune should not be confused with another of the same name that was in use by Jacobean masquewrights, and was apparently based on Arbeau's *moresques* melody (see Ward 1986, 312–13, for details).

11 See Hilton 1981 for a detailed investigation of the French form, and Marsh 1985 for English counterparts.

12 I am most grateful to Alan Terry for supplying the transcription, which may be found in full in appendix C.

11 PRIVATE PREMISES

1 For example, the entries in the table concerned with Stowe House in Buckinghamshire were discovered several years ago by Michael Heaney in the Grenville and Temple families' account books now housed in the Huntington Library in Los Angeles. Their contents appear entirely consistent with accounts from nearby country estates, such as Shalstone Manor and Aynho House.

2 Much of the social history and detail in this case study come from Nicholas Cooper's *Aynho: A Northamptonshire Village* (Cooper 1984), which should be consulted for greater detail concerning the village's affairs from the Middle Ages to the twentieth century. The particular details on such matters as land tenure, inheritance, enclosure, agricultural profitability, farming methods, improvements, and so forth, can be compared with general accounts in *The Agrarian History of England and Wales*, volume 5, 1640–1750 (Thirsk 1984–5), to confirm that in most respects Aynho is a fair representative of this region.

3 These figures are a compilation of a census of households conducted in 1740 and rent, rate, and tithe rolls from 1744.

4 Not all the modes of tenure are noted in the rector's census of the village of 1740, on which these statistics are based, so the freehold acreage could be slightly higher.

12 ENDINGS

1 Some of the basic concepts here, in particular the idea of subaltern classes as structured by paradigms that contrast directly with those of elites, have been explored by a line of Italian folklorists and social scientists following a course mapped by Benedetto Croce (see especially Gramsci 1950, De Martino 1961, and Padiglione 1978).

2 The nature of emics is extremely complex and I do not mean to pursue the technical problems here (see Harris 1968, 568–604, for a useful, though dated, overview of critical issues). However, a little clarification by analogy may help the nonspecialist. Two privates in the same company in the army – one six foot tall, the other five foot four – may be considered by their sergeant to be (emically) wearing the same uniform even though the sleeves of the one's battle dress are three inches longer than those of the other. The objective measure of sleeve length is observable, but not a difference that makes a difference to the sameness of the uniforms. Likewise a caper one foot off the ground may be considered by a teacher to be the same as one six inches off the ground even though they are observably different.

APPENDIX A METHODOLOGICAL ISSUES

1 The current research by the editors of the various volumes for the Records of Early English Drama (REED) project is an excellent case in point. These editors have turned up numerous new references to morris in their general search for primary documents to performance practice in early modern England. This project stops at 1642, however, and so does not cover significant segments of morris history.
2 The actual shape of a typical growth curve is open to question. The battleship curve as illustrated here is fully convex, but standard treatments of the diffusion of innovations suggest that in many cases there might well be moments at the beginning (and end) of the curve, which could be a logistic (a species of S-shaped curve), representing a slow start followed by a sudden 'take off' growth (Rogers 1983, 11, Cavalli-Sforza and Feldman 1981, 30). Exponential, stepwise, linear, and other patterns of growth and decline are all possible. Dethlefsen and Deetz's gravestone data could equally well be approximated to a logistic, but there, as in this work, small datasets (and fragmentary evidence) make curve-fitting highly speculative.

Bibliography

Manuscript Sources

ENGLAND

Aylesbury
Buckinghamshire Record Office
    PR 140/5/1 Marlow churchwardens' account book 1593–1674

Cambridge
University Library
    Dd.4.23 T[homas] R[obinson] MS

Chelmsford
Essex County Record Office
    D/P 11/5/1 Great Dunmow churchwardens' accounts

Kingston upon Thames
Surrey Record Office
    KG 2/2/1 Kingston upon Thames churchwardens' accounts

London
Public Record Office, Chancery Lane
    E 36/217 Richard Gibson's Account Book
    SP 14/64 Letters of the Salisbury Tailors
    Prerogative Court of Canterbury Records
        24–5 Alice Wetenhale's Will 1458
        31 Richard Jackson's Will 1510
British Library
    Additional MSS

61468 Blenheim papers
41996 Seventeenth-century dance notation
Harleian MSS
    247 Mumming before Richard II
Society of Antiquaries
    MS 129 Inventory of the effects of Henry VIII temp. Edward VI

Northampton
Northamptonshire Record Office
    ML 1306 Aynho House domestic accounts 1691–1722
    ML 1307 Aynho House domestic accounts 1722–35

Oxford
Bodleian Library
    MS Aubrey 21   'The Country Revel' (ff. 4–22) John Aubrey 1671
    MS Eng. hist. c.479 'A note of such golde plate & jewelles as Sir William Hericke hath
                          took into his charge.'
    MS Top Oxon d200 Percy Manning's papers
University Museum
    Smith MSS The Whitsun Ale Accounts for 1721

Reading
Berkshire Record Office
    D/ED C1 The Trumbull Lute Book

Trowbridge
Wiltshire County Record Office
    G23/1/252 Salisbury Tailors' Guild Account Book

Warwick
Warwickshire Record Office
    QS 40/1 Order Book, 1650–7

IRELAND

Dublin
Trinity College
    D.1.21/1 William Ballet's Lute Book

UNITED STATES

San Marino, California
Huntington Library
    Stowe MSS STG Elections box 1 folder 4 Accounts of 1741 elections

Printed Works

A. 1593. *The Passionate Morrice.* In *Tell-troths New-Yeares Gift ... etc,* Frederick J. Furnivall, ed. London. New Shakspere Society, series 6, no. 2 (1876): 47–105.

Abbott, Andrew, and John Forrest. 1986. 'Optimal Matching Methods for Historical Data.' *Journal of Interdisciplinary History* 16:473–96.

An Agreeable Companion. 1742. London.

Alford, Violet. 1933. 'Midsummer and Morris in Portugal.' *Folklore* 44:218–35.

– 1962. *Sword Dance and Drama.* London.

Anglo, Sydney. 1960. *The Court Festivals of Henry VII: A Study Based Upon the Account Books of John Heron, Treasurer of the Chamber.* Manchester.

Arbeau, Thoinot (pseudonym of Jehan Tabourot). 1596. *Orchesographie, Metode, et Teorie en Forme de Discours et Tablature.* Lengres.

Archer, Ian. 1991. *The Pursuit of Stability: Social Relations in Elizabethan London.* Cambridge.

Ashton, John. 1904. *Social Life in the Reign of Queen Anne.* London.

Atkinson, Tom. 1963. *Elizabethan Winchester.* London.

Avery, E.L., ed. 1960. *The London Stage 1660–1800.* Carbondale, IL.

Bacon, Lionel. 1974. *A Handbook of Morris Dances.* London.

Barfield, Samuel. 1901. *Thatcham, Berks, and its Manors.* James Parker, ed. 2 vols. Oxford and London.

Barley, M.W. 1985. 'Rural Building in England.' In *The Agrarian History of England and Wales.* Joan Thirsk, gen. ed. 1984–5.Vol. 5 *1640–1750,* 2 parts. Cambridge, 2:590–685.

Barlow, Jeremy, ed. 1985. *The Complete Country Dance Tunes from* Playford's Dancing Master *(1651–ca.1728).* London.

Baskervill, Charles R. 1929. *The Elizabethan Jig.* Chicago.

Bateson, Gregory. 1972. *Steps to an Ecology of Mind.* New York.

Battaglia, Salvatore et al. 1961–. *Grande Dizionario della linga italiano.* Turin.

Baxandall, Michael. 1980. *The Limewood Sculptors of Renaissance Germany.* New Haven, CT.

Beaumont, Francis. 1613. *Masque of the Inner Temple and Gray's Inn.* In *The Dramatic Works in the Beaumont and Fletcher Canon,* Fredson Bowers, gen. ed. 10 vols. Cambridge (1966) 1:111–44.

Beaumont, Francis, and John Fletcher. 1613. *The Knight of the Burning Pestle.* In *The Dramatic Works in the Beaumont and Fletcher Canon,* Fredson Bowers, gen. ed. 10 vols. Cambridge (1966), 1:1–110.

Beveridge, Lord. 1939. *Prices and Wages in England from the Twelfth to the Nineteenth Century.* Vol. 1. London.

Billington, Sandra. 1978. 'Routs and Reyes.' *Folklore* 89:184–200.

Blair, Lawrence. 1940. *English Church Ales.* Ann Arbor.

Blankenfeld, Barton John. 1985. 'Puritans in the Provinces: Banbury, Oxfordshire 1554–1660.' PhD dissertation, Yale University.

Boas, Frederick. S., ed. 1909. 'James I at Oxford in 1605.' *Malone Society Collections* I.3:247–59.

– ed. 1922. *The Christmas Prince*. Oxford: Malone Society reprints no. 47.

Bond, Donald F., ed. 1965. *The Spectator*. 5 vols. Oxford.

Bowers, Fredson. 1989. 'Textual Introduction' [*The Two Noble Kinsmen*.] In *The Dramatic Works in the Beaumont and Fletcher Canon*, Fredson Bowers, gen. ed., Cambridge, 7:147–68.

Brand, John. 1849. *Observations on the Popular Antiquities of Great Britain Chiefly Illustrating the Origin of our Vulgar and Provincial Customs, Ceremonies, and Superstitions*. 3 vols. London.

Brannen, Anne. 1992. 'The Bassingbourn St. George Play: A Contextual Study.' PhD dissertation, University of California, Berkeley.

Brathwait, Richard. 1618. 'Upon Kempe and his Morice.' In *The Good Wife, or, A Care One Amongst Women*. London. *STC* 3568.5

Breton, Nicholas. 1602. *The Mothers Blessing*. In *The Works in Prose and Verse of Nicholas Breton*, Alexander B. Grosart, ed. (1879), 2 vols. London. 1: section m.

– 1605. *A Poste with a Packet of Mad Letters*. In *The Works in Prose and Verse of Nicholas Breton*. 2: section h.

Brett, Philip, ed. 1967. *Consort Songs*. Musica Britannica 22. London.

Bronson, Bertrand Harris. 1966. *The Traditional Tunes of the Child Ballads*. 12 vols. Princeton.

Brown, Howard Mayer. 1963. *Music in the French Secular Theater, 1400–1550*. Cambridge, MA.

Brown, Rawdon, ed. 1869. 'Setting of the Midsummer Watch.' In *Calendar of State Papers and Manuscripts relating to English Affairs, Existing in the Archives and Collections of Venice*. London, 3:136–7.

Buckland, Theresa. 1982. 'English Folk Dance Scholarship: A Review.' *Traditional Dance* 1:3–18.

Burton, Henry. 1628. *A Tryall of Private Devotions*. London. *STC* 4157.

– 1641. *A Divine Tragedie Lately Acted*. 2nd ed. n.p. Wing B6161.

Burton, Samuel. 1620. *A Sermon Preached at the Generall Assises in Warwicke, the Third of March, being the First Friday in Lent, 1619*. London. *STC* 4164.

Caroso, Fabritio. 1581. *Il Ballarino*. Venice.

– 1600. *Nobiltà Di Dame*. Venice.

Castiglione, Baldessare. 1528. *The Book of the Courtier*. Translated by Charles Singleton. New York (1959).

Cavalli-Sforza, Luigi L., and Marcus W. Feldman. 1981. *Cultural Transmission and Evolution: A Quantitative Approach*. Princeton, NJ.

Cavanaugh, M. Jean Carmel, ed. 1942. Technogamia *by Barten Holyday: A Critical Edition*. Washington, DC.

Cavendish, William. 1660. *A Treatise on Government.* In *A Catalogue of Letters and Other Historical Documents Exhibited in the Library at Welbeck,* S.A. Strong, ed. (1903) London, 173–236.

Cawte, E.C. 1963. 'The Morris Dance in Herefordshire, Shropshire and Worcestershire.' *Journal of the English Folk Dance and Song Society* 9:197–212.

– 1978. *Ritual Animal Disguise.* Ipswich.

Cawte, E.C., Alex Helm, R.J. Marriott, and Norman Peacock. 1960. 'A Geographical Index of the Ceremonial Dance in Great Britain.' *Journal of the English Folk Dance and Song Society* 9:1–41.

Chambers, E.K. 1903. *The Mediaeval Stage.* 2 vols. Oxford.

– 1923. *The Elizabethan Stage.* 4 vols. Oxford.

Chandler, Keith. 1993a. *'Ribbons, Bells and Squeaking Fiddles': The Social History of Morris Dancing in the English South Midlands, 1660–1900.* London.

– 1993b. *Morris Dancing in the English South Midlands, 1660–1900: A Chronological Gazeteer.* London.

Chappell, William. 1859. *The Ballad Literature and Popular Music of the Olden Time.* London.

Chaves, Luís. 1941. 'Danças Religiosas.' *Revista de Guimarães* 51:372–87.

– 'Danças, bailados & mímicas guerreiras.' *Revista do Instituto Português de Arqueologia, História e Etnografia* 2:411–32.

Child, Francis James. 1965. *The English and Scottish Popular Ballads.* 5 vols. New York.

The Citie's Loyalty Displayed. 1661. London. Wing C4330.

Clark, Andrew, ed. 1891. *The Life and Times of Anthony Wood, Antiquary, of Oxford, 1632–1695.* Oxford.

Clark, Peter. 1983. *The English Alehouse.* London.

Clopper, Lawrence, ed. 1979. *Chester.* Records of Early English Drama. Toronto.

Coleman, D.C. 1958. *The British Paper Industry 1495–1860: A Study in Industrial Growth.* Oxford.

Collinson, Patrick. 1967. *The Elizabethan Puritan Movement.* Berkeley.

– 1988. *The Birthpangs of Protestant England.* Basingstoke.

Cooper, Nicholas. 1984. *Aynho: A Northamptonshire Village.* Banbury.

Cooper, Thomas. 1552. *Bibliotheca Eliotae, Eliotis librarie, ... enriched ... by Thomas Cooper.* London. *STC* 7662.

Coryate, Thomas. 1776. *Coryat's Crudities.* London.

Cox, Charles. 1913. *Churchwardens' Accounts from the Fourteenth Century to the Close of the Seventeenth Century.* London.

Cox, Robert. 1656. *Acteon & Diana with a Pastoral Storie of the Nimph Oenone.* 2nd ed. London. Wing C6711.

Cressy, David. 1989. *Bonfires and Bells.* London.

Cunnington, B. Howard. 1932. *Records of the County of Wilts.* Devizes.

Dalton, Michael. 1618. *The Countrey Justice.* London. *STC* 6205.

D'Ancona, Alessandro. 1891. *Origini del Teatro Italiano*. 2 vols. Turin.

Darby, H.C., ed. 1973. *A New Historical Geography of England*. Cambridge.

D'Avenant, William. 1668. *The Rivals*. London. Wing D336.

– 1872–4. *The Dramatic Works of William D'Avenant*. James Maidment and W.H. Logan, eds. 5 vols. Edinburgh.

Dean-Smith, Margaret. 1957. *Playford's English Dancing Master*. London.

Deetz, James. 1967. *Invitation to Archaeology*. Garden City, New York.

Dekker, Thomas. 1600. *The Shoemakers' Holiday*. In *The Dramatic Works of Thomas Dekker*, 1:7–104.

– 1953–61. *The Dramatic Works of Thomas Dekker*, Fredson Bowers, ed. 4 vols. Cambridge, England.

Dekker, Thomas, and John Ford. [*c* 1623]. *The Sun's Darling*. In *The Dramatic Works of Thomas Dekker*. 4:1–75.

Dekker, Thomas, William Rowley, and John Ford. 1621. *The Witch of Edmonton*. In *The Dramatic Works of Thomas Dekker*. 3:481–568.

De Martino, Ernesto. 1961. *La terra del rimorso. Contributo a una storia religiosa del sud*. Milan.

Dethlefsen, Edwin, and James Deetz. 1966. 'Death's Heads, Cherubs and Willow Trees: Experimental Archaeology in Colonial Cemeteries.' *American Antiquity*. 31.4:502–10.

Douce, Francis. 1807. 'A Dissertation on the Ancient English Morris Dance.' In *Illustrations of Shakespeare, and of Ancient Manners*, London, 431–82.

Douch, H.L. 1953 'Household Accounts at Lanherne.' *Journal of the Royal Institution of Cornwall* ns 2.1 (1953):25–32.

Douglas, Audrey. 1989. 'Midsummer in Salisbury: the Tailors' Guild and Confraternity, 1444–1642,' *Renaissance and Reformation* 25.1:35–51.

Douglas, Gavin. 1839. *The Aeneid of Virgil, Translated into Scottish Verse by Gavin Douglas*. 2 vols. Edinburgh.

Duffy, Eamon. 1992. *The Stripping of the Altars*. New Haven.

Dundes, Alan, ed. 1965. *The Study of Folklore*. Englewood Cliffs, NJ.

Eliade, Mircea. 1949. *Le Mythe de l'Eternel Retour: Archétypes et Répétition*. Paris.

Emmerson, George S. 1972. *A Social History of Scottish Dance*. Montreal.

Essex, John, trans. 1710. *For the Further Improvement of Dancing, A Treatise of Chorography or ye Art of Dancing Country Dances after a New Character*. London.

Farley, Henry. 1621. *St Paules-church her bill for the Parliament*. London. *STC* 10690.

Ferguson, Arthur B. 1986. *The Chivalric Tradition in Renaissance England*. Washington, DC.

Fetherston, Christopher. 1582. *A Dialogue against Light, Lewde and Lascivious Dancing*. London. *STC* 10835.

Feuillerat, Albert, ed. 1914. *Documents Relating to the Revels at Court in the Time of King Edward VI and Queen Mary*. Louvain.

Feuillet, Raoul Auger. 1706a. *Recueil de Contredances*. Paris.

— 1706b. *Orchesography. Or, the Art of Dancing.* John Weaver, trans. London.

Figueiredo, A. Cardoso Borges de. 1886. *Coimbra antiga e moderna.* Lisbon.

Finberg, H.P.R., ed. 1967. *The Agrarian History of England and Wales.* Vol. 4 *1500–1640.* Cambridge.

Firth, C.H. 1903. *An English Garner: Stuart Tracts 1603–1693.* Westminster.

Firth, C.H., and R.S. Rait. eds. 1911. *Acts and Ordinances of the Interregnum, 1642–1660.* London.

Fischer, David H. 1970. *Historians' Fallacies: Toward a Logic of Historical Thought.* New York.

Fletcher, John. 1619. *Women Pleas'd.* In *The Dramatic Works in the Beaumont and Fletcher Canon,* Fredson Bowers, gen. ed. Cambridge (1982), 5:441–538.

Fletcher, John, and William Shakespeare. 1613. *The Two Noble Kinsmen.* In *The Dramatic Works in the Beaumont and Fletcher Canon,* Fredson Bowers, gen. ed. Cambridge (1989), 7:169–261.

Florio, John. 1611. *Qveen Anna's New World of Words, or Dictionarie of the* Italian *and* English *Tongues.* London. *STC* 11099.

Fonta, Laure, ed. 1888. *Orchesographie par Thoinot Arbeau.* Paris.

Ford, James A. 1962. *A Quantitative Method for Deriving Cultural Chronology.* Washington, DC.

Forrest, John. 1984. *Morris and Matachin: A Study in Comparative Choreography.* Sheffield.

— 1985a. 'Here We Come A-Fossiling.' *Dance Research Journal* 17:27–34.

— 1985b. 'Morris Music: Some Questions.' *Morris Dancing in the South Midlands,* vol.10.

— 1988a. *Lord I'm Coming Home.* Ithaca.

— 1988b. 'Who Calls the Tune? New Methods for Exploring the Relationships between Dances and Their Music.' *Folk Music Journal* 5:448–68.

— 1996. 'The Structure and Notation of Traditional Dance Music: A New Mexican Example.' *Folk Music Journal* 7:167–87.

Forrest, John, and Andrew Abbott. 1990. 'The Optimal Matching Method for Studying Anthropological Sequence Data: An Introduction and Reliability Analysis.' *Journal of Quantitative Anthropology* 2:151–70.

Forrest, John, and Michael Heaney. 1991. 'Charting Early Morris (1450–1750).' *Folk Music Journal* 6:169–86.

Foster, C.W., ed. 1912. *Lincoln Episcopal Registers in the Time of Thomas Cooper, S.T.P., Bishop of Lincoln A.D. 1571 to A.D. 1584.* Lincoln.

Fox Strangeways, A.H., and Maud Karpeles. 1955. *Cecil Sharp.* 2nd ed. Oxford.

Frazer, James George. 1907–15. *The Golden Bough.* 3rd ed. 12 vols. London.

Frere, Walter Howard, ed. 1910. *Visitation Articles and Injunctions of the Period of the Reformation.* 3 vols. London.

Gairdner, James, ed. 1880. *Letters and Papers, Foreign and Domestic, of the Reign of Henry VIII.* London.

— 1893. 'The Spousells of the Princess Mary, Daughter of Henry VII, to Charles Prince of

Castile, A.D. 1508.' *Camden Miscellany* 9, Camden Society, ns 53.

Galloway, David, ed. 1984. *Norwich 1540–1642.* Records of Early English Drama. Toronto.

Gardiner, Dorothy. 1954. *Historic Haven: The Story of Sandwich.* Derby.

Garry, Francis N.A., and A.G. Garry. 1893. *The Churchwardens' Accounts of the Parish of St. Mary's, Reading, Berkshire, 1550–1662.* Reading.

Gay, John. 1986. *The Beggar's Opera.* Bryan Loughrey and T.O. Treadwell, eds. London.

Gazophylacium Anglicanum: Containing the Derivation of English Words, Proper and Common. 1689. London. *STC* G426.

George, David, ed. 1991. *Lancashire.* Records of Early English Drama. Toronto.

Gilpin, George, trans. 1580. *The Beehive of the Romishe Churche.* London. *STC* 17446.

Gosson, Stephen. 1579. *The School of Abuse.* London. *STC* 12097.

– 1582. *Plays Confuted in Five Actions.* London. *STC* 12095.

Gramsci, Antonio. 1950. *Letteratura e vita nazionale.* Turin.

Green, David. 1951. *Blenheim Palace.* London.

Greene, Robert. 1591. *Greene's Farewell to Folly.* In *The Life and Complete Works in Prose and Verse of Robert Greene,* A.B. Grosart, ed. New York (1881–6). 9:225–348.

– 1592. *A Qvip for an Vpstart Courtier.* In *The Life and Complete Works in Prose and Verse of Robert Greene,* A.B. Grosart, ed. New York (1881–6), 11:205–94.

Grimm, Jacob. 1811. *Über den altdeutschen Meistergesang.* Göttingen.

– 1822–37. *Deutsche Grammatik.* 2nd ed. Göttingen.

Grimm, Jacob, and Wilhelm Grimm. 1812–15. *Kinder- und Hausmärchen.* Berlin.

Hägerstrand, Torsten. 1967. *Innovation Diffusion as a Spatial Process.* Allan Pred with Greta Haag, trans. Chicago.

Haigh, Christopher. 1975. *Reformation and Resistance in Tudor Lancashire.* New York.

– 1982. 'The Recent Historiography of the English Reformation.' *Historical Journal* 25:995–1007.

Hall, Edward. 1809. *Chronicle Containing the History of England.* [1550]. London.

Hall, Thomas. 1661. *Funebria Florae, the Downfall of May-games.* 2nd ed. London. Wing H434.

Halm, Philipp Maria. 1928. *Erasmus Grasser.* Augsburg.

Harbage, Alfred. 1941. *Shakespeare's Audience.* New York.

– 1964. *Annals of English Drama, 975–1700: An Analytical Record of all Plays, Extant or Lost, Chronologically Arranged and Indexed by Authors, Titles, Dramatic Companies, &c.* 2nd ed., revised by S. Schoenbaum. Philadelphia.

Harris, Marvin. 1968. *The Rise of Anthropological Theory: A History of Theories of Culture.* New York.

Harsnet, Samuel. 1603. *A Declaration of Egregious Popish Impostures.* London. *STC* 12880.

Harvey, Richard. 1590. *Plaine Percevall the Peace-maker of England.* London. *STC* 12914.

Haskins, Charles. 1912. *The Ancient Trade Guilds and Companies of Salisbury.* Salisbury.

Heaney, Michael. 1989. 'Kingston to Kenilworth: Early Plebeian Morris.' *Folklore* 100:88–104.

Heaney, Michael, and John Forrest. 1991. *Annals of Early Morris.* Sheffield.

Higins, John. 1585. *The Nomenclator, or Remembrancer of Adrianus Junius ... and now in English, by John Higins.* London. *STC* 14860.

Hill, Christopher. 1956. *Economic Problems of the Church.* Oxford.

Hilton, Wendy. 1981. *Dance of Court and Theater.* Princeton.

Hogarth, William. 1753. *Analysis of Beauty.* London.

Holland, Philemon, trans. 1601. *The Historie of the World, Commonly Called, The Natural Historie of C. Plinius Secundus, translated into English by Philemon Holland.* London. *STC* 20029.

Holyday, Barten. 1618. *ΤΕΧΝΟΓΑΜΙΑ: or the Marriages of the Arts.* London. *STC* 13617.

House of Commons. 1867–8. *Second Report of the Commissioners appointed to inquire into the rubrics, orders, and directions for regulating the course and conduct of public worship, &c., according to the use of the United Church of England and Ireland; with minutes of evidence and appendices.* Vol. 23. London.

Hutton, Ronald. 1994. *The Rise and Fall of Merry England: The Ritual Year 1400–1700.* Oxford.

– 1996. *The Stations of the Sun.* Oxford.

Ironside, Gilbert. 1637. *Seven Questions of the Sabbath Briefly Disputed, after the Manner of the Schooles.* Oxford. *STC* 14268.

Isaac, Mr, 1716. *The morris, a new dance for the year 1716.* n.p.

James VI and I. 1982. 'The King's Majesties Declaration to his Subjects Concerning Lawfull Sports to be Used.' In *Minor Prose Works of King James VI and I.* James Craigie, ed. Edinburgh, 101–9.

Johnson, A.H. 1914–15. *The History of the Worshipful Company of the Drapers of London.* 2 vols. Oxford.

Johnson, D.A., and D.G. Vaisey, eds. 1964. *Staffordshire and the Great Rebellion.* Stafford.

Johnston, Alexandra F. 1994. 'Summer Festivals in the Thames Valley Counties.' In *Custom, Culture and Community in the Later Middle Ages*, Tom Pettit and Leif Søndergaard, eds. Odense.

– 1998. 'The Robin Hood of the Records.' In *Playing Robin Hood: The Legend as Performance in Five Centuries.* Lois Potter, ed. Newark, 27–44.

– Forthcoming. *Berkshire, Buckinghamshire, Oxfordshire.* Records of Early English Drama. Toronto.

Johnston, Alexandra F., and Sally-Beth MacLean. 1997. 'Reformation and Resistance in Thames/Severn Parishes: The Dramatic Witness.' In *The Parish in English Life 1400–1600*, Katherine L. French, Gary G. Gibbs, and Brent A. Kümin, eds. Manchester, 178–200.

Jonson, Ben. 1599. *Every Man out of his Humour.* In *The Works of Ben Jonson*, 3:405–601.

– 1603. *A Particvlar Entertainment of the Queene and Prince their Highnesse to Althrope ... etc.* In *The Works of Ben Jonson*, Oxford (1941), 7:119–132.

– 1621. *Gypsies Metamorphosed.* In *The Works of Ben Jonson,* 7:539–622.

– 1925–52. *The Works of Ben Jonson,* C.H. Herford, Percy and Evelyn Simpson, eds. 11 vols. Oxford.

Judge, Roy. 1984. 'D'Arcy Ferris and the Bidford Morris.' *Folk Music Journal* 4:443–80.

Kelly, William. 1865. *Notices Illustrative of the Drama and other Popular Amusements … Extracted from the Chamberlain's Accounts and Other Manuscripts of the Borough of Leicester.* London.

Kemp, William. 1840. *Kemps Nine Daies Wonder, Performed in a Daunce from London to Norwich* [1600]. Alexander Dyce, ed. London.

Kennedy, W.P.M. 1924. *Elizabethan Episcopal Administration: An Essay in Sociology and Politics.* 3 vols. London.

Kerry, Charles. 1861. *The History and Antiquities of the Hundred of Bray in the County of Berks.* London.

– 1883. *A History of the Municipal Church of St. Lawrence, Reading.* Reading.

Kipling, Gordon. 1977. *The Triumph of Honour: Burgundian Origins of the Elizabethan Renaissance.* Leiden.

Klausner, David N., ed. 1990. *Herefordshire, Worcestershire.* Records of Early English Drama. Toronto.

Krohn, Kaarle. 1926. *Die Folkloristische Arbeitsmethode.* Oslo.

Kuhn, Thomas. 1962. *The Structure of Scientific Revolutions.* Chicago.

LaBorde, Le Comte de, ed. 1849–52 *Les Ducs de Bourgogne Études sur les Lettres, Les Arts et L'Industrie Pendant le XVe Siécle.* Vol.2. Paris.

La Marche, Olivier de. 1883–8. *Mémoires.* 4 vols. Paris.

Lancashire, Ian. 1980. 'Orders for Twelfth Day and Night circa 1515 in the Second Northumberland Household Book.' *English Literary Renaissance* 10: 7–45.

Laneham, Robert. 1968. *A Letter.* Menston, Yorks.

Langland, William. 1975. *Piers Plowman: The B Version.* George Kane and E. Talbot Donaldson, eds. London.

Latimer, Hugh. 1845. 'The Sermon of Master Doctor Latimer, Preached on the Third Sunday in Advent, 1552.' In *Sermons by Hugh Latimer,* George Elwes Corrie, ed. Cambridge, 65–83.

Leitner, Quirin von, ed. 1800–2. *Freydal des Kaisers Maximilian I. Turniere und Mummereien Herausgegeben.* Vienna.

Lemor, Robert, ed. 1865. *Calendar of State Papers, Domestic Series, of the Reign of Elizabeth, 1581–1590.* London.

Lingua, or, The Combat of the Tongue, and the Five Senses for Superiority. 1607. London. *STC* 24104.

Lowe, Barbara. 1957. 'Early Records of the Morris in England.' *Journal of the English Folk Dance and Song Society* 8.2:61–82.

Loyd, M. 1646. *The King Found at Southwel, and the Oxford Gigg Playd, and Sung at Witney Wakes.* London. Wing 2662.

Lucas, E.V. 1912. *London Lavender*. London.

Machyn, Henry. 1848. *The Diary of Henry Machyn Citizen and Merchant-Taylor of London, from A.D. 1550 to A.D. 1563*. John Gough Nichols ed. London.

MacLean, Sally-Beth. 1987. 'King Games and Robin Hood: Play and Profit at Kingston upon Thames.' *Research Opportunities in Renaissance Drama* 29:85–93.

– 'Leicester and the Evelyns.' *Review of English Studies*. ns 39 (November 1988), 487–93.

Markham, Gervase. 1986. *The English Housewife* [1615], Michael R. Best, ed. Kingston and Montreal.

Marprelate, Martin (pseudonym). 1589a. 'Hay Any Worke for Cooper.' London. Reprinted in *The Marprelate Tracts [1588–1589]*. Menston (1967).

– 1589b. 'The Just Censure and Reproof of Martin Junior.' Reprinted in *The Marprelate Tracts*.

Marsh, Carol. 1985. 'French Court Dance in England, 1706–1740: A Study of the Sources.' PhD dissertation, City University of New York.

[Marston, John]. 1601. *Iacke Drums Entertainment: Or the Comedie of Pasquill and Katherine*. London. *STC* 7243.

– 1610. *Histrio-Mastix Or, The Player Whipt*. London. *STC* 17475.

'A Merry Wedding; or, O Brave Arthur of Bradley.' [*c* 1600]. In *Robin Hood*. Joseph Ritson, ed. 3rd ed. London (1885), 359–63.

Mill, Anna Jean. 1927. *Mediaeval Plays in Scotland*. Edinburgh.

Minsheu, John. 1617. 'Ηγεμὼν εἰς τας γλῶσσας, id est, Ductor in Linguas, The Guide into Tongues*. London. *STC* 17944.

Moresinus, Thomas. 1594. *Papatus, seu depravatae religionis Origo et Incrementum*. Edinburgh. *STC* 18102.

Morley, Thomas. 1594. *Madrigalls to Foure Voices: The Firste Booke in English Madrigal Verse 1588–1632*, E.H. Fellowes, ed. 3rd ed. Oxford (1967), 139–44.

'Morris-dancing and May-day Games.' 1886. *Walford's Antiquarian* 9:198–200.

Mountgomery, John. attrib. 1585. 'A Booke conteyning the Manner and Order of a watch to be used in the Cittie of London, upon the even at Night of Sainct John Baptist and Sainct Peeter, as in tyme past hath bene accustomed.' In *The Harleian Miscellany*, Thomas Park, ed. 10 vols. London (1812), 9: 389–408.

Mugnier, F. 1887. *Le Théâtre en Savoie*. Chambéry.

Müller-Meiningen, Johanna. 1984. *Die Moriskentänzer und andere Arbeiten des Erasmus Grasser für das Alte Rathaus in München*. Munich and Zurich.

Munday, Anthony. 1965. *The Downfall of Robert, Earl of Huntingdon*. Oxford: Malone Society reprints, 109.

Myers, A.R. 1981. 'The Book of the Disguisings for the Coming of the Ambassadors of Flanders, December 1508.' *Bulletin of the Institute of Historical Research* 54: 120–9.

Nashe, Thomas. 1589. *The Returne of Pasquill*. In *The Works of Thomas Nashe*, 1:65–103.

– 1590. *An Almond for a Parrat*. In *The Works of Thomas Nashe*, 3:341–76.

– 1591. 'Somewhat to reade for them *that list*.' Preface to Sidney's *Astrophel and Stella* in *The Works of Thomas Nashe*, 3:329–33.

– 1596. *Have with you to Saffron Walden*. In *The Works of Thomas Nashe*, 3:11–139.

– 1600. *A Pleasant Comedie, called Summers Last Will and Testament*. In *The Works of Thomas Nashe*, 3:231–95.

– 1958. *The Works of Thomas Nashe*, Ronald B. McKerrow, ed. 5 vols. Oxford. Reprint, Oxford, 1966.

Neal, Mary ed. 1910. *The Espérance Morris Book*. Part 1. 5th ed. London.

Needham, Joseph. 1936. 'Geographical Distribution of English Ceremonial Dance Traditions.' *Journal of the English Folk Dance and Song Society* 3:1–45.

Negri, Carlo. 1604. *Nuove Invenzione di balli*. Milan.

Nelson, Malcolm A. 1973. *The Robin Hood Tradition in the English Renaissance*. Salzburg.

Nichols, John. 1823. *The Progresses and Public Processions of Queen Elizabeth*. 3 vols. London.

Nicol, E.J. 1953. 'Some Notes on the History of the Betley Window.' *Journal of the English Folk Dance and Song Society* 7:59–66 and frontispiece.

Nicolas, Sir Nicholas Harris, ed. 1830. *Privy Purse Expenses of Elizabeth of York*. London.

Padiglione, Vincenzo. 1978. 'In margine al dibattito sul folklore.' In *Antropologia storicismo e marxismo*, Franco Ferrarotti, ed. Milan, 132–48.

Pansier, P. 1919. 'Les Débuts du théâtre à Avignon à la fin du XVe siècle.' *Annales d'Avignon et du comtat Venaissin* 6:5–52.

Partridge, Eric. 1958. *Origins: A Short Etymological Dictionary of Modern English*. New York.

Paul, James Balfour, ed. 1900–2. *Compota Thesaurariorum regum Scotorum: Accounts of the Lord High Treasurer of Scotland*. 4 vols. Edinburgh.

Peck, Francis. 1740. *New Memoirs of the Life and Poetical Works of Mr John Milton*. London.

Peele, George. 1911. *King Edward the First*. W.W. Greg, ed. London.

Pennell, Arthur E., ed. 1980. *An Edition of Anthony Munday's John a Kent and John a Cumber*. New York.

Peyton, S.A., ed. 1928. *The Churchwardens' Presentments in the Oxfordshire Peculiars of Dorchester, Thame and Banbury*. Oxford.

Phillips, Edward. 1658a. *The New World of English Words*. London. Wing P2068.

– 1658b. *The Mysteries of Love and Eloquence; or, The Arts of Wooing and Complementing*. London. Wing P2066.

Playford, John. 1651. *The English Dancing Master: or Plaine and Easie Rules for the Dancing of Country Dances, with the Tune to Each Dance*. London. Wing P2477.

– 1670. *Apollo's Banquet: Short Rules and Directions for Practitioners on the Violin with a Collection of Old Country Dances*. London.

– [1689]. *A New Addition to the Dancing-Master*. Third supplement to the seventh edition. London. Unique copy in BL K.1.a.14.

Price, F.D., 1938. 'Stow, Campden and Winchcombe Deaneries in 1576.' Part 8. *Evesham Journal* 19 Feb: 11.

Prunières, Henri. 1914. *Le Ballet de Cour en France avant Benserade et Lully*. Paris.

Prynne, William. 1633. *Histrio-Mastix*. London. *STC* 20464.

'The Puisne's Walks about London.' 1620. In *Reliquiae Antiquae*. Thomas Wright and James Orchard Halliwell, eds. London (1843), 2:70–2.

Rablet, Richard. 1614. *Cobbes Prophecies*. London. *STC* 5452.

Raine, James, ed. 1855. *Testamente Eboracensia: A Selection of Wills from the Registry at York*. Part 2. Surtees Society 30, no.179: 220–9.

Ramsey, Laurence. 1577. *The Practise of the Divell*. London. *STC* 20665.

Randolph, Thomas. 1632. *Amyntas, Or, The Impossible Dowry*. In *Poetical and Dramatic Works of Thomas Randolph*, W. Carew Hazlitt, ed. London (1875), 1:269–371.

Ratcliff, S.C., and H.C. Johnson, eds. 1937. *Quarter Sessions Order Book, Easter 1650– Epiphany 1657*. Warwick.

The Rates of Merchandizes as they are Rated and Agreed on by the Commons House of Parliament ... from the First Day of July, Anno Dom. 1642. 1657. London. Wing R297.

Ribeiro, João Pedro. 1829. *Dissertaações chronologicas e criticas sobre a historia e jurisprudencia ecclesiastica e civil de Portugal*. Vol. 4, pt. 2.

Richmond, Colin. 1993. 'An Outlaw and Some Peasants: The Possible Significance of Robin Hood.' *Nottingham Mediaeval Studies* 37:90–101.

Ritson, Joseph, ed. 1832. *Robin Hood*. London.

Robertson, J., and D.J. Gordon, eds. 1954. *Calendar of Dramatic Records in the Books of the Livery Companies of London, 1485–1640*. Oxford.

Rogers, Everett M. 1983. *Diffusion of Innovations*. 3rd ed. New York.

Rowlands, Samuel. 1880. 'The Knave of Harts, Haile felow Well Met.' In *The Complete Works of Samuel Rowlands*. Vol. 2 [5th item]. Glasgow.

Rudé, George. 1964. *The Crowd in History*. New York.

Rudder, Samuel. 1779. *A New History of Gloucestershire*. Cirencester.

Rugg, Thomas. 1961. *The Diurnal of Thomas Rugg 1659–1661*. William L. Sachse, ed. London.

S[...], F. 1885. 'Morrice Dancing.' *Shropshire Notes and Queries*, 1st ser 1 (May 1885): 53–4.

Sabol, Andrew. 1978. *Four Hundred Songs and Dances from the Stuart Masque*. Providence.

[Salisbury, Marquis of]. 1899. *Calendar of the Manuscripts of the Most Hon. the Marquis of Salisbury, K.G., &c., Preserved at Hatfield House, Hertfordshire*. Vol. 8. London: Historical Manuscripts Commission.

Sampson, William. 1625. *The Vow Breaker, or, The Fayre Maide of Clifton*. Hans Wallrath, ed. Louvain (1914).

Sharp, Cecil J. 1909–22. *The Country Dance Book*. 6 parts. London.

Sharp, Cecil J., and Herbert MacIlwaine (Parts 1–3), and George Butterworth (Part 5). 1907–13. *The Morris Book*. 1st ed. 5 parts. London.

– 1912–24. *The Morris Book*. 2nd ed. 3 parts. London.

Sharp, Lauriston. 1952. 'Steel Axes for Stone Age Australians.' *Human Organization* 11.2: 17–22.

Sharpe, Reginald R., ed. 1907. *Calendar of Letter-Books Preserved Among the Archives of the*

Corporation of the City of London at the Guildhall: Letter-Book H Circa A.D. 1375–1399. London.

Shorter, A.H. 1971. *Paper Making in the British Isles.* Newton Abbot.

Simeone, W.E. 1951. 'The May-games and the Robin Hood Legend.' *Journal of American Folklore* 64:265–74.

Smith, J.R., 1973. 'Suppression of Pestiferous Dancing in Essex.' *English Dance and Song* 36.1:9–10

Solt, Leo F. 1990. *Church and State in Early Modern England, 1509–1640.* Oxford.

Somerset, J. Alan B., ed. 1994. *Shropshire.* Records of Early English Drama. 2 vols. Toronto.

Sommi, Leone de'. 1968. *Quattro Dialoghi in Materia di Rappresentazioni Sceniche.* Milan.

[Spelman, Henry]. 1622. *Vox graculi, or, Jacke Dawes prognostication … for this yeere 1623.* London. *STC* 6386.

Spinelli, Lodovico. 1521. 'Copia di una lettera di Lodovico Spinelli secretario di l'Orator veneto in Anglia, data in Londra a dì primo Lujo 1521 …' In *I diarii di Marino Sanuto,* Marino Sanuto. 1891 31:95–6. Venice.

Stokes, James. 1986. 'The Wells Cordwainers' Show: New Evidence Concerning Guild Entertainment in Somerset.' *Comparative Drama* 19:332–46.

– ed. 1996. *Somerset.* Records of Early English Drama. 2 vols. Toronto.

Stone, Percy G. 1912. 'The Ledger Book of Newport, I.W., 1567–1799.' *The Antiquary* 48:178–85.

Stow, John. 1908. *A Survey of London.* Reprinted from the text of 1603, with Introduction and Notes by Charles Lethbridge Kingsford. Oxford.

Stubbes, Phillip. 1583. *Anatomie of Abuses.* London. *STC* 23376.

Sumberg, Samuel L. 1941. *The Nuremberg Schembart Carnival.* New York.

Thirsk, Joan, gen. ed. 1984–5. *The Agrarian History of England and Wales.* Vol. 5 1640–1750, 2 parts. Cambridge.

Thompson, Stith. 1953. 'The Star Husband Tale.' In *The Study of Folklore,* Alan Dundes, ed. Englewood Cliffs, NJ (1965).

Tietze-Conrat, E. 1957. *Dwarfs and Jesters in Art.* Translated Elizabeth Osborn. New York.

Tollet, George. 1793. 'Mr Tollet's opinion concerning the Morris Dancers upon his window.' In *The Plays of William Shakespeare in fifteen volumes with the corrections and illustrations of various commentators to which are added notes by Samuel Johnson and George Steevens.* Samuel Johnson and George Steevens, eds. 2nd ed. London, 5:425–34.

Townshend, Aurelian. 1631. *Albion's Triumph, Personated in a Maske at Court by the Kings Maiestie and his Lords, the Sunday after Twelfe Night, 1631.* In *Aurelian Townshend's Poems and Masks.* E.K. Chambers, ed. Oxford (1912), 55–78.

Twemlow, J.A. ed. 1935 *Liverpool Town Books.* Liverpool.

A Treatise of Daunses, Wherein it is Shewed, that they are Accessories to Whoredome. 1581. London. *STC* 24242.5

Underdown, David. 1985. *Revel, Riot, and Rebellion: Popular Politics and Culture in England 1603–1660.* Oxford.

Verney, Margaret Maria, ed. 1930. *Verney Letters of the Eighteenth Century from the MSS. at Claydon House.* London.

Walsh, John. *c* 1730. *The Third Book of the Most Celebrated Jiggs, Lancashire Hornpipes, Scotch and Highland Lilts, Northern Frisks, Morris's and Cheshire Rounds, with Hornpipes the Bagpipe Manner.* London.

– 1735. *The Third Book of the Compleat Country Dancing Master.* London.

Waith, Eugene M. 1989. '(Appendix A) The Morris Dance in 3.5.' In William Shakespeare and John Fletcher. *Two Noble Kinsmen,* Eugene Waith, ed. Oxford.

Ward, John M. 1986. 'The Morris Tune.' *Journal of the American Musicological Society* 39: 294–331.

Ward, Robert. 1909. *Fucus; sive Histriomastix.* G.C. Moore-Smith, ed. Cambridge.

Wase, Christopher. 1654. *Grati Falisci Cynegeticon, or, A Poem of Hunting, by Gratius the Faliscan, Englished and Illustrated by Christopher Wase.* London.

Wasson, John, ed. 1986. *Devon.* Records of Early English Drama. Toronto.

Weelkes, Thomas. 1597. *Madrigals to 3. 4. 5. & 6. Voyces.* In *English Madrigal Verse 1588–1632,* E.H. Fellowes, ed. 3rd ed. Oxford (1967), 279–84.

– 1600. *Madrigals of 5. and 6. parts, apt for the Viols and Voices.* In *English Madrigal Verse 1588–1632,* E.H. Fellowes, ed. 3rd ed. Oxford (1967), 290–4.

– 1608. *Ayres or Phantasticke Spirites for Three Voices.* In *English Madrigal Verse 1588–1632,* E.H. Fellowes, ed. 3rd ed. Oxford (1967), 294–304.

Welsford, Enid. 1927. *The Court Masque.* Cambridge.

Wickham, Glynne. 1959. *Early English Stages.* 3 vols. London.

Winkless, D., ed. 1987. 'Five Tracy Diaries of the Eighteenth and Nineteenth Centuries.' In *The Sudeleys – Lords of Toddington.* London, 200–21.

Wiles, David. 1981. *The Early Plays of Robin Hood.* Ipswich.

Willan, T.S., ed. 1962. *A Tudor Book of Rates [The Rates of the Customes House, 1582].* Manchester.

Withington, Robert. 1918. *English Pageantry: An Historical Outline.* 2 vols. Cambridge, MA.

Wittgenstein, Ludwig. 1953. *Philosophical Investigations.* Oxford.

Wood, Anthony. 1891. *The Life and Times of Anthony Wood, Antiquary, of Oxford, 1632–1695, described by himself, collected from his diaries and other papers by Andrew Clark.* 5 vols. Oxford.

Wood, Melusine. 1937. 'Some Notes on the English Country Dance before Playford.' *Journal of the English Folk Dance and Song Society* 3.2:93–9.

Wright, Daniel. *c* 1713. *An Extraordinary Collection of Pleasant & Merry Humours, Never Before Published.* London.

Wright, Thomas. 1869. *Churchwardens' Accounts of the Town of Ludlow in Shropshire, from 1540 to the End of the Reign of Queen Elizabeth.* London.

Young, John. *c* 1727. *The Dancing Master … The Third Volume.* London.

Index